Descendants
of
Daniel
Wolf

1732–1807

Compiled by *Charles C. Wolf*

HERITAGE BOOKS
2010

HERITAGE BOOKS

AN IMPRINT OF HERITAGE BOOKS, INC.

Books, CDs, and more—Worldwide

For our listing of thousands of titles see our website
at
www.HeritageBooks.com

Published 2010 by
HERITAGE BOOKS, INC.
Publishing Division
100 Railroad Ave. #104
Westminster, Maryland 21157

International Standard Book Numbers
Paperbound: 978-1-55613-922-2
Clothbound: 978-0-7884-8443-8

TABLE OF CONTENTS

INTRODUCTION

Research involving this Wolf family line started about 1975 as a project to prepare a Family History identifying the ancestors of the author's two daughters. Following it's successful completion, the genealogy bug had been born and it was decided to attempt to identify the descendants of their paternal great great great great grandfather Daniel Wolf (1), the subject of this genealogy. Once underway, it followed naturally to wish to publish this information for the use of other family members and researchers.

When using this book it must be remembered that data was obtained over a period of years and, of necessity, information obtained in the early years has not necessarily been up-dated to the date of publication. Unless the material came in unsolicited, no further research was done on families once they were brought up to the current date.

Information on early generations in Frederick and Washington Counties, MD was gathered personally by the author from state and county records and from Federal Census records. In general other information was gathered through the mail, with limited local personal contact.

It is interesting to note that, except for closely related family members, few of those providing information were known personally by the author, even those living in his home town. Contact with related family members was fortunately established by Queries in genealogical publications, newspaper advertisements and telephone calls. The contacts established in this way have been invaluable in preparing this book.

The author expresses his deep appreciation and sincere thanks to all those who provided information for this book. It should be noted that some contributors provided complete lines which they had researched and it is appropriate to identify them specifically, listed alphabetically.

Bailey, Mrs. Roland, 1301 Richard St., Miamisburg, OH 45342 -Provided information for the descendants of Elizabeth Hahn (#21), daughter of Elizabeth (Wolf) Hahn (#4) and wife of Daniel Sharritt.

Bakehouse, Mrs. Glen, R 1, Box 185, Hedrick, IA 5263-9685

Burgert, Annette K., 691 Weavertown Road, Myerstown, PA 17067 -Author of "The Hochstadt Origins of Some of the Early Settlers at Host Church", 1977. This identified the parentage of Daniel (#1).

Caldwell, Milton C. Sr., 7219 Belle Plain Drive, Dayton, OH 45424. Provided information for the descendants (other than George Isaac Wolf) of Jacob Wolf Jr. (#10), son of Jacob (#2).

Gantz, Mrs. Donald W. Sr., 204 Phylane Drive, Hagerstown, MD 21740 - Provided information for the descendants of Tracy Wolf (#28), daughter of Frederick Wolf (#5) and wife of Jacob Blecher, as contained in the "Blecker History" prepared by Arnold Blecker, 1797 San Bernardino Ave., Pomona, CA 91767, dated July 1969.

Ross, Keith E., 29 Oak Drive, N. Manchester, IN 46962 - Provided information for the descendants of Susan Wolf (#9), daughter of Jacob (#2) and wife of John S. Mantle/Montel, as contained in his "Descendants of Christopher Mantle and Elizabeth Soeston - Montel Family".

Schinbeckler, Mrs. Keith (Deceased), formerly RR 8, Columbia City, IN 46725 - Contributed much during the original research on this project.

Seubold, Mrs. Helen W., C.G., 12000 Old Georgetown Road, Rockville, MD 20852 - Provided information for the descendants of Elizabeth Wolf (#26), daughter of Frederick Wolf (#5) and wife of Daniel Schlosser as contained in "The Family of Henry Schlosser of Frederick County, MD", Part IV, published in the "Maryland and Delaware Genealogist" 1975-1977.

Starkweather, Mrs. Norma Shroyer, 722 Copeland St., Madison, WI 53711 - Provided information for the descendants of Sarah Wolf (#11), daughter of Jacob (#2) and wife of George Shroyer, as contained in her unpublished "Shroyer Family".

Stutesman, John Hale, 305 Spruce St., San Francisco, CA 94118 -Provided information for the family of Frederick Wolf, son of Jacob and brother of Daniel (#1), and from whom his wife (now deceased) was descended. Much of the early generations information resulted from an early contact with him. See "Frederick Wolf and Kin, Montgomery County, OH", published in the Ohio Genealogical Society Report (1980) Volume XX #4.

Walters, Mrs. Cora M., 5930 Barcus Way, South Bend, IN 46614 -Provided information for the descendants of George Isaac Wolf (#76), son of Jacob Wolf Jr. (#10).

Wolfe, Dorcas, 19 SE Broad, Des Moines, IA 50315 - Provided information for the descendants of Albert Harold Wolfe (#1623), son of Frank Peter Wolfe (#921).

Wolfe, Merritt W., 303 E. Linwood Ave., Akron, OH 44301 (After July 1, 1993 - 4820 South Colonial Oaks Drive, Marion, IN 46593) - Provided information for the descendants of Christina Wolf (#6), daughter of Daniel (#1) and wife of Abraham Paulus, as contained in his "Abraham Paulus Family History". Rather than completely duplicate the information in his Paulus history, the Paulus line is carried generally through generation No.6 of this book. Later generations can be found in the Paulus history. It is interesting to note that his Wolfe line bears no relationship to the Wolf line of this book.

Wolff, Raymond Alvin, 18 W. 55th St., New York, NY 10019 - Author of "The Wolf Wolfe Wolff Families of Pennsylvania" 1971. Although there is a possibility of a relationship between this Wolf line and that of Daniel(#1), no evidence has as yet been found. However his help, advice and research in the preparation of this book has been invaluable.

There are, of course, others too numerous to mention, who provided the bulk of the information in this book and they are sincerely thanked for their contributions.

Charles C. Wolf
13233 Glendale Drive
Hagerstown, MD 21742

This genealogy of Daniel Wolf is organized somewhat differently than the normal order of presentation. No documentation has been found to prove the ancestry of Daniel, although circumstantial evidence leads to a reasonable conclusion. For this reason the first chapter will discuss Daniel and his family as shown by documentation. The second chapter will then discuss Daniel's probable ancestry as indicated by evidence which, although circumstantial, is felt to be conclusive.

The book is written as a Descending Genealogy, that is it traces descendants of Daniel Wolf (#1). The system used is known as the NGS Quarterly System (also known as the Modified Register System). Three types of numbers are used: one to uniquely identify the individual, one to indicate the generation into which that person falls, and one to denote the birth order within the family. The NGSQ System assigns a number to each infant, distinguishing between individuals who are carried forward and those who are not by a plus sign (+) preceding the number of anyone who is to be separately treated. For those carried forward only a birth date is given, if known.

The arabic number to the left of each person's name uniquely identifies that individual by a number that will not be assigned to anyone else in the genealogy. When anything is known about each child who is not carried forward, that information directly follows the name.

In parentheses, immediately after the given name of the individual, there appears a number called the generation number. The parenthetical outline of an individual's lineage, which is inserted as soon as that individual is introduced in his or her own section, cites only the direct line within the family that the genealogy focuses upon.

When each list of children is presented, birth order is designated by the use of small roman numerals, placed between the individual's arabic identification number and the individual's name. Should there be multiple marriages by an ancestor they are treated as separate families with the roman numerals beginning again for the second set of children.

In case additional children are identified after the numbering system has been developed, special numbering is assigned. For instance, if two additional children are found to fall between #601 and #602, #601a and #601b are assigned.

Reference citations used for each chapter are indicated by a reverse slash and number, such as \26.

Variations in surname spelling pose difficulties. Ascertaining the correct spelling for every person in every generation is an impossible task. Wolf was clearly the preferred spelling at the time of landing in America, as shown by the signatures on the ship's lists. In some branches of the family it has remained so to the present generation. The addition of the "e" to give Wolfe begins to appear in later generations.

Spelling changes in any given family seem to have been made by personal preference. Searching written records has been of little help, particularly in the eary generations, as transcribing documents was usually performed by another, quite possibly of English descent, who used his best judgement in spelling names. As a result, early records show Wolf, Wolfe, Wolff and Woolf at various times for obviously the same family. These same comments apply for all surnames in this genealogy, such as Mantle/Montel and Sharritz/Sharritt. As a result of these inconsistencies, spelling may be incorrect in early generations, but should be accurate for recent generations. There are undoubtedly errors for which the author apologizes.

Because of these difficulties, the index has been prepared using Wolf and Wolfe as a single listing, rather than as separate listings, the same principle applying to other surnames.

CHAPTER 1

DANIEL WOLF

1 - DANIEL(1) WOLF
    The earliest date which can be substantiated concerning Daniel
and his family is the birthdate of son Jacob, 8 September 1770, as
inscribed on his cemetery tombstone.\1 Subsequent data shows the
birth of daughters Elizabeth 12 November 1773 and Christina 13 April
1777, both listed in the baptismal records of Klopp's Church, Lebanon
County, PA.\2 Son Frederick was born 6 March 1776\3 in PA.\4 No
birthdate for daughter Catharine has been found.
    In view of this documentation as to the birth of his children it
is reasonable to conclude that he is the Daniel Wolf listed in the tax
records for Bethel Township, Berks County, PA from 1768 to 1784.

Bethel Township, Berks County, PA Tax Records\5

	1767	1768	1779	1780	1781	1784	1785
Daniel Wolf	----	50A	140A	150A	150A	153A	----

    No transactions for this property have been found in Berks County
land records.
    From Berks County, PA Daniel and his family moved to Frederick
County, MD. The first record of Daniel in Maryland is his purchase in
1784 of a 107 1/2 acre property from Peter Wolf.\6 The deed was made
26 May 1784 and recorded 8 June 1784. Consideration was 700 pounds.
Daniel and Peter are described as being of Frederick County. There is
no evidence to indicate Daniel's coming to Frederick County before
this time.
    This property was purchased 4 February 1777 by Peter from Jesse
Wharton of St. Mary's County, MD.\7 Consideration was 212 pounds. This
property had been conveyed to Jesse Wharton by Henry Neale of St.
Mary's County for William and Henry Digges, heirs of Edward Digges,
deceased. It was witnessed by Jeremiah Jordon and John Shanks. This
would have been the first possession of this property by a resident
property owner as the previous owners were of St. Mary's County, as
previously noted.
    The property lies about five miles south-southwest of Emmitsburg,
and is described in the deed as lying and being on the mouth of Tom's
Creek (where it flows into the Monocacy River), known as Part of
Digges Lott (metes and bounds description given). Except for a small
parcel used for a road relocation, this property today is the same as
in 1777 when it was purchased by Peter Wolf.

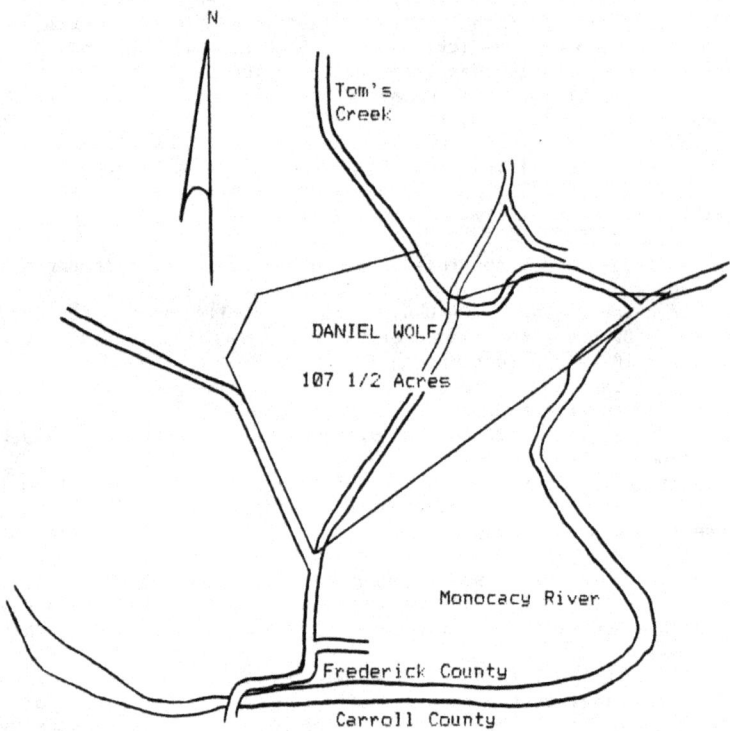

Figure 1
Property of Daniel Wolf in Frederick County, Maryland

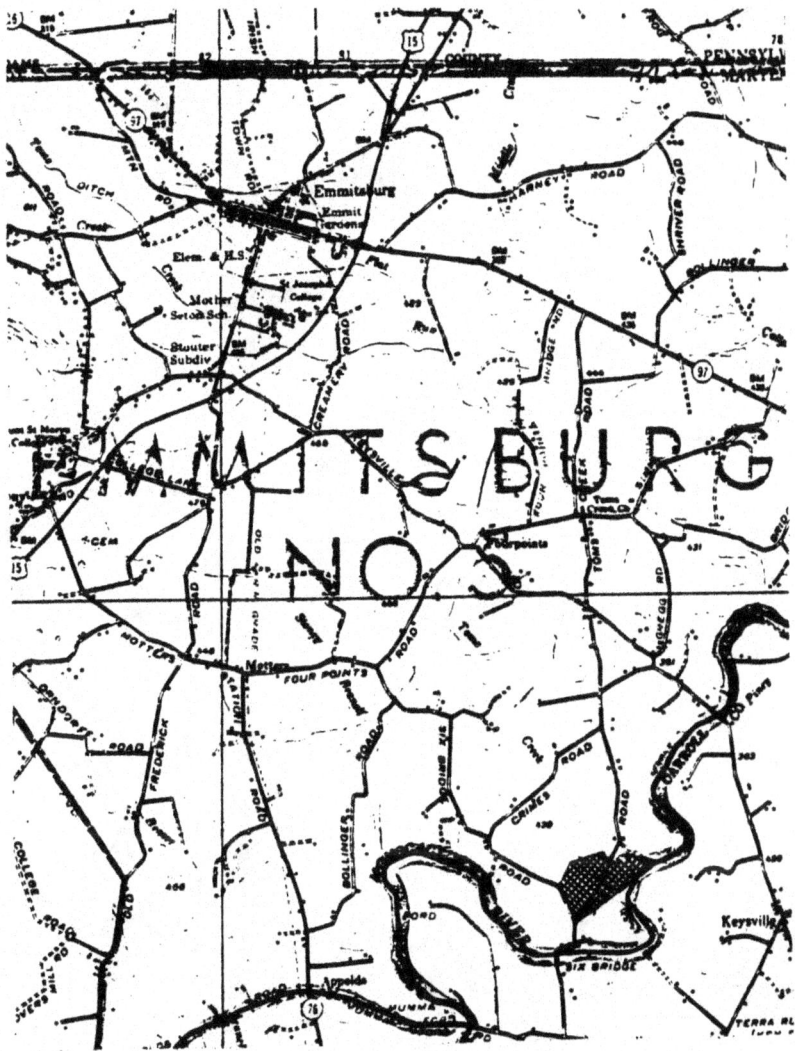

Figure 2
Location of Daniel Wolf property in Frederick County, MD

In the 1790 Federal Census the Daniel Wolf family is listed on Page 65 of the Frederick County, MD census summary as follows:

Males 16 and up   - 2
Males under 16   - 2
Females   - 4

This data indicates one more male than is known to have been in the family. It may have been Frederick Kimmerling or a son who died before settlement of Daniel's estate in 1807.

In the 1800 Federal Census the family is listed in Division Four, Page 882, Line Five of the Frederick County, MD census:

Males 45 and up   - 1
Males 26 - 45   - 1
Females 45 and up   - 1

This data indicates Daniel, his wife Maria Elizabeth and probably son Jacob.

In 1800 Daniel purchased the property, household goods and livestock of his son-in-law Leonard Hahn (married to Elizabeth) in Emmitsburg, Frederick County, MD. A record of sale from Leonard Hawn to Daniel Wolf, made 11 April 1800, recorded 15 April 1800 shows a consideration of 50 pounds for two cows, two sheep, five hogs, two bedsteads and bedding, one chest and all other household and kitchen furniture.\8 A deed made 12 April 1800, recorded 15 April 1800 shows a consideration of 80 pounds for a certain lot of ground in Shields' Addition to Emmitsburg, being a front lot known as Number 16.\9 Later this same year (1800) he sold the property purchased in 1784. It is probable that Daniel, with his wife and one son (1800 census) moved to the Emmitsburg property at that time. It could be suggested that Leonard Hahn might have been incapacitated or in ill health, causing this move.

Daniel sold the property purchased in 1784 to William Jr., Frederick and Joseph Biggs, all of Frederick County for 860 pounds. The deed was made 25 December 1800 and recorded 19 January 1801. Maria Elizabeth, wife of Daniel, released her dower rights.\10

Leonard Hahn died 1805/1806 as evidenced by the filing 27 February 1806 of the first account of his estate settlement by the Administrator, Robert L. Annan. The final account was filed 12 February 1807.\11 The estate was insufficient to satisfy the debts. Apparently at about this same time, Daniel sold the Emmitsburg property to John Weaver, accepting a bond from Weaver in lieu of a cash payment. As this bond was apparently not paid prior to Daniel's death, no deed was drawn or recorded for this sale. A subsequent lawsuit and Sheriff's sale of the property were required of Daniel's heirs after his death to recover the debt covered by the bond.

At about this time (1806), an emigration from Washington County, MD to Ohio was apparently being planned. 20 April 1789 Frederick Wolf Sr., of Berks County, PA had purchased from John Thomas for 1300 pounds a 200 acre tract, "The Resurvey on the Grove and Part of Tellfoot Enlarged" near Boonsboro, Washington County, MD.\12 He remained there until 1806. He sold this property 14 April 1806 to John Waggoner for 3000 pounds.\13 He and his family then emigrated to German Township, Montgomery County, OH. Daniel's death in Washington County in 1807 indicates that he sold the Emmitsburg property and went to Washington County in 1806. As most of Daniel's family emigrated to the same area of Ohio after his death it is logical to assume that Daniel had come to Washington County to join the Frederick Wolf family in the move to Ohio.

Daniel's death in 1807 has been established from the date of 7 August, 1807 of the posting of bond for the administration of his

4

estate as he died intestate.\14 Bond of 2000 pounds "current Money" was posted by "Jacob Woolf, Frederick Woolf, Jacob Woolf and John Wagoner of Washington County". Jacob and Frederick Woolf were appointed Administrators. They were undoubtedly Daniel's two sons. The other Jacob Woolf has not been positively identified.

An inventory and appraisement of Daniel's personal estate was taken 17 August 1807 by John Ringer and Wendell Shecter\15. It shows as follows:

one stove and pipe 12. 8 books of sundry kinds 50	$12.50
1 Bible 3 dollars and ?	1.50
2 Bags dry'd apples 1.50 and 5 linen bags 1.25	2.75
2 washing lines 75 cents and one cow chain 50 cents	1.25
2 flower barrels 25 cents and one small kettle 25	.50
One coffy mill 50 cents one ? and 3 tin cups 25	.75
1 pewter tea pott 12 1/2 cents and one pair of tongs	1.12
1 Stillyard? 2 dollars Curry comb and frying pan 37 1/2 cents	2.37
Six dishes and 2 small pitchers 15. 4 Knives and 5 forks 10	.25
1 funnel two glasses and one knife	.18
2 Cups and saucers 15 cents and one small bell 25	.40
2 Buckets and one watering pott 25	.25
2 Glass bottles 25 cents 2 saddles? and 1 fork 15 cents	.40
Cutting knife steel and ?	1.50
1 Benching tub 2 dollars and one cyder barrel 50 cents	2.50
one gray mare 12 Halter chain neck ? and bridle 1	13.00
one collar 25 cents and small keg 18 cents	.43
one hobble chain 25 cents and a small ? 50	.75
six pair of overalls 50 2 pair ditto 75 cents and 2 halfs 25	1.50
1 Great coat 50 cents and 3 other coats 1.50	2.00
3 pair of britches and one pair of overalls	.75
4 jackets 30 cents and 7 shirts 3.50	3,80
5 pair of stockings and one pair of mittens	1.50
one mans saddle 50 cents and one womans saddle 50	1.00
Two pewter dishes and 3 basons 1.50	1.50
12 pewter plates and 13 spoons 1.25 9 spoons 18	1.43
one sweeping brush and sundry ?	.25
one looking glas and lamp	.15
1 bag of soap 7 1/2 ? at 9 cts	.67
2 Gimblets and other small articles 15	.15
2 pair of shoes 25 cents and 7 dozen and ten buttons 25	.50
5 bread baskets small vials? & 18 ? one mawl ring and a piece?	.12
one half bushel with sundry irons	.35
one small ? 50 cents 2 Coffy potts 16 cents	.66
5 Table cloths 3. 5 sheets and one chaff? bag 5.50	8.50
2 towels and one wallich? 18 cents and 1 chest? 25 cents	.43
One other chest? 2. 1 wallbag? two combs and a ?	.12
one spinning wheel 50. One coverlet? and coverlet? 6.	6.50
one Bed Bedstead ? 6.50. One bread ? and ? 25	6.75
one gammon of meat 16 ? 9	1.44
one spade and hoe 1.25 one chain and one ? of ? iron 33	1.50

	$90.90

On 2 September 1807 Jacob and Frederick Wolf filed the inventory, including the following debts owed to the estate:

A List of Shuate Debts due the Estate of Daniel Wolf Deceased

Frederick Wolf for money lent	$100.28
Peter Necum for money lent	4.00
John Wagoner bond with interest	299.60
Jacob Wolf money lent with interest	151.70

```
Michael Thomas money lent                                    24.00
Michael Gittle open acc.                                    143.86
Frederick Kimmerling open acc.                              315.88
Abraham Powles                                              112.43
Peter Wolf money lent                                         3.94
John Weaver bond due the 1st ? ?                             70.66
John Weaver 3 bond in suit for L26.10.0)
Cash on hand at the time of his death   )                   765.66
                                                           -------
                                                          $1992.01
```

"Vendue of the personal estate of Daniel Wolf late of Washington County, Maryland, Deceased sold the 19th day of September 1807 by Jacob and Frederick Wolf Administrators".\16

Purchasers	Articles Sold	
Nicholas Houp	Steel ? cutting box	$ .12
Upton Powell	Bucket and watering pott	.18
Wendall Schechter	One spade	.57
Henry Locher	One hoe	.45
Nicholas Houp	Cutting knife and rake	.80
Upton Powell	One small tea kettle	1.01
Henry Stonecypher	Flatt iron	.10
Michael Hoof	3 gimlets and whett stone	.66
Phillip Snyder	Hubbles	.31
Henry Locher	1 cow chain	.31
Jacob Wolf	Buttons, brush etc	.30
Upton Powell	?	.62
Old Mrs. Wolf	Coffee mill and cannister	.27
Ditto	7 lb soap	.15
Nicholas Houp	Stillyard	2.05
Jacob Wolf	Tongs	.75
Henry Locher	Clothes-line	.41
Abraham Powles	2 glasses and line	.27
Frederick Wolf	Bell and funnel	.35
Ditto	Brush and shovel	.30
Upton Powell	5 dishes etc	.14
Ditto	Half ? hill and onions	.30
Old Mrs. Wolf	Coffee pott and cups	.07
Michael Hoof	1 keg	.26
Frederick Wolf	Bag and dried apples	.26
Michael Hoof	1 barrel	.77
Upton Powell	2 barrels	.12
Old Mrs. Wolf	1 iron pott	.26
Henry Stonecypher	5 bread baskets	.10
Nicholas Houp	1 coat and jacket	.30
Frederick Wolf	2 pair britches	.30
Daniel Ittenire	3 jackets	.20
Upton Powell	1 pair overalls	.26
Daniel Stonecypher	2 hatts	.07
Frederick Wolf	2 coats	.20
Jacob Wolf	1 large coat	.90
Upton Powell	5 pair linnen overalls	.31
John Ittenire	Box and razors	.22
Jacob Wolf	3 pair of overalls	1.83
Henry Locher	Tankard and bason	.33
Upton Powell	3 pair stockings	.55
Abraham Powlas	1 pair of mittens	.20
Old Mrs. Wolf	1 small chest	.57
Henry Lochner	1 pewter bason	.75

6

Abraham Powlas	1 pewter dish	1.11
Old Mrs. Wolf	Sundry pewter plates	2.00
Ditto	One hand kerchieff	.25
Jacob Wolf	2 muslin shirts	1.75
Upton Powell	1 ditto	.65
Ditto	1 ditto	.20
Ditto	1 ditto	.20
Frederick Wolf	2 ditto	1.15
Old Mrs. Wolf	2 ditto	1.00
Michael Hoof	4 bags	2.05
Abraham Powlas	Bag and dry apples	1.02
Michael Hoop	1 bag	.65
Old Mrs. Wolf	1 pallioh?	.06
Ditto	2 table cloths	1.00
Ditto	2 sheets	2.00
Upton Powell	1 sheet	1.01
Abraham Powlas	1 ditto	1.06
Frederick Wolf	1 table cloth	.30
Jacob Wolf	1 ditto	.44
Frederick Wolf	1 ditto	.70
Ditto	1 sheet	1.15
Ditto	Sundry books	1.50
Old Mrs. Wolf	1 bucket	.20
Ditto	1 bible	3.00
Ditto	3 books	.30
Upton Powell	1 chair	.36
Jacob Fretman	1 spinning wheel	.86
Frederick Wolf	1 gamman 16lb @ 10c	1.60
Henry Ittenier	1 looking glass	4.00
Old Mrs. Wolf	Bed & beadsted etc	12.50
John Ittenier	1 tin plate stove & pipe	19.75
Old Mrs. Wolf	2 tin cups	.07
Frederick Wolf	1 bottle	.14
Jacob Wolf	1 man's saddle	1.25
Old Mrs. Wolf	1 woman's saddle	.10
Ditto	One mare and bridle	12.01
Ditto	Chain and neck Baion?	.03
Wendall Schechter	Neck collar	.06
Jacob Wolf	Halter chain	1.00
John Ittenire	1 large tub	2.40
Upton Powell	2 pair of shoes	.26
Ditto	2 jugs	.12
Old Mrs. Wolf	1 lamp	.04
David Gray	1 frying pan	.04
Frederick Wolf	1 axe	1.50
Ditto	1 dough trough	.25

Total $102.19

Total sale amount to one hundred and two dollars and nineteen cents errors excepted this day of September 1807.

David Gray, Clk

Final distribution of the estate was made by Jacob and Frederick Wolf, Administrators, 6 October 1807.\17 Balance due the estate was L669.1.11 current money, L223.0.7, or 1/3, to the widow and L89.4.3 to each of the five children named in the distribution:

Catharine Kimmollan

Elizabeth Hawn

Christina Powlis
Jacob Woolf
Frederick Woolf

In August 1809 a judgement was issued in Frederick County against John Weaver in favor of Jacob and Frederick Wolf, administrators of the estate of Daniel Wolf (deceased) in the amount of 53 pounds against a debt of 50 pounds, undoubtedly for the bond posted by John Weaver for the purchase of the Emmitsburg property. To settle this judgement the property known as Lot No. 16 in Shields' Addition to Emmitsburg was sold at public sale. Frederick Wolf was the highest bidder and purchased the property for 90 dollars. The deed was made December 26, 1809, recorded April 24, 1810 by George Creager Jr., Sheriff of Frederick County, to Frederick Wolf, of Washington County.\18 This gave Frederick Wolf title to the property, acting for the heirs of Daniel Wolf

April 27, 1811 "Frederick Wolf, of Washington County", executed a deed, "acting as Attorney for the heirs of Daniel Wolf, late of Washington County (deceased). By virtue of a written instrument dated April 18, 1810, signed by Elizabeth Wolf, widow of Daniel Wolf, late of Washington County, Frederick Kemberlane and Catharine his wife, Jacob Wolf and Susannah his wife, Abraham Paulus and Christiana his wife, and Elizabeth Hawn, widow of Leonard Hawn, late of Frederick County, (deceased), the said heirs being of Montgomery County, state of Ohio in German Township, to Joseph Hughes, consideration 300 dollars. That lot containing 1/4 acre in Emmitsburg, lying on the south side of the street leading to Baltimore in Shields' Addition, known as Lot No. 16".\19 Molilina (Magdalena), wife of Frederick, released her dower rights. The deed was recorded May 11, 1811. This transaction completed the administration of the estate of Daniel Wolf.

Daniel Wolf's wife has only been identified by her given names, Maria Elizabeth, from her release of her dower rights in the deed of 25 December 1800\10 and from her will\20. No records have been found to indicate her date or place of birth.

Land and census records show that Daniel's widow, Elizabeth, son Jacob, and the three daughters emigrated to German Township, Montgomery County, Ohio following Daniel's death and the settlement of his estate. Son Frederick remained in Washington County, Maryland appearing in the 1810 thru 1850 census records of that county. Daniel's widow, Elizabeth, son Jacob and son-in-law Abraham Paulus appear in the Montgomery County, Ohio 1810 tax list along with Frederick Wolf Sr. and his sons Frederick Jr. and Philip. These records indicate Daniel's three daughters came with their mother or joined her shortly thereafter.

In 1810 Elizabeth bought from Philip Gunckel for 200 dollars a tract of 80 acres in Section 7, Township 2, Range 5 East, just northeast of Germantown, Montgomery County, Ohio. The deed was made 18 September 1810 and recorded 15 October 1810.\21 (At the same time Frederick Wolf Jr. bought 81 acres in the Northwest Quarter of Section 7, possibly adjoining the land Elizabeth bought.)

Elizabeth died, probably early in 1815, as her will was made 10 April 1814 and filed for probate 1 May 1815.\20 She made the following bequests:

Son- Jacob- One dollar.
Son- Frederick- One dollar.
Daughter- Catherine-" wife of Frederick Kimmerling, fifty acres of land the same on where the said Frederick Kimmerling now resides during both their lives all the use benefits and advantages whatsoever

8

it being the East part of the eighty acres I purchased Frederick Wolf Junr. to be run off in a straight line North and South but that I may be understood they shall be disbarred from selling the same until their decease and after their decease the aforesaid fifty acres of land to be the property of my said daughters heirs their heirs and assigns forever the same as if had bought it from me and paid for".

Daughter- Elizabeth Haun- "widow thirty acres of land the same on where she at present resides she my said daughter Elizabeth to have and to hold the same thirty acres of land during her life all the use benefits profits and advantages whatsoever they may be except as heretofore excepted. She my said daughter Elizabeth shall also be debarred from selling the aforesaid thirty acres of land but that I may understood again after her death then and after the land shall be the property of my said daughter Elizabeth heirs their heirs and assigns forever. The aforesaid thirty acres being the remainder part of the above eighty acres".

Daughter- Christianna- "wife of Abraham Paulus the sum of one hundred and twelve dollars which shall be paid out of my personal estate if so much left and if overplus out of my personal estate then my daughter Elizabeth shall have the money if left and bed and bedstaed and all the clothes belonging to and all my clothes. The other household shall be divided among my three daughters".

Executors- "trusty friends Frederick Kimmerling and Abraham Paulus".

Witnesses- Frederick Wolf, George Wolf.

Elizabeth signed with her mark.

It is not known where Maria Elizabeth Wolf is buried.

Children of Daniel and Maria Elizabeth (   ) Wolf were as follows:\17
```
+   2    i Jacob Wolf, born 8 September 1770.
+   3   ii Catharine Wolf.
+   4  iii Elizabeth Wolf, born 12 November 1773.
+   5   iv Frederick Wolf, born 6 March 1776.
+   6    v Christina Wolf, born 13 April 1777.
```

NOTES AND REFERENCES

1. Old German Cemetery, German Township, Montgomery County, OH.
2. Klopp's Church (now St. Paul's United Church of Christ), Bethel Township, Lebanon County, PA.
3. Tombstone, Old Reformed Church Cemetery, Boonsboro, Washington County, MD.
4. 1850 Federal Census, Washington County, Md, 210.
5. Pennsylvania Archives, 3rd Series, Volume XVIII, 3-814.
6. Frederick County, MD, Land Records, Book WR4, 556.
7. Ibid., RP1, 50.
8. Ibid., WR19, 442.
9. Ibid., WR19, 443.
10. Ibid., WR20, 430.
11. Frederick County, MD, Administration Accounts, RB1, 173.
12. Washington County, MD, Land Records, Book F, 189.
13. Ibid., S, 211.
14. Maryland State Archives, Administration Bonds, 294.
15. Ibid., Inventories, Volume C, 484.
16. Ibid., Account of Sales, 157.

17. Washington County, MD, Accounts Distribution Book 1806-1816.
18. Frederick County, MD, Land Records, Book WR37, 112.
19. Ibid., WR39, 492.
20. Montgomery County, OH, Register of Wills, Book A, 95.
21. Ibid., Land Records, Book B, 345.

CHAPTER 2

ANCESTRY OF DANIEL WOLF

As previously stated no documentation has been found to prove the ancestry of Daniel Wolf although circumstantial evidence leads to a reasonable conclusion. This chapter will discuss that evidence.

It was noted in Chapter 1 that Daniel and his family had a known association with two other Wolfs, Peter and Frederick.

PETER WOLF

Daniel Wolf purchased in 1784 the property of Peter Wolf in Frederick County, MD.\1 This fact alone does not prove a relationship but there are further indications of a relationship in the will of Peter and in the estate administration for Daniel. Peter purchased the Frederick County, MD property 4 February 1777 from Jesse Wharton of St. Mary County, MD, a non-resident property owner.\2 He sold it to Daniel 26 May 1784, Peter's wife Mary renouncing her dower rights.\1 Peter died in Frederick County in 1785 his will having been made 23 August 1785 and filed for probate 4 November 1785.\3 The original will, with Peter's signature, is filed in the Maryland State Archives in Annapolis, MD.\4 Provisions of the will are: "Item I give and bequeath unto my loving wife Mary one third of my personal estate, one third of the grain, one cow, and all her wearing apparel with one feather bed, bedstead and beding (sic) thereto belonging during her life. And also it is my will and desire that the remaining part of my estate be equilly (sic) divided amongst my children as follows, George Wolfe, my daughter Mary who intermarried with a certain John Nickham, and Peter Wolfe to them and their heirs forever excepting twenty pounds specie I give and beqeath unto my stepson John Keeney. Morever insomuch as I have already given unto my son George Wolfe the sum of thirty seven pounds sixteen shillings and six pence specie and also to my son in law John Nickham the sum of thirty pounds eighteen shillings and ten pence specie, and it is my will and I do hereby order and direct that my said son George Wolfe and my son in law John Nickham be charged with the same. Lastly I do hereby constitute and appoint my said loving wife executrix and my step son John Keeney executor of this my last will and testament." The will was witnessed by John Carmack, Jacob Ovelman and Nicholas Manshouse.

At this time Peter's wife Mary and step son, John Keeney, were bonded in the amount of 1000 pounds as executors of Peter's will.\5 Bound were Mary, who signed with her mark, John Keney (sic), Joseph Wood and John Carmack. All were of Frederick County. No Administration Accounts wer filed for this estate indicating it was relatively small.

1790 Frederick County census records show a Mary Wolfe as the head of a family comprised of one male 16 and up, one male under 16 and four females. This is probably Peter's widow, Mary, along with her son, John Keeney, and his wife and children. These records also show a George Wolf as head of a household of two males 16 and up, probably George and Peter, sons of Peter Wolf and who had not married. Also in the 1790 census is a family headed by a John Nickum and comprised of three males 16 and up, three males under 16 and three females. John and Mary Wolf Nickham are probably part of this family group. A John Nickham family appears in the 1800 census of Adams County, PA, which

11

adjoins Frederick County, MD on the north, with eleven children.
George and Peter Wolf, Mary Wolf and John Keeney have not been identified in the 1800 census and probably left Frederick County before that
time (Peter's widow Mary may of course have died in the meantime).

Daniel's estate administration also shows indications of a
connection to the Peter Wolf family. It has been shown in his estate
administration that Daniel was owed $4.00 by Peter Necum (Nick-
ham/Nickum) and $3.94 by Peter Wolf. Peter Wolf's daughter Mary had
married John Nickham as shown in Peter's will. It is reasonable to
feel that Peter Necum is related to John Nickham, very possibly a
son., although this has not been proven. The debt of $4.00 was prob-
ably of Peter who was the son of Peter. These two items indicate a
closer tie between Daniel and Peter Wolf than does the property
transaction alone.

Children of Peter and Mary Keeney (   ) Wolf were as follows:\3

    i John Keeney, step son of Peter, son of Mary.
   ii George Wolf.
  iii Mary Wolf, married John Nickham 1784.
   iv Peter Wolf.

FREDERICK WOLF

The first documented information of Frederick Wolf is 8 May 1771
when an order was issued from "John Lukens Esquire" to survey a 184
acre tract for Frederick Wolf. This tract was surveyed 23 May 1771\6
and patented to Frederick 22 November 1771.\7 It is situated in Berks
County, PA on Swatara Creek which flows through the northern part of
the tract and divides it between Bethel and Tulpehocken Townships,
only a small portion being in Bethel Township. The tract was named
"Hanover Square" and is located just about due north of Rehrersburg,
Tulpehocken Township, Berks County, PA.

Frederick Wolf is listed in the tax records for Tulpehocken
Township, Berks County, PA from 1767 through 1785, described as a
blacksmith. He was taxed for 170/172 acres after the issue of the
warrant in 1771.\8 No record has been found for the disposition of
this property. 20 April 1789 he purchased from John Thomas for 1300
pounds a 200 acre tract, part of "Tellfoot Enlarged", near Boonsboro,
Washington County, MD.\9 The deed described Frederick as "of Berks
County, PA". Frederick then sold this property 14 April 1805 to John
Waggoner for 3000 pounds.\10 He and his family, with married sons and
daughters, migrated to German Township, Montgomery County, OH. He died
there 1814/15. His will was made 22 December 1813 and filed for
probate 1 May 1815. It names oldest son Frederick, son Phillip and
daughters Christena Thomas, Margratha Heck, married to John Heck,
Maryabel, Barbara, Elizabeth and Eva Wolf.\11

As noted in Chapter 1, shortly after Daniel's death his widow
Elizabeth, with her son Jacob and her three daughters, all with their
families, also migrated to German Township, Montgomery County, OH,
settling near to the Frederick Wolf family and purchasing in 1810
property from and adjacent to Frederick Wolf Jr.\12 When she made her
will 10 April 1814 Frederick Wolf Jr. and his son George were wit-
nesses to her signature (mark).\13 It was filed for probate 6 May
1815.

One other connection between Daniel and Frederick has been noted.
Frederick, as previously shown, sold his Washington County, MD property to John Waggoner. John Waggoner was also shown as one posting

bond for the administration of Daniel's estate.\5 He also is shown in
the inventory as having owed Daniel $229.60 on a bond.\14
    Frederick Wolf married 21 July 1751 Eva Barbara Meyer.\15

Children of Frederick and Eva Barbara Meyer Wolf:\16

        i Daniel Wolf, born 27 December 1756, bp. 16 January 1757,
          sponsors Daniel Wolf and Anna Barbara (this child probably
          died young).\17
       ii Barbara Wolf, died 1844. Did not marry.
      iii Frederick Wolf (Jr), died 1823 in Wayne County, IN.
       iv Phillip Wolf, married Sarah Maurer.
        v Eva Wolf.
       vi Catherine Wolf, confirmed 1768 at Host Church.\17
      vii Christina Wolf, born 2 April 1772, died 23 April 1833,
          married Gabriel Thomas.
     viii Maryabel Wolf.
       ix Elizabeth Wolf, d. 1844. Did not marry.
        x Anna Margaret Wolf, born 26 August 1774, bp. 27 February
          1775,\18 married John Jacob Heck.

    Knowing of the association and probable relationship of the three
Wolfs— Peter, Daniel and Frederick— and the Tulpehocken Township,
Berks County, PA reference for Frederick, it is logical to search this
area for a possible Wolf family including these three individuals.
Such a family is listed in "Hochstadt Origins of some of the Early
Settlers at Host Church" by Annette K. Burgert.\19 It is the family of
Jacob and Anna Margaretha Wolf from the Hochstadt area in the Palatinate of Germany.\20 The first of this family to emigrate to this
country were Peter and Friederich Wolf, sons of Jacob, on the ship
"Royal Union", 15 August 1750.\21 They were followed about a year
later by Jacob, sons Daniel and George and , presumably, Anna Margaretha and the daughters on the ship "Queen of Denmark", 4 October
1751.\21

    Children of Jacob and Anna Margaretha Wolf.\20

        i Johan Peter Wolf, bp. 6 October 1726, confirmed 1740,
          sponsors Peter Mayer and Anna Catherina Mayer.
       ii Maria Elizabeth Wolf, bp. 3 October 1728, married 16 Octo-
          ber 1753 George Jacob Ulrich,\17 died 4 March 1805.\22
      iii Johan Friederich Wolf, bp. 7 June 1730, confirmed 1744,
          sponsors Johan Friederich and Anna Barbara Lang, married
          21 July (Anna) Eva Barbara Meyer.\15
       iv Johan Daniel Wolf, bp. 18 February 1732, confirmed 1747,
          sponsors Johan Daniel Meyer and Anna Catherina.
        v Johan George Wolf, bp. 10 February 1734, confirmed 1748,
          sponsors George Becker and Anna Margaretha Becker.
       vi Anna Margaretha Wolf, born 7 January 1736, sponsors Johan
          Jacoob Frey and Anna Margaretha Becker.
      vii Eva Elisabetha, born 15 January 1738.
     viii Anna Margaretha Wolf, born 28 December 1739, sponsors
          Jacob Freyel and Anna Margaretha.
       ix Maria Barbara Wolf, born 19 April 1741, sponsors Maria
          Barbara Martel and George Michael Stoll. Confirmed at Host
          Church 1753.
        x Maria Catherina Wolf, b. 4 September 1744.

In order to reinforce the preceding evidence that Peter, Daniel and Frederick are indeed the Wolfs whose names appear on the named ship's lists an analysis of signatures has been undertaken.

ANALYSIS OF SIGNATURES

Signature of Peter Wolf on Ship List 149C.

Signature of Peter Wolf on his will(original).

Signature of Peter Wolf as transcribed into Will Book GM-2, 173, Frederick County, MD. (This signature shows that the recorders intent was to duplicate the original signature when he made the entry into the will book.)

Signature of Daniel Wolf on Ship List 174C.

Signature of Daniel Wolf as transcribed into Deed Book WR-20, 430, Frederick County, MD.

Signature of Frederick Wolf on Ship List 149C.

Signature of Frederick Wolf on his will (original).

A comparison of the known original signatures shows clearly that Peter, Daniel and Frederick are the Wolfs appearing on the specified ship lists. Although the deed book signature of Daniel is a transcription and not original, it is apparent that the recorder made every effort to duplicate the original signature. It would thus appear that the identification of Daniel is realistic and accurate.

Although circumstantial, the preceding factual information leads to a reasonable conclusion that Peter, Daniel and Frederick were brothers and sons of Jacob and Anna Margaretha Wolf.

NOTES AND REFERENCES

1. Frederick County, MD Land Records, Book WR4, 556.
2. Ibid., RP1, 50.
3. Frederick County, MD Register of Wills, Book GM-2, 173.
4. Maryland State Archives, Original Wills, Box 10.
5. Ibid., Original Administration Bonds, Box 3.
6. Pennsylvania Land Records, Survey Book D-84, 23.
7. Ibid., Patent Book AA-12, 31.
8. Pennsylvania Archives, Third Series, Volume XVIII, 3-814.
9. Washington County, MD Land Records, Book F, 189.
10. Ibid., Book S, 211.
11. Montgomery County, OH, Will Book A, 111.
12. Ibid., Land Records, Book B, 345.
13. Ibid., Will Book A, 95.
14. Maryland State Archives,Inventories, Volume C, 484.
15. "Early Lutheran Baptisms and Marriages in Southeastern Pennsylvania, The Records of Rev. John Casper Stoever from 1730 to 1779" (Genealogical Publishing Co., Inc., Baltimore, 1982.
16. Montgomery County, OH, Will Book A, 111, except as otherwise identified.
17. Baptismal Records, St. John's Host United Church of Christ, Bernville, PA 19506.
18. Klopp's Church (now St. Paul's United Church of Christ), Bethel Township, Lebanon County, PA.
19. "The Hochstadt Origins of Some of the Early Settlers at Host Church", Annette K. Burgert, 691 Weavertown Rd., Myerstown PA, 17067, March, 1977. Because of the excellence of this research and its importance to this genealogy, it is felt desirable to reproduce here a portion of the Preface of this publication.
"Since 1977 marks the 250th anniversary of the founding of Host Church, it would be an appropiate time to pay tribute to the early settlers there by finding and recording the information of the founding families.
The compiler has a deep interest in the early history of this church, descending from four of the early families found in the early

records, Leiss, Meyer, Gerhart and Dundore. From the information supplied by Dr. Fritz Braun in the letter to Mrs. Marie Graeff, mentioned on page 79 of the recently published History of St. John's (Host) Church, it appeared that the Meyer family resided in the Hochstadt area in the Palatinate before coming to Pennsylvania. Finding this evidence resulted in the decision to search the Oberhoch-stadt-Niederhochstadt records for further information on this family. This led to the discovry of the origins of many other early settlers from the same area; more tha 25 of the names mentioned in the Host Church record prior to 1760 were also found in th Oberhochstadt-Niederhochstadt records.

Since finding the place of origin in Germany is one of the most difficult tasks facing a family researcher, and knowing of these difficulties from my own research, I would like to make this information available to other researchers tracing these early families at Host.

Oberhochstadt and Niederhochstadt are two small villages located near Landau in Rheinland-Pfalz. The emigration from these villages appears to have started in 1732, although there may have been earlier emigrants from the area. The emigration continued over a period of more than 20 years and was large in proportion to the population of the villages. An interesting fact about this particular migration is the large number of emigrants from this area that can be found mentioned in the Host Church record. Contrary to other migratory patterns, where large groups came on the same ship but then settled in wide spread areas in Pennsylvania, these immigrants came a few at a time on several ships, but most seem to have settled, at least temporarily, near Host Church.

The church record at Niederhochstadt starts in 1708 and many of the early Oberhochstadt records are entered in this book. There are gaps in the records; in the death records ther are no entries from March 1712 to 1729. Marriages are recorded for the years 1708 to 1716, then skip to 1730. The church record at Oberhochstadt starts with a few baptisms for the period 1727-1729; under the baptism of a child in 1729 is the following notation: "this child was baptised at the new church in Oberhochstadt". The regular record appears to start in 1730."

20. Oberhochstadt Church records.

21. Strassburger and Hinke, "Pennsylvania German Pioneers", Volume 1.

22. Summer Hill records, Schuylkill County, PA.

16

CHAPTER 3

SECOND GENERATION

2 - JACOB(2) WOLF [Daniel(1)]

Jacob Wolf was the son of Daniel and Maria Elizabeth Wolf.\7 He was born 8 September 1770 and died 29 September 1851.\1 No documentation has been found to identify his place of birth but it undoubtedly was Berks County, PA as his father was taxed in Bethel Township of that county from 1768 through 1784.\2 He presumably went to Frederick County, MD in 1784 with the family when his father, Daniel, purchased the property of his brother Peter Wolf.\3 In the 1790 Federal Census of Frederick County he appears as M over 16 and in 1800 as M 26-45 with the Daniel Wolf family. He married Susannah Smith in Frederick County, MD, license issued 5 June 1801.\4

Although no place of residence after the marriage has been established, Jacob and Susannah probably lived in Frederick County until 1806/07 when an emigration to Ohio was apparently planned, accompanying Frederick Wolf (Daniel's brother) and his family. Frederick sold his Washington County, MD property 14 April 1806\5 and apparently Daniel and his family left Frederick County and went to Washington County to join the Frederick Wolf family in the trip to Ohio. However, Daniel died intestate in Washington County in 1807, delaying the family's leaving for Ohio until after the settlement of Daniel's estate for which sons Jacob and Frederick were administrators.\6 Final distribution by Jacob and Frederick was made 6 October 1807.\7

Land and census records show that after the settlement of Daniel's estate his widow, Elizabeth, along with son Jacob, her three married daughters (two married and one widowed) and their families emigrated to German Township, Montgomery County, OH. Son Frederick remained in Washington County, MD appearing in the 1810 through 1850 censuses of that county.\8 Jacob, his mother Elizabeth and his sister Christina's husband Abraham Paulus appear in the Montgomery County 1810 tax list along with Frederick Wolf and his sons Frederick Jr. and Phillip. Elizabeth's other two daughters, with their families, were living on the property purchased by their mother in 1810.

30 August 1810 Jacob purchased from Frederick and Susannah Foutz for 200 dollars a tract of 100 acres on Twin Creek, German Township, Montgomery County, OH described as part of the northwest quarter of Section No. 7, Township 3, of Range 4 East Quarter granted to Frederick Foutz 15 March 1809. The description was: Beginning at the northwest corner of the quarter and running with the section line north 85 deg east 24 chains and 84 links, then running south 5 deg east 40 chains and 25 links to yhe quarter section line, then with the quarter section line south 85 deg west 24 chains and 84 links to the section line, then with the line north 5 deg west to the beginning. The deed was entered 18 September 1810 and recorded 15 October 1810.\9 The farm lies on the north side of OH Route 725 and is adjacent to and on the east side of Preble County Line Road. A road that previously ran along the east side of the property between Jacob and Frecerick Foutz (from whom he bought the property) is no longer in existence.

Jacob and Susannah lived on this property until his death. He died 29 September 1851 and is buried in Old German Cemetery, German Township, Montgomery County, OH. The tombstone inscription says Jacob

17

was 81 years, 21 days at death. Jacob died intestate and 13 December 1851, George W. Moyer, married to Jacob's daughter Elizabeth, was appointed administrator.\10 George W. Moyer, Jacob Lindenmuth and William R. Emrick, all of Montgomery County, posted bond of $400. 26 December George Moyer advertised in the "Western Emporium" his appointment as administrator of the estate of "Jacob Wolf, late of Montgomery County, Ohio, deceased".

An inventory and appraisal of the estate and property of Jacob was made and submitted 10 January 1852 by Frederick Oldfather, Henry Witters and John Willson after "We first set off to Susan Wolf his widow the following property without appraisal the same as directed by statute":\10

    Two spinning wheels
    One reel
    One tin plate stove
    One large Bible and other books
    One cow
    Two bedsteads and beding
    Lot of cooking utensils
    One table
    Six chairs
    Six knives and forks
    Six plates tea cups and saucers spoons etc.

    Signed 10 January 1852
    Frederick Oldfather)
    Henry Witters   )Appraisers
    John Willson   )

The appraisal was as follows:

1 lot of old iron	$ .11
11 harrow teeth	.31
2 chains	.10
1 hammar	.371/2
Mattock and hoe	.50
1 axe	.25
Shovel and spade	.371/2
Lot of leather	.50
1 tub	.05
1 table	.02
1 grindstone	.371/2
3 tubs	.10
Dutch oven and pot	.121/2
Handsaw and hoop	.25
Dutch oven	.10
1 basket	.50
1 churn	.05
1 meat tub	1.00
2 lard stands	.20
1 churn	1.50
Pinchers bridlebit and iron	.25
1 drawing knife	.25
1 bedstead	.25
1 pair steelyards	.30
2 bags	.20
1 lantern	.05
1 lot of iron	.20
Flax hackle	.50

```
1 pair cards                                                       .10
Coffee mill and tea kettle                                         .02
1 chest                                                            .25
1 bed cord                                                         .15
1 barrel and vinegar                                              3.50
1 side saddle                                                     3.00
2 chairs                                                           .25
1 clock                                                           2.50
1 corner cupboard                                                 5.00
1 bureau                                                          3.50
1 steel                                                            .371/2
1 log chain                                                       2.00
1 kettle                                                          1.00
Do kettle                                                         1.00
1 copper kettle                                                   7.00
2 barrels                                                          .371/2
1 wheel barrow                                                     .371/2
Cutting box and flail                                              .371/2
1 half bushel measure                                              .25
1 hogs head                                                        .20
1 wheat fan                                                       2.00
Rasp and gimlet                                                    .25
1 calf                                                             .25
68 1/2 bushels of wheat at 50 cts. per bushel                    34.25
13 bush of rye at 40 cts.                                         5.20
21 bush of oats at 18 cts.                                        3.78
102 bu corn at 20 cts.                                           20.40
3 1/3 acres of wheat in the ground delivered in the bushel       23.00
3 1/2 acres do                                                   19.00
1/3 of 5 1/2 acres of rye in the ground delivered in the bu       5.00
Lot of hay                                                        9.00
Watter pot and chain                                               .15
Dough tray                                                         .37
Fat stand                                                          .05
                                                               -------
10 January 1852              Total                             $163.45
```

The following are the debts etc. owing to said estate:
One note on Daniel S. Witters for $40 dated Aug 27th
1850 due one day after date   40.00
One note on Ephraim Williams for $10 dated Sept
20th 1850 due 3 months after date   10.00
Note on Daniel S. Witters for $14.50 dated Jan
10th 1850 due one day after date   14.50
Note on Frederick Wolf for $30.00 dated Jan 26th
1833 due from date. Very doubtful   30.00
Note of bail on Frederick Wolf for $8.08 dated Aug
1st 1834 due Aug 1st 1835. Very doubtful   8.08
Receipt on James M. Grimes docket against
Frederick Wolf for $27.20 dated June 20th 1828.
Very doubtful   27.20

Cash on hand   59.29

Frederick Oldfather)
Henry Witters   ) Appraisers
John Willson   )

Schedule

The following is a schedule of property etc.
belonging to the estate of Jacob Wolf deceased
set off by the undersigned for the support of
Susan Wolf his widow:

2 hogs at $6.00	12.00
Lot of potatoes	1.00
12 bushels of wheat at 50 cts. per bushel	6.00
50 bushels of corn at 20 cts. per bushel	10.00
Half ton of hay	3.00
$20.00 in cash	20.00

	52.00

January 10th 1852   John Willson   )
                          Frederick Oldfather) Appraisers
                          Henry Witters   )

"A bill of the property sold by George W. Moyer administrator of the
estate of Jacob Wolf, deceased, at public vendue, January the 16th
1852."

David Bear	1 lot of old irons	.01
Daniel S. Witters	11 harrow teeth	.31
Jacob Longman	2 chains	.03
Henry Witters	1 hammar	.20
Christian Cline	Mattock and hoe	.50
Daniel S. Witters	Dung hook	.10
Peter Moyer	1 axe	.09
Daniel S. Witters	Lot of leather	.51
	1 tub taken by the widow	
	at appraisement	.05
Jacob Longman	1 table	.03
John Burr	Grindstone	.05
	3 tubs taken by the widow	
	at appraisement	.10
Henry Witters	Dutch oven, fat saw and hoop	.10
Henry Witters	Dutch oven and basket	.54
	Taken by the widow at appraisement	
	1 churn	.05
	1 meat tub	1.00
	2 lard stands	.20
	1 churn	1.50
Daniel S. Witters	Pinchers, bridlebit and iron	.35
David Longman	Drawing knife	.16
Daniel S. Witters	1 bedstead and steelyards	.71
	2 bags taken by the widow at	
	appraisement	.20
	also lantern	.05
Jacob Moore	Lot of irons	.53
Daniel S. Witters	Flax hackle	.26
Ezra Lantis	1 pair cards	.12
Joseph Willson	Coffee mill, tea kettle and chest	.40
Ephraim Williams	Bed cord	.20
David S. Smith	Barrel and vinegar	2.76
Susan Wolf	One side saddle	3.00
Ephraim Williams	2 chairs	.25
SusanWolf	One clock	1.50
	Corner cupboard taken by the	

	widow at appraisement	5.00
	Also bureau	3.50
	And steel	.371/2
Daniel S. Witters	Log chain	1.85
	One kettle taken by the	
	widow at appraisement	1.00
Jacob Lindenmuth	1 kettle	1.45
Catharine Fouts	Copper kettle	7.31
David Bear	2 barrels	.18
Phillip Izor	Wheel barrow	.35
Wm. Wright	Cutting box and flail	.10
Daniel S. Witters	Half bushel	.21
Ephraim Williams	1 Hogshead	.37
Samuel Brandenburg	Wheat fan	.78
Peter Moyes	Rasp and gimlet	.17
	1 calf taken by the widow	
	at appraisement	.75
Ephraim Williams	25 bushels wheat at .56	14.00
David Fisher	25 bushels do at .55	13.75
David Fisher	18 1/2 bush wheat at .55 1/2	10.27
Jacob Duckwalt	13 bush rye at .39	5.07
Daniel S. Witters	13 oats bush at .18	2.34
	8 bu oats taken by the widow	
	at appraisement .18 per bu	1.44
Cornelius Brown	25 bushels corn at .20 per bu	5.00
Robert Mathews	25 bushels corn at .20	5.00
David S. Smith	25 bush corn at .19	4.75
Michael Lindenmuth	27 bu corn at .20	5.40
Frederick Oldfather	Three 1/3 acres of wheat in ground	20.30
Frederick Oldfather	Do 3 1/2 acres of wheat in ground	13.85
Daniel S. Witter	One third of 5 1/2 acres of rye	3.15
David Longman	Lot of hay	8.65
Alferd Neff	Water pot and chain	.05
	Dough tray taken by the widow	
	at appraisement	.37
Robert Mathews	Fat stand	.05

		$152.90

This bill is correct

Jan. 16th 1852   John Willson Clerk of Sale

Sworn to and subscribed by George W. Moyer, Administrator of the estate of Jacob Wolf , deceased, the 28th day of January 1852.

The first account of the estate settlement was made by George Moyer 8 August 1853 and the final account 26 July 1854 at which time it was sworn to and subscribed. The final account was as follows:\10

George W. Moyer Administrator on the estate of Jacob Wolf deceased in account with said estate on final settlement with the court,

To balance in my hands as Administrator on former
    settlement with the court made August 8, 1853
    See record P No. 1 Pages 223 $124.80
To cash received on notes of Frederick Wolf   48.00

                    Amount $172.80

Money Paid

By cash paid George Brown Clerk Costs No. 1 $ 2.99
  "   "   Extra allowance to Administrator   10.00
  "   "   Probate Court fees this settlement   2.50

                    Amount of credits   15.49

          Balance in Administrators hands $157.51

     In the latter part of 1852 Jacob's 100 acre property purchased in
1810 was sold as part of the estate settlement. The following actions
were taken:\11
     1- 7 June 1852- As a result of an action by Moses R. Walker, a
merchant of Preble County, against Frederick Wolf for 200 dollars
damages, a writ of attachment on lands of Frederick Wolf was issued in
Montgomery County Court.
     8 June 1852- The sheriff attached property described by meets
and bounds and as being the undivided one equal eighth of a property
of 100 acres. The description identifies this property as the Jacob
Wolf home property acquired in 1810. Judgement was issued against
Frederick Wolf for $105.40 and $13.18 costs.
     27 August 1853- The property (Frederick's share) was sold at
public sale to Michael Miller for $133.34.
     2- 7 September 1852- Jacob Wolf of Carrol County, IN and Barbara
his wife sold to Michael Miller of Preble County, OH for $200 property
described as all of the interest of Jacob Wolf in land formerly
belonging to Jacob Wolf in German Township, Montgomery County, OH, it
being the intent to convey all the interest of Jacob and Barbara in
the tract of land belonging to Jacob Wolf Sr., in which Jacob Wolf Sr.
resided at the time of his death, the whole tract containing 100
acres. Description given.
     Received 3 October 1853, recorded 24 October 1853.
     3- 15 September 1852- Susan Wolf, widow of Jacob Wolf deceased,
of Montgomery County, OH - George Moyer and Elizabeth his wife of
Montgomery County, OH - John Montel and Susan his wife of
Cosiusko(sic) County, IN - Ephraim Williams and Christiana his wife
and Daniel S. Witters and Catharine his wife of Montgomery County, OH,
heirs at law to the estate of Jacob Wolf deceased, sold to Michael
Miller of Preble County, OH for $1600 property described as the entire
dowry claim of Susan Wolf and the claim of the grantors as embracing
one half of the desscribed tract, the whole tract containing 100
acres, excepting one half acre sold off the tract for a graveyard and
church. Description given.
     Received 3 October 1853, recorded 22 October 1853.
     4- 13 October 1852- Daniel Wolf and Anna his wife of Elkhart
County, IN sold to Michael Miller for $200 part of the property which
description identifies it as the property of Daniel's deceased father
Jacob Wolf, the whole tract containing 99 1/2 acrs. The deed was
executed in Elkhart County, IN.
     Received 30 October 1853, recorded   October 1853.
     5- 24 December 1852- George Shroyer and Sarah his wife of Kos-
ciusko County, IN sold to Michael Miller for $150 part of the property
which description identifies it as the property of Sarah's deceased
father Jacob Wolf, the whole tract containing 99 1/2 acres. The deed
was executed in Kosciusko County, IN.
     Received 3 October 1853, recorded 25 October 1853.

     Jacob's widow, Susanna Smith was born 1 February 1781 and died 8

November 1866.\12 She is buried in Syracuse Cemetery, Turkey Creek Township, Kosciusko County, IN. After Jacob's death Susanna apparently went to live with her daughter, Sarah, who married George Shroyer, as she is listed with that family in the 1860 Federal Census, Plain Township, Kosciusko County, IN; Susan Wolf, aged 79, a widow. No place of birth is specified.

Children of Jacob and Susanna (Smith) Wolf were as follows:\11

+ 7   i Frederick Wolf, born 29 June 1802
+ 8   ii Elizabeth Wolf, born 26 January 1805
+ 9 iii Susan Wolf, born 24 March 1806
+ 10   iv Jacob Wolf Jr., born 10 October 1807
+ 11   v Sarah Wolf, born 5 January 1810
+ 12   vi Daniel Wolf, born c 1815
+ 13 vii Catharine Wolf, born c 1818
+ 14 viii Christina Wolf, born c 1822

3 - CATHARINE(2) WOLF [Daniel(1)]

Catharine Wolf was the daughter of Daniel and Maria Elizabeth Wolf.\7 She probably was born between 1770 and 1773.\13 Although no documentation has been found to identify her place of birth, it undoubtedly was Berks County, PA as her father was taxed in Bethel Township of that county from 1768 through 1784.\2 She presumably went to Frederick County, MD in 1784 with the family when her father, Daniel, purchased the property of his brother, Peter Wolf.\3 In the 1790 Federal Census of Frederick County she is one of four females listed in the Daniel Wolf household along with her mother and two sisters. Some time before 1800 she married Frederick Kimmerling.\17 As no marriage license has been found to have been issued, the marriage was probably authorized by publishing church bans and held in Frederick County, MD. Catharine died in Montgomery County, OH about 1840.\18 Her place of burial is unknown.

Frederick Kimmerling was born 21 August 1763\15 in Pennsylvania.\16 His parents are not known. The first documentation of Frederick is a bill of sale made 16 March 1799 and recorded in Frederick County, MD.\14 Frederick sold to Christian Shealy for "96 pounds, five shillings current money" what appears to be all of his personal property. Sold were "two black cows, one red and white spotted cow, five head sheep, three feather beds with the bedsteads, one walnut table two poplar chests, one walnut chest, three pewter dishes, eighteen pewter plates, three iron potts, one iron kittle, two pair blacksmith bellows, two large anvils, one vise, one iron horn, one mandrel, two sledge hammers, three hand hammers, five small hammers, eight pair tongs, two spinning wheels, one big wheel, one jack reel, one tin plate stove, two washing tubs, one dutch oven, five bucketts, one teakittle". From this listing of items sold it would appear that Frederick was a blacksmith with a well established business and household. (He apparently did not own the property where he lived at the time as no record of ownership of such property has been found.)

This disposal of his personal property is somewhat puzzling. It would seem possible that he was planning to leave the area, possibly to go to Ohio, an emigration subsequently made in 1808. However, 14 December 1799 he purchased in Frederick County, MD, from John Clabaugh for "350 pounds current money" a parcel of 35 acres described as "part of a tract of lands called "Brookes Discovery on the Rich Lands" beginning for said part hereby bargained and sold at the beginning of a tract or parcel of land containing one hundred and five acres conveyed to William Ferguson by Samuel Ferguson the eighth day of May

one thousand seven hundred and eighty nine and running thence S 59 deg
E 20 perches, S 74 deg E 52 perches, N 36 deg E 3 perches, S 56 1/2
deg E 46 perches and 4 ft, S 38 deg W 36 perches, N 24 deg W 3
perches, W 62 perches, N 49 deg W 52 perches, then by a straight line
to the beginning".\19 This property has not been located but apparently in 1800 was in the Taneytown No. (5) Election District of Frederick County. His household is listed in that district in the 1800
census of Frederick County, showing 1 M 26-45, 1 M 16-26, 1 F 26-45,
and 1 F 0-10. It is possible that the M 16-26 is Frederick Wolf,
brother of his wife Catharine.\20

Apparently the title to this property was not clear as 16 August
1802 a deed was issued to Frederick Kimmerling by Hugh Ferguson of
Ohio County, VA and William Ferguson of Frederick County, MD for the
same property. Price was five pounds current money.\21 Frederick sold
this property 21 April 1807 to Abraham Hill of Frederick County for
300 pounds current money.\22 On the same day Frederick's wife
Catharine appeared and relinquished her right of dower in the property.

This sale was undoubtedly made in preparation for the emigration
to Ohio with the Frederick and Daniel Wolf (brothers) families. The
History of Montgomery County, OH (1822) says "An early immigrant to
German Township from Frederick County, MD was Frederick Kimmerling. He
resided in Frederick County, MD before coming to Ohio in 1808. His
wife and four children located with him in German Township, Montgomery
County, OH". The Frederick Kimmerling family, along with his mother-in
-law Maria Elizabeth Wolf and the families of three of the other
children of Daniel and Maria Elizabeth - Jacob and Susanna Wolf,
Abraham and Christina Wolf Paulus, and Elizabeth Wolf Hahn, widow of
Leonard Hahn all went to German Township, Montgomery County, OH after
Daniel's death in 1807. It is thought that when Daniel died in Washington County, MD the family was on their way from Frederick County,
MD to Ohio. Son Frederick remained in Washington County, MD, engaging
in the blacksmith trade and died there in 1851.

The Kimmerling family resided on the property purchased by Maria
Elizabeth Wolf in 1810. She willed to her daughter Catharine Kimmerling "50 acres of land the same on where the said Frederick Kimmerling
resides".\23 Title was acquired by her grandsons Frederick Jr. and
Abraham Kimmerling in 1841.\24 It was still in Kimmerling possession
in 1883.\25 The family appears in the 1820 census in German Township,
Montgomery County, OH listed as Frederick Kimmel with 1 M 45 & up, 1 M
16-26, 1 M 16-18, 2 M 10-16 and 1 F 45 & up. The family does not
appear in the 1830 census but in 1840 is listed as the family of
Frederick Kimmerling with 1 M 70-80, 1 M 30-40, 1 M 5-10, 1 F 30-40
and 1 F 5-10. In 1850 Frederick is living with his son, Frederick Jr.,
and his family. He is listed as Frederick Kimmerling, age 86, born in
Pennsylvania.\16

Frederick died 2 August 1851, probably in German Township,
Montgomery County, OH. His tombstone is located, with others of the
family in Germantown Cemetery, German Township, Montgomery County,
OH.\26 Catharine died about 1840.\27 It is not known where she is
buried.

The Kimmerlings belonged to the Lutheran congregation in Germantown.\25

Children of Frederick and Catharine (Wolf) Kimmerling were as
follows:\28

   15   i Daughter, born ca 1800 in Frederick County, MD\17
+ 16   ii Frederick Kimmerling Jr.\18 born 2 February 1804
   17 iii Abraham Kimmerling\18 born 1800-1808 in Frederick County,

MD
18   iv Son, born 1800-1808 in Frederick County, MD\29
19   v Son, born 1808-1810 in Montgomery County, OH

4 - ELIZABETH(2) WOLF [Daniel(1)]

Elizabeth Wolf was the daughter of Daniel and Maria Elizabeth Wolf.\7 She was born 12 November 1773\30 in Pennsylvania\16, undoubtedly Berks County as her father was taxed in Bethel Township of that county from 1768 through 1784.\2 She presumably went to Frederick County, MD in 1784 with the family when her father, Daniel, purchased the property of his brother, Peter Wolf.\3 In the 1790 Federal Census of Frederick County she is one of four females listed in the Daniel Wolf household along with her mother and two sisters. About 1795 she married Leonard Hahn.\19 As no marriage license has been found to have been issued, the marriage was probably authorized by publishing church bans and held in Frederick County, MD.

Leonard Hahn was the son of Ludwick and Catrine Hahn. In the will of his father, made 9 April 1808 and filed for probate 12 April 1813, Leonard is mentioned as a deceased son.\31 Heirs of Leonard were specifically excluded from benefits under the will.

In 1797 Leonard purchased from Michael Springer for 118 pounds Lot Number 16 in Shields' Addition to Emmitsburg, Frederick County, MD. The deed was executed 3 April 1797 and recorded 11 April.\32 The 1800 census for Frederick County shows a Leonard Hahn family as 1 M 26-45, 1 M 0-10, 1 F 26-45 and 2 F 0-10, these being Leonard, wife Elizabeth, son Jacob, and daughters Catherine and Elizabeth. In 1800 Leonard sold the Emmitsburg property and his personal property to his father-in-law Daniel Wolf. A record of sale from Leonard Hawn to Daniel Wolf, made 11 April 1800 and recorded 15 April, shows a consideration of 50 pounds for two cows, two sheep, five hogs, two bedsteads and bedding, one chest and all other household and kitchen furniture.\33 Adeed made 12 April 1800 and recorded 15 April shows a consideration of 80 pounds for a certain lot of ground in Shields' Addition to Emmitsburg, being a front lot known as Number 16.\34 As later that year Daniel sold his property acquired in 1784 it is probable that Daniel, with his wife and one son, moved to the Emmitsburg property at that time. It could be suggested that Leonard might have been incapacitated or in ill health, causing this move.

Leonard died intestate 1805/1806. Robert L. Annan was appointed administrator of the estate. His First Account was filed 27 February 1806\35 and the Final Account 12 February 1807.\36 Assets and expenses of the estate were equal, amounting to L81:15:10. The only significant payment was to Frederick Wolf for L6:9:4 1/2.

Elizabeth and her children along with her mother, widowed Maria Elizabeth Wolf and the families of three of the other children of Daniel and Maria Elizabeth - Frederick and Catharine Kimmerling, Jacob and Susanna Wolf, and Abraham and Christina Paulus all went to German Township, Montgomery County, OH after after her father Daniel's death in 1807. Son Frederick remained in Washington County, MD, engaging in the Blacksmith trade.

Widowed Elizabeth Wolf Hahn resided on the property purchased by her mother in German Township, Montgomery County, OH in 1810. The family appears in the 1820 Federal Census of that township listed as Elizabeth Hon, head with 1 F 45 & up, 2 M 16-18, 1 F 16-26 and 1 F 10-16. The family doesn't appear again until the 1850 census, listed as Elizabeth Haun 76 born in PA, Catharine Haun 53 born in MD, Jacob Haun 50 born in MD and Rachel Sharred 15 born in OH. Rachel was the daughter of Mary Hahn, daughter of Leonard and Elizabeth, who had married Joel Sharrit.

Elizabeth's mother Maria Elizabeth Wolf, widow of Daniel, willed to Elizabeth in 1814 "30 acres of land the same on which she at present resides".\23 The other 50 acres of the property was willed to Catharine, wife of Frederick Kimmerling. Elizabeth apparently died 1852/1853 as 26 March 1853 her heirs sold this property to Asher Davis for $1000.\37 The deed was recorded 17 August 1854. The sale of this property was advertised as follows in the Western Emporium, Thursday 14 October 1852, Germantown, OH:

Land for Sale

The undersigned offers at private sale, a 30 acre lot of land, lying about a mile Northeast of Germantown, between the farms of John C. Ayres and F. Kimmerling, belonging to the heirs of Elizabeth Hohn, deceased. About 20 acres of the lot is cleared, and the remainder good wood land. It contains a log house and a stable with a threshing floor, a good well, and a first -rate orchard - mostly grafted fruit.

TERMS-$1200: $300 cash in hand, and the remainder in one year. Any one wishing to purchase said lot will call on the subscriber, one mile West of Miamisburg.   D. Hohn

It is not known where Elizabeth Hahn is buried.

Children of Leonard and Elizabeth (Wolf) Hahn were as follows:\37

20   i Catherine Hahn, born 7 August 1795 in Frederick County, MD, died 25 February 1866 in Montgomery County, OH. Buried in Germantown Cemetery, Germantown, Montgomery County, OH. Did not marry.

+ 21 ii Elizabeth Hahn, born 16 January 1800. *

22 iii Jacob Hahn, born 16 April 1800 * in Frederick County MD, died 20 May 1863 in Montgomery County, OH. Buried in Germantown Cemetery, Germantown, Montgomery County, OH Did not marry.

+ 23 iv Daniel Hahn, born 3 October 1801.

+ 24   v Mary Hahn, born 1802/1806.

*These dates were read from cemetary tombstones and one or both have obviously been misread.

5 - FREDERICK(2) WOLF [Daniel(1)]

Frederick Wolf was the son of Daniel and Maria Elizabeth Wolf.\7 He was born 6 March 1776 and died 6 August 1853.\38 His exact place of birth is not known but it was probably Bethel Township, Berks County, PA as the 1800 Federal Census of Washington County, MD identifies his place of birth as Pennsylvania and his father was taxed in Bethel Township of Berks County from 1768 through 1784.\2 He presumably went to Frederick County, MD in 1784 with the family when his father, Daniel, purchased the property of his brother, Peter Wolf.\3 In the 1790 Federal Census of Frederick County he appears in the Daniel Wolf family as M under 16. In 1800 it is felt he was living with his brother-in-law, Frederick Kimmerling, near Taneytown, (then) Frederick County, MD appearing as M 16-26 in that census. He married Magdalene Smith in Washington County, MD, license issued 27 January 1801.\39 Magdalene was born 6 June 1784 and died 9 February 1844\40 in Washington County, MD. Magdalene was the daughter of Yost/Joseph and Margaret Schmidt/Smith.\41 Her mother is thought to have been Margaret Dennis, daughter of Valentine and Barberry Dennis.

Frederick's first land acquisition was 14 April 1804 when he purchased Lot Number 40 in Boonsboro, Washington County, MD from

26

Michael Pickenpaw for "120 pounds current money". The deed was recorded 7 June 1804.\42 This lot was located on Larkin Avenue running from Main Street to Center Street. In the deed Frederick is described as "blacksmith of Washington County". The property was part of a tract called Fellowship. He sold this property 25 May 1815 to the heirs of Frederick Welty for $1100.\43 His wife Magdalene released her dower rights.

During this period Frederick's father, Daniel, died intestate in Washington County in 1807, apparently on his way to German Township, Montgomery County, OH, with all of his family except Frederick, to join his (Daniel's) brother Frederick who, with his family, including married sons and daughters, had gone to Ohio about 1806. Frederick and his brother Jacob were appointed administrators of their father's estate.\6 The estate had been settled by 7 October 1807 when final distribution was made\7 except for a bond in the amount of 50 pounds given by John Weaver for the purchase of Daniel's Emmitsburg property. Frederick acted as "Attorney for the heirs of Daniel Wolf" for the subsequent public sale of the property. He purchased and then resold the property for the heirs 27 April 1811.\44

Frederick's widowed mother, Maria Elizabeth, with her son Jacob, widowed daughter Elizabeth Hahn, and married daughters Catharine Kimmerling and Christina Paulus with their families continued the trip to Montgomery County, OH about 1808/1809 giving Frederick the authority to act as their attorney as evidenced by an instrument 18 April 1810 giving Frederick the authority to act as their attorney. They were all described as "being of Montgomery County, state of Ohio in German Township".

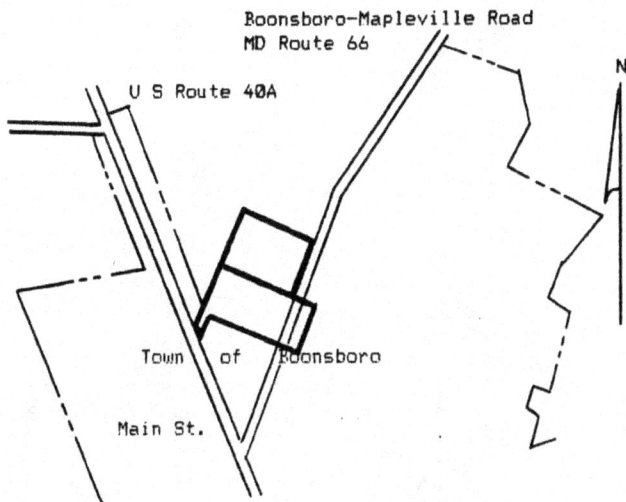

Property of Frederick Wolf, 1814 and 1826 to 1846, in Washington County, MD, near Boonsboro (now within the town limits of Boonsboro). Washington County Land Records, Book Z, 526 and Book HH, 893.

Prior to selling his Boonsboro lot (Number 40) in 1815 Frederick had purchased on 4 May 1814 for $516.50 a tract of six acres, 75 perches from Daniel Stonesifer, recorded 21 May 1814.\45 This property was on the outskirts of Boonsboro and was described as being part of a tract called Iron Field, with the description beginning at a stone in the wagon road leading from the Peter Johns (Schang) old plantation to Boonsberry (sic). A metes and bounds description was given.

He purchased a second tract, adjacent to the Stonesifer tract, 28 March 1826 from Mathias Shaffner for $1,037.50, recorded the same day.\46 It was described as part of a tract called Nelson's Folly, granted Robert Turner for 575 acres, adjacent to the Turnpike (Hagerstown) Road on the Northeast side. It contained nine acres, 64 perches. A metes and bounds description was given.

Frederick lived on this property until his wife Magdalene died in 1844 and then sold both tracts 31 January 1846 to his son-in-law Jacob Blecher, married to daughter Tracy, for $1,600, recorded the same day.\47 He appears as a family head in Washington County Federal Census records from 1810 through 1840. In 1840 his household apparently consisted of Frederick and Magdalene, sons Simon and Jacob, daughter Margaret Ann and granddaughter Elizabeth Stinger. In 1850 he appears in the household of his son Simon, aged 74 and born in Pennsylvania. Also appearing in this household, in addition to Simon's family, is Elizabeth C. Stinger, aged 13, the daughter of Frederick's deceased daughter Sarah, who had married John Stinger.

Frederick was a blacksmith, possibly learning this trade from his brother-in-law Frederick Kimmerling, with whom he is thought to have been living in 1800, or from another Frederick Wolf, a relative. Land records show that a Frederick Wolf, blacksmith, purchased Lot Number 10 in Boonsboro 24 November 1792\48 selling it to Jacob Piper, blacksmith, 12 October 1799.\49 The deed shows that this Frederick's wife was named Barbara who renounced her dower rights. This Frederick could be either Daniel's brother Frederick or Frederick's son, both of whom had wives named Barbara. The Bast "History of Boonsboro" says that a Mr. Wolf was the first blacksmith in Boonsboro followed by a Mr. Piper in 1795 and Henry Nyman in 1802. It then says that "Frederick Wolf had a shop on N. Main St." Frederick's son Simon was also a blacksmith, as was Simon's son Charles M. Wolf.

Frederick was apparently a man of some standing in the community. He, with William Good Jr., John Brantner and Jacob Summers, was appointed a commissioner to sell Lot Number 13 in Boonsboro, being part of the estate of Jane Short, mother of Alexander Kennedy and others. It was sold at public sale 21 January 1809, recorded 7 September 1812.\50 He also served as executor of the will of his father-in-law, Yost Schmidt who died in 1826.\51

Frederick died in 1853 and is buried in the old Reformed Church Cemetery in Boonsboro. His tombstone says "In Memory of Frederick Wolf who died August 6, 1853 aged 77 years and 5 months". His wife Magdalene preceded him in death and is buried in Lydia Shunk's Graveyard, established about 1740, which was restored in 1971 by the Boonsboro Historical Society. This graveyard was associated with a church variously known as Shunk's or Schang's Church. It was the earliest church in the Boonsboro area. Her tombstone says "In Memory of Magdalene Wolf wife of Frederick Wolf. Was born June 6, 1784 and departed this life Feb. 7, 1844 aged 59 years 8 months and 5 days. Was married 43 years and 8 days".

No documentation has been found of Frederick and Magdalene's children. Those listed are felt to be accurate but are based on circumstantial evidence which is felt to be substantial. Such evidence is Frederick's appearing, at age 74, in the household of Simon Wolf in the 1800 census for Washington County and the burial of Sarah Stinger and Tracy Blecher next to Magdalene in the Schang's Church Cemetery.

Children of Frederick and Magdalene (Schmidt) Wolf were as follows:

+ 25   i Daniel Wolf, born 18 January 1802
+ 26 ii Elizabeth Wolf, born about 1807
+ 27 iii Joseph Wolf, born 29 July 1809
+ 28 iv Tracy Wolf, born 28 September 1811
+ 29   v Sarah Wolf, born 1 August 1814
+ 30 vi Sophia Wolf, born about 1817
+ 31 vii Simon Wolf, born 6 January 1820
+ 32 viii Jacob Wolf, born 5 February 1823
+ 33 ix Margaret Ann Wolf, born 17 December 1825

6 - CHRISTINA(2) WOLF [Daniel(1)]
Christina Wolf was the daughter of Daniel and Maria Elizabeth Wolf.\7 She was born 13 April 1777.\30 (Her tombstone has been read as 13 February 1779, probably incorrectly due to the age.) She was undoubtedly born in Berks County, PA as her father was taxed in Bethel Township of that county from 1768 through 1784.\2 She presumably went to Frederick County, MD in 1784 when her father, Daniel, purchased the property of his brother Peter Wolf.\3 In the 1790 Federal Census for Frederick County she is one of four females listed in the Daniel Wolf household, along with her mother and two sisters. About 1800 she married Abraham Paulus.\19 As no marriage license has been found to have been issued, the marriage was probably authorized by publishing church bans and held in Frederick County, MD.

Abraham Paulus was born 2 November 1777\51 in Maryland.\52 His parents are not yet known. Abraham, Christina and their first two children undoubtedly lived in Frederick County, MD until leaving to emigrate to Ohio with the families of her father Daniel Wolf and Frederick Wolf Sr., Daniel's brother. Although Daniel died in Washington County, MD in 1807, on the way to Ohio, the trip continued after the settlement of the estate.

The first documentation of this family resulted from the settlement of her father's estate.\19 After arriving in Ohio, Abraham 23 March 1808 purchased from his wife's uncle, Frederick Wolf Sr., for $100 a tract of 50 acres in the Northeast Quarter of Section 8, Township 2, Range 5 East in German Township, Montgomery County, OH. This property is listed in the name of Abraham Paulus on the 1810 Tax List for German Township. They continued to live on this property until 2 March 1831 when they sold it to Isaac Thing for $750. Abraham purchased 160 acres west of Verona, Harrison Township, Preble County, OH in partnership with Daniel Sharrit, a cousin by marriage.

Christina died 25 September 1845 and Abraham 21 October 1851.\53 Both are buried in the Euphemia-Rose Lawn Cemetery in Lewisburg, Preble County, OH.

Children of Abraham and Christina (Wolf) Paulus were as follows:
+ 34   i Simeon Paulus, born 14 August 1803.
+ 35 ii Daniel Paulus, born 12 January 1807.
  36 iii Christina Paulus, born 19 December 1809 * near Germantown, German Township, Montgomery County, OH, died 28 November 1901 near Verona, Harrison Township, Preble County, OH.
  37 iv Lydia Paulus, born 27 February 1810 * near Germantown, German Township, Montgomery County, OH, died 12 October 1900 near Verona, Harrison Township, Preble County, OH.
        *One or both of these birth dates has obviously been

read incorrectly.

Neither Christina nor Lydia Paulus married. They remained on the old homestead in the Verona, OH area in the northeast corner of Preble County for the rest of their lives. As years passed portions of the farm were sold off, Lydia and Christina owning 59 acres in 1871. They lived in the original log house until their death. Both are buried in the Verona Cemetery.

+ 38   v Mary Paulus, born 25 December 1813.

NOTES AND REFERENCES

1. Tombstone in Old German Cemetery, German Township, Montgomery County, OH. Birthdate calculated from age at death.
2. Pennsylvania Archives, 3rd Series, Volume XVIII, 3-814.
3. Frederick County, MD Land Records, Book WR4, 556.
4. Ibid., Marriage License Index.
5. Washington County, MD, Land Records, Book F, 189.
6. Maryland State Archives, Administration Bonds, 294.
7. Washington County, MD , Accounts Distribution Book 1806-1816.
8. Federal Census, Washington County, MD.
9. Montgomery County, OH, Land Records, Book B, 344.
10. Ibid., Probate Court, Case Number 2432.
11. Ibid., Land Records.
12. Cemetery Tombstone, Syracuse Cemetery, Kosciusko County, IN
13. Catharine is the only one of the children of Daniel and Maria Elizabeth Wolf whose birth date is not known. As the other four children were born in 1770, 1773, 1776 and 1777, it would appear she was probably born 1770-1773.
14. Frederick County, MD, Land Records, Book WR18, 102.
15. Tombstone in Old German Cemetery, German Township, Montgomery County, OH.
16. 1850 Federal Census, German Township, Montgomery County, OH.
17. 1800 Federal Census, Frederick County, MD.
18. In 1841 the property willed to her by her mother was transferred to her two sons, Frederick Jr. and Abraham. The will had prohibited her from disposing of the property during her lifetime. At her death it was to go to her heirs.
19. Frederick County, MD, Land Records, Book WR19. 358.
20. Frederick Wolf has not otherwise been accounted for in the 1800 Federal Census. As he married in 1801 and subsequently became established as a blacksmith in Boonsboro, Washington County, MD he probably learned his trade from his brother-in-law, Frederick Kimmerling who, as shown previously, was apparently a blacksmith.
21. Frederick County, MD, Land Records, Book WR24, 60.
22. Ibid., Book WR31, 22.
23. Montgomery County, OH Register of Wills, Book A, 95.
24. Ibid., Court Records.
25. "Twin Valley, Its Settlement and Subsequent History 1798-1882". Reverend John P. Hentz, Dayton, OH, Christian Publishing House 1883, page 106.
26. In Germantown Cemetery there is an obelisk naming several members of the Kimmerling family, including Frederick Sr. In addition there is a stone for Frederick Sr. lying flat. Based on these facts it is felt that he was buried elsewhere and the stone lying flat was

probably moved to Germantown Cemetery and the obelisk installed for burials of the next generation

27. Montgomery County, OH, Court Records.

28. 1820 Federal Census, German Township, Montgomery County, OH except as otherwise noted.

29. History of Montgomery County, OH (1882) says "Frederick Kimmerling resided in Frederick County, MD before coming to Ohio in 1808. His wife and four children located with him in German Township, Montgomery County, OH".

30. Klopp's Church (now St. Paul's United Church of Christ), Bernville, PA 19506, Bethel Township, Lebanon County, PA.

31. Frederick County, MD, Register of Wills, Book RB1, 380.

32. Ibid., Land Records, Book 15, 237.

33. Ibid., Book WR19, 442.

34. Ibid., Book WR19, 443.

35. Ibid., Administration Accounts, Book RB1, 24.

36. Ibid., Book RB1, 173.

37. Montgomery County, OH, Land Records, Book DBX2, 43.

38. Tombstone in Reformed Church Cemetery, Boonsboro, Washington County, MD.

39. Washington County, MD, Marriage License Index.

40. Tombstone in Schang's Church Cemetery, Boonsboro, Washington County, MD.

41. Washington County, MD, Register of Wills, Book C, 311. Will of Yost Schmidt.

42. Ibid., Land Records, Book P, 662.

43. Ibid., Book AA, 403.

44. Frederick County, MD, Land Records, Book WR39, 492.

45. Washington County, MD, Land Records, Book Z, 526.

46. Ibid., Book HH, 893.

47. Ibid., Book IN1, 46.

48. Ibid., Book H, 28.

49. Ibid., Book M, 210.

50. Ibid., Book Y, 328.

51. Information for the Abraham and Christina (Wolf) Paulus family and descendants from Merritt Wolfe and Joanne Schembeckler, (deceased).

52. Tombstone in Euphemia-Rose Lawn Cemetery, Lewisburg, Harrison Township, Preble County, OH.

53. 1850 Federal Census, Preble County, OH.

CHAPTER 4

THIRD GENERATION

7 - FREDERICK(3) WOLF [Jacob(2), Daniel(1)]

Frederick Wolf was the first child of Jacob and Susanna (Smith) Wolf.\1 He was born 29 June 1802 in Frederick County, MD\2 where his parents married and lived before going to Ohio 1807/1808. In 1810 his father Jacob purchased a tract of 100 acres on Twin Creek, German Township, Montgomery County, OH\3 where Frederick was raised.

Frederick was married 6 January 1825 by J. P. John Saylor in Preble County, OH to Sophia Clark.\4 Sophia was born about 1808 in Bowling Green, KY\2, daughter of Daniel Clark. The family established their home near Eaton in Jackson Township, Preble County, OH, appearing in the 1830, 1840 and 1850 Federal Census listings in that county. In 1850 Frederick is shown as a farmer, aged 49 and born in Maryland.

In 1851 Frederick's father Jacob died and the estate administration indicates Frederick had some financial problems early in life. At that time he owed his father $65.28 on notes incurred in 1828, 1833 and 1834. When his father's property was sold in 1852, Frederick's share was sold at public sale to satisfy a court action by Moses B. Walker, a merchant of Preble County, against Frederick for 200 dollars.\1

Sophia died at Athens, Menard County, IL 1 October 1858.\5 It is not known where she is buried. Frederick has not been found in the 1860 census but in 1870 he is listed two times in West Lincoln Township, Logan County, IL - with son Frederick Jr.\6 and also with daughter Rebecca Jane, wife of George Wirtman.\7

Frederick died of consumption 9 June 1879 in Lincoln, Logan County, IL at the age of 76 years, 11 months, 10 days. The Death Certificate says his usual occupation was as a farmer and confirms that he was born in Maryland. It is not known where he was buried. Funeral Director was John Evans.\8

Children of Frederick and Sophia (Clark) Wolf, all born in Jackson Township, Preble County, OH:\2

    39   i Sarah E. Wolf, born about 1827
+   40   ii Lewis Clark Wolf, born 26 August 1828
    41   iii Nancy Wolf, born about 1829. Married 13 January in Preble
             County, OH Thomas Y. Graham
+   42   iv Frederick Clark Wolf, born December 1831
+   43   v Daniel Clark Wolf, born about 1834
    44   vi Susan Wolf, born about 1836, died 1839
    45   vii Sophia Wolf, born about 1837
+   46   viii Rebecca Jane Wolf, born about 1839
    47   ix Cornelius Wolf, born about 1841, died of typhoid fever in
             Cincinnati, OH 25 September 1862 while in the army during
             the Civil War. He did not marry.
    48   x Jacob Wolf, born about 1843
+   49   xi Washington Clark Wolf, born 11 November 1845
+   50   xii Malinda Ann Wolf, born 23 October 1847
+   51   xiii Oliver Wolf, born about 1849

8 - ELIZABETH(3) WOLF [Jacob(2), Daniel(1)]

Elizabeth Wolf was the second child of Jacob and Susannah (Smith) Wolf.\1 She was born 26 January 1805\9 in Frederick County MD\10 where

33

her parents married and lived before going to Ohio 1807/1808. In 1810 her father Jacob purchased a tract of 100 acres on Twin Creek, German Township, Montgomery County, OH\3 where Elizabeth was raised.

Elizabeth married 12 February 1821 in Montgomery County George Moyer.\11 George was born 9 August 1800\9 in Virginia.\10 They lived in Section 18, German Township, Montgomery County on a farm just south of Elizabeth's parents, Jacob and Susannah Wolf. George served as administrator of Jacob's estate after he died in 1851.

George died 12 July 1857 and Elizabeth 12 January 1863.\9 Both were buried in Old German Cemetery, German Township, Montgomery County, OH\12 but the stones were moved to Schaeffer Church Cemetery, Route 725, German Township.

Children of George and Elizabeth (Wolf) Moyer, all born in German Township, Montgomery County, OH:\10

52   i Catherine Moyer, born about 1822
53   ii Peter Moyer, born about 1826, died 1893
54 iii George Moyer, born about 1828
55   iv Elias Moyer, born 1831, died 21 July 1845
56   v Elizabeth Moyer, born about 1833
57   vi John Moyer, born about 1834
58 vii Daniel Moyer, born 4 June 1837, died 4 June 1837
59 viii Christena Moyer, born about 1838
60   ix William Moyer, born about 1841. Living with the family of
        his brother-in-law, Daniel Clark Wolf (#12), in Elkhart
        County, IN in 1880\72
61   x Mary Moyer, born 1842, died 25 March 1842
62   xi Sarah Jane Moyer, born 26 June 1847, died 25 October 1849

      9 - SUSAN(3) WOLF [Jacob(2), Daniel(1)]
Susan Wolf was the third child of Jacob and Susannah (Smith) Wolf.\1 She was born in Frederick County, MD 24 March 1806\2 where her parents married and lived before going to German Township, Montgomery County, OH 1807/1808. In 1810 her father Jacob purchased a tract of 100 acres on Twin Creek, German Township, Montgomery County, OH\3, where Susan was raised.

Susan married 18 November 1822 John S. Mantle/Montel who was born 17 April 1800 in Augusta County, VA. He was the son of Christopher Mantle, who was born in Hesse of Hesse Cassel in the Prussian Province of Hesse-Nasser on Upper Rhein, and Elizabeth Soeston, whose parents came from Germany.

Christopher came to America as a grenadier in Chasseure under Lieutenant Von Donop for the British. He disembarked on Long Island 1 August 1776. He saw action in New York on 27 August and 15 September at White Plains. On the way to Yorktown he was taken prisoner. On 7 September he took the Oath of Allegiance to the United States of America. 15 September he enlisted as a private in Colonel Moses Hasen's regiment. 17 June he was discharged at Newburgh, NY. He returned to Pennsylvania and 20 July 1784 married Elizabeth Soeston. They settled in Augusta County, VA near Middle River. In 1808 they moved to Section 32, Lanier Township, Preble County, OH. He died 14 October 1829 and is buried in Old Holdeman Cemetery. Elizabeth died 22 March 1860.

By 1850 John and Susan (Wolf) Montel were living in Clay Township, Kosciusko County, IN, the family appearing in the 1850 census of that county. Susan died 27 June 1861 and John 17 March 1889, both in Kosciusko County.

Children of John S. and Susan (Wolf) Montel:\14
63   i Daniel Montel, killed in Civil War

34

```
+  64   ii Abraham Montel, born 28 December 1825
+  65  iii Sarah Montel, born 13 December 1827
+  66   iv Solomon Montel, born 29 March 1829
   67    v Jacob Montel, born about 1831
+  68   vi Adaline Montel, born 1832
+  69  vii George Montel, born 1834
   70 viii Catharine Montel, born about 1836
   71   ix David Montel, born about 1839
+  72    x Susannah Montel, born 1842
+  73   xi John W. Montel, born 1 July 1845
           In addition two children died in infancy.
```

10 - JACOB JR(3) WOLF [Jacob(2), Daniel(1)]

Jacob Wolf Jr. was the fourth child of Jacob and Susannah (Smith) Wolf.\1 He was born 10 October 1807\15 in Frederick County, MD\16 where his parents married and lived before going to Ohio 1807/1808. In 1810 his father Jacob purchased a tract of 100 acres on Twin Creek, German Township, Montgomery County, OH\3 where Jacob Jr. was raised.

Jacob was married by J. P. James M. Grimes 8 September 1829 in Preble County, OH to Barbara Izor.\4 Barbara was born 25 May 1809\15 in Erie County, PA\16 daughter of Peter and Elizabeth Izor. They lived in Montgomery County, OH until about 1833, then Preble County until moving to Jackson Township, Carroll County, IN in 1836. In the 1850 Federal Census of Carroll County Jacob is shown as a farmer with $5500 real estate and $3500 personal property.

Jacob died 12 March 1869 and Barbara 25 November 1889.\15 Both are buried in Camden Cemetery, Carroll County, IN.

Children of Jacob Jr. and Barbara (Izor) Wolf:

```
+  74    i Simon P. Wolfe, born 4 July 1830
+  75   ii Frances (Franny) Wolf, born 12 February 1832
+  76  iii George Isaac Wolf, born 12 June 1834
+  77   iv Jacob Wolf III, born about 1836
+  78    v Daniel Wolf, born 16 June 1840
+  79   vi Magdalena (Lanny) Wolf, born 27 December 1842
   80  vii Barbara Anna Wolf, born about 1847 in Jackson Township,
           Carroll County, IN, died about 1905. Married 17 September
           1868 George Miller, son of Dan and Franny Izor Miller. No
           children.
+  81 viii Malinda J. Wolf, born 26 July 1852
```

11 - SARAH(3) WOLF [Jacob(2), Daniel(1)]

Sarah Wolf was the fifth child of Jacob and Susannah (Smith) Wolf. She was born 5 January 1810\17 in German Township, Montgomery County, OH\10 and raised on the 100 acre property her father Jacob had purchased in 1810 on Twin Creek in German Township.\3

Sarah was married before 1830 to George Shroyer. He was born 5 June 1808\17 in Rockingham County, VA son of Johan George and Katharine (Butts) Shreuer/Shroyer. George and Sarah lived in Preble County, OH, where their first five children were born, until about 1842 when they moved to Benton Township, Elkhart County, IN where their other two children were born.\18 In the 1850 census of Elkhart County George's occupation was given as cooper. Value of real estate was 200 dollars. They moved to Plain Township, Kosciusko County, IN prior to 1860 when they appear in the 1860 census at that location. With them in 1860 is Susan Wolf, mother of Sarah and widow of Jacob who had died in 1851.

Sarah died 28 August 1861 at Benton, IN and is buried in the cemetary at Leesburg, Kosciusko County, IN. George remarried 28

December 1865 at Benton, IN to Pheby (Counts) Bennett with whom he had two more children. He died 11 June 1880 at Warsaw, Kosciusko County and is also buried in Leesburg Cemetery.

Children of George and Sarah (Wolf) Shroyer:\18
+ 82   i Suzanne Shroyer, born about 1830
   83   ii John W. Shroyer, born about 1832 in Preble County, OH.
            Married 1 July 1858 Polly Detmore, born about 1842
+ 84 iii Daniel W. Shroyer, born 12 November 1832
   85   iv Lewis W. Shroyer, born about 1837 in Preble County, OH.
            Married 12 January 1859 Ann Detmore, born about 1844
+ 86   v George W. Shroyer, born about 1839
+ 87   vi Hiram William Shroyer, born 16 July 1843
   88 vii Jacob Shroyer, born about 1846 in Benton, IN
   Children of George and Pheby (Counts) (Bennett) Shroyer:
            i Oliver James Shroyer, born 10 April 1866 in Benton, IN,
               died about 1960. Married 1) Bessie Jarrette 27 December
               1896, 2) Mabel L. Hatch 11 April 1905
           ii Clara Shroyer, born in Benton, IN. Did not marry

12 - DANIEL(3) WOLF [Jacob(2), Daniel(1)]

Daniel Wolf was the sixth child of Jacob and Susannah (Smith) Wolf. He was born 27 November 1814 in German Township, Montgomery County, OH.\19 He was raised on the 100 acre property his father Jacob purchased in 1810 on Twin Creek, German Township, Montgomery County, OH.\3 He married 14 March 1839 Anna Michael in Preble County, OH.\4 Anna was born 29 April 1820 in Ohio.\19 They lived in Preble County, OH until about 1852 when they moved to Benton Township, Elkhart County, IN where Anna died 7 December 1867. Daniel died 26 September 1899, probably in Turkey Creek Township, Kosciusko County, IN as he is buried in Syracuse Cemetery along with his wife Anna, his mother Susanna, and other members of his family.\72

Children of Daniel and Anna (Michael) Wolf:\19
   89   i Rebecca Wolf, born 5 May 1841 in Preble County, OH, died 27
            August 1861. Buried in Syracuse Cemetery, Turkey Creek
            Township, Kosciusko County, IN
   90   ii Sarah J. Wolf, born about 1843 in Preble County, OH
+ 91 iii Jacob Wolf, born 1845
+ 92   iv Mary S. Wolf, born 1848
+ 93   v Catherine Wolf, born 1850
   94   vi Susan Wolf, born 28 November 1852 in Benton Township, Elk-
            hart County, IN, died 6 April 1934. Buried in Syracuse
            Cemetery, Turkey Creek Township, IN
   95 vii John A. Wolf, born 24 October 1855 in Benton Township,
            Elkhart County, IN. Buried in Syracuse Cemetery, Turkey
            Creek Township, Kosciusko County, IN
+ 96 viii George W. Wolf, born 1859

13 - CATHARINE(3) WOLF [Jacob(2), Daniel(1)]

Catharine Wolf was the seventh child of Jacob and Susannah (Smith) Wolf. She was born about 1818 in German Township, Montgomery County, OH.\19 She was raised on the 100 acre property her father Jacob purchased in 1810 on Twin Creek, German Township, Montgomery County, OH. She married Daniel S. Witters 25 November 1835 in Montgomery County. Daniel was born 12 June 1814 in Ohio. They lived first in Ohio where their first four children were born and by 1860 had moved to Benton Township, Elkhart County, IN. Daniel died 24 December 1899. It is not known where or when Catharine died.

Known children of Daniel and Catharine (Wolf) Witters, all born

in Ohio:\19
```
97     i Sarah A. Witters, born about 1840
98    ii Lucinda Witters, born about 1844
99   iii Catharine E. Witters, born about 1851, twin
100   iv James F. Witters, born about 1851, twin
```

14 - CHRISTINA(3) WOLF [Jacob(2), Daniel(1)]
Christina Wolf was the eighth child of Jacob and Susannah (Smith) Wolf. She was born about 1822 in German Township, Montgomery County, OH.\20 She was raised on the 100 acre property her father Jacob purchased in 1810 on Twin Creek in German Township. She married Ephraim Williams 8 August 1844 in Montgomery County, OH. He was born about 1820 in Maryland.\20 They lived in Jackson Township, Montgomery County, OH at the time of the 1850 Federal Census, Ephraim listed as a laborer. It is not known where or when they died.
Known children of Ephraim and Christina (Wolf) Williams, all born in Ohio:
```
101     i Susan Williams, born about 1845
102    ii Catharine Williams, born about 1846
103   iii Jacob Williams, born about 1847
```

16 - FREDERICK JR(3) KIMMERLING [Catharine(2) Wolf, Daniel(1)]
Frederick Kimmerling Jr. was probably the second child of Frederick and Catharine (Wolf) Kimmerling as an unidentified female 0-10 appears as the only child in the family in the 1800 Federal Census for Frederick County, MD. He was born 2 February 1804\21 near Taneytown, Frederick County, MD (now in Carroll County). He was one of four children born in Frederick County before the family went to German Township, Montgomery County, OH in 1807/1808.\22
Frederick married about 1828 Catherine _____ whose maiden name was possibly Holtry. She was born 26 October 1806.\21 They apparently lived on the property purchased in 1810 by his grandmother Elizabeth Wolf and willed to his mother Catharine in 1815 by her mother. They apparently are included in the household of his father Frederick in the 1840 Federal Census of German Township, Montgomery County, OH. His mother had died by this time and and in 1841 the property was transferred to Frederick Jr. and his brother Abraham as "legal heirs of Catharine Kimmerling". By the 1850 census he was listed as the head of the household and his father, 86, was living with them, still in German Township. He was listed as a farmer with real estate valued at $1500.\10 In 1860 it was valued at $4000.\23
Frederick died 15 February 1880 and Catherine 11 February 1882 (75 years 3 months 16 days). Both are buried in Germantown Cemetery, German Township, Montgomery County, OH. The Kimmerlings belonged to the Lutheran Congregation in Germantown.\24
Known children of Frederick Jr. and Catherine (_____) Kimmerling:
```
+ 104     i Maria Kimmerling, born 1830
+ 105    ii Emanuel Kimmerling, born about 1833
```

21 - ELIZABETH(3) HAHN [Elizabeth(2) Wolf, Daniel(1)]
Elizabeth Hahn was the second child of Leonard and Elizabeth (Wolf) Hahn. She was born 16 January 1800\21 in Emmitsburg, Frederick County, MD\10, one of five children born in Emmitsburg before her widowed mother went to Ohio in 1807/1808 with her widowed mother, Maria Elizabeth Wolf, and the families of three of the other children of Daniel and Maria Elizabeth Wolf - Frederick and Catharine Kimmerling, Jacob and Susannah Wolf, and Abraham and Christina Paulus. Elizabeth's father, Leonard Hahn, had died 1805/1806 in Emmitsburg\25

and after going to Ohio she was raised by her widowed mother on the property purchased in 1810 by her maternal grandmother, Maria Elizabeth Wolf, in German Township, Montgomery County, OH. The 30 acre portion on which they lived was willed to her mother in 1814. It was sold by the heirs in 1853, her mother having died 1852/1853.\26

Elizabeth married 4 October 1821 Daniel Sharritt in Montgomery County, OH. Daniel was born 19 December 1795 in Wythe County, VA\27, son of John Schoritz/Sharritt and Mary Cassell. Daniel died 21 November 1862 and Elizabeth 23 March 1885 in German Township, Montgomery County, OH. Both are buried in Germantown Cemetery, German Township, Montgomery County, OH.\27

The family appears in the 1850, 1860 and 1870 censuses of German Township. In 1870 Elizabeth is listed as family head, Daniel having died in 1862. Living with her was son Samuel and his wife and children.\28

Children of Daniel and Elizabeth (Hahn) Sharritt, all born in German Township, Montgomery County, OH:\10
+ 106   i Mary Magdalene Sharritt, born 22 June 1822
+ 107   ii Elizabeth Helena Sharritt, born 1824
+ 108 iii John Sharritt
+ 109   iv Samuel Sharritt, born 28 October 1827
+ 110   v William Sharritt, born 1829
+ 111   vi Leonard Sharritt, born 16 December 1831
  112 vii Sarah Sharritt, born about 1832, died before 1924
+ 113 viii Hiram Sharritt, born 1834
+ 114   ix Sophia Sharritt, born about 1838
+ 115   x Daniel Sharritt Jr., born 30 May 1840
+ 116   xi Jacob Sharritt, born about 1843, died before 1924

23 - DANIEL(3) HAHN [Elizabeth(2) Wolf, Daniel(1)]
Daniel Hahn was the fourth child of Leonard and Elizabeth (Wolf) Hahn. He was born 3 October 1801\29 in Emmitsburg, Frederick County, MD\10, one of five children born in Maryland before his widowed mother went to Ohio in 1807/1808 with her widowed mother, Maria Elizabeth Wolf, and the families of three of the other children of Daniel and Maria Elizabeth Wolf - Frederick and Catharine Kimmerling, Jacob and Susannah Wolf, and Abraham and Christina Paulus. Daniel's father, Leeonard Hahn, had died in 1805/1806 and, after going to Ohio, he was raised by his widowed mother, Elizabeth, on the property purchased in 1810 by his maternal grandmother in German Township, Montgomery County, OH. The 30 acre portion on which they lived was willed by his grandmother to his mother in 1814. It was sold by the heirs in 1853, his mother having died 1852/1853.\26

Daniel married Anna Maria _____ who was born 6 April 1807\29 in Pennsylvania.\30 In 1860 they were living in Miami Township, Montgomery County, OH, Daniel listed as a farmer with real estate valued at $6420.\30 Anna Maria died 29 November 1868 and Daniel 14 August 1871.\29 Both are buried in Ellerton Cemetery, Jefferson Township, Montgomery County, OH.

Known children of Daniel and Anna Maria (_____) Hahn:\30
  117   i Elias Hahn, born about 1838 in Ohio
  118   ii Loretta Hahn, born about 1842 in Ohio (may be wife of Elias)

24 - MARY(3) HAHN [Elizabeth(2) Wolf, Daniel(1)]
Mary Hahn was the fifth child of Leonard and Elizabeth (Wolf) Hahn. She was born about 1802-1805 in Emmitsburg, Frederick County, MD,\10 one of five children born in Maryland before her widowed mother

went to Ohio in 1807/1808 with her widowed mother, Maria Elizabeth
Wolf, and the families of three of the other children of Daniel and
Maria Elizabeth Wolf - Frederick and Catharine Kimmerling, Jacob and
Susannah Wolf, and Abraham and Christina Paulus. Mary's father Leonard
Hahn had died 1805/1806 in Emmitsburg\25 and, after going to Ohio,
Mary was raised by her widowed mother, Elizabeth, on the property
purchased in 1810 by her maternal grandmother in German Township,
Montgomery County, OH. The 30 acre portion on which they lived was
willed by her grandmother to her mother in 1814. It was sold by the
heirs in 1853, her mother having died 1852/1853.\26
    Mary married Joel Sharritt 23 April 1829 in Montgomery County,
OH. Joel was born 22 February 1809 in Wythe County, VA\27 son of John
Schoritz/Sharritt and Mary Cassell. Mary died about 1840 in Montgomery
County, OH. It is not known where she is buried. Joel re-married 6
April 1841 in Montgomery County to Susanna Russell who was born about
1820 in Pennsylvania. In 1880 Joel and Susanna were living in Sunbury,
German Township, Montgomery County.\31 It is not known where or when
they died or where they are buried.
    Children of Joel and Mary (Hahn) Sharritt, order of birth uncer-
tain:
    119   i Margaret Sharritt. Married before 1853 August Weaver
    120   ii Daniel Sharritt
    121 iii Leah Sharritt. Married before 1853 Reuben Smith
    122   iv Rachel Sharritt, born about 1835. Married William Taylor 27
              January 1851 in Montgomery County, OH. In the 1850 census
              of Montgomery County, OH Rachel appears in the household of
              her grandmother, Elizabeth Wolf Hahn.
    123   v Elizabeth Sharritt, a minor in 1853

    25 - DANIEL(3) WOLF [Frederick(2), Daniel(1)]
    Daniel Wolf was the first child of Frederick and Magdalene
(Schmidt/Smith) Wolf. He was born 18 January 1802\32 in Boonsboro,
Washington County, MD. Apparently his parents followed the Old German
custom of naming the first son after his paternal grandfather Daniel
Wolf, Frederick's father. Daniel was raised in Boonsboro where his
father was one of the first blacksmiths in the area. Daniel married in
Washington County Elizabeth Bennett, daughter of Aquilla and Mary
Bennett of Boonsboro. License was issued 28 December 1822.\33
Elizabeth was born about 1802,\34 also in Washington County.
    In 1829 Elizabeth's father, Aquilla Bennett, sold his property in
Boonsboro (lot number 22) for $300 to Daniel Slusser, Aquilla's wife
Mary releasing her dower right. The deed was made 13 September 1828
and recorded 28 February 1829.\35 Aquilla and his family, including
daughter Elizabeth and her husband Daniel Wolf, then emigrated to
Richland (now Ashland) County, OH. 29 April 1831 Aquilla purchased
from Benjamin Johns for $1100 the NW and SW Quarters (160 acres) of
Section 18, Township 21 North of Range 16 East in what is now Vermil-
lion Township, Ashland County, OH.\36 3 November 1832 his sons John
and Peter each purchased half of the East half of the Section. Daniel
and his family lived on the property of his father in law Aquilla
Bennett and 9 September 1839 Aquilla sold the NW quarter (80 acres) of
the Section to his daughter Elizabeth Wolf for ten dollars.\36 After
Daniel's death in 1862 Elizabeth sold this property 1 February 1866 to
Michael Gongway for $3300.\37 Section 18 is on the western edge of
Vermillion Township, adjacent to Mifflin Township, and is between
Mifflin and Hayesville, due south of Ashland.
    Census records show Daniel to have been a farmer.\34 In 1850 his
real estate was valued at $2,000 and in 1860 $4,000, with personal

39

property of $1,300. He became guardian of Amanda, Franklin and Samantha, children of his son Daniel Jr. who died in 1852. Franklin, 10, appears in his household in 1860. A biography of grandson Franklin states that Daniel was also a blacksmith by trade. In this he followed the occupation of his father Frederick.

Daniel died intestate 25 October 1862, at 60 years 9 months 7 days, and is buried in Mifflin Cemetery, Mifflin Township, Ashland County, OH.\38 His son Frederick was appointed Administrator of the estate. The inventory of his personal property was made 22 November 1862 by John Charles, Joseph Doty and John Sigler.\39 The inventory showed typical farm items and included rye, wheat, oats, barley and corn. It also included blacksmith tools. The total amounted to $625.19 plus $99.80 selected by the widow, Elizabeth, which by statute was not to exceed $100. The items selected by the widow were:

1	Lot Broom Corn	$ .50
1	Cupboard	8.00
9 1/2	Bushels Wheat	9.50
1	Bay Mare	50.00
2	Hogs	7.50
81	Bushels Oats	24.30
	Total	$99.80

In addition "The deceased having left a widow we set off to her the following property without appraising the same as directed by statute".

"4 beds and bedsteads and bedding, 2 tables, 1 side saddle, 10 chairs, all the carpets, 1 cupboard, all the dishes, knives and forks, 2 stoves, pots and cooking utensils and kitchen furniture, 1 copper kettle, 1 iron kettle and clock, 2 cows, 3 sheep, 1 mare, buggy and harness and all the clothing and ornaments of the widow of the deceased. December 2, 1862".

Also "The following is a schedule of property, belonging to the estate of Daniel Wolf deceased, set off by the undersigned for the support of Elizabeth Wolf his widow for one year from the date of the death of said decedent, to wit"

15 Bushels Wheat	$11.25
30 Bushels Corn	11.25
3 Ton of hay and corn fodder in the barn	10.00
50 Bushels Oats	12.50
10 Bushels Potatoes	2.00
2 Fat Hogs	10.00
1 Sow and 5 Pigs	3.00
Cash	25.00
Total	$85.00

December 1862

Items of special interest in the inventory were:

1 Two horse wagon	$15.00
1 Lot of blacksmith tools	2.00
13 Acres of wheat in the ground	52.00
1 Acre of barley in the ground	4.00

```
1 Spotted cow                                            7.00
1 Black cow                                              8.00
1 Heifer     taken by widow                             8.00
2 Spring calves                                          6.00
1 Sorel mare                                            55.00
1 Spring colt                                           20.00
1 Sow and pigs and 2 hogs                               11.50
4 Hogs and 1 lot of corn fodder                         23.00
1 Note on Michael Wolf dated 28 October 1856 1 yr.
  after date calling for one hundred and forty dollars
  with a credit on the same for ninety dollars dated
  10 October 1861                                       88.73
1 Note on Henry Sunday dated 12 August 1854 six
  months after date calling for twelve dollars and
  56 cents with a credit on the same of five dollars
  dated 12 February 1855                                11.10
  Cash amounting to                                     38.73
```

Frederick filed his final account 27 January 1865. Some items of
interest were:

14 February 1863 Amount allowed me by the Probate
Judge for settling account of the deceased as guardian of
Franklin, Amanda and Samantha Wolf $ 5.00

December 1862 By amount taken by widow at appraisement as per Voucher No. 52   29.25

Amount paid Michael Wolf guardian of
Franklin Wolf Voucher No. 53   32.78

```
Total amount paid out by Administrator                 866.49
Total amount received by Administrator                 734.03
                                                      -------
Amount due the Administrator                          $132.46
```

Elizabeth died 18 October 1880 in Keokuk, Lee County, IA. It is
not known where she is buried.

Children of Daniel and Elizabeth (Bennett) Wolf:
+ 124   i Sarah Wolf, born about 1824
+ 125   ii Daniel Wolf Jr., born about 1826
  126 iii Unidentified son, born about 1828 in Washington County, MD
+ 127   iv Michael Wolf, born 30 September 1829
  128   v Unidentified daughter born in Richland (now Ashland)
           County, OH
+ 129   vi Frederick R. Wolf, born 13 January 1836
  130 vii Magdalena Wolf, born about 1838 in Vermillion Township,
           Ashland County, OH. Married 23 February 1860 Jacob Bisman
           in Ashland County.
  131 viii Simon Wolf, born about 1840 in Vermillion Township, Ash-
           land County, OH.
  132   ix Matilda Wolf, born about 1842 in Vermillion Township, Ash-
           land County, OH. Married 7 August 1859 John F. Eighinger in
           Ashland County.
  133   x Maria Wolf, born about 1845 in Vermillion Township, Ash-
           land County, OH

   26 - ELIZABETH(3) WOLF [Frederick(2), Daniel(1)]
   Elizabeth Wolf was the second child of Frederick and Magdalene
(Schmidt/Smith) Wolf. She was born about 1807\40 in Boonsboro,
Washington County, MD. As with their first child, apparently her

41

parents followed the Old German custom and named the first daughter
after her paternal grandmother, Maria Elizabeth, Frederick's mother.
She was raised in Boonsboro where her father was one of the first
blacksmiths in the area. Elizabeth married in Washington County Daniel
Schlosser, son of Henry and Catharine (Delauter) Schlosser. License
was issued 14 May 1828.\33 Daniel was born 3 February 1807 near
Middletown, Frederick County, MD.\41
     Daniel was a wagonmaker in Boonsboro where all of their children
were born. Elizabeth died early in 1866. It is not known where she is
buried. The following year Daniel sold his land in Washington County
and moved to Indiana where his sister, brothers and two sons were
living. He settled on a farm 2 1/2 miles west of Williamsport in
Warren County. Daniel died 3 February 1875 in West Lebanon, Warren
County, IN.
     Children of Daniel and Elizabeth (Wolf) Schlosser, all born in
Boonsboro, MD\41
     134   i Sarah A. Schlosser, born 2 February 1829, died 26 April
              1898 Buried in West Lebanon Cemetery, Warren County, IN.
              Did not marry.
     135   ii Susan Schlosser, born 29 September 1830, died 31 December
              1838. Buried in Boonsboro Cemetery, Washington County, MD.
              Did not marry.
+·136   iii Henry Lawson Schlosser, born 1 February 1832
+ 137   iv Frederick A. Schlosser, born about 1834
     138   v Unnamed Schlosser, born and died 1830-1840
     139   vi Mary Catharine Schlosser, born 13 February 1839, died
              1840-1850
     140   vii Elizabeth Jane Schlosser, born about 1841, died 1898-1912.
              Married in Washington County, MD John N. Fritz. License
              issued 6 April 1865\33
+ 141   viii Ann Rebecca Schlosser, born about 1843
+ 142   ix Maria Schlosser, born 28 November 1845
     143   x Daniel Z. Schlosser, born 23 May 1848, died 25 September
              1916. Buried in West Lebanon Cemetery, Warren County, IN
+ 144   xi Margaret S. Schlosser, born 31 January 1850

     27 - JOSEPH(3) WOLF [Frederick(2), Daniel(1)]
     Joseph Wolf was the third child of Frederick and Magdalene
(Schmidt/Smith) Wolf. He was born 29 July 1809\42 in Boonsboro,
Washington County, MD. As with his older brother and sister, his
parents followed the Old German custom of naming the second son after
his maternal grandfather Yost/Joseph Schmidt, Magdalene's father. He
was raised in Boonsboro where his father was one of the first blacksmiths in the area. Joseph married in Washington County Anna Kretzer,
daughter of George and _____ Kretzer. License was issued 14 January
1832.\33 Anna was born 20 March 1810\42 in Maryland.
     The family appears in the 1840 census for Washington County, MD
but by 1850 has gone to Ohio. In 1850 Joseph, Anna and their three
children are listed in the household of Gottlieb Lundeny, mechanic,
born in Germany, in Butler Township, Montgomery County, OH. Joseph was
listed as a laborer. Also in this household was George Cretser, 80,
Anna's father. In 1860 Joseph was head of a household in the same
township. With them were their two younger children, unmarried. In
1870 they had moved to Harrison Township, Montgomery County, OH. Anna
had died and Joseph was head of a household consisting of himself,
John H., 43 and unmarried, and the family of married daughter Elizabeth.
     Anna died 9 May 1868, 58 years 1 month 20 days, and Joseph 30 May

1872, 62 years 10 months 1 day.\42 Both are buried in Willowview
Cemetery, Harrison Township, Montgomery County, OH.
   Children of Joseph and Anna (Kretzer) Wolf, all born in Washington County, MD:\43
+ 145   · i Elizabeth Wolf, born about 1832
  146   ii John H. Wolf, born   February 1833, died October 1887, 54
          years 8 months 12days.\42 Buried in Willowview Cemetery,
          Harrison Township, Montgomery County, OH. Did not marry.
  147 iii Anna C. Wolf, born about 1838

   28 - TRACY(3) WOLF [Frederick(2), Daniel(1)]
   Tracy Wolf was the fourth child of Frederick and Magdalene
(Schmidt/Smith Wolf). She was born 5 June 1807\44 in Boonsboro,
Washington County, MD where her father was one of the first blacksmiths in the area. Tracy married in Washington County Jacob Blecher.
They were married 14 February 1832 by Revd. George Geeting.\45 Jacob
was born 5 June 1807\46 in Maryland.
   They lived in the Boonsboro area of Washington County. Jacob was
listed as a farmer in the 1850 and 1860 censuses and as a retired
farmer in 1870. After the death of Tracy's mother in 1844 Jacob
purchased for $1,000 31 January 1846 the Boonsboro property of his
father in law, Frederick Wolf.\47
   Tracy died 14 October 1840 (one month after the birth of Tracy,
her sixth child) and is buried in Lydia Shunk's Graveyard with her
mother and sister, Sarah (Wolf) Stinger.\44
   After Tracy's death Jacob remarried in Washington County to
Barbara Ann Schriver. License was issued 13 March 1842.\33 Barbara was
born 12 April 1811, daughter of Henery and Catherine Schriver. Jacob
died 29 November 1871 and Barbara Ann 5 May 1889.\46 Both are buried
in Boonsboro Cemetery, Washington County, MD.
   Children of Jacob and Tracy (Wolf) Blecher, all born in Washington County, MD:\48
+ 148   i Elizabeth Blecher, born 7 November 1832
+ 149   ii Mary Ann Blecher, born 20 November 1833
  150 iii Magdalena Blecher, born 31 August 1834, died 18 September
          1835 in Washington County. Did not marry
. 151   iv John Blecher, born 20 June 1836, died 30 November 1838 in
          Washington County. Did not marry.
+ 152   v Jacob B. Blecher, born 30 March 1838
  153   vi Tracy Blecher, born 3 September 1840, died 30 June 1841 in
          Washington County. Did not marry.
   Children of Jacob and Barbara Ann (Schriver) Blecher, all born in
Washington County, MD:\48
          i Daniel Henry Blecher, born 16 April 1843, died 16 September
          1937 at Mt. Morris, IL. Married 1) 18 December 1867 Mary
          Catharine Antsbarger, born 19 October 1842, died 21 Decem-
          ber 1871. Child Catharine E. Blecher, died 23 January 1871
          at 1 year 27 days, 2) 9 January 1879 Elizabeth Ann Miller.
         ii George Dallas Blecher, born 26 December 1844, died 19 March
          1846 in Boonsboro, MD.
        iii William Blecher, born 21 September 1846, died 23 February
          1848 in Boonsboro, MD.
         iv Josiah Blecher, born 3 June 1849, died 14 August 1913 in
          Hagerstown, Md. Married 30 December 1880 Mary Elizabeth
          Thum, born 13 June 1855, died 24 August 1929.
          v Ann C. Blecher, born about 1850

                            43

29 - SARAH(3) WOLF [Frederick(2), Daniel(1)]
    Sarah Wolf was the fifth child of Frederick and Magdalene
(Schmidt/Smith) Wolf. She was born 1 August 1814\44 in Boonsboro,
Washington County, MD. She was raised in Boonsboro where her father
was one of the first blacksmiths in the area. Sarah married in Washington County John Stinger. They were married 4 June 1833 by Revd. J.
Rebaugh.\45 John was born 11 August 1808 in Frederick County, MD,\49
son of Charles and Louise (Tausend) Stinger. Charles Stinger, with his
wife and four children, emigrated to America about 1804 Their last
five children were born in Frederick County. Charles was born in
Karlsbrunn, Saraland, Germany 9 August 1769\50 and died in Frederick
County 20 April 1835.\51
    Sarah died 15 May 1836 in Boonsboro, possibly in childbirth, as
their only child, Elizabeth C. Stinger was born about 1836. Sarah is
buried in Lydia Shunk's Graveyard, Boonsboro, MD with her mother and
sister Tracy (Wolf) Blecher.
    After Sarah's death John went west where in 1850 he was living
with William E. and Wilhelmina (Stinger) Little, his sister, in Mt.
Morris, IL. Another sister Louise Catherine Stinger was also living
with the family.\53 It is interesting to note that John was listed in
the census as a blacksmith, the same trade as his father in law,
Frederick Wolf. By 1860 he had moved to Leaf River, IL and was living
with his sister Catharina Margaret Stinger. Between 1860 and 1870 he
had remarried and in 1870 he and wife Elizabeth were living in Leaf
River with his sister Catharina (stinger) Zeigler.
    John died 22 October 1872 and his second wife Elizabeth 28
February 1882 at the age of 68 years.\54 Both are buried in Plainview
Cemetery in Mt. Morris, IL. No children of this marriage are known.
    Child of John and Sarah (Wolf) Stinger:
154   i Elizabeth C. Stinger, born about 1836 in Boonsboro, Wash-
          ington County, MD, As her mother died about the time of her
          birth Elizabeth was raised by her mother's parents, Freder-
          ick and Magdalene Wolf. In 1844 her grandmother died and in
          1850 she and her grandfather are shown as living with the
          family of Frederck's son Simon Wolf in Boonsboro, MD. In
          1860 Frederick had died and Elizabeth is still living with
          the family of her uncle Simon. As Simon died early in 1870,
          Elizabeth joined the household of Leonard Emmert, listed as
          a domestic servant. Leonard's wife was a sister of Simon's
          wife Elizabeth Warwell. At this time she was 33 years old
          and had not married. No further trace of Elizabeth.\55

30 - SOPHIA(3) WOLF [Frederick(2), Daniel(1)]
    Sophia Wolf was the sixth child of Frederick And Magdalene
(Schmidt/Smith Wolf). She was born 12 June 1807\46 in Boonsboro,
Washington County, MD. She was raised in Boonsboro where her father
was one of the first blacksmiths in the area. Sophia married in
Washington County John Spielman Jr. They were married 11 April 1836 by
Revd. J. Rebaugh.\55 John was born 17 December 1810\46 in Maryland,
son of John Spielman.
    They lived in Boonsboro, appearing in census records through
1880. John was listed as a stonemason. His real estate was valued at
$1200 in 1860, They attended and their children were baptized at Salem
Lutheran Church in Boonsboro. John died 10 April 1884, 73 years 3
months 23 days, and Sophia 5 July 1885, 78 years 23 days. Both are
buried in Boonsboro Cemetery.
    Children of John Jr. and Sophia (Wolf) Spielman, all born in
Boonsboro, MD:\58

155   i Lawson Spielman, born about 1838. Married 26 January 1860
         in Washington County Sarah Ann Hathaway\57
156   ii John Calvin Spielman, born 17 January 1841, died 15 August
         August 1852 in Boonsboro, Washington County, MD. Buried in
         Boonsboro Cemetery\46
157 iii Mary Magdalene Spielman, born 11 December 1842
158   iv Sarah Elizabeth Spielman, born 10 October 1844. Married 19
         December 1861 in Washington County Jacob Roadenzer\33
159   v Georgina Frances Spielman, born about 1847
160   vi Ellen Sophia Spielman, born about 1848
161 vii Robert Spielman, born 25 May 1849
162 viii Catherine Tracy Spielman, born 2 March 1851
163   ix John Luther Wolf Spielman, born 4 June 1854
164   x Emory Allen Spielman, born 24 July 1856, died 7 January
         1899 in Washington County. Married 19 October 1884 Lizzie
         Barmand\57
165   xi Margaret Elizabeth Spielman, born 24 May 1858, died 30
         November 1858.\46 Did not marry.

        31 - SIMON(3) WOLF [Frederick(2), Daniel(1)]
Simon Wolf was the seventh child of Frederick and Magdalene
(Schmidt/Smith). He was born 6 January 1820\59 in Boonsboro, MD. He
was raised in Boonsboro, Washington County, MD where his father was
one of the first blacksmiths in the area. Simon married in Washington
County Elizabeth Warwell, license issued 23 August 1843.\33 She was
born 22 March 1822\59 in Maryland, daughter of Daniel Warwell.
        They lived in Boonsboro, MD, Simon appearing as a family head in
the 1850 and 1860 censuses and listed as a blacksmith, the trade
practiced by his father. In 1850, in addition to his family, his
father Frederick, niece Sarah Stinger and Christ Otto, who was born in
Germany, appear in the household. Simon died 26 February 1870 in
Boonsboro. In the 1870 census Elizabeth is listed as family head with
nine children. She died 29 August 1872. Both Simon and Elizabeth are
buried in the Boonsboro Reformed Church Cemetery.\59
        Children of Simon and Elizabeth (Warwell) Wolf, all born in
Boonsboro, Washington County, MD:\55
  166   i Daniel Frederic Wolf, born 24 July 1844, died 15 September
          1845.\59 Buried in Boonsboro, MD Reformed Church Cemetery.
+ 167   ii George W. Wolf, born 22 March 1846
  168 iii Mary Ellen Wolf, born 1848, died 19 June 1888. Buried in
          Beautiful View Cemetery, Hagerstown, MD. Did not marry.
  169   iv Josiah Wolf, born 10 October 1850 in Boonsboro, Md, died 24
          February 1911. Married Fannie Beachley 10 October 1871 at
          Evangelical Lutheran Church, Middletown, Frederick County
          Md.\60 Fannie was born 12 November 1850,died 25 September
          1910. Both died and are buried in Frederick Co., MD.
  170   v Charles M. Wolf, born 1 July 1853, died 9 November 1925.\46
          Married (License) 11 February 1875 Annie A. Martz,\33
          born 15 February 1856 in Maryland, died 28 December
          1937.\46 As listed in the 1880 and 1900 censuses, he was a
          blacksmith in Boonsboro, Washington County, as were his
          father and grandfather. Both died in Washington County, MD
          and are buried in the Boonsboro Cemetery. No children.
+ 171   vi Franklin Wolf, born 21 September 1855
  172 vii William Carlton Wolf, born 12 March 1858, died 1 April
          1865\59 in Boonsboro. Buried in Boonsboro, MD Reformed
          Church Cemetery. Did not marry.
+ 173 viii Mary Jeannette Wolf, born about 1860

+ 174   ix Ann Cora Wolf, born 27 November 1861\66
  175   x Fannie M. Wolf, born about 1864. Housekeeper for the George
          W. Smith Jr. family in the 1880 and 1900 censuses. Did not
          marry.
+ 176   xi Harvey J. Wolf, born 18 April 1865
  177   xii Alice Gertrude Wolf, born about 1869

     32 - JACOB(3) WOLF [Frederick(2), Daniel(1)]
     Jacob Wolf was the eighth child of Frederick and Magdalene
(Schmidt/Smith) Wolf. He was born 5 February 1823\46 in Boonsboro,
Washington County, MD. He was raised in Boonsboro where his father was
one of the first blacksmiths in the area. Jacob worked as a farm
laborer, appearing in the 1850 census of Washington County in the
household of Isaac Newcomer.\61
     He married Mary Ellen Albaugh in Washington County, license
issued 19 December 1851,\33 Mary Ellen was born in Maryland 4 December
1827,\46 the daughter of Daniel and Catharine (Devilbiss) Albaugh. As
her parents first appear in the Washington County census records in
1850, she apparently was born elsewhere in Maryland, probably in
Frederick County where her parents were married 29 July 1825\57 and
came to Boonsboro with them 1840 - 1850. In the 1850 census she is
shown with her parents, aged 22 and unmarried. Daniel was listed as a
shoemaker in 1850 and 1860. The Albaughs were members of the Church of
Christ in Boonsboro. Daniel was one of the founders of the church 27
February 1848 and was the first elder.\62
     In the 1860 census Jacob and Mary Ellen appear as a family unit
in Boonsboro District with their first three children.\63 Mary Ellen
died 6 February 1863\46 at the age of 36, having born two more
children. She died shortly following the birth of her fifth child.
Following her death the younger children were placed with relatives to
be raised. Jacob no longer maintained a household and in the 1870
census he appears as Jacob Wolf, 42, farm labore in the household of
Noah G. Thomas. Sometime after 1870 he, along with son Carlton and
possibly daughter Orpha, went to live with his eldest son, Van Luther,
in whose household in Beattys, Springfield Township, Delaware County,
PA they are listed in the 1880 census. Jacob is described as having
"paralysis", probably having suffered a stroke.
     Jacob died 23 December 1880\46 while living with son Van Luther.
Both he and Mary Ellen are buried in Boonsboro, MD Cemetery. (It is
thought that they were originally buried in the Trinity Evangelical
Lutheran Church Cemetery whose graves were moved to Boonsboro Cemetery
to provide for a church parking lot.)
     Children of Jacob and Mary Ellen (Albaugh) Wolf, all born in
Boonsboro, Washington County, MD:
+ 178   i Van Luther Wolf, born December 1852
  179   ii Orpha Wolf, born about 1855. She appears in the 1860 census
          with the family. In the 1870 census, after her mother's
          death, she appears with the Jacob E. Welty family, listed
          as a domestic, aged 15. Jacob Welty's wife was Orpha's
          aunt, Emma E. Albaugh, sister of Orpha's deceased mother,
          Mary Ellen. Nothing further is known of Orpha. She may have
          left Washington County with her father and brother, Carl-
          ton, to go with her elder brother, Van Luther, in Beatys,
          Springfield Township, Delaware County, PA,
+ 180   iii Carlton Emmert Wolf, born 5 August 1857
+ 181   iv Catherine Wolf, born 1861
+ 182   v John Albaugh Wolf, born 13 January 1863

                              46

33 - MARGARET ANN(3) WOLF [Frederick(2), Daniel(1)]

Margaret Ann Wolf was the ninth child of Frederick and Magdalene (Schmidt/Smith) Wolf. She was born 18 December 1825\64 in Boonsboro, Washington County, MD. She was raised in Boonsboro where her father was one of the first blacksmiths in the area. Margaret Ann married Benjamin Alexander Edmonds in Washington County, license issued 20 December 1842.\33 Benjamin was born 15 September 1821\64 in Virginia\55 (now West Virginia), son of Nathan and Mary (Nusbaum) Edmonds. Nathan was a miller, having a mill in Frederick County in the mid 1800s.\64 Benjamin followed in his father's footsteps, operating mills in Chewsville\62 and Sharpsburg\65, Washington County, MD. He is listed as a miller in both the 1850 and 1870 censuses for Washington County. By 1880 he has given up milling and his occupation is given as "Boot and shoe" in the town of Sharpsburg, the same as that of his son, Jacob R. Edmonda. Margaret Ann died 27 February 1886 and Benjamin 3 June 1888, both in Washington County. They are buried In Rose Hill Cemetery, Hagerstown, Washington County, MD.\64

Children of Benjamin Alexander and Margaret Ann (Wolf) Edmonds, all born in Washington County, MD:

```
183     i Alexander Calvin Edmonds, born about 1844. He was in
          government service in Washington DC\62
+ 184    ii Nathaniel F. Edmonds, born 22 January 1846
+ 185   iii Jacob R. Edmonds, born 22 February 1849
  186    iv William Newton Edmonds, born 17 January 1852, died 2 March
          1856.\64 Buried in Rose Hill Cemetery, Hagerstown, MD
```

34 - SIMEON(3) PAULUS [Christina(2) Wolf, Daniel(1)]

Simeon Paulus was the first child of Abraham and Christina (Wolf) Paulus. He was born 14 August 1803\67 in Frederick County, MD where his parents married and lived before going to Ohio 1807/1808. In 1808 his father purchased from Christina's uncle, Frederick Wolf Sr., a tract of 50 acres in German Township, Montgomery County, OH, where Simeon was raised.

Simeon married 8 November 1828 in Montgomery County Barbara Gebhart who was born 31 August 1810\67 in Pennsylvania. Simeon died 27 July 1880 and Barbara 8 June 1889.\67 Both are buried in Fair Cemetery, Lake Road, near Lakeville, St. Joseph County, IN.

Children of Simeon and Barbara (Gebhart) Paulus, all born in Preble Co., OH:

```
+ 187     i John Paulus, born 10 July 1831
+ 188    ii Christina Paulus, born 5 February 1833
+ 189   iii Abraham Paulus, born 31 March 1835
+ 190    iv Mariah Paulus, born 30 January 1840
+ 192    vi Daniel Paulus, born 30 March 1841
  193   vii Catharine Paulus, born 21 August 1843
  194  viii Joseph Paulus, born 27 April 1845, died 12 May 1875 in IN
+ 195    ix Simon Peter Paulus, born 6 April 1848
  196     x Margaret Ann Paulus, born and died 1850 in Preble Co., OH.
+ 197    xi Emeline Paulus, born 22 November 1852
```

35 - DANIEL(3) PAULUS [Christina(2) Wolf, Daniel(1)]

Daniel Paulus was the second child of Abraham and Christina (Wolf) Paulus. He was born 12 January 1807,\68 either in Frederick County or Washington County, MD while his parents were on their way from Frederick County to Ohio. In 1805 his father purchased from Christina's uncle, Frederick Wolf Sr., a 50 acre tract in German Township, Montgomery County, OH where Daniel was raised.

Daniel married 3 March 1828 in Montgomery County Louisiana Treon.

She was born 9 February 1810 in Lebanon County, PA, daughter of Jonathan Frances and Maria Catharine (Leitner) Treon. Daniel was a farmer and they lived in Champaign County, IL, Greenville, OH and then Union City, IN. Louisiana died 1 December 1877 and Daniel 17 September 1902 in Union City, IN. Both are buried in Union City, IN Cemetery.

Children of Daniel and Louisiana (Treon) Paulus:

+ 198   i Christina Paulus, born 11 August 1829
+ 199   ii Catharine Paulus, born 30 December 1830
+ 200   iii Rachel Paulus, born 25 February 1832
+ 201   iv Henry Paulus, born 31 May 1833
+ 202   v Elma Elizabeth Paulus, born 19 October 1834
+ 203   vi Lydia Paulus, born 10 April 1836
+ 204   vii Samuel Paulus, born 14 March 1838
+ 205 viii Lucy Ann Paulus, born 18 January 1840
+ 206   ix Sarah Paulus, born 14 November 1841
+ 207   x Abraham Paulus, born 9 September 1843
+ 208   xi Jonathan Francis Paulus, born 30 August 1844
+ 209   xii Mary Jane Paulus, born 6 February 1849
  210   xii Caroline Paulus, born 7 January 1851 in Ohio, died 31
            January 1865. Did not marry.

38 - MARY(3) PAULUS [Christina(2) Wolf, Daniel(1)]

Mary Paulus was the fifth child of Abraham and Christina (Wolf) Paulus. She was born 25 December 1813\70 in German Township, Montgomery County, OH. She was raised on the 50 acre property purchased in German Township in 1808 by her father from her mother's uncle, Frederick Wolf Sr.

Mary married 27 September 1835 in Preble County, OH William M. Baugher, born 13 September 1811 in Virginia. Mary died 3 August 1889\70 in Wilmot, Noble County, IN and is buried in Salem Cemetery at Wilmot. William died 16 May 1895 in Indiana.

Children of William M. and Mary (Paulus) Baugher:

+ 211   i Allen Baugher, born 9 November 1837
+ 212   ii Francis M. Baugher, born 15 January 1843
+ 213   iii Calvin Baugher, born 16 July 1846
+ 214   iv Marvin Baugher, born February 1849
+ 215   v Sarah Baugher, born 29 January 1852

NOTES AND REFERENCES

1. Estate administration for Jacob Wolf, Montgomery County, OH Probate Court, Case Number 2432.

2. 1850 Federal Census, Jackson Township., Preble County, OH.

3. Montgomery County, OH, Land Records, Book B, 344.

4. Preble County, OH, Marriage Records 1808-1830. Don Short.

5. Biographical sketch of son Washington C. Wolf, History of Otoe County, NB, page 458.

6. 1870 Federal Census, West Lincoln Township, Logan County, IL. Page 272.

7. Ibid. Page 277.

8. State of Illinois, Department of Public Health, Death Certificate.

9. Tombstone, Schaeffer Church Cemetery, Route 725, German Township, Montgomery County, OH.

10. 1850 Federal Census, German Township, Montgomery County, OH.

48

11. Montgomery County, OH, marriage records.

12. Brien, Lindsay M., Cemetery Inscriptions of Montgomery County.

13. 1850 Federal Census, Clay Township, Kosciusko County, IN.

14. Information for John S. and Susan Wolf Montel descendants from "Descendants of Christopher Mantle and Elizabeth Soeston -Montel Family" by Keith E. Ross, 29 Oak Drive, North Manchester, IN 46962, March 1983 and subsequent updates.

15. Tombstone, Camden Cemetery, Carroll County, IN.

16. 1850 Federal Census, Jackson Township, Carroll County, IN.

17. Tombstone, Leesburg, IN Cemetery.

18. 1850 Federal Census, Benton Township, Elkhart County, IN.

19. 1860 Federal Census, Benton Township, Elkhart County, IN.

20. 1850 Federal Census, Jackson Township, Montgomery County, OH.

21. Tombstone, Germantown Cemetery, Montgomery County, OH.

22. History of Montgomery County, OH,

23. 1860 Federal Census, German Township, Montgomery County, OH.

24. "Twin Valley, It's Settlement and Subsequent History 1798-1882". Revd. John P. Hentz, Dayton, OH, Christian Publishing House 1883, page 106.

25. Frederick County, MD, Administration Accounts, Bookk RB1, 173.

26. Montgomery County, OH, Land Records, Book DBX2, 43.

27. Tombstone, Germantown Cemetery, Montgomery County, OH and the family bible which says Daniel was born 12 December 1794.

28. 1850, 1860, 1870 Federal Census, German Township, Montgomery County, OH.

29. Tombstone, Ellerton Cemetery, Jefferson Township, Montgomery County, OH.

30. 1860 Federal Census, Miami Township, Montgomery County, OH.

31. 1880 Federal Census, German Township, Montgomery County, OH.

32. Tombstone, Mifflin Cemetery, Ashland County, OH.

33. Washington County, MD, Marriage License Index.

34. 1850, 1860 Federal Census, Vermillion Township, Ashland County, OH.

35. Washington County, MD, Land Records, Book KK, 557.

36. Ashland County, OH Tract Book.

37. Ibid., Land Records, Book 25, 314.

38. Ashland County, OH Cemetery Book, Page 260. Unigraphic, Inc., Evansville, IN, 1979.

39. Ashland County, OH, Inventories, Number 1286, Book 7, 73. Filed 9 March 1863.

40. 1860 Federal Census, Washington County, MD.

41. Information for Daniel Schlosser and his descendants is from "Family Lineage Article: The Family of Henry Schlosser of Frederick County, MD, Part IV", Mrs. Helen W. Seubold, 12000 Old Georgetown Road, Rockville, MD 20852.

42. Tombstone, Willowview Cemetery, Harrison Township, Montgomery County, OH.

43. 1850 Federal Census, Montgomery County, OH.

44. Tombstone, Schang's Church Cemetery, Boonsboro, Washington County, MD. This graveyard was established about 1740 and restored in 1971 by the Boonsboro Historical Society. It was associated with a church variously known as Shunk's or Schang's Church. It was the earliest church in the Boonsboro area.

45. Williamsport, MD "Republican Banner", 18 February 1832.

46. Tombstone, Boonsboro Cemetery, Washington County, MD.

47. Washington County, MD, Land Records, Book M, 210.

48. Information for Jacob Blecher and his descendants is from the Blecher history by Arnold Blecker, 1797 San Bernardino Ave., Pomona, CA 91767, July 1969.

49. Birth records, German Reformed Church, Frederick County, MD, page 170.

50. Familienbach Karlsbrunn, page 266.

51. Diary of Jacob Engelbrecht, Volume 2, page 209.

52. Stinger information provided by Donald L. Smith, 4317 Mapel Lane, Carmichael, CA 95608.

53. 1850 Federal Census, Mt. Morris, Ogle County, IL.

54. Ogle County Cemetaries, page 281.

55. 1850, 1860, 1870 Federal Census, Washington County, MD.

56. Williamsport, MD "Republican Banner", 14 May 1836

57. Frederick County, MD, Marriage Record Index

58. Baptismal Records, Salem Lutheran Church, Boonsboro, MD

59. Tombstone, Reformed Church Cemetery, Boonsboro, MD

60. LDS IGI Index, April 1988, page 8511

61. 1850 Federal Census, Washington County, MD, page 208

62. "History of Washington County, MD", J. C. T. Williams

63. 1860 Federal Census, Washington County, MD, page 188

64. Tombstone, Rose Hill Cemetery, Hagerstown, MD

65. "History of Carrollton Manor", page 436

66. 1870 Federal Census, Washington County, MD

67. Tombstone, Fair Cemetery, Oak Road, near Lakeville, St. Joseph County, IN

68. Tombstone, Union City Cemetery, Union City, IN

69. "Marriages in Darke County, OH", Greenville, OH Library

70. Tombstone, Salem Cemetery, Wilmot, Noble County, IN

71. "Names in Stone", Jacob Mehrling Holdcraft, Ann Arbor, Michigan, 1966. "Cemetery Inscriptions of Frederick County, MD".

72. Tombstones, Syracuse Cemetery, Turkey Creek Township, Kosciusko County, IN

CHAPTER NO. 5

FOURTH GENERATION

40 - LEWIS CLARK(4) WOLF [Frederick(3), Jacob(2), Daniel(1)]
Lewis Clark Wolf, second child of Frederick Sr. and Sophia (Clark) Wolf, was born 26 August 1828 in Jackson Township, Preble County, OH. He married 26 September 1850 in Preble County Eliza Jane Harris, born 1 January 1827 in Preble County, daughter of Nathaniel and Sarah (Davis) Harris.

By 1860 the family had moved to Logan County, IL where they appear in Lincoln Precinct in the 1860 Federal Census of Logan County. Lewis died in 1884 and was buried 8 April 1884 in Carthage, Jasper County, MO. Eliza Jane died 7 May 1904 in Lamar, Barton Co., MO.

Known children of Lewis Clark and Eliza Jane (Harris) Wolf:
+ 216   i Nathaniel Harris Wolf, born 28 November 1851
  217   ii John H. Wolf, born about 1859 in IL

42 - FREDERICK CLARK(4) WOLF [Frederick(3), Jacob(2), Daniel(1)]
Frederick Clark Wolf, fourth child of Frederick and Sophia (Clark) Wolf, was born December 1831 in Jackson Township, Preble County, OH. He married after 1850\1, his wife's name unknown. By 1858 they were living in IL where their three children were born. By 13 September 1866 his wife had died as on that date he married the widow Sarah (Wade) Fraikes. Sarah was born September 1833 in IL,\2 daughter of George W. and Ively Wade. In 1870 they were living in West Lincoln, Logan County, IL. Living with them were his father Frederick and Sarah's father and brother. The Federal Census lists Frederick as a farmer with real estate valued at $3000.\3 It is not known when they died or where they are buried.

Children of Frederick Clark and _____ Wolf, all born in IL:
  218   i Ellen Wolf, born about 1858
  219   ii Alice Wolf, born about 1860
+ 220   iii Martha Wolf, born about 1863
    Child of _____ and Sarah (Wade) Fraikes:
      i Angeline Fraikes, born about 1861, daughter of Sarah (Wade) Fraikes and step-daughter of Frederick Clark Wolf
    Children of Frederick Clark and Sarah (Wade)(Fraikes) Wolf:
+ 222   ii Fred Wade Wolf, born 14 May 1875

43 - DANIEL CLARK(4) WOLF [Frederick(3), Jacob(2), Daniel(1)]
Daniel Clark Wolf, fifth child of Frederick and Sophia (Clark) Wolf, was born about 1834 in Jackson Township, Preble County, OH. He married about 1860 in Logan County, IL Nancy A. _____ (possibly Elder) who was born about 1842 in IL. They lived in Lincoln Precinct, Logan County, IL and sometime prior to 1880 went to South Branch Township, Otoe County, NE. In 1880 his brother Washington Clark Wolf was living there with them.\4 It is not known where or when they died.

Known children of Daniel Clark and Nancy (_____) Wolf, all born in IL:\48
  223   i George W. Wolf, born about 1861
  224   ii Alvin H. Wolf, born about 1863
  225   iii Flora L. Wolf, born about 1869
  226   iv Washington M. Wolf, born about 1873

51

46 - REBECCA JANE(4) WOLF [Frederick(3), Jacob(2), Daniel(1)]
Rebecca Jane Wolf, eighth child of Frederick and Sophia (Clark) Wolf, was born about 1839 in Jackson Township, Preble County, OH. She married George Wirtman, born about 1828 in PA.\5 In 1870 they were living in West Lincoln Township, Logan County, IL. Living with them at that time was her father Frederick.\3 George was listed as a brickmason with real estate valued at $800. It is not known where or when they died.
Known children of George and Rebecca Jane (Wolf) Wirtman, all born in IL:\5
227   i George Wirtman Jr., born about 1863
228   ii William Wirtman, born about 1864
229 iii Samuel Wirtman, born about 1868
230   iv Charles Wirtman, born about 1869

49 - WASHINGTON CLARK(4) WOLF [Frederick(3), Jacob(2), Daniel(1)]
Washington Clark Wolf,\6 eleventh child of Frederick and Sophia (Clark) Wolf, was born 11 November 1845 in Jackson Township, Preble County, OH. Accompanying his parents to IL, he lived with them until thirteen years old. When his mother died in 1858 he began working for himself and in 1860 was living with the family of his brother Daniel Clark Wolf in Logan County, IL. At the age of sixteen he enlisted in the 2nd Illinois Cavalry in 1861 and became a member of Company B. He was mustered in at Camp Butler and served under General Banks. He took part as an active combatant in the siege of Vicksburg, the raid up the Red River, the battle of Memphis, Jacksonville and Baton Rouge and was mustered out, after a service of three years, at Camp Butler, receiving an honorable discharge. After leaving the Union Army he returned to the avocation of husbandry in Township 19, Logan County, IL.
He married 8 August 1865 in Logan County Matilda Donovan, born 15 November 1848 in Logan County, daughter of David and Sarah (Martin) Donovan. She died 24 November 1867 in Lincoln Township, Logan County, IL shortly after the birth of their only child. In 1870 Washington was living in the household of Stephen and Rachel Price, occupation farm worker.
He went to Otoe County, NE in 1879 and in 1880 was again living in the household of his brother Daniel Clark Wolf. He remarried 11 November 1885 to Mary (Flinn) Farrell, widow of Francis Farrell. She was born 22 May 1845, daughter of Charles and Bridget (Butler) Flinn. Mary had been born in Queens County, Ireland and came to this country alone when sixteen years old.
Washington was a stock-raiser and owned 480 acres of land in Sections 30 and 31 of South Branch Township. He was also Supervisor of Roads and held other offices. He and his wife Mary were members of the Catholic Church at Palmyra. Washington died 28 February 1919 in Otoe County. It is not known when his wife Mary died. They had no children.
Child of Washington Clark and Matilda (Donovan) Wolf:
231   i Charles Edward Wolf, born about 1866 in Logan County, IL

50 - MALINDA ANN(4) WOLF [Frederick(3), Jacob(2), Daniel(1)]
Malinda Ann Wolf, twelfth child of Frederick and Sophia (Clark) Wolf, was born 23 October 1847 in Jackson Township, Preble County, OH. She married 26 September 1866 at Lincoln, Logan County, IL her first cousin Hiram William Shroyer (#87), son of George and Sarah (Wolf) Shroyer. Sarah was her father's sister. Hiram was born 16 July 1843 in Benton Township, Elkhart County, IN. Hiram died 11 March 1918 and Malinda 14 April 1931 at Mishawaka, St. Joseph County, IN. Both are buried in Forest Lawn Cemetery at Mishawaka.

Children of Hiram William and Malinda Ann (Wolf) Shroyer:
```
232    i Oliver Shroyer, born 27 July 1867, died in 1868 in IL
233   ii Daughter, born 12 April 1869, died at birth
+ 234  iii Anna Evalee Shroyer, born 18 March 1870
235   iv Ludie Alice Shroyer, born 17 March 1872, died January 1928 at
          Mishawaka, IN. Married November 1922 Harry Biersworth.
+ 236   v Harry Franklin Shroyer, born 30 April 1874
237   vi Son, born 13 September 1876, died at birth
+ 238  vii Nellie Gray Shroyer, born 22 September 1877
239  viii Otis Shroyer, born 10 January 1881, died at 6 months
240   ix George Shroyer, born 10 January 1881, died at 3 months
+ 241   x Harvey Howard Shroyer, born 13 February 1882
+ 242   xi Irene Sprague Shroyer, born 29 December 1884
243   xii Daughter, born 31 October 1886, died at birth
244  xiii Carlton Earl Shroyer, born 22 March 1888 at Mishawaka, IN,
          died 24 February 1964 at South Bend, IN. Married Edna Groff
```

51 - OLIVER(4) WOLF [Frederick(3), Jacob(2), Daniel(1)]
Oliver Wolf, thirteenth child of Frederick and Sophia (Clark)
Wolf, was born about 1849 in Jackson Township, Preble County, OH. He
married Alice Acker(326), born 1854, daughter of Michael and Suzanne
(Shroyer) Acker. They were cousins, Oliver's father Frederick being a
brother of Alice's grandmother, Sarah (Wolf) Shroyer.\7 Oliver died in
1929 in Elkhart Township, Elkhart County, IN and Alice in 1956 at
Mishawaka, IN. She is buried at Goshen, Elkhart County, IN.
    Child of Oliver and Alice (Acker) Wolf:
+ 245   i Ervin J. Wolf, born February 1875

64 - ABRAHAM(4) MONTEL [Susan(3) Wolf, Jacob(2), Daniel(1)]\8
Abraham Montel, second child of John S. and Susan (Wolf) Montel,
was born 28 December 1825 in OH. He married 23 September 1849 Magdalene Frantz, born 28 February 1827, daughter of Nicholas and Catharine
(Crist) Frantz. Abraham died 6 June 1900 and Magdalene 2 October 1900.
    Children of Abraham and Magdalene (Frantz) Montel:
```
246     i Anne Montel, born 20 June 1850, died 2 October 1916. Did
not marry.
+ 247   ii Samuel Montel, born 3 May 1852
+ 248  iii Jacob Montel, born 25 September 1854
+ 249   iv Susanna Montel, born 16 September 1857
250     v Catharine Montel, born 24 May 1860, died 2 September 1862
+ 251   vi Mary Montel, born 2 March 1864
+ 252  vii Lydia Montel, born 1866
253  viii Nicholas Montel, born 24 July 1870, died 24 August 1872
```

65 - SARAH(4) MONTEL [Sarah(3) Wolf, Jacob(2), Daniel(1)]\8
Sarah Montel, third child of John S. and Susan (Wolf) Montel, was
born 13 December 1827 in OH. She married John Butterbaugh, born 23
July 1815, son of George and Catharine (Olinger) Butterbaugh. Sarah
died 3 July 1886 and John 3 April 1895.
    Children of John and Sarah (Montel) Butterbaugh:
```
254     i George Butterbaugh, born 1850, died 16 November 1853
+ 255   ii William H. Butterbaugh, born 18 April 1851
256    iii Susanna Butterbaugh, born10 June 1853, died 1924. Did not
           marry
257     iv Sarah J. Butterbaugh, born 1 November 1856, died 11 Novem
           ber 1867
258      v Mahlon Butterbaugh, born 1859, died 1949, married Rachel
           Ann _____, born 1864, died 1947
```

259   vi Martha E. Butterbaugh, died 22 September 1861
260 vii Mary A. Butterbaugh, died 29 September 1862
261 viii Louisa J. Butterbaugh, born 1 September 1863, died 26 Octo
        ber 1881. Did not marry.
262   ix Cornelius Butterbaugh, born 6 September 1866, died 1867

   66 - SOLOMON(4) MONTEL [Susan(3) Wolf, Jacob(2), Daniel(1)]\8
   Solomon Montel, fourth child of John S. and Susan (Wolf) Montel,
was born 29 March 1829 in OH. He married 1 June 1852 in Kosciusko
County, IN Catharine Snook, born 14 August 1833. Solomon died 21 March
1907 and Catharine 13 February 1909.
   Children of Solomon and Susan (Wolf) Montel:
263   i John Montel, born 1853
264   ii Susan Montel, born 1855, died 9 August 1869
265 iii Jacob Montel, born 1858

   68 - ADALINE(4) MONTEL [Susan(3) Wolf, Jacob(2), Daniel(1)]\8
   Adaline Montel, sixth child of John S. and Susan (Wolf) Montel,
was born in 1832 in OH. She married 8 November 1849 George Tridle II,
born in 1825. George died in 1853 and Adaline in 1855.
   Children of George II and Adaline (Montel) Tridle:
266   i Margaret Tridle
+ 267   ii George Tridle III, born 16 May 1854

   69 - GEORGE(4) MONTEL [Susan(3) Wolf, Jacob(2), Daniel(1)]\8
   George Montel, seventh child of John S. and Susan (Wolf) Montel,
was born in 1834 in OH. He married 16 November 1856 Sarah Ann Yount,
born 27 April 1839. Sarah died 10 December 1865.
   Children of George and Sarah Ann (Yount) Montel, order of birth
uncertain:
268   i Margaret B. Montel
269   ii Lucinda Montel
270 iii Mahlon Montel
271   iv Ellen Montel
272   v Oda Montel, married Joseph Smith
273   vi Albert Montel

   72 - SUSANNAH(4) MONTEL [Susan(3) Wolf, Jacob(2), Daniel(1)]\8
   Susannah Montel, tenth child of John S. and Susan (Wolf) Montel,
was born in 1842 in OH. She married 7 August 1861 Henry Rager. It is
not known when they died.
   Children of Henry and Susannah (Montel) Rager:
+ 274   i Benson Rager
275   ii Emma Jane Rager, born 7 March 1867, died 4 January 1938,
         married 1) Dr. Allen T. Dorsey, 2) 25 February 1897 Dennis
         Dulaney, 3) _____ Caskey
276 iii Charles Rager, born 28 February 1869

   73 - JOHN W.(4) MONTEL [Susan(3) Wolf, Jacob(2), Daniel(1)]\8
   John W. Montel, eleventh child of John W. and Susan (Wolf)
Montel, was born 1 July 1845 in OH. He married Ellen Alvira Eppler,
born in 1844. Ellen died in 1920 and John in 1929.
   Children of John W. and Ellen Alvira (Eppler) Montel:
277   i Artie May Montel, married Jacob Shank
278   ii William S. Montel
+ 279 iii Oris Clyde Montel

74 - SIMON P.(4) WOLFE [Jacob Jr(3), Jacob(2), Daniel(1)]\9
     This branch of the Wolf family is one which added the "e" to
Wolf.
     Simon P. Wolfe, first child of Jacob Jr and Barbara (Izor) Wolf,
was born 4 July 1830 in German Township, Montgomery County, OH. The
family moved to Jackson Township, Carroll County, IN in 1836 where
Simon was raised on the family farm. He married 26 July 1854 in
Carroll County Mary Anna Wagner, born 20 December 1836 in Perry
County, PA, daughter of John and Jane (Varns) Wagner. Immediately
after their marriage Simon and Mary Anna moved to Deer Creek Township,
Cass County, IN, locating upon a farm where all of their children were
born. Simon was Secretary of the Banner Grange in that township. They
then moved to Allen Co., KS. Simon died 26 February 1896 and Mary 3
July 1902 in Humboldt, Allen County, KS. Both are buried in DeWitt
Cemetery in Humboldt.
     Children of Simon P. and Mary Ann (Wagner) Wolfe, all born in
Deer Creek Township, Cass County, IN:
  280   i Charles Simpson Wolfe, born 12 August 1855, died 29 Decem-
             ber 1857. Buried in Paint Creek Cemetery with his maternal
             grandparents, John and Jane (Varns) Wagner.
+ 281   ii Josephine Florida Wolfe, born 22 November 1856
+ 282   iii Caroline Barbara Wolfe, born 8 January 1859
+ 283   iv Margaret Jane Wolfe, born 5 September 1860, twin
  284   v Mary Frances Wolfe, born 5 September 1860, twin. Died 9
             November 1860
+ 285   vi Edward Carrol Wolfe, born 19 April 1862
  286   vii William Alfred Wolfe, born and died 10 August 1864
  287   viii Frank Livingston Wolfe, born 12 March 1867, died 28 Decem-
             ber 1932. Married 20 December 1888 Cimie Husted
  288   ix Dora May Wolfe, born 8 May 1870, died 15 May 1870
  289   x Lucia Victorine Wolfe, born 16 August 1872, died 16 January
             1941 in Akron, OH. Married 1 May 1892 in Grand Junction, MI
             Oliver Arms
+ 290   xi Flora Marie Wolfe, born 27 February 1875
+ 291   xii Amy Pearl Wolfe, born 29 March 1877
+ 292   xiii John Arthur Wolfe, born 12 February 1880
+ 293   xiv Harold Garfield Wolfe, born 14 May 1883

     75 - FRANCES(4) WOLFE [Jacob Jr(3), Jacob(2), Daniel(1)]\9
     Frances Wolfe, second child of Jacob Jr and Barbara (Izor) Wolfe,
was born 12 February 1832 in German Township, Montgomery County, OH.
The family moved to Preble County, OH about 1833 and then to Jacksoh
Township, Carroll County, IN in 1836 where Frances was raised on the
family farm. She married 20 December 1855 (license issued 17 December)
in Camden, Carroll County, IN Conrad Plank, born 23 August 1832 in
Adams County, PA, son of John and Catharine Plank. The ceremony was
performed by D. Smith, pastor of the Evangelical Lutheran Church of
Camden. It is interesting to note that the marriage license gives
Frances' name as Frana and Firena, while the minister's certification
gives Franny.
     At the age of 19 Conrad was apprenticed to learn the carpenter's
trade but after his marriage he engaged in farming and followed this
up to his sudden death, caused by being thrown from his carriage by an
unmanageable horse. The Plank farm contained 240 acres in Section 7
of Deer Creek Township. They were members of the Lutheran Church.\10
Conrad died 17 June 1885 and Frances 25 October 1886 in Deer Creek
Township, Cass County, IN.
     Children of Conrad and Frances (Wolf) Plank, all born in Deer

Creek Township, Cass County, IN:
```
294     i Clarissa Adelaide Plank, born 23 June 1857, died 14 April
          1862
+ 295   ii John J. Plank, born 20 April 1861
  296  iii Malinda Alice Plank, born 5 May 1863. Married _____ Erwin
  297   iv George C. Plank, born 8 March 1865
```

76 - GEORGE ISAAC(4) WOLFE [Jacob Jr(3), Jacob(2), Daniel(1)]\11
George Isaac Wolfe, third child of Jacob Jr and Barbara (Izor)
Wolf, was born 12 June 1834 in Preble County, OH. When he was two
years old his parents moved to Carroll County, IN where he was raised
on the family farm. He married 24 March 1859 Margaret Tolen\12, daughter
of Peter and Nancy A. (Welch) Tolen. They were married on the farm of
Nancy's parents, one mile west of Deacon, Cass County, IN, by Rev.
McReynolds, pastor of the Lutheran Church of Walton.
They began their married life 1 April 1859 on a farm which they
rented. In 1867 he purchased the 80 acre farm from Joseph Daggett for
$1000. It was located three miles north of Young America, Cass County,
IN. At that time only 20 acres were cleared. They remained on this
property for sixty two years. In 1921 they sold the farm and moved to
a property purchased from John Smith located on the north edge of
Young America. This property adjoined that of their son, Charles
Wolfe. At the time of this move they had six children, twenty five
grandchildren and twenty greatgrandchildren living. The Tolens were
originally Lutheran but in 1871 became affiliated with the German
Baptist (Dunkard) Church.\13
George died 28 November 1924 in Young America and Margaret in
1926 in Galveston, Cass County, IN. Both are buried in the Center U.
B. Cemetery in Galveston.
Children of George Isaac and Margaret (Tolen) Wolf:
```
  298    i Child died in infancy
  299   ii Child died in infancy
+ 300  iii Mary E. Wolf, born about 1864
+ 301   iv Sarah C. Wolf, born 1865
+ 302    v Caroline Evalina Wolf, born 2 November ____
+ 303   vi Lydia Ladoskey Wolf, born 19 May 1870
+ 304  vii Anna Margaret Wolf, born 8 October 1871
  305 viii Carrie I. Wolf, born November 1878 in Deer Creek Township,
           Cass County, IN, died 13 December 1920 in Galveston, Cass
           County. Buried in Center U.B.Cemetery, Young America, Cass
           County. She was an invalid and did not marry.
+ 306   ix Charles Henry Wolf, born 4 July 1881
```

77 - JACOB III(4) WOLF [Jacob Jr(3), Jacob(2), Daniel(1)]\9
Jacob Wolf III, fourth child of Jacob Jr and Barbara (Izor) Wolf,
was born about 1836 in Preble County, OH. The year of his birth his
parents moved to Jackson Township, Carroll County, IN where he was
raised on the family farm. He married Mary Insley. Jacob died about
1904 in Moberly, MO.
Children of Jacob III and Mary (Insley) Wolf, order of birth
uncertain:
```
  307    i Clarence Wolf
  308   ii Gilbert Wolf
  309  iii Henry Wolf
  310   iv Louis Wolf
  311    v _____ Wolf
```

78 - DANIEL(4) WOLF [Jacob Jr(3), Jacob(2), Daniel(1)]\9

Daniel Wolf, fifth child of Jacob Jr and Barbara (Izor) Wolf, was born 16 January 1840 in Jackson Township, Carroll County, IN where he was raised on the family farm. He married 1) 10 April 1864 in Carroll County Polly Young\14 who died about 1869. He married 2) October 1883 Sarah Eleanor Cree who was born 2 March 1844 in Preble County, OH, daughter of Samuel Walker and Elizabeth (Welty) Cree. There were no children by this second marriage. Daniel died 7 February 1907 in Jackson Township and Sarah 8 May 1918 in Rockford, Carroll County, IN

Child of Daniel and Polly (Young) Wolf:
+ 312   i Isaac Wolf, born 17 April 1865

79 - MAGDALENA L.(4) WOLF [Jacob Jr(3), Jacob(2), Daniel(1)]\9
Magdalena L. Wolf, sixth child of Jacob Jr and Barbara (Izor) Wolf was born 27 December 1844 in Jackson Township, Carroll County, IN where she was raised on the family farm. She was married by Rev. S. P. Snyder 13 February 1862 in Carroll County to Robert Cree,\15 born 25 December 1838 in IN, son of Samuel Walker and Elizabeth (Welty) Cree. Magdalene died 2 June 1917 and Robert 28 October 1928 in Rock Creek Township, Carroll County. He died of a fractured hip and embolism of the lung.\16 They are buried in the IOOF Cemetery, Rockfield, Carroll County.

Children of Robert and Magdalene (Wolf) Cree:
+ 313   i Anna C. Cree, born 20 June 1863
+ 314   ii Clarisse Cree, born 5 July 1865
+ 315 iii Margaret Cree, born 23 October 1868
+ 316   iv George Robert Cree, born 17 July 1871
+ 317   v Henry Cree, born 17 December 1874
+ 318   vi Albert Cree, born 12 October 1879
+ 319 vii Ezra Cree, born 19 July 1883

81 - MALINDA J.(4) WOLF [Jacob Jr(3), Jacob(2), Daniel(1)]\9
Malinda J. Wolf, eighth child of Jacob Jr and Barbara (Izor) Wolf, was born 26 July 1852 in Jackson Township, Carroll County, IN where she was raised on the family farm. She was married 26 December 1872 in Carroll County by G. L. Stevens\17 to John Andrew Cree, born 20 November 1850 in Indiana, son of Samuel Walker and Elizabeth (Welty) Cree. John died 26 October 1928 in Democrat Township, Carroll County of "chronic endocarditis" and Malinda 1 October 1934 in Jackson Township of "acute dilation of heart". Both are buried in Camden Cemetery, Camden, IN.\18

Children of John Andrew and Malinda J. (Wolf) Cree:
+ 320   i Carl Cree, born 16 April 1875
  321   ii Delsinia Lilly Cree, born 7 July 1879, died 2 March 1950.
          Married 8 February 1905 Berlie A. Rice
+ 322 iii Clarence Cree, born 16 January 1882
+ 323   iv Goldalee Cree, born 22 November 1889
  324   v Earl Cree, born 23 December 1893, died 23 November 1952.
          Married 1) Mary Melton, 2) unknown and 3) Anna R. Shafer

82 - SUZANNE(4) SHROYER [Sarah(3) Wolf, Jacob(2), Daniel(1)]\7
Suzanne Shroyer, first child of George and Sarah (Wolf) Shroyer, was born about 1830 in Preble County, OH and died 11 March 1918 in Goshen, Elkhart County, IN. She married 12 March 1848 Michael Acker, born about 1824.

Children of Michael and Suzanne (Shroyer) Acker:
  325   i Thomas Acker, born in 1849
  326   ii Alice Acker, born in 1854. Married her cousin Oliver Wolf
          (number 51, see his section for details and family.)

84 - DANIEL W.(4) SHROYER [Sarah(3) Wolf, Jacob(2), Daniel(1)]\7
Daniel W. Shroyer, third child of George W. and Sarah (Wolf)
Shroyer, was born 12 November 1833 in Preble County, OH. He married 30
November 1854 Matilda Huffman, born 25 June 1836 in Indiana. Matilda
died 8 October 1904 and Daniel 15 November 1911 in Kosciusko County,
IN. Both are buried in Oakwood Cemetery.
    Children of Daniel W. and Matilda (Huffman) Shroyer:
    327   i Sarah Ann Shroyer, born in 1855, died 24 April 1916, buried
              in Oakwood Cemetery. Did not marry.
 + 328   ii Hiram T. Shroyer, born 1 August 1858
 + 329   iii William Shroyer, twin, born 11 June 1865
    330   iv Albert Shroyer, twin, born 11 June 1865, died 29 August
              1865
 + 331   v Lewis E. Shroyer, born 27 October 1867
    332   vi Johnny Shroyer, born 16 September 1870 in Kosciusko County,
              IN, died 28 October 1874, buried in Leesburg Cemetery,
              Kosciusko County.
    333   vii Luella Shroyer, born 21 January 1873 in Kosciusko County,
              IN, died in 1945. Married 29 June 1907 Frank Wilcox, born
              1864, died 1926.

    86 - GEORGE W.(4) SHROYER [Sarah(3) Wolf, Jacob(2), Daniel(1)]\7
    George W. Shroyer, fifth chid of George and Sarah (Wolf) Shroyer,
was born in 1839 in Preble County, OH. He married 30 July 1863 Elizabeth Thompson, born in 1839. George died in 1865 in Benton, Elkhart
County, IN and is buried in Leesburg Cemetery, Kosciusko County, IN.
    Child of George W. and Ilizabeth (Thompson) Shroyer:
    334   i Susan Matilda Shroyer, born 5 January 1864, died 27 Septem-
              ber 1865

    87 - HIRAM W.(4) SHROYER [Sarah(3) Wolf, Jacob(2), Daniel(1)]\7
    Hiram William Shroyer, sixth child of George and Sarah (Wolf)
Shroyer, was born 16 July 1843 at Benton, Elkhart County, IN. He
married 26 September 1866 at Lincoln, Logan County, IL, his first
cousin, Malinda Ann Wolf, daughter of Frederick and Sophia
(Clark) Wolf. (See number 50, Malinda Ann Wolf for details of this
family.)

    91 - JACOB(4) WOLF [Daniel(3), Jacob(2), Daniel(1)]
    Jacob Wolf, third child of Daniel and Anna (Michael) Wolf, was
born in 1845 in Preble County, OH. He married about 1880 Lydia _____,
born 1848 in Indiana. In 1900 and 1910 Jacob was a mail carrier in
Syracuse, Kosciusko County, IN. Jacob died in 1912 and Lydia in 1923.
Both are buried in Syracuse Cemetery, Turkey Creek Township, Kosciusko
County. His stone is marked GAR.\19
    Children of Jacob and Lydia (_____) Wolf:\20
    335   i Mary L. Wolf, born June 1880
    336   ii Daniel R. Wolf, born in 1882 in Indiana, died in 1942.
              Married Georgia F____, born in 1893 in Indiana, died in
              1940. In 1900 and 1910 Daniel was a baker in Syracuse,
              Kosciusko County, IN. Both are buried in Syracuse Cemetery.
    337   iii Edna E. Wolf, born June 1885 in Indiana

    92 - MARY S.(4) WOLF [Daniel(3), Jacob(2), Daniel(1)]
    Mary S. Wolf, fourth child of Daniel and Anna (Michael) Wolf, was
born about 1848 in Preble County, OH. She married about 1868 _____
Ball.
    Child of _____ and Mary S. (Wolf) Ball:

338   i Effa Ball, born about 1869 in Indiana. In 1880 she was
living with her grandparents, Daniel and Anna Wolf, in
Benton Township, Elkhart County, IN.\21

93 - CATHERINE(4) WOLF [Daniel(3), Jacob(2), Daniel(1)]

Catherine Wolf, fifth child of Daniel and Anna (Michael) Wolf, was born in 1850 in Preble County, OH. She married Alphonse Odell, born in 1853. Catherine died in 1917 and Alphonse in 1918. Both are buried in Syracuse Cemetery, Turkey Creek Township, Kosciusko County, IN.\19

Children of Alphonse and Catherine (Wolf) Odell:
339   i Violette Odell, born in 1880, stone in Syracuse Cemetery,
Turkey Creek Township, Kosciusko County, IN with date of
death not completed.
340   ii Vera Odell, born in 1889, died in 1973, buried in Syracuse
Cemetery

96 - GEORGE W.(4) WOLF [Daniel(4), Jacob(2), Daniel(1)]

George W. Wolf, eighth child of Daniel and Anna (Michael) Wolf, was born in 1859 in Benton Township, Elkhart County, IN. He married Almeda _____, born in 1864. George died in 1938 and Almeda in 1942. Both are buried in Syracuse Cemetery, Turkey Creek Township, Kosciusko County, IN.\19

Children of George W. and Almeda (_____) Wolf:\20
341   i Kimber Wolf, born 1887 in Indiana, died 1958, buried in
Syracuse Cemetery
342   ii Ralph Wolf, born 1889 in Indiana, died 1918, buried in
Syracuse Cemetery. Stone marked OES
343   iii Ruth Wolf, born about 1893 in Indiana

104 - MARIA(4) KIMMERLING [Frederick Jr(3), Catherine(2) Wolf, Daniel(1)]

Maria Kimmerling, first child of Frederick Jr and Catherine (_____) Kimmerling, was born in 1830 in German Township, Montgomery County, OH. She married Leonard Dechant, born in 1827. Leonard died in 1894 and Maria in 1915. Both are buried in the Kimmerling plot in Germantown Cemetery, Montgomery County, OH along with two children.\22

Known children of Leonard and Maria (Kimmerling) Dechant:
344   i Charles F. Dechant, born 1848, died 1850, buried in Germantown Cemetery
345   ii Alice V. Dechant, born 1850, died 1905, buried in Germantown Cemetery

105 - EMANUEL(4) KIMMERLING [Frederick Jr(3), Catherine(2) Wolf, Daniel(1)]

Emanuel Kimmerling, second child of Frederick Jr and Catherine (_____) Kimmerling, was born about 1833 in German Township, Montgomery County, OH. He married about 1859 Helen N. _____ who was born about 1842 in OH. They lived initially with his parents\23 on the property purchased by his greatgrandmother, Elizabeth (Wolf) Kimmerling in 1810 and willed to her daughter Catherine in 1815. In 1841 the property was transferred to his father and his father's brother, Abraham, as "legal heirs of Catherine Kimmerling". In 1860 they established their own household, still in German Township of Montgomery County. In the 1860 Federal Census the family is listed twice - with his father, Family #1037, and as head of Family #77 in Germantown. His occupation is listed as Bricklayer.

Child of Emanuel and Helen N. (_____) Kimmerling:

346   i Charles F. Kimmerling, born about 1860 in German Township,
           Montgomery County, OH

     106 - MARY MAGDALENA(4) SHARRITT [Elizabeth(3) Hahn, Elizabeth(2)
Wolf, Daniel(1)]\24
     Mary Magdalena Sharritt, first child of Daniel and Elizabeth
(Hahn) Sharritt, was born 22 June 1822 in Montgomery County, OH. She
married John Pontious, born 9 February 1819, son of Abraham and Eva
Catherine (Stettler) Pontious. Mary Magdalene died 9 January 1886 and
John 14 November 1900.
     Children of John and Mary Magdalene (Sharritt) Pontious, order of
birth uncertain:
+ 347   i Amanda Pontious
+ 348   ii Serenius Pontious, born 20 November 1844
  349   iii Malinda Pontious
+ 350   iv Sarah Pontious
+ 351   v Samuel Pontious
+ 352   vi Ellen Pontious
  353   vii Allen Pontious, living in 1924
  354   viii John Pontious, living in 1924

     107 - ELIZABETH HELENA(4) SHARRITT [Elizabeth(3) Hahn, Eliza-
beth(2) Wolf, Daniel(1)]\24
     Elizabeth Helena Sharritt, second child of Daniel and Elizabeth
(Hahn) Sharritt, was born in 1824 in Montgomery County, OH. She
married John W. Hipple. Elizabeth died 24 July 1904.
     Children of John W. and Elizabeth Helena (Sharritt) Hipple, order
of birth uncertain:
+ 355   i Andrew J. Hipple
+ 356   ii Daniel Hipple
+ 357   iii Salome Hipple
+ 358   iv Minerva Hipple
  359   v William L. Hipple, living in 1924
  360   vi John I. Hipple, living in 1924
  361   vii Mary Hipple, living in 1924. Married _____ Myers
  362   viii Ella Hipple, living in 1924. Married _____ Schroeder

     108 - JOHN(4) SHARRITT [Elizabeth(3) Hahn, Elizabeth(2) Wolf,
Daniel(1)]\24
     John Sharritt, third child of Daniel and Elizabeth (Hahn) Shar-
ritt, was born in Montgomery County, OH. He died before 1924.
     Children of John and _____ Sharritt, order of birth uncertain:\24
+ 363   i Peter Sharritt
+ 364   ii Henry Sharritt
+ 365   iii George Sharritt
+ 366   iv Catherine Sharritt
  367   v Amanda Sharritt, living in 1924. Married _____ Clensey
  368   vi Jane Sharritt, living in 1924. Married _____ Peffly
  369   vii Savilda Sharritt, living in 1924. Married _____ Temple
  370   viii Dolly Sharritt, living in 1924. Married _____ Curliss
  371   ix Frank Sharritt, living in 1924
  372   x Monroe Sharritt, living in 1924

     109 - SAMUEL(4) SHARRITTS [Elizabeth(3) Hahn, Elizabeth(2) Wolf,
Daniel(1)]\24
     This family added an "s" to Sharritt.
     Samuel Sharritts, fourth child of Daniel and Elizabeth (Hahn)
Sharritt, was born 28 October 1827 in Montgomery County, OH. He

married 30 October 1853 in Montgomery County Margaret Stettler, born March 1834 in Miami Township, Montgomery County, daughter of Thomas and Elizabeth (_____) Stettler. Margaret died 24 November 1906 in Miami Township, Montgomery County and Samuel 23 November 1914 in Germantown, Montgomery County. Both are buried in Germantown Cemetery, Montgomery County.\25

Children of Samuel and Margaret (Stettler) Sharritts, all born in Montgomery County, OH:

373   i Mary Elizabeth Sharritts, born 2 June 1857, died May 1931. Married Samuel W. Libecap, born 1854, died 1933. Both are buried in Germantown Cemetery, Montgomery County, OH

374   ii Sarah Sharritts, born about 1859, died before 1870

375 iii Charles Edward Sharritts, born 24 July 1862, died 17 November 1939. Married Isabel _____.

+ 376 iv Alice Arretta Sharritts, born 22 August 1864

377   v Horace Clayton Sharritts, born October 1869

110 - WILLIAM(4) SHARRITT [Elizabeth(3) Hahn, Elizabeth(2) Wolf, Daniel(1)]\24

William Sharritt, fifth child of Daniel and Elizabeth (Hahn) Sharritt, was born in 1829 in Montgomery County, OH. He married Mary Martz, born in 1830. Mary died in 1902 and William in 1921. Both are buried in Germantown Cemetery, Montgomery County, OH.\22

Children of William and Mary (Martz) Sharritt:

378   i Florence V. Sharritt, born 1860, died 26 June 1923. Married _____ Boyer

379   ii Lemuel L. Sharritt, born 31 July 1863, died 4 July 1878

111 - LEONARD(4) SHARRITT [Elizabeth(3) Hahn, Elizabeth(2) Wolf, Daniel(1)]\24

Leonard Sharritt, sixth child of Daniel and Elizabeth (Hahn) Sharritt, was born 16 December 1831 in Miami Township, Montgomery County, OH. He married 17 December 1854 in Montgomery County Elizabeth Zecher, born in 1833. Leonard died 1 December 1908 and Elizabeth in 1923. Both are buried in Germantown Cemetery, Montgomery County. They were members of the United Brethren Church.\26

Children of Leonard and Elizabeth (Zecher) Sharritt, order of birth uncertain:

+ 380   i Aaron Sharritt

381   ii Ella Sharritt, died after 1924. Married _____ Lambert

382 iii Emma Sharritt, died after 1924. Married _____ Bartles

383   iv Laura Sharritt, died after 1924. Married _____ Whipp

384   v Edwin Sharritt, died after 1924

385   vi Sally Sharritt, died after 1924. Married _____ Friedline

386 vii Cora Sharritt, died after 1924. Married _____ Smith

387 viii David C. Sharritt, died 5 May 1860. Buried in Germantown Cemetery, Montgomery County, OH\25

113 - HIRAM(4) SHARRITT [Elizabeth(3) Hahn, Elizabeth(2) Wolf, Daniel(1)]\24

Hiram Sharritt, eighth child of Daniel and Elizabeth (Hahn) Sharritt, was born in 1834 in Miami Township, Montgomery County, OH. He married 27 March 1862 in Montgomery County Melazina Buehler, born in 1834. Melazina died in 1903 and Hiram in 1921. Both are buried in Germantown Cemetery, Montgomery County.\25

Children of Hiram and Melazina (Buehler) Sharritt, all buried in Germantown Cemetery, Montgomery County, OH\22

388   i Florence M. Sharritt, born 1865, died 1879

```
389    ii  Ida Sharritt, born 1867, died 1954. Did not marry
390   iii  Minnie May Sharritt, born 8 March 1869, died 23 July 1869
391    iv  Oma Sharritt, born 1871, died 1963. Did not marry
392     v  L. Jesse Sharritt, born 1873, died 1956. Married S. Enola,
            born 1868, died 1952
```

114 - SOPHIA(4) SHARRITT [Elizabeth(3) Hahn, Elizabeth(2) Wolf,
Daniel(1)]\24
Sophia Sharrett, ninth child of Daniel and Elizabeth (Hahn)
Sharritt, was born about 1838 in Miami Township, Montgomery County,
OH. She married John Shumaker. Sophia died before 1924.
Children of John and Sophia (Sharrett) Shumaker, order of birth
uncertain:

```
+ 393    i  Daniel Shumaker
  394   ii  Laura Shumaker, died after 1924. Married _____ Woodward
  395  iii  Alonzo Shumaker, died after 1924
  396   iv  William Shumaker, died after 1924
  397    v  Emma Shumaker, died after 1924. Married _____ Norris
  398   vi  Mary Shumaker, died after 1924
  399  vii  Jennie Shumaker, died after 1924. Married _____ Harrington
  400 viii  Elizabeth Shumaker, died after 1924. Married _____ Bell
  401   ix  Ella Shumaker, died after 1924. Married _____ Smith
```

115 - DANIEL JR(4) SHARRITT [Elizabeth(3) Hahn, Elizabeth(2)
Wolf, Daniel(1)]\24
Daniel Sharritt Jr, tenth child of Daniel and Elizabeth (Hahn)
Sharritt, was born 30 May 1840 in Miami Township, Montgomery County,
OH. He married Ann Agnes Ingram. He died 6 December 1920 and Ann Agnes
at a later date. They were Lutherans, members of Emmanuel's Church in
Germantown, Montgomery County. Daniel is buried in Germantown Ceme-
tery.\26
Children of Daniel Jr and Ann Agnes (Ingram) Sharritt:\26

```
  402    i  Martha Sharritt, born 1 August 1879, died 4 November 1962.
            Married Frank Wolpers
+ 403   ii  Harvey Sharritt
```

116 - JACOB(4) SHARRITT [Elizabeth(3) Hahn, Elizabeth(2), Wolf,
Daniel(1)]\24
Jacob Sharritt, eleventh child of Daniel and Elizabeth (Hahn)
Sharritt, was born about 1843 in Miami Township, Montgomery County,
OH. He died before 1924.
Children of Jacob and _____ Sharritt:

```
  404    i  Edward Sharritt
  405   ii  Harley Sharritt
```

124 - SARAH(4) WOLF [Daniel(3), Frederick(2), Daniel(1)]
Sarah Wolf, first child of Daniel and Elizabeth (Bennett) Wolf,
was born about 1824 in Boonsboro, Washington County, MD. About 1830
her parents went to Richland (now Ashland) County, OH with the family
of her maternal grandfather, Aquilla Bennett. She married 31 December
1848 in Ashland County John Bennett,\27 very probably a nephew of her
mother and thus a first cousin.
Known child of John and Sarah (Wolf) Bennett:

```
  406    i  Henry Bennett, born about 1852 in OH. In 1860 he was living
            with his grandfather Daniel Wolf.\28
```

125 - DANIEL JR(4) WOLF [Daniel(3), Frederick(2), Daniel(1)]
Daniel Wolf Jr, second child of Daniel and Elizabeth (Bennett)

Wolf, was born about 1826 in Boonsboro, Washington County, MD. About 1830 his parents went to Richland (now Ashland) County, OH with the family of his maternal grandfather Aquilla Bennett. He married 16 March 1848 in Ashland County Sophia Deeter.\27 born about 1825 in Maryland, daughter of Daniel and Sophia (_____) Deeter. Daniel was a blacksmith, a trade followed by his father Daniel and grandfather, Frederick Wolf, who was one of the first blacksmiths in the Boonsboro, MD area. Daniel died in 1852 and Sophia in 1854, probably in Ashland County. Places of burial are unknown. After the death of Daniel and Sophia his father, Daniel Sr, was appointed guardian of the three minor children.

Children of Daniel Jr and Sophia (Deeter) Wolf, all born in Ashland County, OH:\29

```
  407    i  Amanda Wolf, born about 1849
+ 408   ii  Franklin Wolf, born 7 January 1850
  409  iii  Samantha Wolf, born about 1852
```

127 - MICHAEL(4) WOLF [Daniel(3), Frederick(2), Daniel(1)]
    Michael Wolf, fourth child of Daniel and Elizabeth (Bennett) Wolf, was born 30 September 1829 in Vermillion Township, Richland (now Ashland) County, OH. He married 24 March 1850 in Ashland County 1) Leah Casey,\27 born about 1832 in Ohio. Michael was a farmer and in 1855 he and his famoly moved to Washington County, IA and in 1871 to Grant Township, Union County, IA where he entered land from the government.
    Leah died in 1866 in Washington County and Michael remarried 19 November 1867 2) Carolyn M. McCauley, born in 1835. No children by this marriage have been identified. Michael's last years were spent in Keokuk, Lee County, IA where he died 21 December 1880.\30
    Children of Michael and Leah (Casey) Wolf:

```
  410    i  Romina E. Wolf, born about 1851 in Ashland County, OH
+ 411   ii  Simon Peter Wolf, born 27 March 1853
  412  iii  Mary E. Wolf, born about 1855, died 18 April 1881 in
              Washington County, IA. Did not marry
  413   iv  Amanda A. Wolf, born about 1857 in Washington County, IA,
              died 1921 in Union County, IA
  414    v  Matilda Wolf, born about 1860 in Washington County, IA
  415   vi  Emma Wolf, born about 1862 in Washington County, IA
  416  vii  Nettie Wolf, born about 1865 in Washington County, IA
  417 viii  John F. Wolf, born about 1866 in Washington County, IA
```

129 - FREDERICK R.(4) WOLFE [Daniel(3), Frederick(2), Daniel(1)]
    This branch of the Wolf family is one which added the "e" to Wolf.
    Frederick (F.R.) Wolfe, sixth child of Daniel and Elizabeth (Bennett) Wolf, was born 13 January 1836 in Vermillion Township, Richland (now Ashland) County, OH. His parents were natives of Washington County, MD, having emigrated to Ohio in 1829. He remained on his parents' farm until he was 21 and then went to Iowa, locating in Washington County in 1857. He returned to Ohio and married 7 January 1864 in Ashland County Rebecca M. Nickol, born 4 August 1843 in Pennsylvania, daughter of John and Jennie (Thompson) Nickol. After their marriage they moved to Union County, IA farming 280 acres in Section 25 of Grant Township. He devoted attention to stock-raising, making a specialty of short-horn cattle and Clydesdale horses. He was a Democrat and he and his wife were members of the Methodist Episcopal Church. It is not known when they died.\30
    Children of Frederick (F.R.) and Rebecca M. (Nickol) Wolfe, all

born in Union County, IA,\30 order of birth uncertain:
```
 418     i William M. Wolfe
 419    ii Jessie M. Wolfe
+420   iii Charles F. Wolfe
 421    iv Lillie M. Wolfe
 422     v Lovina L. Wolfe
 423    vi Bertie A. Wolfe
+424   vii John A. Wolfe
```

136 - HENRY LAWSON(4) SCHLOSSER [Elizabeth(3) Wolf, Frederick(2), Daniel(1)]\31

Henry Lawson Schlosser, third child of Daniel and Elizabeth (Wolf) Schlosser, was born 1 February 1832 in Boonsboro, Washington County, MD where his father was a wagonmaker. He married 1) 30 November 1856 in Cedar Rapids, Lynn County, IA Rebecca Ellen Roberts, born 22 February 1839. Rebecca died 24 May 1874 as did her ninth child Eva, thirteen days after Eva's birth. They are both buried in West Lebanon Cemetery, Warren County, IN.

Henry married 2) 11 April 1877 Mrs. Elizabeth Neil, born 31 December 1855, daughter of Robert and Margaret (_____) Nise. Henry died 12 March 1912 in Dunlap, Morris County, KS and Elizabeth 12 January 1939 in Long Beach, CA.

Children of Henry Lawson and Rebecca Ellen (Roberts) Schlosser:
+425   i Mary Catherine Schlosser, born 10 October 1857
 426   ii Elias William Schlosser, born 24 December 1859, died 11
           September 1860
+427   iii Ida May Schlosser, born 27 July 1861
+428   iv Sarah Elizabeth Schlosser, born 3 December 1863
 429   v Margaret Ann Baldane Schlosser, born 3 February 1865 in
           Warren County, IN, died 11 June 1961 in Long Beach, CA.
           Married 30 December 1885 Thomas Beasley
 430   vi Fanny Eliza Adaline Schlosser, born 14 February 1868.
           Married James Schaffer. They lived in Coffeeville, then
           Caney, KS
 431   vii Bessie Vonvoria Schlosser, born 9 August 1869, died 2 July
           1938. Married William Vogel. They lived in Fletcher, OK
 432 viii Maude Agnes Schlosser, born 11 August 1872. Married C. L.
           Holland. They lived in Tulsa, OK, then Long Beach, CA
 433   ix Eva Schlosser, born 11 May 1874, died 24 May 1874, buried
           in West Lebanon Cemetery, Warren County, IN with her mother
Children of Henry Lawson and Elizabeth C. (Nise)(Neil) Schlosser:
 434   i Edith Olive Schlosser, born 26 January 1878. Married 18
           February 1902 Louis Irwin. They lived in Long Beach, CA
 435   ii Henry Garfield Schlosser, born 14 May 1880, died 19 August
           1882
 436   iii Frederick Blain Schlosser
 437   iv Earl Franklin Schlosser, born 26 June 1883
 438   v Coy Wilson Schlosser, born 8 July 1886. Married Lettie
           Lutz. They lived in Chanute, KS
 439   vi Robert Dale Schlosser, born 25 November 1889. Married 24
           December 1913 Ruby Louise Hays. They lived at Lakewood, KS
 440   vii Homer Leland Schlosser, born 13 September 1898, died 17
           August 1950 at Chanute, KS. Married 1) Thelma Noyes, 2)
           Bonnie _____

137 - FREDERICK A.(4) SCHLOSSER [Elizabeth(3) Wolf, Frederick(2), Daniel(1)]\31

Frederick A. Schlosser, fourth child of Daniel and Elizabeth

(Wolf) Schlosser, was born about 1834 in Boonsboro, Washington County, MD. He married 3 May 1857 in Warren County, IN Malinda A. Jackson. He died 5 February 1871 in Warren County. Malinda married 2) Franklin Groff 8 July 1874 (license) in Warren County.

Children of Frederick A. and Malinda A. (Jackson) Schlosser, all born in Warren County, IN:
441   i Franklin L. Schlosser, born August 1859
442   ii Frederick S. Schlosser, born about 1864
443   iii Thomas D. Schlosser, born about 1866
444   iv Elizabeth R. Schlosser, born about 1870

141 - ANN REBECCA(4) SCHLOSSER [Elizabeth(3) Wolf, Frederick(2), Daniel(1\31

Ann Rebecca Schlosser, eighth child of Daniel and Elizabeth (Wolf) Schlosser, was born about 1843 in Boonsboro, Washington County, MD. She married 11 January 1867 (License 16 October 1866)\35 in Boonsboro Jacob F. Kinna, born 18 April 1840, son of Samuel and Susanna (Poffenberger) Kinna. Ann died before 1875. Jacob was living in Ordway, Brown County, SD in 1890.

Children of Jacob F. and Ann Rebecca (Schlosser) Kinna:
445   i Charles H. Kinna, born 26 June 1866
446   ii Clayton F. Kinna, born 25 November 1868
447   iii Elizabeth C. Kinna, born 27 October 1870

142 - MARIA(4) SCHLOSSER [Elizabeth(3) Wolf, Frederick(2), Daniel(1)\31

Maria Schlosser, ninth child of Daniel and Elizabeth (Wolf) Schlosser, was born 28 November 1845 in Boonsboro, Washington County, MD. She married 16 October 1873 (license) in Warren County, IN Joseph E. McAlister. Joseph died 13 August 1931 and Maria 5 November 1935 in Danville, Vermillion County, IL. She is buried in West Lebanon Cemetary, Warren Copunty, IN.

Children of Joseph and Maria (Schlosser) McAlister:
448   i Nettie McAlister
449   ii Margaret McAlister

144 - MARGARET S.(4) SCHLOSSER [Elizabeth(3) Wolf, Frederick(2), Daniel(1)\31

Margaret S. Schlosser, eleventh child of Daniel and Elizabeth (Wolf) Schlosser, was born 31 January 1850 in Boonsboro, Washington County, MD. She married 30 December 1868 (license) in Warren County, IN Jacob Howard Ringer, born 25 July 1844 in Washington County, son of Peter and Elmira (_____) Ringer. Margaret died 29 July 1920 and Jacob 23 January 1925 in Williamsport, IN. Both are buried in West Lebanon Cemetery, Warren County, IN.

Children of Jacob Howard and Mary S. (Schlosser) Ringer:
+ 450   i Victor Howard Ringer, born 13 February 1870
  451   ii William Daniel Ringer, born 1874, died 28 November 1898

145 - ELIZABETH(4) WOLF [Joseph(3), Frederick(2), Daniel(1)]

Elizabeth Wolf, first child of Joseph and Anna (Kretzer) Wolf,\32 was born about 1832 in Washington County, MD and went to Ohio with her family between 1840 and 1850. She married 1850-1860 in Ohio Jeremiah Kirkwood, born about 1829 in Ohio.

Known children of Jeremiah and Elizabeth (Wolf) Kirkwood, born in Montgomery County, OH:\33
452   i Laura B. Kirkwood, born about 1859
453   ii Robert W. Kirkwood, born about 1866

148 - ELIZABETH(4) BLECKER [Tracy(3) Wolf, Frederick(2), Daniel(1)]\34
    Elizabeth Blecker, first child of Jacob and Tracy (Wolf) Blecker, was born 7 November 1832 in Washington County, MD. She married 20 September 1853 (license) in Washington County Edward Keedy \35, born 1 July 1828 in Washington County, died 1 March 1897.
    Children of Edward and Elizabeth (Blecker) Keedy:
  454   i Jacob E. Keedy, born 16 April 1857 in Washington County, MD, died 19 march 1863 in Washington County. Buried in Boonsboro, MD Cemetery.
  455   ii Charles Keedy. Married Vallie Miller
+ 456   iii Howard Keedy
+ 457   iv Alice Keedy
+ 458   v Daniel Blecker Keedy
  459   vi William H. Keedy, born 6 Julne 1867 in Boonsboro, Washington County, MD, died 26 July 1922 in Mount Morris, Ogle County, IL. Married February 1902 Edith Young
+ 460   vii Frank C. Keedy, born 8 August 1869
+ 461 viii Annie Keedy
  462   ix Susie Keedy. Did not marry

    149 - MARY ANN(4) BLECKER [Tracy(3) Wolf, Frederick(2), Daniel(1)]\34
    Mary Ann Blecker, second child of Jacob and Tracy (Wolf) Blecker, was born 20 November 1833 in Washington County, MD. She married 1 February 1859 in Washington County Jacob Chalmers Byers,\35 who was born about 1833 In West Virginia. They lived in the Benevola area of Washington County in 1870. Living with them at that time was Carty (Carlton Emmert) Wolf, age 11,\36 son of Mary Ann's widower uncle, Jacob Wolf (#32).
    Known children of Jacob Chalmers and Mary Ann (Blecker) Byers, all born in Washington County, MD:
  463   i William M. Byers, born 28 February 1860, died 11 August 1863 in Washington County. Buried in Boonsboro, MD Cemetery
  464   ii Ann E. Byers, born about 1863. Married 12 August 1878 (license) in Washington County, MD James W. Scott
  465   iii Charles D. Byers, born about 1866
+ 466   iv George Edward Byers, born about 1868
+ 467   v Jacob C. Byers, born about 1870

    152 - JACOB B.(4) BLECKER [Tracy(3) Wolf, Frederick(2), Daniel(1)]\34
    Jacob B. Blecker, fifth child of Jacob and Tracy (Wolf) Blecker, was born 30 March 1838 in Washington County, MD. He married 5 March 1867 (license) Alice Virginia Young,\35 born 5 July 1847. In the 1860, 1870 and 1880 Federal Censuses Jacob is listed as a shoemaker in Boonsboro, Washington County. Alice died 14 July 1889 and Jacob 15 July 1895.
    Children of Jacob B. and Alice Virginia (Young) Blecker, all born in Boonsboro, Washington County, MD.:
  468   i Emma Tracy Blecker, born 18 January 1868, died 30 October 1892. Married 7 September 1891 (license) in Washington County Frank E. Newcomer, born 1868, died 1891. Buried in the Boonsboro, MD Cemetery. No children
+ 469   ii Annie Virginia Blecker, born 20 October 1871
  470   iii Katie May Blecker, born 9 August 1873, died 29 March 1933. Married Harry B. Friend. No children

+ 471   iv Mary Elizabeth Blecker, born 1 December 1875
+ 472   v Effie Young Blecker, born 25 September 1878

   167 - GEORGE W.(4) WOLF [Simon(3), Frederick(2), Daniel(1)]
   George W. Wolf, second child of Simon and Elizabeth (Warwell)
Wolf, was born 22 March 1846 in Boonsboro, Washington County, MD. He
married 10 December 1873 (license) in Washington County Alice E.
Myers, born about 1853 in Maryland, daughter of _____ and Margaret
(_____) Myers. George died 19 November 1881 and is buried in the
Boonsboro, MD Cemetery.\37
   Child of George W. and Alice E. (Myers) Wolf:
   473   i Sarah E. Wolf, born about 1880 in Boonsboro,MD

   171 - FRANKLIN(4) WOLF [Simon(3), Frederick(2), Daniel(1)]
   Franklin Wolf, sixth child of Simon and Elizabeth (Warwell) Wolf,
was born 21 September 1855 in Boonsboro, Washington County, MD. He
married 14 September 1875 (license) in Washington County Laura Henrietta Martz,\35 born December 1856 in Boonsboro, daughter of David H.
and Mahala (Reeder) Martz. Franklin was a shoemaker and in the early
1900s had his residence and place of business on Franklin Street in
Hagerstown, Washington County, MD. Franklin died 4 February 1924 and
is buried in Rose Hill Cemetery, Hagerstown, MD.
   Children of Franklin and Laura Henrietta (Martz) Wolf:
+ 474   i Sherman E. Wolf, born 31 July 1876
+ 475   ii Florence Estella Wolf, born 25 October 1879
+ 476   iii Nora Pearl Wolf, born May 1881
+ 477   iv Truman Leo Wolf, born 1 May 1887
+ 478   v David Earl Wolf Sr, born 26 june 1891
+ 479   vi Carol Reno Wolf, born February 1894

   173 - MARY JEANNETTE(4) WOLF [Simon(3), Frederick(2), Daniel(1)
   Mary Jeannette Wolf, eighth child of Simon and Elizabeth (War-
well) Wolf, was born about 1860\36 in Boonsboro, Washington County,
MD. She married in Washington County Charles Alfred Trone, son of
Lewis Roman and Susanna (Heise) Trone.
   Children of Charles Alfred and Mary Jeannette (Wolf) Trone:
+ 480   i Lucinda Katheryne Trone, born 1 July 1891
+ 481   ii Anna Ruth Trone, born 30 September 1895

   174 - ANN CORA(4) WOLF [Simon(3), Frederick(2), Daniel(1)]
   Ann Cora Wolf, ninth child of Simon and Elizabeth (Warwell) Wolf,
was born 27 November 1861\36 in Boonsboro, Washington County, MD. She
married 30 August 1882 in Hagerstown, Washington County Dr. Richard
Tydings Harman, born 24 August 1820,\35 son of Abram and Catherine Ann
(Diseman) Harman. She was his fourth wife. He married previously 1)
Amelia Eveline (Jewel) Camp, 2) Callie Saylor and 3) Susan R. McMullen
who died 9 September 1877 at 44 years and is buried in Rose Hill
Cemetery, Hagerstown, Washington County. Dr Harman was Doctor of
Homeopathy, having studied at Hanneman Hospital, Philadelphia, PA. Dr.
Harman died 10 October 1892 and is buried at Ocala, Marion County, FL.
Ann Cora died 21 January 1948 and is buried in the Funkstown Cemetery,
Washington County, MD.
   Child of Dr. Richard Tydings and Ann Cora (Wolf) Harman:
+ 482   i Edith Mentzer Harman, born 3 August 1883

   176 - HARVEY J.(4) WOLF [Simon(3), Frederick(2), Daniel(1)]
   Harvey J. Wolf, eleventh child of Simon and Elizabeth (Warwell)
Wolf, was born 18 April 1865 in Boonsboro, Washington County, MD. He

married 5 November 1889\35 at Beaver Creek, Washington County, MD Cora Pearl DeLauder, who was born 21 March 1870 near Myersville, Washington County, daughter of Samuel and Martha Ann (Weddle) DeLauder. Harvey was a farmer in the Leitersburg area of Washington County and died 12 February 1925 of blood poisoning from a cut from a miilk can. Cora died 21 September 1951. Both are buried in the cemetery near St. Paul's Church, Leitersburg.

Children of Harvey J. and Cora Pearl (DeLauder) Wolf:

+ 483   i   Walter Cleveland Wolfe, born 8 June 1891
+ 484   ii Blanche Belle Wolfe, born 28 September 1892
+ 485   iii Fannie Elizabeth Wolfe, born 22 July 1896
+ 486   iv Edith Marie Wolfe, born 2 July 1902
+ 487   v   Charles Eugene Wolfe, born 14 November 1904

178 - VAN LUTHER(4) WOLF [Jacob(3), Frederick(2), Daniel(1)]

Van Luther Wolf, first child of Jacob and Mary Ellen (Albaugh) Wolf, was born December 1852 in Boonsboro, Washington County, MD. Van was raised in Washington County, appearing in the 1860 Federal Census with the family.\38 His mother died in 1863 when he was eleven years old and he and the rest of the children were placed with relatives to be raised. By 1870 he had left Washington County, family tradition saying he went west but didn't like it and returned to the east. He was married 9 March 1876 by Rev B. D. Hotchem in the Marple Presbyterian Church in Broomall, Delaware County, PA to Jane L. Fry, born 21 June 1856 in Pennsylvania. Broomall was a small community a few miles west of Philadelphia.

Van engaged in the carriage building business in Delaware County, PA and by 1880 was located in Beattys, an area on either side of Crum Creek in the northwest section of Springfield Township, Delaware County. The 1880 Federal Census lists him as a wheelwright. Living with his family are his father Jacob, "paralysis", and his brother Carlton Emmert Wolf, also listed as a wheelwright.\39 He acquired property in Media, Delaware County from 1888 to 1890 and sold these properties from 1891 to 1903, in the 1903 sale being described as "of Philadelphia, PA". Later they lived in Philadelphia and Staten Island, NY. They were residents of Pitman, NJ from 1919 until his death in 1927, their residence being 257 Lake Avenue.\40 After Van's death Jane (Jennie) lived in Hagerstown, MD, where relatives of her husband lived, until 1929 when she moved to the Brethren Home, Huntsdale, Dickinson Township, Cumberland County, PA. She died there 6 August 1939 of bronco-pneumonia.\41 Van and Jane are buried in Media Burial Grounds, Delaware County, PA along with their only child, Gertrude.\42

Child of Van Luther and Jane L. (Fry) Wolf:

488   i   Gertrude E. Wolf, born in 1876, died in 1896 in Delaware County, PA. Buried in Media Burial Grounds, Delaware County with her parents.\42 Did not marry.

180 - CARLTON EMMERT(4) WOLF [Jacob(3), Frederick(2), Daniel(1)]

Carlton Emmert Wolf, third child of Jacob and Mary Ellen (Albaugh) Wolf, was born 5 August 1857 in Boonsboro, Washington County, MD. He was raised in Washington County, appearing in the 1860 Federal Census with the family, age three.\38 His mother died in 1863 when he was not yet six years old and he was raised by the family of J. Chalmers Byers whose wife was Mary Ann Blecker, daughter of Tracy (Wolf) Blecker, a sister of Carlton's father Jacob. Mary Ann was thus a first cousin of Carlton. He appears with this family in the 1870 Federal Census in Benevola District #6 of Washington County, MD. J. Chalmers Byers is listed as a retired farmer. Carlton is listed as Carty Wolf, age 11.\36 Sometime before 1880 Carlton and his father Jacob joined the family of Carlton's older brother, Van Luther, in Beattys, Springfield Township, Delaware County, PA. In the 1880 Federal Census Carlton and Van Luther are both listed as wheelwrights, indicating the carriage building trade.\39

Carlton went west to Ogle County, IL, locating on a farm near Mount Morris. He married 11 January 1884 Ella Mary Fridley, born 27 October 1864 in Mount Morris, daughter of John F. and Elizabeth (Hildebrand) Fridley. They farmed until 1907 when he retired because of ill health and the family moved to Mount Morris where he died 15 March 1918.\43 Ella remarride 28 December 1921 at Normal, IL to Carlton's brother John Albaugh Wolf of Hagerstown, MD whose first wife had died in 1917. They lived in Hagerstown until John died in 1931 and she returned to Illinois, where she died in 1946 in Rockford. Carlton and Ella are both buried in Oakwood Cemetery, Mount Morris, IL.

Children of Carlton Emmert and Ella Mary (Fridley) Wolf:
+ 489   i Ada Blanche Wolf, born 1 June 1886
+ 490   ii Emmert Jacob Wolf, born 28 July 1894

181 - CATHERINE(4) WOLF[Jacob(3), Frederick(2), Daniel(1)]
Catherine Wolf, fourth child of Jacob and Mary Ellen (Albaugh) Wolf, was born in 1861 in Boonsboro, Washington County, MD. Her mother died in 1864 when she was not yet three years old and she was raised in the household of Benjamin Alexander Edmonds, a miller appearing in Sharpsburg, Washington County in the 1870 Federal Census. Catherine was 10 years old.\36 Benjamin's wife was Margaret Ann Wolf, younger sister of Catherine's father, Jacob, and was thus Catherine's aunt. In 1880 she was 20, a servant in the household of Nathaniel F. Edmonds who was a son of Benjamin and was thus her first cousin. Nathaniel was a farmer in the Downsville area of Washington County.\44

Catherine married 11 January 1881 in Washington County George W. Highbarger,\35 born in 1856 in Washington County, son of John L. and Elizabeth (_____) Highbarger. They lived in 1882 in Newark, Licking County, OH and Media, Delaware County, PA. Catherine died in 1926 and George in 1932. Both are buried in Boonsboro Cemetery, Washington County, MD.\37

Children of George W. and Catherine (Wolf) Highbarger:
+ 491   i Harry Luther Highbarger Sr, born 1882
  492   ii Carol C. Highbarger. Married Jessie _____. No children
  493 iii Ada May Highbarger, born 1885, died 1948 in Media, Delaware County, PA. Married Frank Green. No children

182 - JOHN ALBAUGH(4) WOLF [Jacob(3), Frederick(2), Daniel(1)]
John Albaugh Wolf, fifth child of Jacob and Mary Ellen (Albaugh) Wolf, was born 13 January 1863\45 in Boonsboro, Washington County, MD 24 days before his mother's death. He was raised in Boonsboro by his mother's brother and wife, John A. and Lydia Albaugh. He is shown in the 1870 and 1880 Federal Censuses of Washington County as the nephew of and living with the John A. Albaugh family. John Albaugh was listed as a variety store owner in 1870\36 and as a farmer in 1880.\44

John married 1) 11 December 1883 in Washington County Nellie K. Fahrney\35, born February 1866 in Washington County, eighth child of Josiah and Lydia Ellen (Drenner) Fahrney. He was a cabinet maker by trade and lived several places after his marriage, primarily in West Grove, Chester County, PA where his children were raised, and in Hagerstown, Washington county, MD where he died.. They also lived for short periods in the midwest and in Oneida, NY. In West Grove he worked in the casket factory and in Hagerstown was a foreman at the

Moller Organ Co.

Nellie died in 1917\37 in West Grove, PA. After her death John married 2) 28 December 1921 in Normal, Ogle County, IL Ella Mary (Fridley) Wolf, widow of his older brother Carlton Emmert Wolf. They lived in Hagerstown until his death 18 March 1931.\45 They were members of the Presbyterian Church. He and his first wife, Nellie, are buried in the Boonsboro Cemetery, Washington County, MD. His second wife, Ella Mary, returned to Ogle County and died in Rockford in 1946. She is buried with her first husband, Carlton Emmert Wolf, in Oakwood Cemetery at Mount Morris, IL. There were no children by this second marriage.

Children of John Albaugh and Nellie K. (Fahrney) Wolf:
+ 494   i Maude Mae Wolf, born 2 March 1886
+ 495   ii Harry Edwin Wolf, born 15 April 1889
+ 496 iii Charles Welty Wolf, born 9 June 1890
  497   iv Ruth Ann Wolf, born 19 June 1893, died in 1971\37 in West
         Chester, Chester County, PA. She practiced nursing all of
         her life, most of her service as a resident nurse at the
         West Grove Hospital, Chester County. In later years she was
         a private duty nurse in West Chester. She did not marry and
         is buried in the Boonsboro Cemetery, Washington County, MD
         with her mother and father.\37
+ 498   v Mary Ellen Wolf, born 26 June 1895

   184 - NATHANIEL F.(4) EDMONDS [Margaret Ann(3) Wolf, Freder-
ick(2), Daniel(1)]
    Nathaniel F. Edmonds, second child of Benjamin Alexander and
Margaret Ann (Wolf) Edmonds, was born 22 January 1846 in Washington
County, MD. He married 28 January 1868 in Washington County Martha E.
Shaw,\35 born 12 September 1850 in Maryland, daughter of Henry and
_____ Shaw. Nathaniel was listed as a farmer in Downsville District in
the 1880 Federal Census of Washington County. He died 5 November 1920
and Martha 6 November 1921, both in Washington County. They are buried
in Bakersville Cemetery, Washington County. His tombstone says he
was a Master Mason.\46
    Children of Nathaniel F. and Martha E. (Shaw) Edmonds, all born
in Washington County, MD:
  499   i Mary E. Edmonds, born about 1868
. 500   ii Benjamin Edmonds, born about 1872. In 1903,04 he was a
         watchman and he and his sister Mary E., both unmarried,
         were living at 6 North Mulberry Street, Hagerstown, Wash-
         ington County, MD\47
  501 iii Margaret L. Edmonds, born about 1874
  502   iv Violetta D. Edmonds, born 9 October 1877, died 6 August
         18__. Buried with her parents in Bakersville Cemetery,
         Washington County, MD\46

   185 - JACOB R.(4) EDMONDS [Margaret Ann(3) Wolf, Frederick(2),
Daniel(1)]
    Jacob R. Edmonds, third child of Benjamin Alexander and Margaret
Ann (Wolf) Edmonds, was born 22 February 1849 in Washington County,
MD. He married 14 November 1871 in Washington County,\35 Georgetta
Hill, born about 1850 in Washington County, daughter of John Hill of
an old Washington County family. Jacob was a shoe dealer in Sharps-
burg, Washington County for 25 years and in 1902 moved to Hagerstown.
They were members of the Reformed Church.\48 He was a nursery agent
and later a traveling salesman, the family living at 33 King Street
and Wayside Avenue in Hagerstown.\47

Jacob died 24 January 1925 in Hagerstown. In his will he left everything to his wife and at her death to daughter Alice E. Edmonds.\49 He is buried in Rose Hill Cemetery in Hagerstown. After Jacob's death Georgetta lived at 912 Hamilton Boulevard and died 2 May 1937. Her will, made 31 March 1925, names her daughter, two living sons and grandchildren.\50 Daughter Alice E. was named executor.

Children of Jacob R. and Georgetta (Hill) Edmonds, all born in Washington County, MD:
+ 503   i Roger T. Edmonds, born 2 May 1873
   504   ii Howard J. Edmonds, born about 1875. He worked for T. B. Woods' Sons, Chambersburg, Franklin County, PA
   505   iii Robert Hill Edmonds, born 24 December 1877, died 1 September 1878 in Washington County. Buried in the Lutheran Graveyard, Sharpsburg, Washington County
   506   iv J. Benjamin Edmonds, born after 1880, died after 1937. He was a clerk for the Cumberland Valley Railroad and lived with his mother at the time of her death at 912 Hamilton Boulevard, Hagerstown, MD. Apparently he did not marry
   507   v Alice E. Edmonds, born after 1880, died after 1937. She did not marry and lived with the family until about 1937 when she moved to 42 Broadway in Hagerstown. She was Executive Secretary of the Washington County Welfare Board

187 - JOHN(4) PAULUS [Simeon(3), Christina(2) Wolf, Daniel(1)]\51
   John Paulus, first child of Simeon and Barbara (Gephart) Paulus, was born 10 July 1831 in Jefferson Township, Montgomery County, OH. He married 24 October 1852 in Smith Township, Whitley County, IN Elizabeth Ann Shaffner, born in 1832.
   Child of John and Elizabeth Ann (Shaffner) Paulus:
   508   i Jacob Paulus, born in 1853 in Indiana

188 - CHRISTINA(4) PAULUS [Simeon(3), Christina(2) Wolf, Daniel(1)]\51
   Chriatina Paulus, second child of Simeon and Barbara (Gephart) Paulus, was born 5 February 1833 in Preble County, OH. She married 23 November 1852 in Euphemia, Preble County Ira A. Keltner, born 25 February 1830 in Ohio, son of Michael and Carrie (Worte) Keltner. Sometime in the early 1860s they migrated to Indiana where they lived thru 1865. They then moved to Iowa living in Linn Township, Dallas County in 1870 and in Washington Township in 1880. Christina became blind in her later years. Ira died 29 March 1916 in Glenwood, Mills County, IA and Christina 28 December 1917 in Sherrard, IL. Both are buried in Martin's Chapel Cemetery, Plattville Township, Mills County, IA.
   Children of Ira A. and Christina (Paulus) Keltner:
   509   i Joseph Keltner, born 1854 in Preble County, OH
   510   ii Barbara Keltner, born 1856 in Preble County, OH
   511   iii Catherine Keltner, born 1861 in Indiana
+ 512   iv Ellen Martha Keltner, born 11 February 1865

189 - ABRAHAM(4) PAULUS [Simeon(3), Christina(2) Wolf, Daniel(1)]\51
   Abraham Paulus, third child of Simeon and Barbara (Gephart) Paulus, was born 31 March 1835 in Darke County, OH. He married 1) 29 March 1863 in Whitley County, IN Sarah Jane Plummer. There were no children by this marriage and they divorced 17 October 1865. Abraham married 2) 14 November 1867 in Columbia City, Whitley County, IN Mary Ellen Crabill. Abraham was a Civil War veteran, having joined the 17th

71

Indiana Infantry 29 February 1864 and was mustered in 9 March 1864. He was mustered out 8 August 1865 at Macon, GA after a period of illness. Abraham died 24 April 1882 in St. Joseph County, IN and is buried in Fair Cemetery, Lakeville, St. Joseph County. Mary Ellen married 2) 23 May 1885 Harvey Powell. There were no children by this marriage.

Children of Abraham and Mary Ellen (Crabill) Paulus, all born in Indiana:

```
513      i William Allen Paulus, born 20 November 1868
514     ii Martin Sylvester Paulus, born 27 March 1870
515    iii Simon Flavius Paulus, born 30 June 1871
516     iv Melvin Lawrence Paulus, born 22 October 1873
517      v Infant Paulus
518     vi Arleva Belle Paulus, born 28 March 1875. Married _____
            Kunkle
519    vii Emma Alace Paulus, born 12 March 1877. Married 6 October
            1895 Charles Hollopeter
```

190 - MARIAH(4) PAULUS [Simeon(3), Christina(2) Wolf, Daniel(1)]\51

Mariah Paulus, fourth child of Simeon and Barbara (Gebhart) Paulus, was born 30 January 1840 in Preble County, OH. She married 9 April 1857 in Ohio Joshua Iler, born 29 June 1831 in Ohio, son of John and Elizabeth (Bantz) Iler. They moved to Van Wert County, OH in 1880 and in 1885 to Noble County, IN where Joshua engaged in agriculture and operated a thrashing machine over a wide area of the county. His farm lay at the north end of Big Lake, near Ormas, IN. Joshua died 5 August 1901 in Noble County, IN and Mariah 4 August 1911 in Indiana. Both are buried in Thorn Cemetery, Washington Township, Noble County.

Children of Joshua and Mariah (Paulus) Iler:

```
+ 520      i John S. Iler, born 17 October 1857
+ 521     ii Robert Iler
+ 522    iii Ezra G. A. Iler, born 17 October 1859
+ 523     iv Alice E. Iler, born 3 April 1868
```

191 - JACOB(4) PAULUS [Simeon(3), Christina (2) Wolf, Daniel(1)]\51

Jacob Paulus, fifth child of Simeon and Barbara (Gephart) Paulus, was born 17 January 1839 in Preble County, OH. He married in 1868 in Whitley County, IN Anna Lavering, born 23 July 1847 in Hancock County, OH, daughter of Harvey and Rebecca (Dye) Lavering. Jacob was in the sawmill business and farmed the Lavering homestead in Thorncreek Township. He served as County Commissioner for three years. They were members of the Methodist Church. Anna died 15 July 1898 and Jacob 31 May 1919 in Whitley County, IN. Both are buried in Eglof Cemetery, Smith Township, Whitley County.

Children of Jacob and Anna (Lavering) Paulus, all born in Whitley County, IN:

```
524      i Lavina Paulus, born 1869. Married 23 August 1896 Samuel S.
            Fogle
525     ii Harvey Paulus, born 26 January 1870, died 17 August 1888 in
            Whitley County
526    iii Allie Paulus, born 1873. Married 5 March 1893 George Clayb-
            augh, a railroad worker, died 25 December 1902
+ 527     iv Joseph Paulus, born December 1875
528      v Clara Paulus, born November 1877. Married 29 October 1910
            at South Bend, St. Joseph County, IN Percy Danser
529     vi Ira Paulus, born April 1879
530    vii Mazie Paulus, born 31 December 1882, died 11 April 1883 in
```

Whitley County, IN. Buried in Eglof Cemetery, Smith Township, Whitley County
531 viii Grover Paulus, born November 1884
532   ix Arvilla Paulus, born 15 October 1886, died 20 January 1892
in Whitley County, IN. Buried in Eglof Cemetery, Smith Township, Whitley County, IN

192 - DANIEL(4) PAULUS [Simeon(3), Christina(2) Wolf,
Daniel(1)]\51
Daniel Paulus, sixth child of Simeon and Barbara (Gephart)
Paulus, was born 30 March 1841 in Preble County, OH. He was drafted to
serve in the Civil War 4 October 1864 and contracted malaria while in
service. He was discharged 5 October 1865 at Victoria, TX. In 1887 he
applied for an invalid pension. He married 13 October 1867 in Whitley
County, IN Elizabeth Waterfall, born 6 February 1846 in Laupen,
Switzerland, christened 13 March 1846 in Kerzerz, daughter of Samuel
and Maria (Helbig) Waterfall. Daniel died 6 March 1917 and Elizabeth 8
March 1920, both in Noble County, IN. Both are buried in Stough
Cemetery, Whitley County.
Children of Daniel and Elizabeth (Waterfall) Paulus:
+ 533   i Emaline Paulus, born 28 August 1868
  534   ii John W. Paulus, born 29 September 1870 in St. Joseph
County, IN, died 23 March 1874 in St. Joseph County. Buried
in Stough Cemetery, Whitley County, IN
+ 5359 iii Laura Ann Paulus, born 16 July 1873
+ 536   iv Finette (Nettie) Paulus, born 16 August 1876
+ 537   v James Julian Paulus, born 28 June 1878
+ 538   vi Samuel Delbert Paulus, born 28 September 1880
  539 vii Rose Paulus, born 17 October 1883 in Noble County, IN, died
6 June 1913 in Lincoln, NB. Buried in Stough Cemetery,
Whitley County, IN. Married Edgar Wright, no children
  540 viii Leeodus Paulus, born 2 November 1885, died 3 January 1905
in Noble County, IN. Buried in Stough Cemetery, Whitley
County, IN
+ 541   ix Christena Marie Paulus, born 16 February 1890

193 - CATHERINE ELIZABETH(4) PAULUS [Simeon(3), Christena(2)
Wolf, Daniel(1)]\51
Catherine Elizabeth Paulus, seventh child of Simeon and Barbara
(Gephart) Paulus, was born 21 August 1843 in Preble County, OH. She
married 23 August 1866 in Columbia City, Whitley County, IN Joseph
Henry Haas, born 11 May 1845 in Bern, Switzerland. They moved to a
farm near Lakeville, St. Joseph County, IN in December 1874. He was a
farmer and veterinarian, raising cattle and tending bees. He spent his
last years in Epworth Hospital, South Bend, IN and died 25 June 1910.
Catherine died 29 October 1915 in St. Joseph County. Both are buried
in Fair Cemetery, near Lakeville, St. Joseph County
Children of Joseph Henry and Catherine Elizabeth (Paulus) Haas:
+ 542   i Daniel Virgil Haas, born 6 November 1866
+ 543   ii Barbara Ellen Haas, born 7 January 1868
+ 544 iii Theodore L. Haas, born 4 June 1870
  545   iv Infant Haas. Buried in Columbia City Cemetery, Whitley
County, IN
+ 546   v Mary Ann Haas, born 23 May 1873
  547   vi Clara Viola Haas, born 13 May 1875 in Lakeville, St. Joseph
County, In, died 17 August 1893. Buried in Fair Cemetery,
near Lakeville
+ 548 vii Joseph Henry Haas, born 15 August 1877

+ 549   viii Martha Elizabeth Haas, born 24 January 1880
  550   ix Infant Haas, born and died 12 February 1882 in Lakeville,
            St. Joseph County, IN. Buried in Fair Cemetery, near Lake-
            ville
+ 551   x Margaret Maycapitolia Haas, born 1 May 1883
+ 552   xi Bertha Marie Haas, born 29 September 1885
  553   xii Maude Blanch Haas, born 3 May 1889 in Lakeville, St. Joseph
            County, IN, died 17 November 1971 in Bremen, Marshall
            County, IN and is buried in Bremen Cemetery. She married 7
            April 1925 in Los Angeles, CA Ferdinand Wilhelm Westphal,
            born 3 September 1877 in Iowa, died 15 December 1958 in
            Indiana

      195 - SIMON PETER(4) PAULUS [Simeon(3), Chhristina(2) Wolf,
Daniel(1)]\51
      Simon Peter Paulus, ninth child of Simeon and Barbara (Gephart)
Paulus, was born 6 April 1848 in Preble County, OH. He married 24
April 1870 in Indiana Anna M. Davis, born September 1850 in Ohio.
Simon Peter started a barber shop in 1873 but after many years his
health forced him to spend time out of doors. He became an insurance
canvasser, a monument canvasser and eventually operated his own marble
shop. He died as a result of an accident 14 November 1907 in Whitley
County, IN and is buried in the Masonic Cemetery, Columbia City,
Whitley County
      Children of Simon Peter and Anna M. (Davis) Paulus, all born in
Whitley County, IN:
  554   i John W. Paulus, born in 1871
  555   ii Jennie Paulus, born 6 September 1873, died 9 October 1894
            in Indiana
  556   iii Unknown Paulus, died young
  557   iv Mamie Paulus, born in 1879
  558   v Unknown Paulus, died young
  559   vi Edith Paulus, born in 1883
  560   vii Unknown Paulus, died young

      197 - EMELINE(4) PAULUS [Simeon(3), Christina(3) Wolf,
Daniel(1)]\51
      Emeline Paulus, eleventh child of Simeon and Barbara (Gephart)
Paulus, was born 22 November 1852 in Preble County, OH. She married 1
November 1879 in St. Joseph County, IN John Wallace, born in 1857.
John died in 1923 and Emeline in 1941, both in Indiana.
      Children of John and Emeline (Paulus) Wallace, all born near
Lakeville, St. Joseph County, IN
  561   i Jake Wallace, born 1878, died 1929 in Indiana
+ 562   ii Martha Ellen Wallace, born 31 October 1881
+ 563   iii Clarence Wallace, born 12 March 1883
+ 564   iv Marie Wallace, born 16 April 1886
  565   v Anne Wallace, born 8 October 1889, died 7 May 1967 in
            Indiana. Married 1) James Hammond, born 7 May 1873, died 26
            November 1937, married 2) Ed Rose
  566   vi Bess Wallace, born 30 October 1891, died November 1967 in
            Indiana. Married Albert Hay, born 1881, died 1969

      198 - CHRISTINA(4) PAULUS [Daniel(3), Christina(2) Wolf,
Daniel(1)]\51
      Christina Paulus, first child of Daniel and Louisiana (Treon)
Paulus, was born 11 August 1829 near Germantown, Montgomery County,
OH. She was married 29 May 1851 in Darke County, IN by JP A. E. Doty

74

to Jacob Wolf, born 8 June 1831 in Harrison Township, Preble County, OH, first child of Daniel and Caroline (Bantz) Wolf.\52 Jacob was raised on his father's farm, 160 acres located in the upper half of Section 11 of Harrison Township. West Baltimore (now Verona), OH was located one mile west of the farm. He probably attended the school located across the road from the east corner of the farm. The land for this school was donated by Abraham Paulus, Christena's grandfather.\53

Jacob purchased five acres of land 26 December 1853 from Christina's aunts, Lydia and Tena Paulus.\54 He was a carpenter and laborer at this time. In 1877 they moved to Jackson Township, Randolph County, IN, north of Union City, near New Lisbon. Their last child was born there. Jacob owned 40 acres of land, their home being near the Little Minnesaw River. Jacob died 10 September 1889 at age 58 and Christina 13 August 1915 at age 86. Both are buried in Lisbon Cemetery, north of Union City, Darke County, IN.

Children of Jacob and Christina (Paulus) Wolf:

567   i Gideon Wolf, born 14 August 1851 near Verona, Preble County, OH, died 17 April 1867. He is said to have died in a logging accident. Buried in Rose Lawn Cemetery, Lewisburg, Preble County, OH.

+ 568   ii Sarah Ellen Wolf, born 3 October 1852
+ 569 iii Nelson Wolf, born 3 June 1854
+ 570   iv Lydia Wolf, born in 1855
+ 571   v Jane Wolf, born 8 September 1857
+ 572   vi Dan Wolf, born 24 April 1859
+ 573 vii Caroline Wolf, born 11 November 1861
+ 574 viii Mary Elizabeth Wolf, born 11 July 1862
+ 575   ix Henry Wolf, born 10 December 1863
+ 576   x John Wolf, born 1 June 1865
+ 577   xi Alice Wolf, born 28 February 1866
+ 578 xii Lucy Wolf, 28 February 1869
579 xiii Ida Wolf, born 11 September 1871 in Preble County, OH, died 8 June 1940 in Union City, IN. Buried in the New Lisbon Cemetery. Did not marry.
+ 580 xiv Clara B. Wolf, born 28 April 1875

199 - CATHARINE(4) PAULUS [Daniel(3), Christina(2) Wolf, Daniel(1)]\51

Catharine Paulus, second child of Daniel and Louisiana (Treon) Paulus, was born 1 January 1831 in Montgomery County, OH. She married 24 November 1850 in Darke County, OH Isaac Siler, born 2 December 1828 in Ohio. Isaac died 2 July 1905 in Ohio and Catharine 20 August 1914 in Dayton, OH. Both are buried in Woodland Cemetery, Dayton.

Children of Isaac and Catharine (Paulus) Siler:
+ 581   i Peter Siler, born October 1851
+ 582   ii Henry Allen Siler, born 1853
+ 583 iii Leonard B. Siler, born February 1855
584   iv Harriet Siler, born 1857 in Ohio
585   v George A. Siler, born June 1858 in Clay Township, Montgomery County, OH
+ 586   vi Sarah Elizabeth Siler, born October 1861
587 vii Elinor Siler, born 1863 in Ohio
588 viii Emma Siler, born 1866 in Ohio
+ 589   ix Frank Siler, born March 1869
590   x Nancy Siler, born 1871 in Greenville, Darke County, OH
591   xi William M. Siler, born July 1875 in Greenville, Darke County, OH

200 - RACHEL(4) PAULUS [Daniel(3), Christina(2) Wolf,
Daniel(1)]\51
Rachel Paulus, third child of Daniel and Louisiana (Treon)
Paulus, was born 25 February 1832 in Monroe Township, Darke County,
OH. She married 11 September 1853 in Darke County Joseph C. Keltner,
his second wife. Joseph was born 11 September 1817 in Montgomery
County, OH, son of Josiah and Susannah(_____) Keltner, both born in
Germany. Joseph's first wife was Diadema Eddington who died 22 October
1852 and by whom he had eight children. Rachel died 20 July 1867 in
Greenville Township, Darke County and is buried in Martin Cemetery,
Greenville Township.
Joseph was both a farmer and a carpenter. He married a third time
29 October 1868 to Hettie Mosier. In 1873 they moved to Anderson,
Madison County, Indiana where he continued his trades until he
retired. He died 7 May 1910 in Anderson and is buried in Maplewood
Cemetery in Anderson with his third wife, Hettie.
Children of Joseph and Rachel (Paulus) Keltner, both born in
Preble County, OH:
+ 592   i Francis M. Keltner, born 1855
+ 593   ii Sanford M. Keltner, born 10 July 1856

     201 - HENRY(4) PAULUS [Daniel(3), Christina(2) Wolf,
Daniel(1)]\51
Henry Paulus, fourth child of Daniel and Louisiana (Treon)
Paulus, was born 31 May 1833 in Monroe Township, Montgomery County,
OH. He married 26 December 1852 in Gordon, Darke County, OH Christina
M. Bope, born 3 June 1831 in Wittenburg, Germany. They lived in
Champagne County, IL and Darke County, OH then in 1871 they moved to
Paulding County, OH near Briceton where they built a new home on the
farm and lived there the rest of their lives. Henry died 19 March 1897
near Briceton and Christina 23 January 1905. Both are buried in St.
Paul's Lutheran Church Cemetery, southwest of Paulding, OH.
Children of Henry and Christina M. (Bope) Paulus:
  594   i George Washington Paulus, born 15 September 1853 in Darke
           County, OH, died 25 February 1859. Buried in St. Matthew
           Lutheran Church Cemetery, Ithaca, Darke County
  595   ii John Henry Paulus, born 10 June 1856 in Darke County, OH,
           died 6 March 1859. Buried in St. Matthew Lutheran Church
           Cemetery, Ithaca, Darke County
+ 596 iii Augustus Daniel Paulus, born 26 September 1858
+ 597   iv Lafayette Paulus, born 10 February 1861
  598   v Louise Ann Paulus, born 30 October 1862 in Darke County,
           OH, died in 1953. She married Warren Pockmier, born 1856,
           died 1944. They are both buried in Warsaw Cemetery, Kos-
           ciusko County, IN
  599   vi Phillip Paulus, born 16 January 1866 in Darke County, OH,
           died 10 September 1867
  600 vii Clara Catherine Paulus, born 18 March 1870 in Darke
           County, OH, died 1943 in Indiana. Buried in Warsaw Ceme-
           tery, Kosciusko County, IN. Did not marry
+ 601 viii Dora Revilla Paulus, born 11 November 1871
+ 602   ix Charles Wilbur Paulus, born 13 March 1875

     202 - ELMA ELIZABETH(4) PAULUS [Daniel(3), Christina(2) Wolf,
Daniel(1)]\51
Elma Elizabeth Paulus, fifth child of Daniel and Louisiana
(Treon) Paulus, was born 19 October 1834 in Montgomery County, OH. She
married 18 July 1896 in Piett County, IL Gideon Wolf, born 8 February

76

1833 in Frederick County, MD, son of Daniel and Caroline (Bantz) Wolf.
Gideon was a younger brother of Jacob Wolf, who was married to her
sister, Christena Paulus. Elma died 28 June 1856 near Gordon, OH,
shortly after the death of their second child and is buried in Rose
Lawn Cemetery, Lewisburg, OH. Gideon remarried Emaline Keltner, born
14 November 1834 in Ohio. Gideon died 16 July 1896 and Emaline 7
December 1924, both in Illinois. They are buried in the Mansfield,
Piatt County, IL Cemetery. There were ten children by this marriage.
     Children of Gideon and Elma Elizabeth (Paulus) Wolf:
+ 603   i Johnnie Wolf, born 1854
+ 604 ii William Henry Wolf, born 25 January 1856

    203 - LYDIA(4) PAULUS [Daniel(3), Christina(2) Wolf,
Daniel(1)]\51
    Lydia Paulus, sixth child of Daniel and Louisiana (Treon) Paulus,
was born 10 April 1836 in Germantown, Montgomery County, OH. She
married 1) 4 October 1855 in Darke County, OH George Fry, born 12
December 1834 in Ohio. George died of typhoid fever 27 March 1873 in
Twin Township, Darke County, OH. Lydia remarried about 1881 Jacob F.
Ware, born 13 December 1820, died 25 August 1903 near Palestine, Darke
County. There were no children by this marriage.
     Children of George and Lydia (Paulus) Fry:
  605   i Mary Fry, born 1857 in Darke County, OH
  606   ii Sarah J. Fry, born 1859 in Mahomet Township, Champaign
         County, IL
  607 iii Franklin Fry, born 1861 in Mahomet Township, Champaign
         County, IL

    204 - SAMUEL(4) PAULUS [Daniel(3), Christina(2) Wolf,
Daniel(1)]\51
    Samuel Paulus, seventh child of Daniel and Louisiana (Treon)
Paulus, was born 14 March 1838 in Montgomery County, OH. He married
aabout 1861 Catharine Keltner, born 1840. Catharine died 9 September
1892 in Richland Township, Darke County, OH and is buried in Beamsville Cemetery, Darke County. Samuel was a Civil War Veteran, having
served 1862-1865. He remarried 12 May 1896 in Paulding County, OH the
widow Mary E. Harris. There were no children by this marriage which
ended in divorce February 1904. Samuel died 29 April 1913 in Gettys-
burg, Darke County and is buried in Beamsville Cemetery with his first
wife, Catharine.
     Children of Samuel and Catharine (Keltner) Paulus:
+ 609   i Rachael Ann Paulus, born 6 September 1862
  610   ii Elmer E. Paulus, born 1864
  611 iii William H. Paulus, born 1869
  612   iv Ella Paulus, born 1872. Married _____ Kuhl
  613   v Ressette Paulus, born 1873
  614   vi Clara Paulus, born 1875. Married _____ Robertson
  615 vii John D. Paulus, born 1877
  616 viii Lafayette Paulus, born 22 March 1878, died 1 December 1958.
         Married Fran C. _____, born 10 April 1883
+ 617   ix Bertha Paulus, born 15 October 1880
  618   x Benjamin Paulus, born 10 June 1881, died 11 March 1883.
         Buried in Beamsville, OH Cemetery
+ 619   xi Bessie Paulus, born 9 April 1883
  620 xii _____ Paulus. Married William Keihl

    205 - LUCY ANN(4) PAULUS [Daniel(3), Christina(2) Wolf,
Daniel(1)]\51

Lucy Ann Paulus, eighth child of Daniel and Louisiana (Treon) Paulus, was born 18 January 1840 near Gordontown, Darke County, OH. She married 7 May 1857 in Champaign County, IL John Hollehan, born 13 May 1823 in County Cork, Ireland. He died 23 August 1880 in Darke County and is buried in Greenville Cemetery, Darke County. Lucy Ann died 9 February 1921 in Mansfield, Champaign County, having suffered diabetes for 15 years, and is buried in Blue Ridge Cemetery

Children of John and Lucy Ann (Paulus) Hollehan:
+ 621   i Joseph Harrison Hollehan, born 29 August 1858
  622 ii John Francis Hollehan, born 26 January 1860 in Pesotum, IL, died 7 April 1942 in Mansfield, IL. Buried in Blue Ridge Cemetery, Mansfield. Married 14 March 1914 Sally Smith
  623 iii Daniel B. Hollehan, born 18 April 1861 in Pesotum, IL, died 3 February 1939 in Chattanooga, TN. Buried in Greenwood Cemetery. Married 1) unknown, 2) Clara _____
  624 iv William Hollehan, born 3 March 1863 in Pesotum, IL, died 6 May 1918 in Mansfield, IL. Buried in Blue Ridge Cemetery in Mansfield
  625 v Peter Hollehan, born about 1864 in Indiana
  626 vi James Thomas Hollehan, born about 1868 in Darke County, OH, died in 1910 in Mansfield, IL. Buried in Blue Ridge Cemetary, Mansfield
+ 627 viii Sarah Ella Hollehan, born about 1870

206 - SARAH(4) PAULUS [Daniel(3), Christina(2) Wolf, Daniel(1)]\51
Sarah Paulus, ninth child of Daniel and Louisiana (Treon) Paulus, was born 14 November 1841 near Gordon, Darke County, OH. She married 18 December 1858 in Champaign County, IL Levi Brooks.
Known children of Levi and Sarah (Paulus) Brooks, all born in Mahomet Township, Champaign County, IL:
  628 i Mary J. Brooks, born 1859
  629 ii Annie Brooks, born 1863
  630 iii John H. Brooks, born 1864
  631 iv William Brooks, born 1867
  632 v Eliza A. Brooks, born 1869

207 - ABRAHAM(4) PAULUS [Daniel(3), Christina(2) Wolf, Daniel(1)]\51
Abraham Paulus, tenth child of Daniel and Louisiana (Treon) Paulus, was born 9 September 1843 in Gordontown, Darke County, OH. He married 7 April 1864 near Shilo, IL Mary Jane Lane, born 1 December 1845 in Colfax, Clinton County, IN, daughter of William and Catherine Jane (Blecker) Lane. They lived in Champaign County, IL, by 1890 farming 160 acres in Newcome Township, 2 1/2 miles south of John D. Wolf's (a cousin) farm located in Brown Township. He retired from farming about 1916 and moved into Fisher, IL. Abraham died 17 October 1926 and Mary Jane 13 December 1931, both in Fisher, Champaign County. They are buried in Willow Brook Cemetery in Fisher.
Children of Abraham and Mary Jane (Lane) Paulus, all but William born in East Bend Township, Champaign County, IL:
+ 633 i William H. Paulus, born February 1865
+ 634 ii Oliver L. Paulus, born 19 April 1868
  635 iii Cora Paulus, born 1871. Married 20 October 1890 Morris Haines
  636 iv Louisiana Paulus, born 1873. Married Vern Sheppard
  637 v Clara M. Paulus, born December 1875. Married 26 June 1902 at Champaign, IL Lee Mulvain

638   vi Joseph F. Paulus, born October 1878. Married 11 February
           1904 at Champaign, IL Ida Taylor
639   vii Stella Paulus, born 1880. Married 22 February 1899 Walker
           Fielder
640   viii Frank F. Paulus, born March 1884
641   ix Ray Paulus, died as an infant
642   x John Paulus, died as an infant

    208 - JONATHAN FRANCIS(4) PAULUS [Daniel(3), Christina (2) Wolf,
Daniel(1)]:\51
    Jonathan   Francis   Paulus,   eleventh child of Daniel and Louisiana
(Treon) Paulus, was born 30 August 1844 near Gordon, Darke County, OH.
He was a Civil War veteran, serving from 9 May 1864 until 28 September
1864. He married 12 November 1868 in Greenville, Darke County, OH
Louisa Katherine Schell, born 15 July 1848. They were divorced in
1905. Louisa died 6 March 1918 and Jonathan 31 October 1928, both in
Union City, Darke County. Jonathan spent his last twelve years in the
U.S. Veterans Home in Marion, IN and is buried in the Union City, IN
Cemetery
    Children of Jonathan Francis and Louisa Katherine (Schell)
Paulus:
+ 643   i Lucy Anna Paulus, born 22 August 1869
+ 644   ii Lillian May Paulus, born 22 April 1872
  645   iii Willie Francis Paulus, born 14 January 1880, died 29 Octo-
           ber 1882 in Darke County, OH

    209 - MARY JANE(4) PAULUS [Daniel(3), Christina(2) Wolf,
Daniel(1)]\51
    Mary   Jane   Paulus, twelfth child of Daniel and Louisiana (Treon)
Paulus, was born 6 February 1849 near Gordon, Darke County, OH. She
married in Greenville, Darke County John Swartz, born 25 June 1845,
son of George and Catherine (Zellers) Swartz. John was a general
laborer and in later years became a cement contractor. Mary Jane died
17 July 1916 and John 23 January 1922. Both are buried in Greenville
Cemetery,Darke County.
    Children of John and Mary Jane (Paulus) Swartz:
  646   i Mary Etta Swartz, born 1867, died 1907
  647   ii Ida Swartz, born 1871

    211 - ALLEN(4) BAUGHER [Mary(3) Paulus, Christina(2) Wolf,
Daniel(1)]\51
    Allen   Baugher, first child of William M. and Mary (Paulus)
Baugher, was born 9 November 1837 in Darke County, OH. He served in
the Civil War and on his return married 24 May 1866 in Noble County,
IN Malissa Wineland, born 8 March 1849, daughter of John and Lida
(_____) Wineland. This marriage ended in divorce 15 June 1899. Malissa
married 2) James Breedlove. Malissa died 2 July 1916 in Kokomo, Howard
County, IN and is buried in the Kokomo Cemetery under the name of
Malissa Baugher. Allen died at the Soldiers Home at Marion, Grant
County, IN 9 August 1916 and is buried at the Soldiers Home Cemetery.
    Children of Allen and Malissa (Wineland) Baugher
+ 648   i Elmer Calvin Baugher, born 4 July 1867
+ 649   ii Ida Alice Baugher, born 17 August 1869
+ 650   iii Edward Elsworth Baugher, born 23 December 1871
  651   iv Harley Monroe Baugher, born 8 September 1874
+ 652   v Eva Sophronia Baugher, born 27 October 1878
+ 653   vi Walter Raymond Baugher, born 23 September 1882
+ 654   vii Estella Opal Baugher, born 27 September 1886

79

655 viii Pearly Otto Baugher, born 22 August 1891 in Monroe Township, Howard County, IN, died 5 May 1954. He was a World
War I veteran

212 - FRANCIS M.(4) BAUGHER [Mary(3) Paulus, Christina(3) Wolf,
Daniel(1)]\51
Francis M. Baugher, second child of William and Mary (Paulus)
Baugher, was born 15 January 1843 in Darke County, OH, going to
Washington Township, Noble County, IN with his parents. He was a Civil
War Veteran, volunteering 20 February 1864 at Wabash, IN and serving
until 23 October 1865. From June through October 1865 he was a guard
of Provost Marshal at Clayborne Parish, LA.
Following his war duty he married Marietta Hanson, daughter of
Charles and Ann (_____) Hanson. During the following years Francis'
health deteriorated and he applied for a pension on the basis of
chronic diarrhea, contracted during the Red River Campaign in Louisiana. He lived in Heila, Whitley County, IN until his death 22 November 1905 at which time his pension was $12 per month. Marietta died 19
April 1915. Both are buried in Salem Community Church Cemetery,
southeast of Wilmot, Noble County, IN.
Children of Francis M. and Marietta (Hanson) Baugher:
657   i Charles W. Baugher, born 12 March 1869, died 1937. Married
26 February 1896 in Noble County, IN Nancy Ann Stults, born
1870. Buried in Thorn Cemetery
658   ii Myrtle A. Baugher, born 27 July 1878
659 iii Jenna P. Baugher, born 27 July 1878
660   vi Thomas H. Baugher, born 7 March 1889

213 - CALVIN(4) BAUGHER [Mary(3) Paulus, Christina(2) Wolf,
Daniel(1)]\51
Calvin Baugher, third child of William and Mary (Paulus) Baugher,
was born 16 July 1846 in Darke County, OH. He married 15 May 1869 in
Noble County, IN Louzina Wheeler, born 18 November 1844 in Randolph
County, IN, daughter of Charles W. and Sarah (Holderman) Wheeler.
Census listings show Calvin as a sawmill worker in 1870, as a teamster
in 1880 and as a machinist in 1900. Louzina died 2 April 1917 and
Calvin 1 May 1925.
Children of Calvin and Louzina (Wheeler) Baugher:
+ 661   i William Baugher, born 31 July 1869
662   ii Elmer E. Baugher, died 20 August 1885
663 iii Unknown Baugher
664   iv Unknown Baugher

214 - MARVIN(4) BAUGHER [Mary(3) Paulus, Christina(3) Wolf,
Daniel(1)]\51
Marvin Baugher, fourth child of William and Mary (Paulus)
Baugher, was born 1849 in Darke County, OH. He married in 1879 Mary
Beers, born 1854. Marvin died in 1926 and Mary in 1940. Both are
buried in Metz Cemetery, Noble County, IN.
Children of Marvin and Mary (Beers) Baugher:
665   i Luther D. Baugher, born November 1879, died January 1960 of
leukemia. Buried in Metz Cemetery, Noble County, IN
666   ii Bessie Baugher, born April 1882
667 iii Chancie Baugher, born August 1887, died 1944. Buried in
Metz Cemetery, Noble County, IN
668   iv Herschel Baugher, born 31 August 1893, died 30 January
1973. Marriedd 8 October 1960 Fredonna _____

215 - SARAH ELLEN(4) BAUGHER [Mary(3) Paulus, Christina(2) Wolf, Daniel(1)\51
Sarah Ellen Baugher, fifth child of William and Mary (Paulus) Baugher, was born 29 January 1852 in Whitley County, IN. She married 13 February 1870 Jonas B. Swihart, born 2 June 1842, son of Samuel and Fanny (_____) Swihart. They lived in Tippecanoe Township, Kosciusko County, IN near North Webster, IN. Jonas died 6 December 1911 and Sarah Ellen 30 May 1928. They are buried in Salem Church Cemetery, south of Wilmot, IN.
Children of Jonas B. and Sarah Ellen (Baugher) Swihart:
669   i Franklin Swihart, born 1873
670   ii Samuel Swihart, born 1876, died 1942
671 iii Mary E. Swihart, born 1879

NOTES AND REFERENCES

1. 1850 Federal Census, Jackson Township, Preble County, OH. Frederick was listed, age 18, in the household of his father.
2. 1900 Federal Census, Logan County, IL.
3. In the 1870 Federal Census of Logan County, IL, Fred Wolf is listed in both the household of his son Frederick Clark Wolf (West Lincoln Township, Page 272, Dwelling 185, Family 189) and of his daughter, Rebecca Jane, wife of George Wirtman (West Lincoln Township, Page 277, Dwelling 260, Family 266).
4. 1880 Federal Census, Otoe County, NE.
5. 1870 Federal Census, Logan County, IL.
6. Biography of Washington C. Wolf, "Portrait and Biographical Album of Otoe and Cass Counties, Nebraska", NGS LIbrary No. F665.P6 1972, Pages 458,9.
7. Information for the George and Sarah (Wolf) Shroyer descendants from the unpublished "Shroyer Family" compiled by Norma Shroyer Starkweather, June 1980.
8. Information for the John S. and Susan (Wolf) Montel descendants from the unpublished "Descendants of Christopher Mantle and Elizabeth Soeston, Montel Family", compiled by Keith E. Ross, 29 Oak Drive, North Manchester, IN 46962, March 1983.
9. Information for the Jacob Jr and Barbara (Izor) Wolf descendants compiled by Milton C. Caldwell Sr, 7219 Belle Plain Drive, Dayton, OH 45424
10. History of Cass County, IN.
11. Information for the George Isaac and Margaret (Tolen) Wolf compiled by Mrs. Cora M. Walters, 5930 Barcus Way, South Bend, IN 46614.
12. Cass County, IN Marriage Book 3, Page 187.
13. Logansport, IN newspaper article, 30 April 1921, on the occasion of the Wolfs moving from their farm after 62 years.
14. Carroll County, IN Marriage Book 5, Page 300.
15. Ibid. Page 155.
16. Ibid. Health Department Book H17, Page 43. This certificate gives a birth date 22 October 1838 and a death date 22 October 1928 at 89y 11m 1d.
17. Ibid. Marriage Book 6, Page 425.
18. Ibid. Health Department Book H17, Pages 43, 110.
19. Kosciusko County, IN Cemetery Records, Volume II, Van Buren and Turkey Creek Townships by Lester H. Binnie, 31 Oak Drive, North

Manchester, IN 46962, 1978.

20. 1900 Federal Census, Kosciusko County, IN.

21. 1880 Federal Census, Elkhart County, IN.

22. Tombstones,Germantown Cemetery, Montgomery County, OH.

23. 1860 Federal Census, Montgomery County, OH.

24. Information for the Daniel and Elizabeth (Hahn) Sharrit descendants from a lawsuit in 1924 against the estate of Florence (Sharrit) Boyer, Montgomery County, OH Common Pleas Court, Case #53757, M9, Page 486. Florence died 26 June 1923 leaving no husband or lineal descendants. Provided by Mrs. Roland Bailey, 1301 Richard Street, Miamisburg, OH 45342.

25. Cemetery Inscriptions of Montgomery County, Brien, Lindsay M.

26. Obituary on microfilm, Germantown, Montgomery County, OH Library.

27. LDS IGI, September 1981, Page 22, 264.

28. 1860 Federal Census, Vermillion Township, Ashland County, OH.

29. 1850 Federal Census, Ashland County, OH.

30. History of Union County, IA, biographical sketch of F. R. Wolfe.

31. Information for the Daniel and Elizabeth (Wolf) Schlosser descendants from "The Family of Henry Schlosser of Frederick County, MD", Part IV, published in "The Maryland and Delaware Genealogist" 1975-1977 by Mrs. Helen W. Seubold, C. G., 12000 Old Georgetown Road, Rockville, MD 20852.

32. 1850 Federal Census, Montgomery County, OH.

33. 1870 Federal Census, Montgomery County, OH.

34. Information for the Jacob and Tracy (Wolf) Blecher descendants from unpublished Blecker history by Arnold Blecker, 1797 San Bernardino Avenue, Pomona, CA 91767, July 1969.

35. Washington County, MD Marriage Records.

36. 1870 Federal Census, Washington County, MD.

37. Tombstones, Boonsboro Cemetery, Washington County, MD.

38. 1860 Federal Census, Washington County, MD.

39. 1880 Federal county Census, Delaware County, PA.

40. Newspaper article in "The Review" (city of issue unknown, possibly Pitman, NJ) on the occasion of the 50th wedding anniversary of Van Luther and Jane (Fry) Wolf. In possession of author.

41. Pennsylvania Death Certificate, File #75114, Registered #203.

42. Tombstones, Media Burial Burial grounds, Media, Delaware County, PA.

43. Obituary in Mount Morris, IL "Index", 21 March 1918. In possession of author.

44. 1880 Federal Census, Washington County, MD.

45. Death Certificate, Division of Vital Records, Maryland Department of Health and Mental Hygiene, Baltimore, MD.

46. Tombstone, Bakersville Cemetery, Washington County, MD.

47. 1903-11 Hagerstown, MD City Directory, Hill Directory Company, Richmond, VA.

48. History of Washington County, MD. J. C> T. Williams.

49. Wahington County, MD Register of Wills, Book 15, 331.

50. Ibid. Book 18, 189.

51. Information for the Abraham and Christina (Wolf) Paulus descendants from the unpublished "Abraham Paulus Family History" by Merritt W. Wolfe, 303 East Linwood Avenue, Akron, OH 44301, July 1990.

52. IT IS EMPHASIZED THAT THERE IS NO RELATIONSHIP BETWEEN THIS WOLF LINE AND THAT OF DANIEL, SUBJECT OF THIS GENEALOGY.

53. Preble County, OH Land Records, Book 33, 277.

54. Ibid. Book 44, 130

FIFTH GENERATION

216 - NATHANIEL HARRIS(5) WOLF [Lewis Clark(4), Frederick(3),
Jacob(2), Daniel(1)]
    Nathaniel Harris Wolf, first child of Lewis Clark and Eliza Jane
(Harris) Wolf, was born 28 November 1851 in Preble County, OH. By 1860
the family had moved to Lincoln Precinct, Logan County, IL and then to
Jasper County, MO where he married 1) 22 October 1871 in Carthage,
Jasper County Martha Jane Ward, born 21 October 1853 in Lima, Allen
County, OH, daughter of James Lewis and Harriet (Dillon) Ward.
    They divorced and Nathaniel married 2) 4 March 1885 Lucinda B.
Osburn, born 13 February 1864 in Illinois. Martha Jane (Ward) Wolf
married 2) 24 January 1888 Thomas James Lewis. Nathaniel died 15
January 1895 in Jasper County, MO. His first wife, Martha Jane, died
27 December 1920 in Coalville, UT and his second wife, Lucinda, died
14 November 1937 in Galena, Cherokee County, KS.
    Children of Nathaniel Harris and Martha Jane (Harris) Wolf, all
born in Jasper County, MO:
  672   i Infant daughter Wolf, born 12 December 1874, died before
           1880 in Jasper County, MO
+ 673   ii Ada Lleumina Wolf, born 1 December 1875
  674 iii Penny S. Wolf, born about 1877
  675   iv Inez Forest Wolf, born 11 March 1878, died 2 June 1902.
           Married George Stockman
    Children of Nathaniel Harris and Lucinda B. (Osburn) Wolf:
  676   i Nathaniel Wolf Jr, born 17 November 1885 in Carthage,
           Jasper County, MO, died 4 April 1956. Married Maud Coats
  677   ii Lewis Frederick Wolf, born 26 November 1886 in Carthage,
           Jasper County, MO.
  678 iii Axie Wolf, born 1888 in Kansas City, MO
  679   iv Theodore Wolf, born 1890 in Carthage, Jasper County, MO

    220 - MARTHA(5) WOLF [Frederick Clark(4), Frederick(3), Jacob(2),
Daniel(1)]
    Martha Wolf, third child of Frederick Clark Wolf, was born
January 1863 in Illinois. Her mother's name is not known, but she
apparently died about 1865. Martha married twice, her first husband's
name is not known. She married 2) in 1896 in Logan County, IL Charles
Lee, born January 1868 in New York. In 1900 they were living in
Lincoln, Logan County, IL.
    Child of Martha (Wolf) _____'s first marriage:
  680   i Grace P. _____, born January 1884
    Children of Charles and Martha (Wolf) (_____) Lee:
  681   i Emma Lee, born April 1897
  682   ii Charles D. Lee, born April 1899
    Children of Charles Lee's first marriage:
         i Elmer Lee, born November 1887
        ii Harry Lee, born October 1890

    222 - FRED WADE(5) WOLF [Frederick Clark(4), Frederick(3),
Jacob(2), Daniel(1)]
    Fred Wade Wolf, child of Frederick Clark and Sarah (Wade)
(Fraikes) Wolf, was born 14 May 1875 in Logan County, IL, died 4

January 1943 in Nashville, Davidson Co., TN and is buried in Spring Hill Cemetery. He was an optometrist in that city. He married Jennie Louemma Nickel, born 1882 in Smith Center, KS, died and buried at Los Angeles, CA, daughter of John Francis and Mary Althea (Griffin) Nickel
    Children of Fred Wade and Jennie (Nickel) Wolf:
    682A   i Clark Wade Wolf, born and died before 1918 in Georgia
    682B   ii Frances Wolf, born and died before 1918 in Georgia
  + 683   iii Mary Turner Wolf, born 14 September 1918

    234 - ANNA EVALEE(5) SHROYER [Malinda Ann(4) Wolf, Frederick(3), Jacob(2), Daniel(1)
    Anna Evalee Shroyer, third child of Hiram William and Malinda Ann (Wolf) Shroyer, was born 18 March 1870 in Mason City, IL. She married 17 March 1895 Joseph Knabenshue. Anna died 21 June 1916 and Joseph 13 April 1923, both in Mishawaka, St. Joseph County, IN.
    Children of Joseph and Anna Evalee (Shroyer) Knabenshue:
  + 684   i Kenneth Knabenshue, born 5 September 1896
  + 685   ii Violet Audry Knabenshue, born 28 September 1899
  + 686   iii Vivian Ann Knabenshue, born 26 September 1901
    687   iv Ila Naomi Knabenshue, born 12 September 1905. Married 25 April 1926 Earl Hollaway

    236 - HARRY FRANKLIN(5) SHROYER [Malinda Ann(4) Wolf, Frederick(3), Jacob(3), Daniel(1)]
    Harry Franklin Shroyer, fifth child of Hiram William and Malinda Ann (Wolf) Shroyer, was born 30 April 1874 in Indiana. He married November 1895 Ola Lowery, born 30 May 1879. Harry died May 1955 in Mishawaka, IN and Ola in 1962.
    Children of Harry Franklin and Ola (Lowery) Shroyer:
    688   i Gladys Shroyer, born 1896. Married 1) William Gore, divorced and married 2) Robert Johnson
    689   ii Son, died young

    238 - NELLIE GRAY(5) SHROYER [Malinda Ann(4) Wolf, Frederick (3), Jacob(2), Daniel(1)]
    Nellie Gray Shroyer, seventh child of Hiram William and Malinda Ann (Wolf) Shroyer, was born 22 September 1877 in Illinois. She married Jasper McKinley, born 1879. Nellie died 1944 in Marion, IN
    Known children of Jasper and Nellie Gray (Shroyer) Mc Kinley:
  * 690   i Jasper McKinley, Jr, born 1907, died in Marion, IN
  + 691   ii Marjory McKinley, born 1909

    241 - HARVEY HOWARD(5) SHROYER [Malinda Ann(4) Wolf, Frederick(3), Jacob(2), Daniel(1)]
    Harvey Howard Shroyer, tenth child of Hiram William and Malinda Ann (Wolf) Shroyer, was born 13 February 1882 in Kosciusko County, IN. He married 2 February 1908 at South Bend, IN Grace Maude Brewer, born 24 January 1885 at Rolling Prairie, IN. Grace died 10 November 1951 at Mishawaka, IN and Harvey 13 January 1977 at Elkhart, IN. They are buried at Mishawaka.
    Children of Harvey Howard and Grace Maude (Brewer) Shroyer:
  + 692   i Alta Irene Shroyer, born 19 July 1908
  + 693   ii Mildred Lucille Shroyer, born 14 February 1910
  + 694   iii Norma Leora Shroyer, born 25 November 1911
  + 695   iv Dean Kermit Shroyer, born 5 June 1913
  + 696   v Dalton Howard Shroyer, born 13 October 1922
  + 697   vi Keith Laverne Shroyer, born 15 February 1927

242 - IRENE SPRAGUE(5) SHROYER [Malinda Ann(4) Wolf, Frederick(3), Jacob(2), Daniel(1))

Irene Sprague Shroyer, eleventh child of Hiram William and Malinda Ann (Wolf) Shroyer, was born 29 December 1884 in Indiana. She married in 1912 Owen Elder, born 1886. Irene died 2 August 1971 in Los Angeles, CA.

Children of Owen and Irene Sprague (Shroyer) Elder:

- 698   i Reba Elder, died young
- 699   ii Daughter, died young
- 700   iii Delmar Owen Elder, born in 1914

245 - ERVIN J.(5) WOLF [Oliver(4), Frederick (3), Jacob(2), Daniel(1)]

Ervin J. Wolf, only child of Oliver and Alice (Acker) Wolf, was born February 1875 in Indiana. He married in 1896 Ada _____, born November 1874 in Ohio. In 1900 they were living in Goshen, Elkhart County, IN.

Children of Ervin J. and Ada (_____) Wolf:

- 701   i Ruby Wolf, died in her teens in Florida
- 702   ii Jeannette Wolf. Married Maynard Hartranft

247 - SAMUEL(5) MONTEL [Abraham(4), Susan(3) Wolf, Jacob(2), Daniel(1)]

Samuel Montel, second child of Abraham and Magdalene (Frantz) Montel, was born 3 May 1852. He married 3 June 1877 Phoebe Metzger, born 19 May 1857, daughter of Joseph and Elizabeth (Studebaker) Metzger. Phoebe died 10 June 1940 and Samuel 21 June 1941.

Children of Samuel and Phoebe (Metzger) Montel:

- + 703   i Mary Alice Montel, born 21 May 1878
- + 704   ii Elizabeth Montel, born 5 July 1880
- + 705   iii Charles Montel, born 22 April 1882
- + 706   iv Edith Montel, born 9 December 1884
- + 707   v Albert Montel, born 23 April 1887
-   708   vi Florence Montel, born 14 September 1889, died 19 July 1890
- + 709   vii Emery Montel, born 9 August 1892
- + 710   viii Ralph Montel, born 28 April 1894
- + 711   ix Frank Montel, 23 January 1897
- + 712   x Glenn Montel, born 16 January 1900

248 - JACOB(5) MONTEL [Abraham(4), Susan(3) Wolf, Jacob(2), Daniel(1)]

Jacob Montel, third child of Abraham and Magdaline (Frantz) Montel, was born 25 September 1854. He married 21 September 1880 Rebecca Metzger, born 10 February 1863, daughter of Joseph and Elizabeth (Studebaker) Metzger. Jacob died 15 April 1923 and Rebecca in 1932.

Children of Jacob and Rebecca (Metzger) Montel:

-   713   i Alva Montel, born 21 August 1881, died 5 January 1962. Did not marry
-   714   ii Emma Montel, born 17 April 1884, died 11 March 1927. Married Egbert Luther Burger, born 25 April 1874, died 2 November 1953, son of William Edgar and Betty Smith (Nininger) Burger. There were no children
- + 715   iii Effie Montel, born 6 July 1886
- + 716   iv Royal Montel, born 24 November 1891
- + 717   v Iva Ann Montel, born 7 March 1893
- + 718   vi Artemus Montel, born 3 January 1902

249 - SUSANNA(5) MONTEL [Abraham(4), Susan(3) Wolf, Jacob(2), Daniel(1)]
Susanna Montel, fourth chid of Abraham and Magdalene (Frantz) Montel, was born 16 September 1857. She married 20 October 1877 David B. Metzger, son of Solomon and Barbara (Brumbaugh) Metzger. Susanna died 1 February 1894 and David 18 March 1917.
Children of David B. and Susanna (Montel) Metzger:
+ 719   i Mary Magdeline Metzger, born 3 February 1879
+ 720   ii Lyman H. Metzger, born 1881
+ 721 iii Sarah Ellen Metzger, born 2 May 1882
+ 722   iv Irvin Metzger, born 18 June 1885
  723   v Melvin Metzger, born 1889
+ 724   vi Susanna Metzger, born 25 January 1894

251 - MARY(5) MONTEL [Abraham(4), Susan(3) Wolf, Jacob(2), Daniel(1)]
Mary Montel, sixth child of Abraham and Magdalene (Frantz) Montel, was born 2 March 1864. She married 8 March 1888 John L. Sausaman, born 18 November 1867. Mary died 17 May 1889 and John in 1944.
Child of John L. and Mary (Montel) Sausaman:
  725   i Frederick Sausaman, born 4 May 1889. Married Ruth Rue Shirk

252 - LYDIA(5) MONTEL [Abraham(4), Susan(3) Wolf, Jacob(2), Daniel(1)]
Lydia Montel, seventh child of Abraham and Magdalene (Frantz) Montel, was born in 1866. She married Henry Shireman, born in 1864. Lydia died in 1914.
Children of Henry and Lydia (Montel) Shireman:
  726   i Esta E. Shireman, born 21 June 1882, died 28 February 1892
  727   ii John H. Shireman, born 5 October 1889, died 7 March 1892
  728 iii Else Shireman. Married Thomas Ceites
+ 729   iv Stella Shireman
  730   v Charles Shireman

255 - WILLIAM H.(5) BUTTERBAUGH [Sarah(4) Montel, Susan(3) Wolf, Jacob(2), Daniel(1)]
William H. Butterbaugh, second child of John and Sarah (Montel) Butterbaugh, was born 18 April 1851. He married 6 March 1884 Viola Derck, born in 1868, daughter of Henry Derck. William died in 1924 and Viola in 1948.
Children of William H. and Viola (Derck) Butterbaugh:
+ 731   i Hazel Butterbaugh, born 8 January 1888
+ 732   ii Nellie Butterbaugh, born 24 October 1890

267 - GEORGE III(5) TRIDLE [Adaline(4) Montel, Susan(3) Wolf, Jacob(2), Daniel(1)]
George Tridle III, second child of George II and Adaline (Montel) Tridle, was born 16 May 1854. He married 17 May 1877 Sarah Ulrey, born 1 January 1855, daughter of John Aaron and Sarah (Snep) Ulrey. George died 21 November 1934 and Sarah 16 February 1947.
Children of George III and Sarah (Ulrey) Tridle:
+ 733   i Elvin Peter Tridle, born 29 December 1879
+ 734   ii Lizzie Tridle, born 22 June 1884
+ 735 iii Glenn Tridle, born 22 May 1890
+ 736   iv Viola Tridle, born 29 July 1891

274 - BENSON(5) RAGER [Susannah(4) Montel, Susan(3) Wolf,
Jacob(2), Daniel(1)
   Benson Rager was the first child of Henry and Susannah (Montel)
Rager.
   Child of Benson and _____ (_____) Rager:
+ 737   i Erdeen Rager

   279 - ORIS CLYDE(5) MONTEL [John W.(4), Susan(3) Wolf, Jacob(2),
Daniel(1)]
   Oris Clyde Montel was the third child of John W. and Ellen Alvira
(Eppler) Montel.
   Child of Oris Clyde and _____ (_____) Montel:
   738   i Ellen Elvira Montel. Married _____ Fuesik

   281 - JOSEPHINE FLORIDA(5) WOLFE [Simon P.(4), Jacob Jr(3),
Jacob(2), Daniel(1)]
   Josephine Florida Wolfe, second child of Simon P. and Mary Ann
(Wagner) Wolfe, was born 22 November 1856 in Deer Creek Township, Cass
County, IN. She married 5 June 1882 in Cass County Allen L. Oyler,
born 15 June 1855 in Cass County, son of Joseph L. and Susannah
(Erbaugh) Oyler. Josephine died 13 January 1913 near Kokomo, Tipton
Township, in Cass County and Allen married 2) 7 June 1916 in Howard
County, IN Maggie Meeker. He died 30 June 1931 at Walton, Cass County.
   Children of Allen L. and Josephine Florida (Wolfe) Oyler, all
born in Tipton Township, Cass County, IN:
+ 738a   i Joseph Raymond Oyler, born 18 July 1883
  738b ii Grace Victorine Oyler, born 28 July 1885, died 9 March 1923
           in Howard County, IN. Married 11 September 1919 in Cass
           County, IN Otis M. Redenbaugh, son of Solomon and Lida
           (Brasidon) Redinbaugh
+ 738c iii Alva L. Oyler, born April 1890
+ 738d iv Ross E. Oyler, born 1 March 1894

   282 - CAROLINE BARBARA(5) WOLFE [Simon P.(4), Jacob Jr(3),
Jacob(2), Daniel(1)]
   Caroline Barbara Wolfe, third child of Simon P. and Mary Ann
(Wagner) Wolfe, was born 8 January 1859 in Deer Creek Township, Cass
County, IN. She married 6 June 1883 at Logansport, IN Robert John
Monteith, born 20 July 1861 in Israel Township, Preble County, OH, son
of John and Nancy (Garver) Monteith. Caroline died 20 January 1928 and
Robert 13 May 1940. They are buried in Vale Cemetery, Clark County,
OH.
   Children of Robert John and Caroline Barbara (Wolfe) Monteith:
+ 739   i Robert William Monteith, born 11 March 1884
+ 740   ii Harold John Monteith, born 26 December 1886
+ 741 iii Paul Evert Monteith, born 9 May 1889
+ 742   iv Charles Oliver Monteith, born 24 May 1891
  743   v Hugh Simon Monteith, born 20 April 1893 in Carroll County,
           IN, died 28 August 1894. Buried in Miller Cemetery, Cass
           County, IN
  744   vi Ira Edgar Monteith, born 22 February 1895 in Carroll
           County, IN, died 10 October 1920 at Spooner, WI
  745 vii Mary Esther Monteith, born 6 September 1896 in Carroll
           County, IN, died 5 January 1908 in Phillips, Price County,
           WI
+ 746 viii Frank Allen Monteith, born 14 December 1899
+ 747   ix Jesse Arthur Monteith, born 14 November 1901

283 - MARGARET JANE(5) WOLFE [Simon P.(4), Jacob Jr(3), Jacob(2), Daniel(1)]
   Margaret Jane Wolfe, fifth child of Simon P. and Mary Ann (Wagner) Wolfe, was born 5 September 1860 in Deer Creek Township, Cass County, IN. She married 20 October 1881 in Cass County William Alexander Caldwell, born 6 November 1858 in Preble County, OH, son of Andrew Thomas and Margaret (Monteith) Caldwell. William died 3 June 1899 in Moundsville, WV. Margaret died 10 October 1924 and is buried in Vale cemetary, Clark County, OH.
   Children of William Alexander and Margaret Jane (Wolfe) Caldwell:
   748   i Ada Elizabbeth Caldwell, born 7 July 1882 in Washington Township, Carroll County, IN, died 18 August 1939 . Married 1 August 1919 in Springfield, OH Smith Donovan, born about 1855, died about 1944. They are buried in Vale Cemetery, Clark County, OH
 + 749   ii Clara Belle Caldwell, born 27 January 1885
   750   iii Herbert Andrew Caldwell, born 22 May 1889 in Washington Township, Carroll County, IN, died 21 January 1891 in Washington Township
 + 751   iv Emmet Edmunds Caldwell, born 13 December 1890
   752   v Mary Pearl Caldwell, born 16 June 1895 in Washington Township, Carroll County, IN, died 24 September 1896 in Washington Township
 + 753   vi David Milo Caldwell, born 16 June 1897
 + 754   vii William Arthur Caldwell, born 27 December 1899

285 - EDWARD CARROL(5) WOLFE [Simon P.(4), Jacob Jr(3), Jacob(2), Daniel(1)]
   Edward Carrol Wolfe, sixth child of Simon ·P. and Mary Anne (Wagner) Wolfe, was born 19 April 1862 in Deer Creek Township, Cass County, IN. He married 30 March 1896 Elizabeth Exie Husted, born 31 January 1877 in Bates County, MO, daughter of Leander and Catherine (Long) Husted. Edward died 28 August 1919 in Marion, IN and Elizabeth 27 October 1941 in Grant County, IN..
   Children of Edward Carrol and Elizabeth Exie (Husted) Wolfe:
 + 755   i Clarence Leroy Wolfe, born 2 March 1897
   756   ii Viola Maude Wolfe, born 30 January 1901 at Amsterdam, MO, died 5 November 1972 in Grant County, IN. Married Leroy Miller, born 30 January 1901, died 5 November 1972
   757   iii Mary Elizabeth Wolfe, born 16 April 1909, died April 1909
 + 758   iv Ruth Catherine Wolfe, born 22 September 1914

290 - FLORA MARIE(5) WOLFE [Simon P.(4), Jacob Jr(3), Jacob(2), Daniel(1)]
   Flora Marie Wolfe, eleventh child of Simon P. and Mary Anne (Wagner) Wolfe, was born 26 February 1875 in Deer Creek Township, Cass County, IN. She married 24 December 1896 William P. Stevens. Flora died 28 May 1969 in Benedict, KS
   Children of William P. and Flora Marie (Wolfe) Stevens:
 + 759   i Charles Burton Stevens, born 14 October 1897
   760   ii Glen Alva Stevens, born 21 January 1900, died 7 July 1970
   761   iii Amye Frances Stevens, born 13 January 1905, died 23 April 1971
 + 762   iv Roy Arthur Stevens, born 21 May 1913

291 - AMY PEARL(5) WOLFE [Simon P.(4), Jacob Jr(3), Jacob(2), Daniel(1)]
   Amy Pearl Wolfe, twelfth child of Simon P. and Mary Anne (Wagner)

Wolfe, was born 29 March 1877 in Deer Creek Township, Cass County, IN. She married 7 September 1903 Calvin Cornelius Richey, born 20 July 1872. Amy died 10 February 1954. They are buried in Oakwood Cemetery, Austin, TX

   Child of Calvin Cornelius and Amy Pearl (Wolfe) Richey:
   763   i Oleta May Richey, born 12 October 1904 at Coffeyville, KS, died 26 August 1977 at Jackson, MS. Married 15 June 1929 at Austin, TX David Harrel

   292 - JOHN ARTHUR(5) WOLFE [Simon P.(4), Jacob Jr(3), Jacob(2), Daniel(1)]
   John Arthur Wolfe, thirteenth child of Simon P. and Mary Anne (Wagner) Wolfe, was born 12 February 1880 in Deer Creek Township, Cass County, IN. He married 2 August 1902 Mae Kiger. He died 6 February 1960.
   Child of John Arthur and Mae (Kiger) Wolfe:
   764   i Juanita Wolfe

   293 - HAROLD GARFIELD(5) WOLFE [Simon P.(4), Jacob Jr(3), Jacob(2), Daniel(1)]
   Harold Garfield Wolfe, fourteenth child of Simon P. and Mary Anne (Wagner) Wolfe, was born 14 May 1883 in Deer Creek Township, Cass County, IN. He married 24 June 1908 Elizabeth Smith. Harold died 24 June 1976 at Akron, OH. Elizabeth married 2) _____ Goodrich.
   Children of Harold Garfield and Elizabeth (Smith) Wolfe:
 + 765   i Lewis Everett Wolfe, born 13 October 1909. Changed his name to Goodrich, name of his step-father
   766   ii Earnest Leroy Wolfe, born 26 June 1912. Changed his name to Goodrich, name of his step-father

   295 - JOHN J.(5) PLANK [Frances(4) Wolf, Jacob Jr(3), Jacob(2), Daniel(1)]
   John J. Plank, second child of Conrad and Frances (Wolf) Plank, was born 20 April 1861. He married Louella F. Tolen.
   Children of John J. and Louella F. (Tolen) Plank, order of birth uncertain:
   767   i Mary Elizabeth Plank, born 2 April 1883, died 25 August 1956. Married _____ Crockett
   768   ii Burt Plank
   769   iii Charles Plank, died in infancy
   770   iv Clara Plank
   771   v Ella Plank
   772   vi Elmer Plank
   773   vii Frank Plank
   774 viii Louanna Plank
   775   ix Pearl Plank
   776   x Rose Plank

   300 - MARY E.(5) WOLF [George Isaac(4), Jacob Jr(3), Jacob(2), Daniel(1)]
   Mary E. Wolf, third child of George Isaac and Margaret (Tolen) Wolf, was born about 1864 in Cass County, IN. She married 1) 22 May 1884 in Cass County, IN Warren Lake Burrows, son of Martin Van and Mary (Campbell) Burrows. He died 4 April 1915 in Galveston, Cass County and is buried there as is Mary. She married 2) Ed Davis. There were no children by the second marriage.
   Children of Warren Lake and Mary E. (Wolf) Burrows:
 + 777   i Otis W. Burrows, born 17 June 1885

+ 778   ii Elta Burrows

     301 - SARAH C.(5) WOLF [George Isaac(4), Jacob Jr(3), Jacob(2),
Daniel(1)]
     Sarah C. Wolf, fourth child of George Isaac and Margaret (Tolen)
Wolf, was born in 1865 in Cass County, IN. She married 7 October 1885
in Cass County William Henry, born in 1859. William died in 1929 and
Sara in 1952. They are buried in Young America Cemetery, Cass County.
     Children of William and Sarah C. (Wolf) Henry:
+ 779   i Bertha Henry, born 8 August 1884
   780   ii Essie Henry, buried in Mt. Hope Cemetery, Logansport, Cass
             County, IN. Married 10 February 1913 in Cass County Bertel
             Harman. Two sons and one daughter not further identified
   781   iii Iva Henry. Married Raymond Jones. No children
   782   iv Eva Henry, born in 1904, died in 1926, buried in Young
             America, Cass County, IN. Married Bruce Beck. No children

     302 - CAROLINE EVALINA(5) WOLF [George Isaac(4), Jacob Jr(3),
Jacob(2), Daniel(1)]
     Caroline Evalina Wolf, fifth child of George Isaac and Margaret
(Tolen) Wolf, was born in Cass County, IN. She married 8 April 1890 in
Galveston, Cass County Abraham Smith, born 5 February 1854, son of
Jacob and Lydia (Studebaker) Smith. Jacob was a farmer and they were
members of the Brethren Church. Caroline died 19 April 1941 in Logansport, Cass County and is buried in Hoover Cemetery, Cass County.
Abraham died 6 January 1945 in Galveston, Cass County.
     Children of Abraham and Caroline Evalina (Wolf) Smith:
   783   i Elsie Armetta Smith, born 2 April 1891 in Cass County, IN,
             died 10 July 1972 in Galveston, Cass County, buried in
             Center V. B. Cemetery, Galveston. Did not marry
+ 784   ii John Jacob Smith, born 17 July 1892
+ 785   iii Ida Margaret Smith, born 15 December 1893
   786   iv Alvin Isaac Smith, twin, born 4 February 1900 in Galveston,
             Cass County, IN
   787   v Alma Iva Smith, twin, born and died 4 February, 1900 in
             Galveston, Cass County, IN. Buried in Mt. Carmel Cemetery,
             Twelve Mile, Cass County
+ 788   vi Martha Belle Smith, born 25 November 1901
   789   vii Mary Alice Smith, born 13 November 1905 in Cass County, IN,
             died 26 August 1975, buried in Center V. B. Cemetery,
             Galveston, Cass County. Married _____ Heise
   790 viii Daniel Lee Smith, born 24 December 1908 in Cass County, IN.
             Married Deanna Mae Ewing.
   791   ix Henry Abraham Smith, born 15 August 1911 at Galveston, Cass
             County, IN. Married 1 May 1930 at Lincoln, Cass County Mary
             Helen Hamilton

     303 - LYDIA LADOSKEY(5) WOLF [George Isaac(4), Jacob Jr(3),
Jacob(2), Daniel(1)]
     Lydia Ladoskey Wolf, sixth child of George Isaac and Margaret
(Tolen) Wolf, was born 19 May 1870 in Deer Creek Township, Cass
County, IN. She married 8 September 1889 in Cass County William Henry
Marion Michael, born 10 March 1867 in Indiana, son of William J. and
Hannah (Cripe) Michael. William Henry was a farmer and they were
members of the Dunkard Church. Lydia died of cancer 13 October 1931 in
Mishawaka, St. Joseph County, IN and William Henry 29 May 1949 in
Denver, Miami County, IN. They are buried in Center Cemetery, Young
America, Cass County, IN

Children of William Henry Marion and Lydia Ladoskey (Wolf) Michael:
+ 792   i Schuyler Otto Michael, born 20 May 1890
+ 793   ii Vada Estella Michael, born 13 March 1892
+ 794 iii Charles Franklin Michael, born 1 May 1894
+ 795   iv George Emerson Michael, born 30 June 1896
+ 796   v Earl Dewey Michael, born 21 August 1898
  797   vi Cecil Everett Michael, born 11 December 1900 in Camden,
           Carroll County, IN. Did not marry
  798 vii Carrie Armell Michael, born 14 December 1903, died 5
           February 1904 in Cass County, IN, buried in Hoover Ceme-
           tary, Cass County
+ 799 viii Cleo Catherine Michael, born 16 August 1907

    304 - ANNA MARGARET(5) WOLF [George Isaac(4), Jacob Jr(3),
Jacob(20, Daniel(1)]
    Anna Margaret Wolf, seventh child of George Isaac and Margaret
(Tolen) Wolf, was born 8 October 1871 in Young America, Cass County,
IN. She married 18 March 1896 in Cass County David Judge McCloskey,
born 28 March 1871 in Carroll County, IN. David was a farmer and they
were members of the United Brethren Church. David died 30 September
1939 and Anna 22 January 1957, both in Deer Creek Township, Cass
County. They are buried in Center Cemetery, Young America, Cass
County.
    Children of David Judge and Anna Margaret (Wolf) McCloskey were:
  800   i Nellie Belle McMcloskey, born 26 June 1898 in Deer Creek
           Township, Cass County, IN, died in 1925 in Indiana, buried
           in Center Cemetery, Young America, Cass County. Married
           11 February 1920 in Cass County Delbert Larimore. There
           were no children
  801   ii Elmer Otis McCloskey, twin, born 17 June 1904, died 11 March
           1905 in Deer Creek Township, Cass County, IN, buried in
           Center Cemetery, Young America, Cass County.
+ 802 iii Oscar Delmar McCloskey, twin, born 17 June 1904

    306 - CHARLES HENRY(5) WOLF [George Isaac(4), Jacob Jr(3),
Jacob(2), Daniel(1)]
    Charles Henry Wolf, ninth child of George Isaac and Margaret
(Tolen) Wolf, was born 4 July 1881 in Galveston, Cass County, In. He
married 6 March 1907 in Cass County Dora Armell Knight, born 21 March
1885 in Walton, Cass County, daughter of William Perry and Lucy
(Williams) Knight. Charles was a blacksmith and they were members of
the Evangelical United Brethren Church. Charles died April 1965 in San
Pierre, Stark County, IN and Dora 20 September 1970 in Brook, Newton
County, IN. They are buried at Goodland, Newton County, IN.
    Children of Charles Henry and Dora Armell (Knight) Wolf:
+ 803   i George William Wolf, born 11 March 1916
+ 804   ii Margaret Wolf, born 11 March 1920
+ 805 iii Charles Henry Wolf Jr, born 21 December 1924

    312 - ISAAC(5) WOLF [Daniel(4), Jacob Jr(3), Jacob(2), Daniel(1)]
    Isaac Wolf, only child of Daniel and Polly (Young) Wolf, was
born 17 April 1865. He married 1) 30 August 1887 Sarah Margaret Williams and 2) Mary C. Kingery, born 22 February in Virginia, daughter
of John and Sarah (Fisher) Kingery. Isaac died 23 July 1934 and is
buried in Rockfield Cemetery, Rockfield, IN. Mary died 22 April 1924
in Jackson Township, Carroll County, IN.

Children of Isaac and Sarah Margaret (Williams) Wolf:
806   i Esther Wolf, twin, born 21 March 1890, died 30 March 1948.
            Married Tony Snoeberger
807   ii Everett Wolf, twin, born 21 March 1890

313 - ANNA C.(5) CREE [Magdalena L.(4) Wolf, Jacob Jr(3),
Jacob(2), Daniel(1)]
        Anna C. Cree, first child of Robert and Magdalena L. (Wolf) Cree,
was born 20 June 1863 in Indiana. She married 12 October 1887 George
Judy, born 7 August 1859, died February 1946. Anna died 24 June 1953.
        Children of George and Anna C. (Cree) Judy:
+ 808   i Ora E. Judy, born 16 January 1891
  809   ii Everett Judy, born 6 March 1896, died 27 December 1947
  810   iii Raymond E. Judy, born 15 March 1903, died 27 March 1972.
            Married 21 December 1929 Bertha W. Hasselrig, born 1 May
            1906

314 - CLARISSA(5) CREE [Magdalena L.(4) Wolf, Jacob Jr(3),
Jacob(2), Daniel(1)]
        Clarissa Cree, second child of Robert and Magdalena L. (Wolf)
Cree, was born 5 July 1865. She married 27 February 1895 Albert Rice,
born 21 April 1870. Clarissa died 25 August 1941 and Albert 25 January
1955.
        Children of Albert and Clarissa (Cree) Rice:
+ 811   i Chester L. Rice, born 21 February 1897
+ 812   ii Luther Rice, born 25 March 1900
  813   iii Jessie Rice, born 27 May 1902. Married 28 February 1941
            Glenn Coy
+ 814   iv Leo P. Rice, born 23 March 1905
+ 815   v Sarah Rice, born 10 November 1908

315 - MARGARET(5) CREE [Magdalena L.(4) Wolf, Jacob Jr(3),
Jacob(2), Daniel(1)]
        Margaret Cree, third child of Robert and Magdalena L. (Wolf)
Cree, was born 23 October 1868. She married 3 November 1887 George E.
Whipperman, born 22 February 1862. Margaret died about 1948 and George
24 July 1955.
        Children of George L. and Margaret (Cree) Whipperman:
+ 816   i Magdaline Whipperman, born 19 January 1889
+ 817   ii Charles Robert Whipperman, born 5 May 1891
+ 818   iii Esther Whipperman, born 27 August 1893
+ 819   iv Adelbert Lee Whipperman, born 5 March 1912

316 - GEORGE ROBERT(5) CREE [Magdalena L.(4) Wolf, Jacob Jr(3),
Jacob(2), Daniel(1)]
        George Robert Cree, fourth child of Robert and Magdalena L.
(Wolf) Cree, was born 17 July 1871. He married 16 October 1895 Mary
Eva Tribbett, born 30 September 1876. Mary died 27 June 1935 and
George 9 August 1965.
        Children of George Robert and Mary Eva (Tribbett) Cree:
+ 820   i Walter Irving Cree, born 21 November 1900
+ 821   ii Lola Grace Cree, born 31 July 1903
  822   iii Ivy Cree, born 23 October 1905, died 12 September 1906
+ 823   iv Robert George Cree, born 19 July 1914

317 - HENRY(5) CREE [Magdalena L.(5) Wolf, Jacob Jr(3), Jacob(2),
Daniel(1)]
        Henry Cree, fifth child of Robert and Magdalena L. (Wolf) Cree,

was born 17 December 1874. He married Eva V. Little, born 14 February 1880, daughter of Stansbury and Susan (Crosby) Little. Henry died 3 January 1951 and Eva 1 June 1967.
Children of Henry and Eva V. (Little) Cree:
+ 824   i Harold N. Cree, born 4 July 1900
  825   ii Bernadine Cree, born and died 27 March 1908

318 - ALBERT(5) CREE [Magdalena L.(4) Wolf, Jacob Jr(3), Jacob(2), Daniel(1)]
Albert Cree, sixth child of Robert and Magdalena L. (Wolf) Cree, was born 12 October 1879. He married 1) 2 January 1907 Nellie Myrtle Ray, born 27 April 1880, daughter of Stephen and Melinda (Boyles) Ray, 2) 5 November 1960 Sarah Adeline Tribett, born 14 June 1879, daughter of George and Pluma (Perry) Tribbett, and 3) Lillie Stiges. Nellie died 13 June 1959, Albert 26 March 1965 and Sarah 30 June 1965.
Children of Albert and Nellie Myrtle (Ray) Cree:
+ 826   i Mildred Cree, born 3 May 1910
  827   ii Orville Edward Cree, born 16 October 1911, died 20 September 1912
+ 828 iii Alice Louise Cree, born 25 September 1919

319 - EZRA(5) CREE [Magdalena L.(4) Wolf, Jacob Jr(3), Jacob(2), Daniel(1)]
Ezra Cree, seventh child of Robert and Magdalena L. (Wolf) Cree, was born 19 July 1883. He married Mabel Hughes. Ezra died 1 August 1969
Children of Ezra and Mabel (Hughes) Cree:
+ 829   i Irene Cree, born 15 February 1910
  830   ii Gatha Cree, born 27 July 1915. Married November 1933 Carl Sagars
  831 iii Betty Isabella Cree, born 7 March 1927. Married James Dillon

320 - CARL(5) CREE [Malinda Jane(4) Wolf, Jacob Jr(3), Jacob(2), Daniel(1)]
Carl Cree, first child of John Andrew and Malinda J. (Wolf) Cree, was born 16 April 1860. He married 27 December 1900 Sarah Adeline Tribbett, born 14 June 1879, daughter of George and Pluma (Perry) Tribbett. Carl died 28 February 1954 and Sarah 30 June 1965.
Children of Carl and Sarah Adeline (Tribbett) Cree:
+ 832   i Evaughn Gaston Cree, born 22 February 1903
+ 833   ii Paul Cree, born 27 March 1906
+ 834 iii Ward Cree, born 19 December 1908
+ 835   iv Virgil Cree, born 24 December 1911
+ 836   v Mary Thelma Cree, born 16 March 1914
  837   vi Lois Cree
+ 838 vii George Andrew Cree, born 9 September 1917
+ 839 viii Gaston Everett Cree, born 30 August 1919
+ 840   ix Lola May Cree, born 15 March 1921
  841   x Merle James Cree, born 18 September 1922

322 - CLARENCE(5) CREE [Malinda Jane(4) Wolf, Jacob Jr(3), Jacob(2), Daniel(1)
Clarence Cree, third child of John Andrew and Malinda J. (Wolf) Cree, was born 16 January 1882. He married 1) 6 August 1902 Stella Marie Cronk, born about 1880 and 2) 30 May 1925 Marie Kelly, born 1895 in Indiana. Clarence died 22 December 1941. There were no children by the second marriage.

Children of Clarence and Stella Marie (Cronk) Cree:
+ 842   i Mabel Cree, born 8 August 1903
+ 843   ii Russel Cree, born 29 April 1909
+ 844 iii Bennie Cree, born 12 September 1912

    323 - GOLDALEE(5) CREE [Malinda Jane(4) Wolf, Jacob Jr(3),
Jacob(2), Daniel(1)]
    Goldalee Cree, fourth child of John Andrew and Malinda Jane
(Wolf) Cree, was born 22 November 1889. She married 1) 15 January 1908
Thomas G. Ronk, 2) Edward Kindle and 3) _____ Wilson.
    Children of Thomas G. and Goldalee (Cree) Ronk:
+ 845   i Eva Lucille Ronk, born 13 December 1908
  846   ii Gladys Marie Ronk, born 13 January 1911
+ 847 iii Forrest Cree Ronk, born 27 June 1914
  848   iv Bessie Louella Ronk, 7 February 1920
  849   v Earnest Lee Ronk, born 22 September 1922

    328 - HIRAM T.(5) SHROYER [Daniel W.(4), Sarah(3) Wolf, Jacob(2),
Daniel(1)
    Hiram T. Shroyer, second child of Daniel W. and Matilda (Huffman)
Shroyer, was born 1 August 1858. He married 9 September 1879 Dora
Hipp, born 17 March 1859. Hiram died 29 October 1909 and is buried in
Oakwood Cemetery. Dora died 23 December 1929.
    Child of Hiram T. and Dora (Hipp) Shroyer:
  850   i Bessie Shroyer, born 31 October 1883. Married 4 January
          1904 Roy Stoneburner

    329 - WILLIAM(5) SHROYER [Daniel W.(4), Sarah(3) Wolf, Jacob(2),
Daniel(1)]
    William Shroyer, third child of Daniel W. and Matilda (Huffman)
Shroyer, was born 11 June 1865. He married 25 December 1893 Catherine
Brumbaugh.
    Child of William and Catherine (Brumbaugh) Shroyer:
  851   i Grace Shroyer. Married Ralph McDonald

    331 - LEWIS E.(5) SHROYER [Daniel W.(4), Sarah(3) Wolf, Jacob(2),
Daniel(1)]
    Lewis E. Shroyer, fifth child of Daniel W. and Matilda (Huffman)
Shroyer, was born 27 October 1867. He married 21 November 1890 Lillie
Makemson, born 6 March 1870. Lewis died 21 February 1947 and Lillie 28
June 1954. They are buried in Oakwood Cemetery.
    Child of Lewis E. and Lillie (Makemson) Shroyer:
  852   i Carl L. Shroyer, born 8 October 1891, died 4 August 1969,
          buried in Oakwood Cemetery

    347 - AMANDA(5) PONTIOUS [John(4), Elizabeth(3) Hahn, Eliza-
beth(2) Wolf, Daniel(1)]
    Amanda Pontious, daughter of John and Mary Magdalena (Sharritt)
Pontious, married William Hartman. Amanda died before 1924.
    Children of William and Amanda (Pontious) Hartman, order of birth
uncertain:
+ 853   i John Hartman, died before 1924
+ 854   ii Sarah Sabina Hartman, born 14 March 1865
  855 iii William Hartman
  856   iv Samuel Hartman
  857   v Vernon Hartman
  858   vi Frank Hartman
  859 vii Malinda Hartman. Married _____ Booker

```
860  viii James Hartman
861    ix Charles C. Hartman
862     x Mary Hartman. Married _____ Long
863    xi Amos Hartman
```

348 - SERENIUS(5) PONTIUS [John(4), Elizabeth(3) Hahn, Eliza-
beth(2) Wolf, Daniel(1)]
      Serenius Pontius, son of John and Mary Magdalena (Sharritt)
Pontious, was born 20 November 1844. He married 8 September 1872
Minerva Shade, born 20 February 1854, daughter of Peter and Sarah
(Strumbeck) Shade. Minerva died 31 August 1925 and Serenius 2 September 1926.
      Child of Serenius and Minerva (Shade) Pontius:
+ 864   i Charles Henry Pontius, born 11 June 1887

350 - SARAH(5) PONTIUS [John(4), Elizabeth(3) Hahn, Elizabeth(2)
Wolf, Daniel(1)]
      Sarah Pontius was the daughter of John and Mary Magdalene (Shar-
ritt) Pontious. She married _____ Drehr. Sarah died before 1924.
      Child of _____ and Sarah (Pontius) Drehr:
+ 865   i Margaret Drehr

351 - SAMUEL(5) PONTIUS [John(4), Elizabeth(3) Hahn, Elizabeth(2)
Wolf, Daniel(1)]
      Samuel Pontius was the son of John and Mary Magdelene Pontious.
He died before 1924.
      Child of Samuel and _____ Pontius:
866   i Milton Pontius

352 - ELLEN(5) PONTIUS [John(4), Elizabeth(3) Hahn, Elizabeth(2)
Wolf, Daniel(1)]
      Ellen Pontius was the daughter of John and Mary Magdalene (Shar-
ritt) Pontious. She died before 1924. She married _____ Dalton.
      Child of _____ and Ellen (Pontius) Dalton:
867   i Ida Dalton. Married _____ Hannahs

355 - ANDREW J.(5) HIPPLE [Elizabeth(4) Sharritt, Elizabeth(3)
Hahn, Elizabeth(2) Wolf, Daniel(1)]
      Andrew J. Hipple was the son of John W. and Elizabeth (Sharritt)
Hipple. He died before 1924.
      Children of Andrew J. and _____ Hipple:
```
868    i Grover Hipple
869   ii Celia Hipple. Married _____ Puls
870  iii Julia Hipple. Married _____ Evans
871   iv Lydia Hipple. Married _____ Butcher
```

356 - DANIEL(5) HIPPLE [Elizabeth(4) Sharritt, Elizabeth(3) Hahn,
Elizabeth(2) Wolf, Daniel(1)]
      Daniel Hipple was the son of John W. and Elizabeth (Sharritt)
Hipple. He died before 1924.
      Children of Daniel and _____ Hipple:
```
872    i Wilson Hipple
873   ii Charles Hipple
874  iii Henry Hipple
875   iv Flossie Hipple. Married _____ Ericson
876    v Arlina Hipple. Married _____ Groby
```

357 - SALOME(5) HIPPLE [Elizabeth(4) Sharritt, Elizabeth(3) Hahn, Elizabeth(2) Wolf, Daniel(1)]
      Salome Hipple was the daughter of John W. and Elizabeth (Sharritt) Hipple. She died before 1924. She married _____ Anderson.
      Children of _____ and Salome (Hipple) Anderson:
877   i Minerva Belle Anderson. Married _____ Hinkle
878   ii Sarah Elizabeth Anderson. Married _____ Broderick

358 - MINERVA(5) HIPPLE [Elizabeth(4) Sharritt, Elizabeth(3) Hahn, Elizabeth(2) Wolf, Daniel(1)]
      Minerva Hipple was the daughter of John W. and Elizabeth (Sharritt) Hipple. She died before 1924. She married _____ Kuhn.
      Children of _____ and Minerva (Hipple) Kuhn:
879   i J. Edward Kuhn
880   ii Louella Kuhn. Married _____ Stamps

363 - PETER(5) SHARRITT [John(4), Elizabeth(3) Hahn, Elizabeth(2) Wolf, Daniel(1)]
      Peter Sharritt was the son of John and _____ Sharritt. He died before 1924.
      Children of Peter and _____ Sharritt:
881   i Elwood Sharritt
882   ii Lester Sharritt
883   iii Charles Sharritt
884   iv Clara Sharritt. Married _____ Garrison
885   v Pearl Sharritt. Married _____ Rose

364 - HENRY(5) SHARRITT [John(4), Elizabeth(3) Hahn, Elizabeth(2) Wolf, Daniel(1)]
      Henry Sharritt was the son of John and _____ Sharritt. He died before 1924.
      Children of Henry and _____ Sharritt:

886   i Francis Sharritt
887   ii Minerva Sharritt. Married _____ Dill
888   iii David Sharritt
889   iv Cleveland Sharritt
890   v Clarence Sharritt
891   vi Clyde Sharritt

365 - GEORGE(5) SHARRITT [John(4), Elizabeth(3) Hahn, Elizabeth(2) Wolf, Daniel(1)]
      George Sharritt was the son of John and _____ Sharritt. He died before 1924.
      Children of George and _____ Sharritt:
892   i John Sharritt
893   ii Cora Sharritt. Married _____ Berkley
894   iii Anna Sharritt. Married _____ Gear

366 - CATHERINE(5) SHARRITT [John(4), Elizabeth(3) Hahn, Elizabeth(2) Wolf, Daniel(1)]
      Catherine Sharritt was the daughter of John and _____ Sharritt. She died before 1924. She married _____ Vogt.
      Children of _____ and Catherine (Sharritt) Vogt:
895   i Benjamin Vogt
896   ii Glenn Vogt
897   iii Lester Vogt
898   iv Effie Vogt. Married _____ Mazak

376 - ALICE ARRETTA(5) SHARRITTS [Samuel(4), Elizabeth(3) Hahn, Elizabeth(2) Wolf, Daniel(1)]
Alice Arretta Sharritts, fourth child of Samuel and Margaret (Stettler) Sharritts, was born 22 August 1864 in Montgomery County, OH. She married 20 September 1881 in Montgomery County 1) Orlando Boyer, born 3 September 1855 in Montgomery County, son of Jacob and Catherine (Biechler) Boyer. They were divorced and Alice Arretta married 2) 6 April 1899 Charles B. Urschel. Orlando is buried in Germantown Cemetery, Montgomery County and Alice Arretta in Hill-Grove Cemetery, Miamisburg, OH.
Children of Orlando and Alice Arretta (Sharritts) Boyer, all born in Montgomery County, OH:
```
899      i Irvin Boyer, born 29 December 1881, died 26 August 1952.
           Did not marry
+ 900    ii Charles Laird Boyer, born 14 June 1883
+ 901   iii Albert Boyer, born 8 July 1885
  902    iv Bessie Luceal Boyer, born 24 May 1887, died 22 July 1905.
           Married Albert M. Becker
  903     v Edna Pauline Boyer, born 26 March 1889, died 25 June 1959.
           Married 1) Will Brown. They divorced and she married 2)
           Irvin Roggee. There were no children by either marriage
  904    vi Arthur Samuel Boyer, born 3 August 1890 in Montgomery
           County, OH, died 9 August 1967
+ 905   vii Elizabeth Idella Boyer, born 29 June 1893
```
Child of Charles B. and Alice Arretta (Sharrits) (Boyer) Urschel:
```
  906     i Mary Viola Urschel, born 21 July 1899, died 12 June 1942.
           Married Fred Mundhenk
```

380 - AARON(5) SHARRITT [Leonard(4), Elizabeth(3) Hahn, Elizabeth(2) Wolf, Daniel(1)]
Aaron Sharritt was the son of Leonard and Elizabeth (Zecher) Sharritt. He died before 1924.
Children of Aaron and _____ Sharritt:
```
  907     i Paul Sharritt
  908    ii Walter Sharritt
```

393 - DANIEL(5) SHUMAKER [Sophia(4) Sharritt, Elizabeth(3) Hahn, Elizabeth(2) Wolf, Daniel(1)]
Daniel Shumaker was the son of John and Sophia (Sharritt) Shumaker. He died before 1924.
Child of Daniel and _____ Shumaker:
```
  909     i Frank Shumaker
```

403 - HARVEY(5) SHARRITT [Daniel Jr(4), Elizabeth(3) Hahn, Elizabeth(2) Wolf, Daniel(1)]
Harvey Sharritt was the son of Daniel Jr and Ann Agnes (Ingram) Sharritt. He married Pearl Gross.
Child of Harvey and Pearl (Gross) Sharritt:
```
  910     i Bruce Sharritt, died 16 May 1970. He was known in show
           business as Eddie Bruce
```

408 - FRANKLIN(5) WOLFE [Daniel Jr(4), Daniel Sr(3), Frederick(2), Daniel(1)]
Franklin Wolfe, second child of Daniel Jr and Sophia (Deeter) Wolfe, was born 7 January 1850 in Vermillion Township, Ashland County, OH. His father died when he was two years old and his mother two years later. After the death of his parents his paternal grandfather, Daniel Wolf Sr, was appointed his guardian and he lived with him until his

grandfather's death in 1862. He remained in Ohio until 1865 when he went to Iowa, living with his uncle, Michael Wolfe, until 1868. He married 1 January 1873 in Washington County, IA Sarah M. McCaleb, born in that county.

In 1874 they moved to Grant Township, Union County, IA where he purchased 40 raw acres to farm. In 1876 he sold this land and purchased a new tract of 80 acres and then 40 more acres. This farm was located adjacent to Shannon City, IA. He also owned land in Thomas County, KS. In 1889 he engaged in merchandising in Shannon City as a dealer in hardware and groceries, continuing in business until 1905.

Shannon City had been established in 1887 as a stopover point on the Chicago Great Western Railroad being built at that time, a rest stop being needed about halfway between the main ststions at Oelwein, IA and Kansas City, MO. However Shannon City never grew beyond a small village, growing to 333 residents in 1920. By this time, though, the automobile was reducing reliance on railroads and the depression of the 1930s started the decline of Shannon City to a population of 99 in 1980.

Franklin held many public offices, among them Justice of the Peace, Highway Commissioner and School Treasurer. He also servrd as Postmaster of Shannon City for five years, being appointed during Grover Cleveland's second administration. The Wolfe family was associated with the Methodist Episcopal Church of Shannon City. Franklin died in 1912 and Sarah in 1924, both in Union County, IA.

Children of Franklin and Sarah M. (McCaleb) Wolfe, all born in Union County, IA:

```
    911     i Clara Wolfe. Married Henry Jacobs
    912    ii Della Wolfe. Married _____ Van Dyne
    913   iii Willis Wolfe
+   914    iv Pearl Wolfe
    915     v Frank Wolfe
    916    vi Grover Wolfe
+   917   vii Vera Wolfe
```

411 - SIMON PETER(5) WOLFE [Michael(4), Daniel Sr(3), Frederick(2), Daniel(1)]

Simon Peter Wolfe, second child of Michael and Leah (Casey) Wolfe, was born 27 March 1853 in Vermillion Township, Ashland County, OH. In 1855 his parents moved to Washington and in 1871 to Grant Township, Union County, IA. After coming to Union County he worked as a farm hand through the summer seasons, while in the winter he taught school for several years. He afterward returned to Washington County in 1875, his time being divided between educational work and general farming.

He married 15 June 1876 in Keokuk, IA Cynthia Annie Anderson, born 31 December 1855 in Marysville, Union County, OH, daughter of David and Susan (Porter) Anderson. Following their marriage he engaged in farming in Keokuk County for seven years, then went to Union County where he purchased 120 acres of land in Section 25 of Grant Township. He farmed this land for eight years, then sold the property and purchased 200 acres in Section 35. After eight years he sold the property and purchased 240 acres in Section 23 of Grant Township. He raised Poland China and Duroc Jersey hogs and for several years engaged in feeding cattle. He was township assessor for two years, township trustee for seven years, school director and secretary of the school board. He was a member of the Odd Fellows Lodge and the Woodmen of the World. The Wolfe family was associated with the Methodist Episcopal Church of Shannon City.

Simon Peter died 27 April 1923 and Cynthia Annie 30 September 1944, both in Shannon City. They are buried in Shannon City's Oakland Cemetery which is located in Ringgold County, IA.

Children of Simon Peter and Cynthia Annie (Anderson) Wolfe:
+ 918   i Myrtle Annie Wolfe, born 29 December 1878
  919   ii Wayland Wolfe, born in Keokuk County, IA. Did not marry
+ 920   iii Fred Simon Wolfe, twin, born 26 September 1883
+ 921   iv Frank Peter Wolfe, twin, born 26 September 1883
  922   v Otha Wolfe, born in Union County, IA. Married Jessie Griep. No children
  923   vi Leland Wolfe, born in Union County, IA
+ 924   vii Nellie Wolfe

420 - CHARLES FREDERICK(5) WOLFE [Frederick (F.R.)(4), Daniel Sr(3), Frederick(2), Daniel(1)]
Charles Frederick Wolfe was the son of Frederick (F. R.) and Rebecca M. (Nickol) Wolfe. He married Eva Nettie Davenport.
Children of Charles Frederick and Eva Nettie (Davenport) Wolfe, all born in Union County, IA:
  925   i Everett Paul Wolfe, born 19 January 1896
  926   ii Vera Margaret Wolfe, born 10 June 1900
  927   iii Helen Marie Wolfe, born 18 October 1902

424 - JOHN A.(5) WOLFE [Frederick (F.R.)(4), Daniel(3), Frederick(2), Daniel(1)]
John A. Wolfe was born about 1882, son of Frederick (F.R.) and Rebecca M. (Nickol) Wolfe. He married Clara Abel. They died in Grant Township, Union County, IA and are buried in Oakland Cemetery, in Union County.
Children of John A. and Clara (Abel) Wolfe, born in Union County, IA:
  928   i Fred A. Wolfe, born about 1909. Married 20 August 1933 at Indianola, Warren County, IA Beulah Flesher, daughter of Fred C. Flesher
  929   ii Dan Wolfe, born about 1910

425 - MARY CATHERINE(5) SCHLOSSER [Henry Lawson(4), Elizabeth(3) Wolf, Frederick(2), Daniel(1)]
Mary Catherine Schlosser, first child of Henry Lawson and Rebecca Ellen (Roberts) Schlosser, was born 10 October 1857 in Cedar Rapids, IA. She married 11 November 1875 DeWitt Clinton Boggs. She died 30 March 1935 in Williamsport, IN and is buried in West Lebanon Cemetery, Warren County, IN.
Children of DeWitt Clinton and Mary Catherine (Schlosser) Boggs:
  930   i Belle Myrtle Boggs
  931   ii Bertha Boggs

427 - IDA MAY(5) SCHLOSSER [Henry Lawson(4), Elizabeth(3) Wolf, Frederick(2), Daniel(1)]
Ida May Schlosser, third child of Henry Lawson and Rebecca Ellen (Roberts) Schlosser, was born 27 July 1861 in Warren County, IN. She married 20 December 1883 in Warren County J. M. (Mont) Fisher. She died in 1946 in Caney, KS.
Children of J. M. (Mont) and Ida May (Schlosser) Fisher:
  932   i Marguerite Fisher
  933   ii Arthur L. Fisher

428 - SARAH ELIZABETH CARLOTTA(5) SCHLOSSER [Henry Lawson(4),
Elizabeth(3) Wolf, Frederick(2), Daniel(1)]:
    Sarah Elizabeth Carlotta Schlosser, fourth child of Henry Lawson
and Rebecca Ellen (Roberts) Schlosser, was born 3 December 1863 in
Warren County, IN. She married Clayton McMillan. She died 9 October
1893.
    Children of Clayton and Sarah Elizabetta Carlotta (Schlosser)
McMillan:
    934   i Daughter. Married _____ Van Notta
    935   ii Daughter. Married _____ Fleming

    450 - VICTOR HOWARD(5) RINGER [Margaret S.(4) Schlosser, Eliza-
beth(3) Wolf, Frederick(2), Daniel(1)]
    Victor Howard Ringer, first child of Jacob Howard and Margaret S.
(Schlosser) Ringer, was born 13 February 1870 in Warren County, IN. He
married 1) 28 April 1897 Alice Jennie Thomas. She died 4 July 1922 and
he married 2) 16 June 1926 Carrie Little. Victor died 13 October 1948
in Williamsport, IN. There were no children by his second marriage.
    Children of Victor Howard and Alice Jennie (Thomas) Ringer:
    936   i William Raimond Ringer
    937   ii Horace T. Ringer
    938 iii Alfred V. Ringer

    456 - HOWARD(5) KEEDY [Elizabeth(4) Blecker, Tracy(3) Wolf,
Frederick(2), Daniel(1)]
    Howard Keedy was the son of Edward and Elizabeth (Blecker)
Keedy.He married Perry Myers.
    Children of Howard and Perry (Myers) Keedy:
    939   i Merrit Keedy
    940   ii Paul Keedy, did not marry
    941 iii Bessie Keedy. Married in 1918 Ralph Mahoy. There were no
            children
+ 942   iv Mae Elizabeth (Babe) Keedy

    457 - ALICE(5) KEEDY [Elizabeth(4) Blecker, Tracy(3) Wolf,
Frederick(2), Daniel(1)]
    Alice Keedy was the daughter of Edward and Elizabeth (Blecker)
Keedy. She married Sam Sprecher.
    Children of Sam and Alice (Keedy) Sprecher:
  ⁹ 943   i Guy Sprecher. Did not marry
    944   ii Ada Sprecher. Married Walter Mitchell. No children

    458 - DANIEL BLECKER(5) KEEDY [Elizabeth(4) Blecker, Tracy(3)
Wolf, Frederick(2), Daniel(1)]
    Daniel Blecker Keedy was the son of Edward and Elizabeth
(Blecker) Keedy. He married Viola Smith.
    Child of Daniel Blecker and Viola (Smith) Keedy:
+ 945   i Lela Keedy

    460 - FRANK C.(5) KEEDY [Elizabeth(4) Blecker, Tracy(3) Wolf,
Frederick(2), Daniel(1)]
    Frank C. Keedy, son of Edward and Elizabeth (Blecker) Keedy, was
born 8 August 1869 in Washington County, MD. He married 8 February 1899
in Mt. Morris, Ogle County, IL Althea Coffman who died in 1943. Frank
died 31 December 1954 in Freeport, IL and is buried in Oakwood Cemetery,
Mt. Morris.
    Children of Frank C. and Althea (Coffman) Keedy:
+ 946   i Martha Keedy

```
     947    ii Mary Keedy. Did not marry
     948   iii Leroy Keedy. Married Molly Snapp. No children
     949    iv Orville Keedy. Did not marry
   + 950     v Pearl Keedy
     951    vi Mabel Keedy, died 1910. Did not marry
```

461 - ANNIE(5) KEEDY [Elizabeth(4) Blecker, Tracy(3) Wolf, Frederick(2), Daniel(1)]
    Annie Keedy was the daughter of Edward and Elizabeth (Blecker) Keedy. She married Martin Zellers.
    Children of Martin and Annie (Keedy) Zellers:
```
     952    i Edward Zellers. Did not marry
   + 953   ii Ernest Zellers
   + 954  iii Floyd Zellers
   + 955   iv Karl Zellers
   + 956    v Wilbur Zellers
```

466 - GEORGE EDWARD(5) BYERS [Mary Ann(4) Blecker, Tracy(3) Wolf, Frederick(2), Daniel(1)]
    George Edward Byers, fourth child of Jacob Chalmers and Mary Ann (Blecker) Byers, was born about 1868. He married Ella _____. He was a farmer.
    Children of George Edward and Ella (_____) Byers:
```
     957    i Irene Byers. Married _____ Mitchell
     958   ii Flora Byers. Married _____ Snow
```

467 - JACOB C.(5) BYERS [Mary Ann(4) Blecker, Tracy(3) Wolf, Frederick(2), Daniel(1)]
    Jacob C. Byers, fifth child of Jacob Chalmers and Mary Ann (Blecker) Byers, was born about 1870. He married Pearl _____. He was a farmer.
    Child of Jacob C. and Pearl (_____) Byers:
```
     959    i Fern Byers
```

469 - ANNIE VIRGINIA(5) BLECKER [Jacob B.(4), Tracy(3) Wolf, Frederick(2), Daniel(1)]
    Annie Virginia Blecker, second child of Jacob B. and Alice Virginia (Young) Blecker, was born 20 October 1871 in Boonsboro, Washington County, MD. She married 24 March 1903 (license) in Boonsboro Jesse Berry Gantz, born about 1868, son of Joseph and Amalia A. (_____) Gantz. Annie died 17 January 1925 and is buried in Boonsboro Cemetery. Jesse died 14 December 1942.
    Children of Jesse Berry and Annie Virginia (Blecker) Gantz:
```
   + 960    i Kathleen Lucille Gantz, born 8 November 1903
   + 961   ii Donald Wallace Gantz Sr, born 18 July 1910
```

471 - MARY ELIZABETH(5) BLECKER [Jacob B.(4), Tracy(3) Wolf, Frederick(2), Daniel(1)]
    Mary Elizabeth Blecker, fourth child of Jacob B. and Annie Virginia (Young) Blecker, was born 1 December 1875 in Boonsboro, Washington County, MD. She married 1) William L. Irwin, born 16 June 1865, died 22 October 1898, both in Boonsboro, and is buried in Boonsboro Cemetery. Mary married 2) 12 February 1900 William Bishop Lamar. She died 1 March 1928 in Freeport, IL and is buried in Oakland Cemetery, at Freeport. William died 21 December 1943.
    Child of William L. and Mary Elizabeth (Blecker) Irwin:
```
   + 962    i Paul Blecker Irwin, born 24 January 1897
```
    Children of William Bishop and Mary Elizabeth (Blecker) Lamar:

+ 963   i Bertha Isabelle Lamar, born 1 May 1901
+ 964   ii Robert Fulton Lamar, born 5 July 1904

472 - EFFIE YOUNG(5) BLECKER [Jacob B.(4), Tracy(3) Wolf, Frederick(2), Daniel(1)]

Effie Young Blecker, fifth child of Jacob B. and Alice Virginia (Young) Blecker, was born 25 September 1878 in Boonsboro, Washington County, MD. She married 12 June 1901 Simon Luther Young, born 7 October 1879. Simon died 1 June 1925 and Effie 7 February 1948. Both died and are buried in Freeport, IL.

Children of Simon Luther and Effie Young (Blecker) Young:
+ 965   i Walter Luther Young, born 10 September 1906
+ 966   ii Evelyn Alice Young, born 24 September 1912

474 - SHERMAN E.(5) WOLF [Franklin(4), Simon(3), Frederick(2), Daniel(1)]

Sherman E. Wolf, first child of Franklin and Laura W. (Martz) Wolf, was born 31 July 1876 in Boonsboro, Washington County, Md. He married 29 December 1895 in Zittlestown, Washington County Dolly May Summers, born 8 October 1876, daughter of Simon P. and Emma (Zittle) Summers. The 1910 Census lists Sherman as a farmer at Road #14, Boonsboro Election District 6. Sherman died 14 May 1930 and Dolly 30 March 1967. They are buried in the Boonsboro Cemetery, Washington County, MD.

Children of Sherman E. and Dolly May (Summers) Wolf:
+ 967   i Leila Emma Wolf, born 8 April 1897
  968   ii Baby Wolf, born and died young in Washington County, MD
  969 iii Mary Wolf, born 3 April 1901 in Washington County, MD, died
            5 August 1946. Married 26 June 1926 Frank Lowry, born 30
            January 1899, died 22 March 1963. No children
+ 970   iv Franklin Ellsworth Wolf,twin, born 5 March 1903
  971   v Melvin E. Wolf, twin, born 5 March 1903, died 19 August
            1916. Buried in Boonsboro Cemetery. All in Washington
            County, MD
+ 972   vi Irene Elizabeth Wolf, born 26 November 1912

475 - FLORENCE ESTELLA(5) WOLF [Franklin(4), Simon(3), Frederick(2), Daniel(1)]

Florence Estella Wolf, second child of Franklin and Laura Henrietta (Martz) Wolf, was born 25 October 1879 in Boonsboro, Washington County, MD. She married 25 June 1907 in Hagerstown, Washington County Chester Tilmore Lohr, born 29 December 1881 in Pennsylvania, son of William Arthur and Barbara Ellen (_____) Lohr. Chester was listed in Hagerstown directories as a fireman 1905-06, engineer 1910-11 and embalmer 1935. They lived on Frederick and East Antietam Streets in Hagerstown. Chester died 13 November 1958 and Florence Estella 30 August 1964, both in Hagerstown. They are buried in Rose Hill Cemetary, Hagerstown.

Children of Chester Tilmore and Florence Estella (Wolf) Lohr, all born in Hagerstown:
  973   i Carroll Earl (Flick) Lohr, born 4 June 1908 in Hagerstown,
            Washington County, MD, died 28 February 1992 in Hagerstown.
            Married 6 July 1926 at Hagerstown Lillian Barr Zellers,
            born 10 October 1906 at St. James, Washington County, died
            30 December 1988, in Hagerstown, daughter of Bruce and
            Bertha (Barr) Zellers. They are buried in Rose Hill Cemetery, Hagerstown. No children
  974   ii Sherman Tilmore Lohr, born 23 December 1909, died 16 March

1910 in Hagerstown, Washington County, MD. Buried in Rose
Hill Cemetery, Hagerstown
+ 975   iii Ellsworth Franklin Lohr, born 15 July 1911
  976   iv Lenora Irene Lohr, born 26 August 1912
+ 977   v Dorothy I. Lohr, born 15 January 1914
+ 978   vi Louise Lauraetta Lohr, born 31 October 1916.

476 - NORA PEARL(5) WOLF [Franklin(4), Simon(3), Frederick(2),
Daniel(1)]
    Nora Pearl Wolf, third child of Franklin and Laura Henrietta
(Martz) Wolf, was born 22 May 1881 in Boonsboro, Washington County,
MD. She married 7 March 1906 in Hagerstown, Washington County Norman
Saddler Earley Sr, born 8 June 1884 in Hagerstown, son of James W.
and Catherine (Angle) Earley. Norman was at times laborer, cabinet
maker and carpenter. They lived on Frederick Street in Hagerstown.
Nora died 23 June 1968 and Norman 9 April 1974, both in Hagerstown.
They are buried in Rose Hill Cemetery, Hagerstown.
    Children of Norman Saddler Sr and Nora Pearl (Wolf) Earley:
+ 979   i Leslie Filmore Earley, born 16 February 1910
+ 980   ii Norman Saddler (Bus) Earley Jr, born 19 November 1916
+ 981   iii Theodore Harold Earley, born 22 January 1919

477 - TRUMAN LEO(5) WOLFE [Franklin(4), Simon(3), Frederick(2),
Daniel(1)]
    Truman Leo Wolfe, fourth child of Franklin and Laura Henrietta
(Martz) Wolf, was born 1 May 1887 in Boonsboro, Washington County, MD.
He married 27 January 1907 in Appletown, Washington County Alice
Minnie Keyfauver, born 29 October 1891 at Eakle's Mill, Washington
County, daughter of Franklin and Mary S. (Poffenberger) Keyfauver.
Truman was a carpenter and they lived on Frederick Street, Hagerstown.
Alice died 12 January 1955 and Truman 28 February 1959, both in
Hagerstown. They are buried in Boonsboro Cemetery, Washington County.
    Children of Truman Leo and Alice Minnie (Keyfauver) Wolfe:
+ 982   i Pauline Mary Wolfe, born 9 October 1908
  983   ii Gladys Mae Wolfe, born 4 January 1911 at Eakle's Mill,
             Washington County, MD. Married William W. Kretzer
  984   iii Daughter Wolfe, born and died about 1913 in Washington
             County

478 - DAVID EARL(5) WOLF SR [Franklin(4), Simon(3), Frederick(2),
Daniel(1)]
    David Earl Wolf Sr, fifth child of Franklin and Laura Henrietta
(Martz) Wolf, was born 26 June 1891 in Boonsboro, Washington County,
MD. He married 5 September 1912 in Hagerstown, Washington County
Lillian Irene English, born 7 July 1891 in Lovettsville, VA, daughter
of Irvin Thomas and Jesse E. (Smith) English. David was an uphol-
sterer, auto top manufacturer and gas station operator in Hagerstown.
They lived on Frederick Street in Hagerstown. David died 20 April 1960
and Lillian 27 March 1972, both in Hagerstown. They are buried in Rose
Hill Cemetery, Hagerstown.
    Children of David Earl Sr and Lillian Irene (English) Wolf:
+ 985   i David Earl Wolf Jr, born 29 December 1916
  986   ii Frances Ruth Wolf, born 15 November 1920 in Hagerstown,
             Washington County, MD. Married 5 September 1947 in Hager-
             stown Martin Edward Wempe, born January 1920 in Maryland.
             There were no children

479 - CAROL RENO(5) WOLF [Franklin(4), Simon(3), Frederick(2), Daniel(1)]
Carol Reno Wolf, sixth child of Franklin and Laura Henrietta (Martz) Wolf, was born February 1894 in Boonsboro, Washington County, MD. He married 12 January 1914 in Boonsboro Myrtle O. Drill. They divorced 14 December 1918. Carol was a private in the Third Engineering Training Regiment during World War I. In private life he was an upholsterer and auto trimmer and lived on Frederick Street, Hagerstown, Washington County. He died 14 December 1931 and is buried in Rose Hill cemetary, Hagerstown.
Child of Carol Reno and Myrtle O. (Drill) Wolf:
987   i Robert R. Wolf

480 - LUCINDA KATHERYNE(5) TRONE [Mary Jeannette(4) Wolf, Simon(3), Frederick(2), Daniel(1)]
Lucinda Katheryne Trone, first child of Charles Alfred and Mary Jeannette (Wolf) Trone, was born 1 July 1891 in Funkstown, Washington County, MD. She married 31 July 1923 John Luther Ashway, born 8 October 1889 in Franklin County, PA, son of George Wesley and Ida (Ritter) Ashway. John died 19 October 1964 in Mechanicsburg, Cumberland County, PA and Lucinda 18 February 1975 in Camp Hill, Cumberland County. They are buried in Norland Cemetery, Chambersburg, Franklin County, PA.
Child of John Luther and Lucinda Katheryne (Trone) Ashway:
+ 988   i Mary Joan Ashway, born 20 July 1928

481 - ANNA RUTH(5) TRONE [Mary Jeannette(4) Wolf, Simon(3), Frederick(2), Daniel(1)]
Anna Ruth Trone, second child of Charles Alfred and Mary Jeannette (Wolf) Trone, was born 30 July 1895 in Funkstown, Washington County, MD. She married 4 December 1914 in Hagerstown, Washington County Edward Mull Schindel, born 30 May 1894 in Hagerstown, son of Norman Eugene and Sarah Emma (Leiter) Schindel. Edward died 15 June 1942 and Anna Ruth 29 July 1979 in Hagerstwon. She is buried in Funkstown Cemetery, Washington County.
Children of Edward Mull and Anna Ruth (Trone) Schindel:
+ 989   i Edward Trone Schindel, born 12 July 1915
+ 990   ii Sarah Jeannette Schindel, born 31 October 1917
+ 991   iii Doris Ann Schindel, born 10 July 1921
+ 992   iv Robert Norman Schindel, born 10 April 1924

482 - EDITH MENTZER(5) HARMAN [Ann Cora(4) Wolf, Simon(3), Frederick(2), Daniel(1)]
Edith Mentzer Harman, only child of Dr. Richard Tydings and Ann Cora (Wolf) Harman, was born 3 August 1883 in Hagerstown, Washington County, MD. She married 23 October 1907 in Hagerstown Elmer Rohrer Sager Sr, born 17 March 1881 at Beaver Creek, Washington County, son of Aaron David and Mary Elizabeth (Rohrer) Sager. Elmer died 6 July 1948 and Edith 15 July 1950, both in Washington DC. They are buried in Funkstown Cemetery, Washington County.
Children of Elmer Rohrer Sr and Edith Mentzer (Harman) Sager:
+ 993   i Anna Elizabeth Sager, born 26 July 1908
+ 994   ii Margaret Jeannette Sager, born 26 July 1910
+ 995   iii Elmer Rohrer Sager Jr, born 1 October 1916

483 - WALTER CLEVELAND(5) WOLFE [Harvey J.(4), Simon(3), Frederick(2), Daniel(1)]
Walter Cleveland Wolfe, first child of Harvey J. and Cora Pearl

(DeLauder) Wolf, was born 8 June 1890 at Leitersburg, Washington County, MD. He married 20 December 1911 in Hagerstown, Washington County Iva Pearl Nigh, born 1 June 1892. Walter died 27 July 1959 in Washington County and Iva Pearl 5 May 1966. They are buried in Rest Haven Cemetery, Hagerstown.

  Child of Walter Cleveland and Iva Pearl (Nigh) Wolfe:

996 i Roy Nevin Wolfe, born 10 October 1912, died 14 March 1990 in Hagerstown, Washington County, MD. Married 1) 25 April 1939 in Hagerstown Anna E. Snyder, born about 1909 in Maryland and 2) Margie I. Morris, born 26 November 1925. Roy is buried in Rest Haven Cemetery, Hagerstown. He was a veteran of World War II, serving in the U.S. Army. He operated linen services and Wolfe's Grocery in Paramount, Washington County. There were no children by either marriage.

  484 - BLANCHE BELLE(5) WOLFE [Harvey J.(4), Simon(3), Frederick(2), Daniel(1)]

  Blanche Belle Wolfe, second child of Harvey J. and Cora Pearl (DeLauder) Wolf, was born 28 September 1892 at Leitersburg, Washington County, MD. She married 18 December 1912 at Cavetown, Washington County Hiram Maurice McKinsey, born 9 May 1892 at Chewsville, Washington County, son of H. J. and Nettie M. McKinsey. Blanche died 27 May 1957 and Hiram 18 August 1959 in Hagerstown, Washington County. They are buried in Smithsburg Cemetery, Washington County.

  Children of Hiram Maurice and Blanche Belle (Wolfe) McKinsey:

997 i Louise Belle McKinsey, born 15 November 1913 at Chewsville, Washington County, MD. Did not marry
+ 998 ii Morris (Jack) Nevin McKinsey, born 22 January 1916
+ 999 iii Julia Marguerite McKinsey, born 18 February 1918
+ 1000 iv Jane McKinsey, born 3 September 1919
+ 1001 v Roland Wolfe McKinsey, born 28 April 1921
1002 vi Harvey McKinsey, died an infant
1003 vii Frederick Leo McKinsey, born 8 October 1925, died 9 November 1926

  485 - FANNIE ELIZABETH(5) WOLFE [Harvey J.(4), Simon(3), Frederick(2), Daniel(1)]

  Fannie Elizabeth Wolfe, third child of Harvey J. and Cora Pearl (DeLauder) Wolf, was born 22 July 1896 at Leitersburg, Washington County, MD. She married 10 September 1913 at Cavetown, Washington County Roy Brown Rinehart, born 7 December 1881. Roy died 21 July 1970 and is buried in Rest Haven Cemetery, Hagerstown, Washington County. Fannie died 5 December 1990 at the Fahrney-Keedy Home near Boonsboro, Washington County and is buried at the Lutheran Church Cemetery, Leitersburg, Washington County.

  Children of Roy Brown and Fannie Elizabeth (Wolfe) Rinehart:

+ 1004 i Helen Elizabeth Rinehart, born 20 March 1914
+ 1005 ii Thelma Marie Rinehart, born 21 December 1915
+ 1006 iii Robert Roy Rinehart, born 26 February 1918
1007 iv Vivian Genevieve Rinehart, born 10 May 1921 at Leitersburg, Washington County, MD. Married 28 June 1948 near Huyetts, Washington County Samuel Earl Younker Jr, born 2 September 1924 at Hagerstown, Washington county, son of Samuel Earl Sr and Ruth (Heil) Younker. Samuel was a veteran of World War II, serving in the U.S. Army, and was employed with Powers Distributing Company. He died 28 May 1990 and is buried in Rest Haven cemetary, Hagerstown.

+ 1008   v Evelyn May Rinehart, born 28 December 1925
+ 1009   vi Raymond Wolf Rinehart, born 14 May 1927

     486 - EDITH MARIE(5) WOLFE [Harvey J.(4), Simon(3), Frederick(2),
Daniel(1)]
     Edith Marie Wolfe, fourth child of Harvey J. and Cora Pearl
(DeLauder) Wolf, was born 2 July 1902 at Leitersburg, Washington
County, MD. She married 28 March 1924 in Hagerstown, Washington County
James Carroll Benchoff Sr, born 9 December 1901 at Edgemont, Washington County. James died 28 January 1965 at Hagerstown and is buried in
Burns Hill cemetary, Waynesboro, Franklin County, PA.
     Children of James Carroll Sr and Edith Marie (Wolfe) Benchoff,
all born at Leitersburg, Washington County, MD:
  1010   i James Carroll Benchoff Jr, born 18 January 1925, died 29
              June 1936 in Hagerstown, Washington County, MD, struck by
              a car
+ 1011   ii Theron Edwin Benchoff, born 9 January 1926
  1012   iii Phyllis Elaine Benchoff, born 7 September 1930. Married 7
              October 1967 in Hagerstown Frederick Arthur Garrett, born
              8 December 1938 at York, York county, PA, son of George
              Alvin and Beryl Elmira (Miller) Barrett. No children

     487 - CHARLES EUGENE(5) WOLFE [Harvey J.(4), Simon(3), Freder-
ick(2), Daniel(1)]
     Charles Eugene Wolfe, fifth child of Harvey J. and Cora Pearl
(DeLauder) Wolf, was born 14 November 1904 at Leitersburg, Washington
County, MD. He married 13 September 1934 at Hagerstown, Washington
County Bertha Elizabeth Bailey, born 17 February 1911 at Leitersburg,
daughter of Robert Albertus and Sarah Theresa (Finck) Bailey. Charles
died 23 May 1966 at Leitersburg and is buried in Rose Hill Cemetery,
Hagerstown.
     Child of Charles Eugene and Bertha Elizabeth (Bailey) Wolfe:
+ 1013   i Joanne Marie Wolfe, born 1 January 1939

     489 - ADA BLANCHE(5) WOLF [Carlton Emmert(4), Jacob(3), Freder-
ick(2), Daniel(1)]
     Ada Blanche Wolf, first child of Carlton Emmert and Ella Mary
(Fridley) Wolf, was born 1 June 1886 in Mt. Morris, Ogle County, IL.
She married 18 March 1908 at Mt. Morris Orion Frank Huffington, born 1
June 1885 in Darwin Township, Clark County, IL, son of Frank Asberry
and Mary Belle (Stevens) Huffington. Orion died 25 February 1965 and
Ada 2 February 1970, both at Rockford, Winnebago County, IL. They are
buried in Willwood Cemetery at Rockford.
     Children of Orion Frank and Ada Blanche (Wolf) Huffington:
+ 1014   i Maurine Ella Huffington, born 28 August 1909
+ 1015   ii Carlton Dale Huffington, born 19 January 1911

     490 - EMMERT JACOB(5) WOLF [Carlton Emmert(4), Jacob(3), Freder-
ick(2), Daniel(1)]
     Emmert Jacob Wolf, second child of Carlton Emmert and Ella Mary
(Fridley) Wolf, was born 28 July 1894 at Mt. Morris, Ogle County, IL.
He married 20 June 1916 at Oregon, Ogle County Uarda May Sears, born
19 July 1894 at Rockford, IL, daughter of Joseph Jr and Lillian Carry
(Gifford) Sears. They divorced in 1945.
     Emmert was employed at the Mt. Morris Post Office from 1913,
serving as Assistant Postmaster from 1919 until his retirement in
1964. He was a member of the Masons, Kiwanis and the Methodist Church.
He was a member of the Kable Concert Band for almost 55 years.

Emmert died 23 February 1968 at Sarasota, Sarasota County, FL and Uarda 9 March 1971 at Oregon, Ogle County. they are buried in Oakwood Cemetery, Mt. Morris.

Child of Emmert Jacob and Uarda May (Sears) Wolf:

1016   i Joseph Sears Wolf, born 21 September 1926 at Amboy, Lee County, IL. Did not marry

491 - HARRY LUTHER SR(5) HIGHBARGER [Catherine(4) Wolf, Jacob(3), Frederick(2), Daniel(1)]

Harry Luther Highbarger Sr, first child of George W. and Catherine (Wolf) Highbarger, was born in 1882 in Newark, Licking County, OH. He married Ada May Flounders, born in 1882. They lived in Darby, Philadelphia and Media, PA then in Hagerstown, Washington County, MD. Ada May died in 1960 and Harry 27 August 1972 in Washington County. They are buried in the Boonsboro, Washington County, Cemetery.

Children of Harry Luther Sr and Ada May (Flounders) Highbarger:

+ 1017   i Harry Luther Highbarger Jr, born 15 March 1907
+ 1018   ii Paul George W. Highbarger, born 5 April 1917

494 - MAUDE MAE(5) WOLF [John Albaugh(4), Jacob(3), Frederick(2), Daniel(1)]

Maude Mae Wolf, first child of John Albaugh and Nellie K. (Fahrney) Wolf, was born 2 March 1886 at Hagerstown, Washington County, MD. She was a school teacher prior to her marriage in 1921 to William Emil Hebscher, born 22 February 1876 in Belgium. William died 28 December 1968 and Maude 25 January 1978, both in Bakersfield, Kern County, CA. They are buried in Greelawn Cemetery, Bakersfield.

Child of William Emil and Maude Mae (Wolf) Hebscher:

+ 1019   i Ruth Anne Hebscher, born 5 October 1924

495 - HARRY EDWIN(5) WOLF [John Albaugh(4), Jacob(3), Frederick(2), Daniel(1)]

Harry Edwin Wolf, second child of John Albaugh and Nellie K. (Fahrney) Wolf, was born 15 April 1889 in Washington County, MD. He married 29 August 1911 at Greenville, Mercer County, PA Helen Lucile Yeisley, born 5 November 1889 in Greenville, daughter of Reverend Wilson and Frances (Roof) Yeisley.

Harry was a school teacher in early life, then Boys Work Secretary of the Hagerstown, Washington County YMCA until his death 11 January 1951. Lucile died 16 October 1980. They died in Hagerstown and are buried in Rest Haven Cemetery, Hagerstown.

Children of Harry Edwin and Helen Lucile (Yeisley) Wolf:

1020   i Genevieve Lucile Wolf, born 24 September 1912. Married 1) Arthur Stanley Cohen, born 20 September 1914, died 28 July 1944 at Hagerstown. Buried in the Jewish Cemetery, Halfway, Washington County, MD and 2) Robert Hoover Brindle, born 1896, died 1971 in Hagerstown. Genevieve died July 1954 in Hagerstown and is buried with her second husband in Rest Haven Cemetery, Hagerstown
+ 1021   ii John Franklin Bernard Wolf, born 12 February 1918

496 - CHARLES WELTY(5) WOLF [John Albaugh(4), Jacob(3), Frederick(2), Daniel(1)]

Charles Welty Wolf, third child of John Albaugh and Nellie K. (Fahrney) Wolf, was born 9 June 1890 in Boonsboro, Washington County, MD. He married 9 June 1917 at Woodview Farm, home of his bride near Jennersville, Chester County, Pa Mary Rachel Reece, born 25 January 1890 on the family farm, daughter of Jacob Coulson and Margaret Emma

(Elston) Reece.

He lived his early life in West Grove, Chester County, PA and a period in Oneida, NY. He was educated in the public schools of these areas and then attended West Chester, PA State Normal Schol, Drexel Institute in Philadelphia and graduated in 1913 from the University of Michigan Law School, Ann Arbor, MI.

He established his law practice in Hagerstown, Washington County, MD 19 October 1915, specializing in civil and corporation law. He was connected with the Hagerstown Fair Association for many years , serving as secretary for more than 20 years. He was a staunch Republican and in the 1920s served a term in the Maryland House of Delegates. From 1938 until his death he served as Court Auditor for the Washington County, MD Court.

He was an excellent woodworker, a skill which he learned from his father, who was a cabinet maker by occupation, and during the summers of his school years he worked in the casket factory in West Grove, this being the period when wooden caskets were in use. He used this skill to advantage by making much furniture for his home, including a solid mahogany dining room suite which is still in use by the family of one of his granddaughters. His hobbies in later years were stamp collecting and fishing which he engaged in at their summer home on Licking Creek near Camp Harding, Washington County, MD. This summer home was sometimes referred to by friends as "Languish on the Licking".

His wife, Mary, was raised on the family farm, Woodview Farm, near Jennersville, Chester County, PA and attended public schools in the area. She also attended· West Chester, PA State Normal School, receiving a Teacher's Certificate from that school. She taught school and in later years served as a secretary. They were members of the Presbyterian Church of Hagerstown.

Charles died 12 May 1948 in Hagerstown and Mary 20 April 1974 at the Fahrney-Keedy Retirement Home near Mapleville, Washington County. They are buried in Rest Haven Cemetery in Hagerstown.

Children of Charles Welty and Mary Rachel (Reece) Wolf:
+ 1022   i Charles Coulson Wolf, born 29 November 1918
+ 1023   ii Betty Ann Reece Wolf, born 22 May 1924

498 - MARY ELLEN(5) WOLF [John Albaugh(4), Jacob(3), Frederick(2). Daniel(1)]

Mary Ellen Wolf, fifth child of John Albaugh and Nellie K. (Fahrney) Wolf, was born 26 June 1895 in West Grove, Chester County, PA. She married 1 May 1915 Jacob Krauss Rhoads, born 29 July 1894 at Boyertown, Berks County, PA. He was a chemist by occupation. Mary Ellen died 15 December 1964 and Jacob 5 November 1965. They are buried in Acacia Cemetery, North Tonawanda, NY.

Child of Jacob Krauss and Mary Ellen (Wolf) Rhoads:
+ 1024   i Donald Wolf Rhoads, born 26 June 1923

503 - ROGER T.(5) EDMONDS SR [Jacob R.(4), Margaret Ann (3) Wolf, Frederick(2), Daniel(1)]

Roger T. Edmonds Sr, first child of Jacob R. and Georgetta (Hill) Edmonds, was born 2 May 1873 at Sharpsburg, Washington County, MD. He attended local public schools and in 1892 the State Normal School at Millersville, Lancaster County, PA. He married 27 February 1896 in Washington County Mamie Funk, daughter of Jeremiah and Nettie (Mong) Funk of Chewsville District of Washington County.

Roger taught school at Sharpsburg, Beaver Creek and in Rohrersville District, later serving for three years as principal of Antietam

Grammar School in Hagerstown, Washington County. During this time he studied law and was admitted to the Washington County Bar in August 1897. He was a Republican and served as Secretary of the Republican County Committee of Washington County. In 1905 he was appointed Court Auditor of Washington County.

Roger died 27 March 1907 in Washington County and Mamie August 1930 at Reading, Berks County, PA. He is buried in Rose Hill Cemetery, Hagerstown.

Children of Roger T. Sr and Mamie (Funk) Edmonds, order of birth unknown:

1025   i   Roger T. Edmonds Jr
1026   ii   George Henry Edmonds
1027 iii   Margaret Edmonds

512 - ELLEN MARTHA(5) KELTNER [Christina(4) Paulus, Simeon(3), Christina(2) Wolf, Daniel(1)]

Ellen Martha Keltner, fourth child of Ira A. and Christina (Paulus) Keltner, was born 11 February 1865 in Indiana. She married Perry C. Honeywell, born 30 June 1860 near Iowa City, Johnson County, IA. She died 21 July 1895 at Glenwood, Mills County, IA and Perry remarried 2) 11 September 1901 Lucinda Sparks. Perry died 28 June 1935 at Pacific City, IA. He and Ellen Martha are buried in Martin's Church Cemetery, Plattville Township, Mills County, IA.

Children of Perry C. and Ellen Martha (Keltner) Honeywell, order of birth unknown:

1028   i   Flora Bell Honeywell, died at birth
1029   ii   Fred Honeywell, died at birth
1030 iii   Elmer Honeywell, born 6 December 1884 in Iowa, died 22
            August 1918 near Villisca, IA
1831   iv   Allie May Honeywell, born 22 January 1887 in Iowa
1032   v   Minnie Honeywell, born 1 April 1891 in Iowa
       Child of Perry C. and Lucinda (Sparks) Honeywell:
1033   i   Clarence Honeywell, died at six weeks

520 - JOHN S.(5) ILER [Mariah(4) Paulus, Simeon(3), Christina(2) Wolf, Daniel(1)]

John S. Iler, first child of Joshua and Mariah (Paulus) Iler, was born 17 October 1857 in Ohio. He married Mazie Lavering, born in 1857 in Indiana. Mazie died 16 September 1950 and John 3 March 1952, both in Indiana.

Children of John S. and Mazie (Lavering) Iler:

1034   i   Ruth Iler. Married Asher Fisher. No children. Lived at
            Columbia City, IN
+ 1035   ii   Carrie Iler, born 8 March 1891

521 - ROBERT(5) ILER [Mariah(4) Paulus, Simeon(3), Christina(2) Wolf, Daniel(1)]

Robert Iler was the second child of Joshua and Mariah (Paulus) Iler.

Child of Robert and _____ Iler:

1036   i   Emerson Iler. Married Elizabeth _____. They lived on a
            farm, RR #5, Union City, OH

522 - EZRA G. A.(5) ILER [Mariah(4) Paulus, Simeon(3), Christina(2) Wolf, Daniel(1)]

Ezra G. A. Iler, third child of Joshua and Mariah (Paulus) Iler, was born 17 October 1859 in Ohio. He married 19 May 1892 in Noble County, IN Mary Simmons, born 24 March 1872 in Indiana. Ezra died 4

January 1907 and Mary 20 November 1968, both in Indiana. They are buried in Rosehill Cemetery, Noble County, IN.
Children of Ezra G. A. and Mary (Simmons) Iler:
1037   i Maude Iler, born 13 April 1893 in Indiana, died 18 October 1963 in Indiana. Married 1) Frank Ashbaugh. Divorced and married 2) Otto Laykauf, died 10 October 1962 in Indiana. She is buried in Lindenwood Cemetery, Ft. Wayne., IN
1038   ii Infant son, born 6 June 1897, died 14 June 1897 in Indiana
+ 1039   iii Margaret Iler, born 10 February 1905

523 - ALICE E.(5) ILER [Mariah(4) Paulus, Simeon(3), Christina(2) Wolf, Daniel(1)]
Alice E. Iler, fourth child of Joshua and Mariah (Paulus) Iler, was born 3 April 1868 in Ohio. She married Jacob Selby, born 3 December 1852. She was his second wife, he having been previously married to Sarah E. Wolf, daughter of Jacob and Christina (Paulus) Wolf. Jacob died 25 May 1943 and Alice 17 December 1954, both in Ohio. Buried in Ithica Cemetery, Ithica, OH
Children of Jacob and Alice E. (Iler) Selby:
+ 1040   i Florence Selby, born 2 October 1897
1041   ii Mable Selby, born 20 December 1904 in Ohio, died 2 August 1973 in Ohio. Buried in Ithica Cemetery, Ithica, OH. Did not marry

527 - JOSEPH(5) PAULUS [Jacob(40, Simeon(3), Christina(2) Wolf, Daniel(1)]
Joseph Paulus, fourth child of Jacob and Anna (Lavering) Paulus, was born December 1875 in Whitley County, IN. He married Emma Cake, born 1881 in Indiana. Joseph died in 1932 and Emma in 1953, both in Indiana. They are buried in Green Hill cemetary, Columbia City, IN
Child of Joseph and Emma (Cake) Paulus:
1042   i Velma Paulus

533 - EMALINE(5) PAULUS [Daniel(4), Simeon(3), Christina(2) Wolf, Daniel(1)]
Emaline Paulus, first child of Daniel and Elizabeth (Waterfall) Paulus, was born 28 August 1868 in St. Joseph County, IN. She married 8 March 1894 Emerson Pressler, born 26 July 1868 in Whitley County,IN, son of Valentine and Diana (Dupler) Pressler. Emerson died 9 September 1948 and Emaline 27 February 1962, both in Indiana. They are buried in Christian Chapel Cemetery, Noble County, IN.
Children of Emerson and Emaline (Paulus) Pressler:
+ 1043   i Harlan E. Pressler, born 2 April 1895
+ 1044   ii Ralph A. Pressler Sr, born 20 October 1896
+ 1045   iii Wilda Pressler, born 1898

535 - LAURA ANN(5) PAULUS [Daniel(4), Simeon(3), Christina(2) Wolf, Daniel(1)]
Laura Ann Paulus, third child of Daniel and Elizabeth (Waterfall) Paulus, was born 16 July 1873 in St. Joseph County, In. She married 22 October 1893 in Indiana Harvey S. Fruchey, born 18 March 1870 in Indiana. Laura Ann died 4 may 1954 and Harvey 11 February 1958, both in Indiana. They are buried in Merriam Cemetery, Columbia City, Whitley County, IN.
Children of Harvey S. and Laura Ann (Paulus) Fruchey:
+ 1046   i Alice I. Fruchey, born 30 March 1895
+ 1047   ii Erma Fruchey, born 11 April 1898
1048   iii Garrett Fruchey, born 22 September 1899 in Indiana, buried

in Christian Chapel Cemetery, Merriam, IN. Married Addie
Ayers, buried in Pierceton Cemetery, Kosciusko County, IN
+ 1049   iv Dan Fruchey, born 2 October 1901
+ 1050   v Benton S. Fruchey, born 3 July 1904
+ 1051   vi Itha Fruchey
  1052   vii Ilene Fruchey, born 21 March 1915 in Indiana. Married 18
            October 1958 Lester Pheister. No children. They lived at
            R#8 Columbia City, IN

    536 - FINETTE(5) PAULUS [Daniel(4), Simeon(3), Christina(2) Wolf,
Daniel(1)]
    Finette (Nettie) Paulus, fourth child of Daniel and Elizabeth
(Waterfall) Paulus, was born 16 August 1876 in St. Joseph County, IN.
She married 3 June 1903 Francis Marion Grable, born 2 September 1876 in
Whitley County, IN, son of George Washington and Sarah (Lamon) Grable.
Francis was a school teacher and farmer. They were members of the Church
of God. He died 29 July 1955 and Nettie 21 May 1964 in Indiana. They are
buried in Christian Chapel Cemetery, Merriam, IN.
    Children of Francis Marion and Finette (Paulus) Grable:
+ 1053   i Earl Kenneth Grable, twin, born 29 September 1905
+ 1054   ii Ernest Keith Grable, twin, born 29 September 1905
+ 1055   iii Esther Virginia Grable, born 8 February 1907
+ 1056   iv David Allen Grable, born 17 September 1911
+ 1057   v Robert G. Grable, born 24 March 1920
  1058   vi Roland Marcel Grable, born 16 January 1922 in Indiana,
            died 5 November 1975 in Indiana. Buried in Crown Hill
            cemetary, Indianapolis, IN. Married 7 June 1947 at Kokomo,
            IN Virginia Louise Cassel, born 28 August 1918. Reported
            to have two children
  1059   vii Albert Grable, died at age 11 from a fall from a tree
  1060 viii William Scott Grable, died at three months

    537 - JAMES JULIAN(5) PAULUS [Daniel(4), Simeon(3), Christina(2)
Wolf, Daniel(1)]
    James Julian Paulus, fifth child of Daniel and Elizabeth (Water-
fall) Paulus, was born 28 June 1878 in Noble County, IN. He married 7
April 1903 _____ Snell. He died in 1957.
    Children of James Julian and _____ (Snell) Paulus:
+ 1061   i Arthur Clayton Paulus
  1062   ii Clarence Paulus. Lived at RR#3, LaGrange, IN
  1063   iii Gladys Paulus. Married Lester Perrine. Lived at RR#1,
            Sturgis, MI
  1064   iv Cecil Paulus. Lived near Ligonier, IN

    538 - SAMUEL DELBERT(5) PAULUS [Daniel(4), Simeon(3), Chris-
tina(2) Wolf, Daniel(1)]
    Samuel Delbert Paulus, sixth child of Daniel and Elizabeth
(Waterfall) Paulus, was born 28 September 1880 in Noble County, IN. He
married 30 November 1911 Lola Augusta Wilkerson, born 20 August 1889,
daughter of Lyman S. and Angeline (Genth) Wilkerson. Samuel traveled
extensively in the United States and in the east he met the publisher
and physical culturist, Bernarr McFadden. Being impressed he named his
first son after him. He was a farmer in Sparta Township during the
years 1913 to 1919. He died 10 July 1926 having driven his car in
front of a train in a dense fog. Lola died 7 September 1934. They are
buried in the Sparta Cemetery, Noble County.
    Children of Samuel Delbert and Lola Augusta (Wilkerson) Paulus:
+ 1065   i Lawrence Bernarr Paulus, born 30 October 1912

```
+ 1066    ii Helen Christina Paulus, born 15 May 1914
+ 1067   iii Thelma Esther Paulus, born 16 January 1916
+ 1068    iv Jay Woodrow Paulus, born 7 October 1917
+ 1069     v Leon Virgil Paulus, born 14 September 1919
+ 1070    vi Evangeline Kathryn Paulus, born 11 January 1922
  1071   vii Richard Paulus, born and died 8 June 1924 in Indiana
+ 1072  viii Russell Weldon Paulus, born 2 November 1925
```

541 - CHRISTENA MARIE(5) PAULUS [Daniel(4), Simeon(3), Christina(2) Wolf, Daniel(1)]
    Christina Marie Paulus, ninth child of Daniel and Elizabeth (Waterfall) Paulus, was born 16 February 1890 in Noble County, IN. She married Harley Monroe Smith, born 1 May 1892. They lived in Ft. Wayne, IN until 1947 when they moved to Long Beach, CA. They died in California, Harley 3 July 1974 and Christina 28 December 1983, and are buried there.
    Children of Harley Monroe and Christina Marie (Paulus) Smith:
```
+ 1073     i Archie Lee Smith, born 5 August 1917
+ 1074    ii Annabelle Lou Smith, born 27 February 1930
```

542 - DANIEL VIRGIL(5) HAAS [Catherine Elizabeth(4) Paulus, Simeon(3), Christina(2) Wolf, Daniel(1)]
    Daniel Virgil Haas, first child of Joseph Henry and Catherine Elizabeth (Paulus) Haas, was born 6 November 1866 in Whitley County, IN. He married 1) 6 July 1889 in St. Joseph County, IN Viola B. Norris, born 3 December 1875 in Indiana, daughter of Calvin and Mary (Reed) Norris. They divorced in 1906. Daniel remarried 2) in 1910 Clara (Felton) Keck, born January 1883. Viola died 19 July 1932 and is buried in Fair Cemetery near Lakeville, IN. Daniel died 3 September 1934 in Mishawaka, IN and is buried in the Bremen, IN Cemetery. Clara was killed in her car at a railroad crossing in Bremen 19 December 1942. There were no children by the second marriage.
    Children of Daniel Virgil and Viola B. (Norris) Haas:
```
+ 1075     i Mable Esther Haas, born 9 November 1890
  1076    ii Lena Arvilla Haas, born 1892, died July 1893 in St. Joseph
             County, IN. Buried in Fair Cemetery, near Lakeville, St.
             Joseph County
  1077   iii Raymond Gene Haas, born 1894, died 1897 in St. Joseph
             County, IN. Buried in Fair Cemetery, near Lakeville, St.
             Joseph County
+ 1078    iv Hazel Violet Haas, born 2 October 1895
+ 1079     v Lulu Lurene Haas, born 7 November 1897
+ 1080    vi Ernest Welcome Haas, born 6 October 1899
+ 1081   vii Joseph Daniel Haas, born 11 May 1901
```

543 - BARBARA ELLEN(5) HAAS [Catherine Elizabeth(4) Paulus, Simeon(3), Christina(2) Wolf, Daniel(1)]
    Barbara Ellen Haas, second child of Joseph Henry and Catherine Elizabeth (Paulus) Haas, was born 7 January 1868 in Whitley County, IN. She married 4 December 1890 at Lapaz, Marshall County, IN Samuel Clabaugh, born 2 February 1867 in Indiana. Samuel died 25 March 1943 in Indiana and Barbara Ellen 6 October 1964 at South Bend, St. Joseph County, IN. They are buried in Fair Cemetery, near Lakeville, St. Joseph County.
    Children of Samuel and Barbara Ellen (Haas) Clabaugh:
```
  1082     i Floyd Oscar Clabaugh, born 13 May 1892 at Bremen, Marshall
             County, IN, died 2 February 1907 at Ft. Wayne, Allen
             County, IN. Buried in Fair Cemetery, near Lakeville, St.
```

Joseph County, IN
+ 1083   ii Agnes Pearl Clabaugh, born 13 December 1895
+ 1084 iii Nellie Rosella Clabaugh, twin, born 20 August 1900
+ 1085   iv Nettie Rosetta Clabaugh, twin, born 20 August 1900
+ 1086   v Bernice Mildred Clabaugh, born 24 September 1903

544 - THEODORE L.(5) HAAS [Catherine Elizabeth(4) Paulus,
Simeon(3), Christina(2) Wolf, Daniel(1)]
     Theodore L. Haas, third child of Joseph Henry and Catherine
Elizabeth (Paulus) Haas, was born 4 June 1870 in Whitley County, IN.
He married Hattie Elizabeth Renas, born 22 December 1873 in Indiana.
Hattie died 6 March 1915 and Theodore 20 October 1957. They are buried
in the Bremen Cemetery, Marshall County, IN.
     Children of Theodore L. and Hattie Elizabeth (Renas) Haas:
  1087   i Millard Martin Haas, born 11 October 1896 in Indiana.
            Married 6 March 1928 at Mishawaka, St. Joseph County, IN
            Grace I. Forsythe, born 2 March 1895 in Michigan. Millard
            served in World War I. There were no children
+ 1088   ii Edith May Haas, born 3 April 1898
+ 1089 iii Orville Henry Haas, born 23 may 1900
+ 1090   iv Matilda Elizabeth Haas, born 19 February 1902
+ 1091   v Welcome Forest Haas, born 1 June 1905
+ 1092   vi Nettie Almira Haas, born 7 September 1907
+ 1093 vii Violet Marie haas, born 25 January 1910

546 - MARY ANN(5) HAAS [Catherine Elizabeth(4) Paulus, Simeon(3),
Christina(2) Wolf, Daniel(1)]
     Mary Ann Haas, fifth child of Joseph Henry and Catherine Eliza-
beth (Paulus) Haas, was born 23 May 1873 in Whitley County, IN. She
married 13 August 1895 James Monroe Ranstead, born 13 November 1867.
He was a farmer and carpenter. Mary Ann died 3 August 1954 and James
12 April 1964.
     Children of James Monroe and Mary Ann (Haas) Ranstead:
+ 1094   i Glen Virgil Ranstead, born 13 March 1896
+ 1095   ii Gladys Pearl Ranstead, born 3 April 1900
+ 1096 iii Catherine E. Ranstead, born 18 April 1902

548 - JOSEPH HENRY(5) HAAS JR [Catherine Elizabeth(4) Paulus,
Simeon(3), Christina(2) Wolf, Daniel(1)]
     Joseph Henry Haas Jr, seventh child of Joseph Henry and Catherine
Elizabeth (Paulus) Haas, was born 15 August 1877 at Lakeville, St.
Joseph County, In. He married 23 December 1902 Ardella Azella Hodges,
born 4 February 1877. Ardella died 21 March 1951 and Joseph 24 July
1955. They are buried in Bremen Cemetery, Marshall County, IN.
     Children of Joseph Henry Jr and Ardella Azella (Hodges) Haas:
+ 1097   i Marguerette Verna Haas, born 25 November 1903
+ 1098   ii Homer Jennings Haas, born 3 June 1905
+ 1099 iii Glenn Martin Haas, born 18 October 1909
  1100   iv Herman Henry haas, born 20 December 1912 in Indiana.
            Married 6 October 1945 in Chattanooga, TN Sarah Elizabeth
            Rudd, born 24 November 1921 in Tennessee. There were no
            children
+ 1101   v Helen Irene Haas, born 20 December 1912

549 - MARTHA ELIZABETH(5) HAAS [Catherine Elizabeth(4) Paulus,
Simeon(3), Christina(2) Wolf, Daniel(1)]
     Martha Elizabeth Haas, eighth child of Joseph Henry and Catherine
Elizabeth (Paulus) Haas, was born 24 January 1880 at Lakeville, St.

Joseph County, IN. She married 27 February 1906 Floyd Emerson Platz, born 18 July 1879. Martha died 5 January 1968. They are buried in Bremen Cemetery, Marshall County, IN.

Child of Floyd Emerson and Martha Elizabeth (Haas) Platz:
1102   i Virginia Emma Platz, adopted, born 2 February 1915

551 - MARGARET MAYCAPITOLIA(5) HAAS [Catherine Elizabeth(4) Paulus, Simeon(3), Christina(2) Wolf, Daniel(1)]
Margaret Maycapitolia Haas, tenth child of Joseph Henry and Catherine Elizabeth (Paulus) Haas, was born 1 May 1883 in Lakeville, St. Joseph County, IN. She married 31 March 1908 Otto Clyde Platz, born 23 April 1883. Margaret died 8 June 1920 and Otto 4 October 1961 in Indiana. They are buried in Fair Cemetery, near Lakeville, St. Joseph County, IN.

Children of Otto Clyde and Margaret Maycapitolia (Haas) Platz, born in Indiana:
1103   i Kenneth J. Platz, born 10 December 1910
1104   ii Mildred May Platz, born 8 December 1914. Married _____ Eslinger

552 - BERTHA MARIE(5) HAAS [Catherine Elizabeth(4) Paulus, Simeon(3), Christina(2) Wolf, Daniel(1)]
Bertha Marie Haas, eleventh child of Joseph Henry and Catherine Elizabeth (Paulus) Haas, was born 29 September 1885 at Lakeville, St. Joseph County, IN. She married 14 June 1905 at Lapaz, Marshall County, IN Hiram W. K. Rose, born 16 April 1882 in Indiana. Hiram died 14 January 1955 in South Bend, St. Joseph County and Bertha 25 October 1983 on the farm of a son, located near Lakeville, St. Joseph County. They are buried in South Lawn Cemetery, South Bend.

Children of Hiram W. K. and Bertha Marie (Haas) Rose:
+ 1105   i Dale Leroy Rose, born 22 October 1907
+ 1106   ii Virginia Mae Rose, born 26 February 1910
+ 1107   iii Carl W. K. Rose, born 16 March 1912
+ 1108   iv Betty Elizabeth Rose, born 22 November 1921

562 - MARTHA ELLEN(5) WALLACE [Emeline(4) Paulus, Simeon(3), Christina(2) Wolf, Daniel(1)]
Martha Ellen Wallace, second child of John and Emeline (Paulus) Wallace, was born 31 October 1881 in St. Joseph County, IN. She married in St. Joseph County Charles Robertson, born 1867. Charles died in 1942 and Martha in 1963 in Inciana.

Child of Charles and Martha Ellen (Wallace) Robertson:
1109   i Duward Robertson, born 11 June 1899, died 7 October 1910

563 - CLARENCE(5) WALLACE [Emeline(4) Paulus, Simeon(3), Christina(2) Wolf, Daniel(1)]
Clarence Wallace, third child of John and Emeline (Paulus) Wallace, was born 12 March 1883 in St. Joseph County, IN. He married Bessie Fisher, born 31 March 1885. Clarence died in 1945 and Bessie in 1956.

Children of Clarence and Bessie (Fisher) Wallace:
+ 1110   i Charles M. Wallace, born 9 February 1906
1111   ii Edna Wallace, born 9 March 1908. Married Harry Boyer
+ 1112   iii Cecil Wallace, born 26 February 1910
+ 1113   iv Ralph Wallace, born 20 May 1912
1114   v Fern Wallace, died in infancy
+ 1115   vi Marvin Wallace, born 20 August 1921
+ 1116   vii Robert Wallace, born 5 April 1927

564 - MARIE(5) WALLACE [Emeline(4) Paulus, Simeon(3), Chris-
tina(2) Wolf, Daniel(1)]
    Marie Wallace, fourth child of John and Emeline (Paulus) Wallace,
was born 16 April 1886 in St. Joseph County, IN. She married 9 July
1911 Otis Hosler. Marie died in 1958 in Indiana.
    Child of Otis and Marie (Wallace) Hosler:
+ 1117   i Maxine Hosler, born 26 October 1919

    568 - SARAH ELLEN(5) WOLF [Christina(4) Paulus, Daniel(3),
Christina(2) Wolf, Daniel(1)]
    Sarah Ellen Wolf, second child of Jacob and Christina (Paulus)
Wolf, was born 3 October 1852 in Harrison Township, Preble County, OH.
She married Jacob Selby, born 3 December 1852. Sarah died 28 February
1894 in Ohio and Jacob remarried Alice E. Iler (see #523), daughter of
Joshua and Mariah (Paulus) Iler. Mariah was the daughter of Simeon
Paulus, brother of Daniel Paulus. Jacob died 25 may 1943. Jacob and
Sarah are buried in the Ithaca, OH Cemetery.
    Children of Jacob and Sarah Ellen (Wolf) Selby:
+ 1118   i Norman Selby, born 24 November 1873
+ 1119   ii Malinda Maude Selby, born 9 March 1878
+ 1120   iii Mount Vernon Selby, born 6 March 1880
  1121   iv Harry Clyde Selby, born 23 October 1883, died 1 November
                1965. Buried in Ithica, OH Cemetery
    Children of Jacob and Alice E. (Iler) Selby:
+ 1040   i Florence Selby, born 2 October 1897
  1041   ii Mable Selby, born 20 December 1904 in Ohio, died 2 August
                1973 in Ohio. Buried in Ithica, OH Cemetery

    569 - NELSON(5) WOLF [Christina(4) Paulus, Daniel(3), Chris-
tina(2) Wolf, Daniel(1)]
    Nelson Wolf, third child of Jacob and Christina (Paulus) Wolf,
was born 3 June 1854 near Verona, Preble County, OH. He married 23
December 1880 in Indiana Margaret Bradford, born 19 September 1855 in
Indiana, daughter of William Bradford. Nelson left home at age 17 to
become a carpenter, which occupation he continued for several years,
and in 1874 he went to Indiana and went into the sawmill business
until 1883. In 1883 he purchased land from his father and engaged in
farming. In 1912 he owned 175 acres in Sections 9, 10 and 20 of Grant
County, IN. Nelson died 9 March 1934 and Margaret 21 August 1934 in
Grant County. They are buried in the IOOF Cemetery at Marion in Grant
County.
    Children of Nelson and Margaret (Bradford) Wolf:
+ 1122   i Norman Wolfe, born 22 September 1881
  1123   ii Rosie Wolfe, born 11 June 1885, died 1886 in Grant County,
                IN
+ 1124   iii Florence Wolfe, born 7 November 1893

    570 - LYDIA(5) WOLF [Christina(4) Paulus, Daniel(3), Christina(2)
Wolf, Daniel(1)]
    Lydia Wolf, fourth child of Jacob and Christina (Paulus) Wolf,
was born in 1855 near Verona, Preble County, OH. She married James
Otto Walker, born 2 December 1845. In the 1880s they moved to Peoria,
IL. They divorced 2 December 1889. Lydia worked at the Windsor Cafe in
Peoria. James worked in the Peoria and Pekin Union Railway Company
switch yards where he was killed 16 February 1890. He was buried in
Peoria by the railway company. Lydia was living in Peoria at the time
of her mother's estate settlement in 1915.

                                115

Children of James Otto and Lydia (Paulus) Walker:
1125   i Stella Walker, born 17 March 1875. Married _____ Ferguson.
          She was living in Chicago in 1896
+ 1126 ii May Walker
1127 iii Otto Walker. Married in Peoria. In 1922 he was living in
          Edgewater, CO

      571 - JANE(5) WOLF [Christina(4) Paulus, Daniel(3), Christina(2)
Wolf, Daniel(1)]
      Jane Wolf, fifth child of Jacob and Christina (Paulus) Wolf, was
born 8 September 1857 near West Baltimore (Verona), Harrison Township,
Preble County, OH. She married David Gebhart Jr, born 12 December
1841, son of David Sr and Margaret (Pence) Gebhart. They lived on a
farm near Lewisburg, OH. David died 20 March 1917 and Jane 9 January
1945. They are buried in Rose Lawn Cemetery, Lewisburg.
      Children of David Jr and Jane (Wolf) Gebhart:
+ 1128   i Norah Gebhart, born 7 April 1874
+ 1129 ii Early Gebhart, born 11 September 1876
1130 iii Otto Gebhart, born 8 May 1878 near Lewisburg, OH, died 26
          September 1887
1131   iv John V. Gebhart, born 27 January 1881 near Lewisburg, OH,
          died 30 January 1955. Married Laura _____. They lived at
          Dayton, OH and had no children
+ 1132   v Opal Gebhart, born 17 April 1889
1133   vi Margaret Gebhart, born 5 September 1893 near Lewisburg,
          OH, died 20 March 1980. Married Donivar D. Stutz, born
          1895, died 1933. They lived on a farm at Arcanum, OH and
          are buried in Ithica, OH Cemetery

      572 - DAN(5) WOLF [Christina(4) Paulus, Daniel(3), Christina(2)
Wolf, Daniel(1)]
      Dan Wolf, sixth child of Jacob and Christina (Paulus) Wolf, was
born 24 April 1859 near Verona, Preble County, OH. He married 28 July
1878 Emily Elizabeth Black, born 1 May 1859. Dan was a farmer most of
his life. In the 1870s he rented and farmed 300 to 400 acres near
Mansfield, IL and about 1900 he moved to and farmed at Warren, MN.
About 1909 they returned to Greenville, OH where he had a part interest in a garage. Dan died 26 January 1919 in Greenville and is buried
in the mausoleum in Greenville Cemetery. Emily remarried in July 1923
to John Ehler. She died in 1937.
      Child of Dan and Emily Elizabeth (Black) Wolf:
+ 1134   i Sarah Catherine Wolf, born 24 November 1880

      573 - CAROLINE(5) WOLF [Christina(4) Paulus, Daniel(3), Chris-
tina(2) Wolf, Daniel(1)]
      Caroline Wolf, seventh child of Jacob and Christina (Paulus) Wolf,
was born 11 November 1861 in Preble County, OH. She married Samuel
Selby, born 15 June 1855 in Darke County, OH. Caroline died 22 June
1897 and Samuel married 2) 23 March 1899 Isa Dora Wolf, born 25
December 1878, died 1946. Samuel died 9 June 1933. Samuel and Caroline
are buried in Blue Ridge Cemetery, Mansfield, IN.
      Children of Samuel and Caroline (Wolf) Selby:
+ 1135   i Clara Selby, born 17 December 1878
1136   ii Weltha Selby, born 16 November 1882, died 20 December
          1962. Married William Kidd, born 31 October 1881, died 22
          July 1962. No children
+ 1137 iii George Selby, born 28 May 1888
1138   iv Cora Selby. Married _____ Hedrick

574 - MARY ELIZABETH(5) WOLF [Christina(4) Paulus, Daniel(3), Christina(2) Wolf, Daniel(1)]

Mary Elizabeth Wolf, eighth child of Jacob and Christina (Paulus) Wolf, was born 11 July 1862 near Verona, Preble County, OH. She married Joseph A. Katzenberger, born 9 July 1854. They lived first at Mt. Heron, then moved to Oakland, CA. Joseph died 30 June 1930 and Mary 28 October 1935. They are buried in Sunset View Cemetery, Oakland, CA.

Children of Joseph and Mary Elizabeth (Wolf) Katzenberger:

  1139   i Charles Alfred Burket, born 15 September 1880
+ 1140   ii Cladola Katzenberger, born 15 April 1884
+ 1141 iii Etta May Katzenberger, born 30 March 1886
+ 1142   iv Charles L. Katzenberger, born 11 August 1889

575 - HENRY(5) WOLFE [Christina(4) Paulus, Daniel(3), Christina(2) Wolf, Daniel(1)]

Henry Wolfe, ninth child of Jacob and Christina (Paulus) Wolf, was born 10 December 1863 near Verona, Preble County, OH. While working on the farm of Joseph Bradford, northeast of Marion, Grant County, IN, he met and married Lola Dale Bradford, youngest daughter of Joseph and Sarah (Woolman) Bradford. They were married 14 April 1889 by Rev. McCarty in a double ceremony with a sister Lucy Bradford and Caleb Dooley at Anderson, Grant County, IN. In the fall of 1897 Henry was suddenly taken ill and died 2 October 1897. Lola died 17 July 1962. They are buried in Fairview Cemetery, Marion, Grant County, IN.

Children of Henry and Lola Dale (Bradford) Wolfe:

+ 1143   i Floyd Stanley Wolfe, born 12 August 1890
+ 1144   ii Clark Talmadge Wolfe, born 26 January 1892
+ 1145 iii Amy Edell Wolfe, born 23 January 1893
+ 1146   iv Arthur Wendell Wolfe, born 20 December 1894
+ 1147   v Jennings Bryan Wolfe, born 4 November 1896

576 - JOHN(5) WOLF [Christina(4) Paulus, Daniel(3), Christina(2) Wolf, Daniel(1)]

John Wolf, tenth child of Jacob and Christina (Paulus) Wolf, was born 1 June 1865 near Verona, Harrison Township, Preble County, OH. He married Laura J. Swallow, born 3 November 1874. Laura died 22 November 1905 and John 26 December 1939. They are buried in New Lisbon Cemetary, Randolph County, IN.

Children of John and Laura J. (Swallow) Wolf:

  1148   i Hazel Wolf, born 12 May 1891, died 28 January 1980. Married 1) Samuel Conklin, born 17 February 1891. They lived on a farm near Union City, IN. She married 2) 30 July 1973 Lester Eley, born 17 June 1908
+ 1149   ii Cora Wolf, born 7 July 1892
+ 1150 iii Stella Wolf, born 28 June 1898
+ 1151   iv Russell Wolf, born 27 July 1900
  1152   v Alice Wolf, born 12 November 1903 in Jackson township, Randolph County, IN. Married 29 June 1920 Roy Mote, born 17 May 1902, died 13 October 1983 in Ohio. They are buried in Lisbon Cemetery, north of Union City, Randolph County

577 - ALICE(5) WOLF [Christina(4) Paulus, Daniel(3), Christina(2) Wolf, Daniel(1)]

Alice Wolf, eleventh child of Jacob and Christina (Paulus) Wolf, was born 28 February 1866 near Verona, Preble County, OH. She married about 1881 Franklin P. Hindsley, born April 1856. Franklin died 1915 and Alice 8 May 1924. They are buried in New Lisbon Cemetery, Randolph County, IN.

Chrildren of Franklin P. and Alice (Wolf) Hindsley:

1153   i   Elsie Mabel Hindsley, born February 1882 in Illinois. Married W. J. Schneider. They lived in Dayton, OH

1154   ii   Lottie Hindsley, born May 1886. Married James Gibbons. They lived in Nashville, TN

1155   iii   Joseph Foster Hindsley, born December 1889, died 25 August 1965. Married Esther Worth. They lived at Ft. Wayne, IN for 50 years where he was employed as a Parts Manager for International Harvester Company, retiring in 1956. They are buried in New Lisbon Cemetery, Randolph County, IN. There were no children

1156   iv   Ross Hindsley, born October 1892. Wife unknown. They lived at RR#1, Union City, IN

1157   v   Estella Hindsley, born February 1899. Married Milton Whitmore. They lived at Dayton, OH

1158   vi   Nelson Hindsley. Wife unknown. They lived at Union City, IN

578 - LUCY(5) WOLF [Christina(4) Paulus, Daniel(3), Christina(2) Wolf, Daniel(1)]

Lucy Wolf, twelfth child of Jacob and Christina (Paulus) Wolf, was born 28 February 1869 near Verona, Preble County, OH. She married about 1888 Alfred H. Trine, born September 1867. Alfred died in 1941 and Lucy 14 November 1945.

Children of Alfred and Lucy (Wolf) Trine:

1159   i   Charles A. Trine, born 15 June 1889, died 12 January 1979. Married Acil Bradford, born September 1891

1160   ii   Mayme Trine, born 27 July 1891, died 11 February 1978. Married Alfred Ray Krieder, born 22 November 1886, died 26 March 1947, son of Oscar L. and Sarah E. Krieder. They lived in Union City, IN

580 - CLARA B.(5) WOLF [Christina(4) Paulus, Daniel(3), Christina(2) Wolf, Daniel(1)]

Clara B. Wolf, fourteenth child of Jacob and Christina (Paulus) Wolf, was born 28 April 1878 in Randolph County, IN. She married 28 September 1895 Frank B. White, born 27 September 1874. They first lived on a farm in Indiana until 1908 when they moved to Ohio where Frank became a glas blower. He worked at Libby Owens Plate Glass Company at Lancaster, OH until retirement. He died 26 March 1936 and Clara 31 October 1942. They are buried in the Utica, OH Cemetery.

Children of Frank B. and Clara B. (Wolf) White:

+ 1161   i   Ada C. White, born 15 August 1896

+ 1162   ii   Inez L. White, born 12 July 1902

1163   iii   Marjorie White, born 2 February 1904 in Indiana, died 2 November 1920. Married October 1920 Bill Nelson. She is buried in the Utica, OH Cemetery

+ 1164   iv   Lucille E. White, born 29 May 1907

+ 1165   v   Evon C. White, born 2 March 1909

+ 1166   vi   Fred W. White Sr, born 20 December 1910

+ 1167   vii   Kathleen I. White, born 19 September 1914

+ 1168   viii   Foster R. White, born 14 July 1916

+ 1169   ix   Frances M. White, born 18 May 1919

581 - PETER(5) SILER [Catharine(4) Paulus, Daniel(3), Christina(2) Wolf, Daniel(1)]

Peter Siler, first child of Isaac and Catharine (Paulus) Siler, was born October 1851 in Ohio. He married in 1882 Sarah A. _____, born April 1855 in Illinois. About 1900 Peter was a house painter living in Mansfield, IL.
   Children of Peter and Sarah A. (_____) Siler, born in Illinois:
   1170   i Winnie Siler, born February 1883
   1171   ii Earl Siler, born June 1890

   582 - HENRY ALLEN(5) SILER [Catharine(4) Paulus, Daniel(3), Christina(2) Wolf, Daniel(1)]
   Henry Allen Siler, second child of Isaac and Catharine (Paulus) Siler, was born in 1853 in Ohio. He married 1) Celinda Weikel, born 10 March 1854 in Ohio. He was a motorman and later a guard at the Dayton, OH City Workhouse. Celinda died 14 April 1905 in Dayton and Henry remarried 2) Harriett _____, born in 1862 in Ohio. Henry died 10 January 1930. Henry and Celinda are buried in Woodland Cemetery in Dayton.
   Children of Henry Allen and Celinda (Weikel) Siler:
   1172   i Jessie G. Siler, born 2 March 1879, died 2 July 1879
   1173   ii Isaac A. Siler, born 18 October 1880, died 18 January 1886
   1174 iii Charles E. Siler, born 20 November 1882, died 5 June 1953.
                Buried in Woodland Cemetery, Dayton, OH
   1175   iv Elizabeth I. Siler, born December 1884, died 9 June 1955.
                Married _____ Link. She was cremated and her ashes buried
                at her father's grave in Woodland Cemetery, Dayton, OH
   1176   v Harry C. Siler, born 20 December 1888, died 11 March 1965.
                Buried in Woodland Cemetery, Dayton, OH

   583 - LEONARD B.(5) SILER [Catharine(4) Paulus, Daniel(3), Christina(2) Wolf, Daniel(1)]
   Leonard B. Siler, third child of Isaac and Catharine (Paulus) Siler, was born February 1855 in Ohio. He married Mary _____, born April 1861 in Germany. In 1900 he was a pattern Maker for the Ohio Rake Company, living in Dayton.
   Children of Leonard B. and Mary (_____) Siler:
   1177   i Earl E. Siler, born June 1879 in Ohio. Married Grace
                _____. He was a salesman living in Dayton, OH
   1178   ii Ruby L. Siler, born August 1880 in Ohio. She was a core
                maker at the Ohio Rake Company
   1179 iii Edna M. Siler, born March 1882 in Ohio. She was a core
                maker at the Ohio Rake Company
   1180   iv Chester F. Siler, born April 1887 in Ohio
   1181   v Walter L. Siler

   586 - SARAH ELIZABETH(5) SILER [Catharine(4) Paulus, Daniel(3), Christina(2) Wolf, Daniel(1)]
   Sarah Elizabeth Siler, sixth child of Isaac and Catharine (Paulus) Siler, was born October 1861 in Ohio. She married Robert J. Watt, born November 1861. He was an iron molder.
   Children of Robert J. and Sarah Elizabeth (Siler) Watt:
   1182   i William W. Watt, born April 1890 in Ohio
   1183   ii Harry C. Watt, born October 1899 in Ohio

   589 - FRANK(5) SILER [Catharine(4) Paulus, Daniel(3), Christina(2) Wolf, Daniel(1)]
   Frank Siler, ninth child of Isaac and Catharine (Paulus) Siler, was born March 1869 in Greenville, OH. He married in 1895 Myrtle Frederick, born May 1876, daughter of Andrew and Louise Frederick.

Children of Frank and Myrtle (Frederick) Siler:
1184   i Mildred Siler, born January 1900 in Ohio
1185   ii Byron Siler, born 1906 in Ohio

592 - FRANCIS M.(5) KELTNER [Rachel(4) Paulus, Daniel(3), Christina(2) Wolf, Daniel(1)]

Francis M. Keltner, first child of Joseph C. and Rachel (Paulus) Keltner, was born in 1855 near Verona, Preble County, OH. He married Rebecca _____ about 1876. Francis was a dentist and began his practice with his brother Samuel about 1885 in Muncie, Delaware County, IN. He died 14 December 1905 in Muncie and Rebecca 14 August 1944 at the Masonic Hospital in Franklin, In. They are buried in Beech Grove Cemetery in Muncie.

Children of Francis M. and Rebecca (_____) Keltner:
1186   i Velma Keltner. Married Rollin E. Greely. They had one son
          and two daughters
+ 1187   ii Edna Keltner, born 1879
1188   iii Harry A. Keltner, born 1881, died 5 August 1909 in Muncie,
          IN. Married Lena E. (_____). He was a machinist at the
          Wheel and Jobbing Company. There were no children
1189   iv Bertha Keltner, born 1884, died 19 March 1965 at Torrence,
          CA. She married Jesse Kramer. She is buried in the Beech
          Grove Cemetery, Muncie, IN
1190   v Caroline R. Keltner, born 1886 in Muncie, Delaware County,
          IN, died 28 May 1932 at Tampa, FL. She married Marshall
          Keene. She is buried in Beech Grove Cemetery, Muncie. They
          had two children who died at birth

593 - SANFORD M.(5) KELTNER [Rachel(4) Paulus, Daniel(3), Christina(2) Wolf, Daniel(1)]

Sanford M. Keltner, second child of Joseph C. and Rachel (Paulus) Keltner, was born 10 July 1856 in Preble County, OH. He married 26 October 1886 Alice May Cockefair of Connersville, IN, born 27 June 1864 at Valley Home, Everton, Fayette County, IN, daughter of Sylvanous and Mary A. (_____) Cockefair. He was educated at Indiana State Normal School in Terre Haute, IN. He taught and was principal at several schools in Anderson, IN. In 1884 he began the study of law under Milton S. Robinson, afterwards becoming a partner in the law firm of Robinson, Lovett and Keltner. He later served as president of Anderson Trust Company, the Anderson Board of Public Works, the Board of Trustees of Indiana State Teachers College at Terre Haute and was a member of the board of the State Teachers College at Muncie. He was a member of the Madison County Bar Association, Methodist Church, Elks, Masons, Redmen, Woodman, Odd Fellows, Knights of Pythias and the Anderson Kiwanis Club. Alice was a member of the Universalist Church. She died of pneumonia 5 December 1930 and was buried in the Everton Methodist Church Cemetery in Fayette County, IN beside her parents. Sanford died 28 July 1940 and is buried in the same cemetery.

Children of Sanford and Alice May (Cockefair) Keltner:
+ 1191   i Ruth Keltner, born 7 January 1888
1192   ii Mary Keltner, born 10 January 1892 near Everton, Fayette
          County, IN. She attended Anderson , IN College and was
          affiliated with the YWCA, Anderson Art League and Anderson
          College Alumnae. She is reported to have been married once
          and divorced. She died 4 October 1969 and is buried in the
          Everton Cemetery, Fayette County, IN

596 - AUGUSTUS DANIEL(5) PAULUS [Henry(4), Daniel(3), Chris-
tina(2) Wolf, Daniel(1)]
     Augustus Daniel Paulus, third child of Henry and Christina Mary
(Bope) Paulus, was born 26 September 1858 in Champaign, IL. He married
Sarah Stombaugh in 1880. They purchased and lived on a farm southwest
of Paulding, Paulding County, OH. Augustus died 13 June 1904 and is
buried in St. Paul's Church Cemetery, Paulding County. In 1912, after
Augustus' death, Sarah and her three children sold the Ohio property
and bought 250 acres of land one mile south of Tilbury, Ontario,
Canada where descendants still live on the farm.
     Children of Augustus Daniel and Sarah (Stombaugh) Paulus:
+ 1193   i Laura Paulus, born 7 February 1881
+ 1194   ii Oscar Paulus, born 9 September 1882
+ 1195   iii Adolph Paulus, born 18 October 1884

     597 - LAFAYETTE(5) PAULUS [Henry(4), Daniel(3), Christina(2)
Wolf, Daniel(1)]
     Lafayette Paulus, fourth child of Henry and Christina Mary (Bope)
Paulus, was born 10 February 1861 in Darke County, OH. He married in
1885 Lydia Ann Anspach, born 2 June 1865, daughter of Levi and Catherine (_____) Anspach. Lafayette's occupations were farming, mortician
and store owner. He died 15 March 1924 in Sidney, Kosciusko County, IN
and Lydia 16 November 1953. They are buried in Sidney.
     Children of Lafayette and Lydia Ann (Anspach) Paulus:
  1196   i _____ Paulus, twin, born and died 11 June 1886
  1197   ii _____ Paulus, twin, born and died 11 June 1886
  1198   iii Arthur Clarence Paulus, born 10 November 1889. Married
              Goldie Leona Hartsock, born 1885, died 1964. There were no
              children. They lived at Garden Grove, CA
  1199   iv Raymond Paulus, born 9 October 1889, died 10 June 1890
  1200   v Florence Paulus, born 21 June 1892, died 3 January 1893
  1201   vi George A. Paulus, born 17 June 1894, died 8 August 1894
+ 1202   vii Edna E. Paulus, born 8 November 1895
+ 1203 viii Lela May Paulus, born 1 October 1896
  1204   ix Trenton Paulus, born 2 May 1898, died 30 September 1898
+ 1205   x Esther Paulus, born 28 October 1899
+ 1206   xi Elra Paul Paulus, born 2 December 1900
  1207   xii Foster Paulus, born 5 September 1902, died 12 October 1902
+ 1208 xiii Warren Augustus Paulus, born 28 September 1903
  1209   xiv Martha Paulus, born 2 January 1905, died 26 December 1907

     601 - DORA REVILLA(5) PAULUS [Henry(4), Daniel(3), Christina(2)
Wolf, Daniel(1)]
     Dora Revilla Paulus, eighth child of Henry and Christina Mary
(Bope) Paulus, was born 11 November 1871 in Paulding County, OH. She
married George DeHoff, born 1876. George died in 1947 and Dora in
1957, both in Winona Lake, Kosciusko County, IN. They are buried in
Warsaw Cemetery, Kosciusko County.
     Children of George and Dora Revilla (Paulus) DeHoff:
  1210   i Ilow DeHoff, born 16 May ____, died March 1952. Married
              Henry Shriver. There were no children

     602 - CHARLES WILBUR(5) PAULUS [Henry(4), Daniel(3), Christina(2)
Wolf, Daniel(1)]
     Charles Wilbur Paulus, ninth child of Henry and Christina Mary
(Bope) Paulus, was born 13 March 1875 in Paulding County, OH. He
married in 1898 Lovina Dearth, born 17 November 1873, daughter of John
and Sarah (_____) Dearth. Charles was a farmer until they moved to

Paulding, OH where he ran a grocery store. Charles died 4 July 1935 and Lovina 22 May 1955.

Children of Charles Wilbur and Lovina (Dearth) Paulus:
+ 1211   i Sinclair Virgil Paulus, born 24 February 1900
  1212   ii Norma Paulus, born 12 December 1901, died 26 December 1975 at Paulding, Paulding County, OH. Married Arthur E. Houchin, born 22 May 1889, died 3 September 1970. There were no children
+ 1213 iii Charles Wilbur Paulus, born 25 March 1910
+ 1214   iv Gordon Lafayette Paulus, born 24 August 1911
  1215   v Ralph Paulus, born 24 December 1914, died 18 March 1920, both in Paulding County, OH. Buried in St. Paul Lutheran Cemetery, Paulding County

603 - JOHNNIE(5) WOLF [Elma Elizabeth(4) Paulus, Daniel(3), Christina(2) Wolf, Daniel(1)]
Johnnie Wolf, first child of Gideon and Elma Elizabeth (Paulus) Wolf, was born 1854 near Verona, Darke County, OH. He married 8 December 1884 Eliza Jane Hubbard, born 1852. Eliza died in 1918 in Illinois. Johnnie is buried at Mansfield, IL.

Children of Johnnie and Eliza Jane (Hubbard) Wolf:
  1216   i Anna E. Wolf, born 1877, died 1898
  1217   ii Eddie H. Wolf, born 1878, died 1896

604 - WILLIAM HENRY(5) WOLFE [Elma Elizabeth(4) Paulus, Daniel(3), Christina(2) Wolf, Daniel(1)]
William Henry Wolfe, second child of Gideon and Elma Elizabeth (Paulus) Wolf, was born 25 January 1856 near Verona, Darke County, OH. He married 1) 30 January 1880 in Illinois Hattie Boner, born 1854, died August 1903 in Preble County, OH. He married 2) in 1905 Bertha M. Newman. William died 13 March 1942 and he and Hattie are buried in Roselawn Cemetery, Lewisburg, Preble County.

Child of William Henry and Hattie (Boner) Wolfe:
+ 1218   i Goldie Belle Wolfe, born 24 November 1880

609 - RACHEL ANN(5) PAULUS [Samuel(4), Daniel(3), Christina(2) Wolf, Daniel(1)]
Rachel Ann Paulus, first child of Samuel and Catherine (Keltner) Paulus, was born 6 September 1862 in Ohio. She married Frank Plessenger, born June 1861. Frank was secretary of the Darke County, OH Agriculture Society and they lived at Beamsville, north of Greenville, OH. They died in 1931, Rachel 20 March.

Child of Frank and Rachel Ann (Paulus) Plessenger:
+ 1219   i Johnny D. Plessenger, born November 1883

617 - BERTHA(5) PAULUS [Samuel(4), Daniel(3), Christina(2) Wolf, Daniel(1)]
Bertha Paulus, ninth child of Samuel and Catherine (Keltner) Paulus, was born 15 October 1880 in Richland Township, Darke County, OH. She married Dale Snyder. They lived at Mason, MI and Lima, OH.

Child of Dale and Bertha (Paulus) Snyder:
  1220   i Kenneth Snyder

619 - BESSIE(5) PAULUS [Samuel(4), Daniel(3), Christina(2) Wolf, Daniel(1)]
Bessie Paulus, eleventh child of Samuel and Catherine (Keltner) Paulus, was born 9 April 1883. She married Forest E. Morton, born in 1881. They lived at Versailles, OH. Forest died in 1945 and Bessie 6

Septembr 1967.
Children of Forest E. and Bessie (Paulus) Morton:
1221   i Webster Morton, born in 1906. Married Thelma L. _____,
        born in 1908, died in 1962. They lived at RR #2, Ver-
        sailles, OH
1222   ii Roscoe Morton, lived at RR #4, Greenville, OH
1223 iii Esther Ruth Morton. Married _____ Myers. They lived at
        Gettysburg, OH and Waterloo, IN
1224   iv Ruby Morton. Lived at Columbus, OH

    621 – JOSEPH HARRISON(5) HOLLEHAN [Lucy Ann(4) Paulus, Daniel(3),
Christina(2) Wolf, Daniel(1)]
    Joseph Harrison Hollehan, first child of John and Lucy Ann
(Paulus) Hollehan, was born 29 August 1858 at Pesotum, IL. He married
29 August 1881 Delilah DeHoff, born 14 October 1860 in Stark County,
OH, daughter of Anthony and Barbara (Metz) DeHoff. Delilah died 8
September 1923 at Ft. Wayne, IN and Joseph 21 April 1937 at Chattanooga, TN. They are buried in Lindenwood Cemetery, Ft. Wayne.
    Children of Joseph Harrison and Delilah (DeHoff) Hollehan:
+ 1225   i Lessie Irene Hollehan, born 30 March 1882
  1226   ii John Hollehan, born 5 October 1893 in Paulding County, OH.
        He was enlisted in the U S Army during World War I and
        arrived in England 26 October 1918, very ill with the flu.
        He was taken to the military hospital at Gravesend, 25
        miles east of London where he died 1 November 1918. He was
        buried at Brookwood Cemetery near Woking, 25 miles SW of
        London. After the war his body was returned and buried in
        the Lindenwood Cemetery, Ft. Wayne, IN

    627 – SARAH ELLEN(5) HOLLEHAN [Lucy Ann(4) Paulus, Daniel(3),
Christina(2) Wolf, Daniel(1)]
    Sarah Ellen Hollehan, seventh child of John and Lucy Ann (Paulus)
Hollehan, was born in 1870 in Darke County, OH. She married Henry
Smith. Henry was a hotel keeper and Sarah was a housemother for a
fraternity at the University of Illinois. She died after 1931.
    Children of Henry and Sarah Ellen (Hollehan) Smith:
1227   i Virgil Smith, born 1889
1228   ii Lydia Smith, born 1891

    633 – WILLIAM H.(5) PAULUS [Abraham(4), Daniel(3), Christina(2)
Wolf, Daniel(1)]
    William H. Paulus, first child of Abraham and Mary Jane (Lane)
Paulus, was born February 1865 in Darke County, OH. He married 1) 5
September 1886 at Dickerson, IL Cora Marshall and 2) Julia Burge, born
January 1872. William lived at Osman, then at Chicago Ridge, IL.
    Children of William H.and Cora (Marshall) Paulus:
1229   i William J. Paulus, born May 1888
1230   ii Roy Paulus, born February 1891
    Children of William H. and Julia (Burge) Paulus:
1231   i Vera Paulus, born July 1896
1232   ii Esther Paulus, born September 1898

    634 – OLIVER(5) PAULUS [Abraham(4), Daniel(3), Christina(2) Wolf,
Daniel(1)]
    Oliver Paulus, second child of Abraham and Mary Jane (Lane)
Paulus, was born 19 April 1868 in East Bend Township, Champaign
County, IL. He married about 1894 Alice _____. They lived in Newcomb
Township, Champaign County, IL. Oliver died 27 June 1928 and Alice in

1957, both in Illinois.
        Child of Oliver and Alice (_____) Paulus:
    1233   i Ruby Paulus, born 1 August 1896, died 28 April 1962.
             Married Winfield Ross. There were no children

    643 - LUCY ANNA(5) PAULUS [Jonathan Francis(4), Daniel(3),
Christina(2) Wolf, Daniel(1)]
        Lucy Anna Paulus, first child of Jonathan Francis and Louisa
Katherine (Schell) Paulus, was born 22 August 1869 in Darke County,
OH. She married 1) 21 March 1886 William Hoke and 2) _____ Denniston.
She died 21 May 1961. There were no children by the second marriage.
        Children of William and Lucy Ann (Paulus) Hoke:
    1234   i Goldie Arnetta Hoke, born 14 January 1888, died 9 May
             1962. Married Ralph Knarre. They had two children
    1235   ii Bessie May Hoke, born 25 June 1891, died 2 November 1962.
             Married John Hiatt. They had two children

    644 - LILLIAN MAY(5) PAULUS [Jonathan Francis(4), Daniel(3),
Christina(2) Wolf, Daniel(1)]
        Lillian May Paulus, second child of Jonathan Francis and Louise
Katherine (Schall) Paulus, was born 22 April 1872 in Darke County, OH.
She married 26 April 1890 Charles Henry Mackey, born August 1870.
Lillian died 29 March 1944 and Charles 24 November 1947. They lived in
Jackson Township, Union County, OH.
        Children of Charles Henry and Lillian May (Paulus) Mackey:
    1236   i Mabel Violla Mackey, born 20 July 1891, died 7 February
             1920. Married 24 August 1914 Harry Clark. There were no
             children
    1237   ii Ethel Anna Mackey, born 24 September 1893. Married 24
             September 1910 _____ Adams, died 10 August 1968. She lived
             at 228 N. Plum Street, Union City, IN in 1971. They had
             one daughter

    648 - ELMER CALVIN(5) BAUGHER [Allen(4), Mary(3) Paulus, Chris-
tina(2) Wolf, Daniel(1)]
        Elmer Calvin Baugher, first child of Allen and Malissa (Wineland)
Baugher, was born 4 July 1867 in Indiana. He married 26 July 1896 Mary
E. Tague, born 14 May 1873. In 1900 they lived on S. Main Street,
Kokomo, Howard County, IN. He was a filer at the Bit Works. Mary died
8 October 1937 and Elmer 15 December 1937
        Children of Elmer Calvin and Mary E. (Tague) Baugher:
    1238   i Ruth Urene Baugher, born 26 June 1904 in Kokomo, Howard
             County, IL, died 10 January 1905
    1239   ii Harold Baugher (adopted), born 1905, died 28 June 1966
  + 1240   iii George Robert Baugher, born 10 October 1911

    649 - IDA ALICE(5) BAUGHER [Allen(4), Mary(3) Paulus, Chris-
tina(2) Wolf, Daniel(1)]
        Ida Alice Baugher, second child of Allen and Malissa (Wineland)
Baugher, was born 17 August 1869 in Noble County, IN. She married
Flavius Moss, born 13 August 1861. She died 5 November 1950.
        Children of Flavius and Ida Alice (Baugher) Moss:
  + 1241   i Marie Moss, born 12 September 1889
    1242   ii _____ Moss, born 31 December 1891, died 11 July 1893
  + 1243   iii Tirzah Moss, born 14 June 1893
    1244   iv Thelma Moss, born 27 September 1904, died 30 November
             1979. Married Alva T. DeLawter. They lived at 800 N.
             Rangeline Road, Anderson, IN

650 - EDWARD ELSWORTH(5) BAUGHER [Allen(4), Mary(3) Paulus, Christina(2) Wolf, Daniel(1)]

Edward Elsworth Baugher, third child of Allen and Malissa (Wineland) Baugher, was born 23 December 1871 in Indiana. He married 1) Alice F. Hoon, born 7 March 1876, daughter of Edward A. Hoon, who was of Prussian parentage and was born on board an emigrant ship just as the vessel was entering the harbor of Philadelphia, thus making him a native of the United States, and Josephine Bauder. Alice died 18 August 1899 and Edward married 2) Gertrude McWilliams, born 28 May 1878 at Holdren, Johnson County, MO. Edward died 25 April 1949 and Gertrude November 1956.

Child of Edward Elsworth and Alice F. (Hoon) Baugher:

1245   i Noble Baugher, born August 1896, died 22 August 1916. Did not marry

Children of Edward Elsworth and Gertrude (McWilliams) Baugher:

+ 1246   i Roi Ellsworth Baugher, born 24 February 1910
+ 1247   ii Gladys Baugher, born 19 December 1912

652 - EVA SOPHRONIA(5) BAUGHER [Allen(4), Mary(3) Paulus, Christina(2) Wolf, Daniel(1)]

Eva Sophronia Baugher, fifth child of Allen and Malissa (Wineland) Baugher, was born 27 October 1878 in Noble County, IN. She married 1) Francis S. Brown, born 1867, 2) Marvin David Sortor, born 10 February 1877, divorced 29 April 1912 and 3) 6 July 1915 William Albert Lee, born 25 October 1872. Marvin Sartor died 1 July 1935. William Lee died 18 December 1958 and Eva 22 August 1960 in Indiana. William and Eva are buried in a small church cemetery in Jackson Township, Jay County, IN. There were no known children by the first marriage.

Child of Marvin David and Eva Sophronia (Baugher) Sortor:

+ 1248   i Sylvian David Sortor (adopted), born 27 August 1905

Child of William Albert and Eva Sophronia (Baugher) Lee:

1249   ii Margaret Lee, born 11 May 1913, adopted

653 - WALTER RAYMOND(5) BAUGHER [Allen(4), Mary(3) Paulus, Christina(2) Wolf, Daniel(1)]

Walter Raymond Baugher, sixth child of Allen and Malissa (Wineland) Baugher, was born 23 September 1882 in Noble County, IN. He married Grace Marie Price, born 27 July 1885. Walter was a fitter at the Bit Works in Kokomo, Howard County, IN and later in the plumbing and heating business in Anderson. Grace died 28 May 1953 and Walter 12 June 1955 in Kokomo.

Children of Walter Raymond and Grace Marie (Price) Baugher:

+ 1250   i Raymond A. Baugher, born 5 January 1915
1251   ii Dorothy Helen Baugher, born 8 September 1916. Married 1) unknown, 2) William Dodson
1252 iii Donald E. Baugher, born and died 11 August 1918
1253   iv Rosemary Baugher, born and died 2 August 1919
+ 1254   v Virginia Ann Baugher, born 1 July 1922

654 - ESTELLA OPAL(5) BAUGHER [Allen(4), Mary(3) Paulus, Christina(2) Wolf, Daniel(1)]

Estella Opal Baugher, seventh child of Allen and Malissa (Wineland) Baugher, was born 27 September 1886 in Monroe Township, Howard County, IN. She married 29 April 1912 Marvin David Sortor, divorced husband of her older sister, Eva. They lived in Anderson, Madison County, IN where Marvin operated a plumbing and heating business. Estella died 14 November 1926 in Anderson and Marvin 1 July 1935. They

are buried in Maplewood Cemetery in Anderson.
      Children of Marvin David and Estella Opal (Baugher) Sortor:
  1255   i Sina Delight Sortor, born 7 April 1913 in Anderson, IN.
                She worked in the garment factory in Portland, IN, eventu-
                ally becoming foreman. After retiring she lived at 628 E.
                Water Street, Portland.
  1256   ii Paul Allen Sortor, born 20 March 1917. He married twice
                and lived in Las Vegas, NV. There were no children
+ 1257   iii Agnes Malissa Sortor, born 13 December 1919
+ 1258   iv Norma Alice Sortor, born 27 December 1922
+ 1259   v Marvin Earl Sortor, born 30 July 1926

     661 - WILLIAM(5) BAUGHER [Calvin(4), Mary(3) Paulus, Christina(2) Wolf, Daniel(1)]
     William Baugher, first child of Calvin and Louzina (Wheeler) Baugher, was born 31 July 1869 in Noble County, IN. He married 1) Minnie Dullinger, born April 1873 and 2) Allie (Brown) Fowler. William died 21 October 1954 in Warsaw, Kosciusko County, IN and Minnie 3 December 1954.
     Children of William and Minnie (Dullinger) Baugher:
+ 1260   i Kenneth V. Baugher, born 8 June 1895
  1261   ii Ferris Cecil Baugher, born February 1897. Married 1
                February 1919 Blanch Bartholemew. There were no children

CHAPTER No. 7

SIXTH GENERATION

673 - ADA LLEUMINA(6) WOLF [Nathaniel Harris(5), Lewis Clark(4),
Frederick(3), Jacob(2), Daniel(1)]
Ada Lleumina Wolf, second child of Nathaniel Harris and Martha
Jane (Ward) Wolf, was born 1 December 1875 at Jasper City, MO. She
married 3 February 1897 Robert S. Calderwood. She died 8 March 1960.
    Child of Robert S. and Ada Lleumina (Wolf) Calderwood:
1262   i Aileen Calderwood. Married _____ Boss

683 - MARY TURNER(6) WOLF [Fred Wade(5), Frederick Clark(4),
Frederick(3), Jacob(2), Daniel(1)]
Mary Turner Wolf, third child of Fred Wade and Jennie Louemma
(Nickel) Wolf, was born 14 September 1918 at Rome, Floyd County, GA.
She married 6 February 1946 at Nashville, TN Earl Sims Turman Sr.,
born 2 June 1906 at Waynesboro, TN, son of Benjamin Franklin and
Katherine (Spinks) Turman. He died in Santee, CA 1 April 1975, was
cremated and his ashes spread at sea. Both were WW2 veterans.
    Children of Earl Sims Sr. and Mary Turner (Wolf) Turman:
1262A   i Earl Sims Turman Jr., born 2 August 1949 at Nashville,
           Davidson County, TN
+ 1262B   ii Mary Jane Turman, born 24 December 1953
+ 1262C iii Benjamin Frederick Turman, born 6 April 1955
  1262D   iv Robert Edward Turman, born 4 July 1956 at Gallatin, Sumner
           Co., TN
+ 1262E   v Kenneth Marshall Turman, born 21 September 1957

684 - KENNETH(6) KNABENSHUE [Anna Evalee(5) Shroyer, Malinda
Ann(4) Wolf, Frederick(3), Jacob(2), Daniel(1)]
Kenneth Knabenshue, first child of Joseph and Anna Evalee
(Shroyer) Knabenshue, was born 5 September 1896 at Warsaw, Kosciusko
County, IN. He married 5 May 1918 Wilma J. Boltenhouse. Kenneth died
14 December 1968 and Wilma 13 November 1969.
    Children of Kenneth and Wilma J. (Boltenhouse) Knabenshue:
+ 1263   i Alice Anne Knabenshue, born 8 September 1920
  1264   ii Dorothy M. Knabenshue, born 11 December 1921. Married 4
           July 1944 Charles Althouse. He died 17 November 1972. No
           children
+ 1265 iii Kenneth A. Knabenshue II, born 12 February 1924
  1266   iv Harry L. Knabenshue, born 25 October 1927, died 26 Decem-
           ber 1950. Did not marry
+ 1267   v Shirley Ann Knabenshue, born 17 September 1935

685 - VIOLET AUDRY(6) KNABENSHUE [Anna Evalee(5) Shroyer, Malinda
Ann(4) Wolf, Frederick(3), Jacob(2), Daniel(1)]
Violet Audry Knabenshue, second child of Joseph and Anna Evalee
(Shroyer) Knabenshue, was born 28 September 1899. She married 22
November 1919 at St. Joseph, Berrien County, MI Verner W. Malhaupt.
Violet died 21 May 1948 and Verner 10 January 1951.
    Children of Verner W. and Violet Audry (Knabenshue) Malhaupt:
+ 1268   i Naomi Bernice Malhaupt, born 15 May 1920
+ 1269   ii Richard Verne Malhaupt, born 2 November 1922
+ 1270 iii Marjorie F. Malhaupt, born 29 September 1924

+ 1271   iv Genevieve I. Malhaupt, born 9 March 1926
+ 1272   v Verna L. Malhaupt, born 23 August 1929

     686 - VIVIAN ANN(6) KNABENSHUE [Anna Evalee(5) Shroyer, Malinda
Ann(4) Wolf, Frederick(3), Jacob(2), Daniel(1)]
     Vivian Ann Knabenshue, third child of Joseph and Anna Evalee
(Shroyer) Knabenshue, was born 26 July 1901. She married 30 April 1919
Alvia Jackman, born 5 February 1898. Vivian died 14 September 1966 and
Alvia 30 July 1970.
     Children of Alvia and Vivian Ann (Knabenshue) Jackman:
+ 1273   i Esther Irene Jackman, born 25 October 1919
+ 1274   ii Virginia M. Jackman, born 24 January 1922
  1275   iii Robert Vance Jackman, born 28 January 1925, died 21
             February 1926
+ 1276   iv Earl Wayne Jackman, born 12 January 1927
+ 1277   v Betty Ann Jackman, born 27 August 1930
+ 1278   vi Alton R. Jackman, born 12 April 1932
  1279 vii Shirley J. Jackman, born 14 January 1937. Married 12
             December 1965 Howard Melichar
+ 1280 viii Joseph L. Jackman, born 26 December 1941

     691 - MARJORY(6) MC KINLEY [Nellie Gray(5) Shroyer, Malinda
Ann(4) Wolf, Frederick(3), Jacob(2), Daniel(1)]
     Marjory   McKinley, second child of Jasper and Nellie Gray
(Shroyer) McKinley, was born in 1909. She married 1) Lex Wilkinson and
2) Joe Dean.
     Child of Joe and Marjory (McKinley) (Wilkinson) Dean:
  1281   i Jody Dean

     692 - ALTA IRENE(6) SHROYER [Harvey Howard(5), Malinda Ann(4)
Wolf, Frederick(3), Jacob(2), Daniel(1)]
     Alta Irene Shroyer, first child of Harvey Howard and Grace Maude
(Brewer) Shroyer, was born 19 July 1908 at Mishawaka, St. Joseph
County, IN. She married 24 December 1933 at Mishawaka Charles Raymond
Brugh, born 4 April 1904 in Fulton County, IN.
     Children of Charles Raymond and Alta Irene (Shroyer) Brugh:
+ 1282   i Barton Lee Brugh, born 8 April 1942
+ 1283   ii Barbara Ann Brugh, born 3 October 1944

     693 - MILDRED LUCILLE(6) SHROYER [Harvey Howard(5), Malinda
Ann(4) Wolf, Frederick(3), Jacob(2), Daniel(1)]
     Mildred Lucille Shroyer, second child of Harvey Howard and Grace
Maude (Brewer) Shroyer, was born 14 February 1910 at Marshall, Calhoun
County, MI. She married 12 August 1928 at Mishawaka, St. Joseph
County,   IN Celestine Edward Day, born 21 February 1907 at Potasi, WI,
died 12 May 1979 at South Bend, St. Joseph County, IN. They divorced
6 December 1959.
     Children of Celestine Edward and Mildred Lucille (Shroyer) Day:
+ 1284   i Joanne Evelyn Day, born 14 August 1930
+ 1285   ii Richard Edward Day, born 4 June 1932
+ 1286 iii Craig Douglas Day, born 6 May 1934
+ 1287   iv Brian Dean Day, born 27 september 1944

     694 - NORMA LEORA(6) SHROYER [Harvey Howard(5), Malinda Ann(4)
Wolf, Frederick(3), Jacob(2), Daniel(1)]
     Norma Leora Shroyer, third child of Harvey Howard and Grace Maude
(Brewer) Shroyer, was born 25 November 1911 at Marshall, Calhoun
County, MI. She married at Mishawaka, St. Joseph County, IN 31 March

1931 Walter Edward Starkweather, born 9 February 1912 at Lancaster, Grant County, WI. He died 8 August 1974 at Madison, WI and is buried at Roselawn Memorial Park.

Children of Walter Edward and Norma Leora (Shroyer) Starkweather:
+ 1288   i Janice Elaine Starkweather, born 17 February 1934
  1289   ii David Walter Starkweather, born 11 September 1935 at
          Madison, WI
+ 1290 iii Peter Edward Starkweather, born 22 March 1937
+ 1291   iv Linda Ann Starkweather, born 4 March 1942

   695 - DEAN KERMIT(6) SHROYER [Harvey Howard(5), Malinda Ann(4)
Wolf, Frederick(3), Jacob(2), Daniel(1)]
   Dean Kermit Shroyer, fourth child of Harvey Howard and Grace
Maude (Brewer) Shroyer, was born 5 June 1913 at Mishawaka, St. Joseph
County, IN, died 10 November 1937 at Logansport, Cass County, IN. He
married 10 November 1934 Gladys Kusmanovitch Bordman.
   Child of Dean Kermit and Gladys Kusmanovitch (Bordman) Shroyer:
+ 1292   i Norburt Raymond Shroyer, born 31 October 1935

   696 - DALTON HOWARD(6) SHROYER [Harvey Howard(5), Malinda Ann(4)
Wolf, Frederick(3), Jacob(2), Daniel(1)]
   Dalton Howard Shroyer, fifth child of Harvey Howard and Grace
Maude (Brewer) Shroyer, was born 13 October 1922 at Mishawaka, St.
Joseph County, IN. He married 2 August 1942 at Mishawaka Charlotte
Pherson, born 17 February 1923 at South Bend, IN.
   Children of Dalton Howard and Charlotte (Pherson) Shroyer:
+ 1293   i Charlene Marie Shroyer, born 29 July 1944
+ 1294   ii Wayne Howard Shroyer, born 14 May 1946
+ 1295 iii Caryn Margaret Shroyer, born 3 December 1948
  1296   iv Robert Shroyer, born 29 January 1952

   697 - KEITH LAVERNE(6) SHROYER [Harvey Howard(5), Malinda Ann(4)
Wolf, Frederick(3), Jacob(2), Daniel(1)]
   Keith Laverne Shroyer, sixth child of Harvey Howard and Grace
Maude (Brewer) Shroyer, was born 15 February 1927 at Mishawaka, St.
Joseph County, IN. He married 7 June 1947 at Mishawaka Barbara Duck-
worth, born 23 July 1930 at Mishawaka. He died 15 September 1984 at
South Bend, St. Joseph County, IN and is buried in Salem Cemetery.
   Children of Keith Laverne and Barbara (Duckworth) Shroyer:
+ 1297   i Larry Shroyer, born 14 March 1948
+ 1298   ii Laura Mae Shroyer, born 15 February 1949
  1299 iii Dennis Shroyer, born 1 April 1950 at South Bend, IN.
          Married 21 January 1984 at Greenwood, Jefferson County,
          IN Suzanne Brown. They divorced
+ 1300   iv Kathleen Shroyer, born 5 October 1951

   703 - MARY ALICE(6) MONTEL [Samuel(5), Abraham(4), Susan(3) Wolf,
Jacob(2), Daniel(1)]
   Mary Alice Montel, first child of Samuel and Phoebe (Metzger)
Montel, was born 21 May 1878. She married 28 February 1903 Elmer C.
Pyle, born 22 August 1879, son of Joseph Byron Pyle. Elmer died in
1918 and Mary Alice 11 August 1960.
   Children of Elmer C. and Mary Alice (Montel) Pyle:
+ 1301   i Virgil Pyle, born 18 May 1903
+ 1302   ii Wilbur Pyle, born 23 November 1906
+ 1303 iii Robert Pyle, born 19 March 1909
+ 1304   iv Emery Pyle, born 30 July 1911
  1305   v Ruby Pyle, born 6 June 1914. Married 21 August 1937 Harold

Swihart, born 22 March 1911

704 - ELIZABETH(6) MONTEL [Samuel(5), Abraham(4), Susan(3) Wolf, Jacob(2), Daniel(1)]
Elizabeth Montel, second child of Samuel and Phoebe (Metzger) Montel, was born 5 July 1880. She married 19 August 1903 Simon P. Neher, born 19 January 1883, son of Joseph W. and Hannah (Cripe) Neher. Elizabeth died 3 February 1918 and Simon 23 January 1956.
Children of Simon P. and Elizabeth (Montel) Neher:
+ 1306   i Harold M. Neher, born 8 April 1904
+ 1307   ii Charles S. Neher, born 1 March 1906
+ 1308 iii Esther L. Neher, born 7 March 1910
+ 1309   iv E. Paul Neher, born 24 July, 1912

705 - CHARLES(6) MONTEL [Samuel(5), Abraham(4), Susan(3) Wolf, Jacob(2), Daniel(1)]
Charles Montel, third child of Samuel and Phoebe (Metzger) Montel, was born 22 April 1882. He married Mary C. Freed, born 1888. Charles died in 1927 and Mary 19 March 1983.
Children of Charles and Mary C. (Freed) Montel:
+ 1310   i Deverl Montel, born 28 July 1912
  1311   ii Lucille Montel. Married Merritt Jenkins
+ 1312 iii Ruby Montel, born 30 October 1916
  1313   iv Fern Montel. Married Richard Woods

706 - EDITH(6) MONTEL [Samuel(5), Abraham(4), Susan(3) Wolf, Jacob(2), Daniel(1)]
Edith Montel, fourth child of Samuel and Phoebe (Metzger) Montel, was born 9 December 1884. She married 12 February 1910 Chester Ray Metzger, born 28 April 1891, son of Jacob Albert and Elizabeth (Ulrey) Metzger. Edith died 10 September 1966 and Chester 16 October 1970.
Children of Chester Ray and Edith (Montel) Metzger:
  1314   i Herbert Metzger, born 4 February 1911
+ 1315   ii Phoebe Lavon Metzger, born 4 September 1912
+ 1316 iii Elizabeth Ruth Metzger, born 14 December 1914
+ 1317   iv Ernest Ray Metzger, born 5 November 1917
  1318   v Arden Eugene Metzger, born 26 March 1925

707 - ALBERT(6) MONTEL [Samuel(5), Abraham(4), Susan(3) Wolf, Jacob(2), Daniel(1)]
Albert Montel, fifth child of Samuel and Phoebe (Metzger) Montel, was born 23 April 1887. He married 27 March 1909 Bertha Miller, born 13 June 1892, daughter of William and Mary (Clipp) Miller.
Children of Albert and Bertha (Miller) Montel:
+ 1319   i Grace M. Montel, born 18 October 1910
+ 1320   ii Joe Montel, born 29 May 1913
+ 1321 iii Everett Montel, born 8 September 1916
+ 1322   iv Harold Ray Montel, born 31 January 1919
+ 1323   v Max Albert Montel, born 26 July 1920
+ 1324   vi Delbert Montel, born 17 February 1924
+ 1325 vii Lois Montel, born 8 October 1926
+ 1326 viii Wayne Montel, born 31 March 1933

709 - EMERY(6) MONTEL [Samuel(5), Abraham(4), Susan(3) Wolf, Jacob(2), Daniel(1)
Emery Montel, seventh child of Samuel and Phoebe (Metzger) Montel, was born 9 August 1892. He married 19 June 1915 Mary Fay Metzger, born 19 February 1896, daughter of Jacob Albert and Elizabeth

(Ulrey) Metzger. Emory died 13 February 1970 and Mary 19 August 1970.
Children of Emery and Mary Fay (Metzger) Montel:
+ 1327   i Retha Elizabeth Montel, born 18 August 1917
+ 1328   ii Lamoin Albert Montel, born 7 August 1919
+ 1329   iii Blanche Mattie Montel, born 12 June 1922
+ 1330   iv John Irvin Montel, born 18 March 1924

    710 - RALPH(6) MONTEL [Samuel(5), Abraham(4), Susan(3) Wolf,
Jacob(2), Daniel(1)]
    Ralph Montel, eighth child of Samuel and Phoebe (Metzger) Montel,
was born 28 April 1894. He married 18 August 1914 Oznola V. Freed,
born 3 March 1898, daughter of Amos and Esther (Bowers) Freed. Ralpf
died 7 August 1955 and Oznola 16 October 1958.
    Children of Ralph and Oznola V. (Freed) Montel:
+ 1331   i Mildred Phoebe Montel, born 19 August 1915, twin
+ 1332   ii Marie Esther, Momtel, born 19 August 1915, twin
+ 1333   iii Elva Oznola Montel, born 20 August 1917
    1334   iv Alice Elizabeth Montel, born 30 March 1919. Married Lloyd
               Hasty
    1335   v Florence Valentine Montel, born 14 February 1921. Married
               Jack Shipley
    1336   vi Mable Louise Montel, born 1 February 1925. Married Truman
               Enyeart
    1337   vii Miriam Donna Montel, born 10 January 1937. Married _____
               Eads
    1338   viii Marion Ralph Montel, born 10 October 1934. Married Mar-
               garet Lewis
+ 1339   ix Merle D. Montel, born 18 May 1939

    711 - FRANK(6) MONTEL [Samuel(5), Abraham(4), Susan(3) Wolf,
Jacob(2), Daniel(1)]
    Frank Montel, ninth child of Samuel and Phoebe (Metzger) Montel,
was born 23 January 1897. He married 1) 5 October 1918 Mary Burger,
born 12 October 1899, daughter of Egbert and Libbie (Rinehart) Burger.
Mary died 19 March 1956 and Frank married 2) 9 April 1972 Thelma
Morphew. Frank died 16 August 1979.
    Children of Frank and Mary (Burger) Montel:
+ 1340   i Beulah May Montel, born 31 December 1919
+ 1341   ii Edward Frank montel, born 10 March 1921
+ 1342   iii Ernest Harold Montel, born 16 May 1922
+ 1343   iv Marjorie Jane Montel, born 2 November 1924
+ 1344   v Walter Lloyd Montel, born 10 November 1926
    1345   vi Charles Montel, born 15 August 1927, died 25 July 1929
+ 1346   vii Elizabeth Ann Montel, born 2 December 1930
    1347   viii Donald Montel, born 1931, died in infancy
    1348   ix Arthur Montel, born 1931, died in infancy
    1349   x Mary M. Montel, born 1932, died in infancy
+ 1350   xi Ruth Eleanor Montel, born 7 February 1934
    1351   xii Frank Montel Jr, born 29 March 1938. Married Sondra Zolman

    712 - GLENN(6) MONTEL [Samuel(5), Abraham(4), Susan(3) Wolf,
Jacob(2), Daniel(1)]
    Glenn Montel, tenth child of Samuel and Phoebe (Metzger) Montel,
was born 16 January 1900. He married 29 July 1922 Nora Van Bebber,
born 28 July 1900, daughter of Jacob Isaac and Jennie Matilda
(Rhoades) Van Bebber. Nora died 13 October 1955 and Glenn 30 January
1975.

Children of Glenn and Nora (Van Bebber) Montel:
1352   i Glenora June Montel, born 23 June 1923. Married 26 June
           1945 George F. Wyncotte
1353   ii Paul Montel, born 12 April 1926, died 30 September 1963.
           Married 28 July 1963 Mary Thompson

     715 - EFFIE(6) MONTEL [Jacob(5), Abraham(4), Susan(3) Wolf,
Jacob(2), Daniel(1)]
     Effie Montel, third child of Jacob and Rebecca (Metzger) Montel,
was born 6 July 1886. She married 25 February 1912 Howard Overholser,
born 24 June 1889, son of Levi and Emmeline (Miller) Overholser.
Howard died 31 August 1974 and Effie 29 November 1975.
     Children of Howard and Effie (Montel) Overholser:
1354   i Dwight Overholser, born 7 December 1912
+ 1355 ii Miriam Overholser, born 4 September 1916

     716 - ROYAL(6) MONTEL [Jacob(5), Abraham(4), Susan(3) Wolf,
Jacob(2), Daniel(1)]
     Royal Montel, fourth child of Jacob and Rebecca (Metzger) Montel,
was born 24 November 1891. He married 1) Elizabeth Eiler, born 5
October 1885, died 12 January 1970. They divorced 1946 and Royal
married 2) 25 December 1950 Cecil Divelbiss, born 4 November 1902,
daughter of Charles D. and Dessie Lahr. Royal died 11 August 1974.
     Children of Royal and Elizabeth (Eiler) Montel:
1356   i   Vera Esther Montel, born 24 January 1912. Married 1)
            unknown and 2) Earl Cooper, they divorced
1357   ii Dessie Montel, born 27 January 1913. Married 6 September
            1947 Clarence Hendricks, born 5 February 1910
1358   iii John Montel, born 24 March 1915, died 24 July 1968.
            Married 1) _____ Grim, 2) _____ Shannon
1359   iv Grace Montel, born 19 July 1918. Married 1) _____ Joy, 2)
            _____ Burney, 3) Marcella Green
1360   v   Donald Montel, born 1 November 1923

     717 - IVA ANN(6) MONTEL [Jacob(5), Abraham(4), Susan(3) Wolf,
Jacob(2), Daniel(1)]
     Iva Ann Montel, fifth child of Jacob and Rebecca (Metzger)
Montel, was born 7 March 1893. She married 1) 30 October 1920 Sherman
Alfred Rhoades, born 15 June 1892, son of Mahlon and Lydia (Wachter)
Rhoades. Sherman died 20 January 1966 and Iva married 2) 4 January
1968 Russell Werking, born 23 March 1894, son of David and Katharine
(Horning) Werking. Iva died 19 June 1985.
     Children of Sherman Alfred and Iva Ann (Montel) Rhoades:
+ 1361   i   Delbert Milton Rhoades, born 28 August 1922
+ 1362   ii Leanna Mae Rhoades, born 13 May 1924
+ 1363   iii Wayne Lowell Rhoades, born 1 September 1926
+ 1364   iv Eva Kathlene Rhoades, born 13 April 1927
+ 1365   v   Dorsey Hurl Rhoades, born 24 November 1931

     718 - ARTEMUS(6) MONTEL [Jacob(5), Abraham(4), Susan(3) Wolf,
Jacob(2), Daniel(1)]
     Artemus (Artie) Montel, sixth child of Jacob and Rebecca (Metz-
ger) Montel, was born 3 January 1902. He married 20 January 1923
Bertha V. Beight, born 25 December 1904, daughter of James and Lydia
Ann (Metzger) Beight. Artemus died 29 March 1975.
     Children of Artemus and Bertha V. (Beight) Montel:
1366   i James H. Montel, born 1923, died 1930
+ 1367   ii Bernice Irene Montel, born 3 August 1925

+ 1368   iii Francis Earl Montel, born 7 July 1926
+ 1369   iv Betty Ann Montel, born 11 April 1928
+ 1370   v Barbara J. Montel, born 30 December 1937

    719 - MARY MAGDELINE(6) METZGER [Susanna(5) Montel, Abraham(4),
Susan(3) Wolf, Jacob(2), Daniel(1)]
    Mary Magdeline Metzger, first child of David B. and Susanna
(Montel) Metzger, was born 3 February 1879. She married 27 September
1914 Frank Wyatt, born 22 July 1878. Mary died November 1931 and Frank
11 November 1960.
    Child of Frank and Mary Magdeline (Metzger) Wyatt:
+ 1371   i Melvin Wyatt, born 5 May 1919

    720 - LYMAN H.(6) METZGER [Susanna(5) Montel, Abraham(4),
Susan(3) Wolf, Jacob(2), Daniel(1)]
    Lyman H. Metzger, second child of David B. and Susanna (Montel)
Metzger, was born 1881. He married 1905 Nova Ethel Frantz, born 1891,
daughter of Michael and Jennie (Witt) Frantz. Lyman died 1938 and Nova
1957.
    Children of Lyman H. and Nova Ethel (Frantz) Metzger:
  1372   i Harold Metzger, born 7 May 1906
  1373   ii Niomi Metzger, born 25 January 1908
  1374   iii Merrill Metzger, born 17 September 1910
  1375   iv Nova Metzger
  1376   v Ruth Metzger
  1377   vi Carl Metzger
  1378   vii Paul Metzger. Married Mildred Aster

    721 - SARAH ELLEN(6) METZGER [Susanna(5) Montel, Abraham(4),
Susan(3) Wolf, Jacob(2), Daniel(1)]
    Sarah Ellen Metzger, third child of David B. and Susanna (Montel)
Metzger, was born 2 May 1882. She married Daniel C. Frantz, born 1876.
Daniel died 1949 and Sarah 1961.
    Child of Daniel C. and Sarah Ellen (Montel) Metzger:
  1379   i Infant son, died 1906

    722 - IRVIN(6) METZGER [Susanna(5) Montel, Abraham(4), Susan(3)
Wolf, Jacob(2), Daniel(1)]
    Irvin Metzger, fourth child of David B. and Susanna (Montel)
Metzger, was born 18 June 1885. He married about 1911 Ella Pearl
Warner, born 20 November 1883. Irvin died 27 June 1950 and Ella 6 June
1964.
    Child of Irvin and Ella Pearl (Warner) Metzger:
+ 1380   i Kathryn Elizabeth Metzger, born 19 August 1912

    724 - SUSANNA(6) METZGER [Susanna(5) Montel, Abraham(4), Susan(3)
Wolf, Jacob(2), Daniel(1)]
    Susanna Metzger, sixth child of David B. and Susanna (Montel)
Metzger, was born 25 January 1894. She married 1) 21 January 1916
Arthur Harley Grimes, born 29 December 1888, died 16 July 1941 and 2)
Gorman Grossnickle, born 25 November 1882, died 12 October 1963.
Susanna died 13 March 1982.
    Children of Arthur Harley and Susanna (Metzger) Grimes:
  1381   i Helen Louise Grimes, born 10 December 1917. Married Alva
              Edwards, born 26 July 1908, died 30 August 1962
+ 1382   ii Robert Dean Grimes, born 12 October 1920
+ 1383   iii Joan Beth Grimes, born 1 March 1924
  1384   iv Mary Ann Grimes, born and died 1931

729 - STELLA(6) SHIREMAN [Lydia(5) Montel, Abraham(4), Susan(3) Wolf, Jacob(2), Daniel(1)]
    Stella Shireman, was the fourth child of Henry and Lydia (Montel) Shireman. She married Floyd Enfield.
    Children of Floyd and Stella (Shireman) Enfield:
    1385   i Ruth Enfield. Married Harold Miller
    1386   ii Henry Enfield
    1387   iii Glenn Enfield
    1388   iv Delores Enfield

731 - HAZEL(6) BUTTERBAUGH [William H.(5), Sarah(4) Montel, Susan(3) Wolf, Jacob(2), Daniel(1)]
    Hazel Butterbaugh, first child of William H. and Viola (Derck) Butterbaugh, was born 8 January 1888. She married 19 April 1905 Alvin Perry, born 27 September 1882. Alvin died 17 March 1958 and Hazel 8 January 1971.
    Child of Alvin and Hazel (Butterbaugh) Perry:
    1389   i Ellouise Perry. Married Richard Sands

732 - NELLIE(6) BUTTERBAUGH [William H.(5), Sarah(4) Montel, Susan(3) Wolf, Jacob(2), Daniel(1)]
    Nellie Butterbaugh, second child of William H. and Viola (Derck) Butterbaugh, was born 24 October 1890. She married 1912 Glen Walther, born 7 March 1891, son of Albert J. and Lydia (Mishler) Walther. Nellie died 28 January 1936 and Glen 27 November 1961.
    Children of Glen and Nellie (Butterbaugh) Walther:
    + 1390   i Louise Walther, born 5 March 1913
    + 1391   ii Maurice Walther, born 12 September 1914
    + 1392   iii Doscas Irene Walther, born 24 December 1917
    + 1393   iv Max Donald Walther, born 2 February 1925

733 - ELVIN PETER(6) TRIDLE [George III(5), Adaline(4) Montel, Susan(3) Wolf, Jacob(2), Daniel(1)]
    Elvin Peter Tridle, first child of George III and Sarah (Ulrey) Tridle, was born 29 December 1879. He married 31 March 1900 Ella Ulrey, born 4 April 1882, daughter of Gaabril and Mary Ann (Kreiter) Ulrey. Ella died 24 February 1965 and Elvin 22 October 1973.
    Child of Elvin Peter and Ella (Ulrey) Tridle:
    + 1394   i Mary Blanche Tridle (adopted), born 14 January 1903

734 - LIZZIE(6) TRIDLE [George III(5), Adaline(4) Montel, Susan(3) Wolf, Jacob(2), Daniel(1)]
    Lizzie Tridle, second child of George III and Sarah (Ulrey) Tridle, was born 22 June 1884. She married 12 January 1907 Elmer C. Ross, born 19 June 1882, son of Robert and Susan (Snell) Ross. Elmer died 30 January 1955.
    Children of Elmer C. and Lizzie (Tridle) Ross:
    + 1395   i Keith Emerson Ross, born 23 April 1909
    1396   ii Everett Max Ross, born 6 April 1916, died 26 January 1917
    + 1397   iii Harold Wayne Ross, born 9 April 1918
    + 1398   iv Dorotha Maxine Ross, born 15 August 1921

735 - GLENN(6) TRIDLE [George III(5), Adaline(4) Montel, Susan(3) Wolf, Jacob(2), Daniel(1)]
    Glenn Tridle, third child of George III and Sarah (Ulrey) Tridle, was born 22 May 1890. He married 25 January 1913 Mattie Pfleiderer, born 20 January 1892. Mattie died 11 August 1974 and Glenn 1 November 1975.

Children of Glenn and Mattie (Pfleiderer) Tridle:
+ 1399   i Loren Leroy Tridle, born 4 April 1914
+ 1400   ii Earl Eugene Tridle, born 16 September 1915

736 - VIOLA(6) TRIDLE [George III(5), Adaline(4) Montel, Susan(3)
Wolf, Jacob(2), Daniel(1)]
     Viola Tridle, fourth child of George III and Sarah (Ulrey)
Tridle, was born 29 July 1891. She married 20 January 1912 Rolla
Heeter, born 23 September 1893, son of John and Martha (Tuckey)
Heeter. Viola died 23 March 1949 and Rolla 15 May 1957.
     Child of Rolla and Viola (Tridle) Heeter:
+ 1401   i Vera Lavon Heeter, born 11 October 1912

737 - ERDEEN(6) RAGER [Benson(5), Susannah(4) Montel, Susan(3)
Wolf, Jacob(2), Daniel(1)]
     Erdeen Rager, was a child of Benson and _____ (_____) Rager. She
married _____ Hinds.
     Child of _____ and Erdeen (Rager):
  1402   i L. Alice Hinds

738a - JOSEPH RAYMOND(6) OYLER [Josephine Florida(5) Wolfe, Simon
P.(4), Jacob Jr(3), Jacob(2), Daniel(1)]
     Joseph Raymond Oyler, first child of Allen L. and Josephine
Florida (Wolfe) Oyler, was born 18 July 1883 in Tipton Township, Cass
County, IN. He married 21 March 1907 in Cass County Myrtle Olive
Peter, daughter of William T. and Nannie (Conner) Peter. He lived
in Galveston, Cass County for 48 years, attending Marion Normal
School, and was a teacher in Tipton Township, Lincoln Township and
Galveston schools. He became a rural mail carrier in 1916 and served
for 30 years before retiring. He was a member of the Galveston E.U.B.
Church. He died 24 June 1959 in Cass County.
     Children of Joseph Raymond and Myrtle Olive (Peter) Oyler:
+ 1403   i Josephine Oyler, born 20 October 1908
  1404   ii Portia L. Oyler, born 1 April 1912 in Cass County, IN.
             Married _____ Thatcher
  1405 iii Margaret Oyler. Married _____ Reeves
  1406   iv Raymond Oyler
  1407   v Phyllis Jean Oyler, born 16 March 1922 in Cass County, IN.
             Married _____ Miller

738c - ALVA L.(6) OYLER [Josephine Florida(5) Wolfe, Simon P.(4),
Jacob Jr(3), Jacob(2), Daniel(1)]
     Alva L. Oyler, third child of Allen L. and Josephine Florida
(Wolfe) Oyler, was born April 1890 in Cass County, IN. He married
Leona Wright.
     Child of Alva L. and Leona (Wright) Oyler:
  1408   i Rex Wright Oyler, born 18 March 1918

738d - ROSS E.(6) OYLER [Josephine Florida(5) Wolfe, Simon P.(4),
Jacob Jr(3), Jacob(2), Daniel(1)]
     Ross E. Oyler, fourth child of Allen L. and Josephine Florida
(Wolfe) Oyler, was born 1 March 1894 in Cass County, IN. He married 10
January 1920 in Cass County Elsie Mae Walker, daughter of Joseph W.
and Nancy (Rhinehart) Walker.
     Child of Ross E. and Elsie Mae (Walker) Oyler:
  1409   i Miriam Laveta Oyler, born 6 August 1920

739 - ROBERT WILLIAM(6) MONTEITH [Caroline Barbara(5) Wolfe, Simon P.(4), Jacob Jr(3), Jacob(2), Daniel(1)]
Robert William Monteith, first child of Robert John and Caroline Barbara (Wolfe) Monteith, was born 11 March 1884 in Deer Creek Township, Cass County, IN. He married 6 April 1910 at Phillips, Price County, WI Ruth Criswell, born 18 July 1888. Robert died 20 December 1941. They are buried in Honey Creek Baptist Church Cemetery, Racine County, WI.
Children of Robert William and Ruth (Criswell) Monteith:
1410　　i Zona Artis Monteith, born 1913. Married Marion Nathan Yoder
1411　　ii Walter Monteith, born 1916. Married Lillian Bere
1412　　iii Howard Casper Monteith, born 1921. Married Inga _____
1413　　iv Homer Francis Monteith, born 1924. Married Shirley Pascavis
1414　　v Paul Evert Monteith, born 1926

740 - HAROLD JOHN(6) MONTEITH [Caroline Barbara(5) Wolfe, Simon P.(4), Jacob Jr(3), Jacob(2), Daniel(1)]
Harold John Monteith, second child of Robert John and Caroline Barbara (Wolfe) Monteith, was born 26 December 1886 in Deer Creek Township, Cass County, IN. He married 22 March 1909 at Burrows, IN Mary Melinda Downing, born 2 July 1890 at Lockport, IN, daughter of Hiram Stuart and Minerva Jane (Tribbett) Downing. Harold died 14 July 1964 and Mary 11 August 1977. They are buried in Vale Cemetery, Clark County, OH.
Children of Harold John and Mary Melinda (Downing) Monteith:
1415　　i Pauline Leora Monteith, born 1910. Married Glenn E. Timberman
1416　　ii William Harold Monteith, born 1915. Married Rosalyn Kilberry

741 - PAUL EVERT(6) MONTEITH, [Caroline Barbara(5) Wolfe, Simon P.(5), Jacob Jr(4), Jacob(2), Daniel(1)]
Paul Evert Monteith, third child of Robert John and Caroline Barbara (Wolfe) Monteith, was born 9 May 1889 in Deer Creek Township, Cass County, IN. He married 27 March 1914 at Springfield, OH Nellie Enola Warren, born 27 August 1894 in Clark County, OH, daughter of Barney Elliot and Nannie M. (Kiger) Warren.
Children of Paul Evert and Nellie Enola (Warren) Monteith:
+ 1417　　i Jess Warren Monteith, born 26 May 1915
+ 1418　　ii Virgil Eugene Monteith, born 24 October 1916

742 - CHARLES OLIVER(6) MONTEITH [Caroline Barbara(5) Wolfe, Simon P.(4), Jacob Jr(3), Jacob(2), Daniel(1)]
Charles Oliver Monteith, fourth child of Robert John and Caroline Barbara (Wolfe) Monteith, was born 24 May 1891 in Carroll County, IN. He married 26 June 1913 at Springfield, OH Rachel E. Rehm, born 1892. Charles died 24 October 1921 and Rachel January 1952. They are buried in Vale Cemetery, Clark County, OH.
Children of Charles Oliver and Rachel E. (Rehm) Monteith:
1419　　i Byron Ellsworth Monteith. Married 1) Cleo _____ and 2) Judy _____
1420　　ii John (Jack) A. Monteith, died 25 October 1921 at Springfield, OH. Buried in Vale Cemetery, Clark County, OH

746 - FRANK ALLEN(6) MONTEITH [Caroline Barbara(5) Wolfe, Simon P.(4), Jacob Jr(3), Jacob(2), Daniel(1)]

Frank Allen Monteith, eighth child of Robert John and Caroline Barbara (Wolfe) Monteith, was born 14 December 1899 in Carroll County, IN. He married 10 December 1927 at Springfield, OH Mary A. Pence. Frank died 17 November 1971 at North Carlisle, Clark County, OH.

Children of Frank Allen and Mary A. (Pence) Monteith:
```
1421    i Donald Edgar Monteith, born 1929. Married Jeanne Lewis
1422   ii Bernice Ellen Monteith, born 1933. Married Roger Eagle
```

747 - JESSE ARTHUR(6) MONTEITH [Caroline Barbara(5) Wolfe, Simon P.(4), Jacob Jr(3), Jacob(2), Daniel(1)]

Jesse Arthur Monteith, ninth child of Robert John and Caroline Barbara (Wolfe) Monteith, was born 14 November 1901 in Carroll County, IN. He married 26 June 1923 at Springfield, OH Florence Alice Carter. Jesse died 18 April 1986 and is buried in Rose Hill Cemetery, Springfield, OH.

Children of Jesse Arthur and Florence Alice (Carter) Monteith:
```
1423     i Anna Ruth Monteith, born 1925. Married James Palmer
1424    ii Jaquelone Jeanne Monteith, born 1932. Married Rev. Ernest
            Gross Jr
1425   iii Douglas Carter Monteith, born 1939. Married Mary Lou
            Snyder
1426    iv Deanna Kay Monteith, born 1940. Married Rev. James Edwards
```

749 - CLARA BELLE(6) CALDWELL [Margaret Jane(5) Wolfe, Simon P.(4), Jacob Jr(3), Jacob(2), Daniel(1)]

Clara Belle Caldwell, second child of William Alexander and Margaret Jane (Wolfe) Caldwell, was born 27 January 1885 in Washington Township, Carroll County, IN. She married 18 September 1907 in Price County, WI John Shick. Clara died 24 August 1965 and is buried in Rose Hill Cemetery, Springfield, OH.

Children of John and Clara Belle (Caldwell) Shick:
```
1427     i Jerold Shick, born about 1911 at Springfield, OH, died
            about 1945 in Greene County, OH
1428    ii Edwin Shick, born July 1913 at Springfield, OH, died about
            1972 in Ross County, OH
1429   iii Carrol Shick, born about 1915 at Springfield, OH, died
            about 1942 at Springfield
```

751 - EMMET EDMUNDS(6) CALDWELL [Margaret Jane(5) Wolfe, Simon P.(4), Jacob Jr(3), Jacob(2), Daniel(1)]

Emmet Edmunds Caldwell, fourth child of William Alexander and Margaret Jane (Wolfe) Caldwell, was born 13 December 1890 in Washington Township, Carroll County, IN. He married 6 May 1913 at Springfield, OH Ina Belle Hylander, born 23 March 1889 in Robertson County, KY, daughter of Charles Luther and Martha Frances (Lewis) Hylander. Ina died 26 November 1938 and is buried in Cedar Hill Cemetery, Newark, OH. Emmet died 3 October 1976 and is buried in Maplewood Cemetery, Anderson, IN.

Children of Emmet Edmunds and Ina Belle (Hylander) Caldwell:
```
+ 1430     i Milton Charles Caldwell Sr, born 17 January 1914 at 308
             Bectle Ave., Springfield, OH
+ 1431    ii Martha Frances Caldwell, born 12 November 1915 at 1314
             Broadway, Springfield, OH
  1432   iii William Glenn Caldwell, born 23 January 1918 at 1425
             Broadway, Springfield, OH, died 22 August 1921, buried in
             Cedar Hill Cemetery, Newark, OH
+ 1433    iv Herbert Eugene Caldwell, born 12 July 1919 at 119 N.
             Williams St., Newark, OH
```

1434   v Miriam Elizabeth Caldwell, born 25 November 1920 at 149 N.
           Williams St., Newark, OH, died 28 July 1940, buried in
           Cedar Hill Cemetery, Newark, OH
+ 1435   vi Doris Virginia Caldwell, born 29 August 1924 at 149 N.
           Williams St., Newark, OH

    753 - DAVID MILO(6) CALDWELL [Margaret Jane(5) Wolfe, Simon
P.(4), Jacob Jr(3), Jacob(2), Daniel(1)]
    David Milo Caldwell, sixth child of William Alexander and Mar-
garet Jane (Wolfe) Caldwell, was born 16 June 1897 at Grand Junction,
MI. He married 24 September 1920 at Springfield, OH Hazel Abigail
Lorton, born 30 March 1898 at Springfield, daughter of George and
Elizabeth (Wise) Lorton. David died 28 October 1920 and is buried in
Vale Cemetery, Clark County, OH. Hazel died 24 March 1983 at Spring-
field.
    Child of David Milo and Hazel Abigail (Lorton) Caldwell:
+ 1436   i Priscilla Maxine Caldwell, born 5 October 1921

    754 - WILLIAM ARTHUR(6) CALDWELL [Margaret Jane(5) Wolfe, Simon
P.(4), Jacob Jr(3), Jacob(2), Daniel(1)]
    William Arthur Caldwell, seventh child of Willaim Alexander and
Margaret Jane (Wolfe) Caldwell, was born 27 December 1899 at Moundsville, WV. He married 15 March 1919 at Newport, KY Gladys Fern Downing, born 14 October 1902 at Lockport, IN, daughter of Hiram Stuart
and Minerva Jane (Tribbett) Downing. Gladys died 8 September 1968 at
Springfield, OH and William 12 June 1978. They are buried in Rose Hill
Cemetery, Springfield.
    Children of William Arthur and Gladys Fern (Downing) Caldwell:
+ 1437   i Dorothy Jane Caldwell, born 18 December 1919
+ 1438   ii Wayne Eugene Caldwell, born 13 July 1922

    755 - CLARENCE LEROY(6) WOLFE [Edward Carrol(5), Simon P.(4),
Jacob Jr(3), Jacob(2), Daniel(1)]
    Clarence Leroy Wolfe, first child of Edward Carrol and Elizabeth
Exie (Husted) Wolfe, was born 2 March 1897 at Amsterdam, MO. He
married 1) 20 April 1918 in Wabash County, IN Josephine Dailey, born
10 July 1901 at Sherbourne, KY, daughter of Henry and Mary Belle
(Yargo) Dailey. They divorced 14 October 1918 in Grant County, IN and
he married 2) 31 December 1922 in Madison County, IN Anna Marie Heinnickel, born 3 October 1901 in Wabash County, daughter of John and
Margaret G. (Bohnstedt) Heinnickel. There were no children by his
first marriage.
    Children of Clarence Leroy and Anna Marie (Heinnickel) Wolfe:
  1439   i Alice Marie Wolfe, born 17 June 1924. Married 29 december
           1945 in Madison County, IN Kenneth Roy Brown, born 13 july
           1923 in Madison County, IN. No children
+ 1440   ii William Edward Wolfe, born 25 March 1927
+ 1441 iii Miriam Louise Wolfe, born 12 September 1934
  1442   iv Jenny Mae Wolfe, born 15 June 1941, died 21 June 1941 in
           Madison County, IN

    758 - RUTH CATHERINE(6) WOLFE [Edward Carrol(5), Simon P.(4),
Jacob Jr(3), Jacob(2), Daniel(1)]
    Ruth Catherine Wolfe, fourth child of Edward Carrol and Elizabeth
Exie (Husted) Wolfe, was born 22 September 1914 at Marion, IN. She
married 23 November 1940 Ralph Hillis Van Osdol, born 26 May 1908.
    Children of Ralph Hillis and Ruth Catherine (Wolfe) Van Osdol:
  1443   i Dale Van Osdol

```
1444    ii Denny Van Osdol
1445   iii Karen Van Osdol
1446    iv Wilma Van Osdol
```

759 - CHARLES BURTON(6) STEVENS [Flora Marie(5) Wolfe, Simon
P.(4), Jacob Jr(3), Jacob(2), Daniel(1)]
        Charles Burton Stevens, first child of William P. and Flora Marie
(Wolfe) Stevens, was born 14 October 1897. He married 5 May 1929 Ruth
Rebecca Wells. Rebecca died about 1978 and Charles 1 November 1981.
        Children of Charles Burton and Ruth Rebecca (Wells) Stevens:
+ 1447   i William Kline Stevens, born 8 October 1930
+ 1448   ii Sylvia Charlene Stevens, born 29 October 1933
+ 1449   iii Thelma Elaine Stevens, born 9 November 1945

762 - ROY ARTHUR(6) STEVENS [Flora Marie(5) Wolfe, Simon P.(4),
Jacob Jr(3), Jacob(2), Daniel(1)]
        Roy Arthur Stevens, fourth child of William P. and Flora Marie
(Wolfe) Stevens, was born 21 May 1913. He married 26 July 1939 Phyllis
Eilene Travis.
        Children of Roy Arthur and Phyllis Eilene (Travis) Stevens:
  1450   i Richard Roy Stevens, born and died 21 May 1941
+ 1451   ii Gordon Arthur Stevens, born 29 July 1942
+ 1452   iii Phyllis Darlene Stevens, born 17 November 1946
  1453   iv Kathleen Rose Stevens, born 25 October 1948

765 - LEWIS EVERETT(6) GOODRICH [Harold Garfield(5) Wolfe, Simon
P.(4), Jacob Jr(3), Jacob(2), Daniel(1)]
        Lewis Everett Goodrich, first child of Harold Garfield and
Elizabeth (Smith) Wolfe, was born 13 October 1909. After becoming an
adult he changed his name to that of his stepfather. His wife's name
is not known.
        Children of Lewis Everett and _____ (_____) Goodrich:
  1454   i Barbara Goodrich
  1455   ii Gayla Goodrich

777 - OTIS W.(6) BURROWS [Mary E.(5) Wolf, George Isaac(4), Jacob
Jr(3), Jacob(2), Daniel(1)]
        Otis W. Burrows, first child of Warren L. and Mary E. (Wolf)
Burrows, was born 17 June 1885. He married 12 October 1912 in Cass
County, IN Cora Munson. They are buried at Galveston, Cass County, IN.
        Child of Otis W. and Cora (Munson) Burrows:
  1456   i Jean H. Burrows, born 15 February 1921

778 - ELTA(6) BURROWS [Mary E.(5) Wolf, George Isaac(4), Jacob
Jr(3), Jacob(2), Daniel(1)]
        Elta Burrows was the second child of Warren L. and Mary E. (Wolf)
Burrows. She married 12 May 1915 in Cass County, IN Harry F. Martin.
They are buried at Galveston, Cass County, IN.
        Children of Harry F. and Elta (Burrows) Martin:
  1457   i Warren Martin
  1458   ii Robert Martin
  1459   iii Mary Jo Ann Martin

779 - BERTHA(6) HENRY [Sarah C.(5) Wolf, George Isaac(4), Jacob
Jr(3), Jacob(2), Daniel(1)]
        Bertha Henry, first child of William and Sarah C. (Wolf) Henry,
was born 8 August 1884 in Cass County, IN. She married 5 June 1907 in
Cass County Ollie Seward, born 14 February 1885 in Indiana. Bertha is

buried in Hope Well Cemetery, Deer Creek Township, Cass County.
    Children of Ollie and Bertha (Henry) Seward:
    1460   i William Seward, born 1909 in Carroll County, IN
    1461   ii Leonard H. Seward, born 2 January 1911 in Cass County, IN
    1462   iii Lee Seward
    1463   iv Paul Seward
    1464   v George I. Seward, born 1 November 1918 in Cass County, IN
    1465   vi Eva Margaret Seward, born 23 September 1920 in Cass
            County, In. Married _____ McHale

    784 - JOHN JACOB(6) SMITH [Caroline Evalina(5) Wolf, George
Isaac(4), Jacob Jr(3), Jacob(2), Daniel(1)]
    John Jacob Smith, second child of Abraham and Caroline Evalina
(Wolf) Smith, was born 17 July 1892 in Galveston, Cass County, IN. He
married 25 November 1914 at Burrows, Carroll County, IN Rachel Hynes,
born 20 October 1893 at Burrows, daughter of John and Jane (Gasaway)
Hynes. John was a farmer and they were affiliated with the Brethren
Church. John died 11 June 1965 at Galveston and Rachel 14 May 1973 at
Flora,IN. They are buried in the Galveston Cemetery.
    Children of John Jacob and Rachel (Hynes) Smith:
+ 1466   i Elizabeth Jane Smith, born 25 April 1916
+ 1467   ii Samuel Hynes Smith, born 24 August 1920
+ 1468   iii Dorothy Rose Smith, born 24 March 1924
+ 1469   iv Edith Anice Smith, born 12 January 1926
+ 1470   v Mamie Alice Smith, born 12 January 1930

    785 - IDA MARGARET(6) SMITH [Caroline Evalina(5) Wolf, George
Isaac(4), Jacob Jr(3), Jacob(2), Daniel(1)]
    Ida Margaret Smith, third child of Abraham and Caroline Evalina
(Wolf) Smith, was born 15 December 1893 at Logansport, Cass County,
IN. She married 5 October 1926 at Chicago, Cook County, IL John C.
(Jack) Harless, born 8 November 1891 at Delphi, Carroll County, In,
son of John and Linnie Mae (Axtell) Harless. John was a railroad car
inspector. He died 5 October 1973 at Monticello, White County, In and
is buried in Mt. Carmel Cemetery, Twelve Mile, Cass County, IN. They
were members of the Brethren Church.
    Chilldren of John C. and Ida Margaret (Smith) Harless:
+ 1471   i Caroline Evalina Harless, born 30 May 1928
+ 1472   ii Alan John Harless, born 7 March 1931
    •

    788 - MARTHA BELLE(6) SMITH [Caroline Evalina(5) Wolf, George
Isaac(4), Jacob Jr(3), Jacob(2), Daniel(1)]
    Martha Belle Smith, sixth child of Abraham and Caroline Evalina
(Wolf) Smith, was born 25 November 1901 at Galveston, Cass County, IN.
She married 17 June 1922 at Galveston Charles Murley Harner, born 26
May 1901 at Shoals, Martin County, IN, son of Clemet and Katherine
(Baker) Harney. Charles died 18 February 1980 at Kathleen, GA and is
buried in the E. U. B. Cemetery at Galveston. He was a farmer, train-
man and factory worker and Martha was a seamstress. They were members
of the Brethren Church.
    Children of Charles Murley and Martha Belle (Smith) Harner:
+ 1473   i Ruby Evangeline Harner, born 21 August 1926
+ 1474   ii Myrel Eugene Harner, born 7 February 1930
+ 1475   iii Everett Dale Harner, born 2 March 1935

    792 - SCHUYLER OTTO(6) MICHAEL [Lydia Ladoskey(5) Wolf, George
Isaac(4), Jacob Jr(3), Jacob(2), Daniel(1)]
    Schuyler Otto Michael, first child of William Henry Marion and

Lydia Ladoskey (Wolf) Michael, was born 20 May 1890 in Carroll County, IN. He married 20 May 1919 at Twelve Mile, Cass County, IN Hazel Marie Wysong, born 10 June 1899 at Monticello, White County, IN, daughter of Josiah and Carrie (McKinley) Wysong. Hazel died 10 December 1962 at Logansport, Cass County and Schuyler 16 April 1970 at Kokomo, Howard County, IN. They are buried in Metea Cemetery, Cass County. Schuyler was an electrician. They were members of the Church of God.
    Child of Schuyler Otto and Hazel Marie (Wysong) Michael:
    1476   i Kathern D. Michael, adopted November 1939, born 22 September 1922 at Logansport, Cass County, IN. Married 22 August 1941 at Logansport Harold E. Martin

    793 - VADA ESTELLA(6) MICHAEL [Lydia Ladoskey(5) Wolf, George Isaac(4), Jacob Jr(3), Jacob(2), Daniel(1)]
    Vada Estella Michael, second child of William Henry Marion and Lydia Ladoskey (Wolf) Michael, was born 13 March 1892 in Deer Creek Township, Cass County, IN. She married 3 January 1909 in Cass County Melvin Earl Snavely, born 20 July 1888 in Howard County, IN, son of I. B. and Isabel (Johnson) Snavely. He was a farmer. Melvin died 6 September 1967 at Royal Center, Cass County and Vada 8 September 1968 in Indiana. They are buried in Galveston Cemetery, Cass County.
    Children of Melvin Earl and Vada Estella (Michael) Snavely:
+ 1477   i Ross Ovid Snavely, born 17 May 1909
+ 1478   ii Ida Snavely, born 2 June 1911
+ 1479 iii Clara Monzel Snavely, born 9 March 1913
+ 1480   iv Edna Leo Snavely, twin, born 20 November 1917
+ 1481   v Ethel Cleo Snavely, twin, born 20 November 1917
+ 1482   vi Lola Frances Snavely, born 25 March 1926

    794 - CHARLES FRANKLIN(6) MICHAEL [Lydia Ladoskey(5) Wolf, George Isaac(4), Jacob Jr(3), Jacob(2), Daniel(1)]
    Charles Franklin Michael, third child of William Henry Marion and Lydia Ladoskey (Wolf) Michael was born 1 May 1894 at New Waverly, Cass County, IN. He married 1 November 1917 at Rochester, Fulton County, IN Hattie May Ellen Teems, born 7 October 1897 at Twelve Mile, Cass County, daughter of John Henry and Sarah E. (Overmyer) Teems. Charles was a carpenter and a veteran of World War I. They were members of the United Brethern Church. He died of cancer 26 May 1974 at Munising, Alger County, MI and Hattie 6 August 1978 at Sturgis, St. Joseph County, MI. They are buried in South Lawn Cemetery, South Bend, St. Joseph County, IN.
    Children of Charles Franklin and Hattie May Ellen (Teems) Michael:
+ 1483   i Cora Mabel Michael, born 6 January 1918
+ 1484   ii Kenneth Rollie Michael, born 11 February 1920

    795 - GEORGE EMERSON(6) MICHAEL [Lydia Ladoskey(5) Wolf, George Isaac(4), Jacob Jr(3), Jacob(2), Daniel(1)]
    George Emerson Michael, fourth child of William Henry Marion and Lydia Ladoskey (Wolf) Michael, was born 30 June 1896 at New Waverly, Cass County, IN. He married 18 June 1924 at St. Joseph, MI Mary Adeline Glassburn, born 27 September 1906 at Bunker Hill, Miami County, IN, daughter of Wilbur and Cora E. (Fishtorn) Glassburn. George was a metal finisher. He died 31 August 1962 and is buried in Corinth Cemetery, Twelve Mile, Cass County.
    Children of George Emerson and Mary Adeline (Glassburn) Michael:
+ 1485   i Ruby Mae Michael, born 21 March 1925
+ 1486   ii Ray Emerson Michael, born 3 February 1932

+ 1487   iii Ronald Lee Michael, born 3 november 1945

796 - EARL DEWEY(6) MICHAEL [Lydia Ladoskey(5) Wolf, George Isaac(4), Jacob Jr(3), Jacob(2), Daniel(1)]
     Earl Dewey Michael, fifth child of William Henry Marion and Lydia Ladoskey (Wolf) Michael, was born 21 August 1898 in Cass County, IN. He married 9 October 1920 in Cass County Arla Gaias Champ, born 10 April 1900 at Twelve Mile, Adams Township, Cass County, daughter of Melvin Simpson and Mary Caroline (Crippen) Champ. They divorced 7 November 1952. Earl was a mechanic. Earl died 19 February 1961 at South Bend, St. Joseph County, IN and is buried in the City Cemetery there.
     Children of Earl Dewey and Arla Gaias (Champ) Michael:
+ 1488   i Raymond Champ Michael, born 2 March 1923
  1489   ii Arnold Duane Michael, born 29 January 1927 and died 26 April 1927 at Lapaz, Marshall County, IN. Buried in the Brethren Cemetery, Twelve Mile, Cass County, IN
+ 1490 iii Aldonna Maxine Michael, born 17 February 1928
+ 1491   iv Phyllis Kathleen Michael, born 20 November 1933

799 - CLEO CATHERINE(6) MICHAEL [Lydia Ladoskey(5) Wolf, George Isaac(4), Jacob Jr(3), Jacob(2), Daniel(1)]
     Cleo Catherine Michael, eighth child of William Henry Marion and Lydia Ladoskey (Wolf) Michael, was born 16 August 1907 at Galveston, Cass County, IN. She married 24 April 1927 at Bremen, Marshall County, IN Avery James Sumpter, born 17 March 1902 at Huntington, Huntington County, IN, son of William and Lucy (Lathrop) Sumpter. Avery was a farmer and they were members of the Baptist Church. He died 8 April 1979 at Chandler, AZ and is buried in the East Rest Haven Cemetery at Tempe, AZ.
     Children of Avery James and Cleo Catherine (Michael) Sumpter:
+ 1492   i Bobby Cleon Sumpter, born 19 September 1927
+ 1493   ii Bobetta Joy Sumpter, born 20 November 1928
+ 1494 iii Opal Naomi Sumpter, born 2 January 1931
+ 1495   iv Reah Jeanette Sumpter, born 28 August 1936
+ 1496   v Lucy Ellen Sumpter, born 21 August 1938
+ 1497   vi Sheila Jeanine Sumpter, born 28 May 1943

802 - OSCAR DELMAR(6) MC CLOSKEY [Anna Margaret(5) Wolf, George Isaac(4), Jacob Jr(3), Jacob(2), Daniel(1)]
     Oscar Delmar McCloskey, third child of David Judge and Anna Margaret (Wolf) McCloskey, was born 17 June 1904 at Walton, Deer Creek Township, Cass County, IN. He married 16 December 1928 in Deer Creek Township Mary Iona Peter, born 1 September 1905 at Walton, Cass County, daughter of Henry Ebenezer and Fannie Margaret (Caldwell) Peter. Oscar was a farmer.
     Children of Oscar Delmar and Mary Iona (Peter) McCloskey:
+ 1498   i David Allen McCloskey, born 27 October 1933
+ 1499   ii Danny Lee McCloskey, born 15 July 1946

803 - GEORGE WILLIAM(6) WOLF [Charles Henry(5), George Isaac(4), Jacob Jr(3), Jacob(2), Daniel(1)]
     George William Wolf, first child of Charles Henry and Dora Armell (Knight) Wolf, was born 11 March 1916 at Young America, Cass County, IN. He married 1) 27 May 1939 at Francesville, Pulaski County, IN Arlene Lisenby, daughter of Frank Lisenby. They divorced about 1946 and George married 2) Bessie _____. Arlene and the children went to California after the divorce.

142

Children of George William and Arlene (Lisenby) Wolf:
1500   i James Wolf, born 10 June 1942
1501   ii Christina Wolf
1502   iii Frank Wolf

804 - MARGARET(6) WOLF [Charles Henry(5), George Isaac(4), Jacob
Jr(3), Jacob(2), Daniel(1)]
    Margaret Wolf, second child of Charles Henry and Dora Armell
(Knight) Wolf, was born 11 March 1920 at Young America, Cass County,
IN. She married 31 August 1939 at Francesville, Pulaski County, IN
Stephen Edward McKinley, born 13 October 1918 at Francesville, son of
Stephen Alexander and Elsie Jane (Wright) McKinley. Stephen was a
farmer and Margaret a school librarian. They were members of the
Presbyterian Church.
    Children of Stephen Edward and Margaret (Wolf) McKinley:
+ 1503   i Mary Ann McKinley, born 10 March 1941
  1504   ii Richard Lee McKinley, born 6 July 1942
+ 1505   iii Delores Lorene McKinley, born 30 April 1948

805 - CHARLES HENRY(6) WOLF JR [Charles Henry(5), George
Isaac(4), Jacob Jr(3), Jacob(2), Daniel(1)]
    Charles Henry Wolf Jr, third child of Charle Henry and Dora
Armell (Knight) Wolf, was born 21 December 1924. He married August
1948 Ruby Rapp.
    Children of Charles Henry Jr and Ruby (Rapp) Wolf:
  1506   i Steven Wolf, born 1950
  1507   ii John Wolf, born 1952
  1508   iii Daniel Wolf, born 1954
  1509   iv David Wolf, born 1963

808 - ORA E.(6) JUDY [Anna C.(5) Cree, Magdalena L.(4) Wolf,
Jacob Jr(3), Jacob(2), Daniel(1)]
    Ora E. Judy, first child of George and Anna C. (Cree) Judy, was
born 16 January 1891. He married 19 February 1919 Elizabeth Twaits. He
died 9 July 1972.
    Children of Ora E. and Elizabeth (Twaits) Judy:
+ 1510   i Helen Mae Judy, born 2 February 1922.
  1511   ii Ellis Edward Judy, born about 1925
  1512   iii Daughter Judy. Married F. D. Thompson

811 - CHESTER L.(6) RICE [Clarissa(5) Cree, Magdalena L.(4) Wolf,
Jacob Jr(3), Jacob(2), Daniel(1)]
    Chester L. Rice, first child of Albert and Clarissa (Cree) Rice,
was born 21 February 1897. He married 1) Edna Frier who died about
1935, 2) Rose Anderson and 3) Maxine Jones. He died 20 November 1966.
    Children of Chester L. and Edna (Frier) Rice:
+ 1513   i Helen Marie Rice, born 1924
  1514   ii Freda Marie Rice. Married _____Shagley

812 - LUTHER(6) RICE [Clarissa(5) Cree, Magdalena L.(4) Wolf,
Jacob Jr(3), Jacob(2), Daniel(1)]
    Luther Rice, second child of Albert and Clarissa (Cree) Rice, was
born 25 March 1900. He married 23 September 1924 Alma Burge. He died
12 November 1962.
    Children of Luther and Alma (Burge) Rice:
+ 1515   i Robert Rice, born 1929
+ 1516   ii Pauline Rice, twin, born 15 June 1930
  1517   iii Paul Rice, twin, born 15 June 1930. Married 19 December

                    1959 Bonnie Ruth Reed
1518   iv Carolyn Sue Rice, born 1939
1519   v Richard Rice
1520   vi Daughter Rice. Married Gene Fillenworth
1521   vii Daughter Rice. Married Phillip Hess
1522   viii Daughter Rice. Married Ralph West

     814 - LEO P.(6) RICE [Clarissa(5) Cree, Magdalena L.(4) Wolf,
Jacob Jr(3), Jacob(2), Daniel(1)]
     Leo P. Rice, fourth child of Albert and Clarissa (Cree) Rice, was
born 23 March 1905. He married 6 December 1925 Edna Saunders.
     Children of Leo P. and Edna (Saunders) Rice:
+ 1523   i Albert Paul Rice
  1524   ii John Edward Rice, born 1927
  1525   iii Melva June Rice, born 1929
  1526   iv Leo P. Rice Jr
  1527   v Carrol Elmer Rice, born 1939. Married 24 January 1960
             Gloria Ann Musall, daughter of Harold Musall
  1528   vi Lois Beth Rice. Married 12 November 1966 Michael J.
             Hill,son of Robert and Lucretia (Downham) Hill

     815 - SARAH(6) RICE [Clarissa(5) Cree, Magdalena L. (4) Wolf,
Jacob Jr(3), Jacob(2), Daniel(1)]
     Sarah Rice, fifth child of Albert and Clarissa (Cree) Rice, was
born 10 November 1908. She married 24 May 1928 John Burge.
     Children of John and Sarah (Rice) Burge:
+ 1529   i Meredith Dean Burge, born about 1929
+ 1530   ii Marjorie Ann Burge, born 2 April 1931

     816 - MAGDALINE(6) WHIPPERMAN [Margaret(5) Cree, Magdalena L.(4)
Wolf, Jacob Jr(3), Jacob(2), Daniel(1)]
     Magdalene Whipperman, first child of George E. and Margaret
(Cree) Whipperman, was born 19 January 1889. She married 5 December
1907 Benjamin M. Sailors, born 14 november 1888. Benjamin died 7
December 1942 and Magdalene 29 April 1973.
     Children of Benjamin M. and Magdalene (Whipperman) Sailors:
+ 1531   i Amiel Sailors, born 12 December 1907
+ 1532   ii Samuel Sailors, born 1 May 1909
+ 1533   iii Irene Sailors, born 21 June 1910
+ 1534   iv Arlo Sailors, born 21 December 1912
  1535   v Lola Bernice Sailors, born about 1918

     817 - CHARLES ROBERT(6) WHIPPERMAN [Margaret(5) Cree, Magdalena
L.(4) Wolf, Jacob Jr(3), Jacob(2), Daniel(1)]
     Charles Robert Whipperman, second child of George E. and Margaret
(Cree) Whipperman, was born 5 May 1891. He married 15 July 1925 Ruth
Bean.
     Child of Charles Robert and Ruth (Bean) Whipperman:
  1536   i Margaret Adeline Whipperman, born 27 July 1927

     818 - ESTHER(6) WHIPPERMAN [Margaret(5) Cree, Magdalena L.(4)
Wolf, Jacob Jr(3), Jacob(2), Daniel(1)]
     Esther Whipperman, third child of George E. and Margaret (Cree)
Whipperman, was born 27 August 1893. She married 3 May 1911 Quincy
Downham, born 24 October 1891. He died 30 December 1939.
     Children of Quincy and Esther (Whipperman) Downham:
+ 1537   i Elmer Downham, born 24 September 1911
  1538   ii Bernadine Ardil Downham, born about 1915

1539   iii Lucretia Downham, born 31 December 1916. Married Robert
          Hill
1540   iv Ione Downham, born about 1917
+ 1541   v George Daniel Downham, born 28 June 1918
1542   vi Otho Carl Downham
1543   vii Mary Margaret Downham, born 23 February 1923
1544 viii Alvina Marie Downham, born 5 November 1925. Married about
          1947 Ralph Donald Stewart
1545   ix Quincine Juanita Downham, born 8 August 1928. Married 8
          June 1947 Robert Lee Brown

   819 - ADELBERT LEE(6) WHIPPERMAN [Margaret(5) Cree, Magdalena
L.(4) Wolf, Jacob Jr(3), Jacob(2), Daniel(1)]
    Adelbert Lee Whipperman, fourth child of George E. and Margaret
(Cree) Whipperman, was born 5 March 1912. He married Ruth Elizabeth
Rhoads.
    Child of Adelbert Lee and Ruth Elizabeth (Rhoads) Whipperman:
1546   i Alberta Lea Whipperman. Married 30 may 1965 Gerald Devon
          Moore

   820 - WALTER IRVING(6) CREE [George Robert(5), Magdalena L.(4)
Wolf, Jacob Jr(3), Jacob(2), Daniel(1)]
    Walter Irving Cree, first child of George Robert and Mary Eva
(Tribbett) Cree, was born 21 November 1900. He married 25 June 1919
Lucretia Beatrice Bechtol, born 28 October 1900. Walter died 24 may
1968.
    Child of Walter Irving and Lucretia Beatrice (Bechtol) Cree:
+ 1547   i Charlotte Elizabeth Cree, born 13 March 1927

   821 - LOLA GRACE(6) CREE [George Robert(5), Magdalena L.(4) Wolf,
Jacob Jr(3), Jacob(2), daniel(1)]
    Lola Grace Cree, second child of George Robert and Mary Eva
Tribbett) Cree, was born 31 July 1903. She married 24 November 1921
Ardis Joseph Landis, born 18 March 1899. Lola died 12 August 1966.
    Children of Ardis Joseph and Lola Grace (Cree) Landis:
1548   i Eugene Landis, born about 1924
+ 1549   ii Wayne Lee Landis, born 13 November 1925
+ 1550   iii Doris Ruth Landis, born 29 October 1929
+ 1551   iv Betty Arlene Landis, born 22 April 1933
+ 1552   v Dortha Jean Landis, born 22 December 1936

   823 - ROBERT GEORGE(6) CREE [George Robert(5), Magdalena L.(4)
Wolf, Jacob Jr(3), Jacob(2), Daniel(1)]
    Robert George Cree, fourth child of George Robert and Mary Eva
(Tribbett) Cree, was born 19 July 1914. He married Bernice Been.
    Children of Robert George and Bernice (Been) Cree:
1553   i Earnest Cree
1554   ii Robert George Cree Jr. Married 1 May 1971 Katherine G.
          Blackhurst
1555   iii Dana Allen Cree. Married 5 June 1977 Debra Ann Poland

   824 - HAROLD N.(6) CREE [Henry(5), Magdalena L.(4) Wolf, Jacob
Jr(3), Jacob(2), Daniel(1)]
    Harold N. Cree, first child of Henry and Eva V. (Little) Cree,
was born 4 July 1900. He married 18 June 1926 Arlene Barnard, born 5
July 1904, daughter of William Monroe and Lydia (Jorden) Barnard.
Harold died 4 January 1965.

Children of Harold N. and Arlene (Barnard) Cree:
1556   i   Wilma Jean Cree, born about 1927 . Married 21 December
           1946 William Zimmerman, born 14 April 1927
+ 1557   ii   Billy Dean Cree, twin, born about 1929
1558   iii   Bobby Don Cree, twin, born about 1929
+ 1559   iv   Wayne Barnard Cree
1560   v   Ralph Cree
1561   vi   Janet Sue Cree, born and died 30 July 1936

826 - MILDRED(6) CREE [Albert(5), Magdalena L.(4) Wolf, Jacob
Jr(3), Jacob(2), Daniel(1)]
    Mildred Cree, first child of Albert and Nellie Myrtle (Ray) Cree,
was born 3 May 1910. She married 24 August 1929 Walter Parrot.
    Children of Walter and Mildred (Cree) Parrot:
+ 1562   i   Dorothy Ione Parrot, born about 1933
1563   ii   Keith Albert Parrot, born 20 July 1937. Married 24 April
           1965 Shelby Thompson

828 - ALICE LOUISE(6) CREE [Albert(5), Magdalena L.(4) Wolf,
Jacob Jr(3), Jacob(2), Daniel(1)]
    Alice Louise Cree, third child of Albert and Nellie Myrtle (Ray)
Cree, was born 25 September 1919. She married about 1947 Claude Linn,
born 11 April 1911, son of Thomas and Mary (Burge) Linn. Claude died
15 December 1968.
    Children of Claude and Alice Louise (Cree) Linn:
1564   i   Rita Kay Linn, born 15 May 1949
1565   ii   Gary Eugene Linn, born about 1952

829 - IRENE(6) CREE [Ezra(5), Magdalena L.(4) Wolf, Jacob Jr(3),
Jacob(2), Daniel(1)]
    Irene Cree, first child of Ezra and Mabel (Hughes) Cree, was born
15 February 1910. She married December 1930 Lewis Penn. Lewis died 4
March 1963 and Irene 16 February 1971.
    Children of Lewis and Irene (Cree) Penn:
+ 1566   i   Phyllis Ellen Penn, born about 1935. Married about 1955
           Donald Myers
1567   ii   Gerald Allen Penn, born 24 July 1942. Married 8 February
           1968 Jane Ellen Downham
1568   iii   Dale Penn
1569   iv   Janice Penn. Married Robert Collins
1570   v   Larry Penn. Married Linda Fae Arnold
1571   vi   Marilyn Penn. Married _____ Guckien
1572   vii   Mary Lou Penn
1573 viii   Roselyn Penn

832 - EVAUGN GASTON(6) CREE [Carl(5), Malinda Jane(4) Wolf, Jacob
Jr(3), Jacob(2), Daniel(1)]
    Evaughn Gaston Cree, first child of Carl and Sarah Adeline
(Tribbett), was born 22 February 1903. She married 1925 Virgil Allen.
    Children of Virgil and Evaughn Gaston (Cree) Allen:
+ 1574   i   Frieda May Allen, born about 1925. Married Harold Buck-
           worth
1575   ii   Juanita Arlene Allen, born about 1927, died 12 February
           1947
1576   iii   Richard Allen
1577   iv   Virgil Keith Allen, born 11 February 1934

833 - PAUL(6) CREE [Carl(5), Malinda Jane(4) Wolf, Jacob Jr(3), Jacob(2), Daniel(1)]
    Paul Cree, second child of Carl and Sarah Adeline (Tribbett) Cree, was born 27 March 1906. He married 28 Seoptember 1929 Phoebe Wanty, born 18 November 1912.
    Children of Paul and Phoebe (Wanty) Cree:
  1578   i Morris Glenn Cree, born 15 August 1930
  1579   ii Lorena Cree, twin, born 17 November 1941
  1580 iii Loren Cree, twin, born 17 November 1941
  1581   iv Carl Wayne Cree, born about 1949, died in the 1960s

834 - WARD(6) CREE [Carl(5), Malinda Jane(4) Wolf, Jacob Jr(3), Jacob(2), Daniel(1)]
    Ward Cree, third child of Carl and Sarah Adeline (Tribbett) Cree, was born 19 December 1908. He married 2 November 192_ Pauline Akins, born 21 June 1912.
    Child of Ward and Pauline (Akins) Cree:
  1582   i Ward Laurel Cree, born 10 March 1943

835 - VIRGIL(6) CREE [Carl(5), Malinda Jane(4) Wolf, Jacob Jr(3), Jacob(2), Daniel(1)]
    Virgil Cree, fourth child of Carl and Sarah Adeline (Tribbett) Cree, was born 24 December 1911. He married 1935 Bethel Taylor, born 8 June 1917.
    Children of Virgil and Bethel (Taylor) Cree:
  1583   i Kenneth Virgil Cree, born 8 May 1942
  1584   ii Ronald Clifton Cree, twin, born about 1945
  1585 iii Rosa Dell Cree, twin, born about 1945

836 - MARY THELMA(6) CREE [Carl(5), Malinda Jane(4) Wolf, Jacob Jr(3), Jacob(2), Daniel(1)]
    Mary Thelma Cree, fifth child of Carl and Sarah Adeline (Tribbett) Cree, was born 16 March 1914. She married Elmo Dotson.
    Children of Elmo and Mary Thelma (Cree) Dotson:
  1586   i Raymond Dotson, born about 1941
  1587   ii Raymona Dotson, born about 1945

838 - GEORGE ANDREW(6) CREE [Carl(5), Malinda Jane(4) Wolf, Jacob Jr(3), Jacob(2), Daniel(1)]
    George Andrew Cree, seventh child of Carl and Sarah Adeline (Tribbett) Cree, was born 9 September 1917. He married Laura Wilson.
    Child of George Andrew and Laura (Wilson) Cree:
  1588   i Larry Dean Cree, born about 1953

839 - GASTON EVERETT(6) CREE [Carl(5), Malinda Jane(4) Wolf, Jacob Jr(3), Jacob(2), Daniel(1)]
    Gaston Everett Cree, eighth child of Carl and Sarah Adeline (Tribett) Cree, was born 30 August 1919. He married 3 June 1943 Mary Brown. Gaston died 24 January 1985.
    Children of Gaston Everett and Mary (Brown) Cree:
  1589   i Charles Cree
  1590   ii Juanita Evaughn Cree, born about 1955
  1591 iii Charles Cree

840 - LOLA MAY(6) CREE [Carl(5), Malinda Jane(4) Wolf, Jacob Jr(3), Jacob(2), Daniel(1)]
    Lola May Cree, ninth child of Carl and Sarah Adeline (Tribbett) Cree, was born 15 March 1921. She married Harold Leroy Clem.

Children of Harold Leroy and Lola May (Cree) Clem:
1592   i Harold Leroy Clem Jr, born 3 January 1941
1593   ii Marilyn Kay Clem, born 1950

     842 - MABEL(6) CREE [Clarence(5), Malinda Jane(4) Wolf, Jacob
Jr(3), Jacob(2), Daniel(1)]
     Mabel Cree, first child of Clarence and Stella Marie (Cronk)
Cree, was born 8 August 1903. She married 31 August 1930 Franklin
Briggs.
     Children of Franklin and Mabel (Cree) Briggs:
1594   i Shirley Ann Briggs, born 4 March 1934
1595   ii Harry Briggs, born 11 October 1936
1596 iii Clarence Thomas Briggs, born 11 March 1938
1597   iv Patricia Mae Briggs, born 9 December 1939

     843 - RUSSEL(6) CREE [Clarence(5), Malinda Jane(4) Wolf, Jacob
Jr(3), Jacob(2), Daniel(1)]
     Russel Cree, second child of Clarence and Stella Marie (Cronk)
Cree, was born 29 April 1909. He married 1) 17 December 1926 Audrey
Campbell and 2) 29 August 1931 Florence Reynolds.
     Child of Russel and Audrey (Campbell) Cree:
1598   i Frances Marie Cree, born 23 April 1927

     844 - BENNIE(6) CREE [Clarence(5), Malinda Jane(4) Wolf, Jacob
Jr(3), Jacob(2), Daniel(1)]
     Bennie Cree, third child of Clarence and Stella Marie (Cronk)
Cree, was born 12 September 1912. He married 21 April 1934 Viola
Becker.
     Child of Bennie and Viola (Becker) Cree:
1599   i Jean Estelle Cree, born 15 February 1939

     845 - EVA LUCILLE(6) RONK [Goldalee(5) Cree, Malinda Jane(4)
Wolf, Jacob Jr(3), Jacob(2), Daniel(1)]
     Eva Lucille Ronk, first child of Thomas G. and Goldalee (Cree)
Ronk, was born 13 December 1908. She married 2 May 1928 Arthur Allen
Melton.
     Children of Arthur Allen and Eva Lucille (Ronk) Melton:
1600   i Willadean Malinda Melton, born 28 April 1928
1601   ii Donald Lloyd Melton, born 18 August 1929
1602 iii Barbara Muriel Melton, born 18 March 1931
1603   iv John Thomas Melton, born 29 December 1932
1604   v Forrest Leroy Melton, born 5 January 1935
1605   vi Mary Lou Melton, born 4 September 1936
1606 vii Patsy Sue Melton, born 15 August 1937

     847 - FORREST CREE(6) RONK [Goldalee(5) Cree, Malinda Jane(4)
Wolf, Jacob Jr(3), Jacob(2), Daniel(1)]
     Forrest Cree Ronk, third child of Thomas G. and Goldalee (Cree)
Ronk, was born 27 June 1914. He married 22 December 1935 Thelma
Edgerley.
     Child of Forrest Cree and Thelma (Edgerley) Ronk:
1607   i Shirley May Ronk, born 15 May 1937

     853 - JOHN(6) HARTMAN [Amanda(5) Pontious, John(4), Elizabeth(3)
Hahn, Elizabeth(2) Wolf, Daniel(1)]
     John Hartman was a son of William and Amanda (Pontious) Hartman.
He died before 1924.

Children of John and _____ (_____) Hartman:
1608   i Floyd Hartman
1609   ii Mina Hartman. Married _____ Johnson

854 - SARAH SABINA(6) HARTMAN [Amanda(5) Pontious, John(4),
Elizabeth(3) Hahn, Elizabeth(2) Wolf, Daniel(1)]
     Sarah Sabina Hartman, second child of William and Amanda (Pon-
tious) Hartman, was born 14 March 1865 at Arcanum, Darke County, OH.
She married 27 March 1887 at Arcanum John Amos Shilt, born 20 April
1866 at Gordon, Darke County, son of Jeremiah and Sarah Ann (Weid)
Shilt. John married 2) Emma Miller. Sarah died 13 August 1917 and John
13 October 1945, both at Dayton, Montgomery County, OH. They are
buried at W. Baltimore, Verona, OH. During his lifetime, John worked
at the Brownell Boiler Works as a laborer, engine tester and janitor.
     Children of John Amoa and Sarah Sabina (Hartman) Shilt:
1610   i Arthur Oscar Shilt, born 2 October 1887 at Arcanum, Darke
            County, OH. He was a maintenance man at the Brownell
            Boiler Works. He married 26 January 1909 at Dayton, OH
            Susie Lena Bell Barlow. Arthur died 20 December 1950 at
            Dayton and is buried at W. Baltimore, Verona, OH
1611   ii Harry Victor Shilt, born 2 October 1889 at Arcanum. He
            married 14 July 1908 at Chicago, IL Louise Rasmussen. He
            died 24 April 1951 and is buried at Chicago
1612   iii Cleo Clyde Shilt, born 8 May 1893 at dayton, Montgomery
            County, OH. He married 16 June 1915 Gertie Blanch Wilson.
            Cleo died 9 July 1961 at South Bend, IN and is buried in
            St. Joseph Memorial Park Cemetery.
1613   iv Walter Frank Shilt, born 5 October 1895 at Dayton, OH.
            Married 1) 8 June 1916 at Dayton Hazel Recking and 2) Ada
            Hannah. He died 26 August 1972 at Dayton and is buried in
            the Centerville Cemetery
1614   v Earl Calvin Shilt, born 13 February 1899 at Dayton, OH.
            Married 1920 Ethel Mitchell. He died 9 December 1941 and
            is buried in St. Joseph Memorial Park Cemetery
1615   vi Emma Elizabeth Shilt, born 2 March 1901 at Dayton, OH,
            died 12 March 1902, buried at W. Baltimore, Verona, OH
1616   vii John Emerson Shilt, born 28 December 1902. Married 2 July
            1924 at Dayton Gladys Johnston. He died February 1931 and
            is buried at Marysville, KY
1617 viii Edward Russell Shilt, born 26 March 1905 at Dayton, OH.
            Married 1) 14 April 1923 at Newport, KY Mattie Purdue and
            2) Sylvia Hartman Alexander. He died 17 June 1971 and is
            buried in Mote Cemetery, Miami County, OH

864 - CHARLES HENRY(6) PONTIUS [Serenius(5), John(4), Eliza-
beth(3) Hahn, Elizabeth(2) Wolf, Daniel(1)]
     Charles Henry Pontius, first child of Serenius and Minerva
(Shade) Pontius, was born 11 June 1887. He married 31 December 1908
Roxanna Bell Hull, born 29 June 1889, daughter of William and Roxanna
(Brandon) Hall. Charles died 16 January 1957 and Roxanna 12 March
1964.
     Child of Charles Henry and Roxanna Bell (Hall) Pontius:
+ 1618   i Alna Charlene Pontius, born 11 August 1921

865 - MARGARET(6) DREHR [Sarah(5) Pontius, John(4), Elizabeth(3)
Hahn, Elizabeth(2) Wolf, Daniel(1)]
     Margaret Drehr, child of _____ and Sarah (Pontius) Drehr, married
1) _____ Stettler and 2) _____ Peshbaugh. She die dbefore 1924.

Child of _____ and Margaret (Drehr) Stettler:
1619   i William Stettler

900 - CHARLES LAIRD(6) BOYER [Alice Arretta(5) Sharritts, Sam-
uel(4), Elizabeth(3) Hahn, Elizabeth(2) Wolf, Daniel(1)]
     Charles Laird Boyer, second child of Orlando and Alice Arretta
(Sharritts) Boyer, was born 14 June 1883 in Montgomery County, OH and
died 23 March 1926. His wife's name is not known.
     Children of Charles Laird and _____ (_____) Boyer:
1620   i Earl Boyer
1621   ii Ray Boyer

901 - ALBERT(6) BOYER [Alice Arretta(5) Sharritts, Samuel(4),
Elizabeth(3) Hahn, Elizabeth(2) Wolf, Daniel(1)]
     Albert Boyer, third child of Orlando and Alice Arretta (Shar-
ritts) Boyer, was born 8 July 1885 in Montgomery County, OH. He
married Ruth _____. Albert died 27 November 1958.
     Child of Albert and Ruth (_____) Boyer:
1622   i Dorothy Boyer

905 - ELIZABETH IDELLA(6) BOYER [Alice Arretta(5) Sharritts,
Samuel(4), Elizabeth(3) Hahn, Elizabeth(2) Wolf, Daniel(1)]
     Elizabeth Idella Boyer, seventh child of Orlando and Alice
Arretta (Sharritts) Boyer, was born 29 June 1893 in Montgomery
County, OH. She married 11 February 1911 at Miamisburg, OH Burnett
Bailey, born 24 August 1892 in Montgomery County, son of Charles
Wesley and Cora Lucinda (Libecap) Baillie. Burnett died 13 April 1968
in Montgomery County and is buried in Hill-Grove Cemetery, Miamisburg.
     Children of Burnett and Elizabeth Idella (Boyer) Bailey:
+ 1623   i Catherine Pauline Bailey, born 11 September 1911
+ 1624   ii James M. Bailey, born 15 July 1913
+ 1625 iii Helen Louise Bailey, born 17 June 1919
+ 1626   iv Roland Burnett Bailey, born 12 September 1931 at Miamis-
             burg, OH. Married 10 June 1954 Jane Ann Beal, born 15
             July 1933 in Warren County, OH. No children

914 - PEARL(6) WOLFE [Franklin(5), Daniel Jr(4), Daniel Sr(3),
Frederick(2), Daniel(1)]
     Pearl Wolfe, fourth child of Franklin and Sarah M. (McCaleb)
Wolfe, was born in Grant Township, Union County, IA. She married
Charles McGregor. It is thought they are buried in Graceland Cemetery,
Creston, Union County, IA.
     Child of Charles and Pearl (Wolfe) McGregor:
1627   i Gayle McGregor, born in Union County, IA

917 - VERA(6) WOLFE [Franklin(5), Daniel Jr(4), Daniel Sr(3),
Frederick(2), Daniel(1)]
     Vera Wolfe, seventh child of Franklin and Sarah M. (McCaleb)
Wolfe, was born about 1893 in Grant Township, Union County, IA. She
married Raymond Borland. Vera died about 1987 at Creston, Union
county.
     Children of Raymond and Vera (Wolfe) Borland:
+ 1628   i Melba Marie Borland, born 2 December 1913
  1629   ii Mildred Borland, born about 1916 at Shannon City, Union
             County, IA. Married Joseph Lindsay

918 - MYRTLE ANNIE(6) WOLFE [Simon Peter(5), Michael(4), Daniel
Sr(3), Frederick(2), Daniel(1)]

Myrtle Annie Wolfe, first child of Simon Peter and Cynthia Annie (Anderson) Wolfe, was born 29 December 1878 at Keota, Keokuk County, IA. She married 8 June 1899 David Edwin Jacobs, born 15 September 1874 at Creston, Union County, IA, son of Ahimas Thomas and Mary E. (Erdman) Jacobs. David died 30 November 1941 at St. Joseph, Buchanan County, MO and Myrtle 13 August 1964 at Grant City, Worth County, MO. They are buried at Grant City.

Children of David Edwin and Myrtle Annie (Wolfe) Jacobs:

1630   i Alfred Clark Jacobs, born before 1904, died in infancy about 1904
+ 1631   ii Fred David Jacobs, twin, born 5 February 1904
+ 1632 iii Frank Edwin Jacobs, twin, born 5 February 1904
1633   iv Lois Mildred Jacobs, born 17 April 1911 at Allendale, Worth County, MO. Married Nolan Bricken. They divorced

920 - FRED SIMON(6) WOLFE [Simon Peter(5), Michael(4), Daniel Sr(3), Frederick(2) Daniel(1)]

Fred Simon Wolfe, third child of Simon Peter and Cynthia Annie (Anderson) Wolfe, was born 26 September 1883 in Iowa. He married 7 March 1906 Hattie Lorena Griep, born 20 November 1886. Fred died 1 April 1957 and Hattie 22 September 1957, both at Shannon City, Union County, IA.

Children of Fred Simon and Hattie Lorena (Griep) Wolfe:

+ 1634   i Claude Wolfe, born 22 June 1907
+ 1635   ii Gladys Marie Wolfe, born 19 June 1910
+ 1636 iii Dorothy Pearl Wolfe, born 15 January 1912

921 - FRANK PETER(6) WOLFE [Simon Peter(5), Michael(4), Daniel Sr(3), Frederick(2), Daniel(1)]

Frank Peter Wolfe, fourth child of Simon Peter and Cynthia Annie (Anderson) Wolfe, was born 26 September 1883 in Iowa. He married 7 February 1906 in Jefferson Township, Union County, IA Lenora Walker, born 26 January 1885. Lenora died 14 November 1959 and Frank 3 June 1969.

Children of Frank Peter and Lenora (Walker) Wolfe:

1637   i Arvilla L. Wolfe, born 1907, died 1957. Did not marry
+ 1638   ii Albert Harold Wolfe, born 14 November 1910
1639 iii Everett Wolfe, born 1922. Married Nellie Linthicum, born about 1920. He was a minister

924 - NELLIE(6) WOLFE [Simon Peter(5), Michael(4), Daniel Sr(3), Frederick(2), Daniel(1)]

Nellie Wolfe, seventh child of Simon Peter and Cynthia Annie (Anderson) Wolfe, was born in Union County, IA. She married Newton Tallman.

Children of Newton and Nellie (Wolfe) Tallman:

1640   i Grace Tallman, born about 1910 in Union County, IA. Married Francis Campbell
1641   ii Leila Tallman, born about 1911 in Union County, IA. Married 16 December 1931 at Fremont, NB Raymond Ballerich and died a short time afterward. There were no children. Raymond worked at the Studebaker Motor Co. in Creston, Union County, IA

942 - MAE ELIZABETH(6) KEEDY [Howard(5), Elizabeth(4) Blecker, Tracy(3) Wolf, Frederick(2), Daniel(1)]

Mae Elizabeth (Babe) Keedy was the fourth child of Howard and Perry (Myers) Keedy. She married Harry Franklin.

Children of Harry and Mae Elizabeth (Keedy) Franklin:
+ 1642   i John Franklin
+ 1643   ii Margaret Franklin
+ 1644 iii Rogene Franklin

945 - LELA(6) KEEDY [Daniel Blecker(5), Elizabeth(4) Blecker,
Tracy(3) Wolf, Frederick(2), Daniel(1)]
    Lela Keedy was the, first child of Daniel Blecker and Viola
(Smith) Keedy. She married Merrit Miller.
    Child of Merrit and Lela (Keedy) Miller:
  1645   i Jean Miller. Married Lee Gibbs

946 - MARTHA(6) KEEDY [Frank C.(5), Elizabeth(4) Blecker,
Tracy(3) Wolf, Frederick(2), Daniel(1)]
    Martha was the first child of Frank C. and Althea (Coffman)
Keedy. She married Eber Long.
    Children of Eber and Martha (Keedy) Long:
+ 1646   i Shirley Long
  1647   ii Daniel Long
  1648 iii Harlan Long. Did not marry
+ 1649   iv Lilian Long

950 - PEARL(6) KEEDY [Frank C.(5), Elizabeth(4) Blecker, Tracy(3)
Wolf, Frederick(2), Daniel(1)]
    Pearl Keedy was the fifth child of Frank C. and Althea (Coffman)
Keedy. She married William Lawrence.
    Children of William and Pearl (Keedy) Lawrence:
  1650   i Carl Lawrence. Married 1) Carolee Rouse and 2) _____
             Bolthouse
  1651   ii Beverly Lawrence

953 - ERNEST(6) ZELLERS [Annie(5) Keedy, Elizabeth(4) Blecker,
Tracy(3) Wolf, Frederick(2), Daniel(1)]
    Ernest Zellers was the son of Martin and Annie (Keedy) Zellers.
He married Ruth Wagner.
    Children of Ernest and Ruth (Wagner) Zellers:
  1652   i Dorothy Zellers
  1653   ii Lola Zellers

954 - FLOYD(6) ZELLERS [Annie(5) Keedy, Elizabeth(4) Blecker,
Tracy(3) Wolf, Frederick(2), Daniel(1)]
    Floyd Zellers was the son of Martin and Annie (Keedy) Zellers. He
married Ella Johnson.
    Children of Floyd and Ella (Johnson) Zellers:
  1654   i Royal Zellers
  1655   ii Laverne Zellers. Married Mary Watts
  1656 iii Keith Zellers
  1657   iv Robert Zellers
  1658   v Donald Zellers
  1659   vi Florence Zellers. Married _____ Schrieber
  1660 vii Doris Zellers

955 - KARL(6) ZELLERS [Annie(5) Keedy, Elizabeth(4) Blecker,
Tracy(3) Wolf, Frederick(2), Daniel(1)]
    Karl Zellers was the son of Martin and Annie (Keedy) Zellers. He
married Katheryn Wolfe.
    Children of Karl and Katheryn (Wolfe) Zellers:
  1661   i Laurence Zellers

956 — WILBUR(6) ZELLERS [Annie(5) Keedy, Elizabeth(4) Blecker, Tracy(3) Wolf, Frederick(2), Daniel(1)]
    Wilbur Zellers was the son of Martin and Annie (Keedy) Zellers. He married Annie Peacock.
    Child of Wilbur and Annie (Peacock) Zellers:
    1663   i Anna Zellers

960 — KATHLEEN LUCILLE(6) GANTZ [Annie Virginia(5) Blecker, Jacob B.(4), Tracy(3) Wolf, Frederick(2), Daniel(1)]
    Kathleen Lucille Gantz, first child of Jesse Berry and Annie Virginia (Blecker) Gantz, was born 8 November 1903 at Boonsboro, Washington County, MD. She married 19 August 1925 at Boonsboro Hugh A. Ford. Hugh died 3 September 1964. Kathleen died 29 November 1967 at Boonsboro and is buried in the Boonsboro Cemetery.
    Child of Hugh A. and Kathleen Lucille (Gantz) Ford:
+ 1664   i Anne Lorraine Ford

961 — DONALD WALLACE SR(6) GANTZ [Jesse Berry(5), Annie Virginia(4) Blecker, Tracy(3) Wolf, Frederick(2), Daniel(1)]
    Donald Wallace Gantz Sr, second child of Jesse Berry and Annie Virginia (Blecker) Gantz, was born 18 July 1910 at Boonsboro, Washington County, MD. He married 24 December 1933 Esther Kathleen Winfield, born 11 October 1911 at Rohrersville, Washington County, daughter of Floyd Lester and Mary Estelle (Hott) Winfield. Donald died 20 February 1983 at Hagerstown, Washington County and is buried in the Boonsboro Cemetery.
    Children of Donald Wallace Sr and Esther Kathleen (Winfield) Gantz:
+ 1665   i Mary Ann Gantz, born 21 May 1936
+ 1666   ii Donald Wallace Gantz Jr, born 19 may 1944

962 — PAUL BLECKER(6) IRWIN [Mary Elizabeth(5) Blecker, Jacob B.(4), Tracy(3) Wolf, Frederick(2), Daniel(1)]
    Paul Blecker Irwin, first child of William L. and Mary Elizabeth (Blecker) Irwin, was born 24 January 1897. His wife's name is not known.
    Child of Paul Blecker and _____ (_____) Irwin:
    1667   i William Paul Irwin, born October 1918, died October 1942.
            Married Zelma Shuffield

963 — BERTHA ISABELLE(6) LAMAR [Mary Elizabeth(5) Blecker, Jacob B.(4), Tracy(3) Wolf, Frederick(2), Daniel(1)]
    Bertha Isabelle Lamar, first child of William Bishop and Mary Elizabeth (Blecker) (Irwin) Lamar, was born 1 May 1901. She married 14 October 1925 Philip Jacob Bardell, born 3 November 1900. Bertha died 13 June 1973.
    Child of Philip Jacob and Bertha Isabelle (Lamar) Bardell:
+ 1668   i Philip William Bardell Sr, born 14 April 1928

964 — ROBERT FULTON(6) LAMAR [Mary Elizabeth(5) Blecker, Jacob B.(4), Tracy(3) Wolf, Frederick(2), Daniel(1)]
    Robert Fulton Lamar, second child of William Bishop and Mary Elizabeth (Blecker0 (Irwin) Lamar, was born 5 July 1904. He married 11 July 1928 Earline Elise Lamkey, born 27 June 1909. Robert died 10 April 1948.

Children of Robert Fulton an153arline Elise (Lamkey) Lamar:
+ 1669   i Joan Elise Lamar, born 1 July 1930
+ 1670   ii Barbara Ann Lamar, born 2 January 1933

965 - WALTER LUTHER(6) YOUNG [Effie Young(5) Blecker, Jacob
B.(4), Tracy(3) Wolf, Frederick(2), Daniel(1)]
    Walter Luther Young, first child of Simon Luther and Effie Young
(Blecker) Young, was born 10 September 1906. He married 14 October
1935 Helen Bertha Klever, born 1 April 1913.
    Children of Walter Luther and Helen Bertha (Klever) Young:
    1671   i Wallace Brian Young, born 7 December 1940
    1672   ii Steven Alan Young, born 22 January 1947

966 - EVELYN ALICE(6) YOUNG [Effie Young(5) Blecker, Jacob B.(4),
Tracy(3) Wolf, Frederick(2), Daniel(1)]
    Evelyn Alice Young, second child of Simon Luther and Effie Young
(Blecker) Young, was born 24 September 1912. She married 21 August
1933 Ferdinand Weipert. Evelyn died 13 March 1944.
    Child of Ferdinand and Evelyn Alice (Young) Weipert:
+ 1673   i Deanna Weipert, born 8 February 1937

967 - LEILA EMMA(6) WOLF [Sherman E.(5), Franklin(4), Simon(3),
Frederick(2), Daniel(1)]
    Leila Emma Wolf, first child of Sherman E. and Dolly May (Sum-
mers) Wolf, was born 8 April 1897 in Boonsboro, Washington County, MD.
She married 22 February 1921 at Boonsboro William Isaiah Lowry, born
12 October 1896.
    Children of William Isaiah and Leila Emma (Wolf) Lowry:
+ 1674   i Leonard Earl Lowry, born 23 February 1923
+ 1675   ii William Elsworth Lowry, born 28 October, 1924

970 - FRANKLIN ELSWORTH(6) WOLFE [Sherman E.(5), Franklin(4),
Simon(3), Frederick(2), Daniel(1)]
    Franklin Elsworth Wolfe, twin, fourth child of Sherman E. and
Dolly May (Summers) Wolf, was born 5 March 1903 at Boonsboro, Washington County, MD. He married 23 December 1920 at Boonsboro Esther
Viola Smith. Esther died 4 July 1945 and Franklin 27 November 1961.
    Children of Franklin Ellsworth and Esther Viola (Smith) Wolfe:
+ 1676   i Luther E. Wolfe, born 6 May 1921
+ 1677   ii Franklin Eugene Wolfe, born 22 January 1926

972 - IRENE ELIZABETH(6) WOLF [Sherman E.(5), Franklin(4),
Simon(3), Frederick(2), Daniel(1)]
    Irene Elizabeth Wolf, sixth child of Sherman E. and Dolly May
(Summers) Wolf, was born 26 November 1912 at Boonsboro, Washington
County, MD. She married 22 March 1933 in the Evangelical Lutheran
Church, Middletown, Frederick County, MD William Ross Adams Sr, born
14 August 1912 at Middletown, son of James Ross and Nora Pauline (Six)
Adams. William died 11 November 1969 at Frederick, Frederick County
and Irene 29 October 1973 at Middletown. They are buried in the
Evangelical Lutheran Cemetery at Middletown.
    Children of William Ross Sr and Irene Elizabeth (Wolf) Adams:
+ 1678   i William Ross Adams Jr, born 16 July 1934
+ 1679   ii Barbara Adams, born 23 May 1937
+ 1680 iii Frances Adams, born 26 March 1945
+ 1681   iv Deborah Jean Adams, born 28 July 1953

975 - ELLSWORTH FRANKLIN(6) LOHR [Florence Estella(5) Wolf, Franklin(4), Simon(3), Frederick(2), Daniel(1)]
  Ellsworth Franklin Lohr, third child of Chester Tilmore and Florence Estella (Wolf) Lohr, was born 15 July 1911 at Hagerstown, Washington County, MD. He married 27 October 1934 at Hagerstown Dorothy Carmen Staley, born about 1915, daughter of William and Rayetta (Stouffer) Staley. Dorothy died in 1984 and Ellsworth 15 January 1989, both in Hagerstown. They are buried in Rose Hill Cemetery, Hagerstown.
  Children of Ellsworth Franklin and Dorothy Carmen (Staley) Lohr:
+ 1682   i Carolyn Lohr, born 24 June 1934
+ 1683   ii Barbara Ellen Lohr, born 3 March 1936
+ 1684   iii Steven Ellsworth Lohr, born 6 January 1955

977 - DOROTHY I.(6) LOHR [Florence Estella(5) Wolf, Franklin(4), Simon(3), Frederick(2), Daniel(1)]
  Dorothy I. Lohr, fourth child of Chester Tilmore and Florence Estella (Wolf) Lohr, was born 15 January 1914 at Hagerstown, Washington County, MD. She married 11 August 1940 at Boonsboro, Washington County, MD Irvin Long Dinkle, born 3 August 1914, at Hagerstown, son of Ralph L. and Lola (long) Dinkle.
  Child of Irvin Long and Dorothy I. (Lohr) Dinkle:
+ 1685   i Ralph Edward Dinkle, born 1 January 1943

978 - LOUISE LAURAETTA(6) LOHR [Florence Estella(5) Wolf, Franklin(4), Simon(3), Frederick(2), Daniel(1)]
  Louise Lauraetta Lohr, sixth child of Chester Tilmore and Florence Estella (Wolf) Lohr, was born 31 October 1916 at Hagerstown, Washington County, Md. She married 15 December 1934 at Hagerstown Charles Earl Hines, born 4 November 1913 at Sharpsburg, Washington County, son of John and Millie (Spong) Hines. Charles is buried in Mountain View Cemetery, Sharpsburg. Louise died 7 February 1991 and is buried in Rose Hill Cemetery, Hagerstown.
  Child of Charles Earl and Louise Lauraetta (Lohr) Hines:
+ 1686   i Charles Eugene Hines, born 27 December 1936

979 - LESLIE FILMORE(6) EARLEY [Nora Pearl(5) Wolf, Franklin(4), Simon(3), Frederick(2), Daniel(1)]
  Leslie Filmore Earley, first child of Norman Saddler and Nora Pearl (Wolf) Earley, was born 16 February 1910 at Hagerstown, Washington County, MD. He married 12 January 1929 at Hagerstown Madalene Rhodes, born 30 October 1909 at Hagerstown, daughter of Percy and Bertha (Brewer) Rhodes. Leslie died 8 August 1983 and Madalene 27 May 1990, both at Hagerstown. They are buried in Rest Haven Cemetery, Hagerstown.
  Children of Leslie Filmore and Madalene (Rhodes) Earley:
+ 1687   i Harold Herman (Buck) Earley, born 17 March 1930
  1688   ii Beverly Ann Earley, born 26 November 1932 at Hagerstown, Washington County, MD, died 6 June 1940 at Hagerstown

980 - NORMAN SADDLER JR(6) EARLEY [Nora Pearl(5) Wolf, Franklin(4), Simon(3), Frederick(2), Daniel(1)]
  Norman Saddler (Bus) Earley Jr, second child of Norman Saddler Sr and Nora Pearl (Wolf) Earley, was born 19 November 1916 at Hagerstown, Washington County, MD. He married Mildred May Ruffner, born 25 June 1918 at Grimes, Washington County, MD, daughter of Peter and Rebecca (Schweitzer) Ruffner. Norman died 6 October 1970 at Hagerstown and Mildred 19 April 1985 at Waynesboro, Franklin County, PA at the home

of her son. They are buried in Rose Hill Cemetery, Hagerstown.
Child of Norman Saddler Jr and Mildred May (Ruffner) Earley:
+ 1689   i Norman Saddler Earley III, born 19 January 1951

    981 - THEODORE HAROLD(6) EARLEY [Nora Pearl(5) Wolf, Franklin(4),
Simon(3), Frederick(2), Daniel(1)]
    Theodore Harold (Ted) Earley, third child of Norman Saddler Sr
and Nora Pearl (Wolf) Earley, was born 22 January 1919 at Hagerstown,
Washington County, MD. He married 16   June 1940 at Ellicott City,
Howard County, MD Virginia Elmira Strait, born 16 March 1920 at
Mercersburg, Franklin County, PA, daughter of Howard and Elmira (Auld)
Strait. Theodore died 4 March 1987 at Hagerstown and is buried in Rose
Hill Cemetery, Hagerstown.
    Children of Theodore Harold and Virginia Elmira (Strait Earley:
+ 1690   i Terry Lee Earley, born 11 January 1941
  1691   ii Theodore James Earley, born 27 April 1942, died 3 April
             1967, both at Hagerstown, Washington County, MD. Did not
             marry
+ 1692   iii David Allen Earley, born 12 January 1945

    982 - PAULINE MARY(6) WOLFE [Truman Leo(5), Franklin(4),
Simon(3), Frederick(2), Daniel(1)]
    Pauline Mary Wolfe, first child of Truman Leo and Alice Minnie
(Keyfauver) Wolfe, was born 9 October 1908 at Eakle's Mill, Washington
County, MD. She married 15 December 1828 at Hagerstown, Washington
County Edward Mealy Alton, born 28 April 1908 in Washington County,
son of William and Anna (_____) Alton. Edward died 25 July 1967 in
Baltimore, MD and is buried in Cedar Lawn Cemetery, Hagerstown.
    Children of Edward Mealy and Pauline Mary (Wolfe) Alton:
+ 1693   i Robert Randolph Alton, born 24 October 1929
+ 1694   ii Janice Marlene Alton, born 10 September 1934
+ 1695   iii Richard Lee Alton, born 26 July 1938

    985 - DAVID EARL JR(6) WOLF [David Earl Sr(5), Franklin(4),
Simon(3), Frederick(2), Daniel(1)]
    David Earl Wolf Jr, first child of David Earl Sr and Lillian
Irene (English) Wolf, was born 29 December 1916 at Hagerstown, Wash-
ington County, MD. He married 28 September 1940 at Blue Ridge Summit,
Franklin County, PA Gladys Lee Hendricks, born 16 March 1920 in
Washington, DC, daughter of Arthur Joseph and Besse Lee (Yountz)
Hendricks.
    Children of David Earl Jr and Gladys Irene (Hendricks) Wolf:
  1696   i David Arthur Wolf, born 1 March 1946 at Columbia, SC.
             Married 1) 30 August 1969 Nancy Stevens Wheeler and 2)
             Shanon Mae Shildknecht
+ 1697   ii Michael Hendricks Wolf, born 3 April 1952

    988 - MARY JOAN(6) ASHWAY [Lucinda Katheryne(5) Trone, Mary
Jeannette(4) Wolf, Simon(3), Frederick(2), Daniel(1)]
    Mary Joan Ashway, first child of John Luther and Lucinda Kather-
yne (Trone) Ashway, was born 20 July 1928 at Funkstown, Washington
County, MD. She married 17 June 1950 at Lemoyne, Cumberland County, PA
George Adair Wolfe, born 7 September 1924 at Harrisburg, Dauphin
County, PA, son of Herman Adair and Daisy (Swab) Wolfe.
    Children of George Adair and Mary Joan (Ashway) Wolfe:
  1698   i Thomas Ashway Wolfe, born 13 March 1952 at Harrisburg,
             Dauphin County, PA
+ 1699   ii Andrew Adair Wolfe, born 6 March 1954

+ 1700   iii Kristen Trone Wolfe, born 31 January 1957
  1701   iv Jennifer Anne Wolfe, born 13 May 1966 at Harrisburg,
              Dauphin County, PA

     989 - EDWARD TRONE(6) SCHINDEL [Anna Ruth(5) Trone, Mary Jean-
nette(4) Wolf, Simon(3), Frederick(2), Daniel(1)]
     Edward Trone Schindel, first child of Edward Mull and Anna Ruth
(Trone) Schindel, was born 12 July 1915 at Funkstown, Washington
County, MD. He married at Hagerstown, Washington County Phyliss Ker-
foot. Edward died before 29 July 1979 in Hagerstown and Phyliss in
1989.
     Children of Edward Trone and Phyliss (Kerfoot) Schindel:
  1702   i Phillip Edward Schindel
  1703   ii Jacqueline Schindel
  1704   iii Thomas Schindel

     990 - SARAH JEANNETTE(6) SCHINDEL [Anna Ruth(5) Trone, Mary
Jeannette(4) Wolf, Simon(3), Frederick(2), Daniel(1)]
     Sarah Jeannette Schindel, second child of Edward Mull and Anna
Ruth (Trone) Schindel, was born 31 October 1917 at Funkstown, Washing-
ton County, MD. She married 1) 15 June 1940 at Funkstown Dudley Curtis
Hoffman Sr, born 16 December 1914 at Baltimore, MD, son of Carrol Busey
Jr and Grace Irene (Bowersock) Hoffman, 2) 19 July 1971 at Baltimore
Raymond Stevens Hoffman, brother of her first husband, born 7 July
1912 at Baltimore, and 3) 26 November 1983 at Elkridge, MD Charles
Howe Eller, born 5 June 1904 at Bloomington, IN, son of Charles Asbury
and Alice Jennings (Howe) Eller. Dudley died 16 November 1969 at
Orlando, FL and Raymond 30 April 1973 at Baltimore. There were no
children by the second and third marriages.
     Children of Dudley Curtis Sr and Sarah Jeannette (Schindel)
Hoffman:
  1705   i Dudley Curtis Hoffman Jr, born 10 January 1942 at Balti-
              more, MD. Married 27 December 1969 at Torrington, CT
              Patricia Lynn Arnold
  1706   ii Barbara Ann Hoffman, born 30 march 1943 at Baltimore
  1707   iii Allen Schindel Hoffman, born 12 October 1954 at Baltimore

     991 - DORIS ANN(6) SCHINDEL [Anna Ruth(5) Trone, Mary Jean-
nette(4) Wolf, Simon(3), Frederick(2), Daniel(1)]
     Doris Ann Schindel, third child of Edward Mull and Anna Ruth
(Trone) Schindel, was born 10 July 1921 at Funkstown, Washington
County, MD. She married 28 December 1942 at Hagerstown John Adam
Doarnberger, born 17 August 1919 at Hagerstown, Washington County, MD.
She died 20 January 1968 at Hagerstown.
     Children of John Adam and Doris Ann (Schindel) Doarnberger:
+ 1708   i John Michael Doarnberger, born 10 November 1943
+ 1709   ii Suzanne Doarnberger, born 24 March 1946
  1710   iii Gretchen Carrol Doarnberger, born 13 February 1948 at
              Hagerstown, Washington County, MD. Married David Russell
              Starliper, born 5 September at Clearspring, Washington
              County, MD
  1711   iv Nancy Ann Doarnberger, born 17 October 1953 at Hagerstown,
              Washington County, MD.
  1712   v Jeffery Schindel Doarnberger, born 14 February 1958 at
              Hagerstown

     992 - ROBERT NORMAN(6) SCHINDEL [Anna Ruth(5) Trone, Mary Jean-
nette(4) Wolf, Simon(3), Frederick(2), Daniel(1)]

Robert Norman Schindel, third child of Edward Mull and Anna Ruth (Trone) Schindel, was born 10 April 1924 at Funkstown, Washington county, MD. He married 1) 12 March 1949 at Frederick, Frederick County, MD Mary Katherine Anthony, born 4 September 1923, divorced 1966 and she remarried David Hugh Smith, 2) 4 November 1972 at Hagerstown Mrs. Karen Paula Mumma, born 4 November 1926, divorced 1978 and they remarried 2 July 1979 at Hagerstown.

Children of Robert Norman and Mary Katherine (Anthony) Schindel:
1713   i Robert Norman Schindel Jr
1714 ii Natalie Schindel
1715 iii Mary Ann Schindel

993 - ANNA ELIZABETH(6) SAGER [Edith Mentzer(5) Harman, Ann Cora(4) Wolf, Simon(3), Frederick(2), Daniel(1)]
Anna Elizabeth Sager, first child of Elmer Rohrer Sr and Edith Mentzer (Harman) Sager, was born 26 July 1908 at Philadelphia, PA. She married 15 October 1938 at the Mercersburg Academy, Mercersburg, Franklin County, PA William J. Miller, born 20 May 1909. They divorced June 1954.

Children of William J. and Anna Elizabeth (Sager) Miller:
+ 1716   i Susan Elizabeth Miller, twin, born 17 September 1944
  1717 ii Constance Anne Miller, twin, born 17 September 1944, died
          29 January 1989

994 - MARGARET JEANNETTE(6) SAGER [Edith Mentzer(5) Harman, Ann Cora(4) Wolf, Simon(3), Frederick(2), Daniel(1)]
Margaret Jeannette Sager, second child of Elmaer Rohrer Sr and Edith Mentzer (Harman) Sager, was born 26 July 1910 at Philadelphia, PA. She married 1 September 1934 at Frederick, Frederick County, MD Carroll Staley James Sr, born 15 January 1908 at Frederick, son of Edward and Virginia Estelle (Staley) James.

Children of Carroll Staley and Margaret Jeannette (Sager) James:
+ 1718   i Carroll Staley James Jr, born 21 July 1936
+ 1719 ii Martha Harman James, born 28 August 1940

995 - ELMER ROHRER JR(6) SAGER [Edith Mentzer(5) Harman, Ann Cora(4) Wolf, Simon(3), Frederick(2), Daniel(1)]
Elmer Rohrer Sager Jr, third child of Elmer Rohrer Sr and Edith Mentzer (Harman) Sager, was born 1 October 1916 at Philadelphia, PA. He married Joan McKay, born 31 January 1925. Elmer died 28 June 1962 at Washington, DC and is buried at Arlington, VA Cemetery.

Children of Elmer Rohrer Jr and Joan (McKay) Sager:
+ 1720   i Richard Aaron Sager, born 23 March 1947.
  1721 ii Anne Tydings Sager, born 11 June 1951. Married 1984
          Barry Muehe

998 - MORRIS NEVIN(6) MC KINSEY [Blanche Belle(5) Wolfe, Harvey J.(4), Simon(3), Frederick(2), Daniel(1)]
Morris (Jack) Nevin McKinsey, second child of Hiram Maurice and Blanche Belle (Wolfe) McKinsey, was born 22 January 1916 at Smithsburg, Washington County, MD. He married 27 September 1940 at Belair, MD Jane Alberta Kershner, born 27 October 1918 at Hagerstown, Washington County, MD, daughter of Charles Joseph and Jessie (Shadrack) Kershner.

Child of Morris Nevin and Jane Alberta (Kershner) McKinsey:
+ 1722   i Judith Lou McKinsey, born 28 December 1941

999 - JULIA MARGUERITE(6) MC KINSEY [Blanche Belle(5) Wolfe,
Harvey J.(4), Simon(3), Frederick(2), Daniel(1)]
    Julia Marguerite McKinsey, third child of Hiram Maurice and
Blanche Belle (Wolfe) McKinsey, was born 18 February 1918 at Smiths-
burg, Washington County, MD. She married 28 September at Hagerstown,
Washington County William Barkdoll Wiles Sr, born 31 March 1917 at
Greensburg, Washington County, son of John Raymond and Nora (Bark-
doll) Wiles. William died 18 October 1983 at Smithsburg and is buried
in Smithsburg Cemetery.
    Child of William Barkdoll Sr and Julia Marguerite (McKinsey)
Wiles:
+ 1723   i William Barkdoll Wiles Jr, born 19 December 1940

    1000 - JANE(6) MC KINSEY [Blanche Belle(5) Wolfe, Harvey J.(4),
Simon(3), Frederick(2), Daniel(1)]
    Jane McKinsey, fourth child of Hiram Maurice and Blanche Belle
(Wolfe) McKinsey, was born 3 September 1919 at Hagerstown, Washington
County, MD. She married 31 December 1937 at Hagerstown William Woodrow
Smith, born 16 February 1914 at Hopewell, Washington County, son of
Martin L. and Annie E. (Cunningham) Smith.
    Child of William Woodrow and Jane (McKinsey) Smith:
+ 1724   i Carol Louise Smith, born 28 December 1938

    1001 - ROLAND WOLFE(6) MC KINSEY [Blanche Belle(5) Wolfe, Harvey
J.(4), Simon(3), Frederick(2), Daniel(1)]
    Roland Wolfe McKinsey, fifth child of Hiram Maurice and Blanche
Belle (Wolfe) McKinsey, was born 28 April 1921 at Leitersburg, Washington County, MD. He married 27 September 1947 at Chewsville, Washington County Sigrid Rebecca Rinehart, born 28 November 1927 at
Chewsville, daughter of Bruce Theron and Kathryn Rebecca (Harshman)
Rinehart.
    Children of Roland Wolfe and Sigrid Rebecca (Rinehart) McKinsey:
+ 1725   i Jody Lynn McKinsey, born 1 August 1951
  1726   ii Roland Rinehart McKinsey, born 21 February 1954. Married
            22 September 1989 at Hagerstown, Washington County, MD
            Nancy (_____) Bachtell
  1727 iii Gary Lee McKinsey, born 1 December 1961

    1004 - HELEN ELIZABETH(6) RINEHART [Fannie Elizabeth(5) Wolfe,
Harvey J.(4), Simon(3), Frederick(2), Daniel(1)]
    Helen Elizabeth Rinehart, first child of Roy Brown and Fannie
Elizabeth (Wolfe) Rinehart, was born 20 March 1914 at Leitersburg,
Washington County, MD. She married 1) 21 September 1935 at Hagerstown,
Washington County Lester Lee Baker, born 1 January 1904 in Washington
County, son of John and Rosie (_____) Baker. They divorced and she
married 2) 1946 Wilbur Glen Harnish, born 4 December 1906 in Pennsyl-
vania. Wilbur died 28 April 1956 and Lester 1985, both Hagerstown.
Both are buried in Rest Haven Cemetery, Hagerstown.
    Child of Lester Lee and Helen Elizabeth (Rinehart) Baker:
+ 1728   i Nancy Lee Baker, born 24 February 1939
    Children of Wilbur Glen and Helen Elizabeth (Rinehart) (Baker)
Harnish:
+ 1729   i Gary Lynn Harnish, born 19 September 1947
+ 1730   ii Debra Dee Harnish, born 12 July 1951

    1005 - THELMA MARIE(6) RINEHART [Fannie Elizabeth(5) Wolfe,
Harvey J.(4), Simon(3), Frederick(2), Daniel(1)]
    Thelma Marie Rinehart, second child of Roy Brown and Fannie

Elizabeth (Wolfe) Rinehart, was born 21 December 1915 at Leitersburg, Washington County, MD. She married 29 February 1936 near Huyetts, Washington County Hampton Erskin Grant, born 23 August 1915 at Staunton, Augusta County, VA, son of William and Esta (Ellyard) Grant. Thelma died 16 January 1960 at Hagerstown, Washington County and is buried in Rest Haven Cemetery, Hagerstown.

Children of Hampton Erskin and Thelma Marie (Rinehart) Grant:
+ 1731   i James Lee Grant, born 29 December 1936
+ 1732   ii Barbara Ann Grant, born 1 June 1939

1006 - ROBERT ROY(6) RINEHART [Fannie Elizabeth(5) Wolfe, Harvey J.(4), Simon(3), Frederick(2), Daniel(1)]

Robert Roy Rinehart, third child of Roy Brown and Fannie Elizabeth (Wolfe) Rinehart, was born 26 February 1918 at Leitersburg, Washington County, MD. He married 1938 at Hagerstown, Washington County Jane Naomi Springer, born 6 December 1919 in Washington County, daughter of William Henry and Bessie Ellen (Jones) Springer. Robert died 9 September 1976 at State Line, Franklin County, PA and is buried in Rose Hill Cemetery, Hagerstown.

Children of Robert Roy and Jane Naomi (Springer) Rinehart:
+ 1733   i Robert Wayne Rinehart, born 10 November 1938
+ 1734   ii Jo Ellen Rinehart, born 22 March 1948

1008 - EVELYN MAE(6) RINEHART [Fannie Elizabeth(5) Wolfe, Harvey J.(4), Simon(3), Frederick(2), Daniel(1)]

Evelyn Mae Rinehart, fifth child of Roy Brown and Fannie Elizabeth (Wolfe) Rinehart, was born 28 December 1925 at Leitersburg, Washington County, MD. She married Arthur Maurice Mohler, born 25 July 1914 at Lebanon, Lebanon County, PA, son of Howard and Elva (Reich) Mohler. Arthur died 6 September 1974 at St Petersburg, Pinelas County, FL and is buried at Sanford, Volusi County, FL.

Children of Arthur Maurice and Evelyn Mae (Rinehart) Mohler:
  1735   i Keith Duane Mohler, born 25 October 1951 at Lebanon,
             Lebanon County, PA. Married 16 February 1983 at Chatta-
             nooga, Marion County, TN Elena Sue Davenport, born 24 July
             1953 at McMinnville, Warren County, TN
  1736   ii Kevin Lynn Mohler, born 21 June 1954 at Lebanon, Lebanon
             County, PA, died 14 September 1958 at Sanford, Volusi
             County, FL. Buried at Sanford

1009 - RAYMOND WOLFE(6) RINEHART [Fannie Elizabeth(5) Wolfe, Harvey J.(4), Simon(3), Frederick(2), Daniel(1)]

Raymond Wolfe Rinehart, sixth child of Roy Brown and Fannie Elizabeth (Wolfe) Rinehart, was born 14 May 1927 at Leitersburg, Washington County, MD. He married 27 August 1948 at Hagerstown, Washington County Betty Jane Shoemaker, born 19 October 1927 at Hagerstown, daughter of Roy and Margerie Ellen (Slifer) Shoemaker.

Child of Roy Wolfe and Margerie Betty Jane (Shoemaker) Rinehart:
+ 1737   i Christine Marilyn Rinehart, born 12 January 1956

1011 - THERON EDWIN(6) BENCHOFF [Edith Marie(5) Wolfe, Harvey J.(4), Simon(3), Frederick(2), Daniel(1)]

Theron Edwin Benchoff, second child of James Carroll and Edith Marie (Wolfe) Benchoff, was born 9 January 1926 at Leitersburg, Washington County, MD. He married 28 May 1949 at Hagerstown, Washington County Dorothy Louise Smith, born 3 February 1929 at Highfield, Washington County, daughter of Robert Funkhouser and Reita Catherine (Gonder) Smith.

Child of Theron Edwin and Dorothy Louise (Smith) Benchoff:
1738   i Phillip Edwin Benchoff, born 25 April 1963 at Hagerstown,
           Washington County, MD

1013 - JOANNE MARIE(6) WOLFE [Charles Eugene(5), Harvey J.(4),
Simon(3), Frederick(2), Daniel(1)]
      Joanne Marie Wolfe, only child of Charles Eugene and Bertha Eliza-
beth (Bailey) Wolfe, was born 1 January 1939 in Washington County, MD.
She married 14 February 1960 at Hagerstown, Washington County Robert Dean
Rodgers Sr, born 27 April 1938 at Waynesboro, Franklin County, PA, son
of Ordean and Evelyn (Miller) Rodgers.
      Children of Robert Dean Sr and Joanne Marie (Wolfe) Rodgers:
1739   i Robert Dean Rodgers Jr, born 9 December 1960 in Washington
            County, MD. Married 4 June 1990 in Washington County
            Kimberly Lynn Doyle, born 29 June 1965 in Maryland
+ 1740   ii Steven Keith Rodgers, born 7 January 1962
1741   iii James Allen Rodgers, born 3 August 1964 in Washington
            County, MD

1014 - MAURINE ELLA(6) HUFFINGTON [Ada Blanche(5) WOLF, Carlton
Emmert(4), Jacob(3), Frederick(2), Daniel(1)]
      Maurine Ella Huffington, first child of Orion Frank and Ada
Blanche (Wolf) Huffington, was born 28 August 1909 at Normal, McLean
County, IL. She married 12 July 1941 at Rockford, Winnebago County, IL
Percy Wayne Staublin, born 29 March 1897 at La Crosse, La Crosse
County, WI, son of Abraham Lincoln and Myra Effie (Willey) Staublin.
This was his second marriage. Percy died 27 March 1989 at Rockford.
      Children of the first marriage of Percy Wayne Staublin, born in
Winnebago County, IL:
            i Jeanne Margaret Staublin, born 1 February 1926. Married 13
               February 1960 John Otto Deringer
           ii Gerald David Staublin, born 31 August 1929. Married 6
               October 1951 Arla Rose Rice

1015 - CARLTON DALE(6) HUFFINGTON [Ada Blanche(5) Wolf, Carlton
Emmert(4), Jacob(3), Frederick(2), Daniel(1)]
      Carlton Dale Huffington, second child of Orion Frank and Ada
Blanche (Wolf) Huffington, was born 19 January 1911 at Normal, McLean
County, IL. He married 25 December 1937 at Rockford, Winnebago County,
IL Lona Mildred Howe, born 3 July 1912, daughter of Franklin Oldt and
Neva Cleo (Coffman) Howe. Carlton died 13 September 1977 at Rockford
and is buried in Wildwood Cemetery at Rockford. He attended the University of Cincinnati and was an agent for the Connecticut Mutual Life
Insurance Company for 43 Years. He attended the Unitarian Church.
      Children of Carlton Dale and Lona Mildred (Howe) Huffington, all
born in Rockford, Winnebago County, IL:
+ 1742   i Dennis Alan Huffington, born 22 August 1941
+ 1743   ii Robert Dale Huffington, born 13 March 1944
+ 1744   iii Carol Diane Huffington, born 20 June 1946
+ 1745   iv Richard William Huffington, born 30 June 1949
+ 1746   v James Franklin Huffington, born 17 June 1951
+ 1747   vi Joanne Lee Huffington, born 14 December 1953
+ 1748   vii Jeffrey Mead Huffington, born 14 December 1953

1017 - HARRY LUTHER JR(6) HIGHBARGER [Harry Luther Sr(5), Cathe-
rine(4) Wolf, Jacob(2), Frederick(2), Daniel(1)]
      Harry Luther Highbarger Jr, first child of Harry Luther Sr and
Ada May (Flounders) Highbarger, was born 15 March 1907 at Darby,

161

Delaware County, PA. He married June A. Kemp, born about 1918 in
Hagerstown, Washington County, MD , daughter of Edward C. and Catherine L. (Hartle) Kemp. Harry was employed by Pangborn Corporation for
27 years and was a World War II veteran. June died 17 February 1986
and Harry 16 October 1990, both in Hagerstown. They are buried in the
Boonsboro Cemetery, Washington County.
    Children of Harry Luther Jr and June A. (Kemp) Highbarger:
  1749   i David E. Highbarger, adopted, born 19 May 1945 at Phila-
        delphia, PA
  1750   ii Vincent Highbarger, born 1946, died 1973, buried in
        Boonsboro Cemetery, Washington County, MD

    1018 - PAUL GEORGE W.(6) HIGHBARGER [Harry Luther Sr(5), Cathe-
rine(4) Wolf, Jacob(3), Frederick(2), Daniel(1)]
    Paul George W. Highbarger, second child of Harry Luther Sr and
Ada May (Flounders) Highbarger, was born 5 April 1917 at Philadelphia,
PA. He married 10 January 1942 in Washington County, MD Ruth Elizabeth
Fleet, born 29 January 1922 at Hagerstown, Washington County, daughter
of Frank Rosser and Bessie Nelson (Cooper) Fleet. Paul was a security
guard for the Pangborn Corporation and a veteran of World War II. He
died 13 June 1974 at the Veterans Administration Medical Center,
Martinsburg, Berkely County, WV and is buried in Cedar Lawn Cemetery,
Hagerstown.
    Child of Paul George W. and Ruth Elizabeth (Fleet) Highbarger:
+ 1751   i Susan Fleet Highbarger, born 11 August 1946

    1019 - RUTH ANNE(6) HEBSCHER [Maude Mae(5) Wolf, John Albaugh(4),
Jacob(3), Frederick(2), Daniel(1)]
    Ruth Anne Hebscher, daughter of William Emil and Maude Mae (Wolf)
Hebscher, was born 5 October 1924 at Philadelphia, PA. She married 18
June 1945 at Kingman, AZ Victor Norman Robinson, born 10 July 1924 at
Bakersfield, Kern County, CA. Victor died 13 June 1974 and Ruth 23
April 1975, both at Bakersfield. They were cremated and their ashes
distributed off the coast of California.
    Children of Victor Norman and Ruth Anne (Hebscher) Robinson:
+ 1752   i William Victor Robinson, born 13 April 1947
+ 1753   ii John Alec Robinson Sr, born 10 July 1949
+ 1754 iii Koyya Ann Robinson, born 13 February 1954
  1755   iv Charles Victor Robinson, born at Bakersfield, Kern County,
        CA 13 August 1958

    1021 - JOHN FRANKLIN BERNARD(6) WOLF [Harry Edwin(5), John
Albaugh(4), Jacob(3), Frederick(2), Daniel(1)]
    John Franklin Bernard Wolf, second child of Harry Edwin and Helen
Lucile (Yeisly) Wolf, was born 12 February 1918 at Hagerstown, Washington County, MD. He married 1936 at Hagerstown Eva Glenview Ebersole, born 12 September 1917, daughter of Franklin Jacob and Eva
Gertrude (Snyder) Ebersole. John (Bernard) was an insurance agent. He
died June 1968 at Hagerstown and is buried in Rest Haven Cemetery,
Hagerstown.
    Child of John Franklin Bernard and Eva Glenview (Ebersole) Wolf:
+ 1756   i Joseph Wayne Wolf, born 8 November 1937

    1022 - CHARLES COULSON(6) WOLF [Charles Welty(5), John
Albaugh(4), Jacob(3), Frederick(2), Daniel(1)]
    Charles Coulson Wolf, first child of Charles Welty and Mary
Rachel (Reece) Wolf, was born 29 November 1918 at Hagerstown, Washing-
ton County, MD. He married 8 February 1941 at Hagerstown Julia Corne-

lia Foreman, born 23 April 1919 at Hagerstown, daughter of Ambrose Loy and Ann Cyril (Willson) Foreman. Charles graduated in 1939 from the University of Michigan with a Bachelor of Science degree in Electrical Engineering. Following graduation he worked for The Potomac Edison Company for over 42 years retiring 1 August 1982 as Director Engineering and Construction. He has been a lifelong member of the Presbyterian Church of Hagerstown, having served as Deacon, Trustee and Elder. His wife Julia has been a lifelong member of the Roman Catholic Church, attending St. Mary's and St. Ann's churches in Hagerstown.

    Children of Charles Coulson and Julia Cornelia (Foreman) Wolf:

+ 1757   i Barbara Louise Wolf, born 11 January 1943
+ 1758   ii Mary Julia Wolf, born 18 March 1946

    1023 - BETTY ANN REECE(6) WOLF [Charles Welty(5), John Albaugh(4), Jacob(3), Frederick(2), Daniel(1)]

    Betty Ann Reece Wolf, second child of Charles Welty and Mary Rachel (Reece) Wolf, was born 22 May 1924 at Hagerstown, Washington County, MD. She married 14 March 1943 at Hagerstown Reuel Augustine Wiebel Jr, born 10 May 1920 in Virginia, son of Reuel Augustne Sr and _____ (_____) Wiebel. They divorced.

    Children of Reuel Augustine Jr and Betty Ann Reece (Wolf) Wiebel:

+ 1759   i Reuel Augustine Wiebel III, adopted, born 19 December 1957
  1760   ii Mary Rebecca Wiebel, adopted, born 27 April 1961. Married
         16 May 1987 at Charlottesville, VA Douglas James Yenson.
         They divorced

    1024 - DONALD WOLF(6) RHOADS [Mary Ellen(5) Wolf, John Albaugh(4), Jacob(3), Frederick(2), Daniel(1)]

    Donald Wolf Rhoads, son of Jacob Krauss and Mary Ellen (Wolf) Rhoads, was born 26 June 1923 at West Grove, Chester County, PA. He married 1) 6 October 1949 Jane Marie Dambach, born 25 September 1920 at Buffalo, NY, died 6 April 1981. Donald remarried 15 April 1982 Evelyn Mae McElmoyle, born 18 September 1923, her third marriage. He was an Aeronautical Engineering graduate of the University of Michigan, retiring from Scott Aviation in 1988.

    Children of Donald Wolf and Jane Marie (Dambach) Rhoads:

  1761   i Jeffrey Scott Rhoads, born 12 September 1953 at Buffalo,
         NY
+ 1762   ii Kim Elizabeth Rhoads, born 9 June 1956
    Stepchildren of Donald Wolf Rhoads:
        i Robert Charles Weitzel, born 17 July 1945
      ii Melody Faye WEitzel, born 1 September 1946
    iii Mark William Thornley, born 27 January 1962

    1035 - CARRIE(6) ILER [John S.(5), Mariah(4) Paulus, Simeon(3), Christina(2) Wolf, Daniel(1)]

    Carrie Iler, second child of John S. and Marie (Lavering) Iler, was born 8 March 1891 in Indiana. She married _____ Wilkerson. She died 3 January 1973 and is buried in Hively Church Cemetery, near Columbia City, IN.

    Children of _____ and Carrie (Iler) Wilkerson:

  1763   i John Wilkerson, died 1976. Married Mildred Bailer
  1764   ii Kenneth Wilkerson. Married Virginia _____
  1765 iii Raymond Wilkerson

    1039 - MARGARET(6) ILER [Ezra G. A.(5), Mariah(4) Paulus, Simeon(3), Christina(2) Wolf, Daniel(1)]

    Margaret Iler, third child of Ezra G. A. and Mary (Simmons) Iler,

was born 10 February 1905 in Indiana. She married Ralph Byrum Day, born 8 September 1901.
    Child of Ralph Byrum and Margaret (Iler) Day:
1766   i Terrence Cline Day, born 10 October 1937. Married Ann
            Nagel, born 12 November 1941, children Joshua Andrew and
            Joel Thomas Day

    1040 - FLORENCE(6) SELBY [Alice E.(5) Iler, Mariah(4) Paulus,
Simeon(3), Christina(2) Wolf, Daniel(1)]
    Florence Selby, first child of Jacob and Alice E. (Iler) Selby,
was born2 October 1897. She married Lee Miller, born 14 November 1895
in Ohio. Lee died 28 September 1971 and Florence 2 October 1987 at
Brookville, OH.
    Child of Lee and Florence (Selby) Miller:
1767   i Kathryn Miller, born 6 June 1918. Married Frank Miller,
            born 16 February 1916 in Maryland, children Stanley and
            Kathy Miller

    1043 - HARLAN E.(6) PRESSLER [Emaline(5) Paulus, Daniel(4),
Simeon(3), Christina(3) Wolf, Daniel(1)]
    Harlan E. Pressler, first child of Emerson and Emaline (Paulus)
Pressler, was born 2 April 1895 in Indiana. He married 9 June 1917
Pearl J. Ott, born 7 November 1892 In Indiana. She died 8 October 1963
in Indiana and is buried in Christ Chapel Cemetery, Noble County, IN.
    Children of Harlan E. and Pearl J. (Ott) Pressler, both born in
Indiana:
1768   i J. D. Pressler, born 3 August 1917. Married Mildred Quick,
            born 14 September 1915 in Illinois, children Ronald Jay
            and John Dee Pressler
1769   ii Betty Pressler, born 30 October 1922. Married Robert
            Hageman

    1044 - RALPH A. SR(6) PRESSLER [Emaline(5) Paulus, Daniel(4),
Simeon(3), Christina(2) Wolf, Daniel(1)]
    Ralph A. Pressler Sr, second child of Emerson and Emaline (Paulus) Pressler, was born 20 October 1896. He married 3 April 1920
Ursula Ott, born 16 June 1895. Ursula died 4 January 1959 and Ralph 5
September 1979.
    Children of Ralph Sr and Ursula (Ott) Pressler:
•1770   i Virginia R. Pressler, born 30 July 1930 in Indiana.
            Married Frederick L. Brown, born 13 January 1929 in
            Indiana, children Frederick L. Jr and Steven A. Brown
1771   ii Ralph A. Pressler Jr

    1045 - WILDA(6) PRESSLER [Emaline(5) Paulus, Daniel(4),
Simeon(3), Christina(2) Wolf, Daniel(1)]
    Wilda Pressler, third child of Emerson and Emaline (Paulus)
Pressler, was born in 1898. She married Gary Skinner. Wilda died in
1941 and Gary in 1955.
    Children of Gary and Wilda (Pressler) Skinner:
1772   i Eugene Skinner
1773   ii Bernard Skinner

    1046 - ALICE I.(6) FRUCHEY [Laura Ann(5) Paulus, Daniel(4),
Simeon(3), Christina(2) Wolf, Daniel(1)]
    Alice I. Fruchey, first child of Harvey S. and Laura Ann (Paulus)
Fruchey, was born 30 March 1895 in Indiana. She married Charles Lesco
Wolfe, born 16 June 1893. Charles died 11 February 1960 in Indiana. He

and Alice are buried in Thorn Cemetery, Noble County, IN.
    Children of Charles Lesco and Alice I. (Fruchey) Wolfe:
1774   i Dorthea S. Wolfe, born 5 August 1915
1775   ii Rowena Annabell Wolfe, born 15 July 1917 in Indiana.
          Married Robert Lewis Shoda, born 1912, died 1981. They are
          buried in Thorn Cemetery, Noble County, IN
1776 iii William Harvey Wolfe, born 16 June 1919 in Indiana.
          Married 3) Rozella Ann Scheiber
1777   iv Paul Lesco Wolfe, born 12 May 1921 in Indiana. Married
          Betty _____, three children
1778   v Jay Wolfe, born 28 July 1923 in Indiana, died 1959 and is
          buried in Thorn Cemetery, Noble County, IN. Married Nellie
          C. _____ , born 1929, died 1971 in Indiana
1779   vi Evelyn Wolfe, born 6 May 1925, died 1941, both in Indiana,
          buried in Thorn Cemetery, Noble County, IN
1780 vii Elizabeth Catherine Wolfe, born 9 March 1927 in Indiana.
          Married Carl Sheets, born 23 May 1919, children Roger
          Lesco, Rodney C. and Karla Kristine Sheets
1781 viii Violet E. Wolfe, born 17 August 1929, died 1942, both in
          Indiana, buried in Thorn Cemetery, Noble County, IN
1782   ix Phyllis Wolfe, born 9 September 1935 in Indiana. Married
          Walter D. Wilson
1783   x Phillip Wolfe, born 9 September 1935, died 1936, both in
          Indiana, buried in Thorn Cemetery, Noble County, IN

    1047 - ERMA(6) FRUCHEY [Laura Ann(5) Paulus, Daniel(4),
Simeon(3), Christina(2) Wolf, Daniel(1)]
    Erma Fruchey, second child of Harvey S. and Laura Ann (Paulus)
Fruchey, was born 11 April 1898 in Indiana. She married 19 June 1920
Stanley Vanitor, born in Indiana. Stanley died 16 October 1951. They
are buried in North Webster Cemetery, Kosciusko County, IN.
    Children of Stanley and Erma (Fruchey) Vanitor:
1784   i Thomas Vanitor, born 7 July 1922, died 28 July 1922 in
          Indiana
1785   ii Ray G. Vanitor, born 6 June 1924 in Indiana. Married
          Eleanor Wallace, children Michael Ray, Jane and Vickie
1786 iii Glen Allen Vanitor, born 19 September 1926. Married
          Delores Dishmun, children Janet, Nancy, Gary, Denise, Mary
          Alice, Glenda Rae, Jill and Gayle
1787   iv Mary Alice Vanitor, born 19 September 1926

    1049 - DAN(6) FRUCHEY [Laura Ann(5) Paulus, Daniel(4), Simeon(3),
Christina(2) Wolf, Daniel(1)]
    Dan Fruchey, fourth child of Harvey S. and Laura Ann (Paulus)
Fruchey, was born 2 October 1901 in Indiana. He married Helen I.
Cooperrider, born 26 September 1910. Helen died 5 October 1959 and Dan
October 1988. They are buried in Stough Cemetery, Whitley County, IN.
    Child of Dan and Helen I. (Cooperrider) Fruchey:
1788   i Kathleen E. Fruchey, born 29 April 1928 in Indiana.
          Married Owen F. Kistler, born 22 April 1924 in Indiana,
          children Michael Aaron and Marsha Kay

    1050 - BENTON S.(6) FRUCHEY [Laura Ann(5) Paulus, Daniel(4),
Simeon(3), Christina(2) Wolf, Daniel(1)]
    Benton S. Fruchey, fifth child of Harvey S. and Laura Ann (Pau-
lus) Fruchey, was born 3 July 1904 in Indiana. He married 29 December
1928 Lovinna Addie Scripter, born 1905 in Indiana. Benton died 5 June
1974.

Children of Benton S. and Lovinna Addie (Scripter) Fruchey, all
born in Indiana:
1789   i Jean Ann Fruchey, born 11 May 1930. Married 1 January 1949
            Billie Jim Brown, born December 1924, children Everett
            Benton, Lucinda Ray, Ladona May, and Jeannette Kay
1790   ii Arlene June Fruchey, born 28 May 1931. Married Richard
            Keith Briggs, children Robert K., Richard Eugene and
            Stephen Brian
1791   iii Mary Jane Fruchey, born 24 June 1933, died 25 June 1933,
            buried in Merriam Cemetery, Columbia City, IN
1792   iv Joseph S. Fruchey. Married 10 September 1955 Marian Crane,
            born 21 December 1936, children Gay Joseph, David Brian
            and Dawn Renee
1793   v Joan Elaine Fruchey, born 17 April 1936. Married 1)
            Charles Gibson, they divirced 1961, child Lois Ann
1794   vi Alma Janet Fruchey, born and died 5 December 1937, buried
            in Christian Chapel Cemetery, Merriam, IN

     1051 - ITHA(6) FRUCHEY [Laura Ann(5) Paulus, Daniel(4),
Simeon(3), Christina(2) Wolf, Daniel(1)]
     Itha Fruchey, sixth child of Harvey S. and Laura Ann (Paulus)
Fruchey, married Ralph McKown, born 14 January 1908 in Indiana.
     Children of Ralph and Itha (Fruchey) McKown, all born in Indiana:
1795   i Jack McKown, born 2 October 1931, died 20 May 1934
1796   ii Larry L. McKown, born 25 July 1935
1797   iii Richard Dale McKown, born 2 April 1947

     1053 - EARL KENNETH(6) GRABLE [Finette(5) Paulus, Daniel(4),
Simeon(3), Christina(2) Wolf, Daniel(1)]
     Earl Kenneth Grable, first child of Francis Marion and Finette
(Nettie) (Paulus) Grable, was born 29 September 1905 in Indiana, died
3 November 1983. He married Irene Scripter. They lived in Dimondale,
MI where he owned a machine shop.
     Children of Earl Kenneth and Irene (Scripter) Grable:
1798   i Earl Edgar Grable, born 21 July 1930, died 25 February
            1976. Married Joanne _____, child Diana Kathleen
1799   ii Joyce M. Grable, born 4 May 1930. Married 6 March 1953
            Earl Johnson, two children.
1800   iii David Grable, born 9 October 1931
1801   iv Phillip Brian Grable, born 17 April 193_
1802   v Val Dean Grable
1803   vi Leslie Grable

     1054 - ERNEST KEITH(6) GRABLE [Finette(5) Paulus, Daniel(4),
Simeon(3), Christina(2) Wolf, Daniel(1)]
     Ernest Keith Grable, second child of Francis Marion and Finette
(Nettie) (Paulus) Grable, was born 29 September 1905 in Indiana. He
married 17 June 1933 Retha May Isenbarger, born 31 October 1909 in
Indiana, daughter of John and Rose (Johnson) Isenbarger.
     Children of Ernest Keith and Retha May (Isenbarger) Grable, born
in Indiana:
1804   i Margie Joann Grable, born 8 April 1934 in Indiana. Married
            1) 1 July 1955 James R. Davis, born 2 January 1936,
            children Leilani Lynette and Kayla Denise. They divorced
            and she married 2) 14 May 1978 Dick Harry Elliott, born 26
            February 1932
1805   ii Ronald Leon Grable, born 22 February 1942. Married Mary
            Nanette Alley, born 7 September 1946, children Brian

Douglas, Amy Melissa, Edward J. and Brent D.

1055 - ESTHER VIRGINIA(6) GRABLE [Finette(5) Paulus, Daniel(4),
Simeon(3), Christina(2) Wolf, Daniel(1)]
   Esther Virginia Grable, third child of Francis Marion and Finette
(Nettie) (Paulus) Grable, was born 8 February 1907 in Indiana. She
married 18 March 1930 Wilbur M. Lane, born 21 March 1908.
   Children of Wilbur M. and Esther Virginia (Grable) Lane:
1806   i Neil Arden Lane, born 3 August 1931
1807   ii Max Leroy Lane, born 22 February 1942. Married, wife's
           name not known, children Claudia, Lawrence and Jennie

1056 - DAVID ALLEN(6) GRABLE [Finette(5) Paulus, Daniel(4),
Simeon(3), Christina(2) Wolf, Daniel(1)]
   David Allen Grable, fourth child of Francis Marion and Finette
(Nettie) (Paulus) Grable, was born 17 september 1911 in Indiana. He
married 24 June 1934 Pauline Ellen Lein, born 17 October 1918. David
died 29 April 1985 and Pauline September 1985. They are buried in
Covington Gardens Cemetery, Ft. Wayne, IN.
   Children of David Allen and Pauline Ellen (Lein) Grable:
1808   i Julia Ann Grable, born 7 October 1935. Married Charles
           William Schade, children Janet Lee, Karen Ellen and
           Stephen Charles
1809   ii Sharon Sue Grable, born 13 September 1940 in Indiana.
           Married Richard Lee Bauman, born 8 November 1935 in Ohio,
           children James Andrew and Renata Kay

1057 - ROBERT G.(6) GRABLE [Finette(5) Paulus, Daniel(4),
Simeon(3), Christina(2) Wolf, Daniel(1)]
   Robert G. Grable, fifth child of Francis Marion and Finette
(Nettie) (Paulus) Grable, was born 24 March 1920 in Indiana. He
married 1) in England, while he was in the service, Jean Milhient
Webb, born and died in England, and 2) Shirley Martha Sharp, born 22
February 1918.
   Child of Robert G. and Jean Milhient (Webb) Grable:
1810   i Roderick Gene Grable, born in England while his father was
           in the service. His mother died in England and he remained
           in England and was raised by his grandparents

1061 - ARTHUR CLAYTON(6) PAULUS [James Julian(5), Daniel(4),
Simeon(3), Christina(2) Wolf, Daniel(1)]
   Arthur Clayton Paulus was the first child of James Julian and ____
(Snell) Paulus. He married 6 December 1924 Hazel Johnson. He died 1
March 1961 in Indiana.
   Children of Arthur Clayton and Hazel (Johnson) Paulus, born in
Indiana:
1811   i Helen May Paulus, born 2 February 1926. Married 1) Henry
           D. Wolf, died 4 October 1968 in Indiana, child Euretta.
           She married 2) Herbert Prior, no children
1812   ii Mary Lou Paulus, born 25 September 1927. Married 17 May
           1947 Ellis Dean Paight, born 17 May 1924, children Linda
           Darlene, Delores Irene, Richard Dean, Beverly Louise
           and Leroy Gene
1813   iii Robert Clayton Paulus Sr, born 25 October 1929. Married 3
           June 1949 Ardith R. Boyd, born 26 March 1931, children
           Robert Clayton Jr, Jack A., Terry L., Mark R., Peggy D.
           and Jayne
1814   iv Donald Arthur Paulus, born 24 January 1931, died 5 July

```
                1931
1815     v Betty Jane Paulus, born 8 March 1940, died 5 April 1948
```

1065 - LAWRENCE BERNARR SR(6) PAULUS [Samuel Delbert(5), Daniel(4), Simeon(3), Christina(2) Wolf, Daniel(1)]

Lawrence Bernarr Paulus Sr, first child of Samuel Delbert and Lola Augusta (Wilkerson) Paulus, was born 30 October 1912 in Sparta Township, Noble County, IN. He was named after Bernarr McFadden, the physical culturist. He married 2 June 1946 Mary J. Herron, born 20 August 1919. He was a veteran of WWII, flying B-24 bombers in the Pacific Campaign.

Children of Lawrence Bernarr Sr and Mary J. (Herron) Paulus, born in Indiana:

1816   i Lawrence Bernarr Paulus Jr, born 3 August 1947. Married 23 January 1971 Charlotte C. Kelsey, born 7 April 1951, children William Daniel and Nicholas Andrew

1817   ii Garrie Jay Paulus, born 22 September 1948. Married Janice Eglof, born 24 July 1951, children Jenny K., Taresa and Cynthia

1818   iii Rose Etta Paulus, born 24 July 1952. Married 1) Frank Freshour, born 3 April 1950. Child Carmen Danielle. They divorced and she married 2) Jay H. Parker, born 4 July 1948, child Crystal Lynn

1819   iv Delbert Floyd Paulus, born 7 January 1954. Married Linda Speece, born 9 October 1947, child Jeffery Martin

1066 - HELEN CHRISTENA(6) PAULUS [Samuel Delbert(5), Daniel(4), Simeon(3), Christina(2) Wolf, Daniel(1)]

Helen Christena Paulus, second child of Samuel Delbert and Lola Augusta (Wilkerson) Paulus, was born 15 May 1914 in Sparta Township, Noble County, IN. She married 15 June 1936 Charles Emil Hickman, born 28 August 1909.

Children of Charles Emil and Helen Christena (Paulus) Hickman:

1820   i Lola Ann Hickman, born 5 October 1937. Married Charles Martin Kerlin, child Christopher Kerlin

1821   ii Mary Lou Hickman, born 29 September 1940. Married 6 May 1959 John C. Padgett, born 16 February 1942, children Mary Christena, Athena Louise and Shawn Renee

1822   iii Carolyn Sue Hickman, born 28 April 1942. Married George Victor Bobilya, born 26 September 1940, child Douglas Kent

1823   iv Lois June Hickman, born 6 June 1946

1067 - THELMA ESTHER(6) PAULUS [Samuel Delbert(5), Daniel(4), Simeon(3), Christina(2) Wolf, Daniel(1)]

Thelma Esther Paulus, third child of Samuel Delbert and Lola Augusta (Wilkerson) Paulus, was born 16 January 1916 in Sparta Township, Noble County, IN. She married 15 August 1935 Harry Alton Reed, born 6 February 1913.

Children of Harry Alton and Thelma Esther (Paulus) Reed:

1824   i Richard Allen Reed, born 6 December 1937. Married 1) 8 November 1957 Mary Ellen Earnhart, born 2 February 1939, children Amanda Kay, Richard Leon and Tamarah Ann and 2) 29 February 1972 Nelletta White, born 19 April 1937, no children

1825   ii Roger Lee Reed, born 27 July 1940. Married 30 July 1966 Deanna Shull, born 14 February 1943, children Hayden Yurie and Kiley Lane

1826   iii Thomas Raymond Reed, born 5 April 1944. Married 8 May 1966

Donna Wilkinson, born 5 January 1946, children Thomas R. II
and Yvonne Irene
1827   iv Paula Jane Reed, born 27 February 1946. Married 15 May
1967 Jay Dean Ridings, born 15 May 1944, child Jeremy Dean
1828   v Rita Mary Reed, born 6 March 1951

1068 - JAY WOODROW(6) PAULUS [Samuel Delbert(5), Daniel(4),
Simeon(3), Christina(2) Wolf, Daniel(1)]
Jay Woodrow Paulus, fourth child of Samuel Delbert and Lola
Augusta (Wilkerson) Paulus, was born 7 October 1917. He married 14
June 1941 Florence Irene Wooten, born 19 November 1921.
Children of Jay Woodrow and Florence Irene (Wooten) Paulus:
1829   i Barbara Louise Paulus, born 21 July 1942. Married 21 June
1964 Wilbur Scott Grosse, born 21 January 1942, children
Linda Louise and Lisa Anne
1830   ii Dale Bernarr Paulus, born 17 June 1945. Married 23 Decem-
ber 1966 Georgia Ann Jackson, born 15 June 1945, children
Stephen Keith and Tracy Yvonne
1831 iii Janice Leah Paulus, born 14 March 1950. Married 2 August
Thomas R. Robson, born 2 January 1947

1069 - LEON VIRGIL(6) PAULUS [Samuel Delbert(5), Daniel(4),
Simeon(3), Christina(2) Wolf, Daniel(1)]
Leon Virgil Paulus, fifth child of Samuel Delbert and Lola
Augusta (Wilkerson) Paulus, was born 14 September 1919. He married 3
May 1941 Jeane Fetters, born 15 January 1923. Leon was a WWII veteran.
Children of Leon Virgil and Jeane (Fetters) Paulus:
1832   i Kay Marie Paulus, born 27 December 1941. Married 10
September 1960 Richard Anderson, born 13 September 1935,
children Curt Douglas and Eric
1833   ii Cheryl Diane Paulus, born 11 August 1943. Married 18 July
1964 Howard Edward Merritt, born 4 April 1938, children
Derek Andrew and Dena Ann
1834 iii Jerrie Duane Paulus, born 26 March 1945
1835   iv Donna Jean Paulus, born 14 January 1947. Married 6 December 1970 Lewis Kyes, born 10 April 1930
1836   v Vickie Leonna Paulus, born 30 July 1956. Married Robert
Cohee, born 4 December 1954, child Fawn Anitra
1837   vi Samuel Charles Paulus, born 20 February 1958

1070 - EVANGELINE KATHRYN(6) PAULUS [Samuel Delbert(5),
Daniel(4), Simeon(3), Christina(2) Wolf, Daniel(1)]
Evangeline Kathryn Paulus, sixth child of Samuel Delbert and Lola
Augusta (Wilkinson) Paulus, was born 11 January 1922 in Indiana. She
married James Edward Baker, born 11 March 1922.
Children of James Edward and Evangeline Kathryn (Paulus) Baker:
1838   i Terry Edward Baker, born 16 February 1945. Married 29
November 1974 Barbara Ann Bloom, born 16 August 1948,
child Ann Marie Kathryn
1839   ii Bert Vincent Baker, born 19 January 1949. Married 15 April
1972 Karen Marie Woehnker, born 20 October 1951, child
Molly Marie

1072 - RUSSELL WELDON(6) PAULUS [Samuel Delbert(5), Daniel(4),
Simeon(3), Christina(2) Wolf, Daniel(1)]
Russell Weldon Paulus, eighth child of Samuel Delbert and Lola
Augusta (Wilkinson) Paulus, was born 2 November 1925 in Indiana. He
married 25 January 1947 Marcell Dunlap, born 20 September 1928.

Russell was in the occupation forces in Europe after WWII.
    Children of Russell Weldon and Marcell (Dunlap) Paulus:
    1840   i Norma Lynn Paulus, born 11 June 1948. Married David
             Dellinger, born 4 October 1942, child Angela
    1841   ii Allen Rex Paulus, born 28 March 1951

    1073 - ARCHIE LEE(6) SMITH [Christena Marie(5) Paulus, Daniel(4),
Simeon(3), Christina(2) Wolf, Daniel(1)]
    Archie Lee Smith, first child of Harley Monroe and Christena
Marie (Paulus) Smith, was born 5 August 1917 in Indiana. He married 16
April 1947 Nadia Geraldine Kessie, born 31 January 1921. He was a WWII
veteran.
    Children of Archie Lee and Nadia Geraldine (Kessie) Smith:
    1842   i Marylin Sue Smith, born 21 August 1949
    1843   ii Janice Louise Smith, born 29 November 1951. Married 11
             October 1975 Robert Charles Crowson. He was of Indian
             descent

    1074 - ANNABELLE LOU(6) SMITH [Christena Marie(5) Paulus,
Daniel(4), Simeon(3), Christina(2) Wolf, Daniel(1)]
    Annabelle Lou Smith, second child of Harley Monroe and Christena
Marie (Paulus) Smith, was born 27 February 1930. She married 18
February 1949 Paul Olney Roberts, born 11 September 1927.
    Children of Paul Olney and Annabelle Lou (Smith) Roberts:
    1844   i Randall Scott Roberts, born 8 February 1950. Married 28
             October 1972 Shirley Anne Meyers, children Christopher
             Brian and Matthew Allen
    1845   ii Richard Paul Roberts, born 6 July 1951
    1846   iii Carol Ann Roberts, born 21 October 1953
    1847   iv Sharon Sue Roberts, born 15 May 1956

    1075 - MABLE ESTHER(6) HAAS [Daniel Virgil(5), Catherine Eliza-
beth(4) Paulus, Simeon(3), Christena(2) Wolf, Daniel(1)]
    Mable Esther Haas, first child of Daniel Virgil and Viola B.
(Norris) Haas, was born 9 November 1890 in St. Joseph County, IN. She
married 27 June 1908 at Ft. Wayne, IN Delbert Neher, born 10 July 1887
in Indiana. Delbert died 31 March 1961.
    Children of Delbert and Mable E. (Haas) Neher:
    1848   i Erma Lucille Neher, born 9 May 1908, died 6 September 1908
             in Indiana
    1849   ii Laura Irene Neher, born 11 July 1909 in Indiana. Married
             James Lee Roy Doub, born 29 December 1906, died 29 Septem-
             ber 1952, children Margaret Alice, Doris Ann, Esther
             Irene, Linda Lou and Marion Delbert
    1850   iii Violet Estella Neher, born 23 July 1910. Married 4 June
             1930 Richard Russell Leeper, born 12 May 1908, children
             Marvin Gene, Herbert Lee and Lewis Duane
    1851   iv Arvilla Elnora Neher, born 16 December 1911. Married Henry
             Park Thomas, born 24 March 1909, child Charles Loel
    1852   v Charles William Neher, born 15 March 1915. Married 28
             September 1940 at Connersville, IN Helen Louise Eberly,
             born 28 June 1907 in Ohio. Charles was a veteran of WWII

    1078 - HAZEL VIOLET(6) HAAS [Daniel Virgil(5), Catherine Eliza-
beth(4) Paulus, Simeon(3), Christena(2) Wolf, Daniel(1)]
    Hazel Violet Haas, fourth child of Daniel Virgil and Viola B.
(Norris) Haas, was born 2 October 1895 in St. Joseph County, IN. She
married 1) 20 September 1915 Ralph Chester Enders, born 20 September

1895. They divorced and she married 2) 18 march 1939 Charles John Fifer, a Mexican Border War Veteran. Hazel died 31 March 1968 in Indiana.

Children of Ralph Chester and Hazel Violet (Haas) Enders, all born in Indiana:

1853   i Barbara L. Enders, born 22 October 1916. Married 1936 Charles E. Pavey, born 3 February 1899, died 21 July 1970 in Indiana, children Laura J., Roger Allen, Nancy Beth and Phillip Dennis

1854   ii Ralph R. Enders, born 18 March 1918. Married 4 September 1937 Edna M. Schultz, born 27 April 1918, children Ralph Frederick and Evelyn M.

1855   iii Lois M. Enders, twin, born 27 September 1920. Married 7 September 1938 Hick Jones, children Lonnie, Jeffrey J., Douglas A. and Darlene K.

1856   iv Louis Dale Enders, twin, born 27 September 1920. A WWII Veteran

1857   v Earl Raymond Enders, born 24 April 1923. Married Elouise Harmon, children Michael B., _____, Marjorie C. and David Chris. Earl was a WWII Veteran

1858   vi Kathleen M. Enders, born 29 April 1934. Married 14 February 1954 John Paul Albright, children Dianna L., Paul G. and Brian J.

Child of Charles John and Hazel Violet (Haas) (Enders) Fifer:

1859   i Patricia Anne Fifer, born 2 May 1940 in Indiana. Married 6 May 1961 Howard E. Stump, born 2 November 1940 in Indiana, children Cheryll, Tamara Sue and Howard Wayne

1079 - LULU LURENE(6) HAAS [Daniel Virgil(5), Catherine Elizabeth(4) Paulus, Simeon(3), Christina(2) Wolf, Daniel(1)]

Lulu Lurene Haas, fifth child of Daniel Virgil and Viola B. (Norris) Haas, was born 7 November 1897 in St. Joseph County, IN. She married 3 August 1920 Otis Otto Mills, born 29 January 1891 in Indiana, died 7 October 1968 in California.

Children of Otis Otto and Lulu Lurene (Haas) Mills, all born in Indiana:

1860   i Otis Gene Mills, born 14 July 1922. Married 13 January 1944 at Ft. Wayne, IN Virginia M. Busse, divorced 1956, children Carol Ann, Sandra K. and Betty Lou. Otis married a second and third time

1861   ii Dorothy Esther Mills, born 8 April 1924, died 2 May 1924, buried in Linden Cemetery, Ft. Wayne, IN

1862   iii Donald Leroy Mills, born 20 September 1925. Married 16 July 1958 Virginia Rutherford, born 23 January 1931, children Lois Ann, Donna Lurene, Barbara Dawn, Cherie Bradean and Margie Ellen. Donald served 22 years in the U S Navy

1863   iv Fred Raymond Mills, born 9 April 1938. Married 16 February 1948 Mary E. Marsh, born 24 September 1931, children Dorothy J., Kathleen D., Martha J,. and Stephanie F. They divorced 1967 and Fred has since married twice

1864   v Robert Virgil Mills, born 8 October 1930. Married 22 March 1954 in California Evelyn Louise Christean. There are three sons by her previous marriage

1080 - ERNEST WELCOME(6) HAAS [Daniel Virgil(5), Catherine Elizabeth(4) Paulus, Simeon(3), Christina(2) Wolf, Daniel(1)]

Ernest Welcome Haas, sixth child of Daniel Virgil and Viola B.

(Norris) Haas, was born 6 October 1899 in St. Joseph County, IN. He married 14 January 1919 Ruby Havener, born 29 August 1900. Ruby died 11 April 1927 and Ernest 23 July 1967, both in Indiana.

Children of Ernest Welcome and Ruby (Havener) Haas:

1865   i Marjorie E. Haas, born 20 November 1919 in Indiana. Married 6 October 1941 at Mishawaka, IN Floyd R. Richardson. Marjorie died 15 April 1943 in childbirth as did the child

1866   ii Willis Raymond Haas, born 11 February 1921 in Pennsylvania. Married 1) 14 August 1940 at Mishawaka, In Lenora H. Miller, born 13 January 1924 in Indiana, died 27 March 1966, no children. Willis married 2) 1966 Patricia _____, child Danny

1867 iii Dale Eugene Haas, born 26 April 1923 in Indiana, did not marry

1868   iv Harry James Haas, born 13 April 1926 in Indiana. Married Bess Littlejohn, born 10 June 1922, children Sue Ann and Jesse James. Harry was a WWII Veteran

1081 - JOSEPH DANIEL(6) HAAS [Daniel Virgil(5), Catherine Elizabeth(4) Paulus, Simeon(3), Christina(2) Wolf, Daniel(1)]

Joseph Daniel Haas, seventh child of Daniel Virgil and Viola B. (Norris) Haas, was born 11 may 1901 in St. Joseph County, IN. He married 1) 8 December 1922 Grace M. Balsley, born 8 January 1902. They divorced 1954.

Children of Joseph Daniel and Grace M. (Balsley) Haas, all born in Indiana:

1869   i Marvene E. Haas, born 20 April 1924, died 5 April 1959. Married 10 August 1947 at Osceola, IN Robert Harvey Wilson, born 14 October 1921 in Indiana, children Barbara Ann and Earl Henry (adopted)

1870   ii Joseph Eugene Haas, born 15 September 1926. Married 19 June 1948 at Osceola, IN Joan E. Bunch, born 15 July 1931 in Indiana, children Dennis E. and Tamara K.

1871 iii Joann M. Haas, born 15 October 1928. Married 29 October 1948 at Osceola, IN Ander Devon Stouder, born 22 May 1926 in Indiana, children Charlene J., Darlene A., Galen D. and Kimberly J.

1872   iv Betty Viola Haas, born 2 December 1929. Married 24 January 1948 at Osceola, IN Robert E. Miller, born 29 march 1927 in Indiana, children Sandra Sue, Keith E., Eric W., Cynthia A., and Robert J.

1873   v Dorothy M. Haas, born 30 September 1931. Married 21 May 1949 at Osceola, IN Richard E. Henderson, born 3 June 1929 in Indiana, children Becky J., Marilyon L., Debra K., Jo Rita, Wanda Ann, Kenneth J., Michael E. and Dorothy S.

1874   vi Patricia A. Haas, born 2 October 1933. Married 7 October 1955 Raoul Jean Beaudette, born 17 September 1933 in Indiana, divorced 1963, children Jeffery Alan, Michelle Rae and David Lee

1083 - AGNES PEARL(6) CLABAUGH [Barbara Ellen(5) Haas, Catherine Elizabeth(4) Paulus, Simeon(3), Christina(2) Wolf, Daniel(1)]

Agnes Pearl Clabaugh, second child of Samuel and Barbara Ellen (Haas) Clabaugh, was born 13 December 1895 in Indiana. She married 15 December 1915 Clyde J. Marks, born 6 May 1891, died 10 december 1968.

Children of Clyde J. and Agnes Pearl (Clabaugh) Marks:

1875   i Marvel L. Marks, born 20 March 1917. Married _____ Kelley

```
1876    ii Harold J. Marks, born 28 September 1919
1877   iii Helen P. Marks, born 5 October 1921. Married _____ Chizran
1878    iv June Eleanore Marks, born 30 June 1924
```

**1084 - NELLIE ROSELLA(6) CLABAUGH [Barbara Ellen(5) Haas, Cathe-
rine Elizabeth(4) Paulus, Simeon(3), Christina(2) Wolf, Daniel(1)]**

Nellie Rosella Clabaugh, twin, third child of Samuel and Barbara
Ellen (Haas) Clabaugh, was born 20 august 1900 in Indiana. She married
12 December 1917 Roy Glen Franklin, born 10 June 1900. Nellie died 9
March 1967. They are buried in Bremen Cemetery, Marshall county, IN.

Children of Roy Glen and Nellie Rosella (Clabaugh) Franklin:

```
1879    i Lula L. Franklin, born 8 July 1918. Married _____ Allsop
1880   ii Omar Eugene Franklin, born 4 September 1923. He was a tail
          gunner in a B-24 bomber, reported missing in action 9 June
          1944 in the South Pacific in WWII
1881  iii Phyllis J. Franklin, born 15 November 1928. Married _____
          Pippenger
1882   iv Betty Lou Franklin, born 2 September 1931. Married _____
          Weigand
1883    v Joyce A. Franklin, born 23 January 1939. Married _____
          Lacher
```

**1085 - NETTIE ROSETTA(6) CLABAUGH [Barbara Ellen(5) Haas, Cathe-
rine Elizabeth(4) Paulus, Simeon(3), Christina(2) Wolf, Daniel(1)]**

Nettie Rosetta Clabaugh, twin, fourth child of Samuel and Barbara
Ellen (Haas) Clabaugh, was born 20 August 1900. She married 30 September 1925 John Stephen Proctor, born 19 January 1902.

Child of John Stephen and Nettie Rosetta (Clabaugh) Proctor:

```
1884    i James Arthur Proctor, born 11 September 1926
```

**1086 - BERNICE MILDRED(6) CLABAUGH [Barbara Ellen(5) Haas,
Catherine Elizabeth(4) Paulus, Simeon(3), Christina(2) Wolf,
Daniel(1)]**

Bernice Mildred Clabaugh, fifth child of Samuel and Barbara Ellen
(Haas) Clabaugh, was born 24 September 1903 in Indiana. She married 20
October 1922 Earl Goon, born 15 February 1901.

Child of Earl and Bernice Ellen (Clabaugh) Goon:

```
1885    i Janice Goon. Married _____ Voit
```

**1088 - EDITH MAY(6) HAAS [Theodore L.(5), Catherine Elizabeth(4)
Paulus, Simeon(3), Christina(2) Wolf, Daniel(1)]**

Edith May Haas, second child of Theodore L. and Hattie Elizabeth
(Renas) Haas, was born 3 April 1898 in Indiana. She married 18 October
1917 George F. Esenwein Sr, born 23 August 1891 in Indiana, died 26
August 1963.

Children of George F. Sr and Edith May (Haas) Esenwein:

```
1886    i Walter Dale Esenwein, born 6 April 1918 in Indiana
1887   ii Evelyn R. Esenwein, born 21 March 1919 in Indiana. Married
          _____ Lehman
1888  iii Frederick Theodore Esenwein, born 7 August 1920
1889   iv Robert Albert Esenwein, born 18 July 1922
1890    v Fern Madeline Esenwein, born 31 January 1928. Married
          _____ Hostettler
1891   vi George F. Esenwein Jr, born 27 August 1929
1892  vii Lewis Dean Esenwein, born 22 January 1935
1893 viii Jannette Sue Esenwein, born 9 October 1939. Married _____
          Hess
```

1089 - ORVAL HENRY(6) HAAS [Theodore L.(5), Catherine Eliza-
beth(4) Paulus, Simeon(3), Christina(2) Wolf, Daniel(1)]
     Orval Henry Haas, third child of Theodore L. and Hattie Eliza-
beth (Renas) Haas, was born 23 May 1900 in Indiana. He married 24
December 1927 at Nappanee, IN Ada Irene Zentz, born 12 December 1899
in Indiana.
     Children of Orval Henry and Ada Irene (Zentz) Haas, all born in
Indiana:
  1894   i Shirley Jean Haas, born 23 November 1928, died 11 October
             1953 in Indiana
  1895   ii Margery A. Haas, born 1930. Married _____ Baumgardener
  1896 iii Marilyn R. Haas, born 20 July 1932. Married _____ Cripe
  1897   iv Kenneth Dean Haas, born 18 November 1934

1090 - MATILDA ELIZABETH(6) HAAS [Theodore L.(5), Catherine
Elizabeth(4) Paulus, Simeon(3), Christina(2) Wolf, Daniel(1)]
     Matilda Elizabeth Haas, fourth child of Theodore L. and Hattie
Elizabeth (Renas) Haas, was born 19 February 1902 in Indiana. She
married 3 October 1925 Clarence Harvey Wiegand, born 3 November 1899
in Indiana, died 29 November 1962 at South Bend, IN.
     Children of Clarence Harvey and Matilda Elizabeth (Haas) Wiegand:
  1898   i Eldina M. Wiegand, born 17 February 1928. Married _____
             Youngs
  1899   ii Carol J. Wiegand, born 14 May 1933. Married _____ Stein-
             hiller

1091 - WELCOME FOREST(6) HAAS [Theodore L.(5), Catherine·Eliza-
beth(4) Paulus, Simeon(3), Christina(2) Wolf, Daniel(1)]
     Welcome Forest Haas, fifth child of Theodore L. and Hattie
Elizabeth (Renas) Haas, was born 1 June 1905 in Indiana. He married 7
July 1934 Gertrude Ellen Spicher, born 8 January 1909.
     Children of Welcome Forest and Gertrude Ellen (Spicher) Haas:
  1900   i David Alan Haas, born 4 January 1939
  1901   ii Karen Jean Haas, born 5 November 1944
  1902 iii Mara Beth Haas, born 7 June 1951

1092 - NETTIE ALMIRA(6) HAAS [Theodore L.(5), Catherine Eliza-
beth(4) Paulus, Simeon(3), Christina(2) Wolf, Daniel(1)]
     Nettie Almira Haas, sixth child of Theodore L. and Hattie Eliza-
beth (Renas) Haas, was born 7 September 1907 in Indiana. She married
18 July 1926 Orville Wagley, born 22 September 1905.
     Children of Orville and Nettie Almira (Haas) Wagley:
  1903   i Donald Eugene Wagley, born 2 September 1927
  1904   ii Billy Dean Wagley, born 14 May 1930
  1905 iii Jack Lee Wagley, twin, born 14 February 1933
  1906   iv Jeannette E. Wagley, twin, born 14 February 1933
  1907   v Richard Lewis Wagley, born 18 April 1944
  1908   vi Dennis Dale Wagley, born 7 May 1952

1093 - VIOLET MARIE(6) HAAS [Theodore L.(5), Catherine Eliza-
beth(4) Paulus, Simeon (3), Christina(2) Wolf, Daniel(1)]
     Violet Marie Haas, seventh child of Theodore L. and Hattie
Elizabeth (Renas) Haas, was born 25 January 1910 in Indiana. She
married 2 July 1930 Raymond W. Rhoade.
     Children of Raymond W. and Violet Marie (Haas) Rhoade, born in
Indiana:
  1909   i Elaine Sybil Rhoade, born 16 February 1931. Married _____
             Hinton

1910   ii James Lee Rhoade, born 13 January 1935
1911   iii Mary Lou Rhoade, born 13 May 1937. Married _____ King
1912   iv Gerald Roger Rhoade, born 11 March 1941

    1094 - GLEN VIRGIL(6) RANSTEAD [Mary Ann(5) Haas, Catherine
Elizabeth(4) Haas, Simeon(3), Christina(2) Wolf, Daniel(1)]
    Glen Virgil Ranstead, first child of James Monroe and Mary Ann
(Haas) Ranstead, was born 13 March 1896. He married October 1921 Sarah
Fisher, born 12 May 1896.
    Children of Glen Virgil and Sarah (Fisher) Ranstead:
1913   i Mary E. Ranstead, born 25 March 1925. Married _____ Close
1914   ii Louise J. Ranstead, twin, born 13 March 1928. Married
           _____ Emerick
1915   iii Phyllis Jean Ranstead, twin, born 13 March 1928, died 15
           December 1928

    1095 - GLADYS PEARL(6) RANSTEAD [Mary Ann(5) Haas, Catherine
Elizabeth(4) Paulus, Simeon(3), Christina(2) Wolf, Daniel(1)]
    Gladys Pearl Ranstead, second child of James Monroe and Mary Ann
(Haas) Ranstead, was born 3 April 1900. She married 4 June 1921 Vernon
McKinley Fisher, born 11 August 1896.
    Children of Vernon McKinley and Gladys Pearl (Ranstead) Fisher:
1916   i Foster Lee Fisher, born 29 May 1922, died 15 December
           1955. He was a WWII veteran
1917   ii James Lincoln Fisher, born 21 September 1923, died 17 July
           1944 in France. He entered the U.S. Army 4 March 1943, was
           wounded on "D" day, 8 June 1944 invading Normandy and was
           awarded a Purple Heart. On 17 July 1944 he was killed in
           action and was buried in the Normandy American Cemetery in
           France
1918   iii Junior Eugene Fisher, born 30 June 1925
1919   iv Donald Virgil Fisher, born 18 June 1927
1920   v Rolland Dale Fisher, born 12 May 1928
1921   vi Shirley J. Fisher, born 5 March 1931. Married _____ Manula
1922   vii Rosemary Fisher, born 11 November 1933. Married _____
           Willett
1923 viii Carl Dean Fisher, born 5 July 1936, died 17 November 1951
1924   ix Marilyn J. Fisher, born 24 May 1938. Married _____ Traver

    1096 - CATHERINE E.(6) RANSTEAD [Mary Ann(5) Haas, Catherine
Elizabeth(4) Paulus, Simeon(3), Christina(2) Wolf, Daniel(1)]
    Catherine E. Ranstead, third child of James Monroe and Mary Ann
(Haas) Ranstead, was born 18 April 1902. She married 1) 13 May 1922
Don Fluckey, born 15 December 1901. There were no children. They
divorced 1928 and she married 2) 22 October 1938 Walter Jennings Lane,
born 24 October 1897 in Indiana, died 14 November 1965, buried in Fair
Cemetery, near Lakeville, IN.
    Child of Walter Jennings and Catherine E. (Ranstead) Lane:
1925   i Ulta M. Lane (adopted). Married _____ Grable

    1097 - MARGUERETTE VERNA(6) HAAS [Joseph Henry Jr(5), Catherine
Elizabeth(4) Paulus, Simeon(3), Christina(2) Wolf, Daniel(1)]
    Marguerette Verna Haas, first child of Joseph Henry Jr and
Ardella Azelta (Hodges) Haas, was born 25 November 1903. She married
16 July 1927 Russell H. Ruff, born 19 January 1897.
    Children of Russell H. and Marguerette Verna (Haas) Ruff:
1926   i Robert Russell Ruff, born 14 July 1928
1927   ii Donald Eugene Ruff, born 9 May 1930

1928 iii Norman Wesley Ruff, born 28 July 1932, died 15 September
           1932
1929   iv Paul Harold Ruff, born 16 December 1934
1930   v Arlene Louise Ruff, born 20 September 1936. Married _____
           Keiper

   1097 - HOMER JENNINGS(6) HAAS [Joseph Henry Jr(5), Catherine
Elizaabeth(4) Paulus, Simeon(3), Christina(2) Wolf, Daniel(1)]
     Homer Jennings Haas, second child of Joseph Henry Jr and Ardella
Azelta (Hodges) Haas, was born 3 June 1905. He married 23 February
1929 Sybil Belle Ranstead, born 9 April 1911.
     Children of Homer Jennings Jr and Sybil Belle (Ranstead) Haas:
1931   i Blanch I. Haas, born 11 October 1928. Married 1) _____
           Yarbough, 2) _____ Jessop, 3) _____ Koon
1932   ii Rowena May Haas, born 7 december 1931. Married _____ Berry
1933 iii Eunice Loretta Haas, born 22 November 1933 _____ Berry
1934   iv Herbert Seymore Haas, born 6 December 1935
1935   v Gertrude M. Haas, born 14 June 1938. Married _____ Shinne-
           man
1936   vi Donnie Lee Haas, born 3 September 1940
1937 vii Lyle Jennings Haas, born 22 October 1943
1938 viii Ervine Ray Haas, born 29 April 1945
1939   ix Ronald H. Haas, born 27 may 1950

   1099 - GLENN MARTIN(6) HAAS [Joseph Henry Jr(5), Catherine
Elizabeth(4) Paulus, Simeon(3), Christina(2) Wolf, Daniel(1)]
     Glenn Martin Haas, third child of Joseph Henry Jr and Ardela
Azelta (Hodges) Haas, was born 18 October 1909. He married 5 July at
Argus, IN Wilma Lucile Huff, born 24 August 1912.
     Children of Glenn Martin and Wilma Lucile (Huff) Haas:
1940   i Theodore Lewis Haas, born 12 February 1932
1941   ii Fred Jay Haas, born 18 February 1933
1942 iii Marjorie Ellen Haas, born 1934. Married _____ Milikin
1943   iv Dorothy Ann Haas, born 6 January 1935. Married _____ Cline
1944   v Ralph G. Haas, born 30 November 1937
1945   vi Evelyn Lucile Haas, born 9 December 1938. Married _____
           Leiter
1946 vii Kay Yvonne Haas, born 25 November 1943. Married _____
           Russell
1947 viii Arthur Lee Haas, born 4 March 1945
1948   ix Nancy Helen Haas, born 15 July 1951. Married _____ Lambert

   1101 - HELEN IRENE(6) HAAS [Joseph Henry Jr(5), Catherine Eliza-
beth(4) Paaulus, Simeon(3), Christina(2) Wolf, Daniel(1)]
     Helen Irene Haas, fifth child of Joseph Henry Jr and Ardelle
Azelta (Hodges) Haas, was born 20 December 1912 in Indiana. She
married 29 October 1933 Kenneth Yost, born 6 February 1916.
     Children of Kenneth and Helen Irene (Haas) Yost:
1949   i Dale Eugene Yost, born 22 May 1934
1950   ii Joyce Alfreda Yost, born 3 February 1939. married _____
           Thornton
1951 iii Alfred Roy Yost, born 23 June 1946
1952   iv Danalene Antoinette Yost, born 14 September 1953

   1105 - DALE LEROY(6) ROSE [Bertha Marie(5) Haas, Catherine
Elizabeth(4) Paulus, Simeon(3), Christina(2) Wolf, Daniel(1)]
     Dale Leroy Rose, first child of Hiram W. K. and Bertha Marie
(Haas) Rose, was born 22 October 1907 in Indiana. He married 9 August

1930 Thelma V. Emyerart, born 4 January 1910 in Indiana.
    Children of Dale Leroy and Thelma V. (Emyerart) Rose:
  1954   i Jack D. Rose, born 8 March 1931
  1955   ii Richard Allen Rose, born 10 november 1932

    1106 - VIRGINIA MAE(6) ROSE [Bertha Marie(5) Haas, Catherine
Elizabeth(4) Paulus, Simeon(3), Christina(2) Wolf, Daniel(1)]
    Virginia Mae Rose, second child of Hiram W. K. and Bertha Marie
(Haas) Rose, was born 26 February 1910 in Indiana. She married 12
October 1920 in Indiana Charles Edward Kurtz, born 9 January 1909 in
Indiana.
    Children of Charles Edward and Virginia Mae (Rose) Kurtz, all
born in Indiana:
  1956   i Janet May Kurtz, born 30 October 1930. Married _____ Hitch
  1957   ii Vivian Jean Kurtz, born 25 February 1938. Married _____
            Sechrist
  1958 iii Rosemary Kurtz, born 6 June 1940. Married _____ Graboski
  1959   iv Larry Dean Kurtz, born 26 September 1943
  1960   v Gary Lynn Kurtz, born 23 July 1945

    1107 - CARL W. K.(6) ROSE [Bertha Marie(5) Haas, Catherine
Elizabeth(4) Paulus, Simeon(3), Christina(2) Wolf, Daniel(1)]
    Carl W. K. Rose, third child of Hiram W. K. and Bertha Marie
(Haas) Rose, was born 16 March 1912 in Indiana. He married 7 April
1934 Ernestine M. Harlin, born 18 October 1911 in Indiana.
    Children of Carl W. K. and Ernestine M. (Harlin) Rose, born in
Indiana:
  1961   i Kathleen Sue Rose, born 13 June 1936. Married _____ Shaw
  1962   ii Jerry Dean Rose, born 21 February 1940. A West Point
            graduate, served in Viet Nam, married with two children

    1108 - BETTY ELIZABETH(6) ROSE [Hiram W. K.(5), Catherine Eliza-
beth(4) Paulus, Simeon(3), Christina(2) Wolf, Daniel(1)]
    Betty Elizabeth Rose, fourth child of Hiram W. K. and Bertha
Marie (Haas) Rose, was born 22 November 1921 in Indiana. She married
1) 20 September 1942 Jo Davis. They divorced and she married 2) 14
June 1947 Joseph Rhoades, born 30 October 1922.
    Child of Jo and Betty Elizabeth (Rose) Davis:
  1963   i Dennis Lee Davis, born 29 January 1944 in Indiana. Dennis
            was adopted by his mother's second husband
    Children of Joseph and Betty Elizabeth (Rose) Rhoades, born in
Indiana:
  1964   i Darl Wayne Rhoades, born 12 April 1949
  1965   ii Patricia Ann Rhoades, born 1 December 1953

    1110 - CHARLES M.(6) WALLACE [Clarence(5), Emeline(4) Paulus,
Simeon(3), Christina(2) Wolf, Daniel(1)]
    Charles M. Wallace, first child of Clarence and Bessie (Fisher)
Wallace; was born 9 February 1906, died 31 August 1946. He married
Ruby Baumgardner.
    Children of Charles M. and Ruby (Baumgardner) Wallace:
  1966   i Jon Eugene Wallace, born 14 December 1932. Married Dixie
            Talbot, children Gary Eugene and Brenda Kay
  1967   ii Joyce Marie Wallace, born 5 July 1935. Married Richard K.
            Harris, children Linda Lea, Debra Kay and Todd Richard
  1968 iii Carl Dean Wallace, born 1 September 1936. Married Jean-
            nette Rymarz, children Carla Sue and Jennifer Lynn
  1969   iv Gene Charles Wallace, born 22 December 1937. Married

Rosemary Dark, children Kimberly Jo, Steven Charles, Julie Lynn and Jeanna Lynn

1112 - CECIL(6) WALLACE [Clarence(5), Emeline(4) Paulus, Simeon(3), Christina(2) Wolf, Daniel(1)]
   Cecil Wallace, third child of Clarence and Bessie (Fisher) Wallace, was born 26 February 1910, died December 1954. He married Arlene Hancock.
   Children of Cecil and Arlene (Hancock) Wallace:
   1970   i Sandra Wallace. Married William Annis, children John Wallace and William T.
   1971   ii Norman Wallace. Married Susan Lzdepski, child James Conrad

1113 - RALPH(6) WALLACE [Clarence(5), Emeline(4) Paulus, Simeon(3), Christina(2) Wolf, Daniel(1)]
   Ralph Wallace, fourth child of Clarence and Bessie (Fisher) Wallace, was born 20 May 1912. He married Martha Feece.
   Child of Ralph and Martha (Feece) Wallace:
   1972   i Karen Wallace. Married 1) James Warner, child Julie. They divorced and she married 2) Richard Warner

1115 - MARVIN(6) WALLACE [Clarence(5), Emeline(4) Paulus, Simeon(3), Christina(2) Wolf, Daniel(1)]
   Marvin Wallace, sixth child of Clarence and Bessie (Fisher) Wallace, was born 20 August 1921. He married Dorothy Barnes.
   Children of Marvin and Dorothy (Barnes) Wallace:
   1973   i Allen Wallace. Married Carol White
   1974   ii Jerry Wallace. Married Judith Thomas, children Sarah and Peter

1116 - ROBERT(6) WALLACE [Clarence(5), Emeline(4) Paulus, Simeon(3), Christina(2) Wolf, Daniel(1)]
   Robert Wallace, seventh child of Clarence and Bessie (Fisher) Wallace,was born 5 April 1927, died 1967. He married Lila Facus.
   Children of Robert and Lila (Facus) Wallace:
   1975   i Glenn Wallace. Married Sharon Neirynck, child Dawn
   1976   ii Roger Wallace

1117 - MAXINE(6) HOSLER [Marie(5) Wallace, Emeline(4) Paulus, Simeon(3), Christina(2) Wolf, Daniel(1)]
   Maxine Hosler, first child of Otis and Marie (Wallace) Hosler, was born 26 October 1919. She married Victor Manguson.
   Children of Victor and Maxine (Hosler) Manguson:
   1977   i Robert Manguson, born 31 January 1939. Wife not known, children Thomas and Timothy, twins; Lori and Deanne
   1978   ii Terry Manguson, born 5 May 1941. Wife not known, children Terrance, Douglas M., Donald E. and Catherine E.
   1979 iii Vicky Manguson, born 4 June 1946. Married _____ Watson, children Robert K., Michael P., Kristin M. and Angela L.

1118 - NORMAN(6) SELBY [Sarah Ellen(5) Wolf, Christina(4) Paulus, Daniel(3), Christina(2) Wolf, Daniel(1)]
   Norman Shelby, first child of Jacob and Sarah Ellen (Wolf) Selby, was born 24 November 1873, died 16 October 1959 in Glendale, CA. His wife's name is not known.
   Child of Norman and _____ (_____) Selby:
   1980   i Howard Selby

1119 - MALINDA MAUDE(6) SELBY [Sarah Ellen(5) Wolf, Christina(4) Paulus, Daniel(3), Christina(2) Wolf, Daniel(1)]
Malinda Maude Selby, second child of Jacob and Sarah Ellen (Wolf) Selby, was born 9 March 1878, died 1938. She married William F. Single, born 1877, died 1956.
Child of William F. and Malinda Maude (Selby) Single:
1981   i Irene Single, born 23 December 1898, died 1938, buried in Ithica Cemetery. Married _____ Harvey

1120 - MOUNT VERNON(6) SELBY [Sarah Ellen(5) Wolf, Christina(4) Paulus, Daniel(3), Christina(2) Wolf, Daniel(1)]
Mount Vernon Selby, third child of Jacob and Sarah Ellen (Wolf) Selby, was born 6 March 1880. His wife's name is not known.
Child of Mount Vernon and _____ (_____) Selby:
1982   i Walter Jacob Selby, born 1 December 1913, died 2 December 1944 in Germany, serving in WWII

1122 - NORMAN(6) WOLFE [Nelson(5) Wolf, Christina(4) Paulus, Daniel(3), Christina(2) Wolf, Daniel(1)]
Norman Wolfe, first child of Nelson and Margaret (Bradford) Wolf, was born 22 September 1881 in Grant County, IN, died 25 January 1967 in Indiana. He married Mary Smith, born 17 May 1882, died 18 May 1956. They are buried in Grant Memorial Cemetery.
Children of Norman and Mary (Smith) Wolfe:
1983   i Gerald Holt Wolfe, born 13 September 1905 in Indiana. Married Velma L. Cadiz, born 20 August 1910, children Norman Edward and Marvin Dean
1984   ii Robert Trenton Wolfe, born 19 July 1907. Married Helen E. Bowman, born 10 november 1910, children Dale L. and Elizabeth A.
1985   iii Maynard LaVerne Wolfe, born 31 March 1911. Married Mary M. Brown, born 27 February 1915, children Nelson LaVerne and Virginia Mae

1124 - FLORENCE(6) WOLFE [Nelson(5), Christina(4) Paulus, Daniel(3), Christina(2) Wolf, Daniel(1)]
Florence Wolfe, third child of Nelson and Margaret (bradford) Wolfe, was born 7 November 1893 in Grant County, IN, died 12 June 1963. She married Fred Streib, born 29 August 1888, died 12 June 1954.
Children of Fred and Florence (Wolfe) Streib:
1986   i Albert Streib, born 31 May 1815. Married Melba Howard, born 27 September 1918, children Terry Albert and Victor Lee
1987   ii Margaret Streib, born 13 August 1919. Married Robert Wahl, children Harry Frederick, Robert T., Tanya Marie and Kirk S.

1126 - MAY(6) WALKER [Lydia(5) Wolf, Christina(4) Paulus, Daniel(3), Christina(2) Wolf, Daniel(1)]
May Walker, second child of James Otto and Lydia (Wolf) Walker married _____ Scheffler.
Child of _____ and May (Walker) Scheffler:
1988   i Leroy Scheffler

1128 - NORAH(6) GEBHART [Jane(5) Wolf, Christina(4) Paulus, Daniel(3), Christina(2) Wolf, Daniel(1)]
Norah Gebhart, first child of David Jr and Jane (Wolf) Gebhart, was born 9 April 1874 in Ohio, died 10 June 1958. She married _____

Riley.
       Children of _____ and Norah (Gebhart) Riley:
 1989   i Harry Riley, born 7 September 1890
 1990   ii Maud Riley, born 27 August 1895. Married _____ Douglas
 1991   iii Vernon Riley, born 31 July 1902

      1129 - EARLY(6) GEBHART [Jane(5) Wolf, Christina(4) Paulus,
Daniel(3), Christina(2) Wolf, Daniel(1)]
      Early Gebhart, second child of David Jr and Jane (Wolf) Gebhart,
was born 11 September 1876 at Springfield, IL, died 12 July 1971. He
married Amanda Brown, born 1877, died 6 February 1959.
      Children of Early and Amanda (Brown) Gebhart:
 1992   i Adrian Gebhart, born 9 April 1904. Married Eva Shell, born
             23 March 1902, died 24 December 1973, child Robert Dale
 1993   ii Odessa Gebhart, born 18 September 1906. Married _____
             Prass, child Nancy
 1994   iii Karl Gebhart, born 2 July 1917. Married Myra Detling, born
             11 February 1925, children Ellen Louise, Mark Edward, Gary
             James and Roger David
 1995   iv Ruth Gebhart, born 17 November 1918, died 24 June 1977,
             buried in Forest Hills Cemetery, Vandalia, OH. Married
             Kenneth Smith, children Mike and Mark

      1132 - OPAL(6) GEBHART [Jane(5) Wolf, Christina(4) Paulus,
Daniel(3), Christina(2) Wolf, Daniel(1)]
      Opal Gebhart, fifth child of David Jr and Jane (Wolf) Gebhart,
was born 17 April 1889, died 16 August 1942. She married Tom Corwin,
born 1886.
      Child of Tom and Opal (Gebhart) Corwin:
 1996   i Lowel D. Corwin

      1134 - SARAH CATHERINE(6) WOLF [Dan(5), Christina(4) Paulus,
Daniel(3), Christina(2) Wolf, Daniel(1)]
      Sarah Catherine Wolf, only child of Dan and Emily Eliza-
beth (Black) Wolf, was born 24 November 1880 at Mansfield, IL, died 29
October 1967 at Dayton, OH. Married James Rufus Knupp, born 11 March
1880. They are buried in Woodlawn Cemetery, Dayton, OH.
      Children of James Rufus and Sarah Catherine (Wolf) Knupp:
 1997   i Ralph Waldo Knupp, born 26 October 1901. Married Marie
             Brown, child Richard
 1998   ii James Dwight Knupp, born 19 october 1903. Married Frances
             Evelyn Smith, children Carol Eileen and Robert Ervin

      1135 - CLARA(6) SELBY [Caroline(5) Wolf, Christina(4) Paulus,
Daniel(3), Christina(2) Wolf, Daniel(1)]
      Clara Selby, first child of Samuel and Caroline (Wolf) Selby, was
born 17 December 1878. She married 21 October 1896 William Mitchell
Moore, born 3 March 1868, died 8 June 1936.
      Children of William Mitchell and Clara (Selby) Moore:
 1999   i Clarence Moore, born 12 August 1897, died 18 June 1951.
             His wife's name is not known, child Sandra
 2000   ii Zora Moore, born 22 October 1899, died 8 November 1966.
             Married 6 February 1918 Glade W. Sunderland, born 26
             January 1897, died 25 April 1958, children Dr. Paul W. and
             Dr. Dale
 2001   iii James T. Moore, born 18 August 1902. Married 14 July 1934
             Edith Scholl, no children
 2002   iv Lyle W. Moore, born 22 September 1904. Married 22 August

1942 Elenore Williams, no children
2003   v Elizabeth Moore, born 20 september 1914. Married 1 August
        1936 Edwin Sale, child Peggy

    1137 - GEORGE(6) SELBY [Caroline(5) Wolf, Christina(4) Paulus,
Daniel(3), Christina(2) Wolf, Daniel(1)]
    George Selby, third child of Samuel and Caroline (Wolf) Selby,
was born 28 May 1888. He married Audie Trotter.
    Children of George and Audie (Trotter) Selby:
2004   i Daughter. Married Harold Stringer
2005   ii Daughter. Married Melvin I. Patterson

    1140 - CLADOLA(6) KATZENBERGER [Mary Elizabeth(5) Wolf, Chris-
tina(4) Paulus, Daniel(3), Christina(2) Wolf, Daniel(1)]
    Cladola Katzenberger, second child of Joseph A. and Mary Eliza-
beth (Wolf) Katzenberger, was born 15 April 1884. She married 1)
Alfred Hicks Sr and 2) _____ Chapin. There were no children by the
second marriage.
    Children of Alfred Sr and Cladola (Katzberger) Hicks:
2006   i Alfred Hicks Jr
2007   ii Kathryn Hicks. Married G. E. Drew

    1141 - ETTA MAY(6) KATZENBERGER [Mary Elizabeth(5) Wolf, Chris-
tina(4) Paulus, Daniel(3), Christina(2) Wolf, Daniel(1)]
    Etta May Katzenberger, third child of Joseph A. and Mary Eliza-
beth (Wolf) Katzenberger, was born 30 March 1886, died 31 March 1911.
She married Earl C. Dangler, born 1882. They are buried in the Greenville, OH Cemetery.
    Children of Earl C. and Etta May (Katzenberger) Dangler:
2008   i Joseph Edward Dangler Sr, born 1905, died 24 September
          1981 at Eagle Lake, TX. Married Martha Fontain. He was
          Postmaster at Seabrook, TX for many years. Children Joseph
          Edward Jr, Nancy and Margaret Elizabeth
2009   ii Grace L. Dangler, was a Registered Nurse
2010 iii Gertrude Dangler. Married A. E. Babcock

    1142 - CHARLES L.(6) KATZENBERGER [Mary Elizabeth(5) Wolf,
Christina(4) Paulus, Daniel(3), Christina(2) Wolf, Daniel(1)]
    Charles L. Katzenberger, fourth child of Joseph A. and Mary
Elizabeth (Wolf) Katzenberger, was born 11 August 1889, died 18 march
1965. Married 1) unknown, 2) 14 February 1942 Mary Lou Taylor, her
second marriage. She married 3) _____ Lender.
    Child of Charles L. and Mary Lou (Taylor) Katzenberger:
2011   i James Daniel Katzenberger, adopted, son of Mary Lou's
          first marriage

    1143 - FLOYD STANLEY(6) WOLFE [Henry(5), Christina(5) Paulus,
Daniel(1), Christina(2) Wolf, Daniel(1)]
    Floyd Stanley Wolfe, first child of Henry and Lola Dale (Brad-
ford) Wolfe, was born 12 August 1890 in Huntington County, IN. Floyd
enlisted in the army during WWI and was called 1 July 1918. He served
at Valpariso University, University of Vermont and the Nela Park
General Electric plant in Cleveland for construction of furnaces to
produce carbon for gas masks. He was honorably discharged 19 February
1919.
    Floyd married Wilma Delight Coy, born 22 July 1894 and afterwards
was employed by the Marion Machine and Foundry Co. and later by the
Paranite Wire Co. until his retirement. He died 17 December 1967 at

the Stratford House Nursing Home, Wabash, IN. Wilma died 15 May 1972 at Marion, IN. They are buried at the IOOF Cemetery, Marion.
Children of Floyd Stanley and Wilma Delight (Coy) Wolfe:
2012   i Hazel Wolfe, born 14 April 1930. Married 1) Leonard Johnson, born 11 June 1927, children Stephen, Luann and Brian. They divorced and she married 2) Robert E. Reed, born 28 May 1931. There were no children by this marriage
2013   ii Bertha Wolfe, born 11 February 1932. Married John Sidney Elofson, born 11 January 1933, children Sharon E., Mark and Connie E.

1144 - CLARK TALMADGE(6) WOLFE [Henry(5), Christina(4) Paulus, Daniel(3), Christina(2) Wolf, Daniel(1)]
Clark Talmadge Wolfe, second child of Henry and Lola Dale (Bradford) Wolfe, was born 26 January 1892 in Washington Township, Grant County, IN. He married Mae Keck, born 19 March 1895, died 12 July 1970 at the Methodist Memorial Home for the aged, Warren, IN. Clark was a WWI veteran, serving 26 April 1917 to 23 May 1919 in the United States, England and France as an airplane repairman.
Children of Clark Talmadge and Mae (Keck) Wolfe:
2014   i Robert Wolfe, born 7 January 1928. Married Roseanne ____, born 3 June 1938, children Bethany Jean, Robert Timothy, Cathie Noel and Steve
2015   ii Alice Jean Wolfe, born 1 August 1934. Married Robert K. Dickerson, born 8 May 1927, children Debra Jean, Robert David and Diana Sue

1145 - AMY EDELL(6) WOLFE [Henry(5), Christina(4) Paulus, Daniel(3), Christina(2) Wolf, Daniel(1)]
Amy Edell Wolfe, third child of Henry and Lola Dale (Bradford) Wolfe, was born 23 January 1893 in Washington Township, Grant County, IN. She married Russell N. Sears and they lived in Marion, IN where he worked at the Indiana Truck Manufacturing Co., later moving to Cortland, NY and Catonsville, MD in 1938 where he worked for Brockway Trucking Co. Amy died 13 September 1974 in Baltimore, MD and Russell 25 September 1989. They are buried in the IOOF Cemetery, Marion, IN.
Children of Russell N. and Amy Edell (Wolfe) Sears:
2016   i Wilford Sears, born 7 December 1917, died 11 May 1920
2017   ii Murl Glen Sears, born 8 February 1920. Married Irene Bronsenne, born 6 March 1923, children Ronald, Bernadine and Jonathan
2018   iii Oleta Pearl Sears, born 2 September 1922 at Marion, IN. She was employed by the Maryland Cup Co. from which she retired 4 October 1984 after which she moved to Alexandria, PA where her sister Wilma lived. She did not marry
2019   iv Wilma Sears, born 20 February 1924. Married William McDaniels, born 19 July 1918, now deceased. Children Karen, Debbie and Arthur

1146 - ARTHUR WENDELL(6) WOLFE [Henry(5), Christina(4) Paulus, Daniel(3), Christina(2) Wolf, Daniel(1)]
Arthur Wendell Wolfe, fourth child of Henry and Lola Dale (Bradford) Wolfe, was born in Washington Township, Grant County, IN, the last child to be born in the log cabin on the Wolfe farm. He was not called into service during WWI as his three brothers volunteered, leaving him to farm the homeplace as his father Henry had died in 1897. He married 21 June 1919 Celia Robinson, born 7 August 1898 in Landess, IN, daughter of Wade and Alice (Tinkel) Robinson.

182

They lived first in Washington Township, then in Van Buren Township on an 80 acre farm in Section 14, purchased in 1923. It was here they struggled through the great depression, with a farm debt, and survived. Later 40 acres in Section 13 and another 40 acres in Section 14 were added to their land holdings. In 1975 they retired from the farm, moving into the Methodist Memorial Home at Warren, IN. Celia died 25 February 1985 and Arthur 14 July 1988. They are buried in the Grant Memorial Cemetery at Marion, IN.

Child of Arthur Wendell and Celia (Robinson) Wolfe:
+ 2020 i Merritt Wendell Wolfe, born 10 May 1920

  1147 - JENNINGS BRYAN(6) WOLFE [Henry(5), Christina(4) Paulus, Daniel(3), Christina(2) Wolf, Daniel(1)]
  Jennings Bryan Wolfe, fifth child of Henry and Lola Dale (Bradford) Wolfe, was born 4 November 1896 in Washington Township, Grant County, IN. He was a veteran of WWI, having served along with his brother Clark in the United States, England and France in maintenance of airplanes. After 25 months of service he was mustered out in Chillicothe, OH and returned to Marion, IN where he worked in a garage, at Indiana Trucking Company and at a commercial truck line. He married Vivian Fay Perkins, born 19 February 1896.
  In later years he was employed at Wolff Lumber Company, east of Marion until he retired. After retiring they moved to Aldersgate Retirement Village near Kissimee, FL until 15 November 1979 when they moved to the Methodist Memorial Home in Warren, IN where Jennings died 31 January 1984 and Vivian 28 January 1986. They are buried in Ogan Cemetery, Wabash County, IN southwest of Wabash.

Child of Jennings Bryan and Vivian Fay (Perkins) Wolfe:
2021 i John Wolfe, born 24 January 1928 in Indiana. Married Willadene Campbell, born February 1932, children James Clifford, Synthia Sue, David Allen and Dianna Lynn

  1149 - CORA(6) WOLF [John(5), Christina(4) Paulus, Daniel(3), Christina(2) Wolf, Daniel(1)]
  Cora Wolf, second child of John and Laura J. (Swallow) Wolf, was born 7 July 1892, died 5 May 1967. She married Frank E. Mann, born 9 September 1884, died 22 May 1954. They are buried in New Lisbon Cemetery, Randolph County, IN.

Children of Frank E. and Cora (wolf) Mann:
2022 i Harold E. Mann, born 1 September 1908. Married Retha Garnet, born 10 July 1909, died 15 January 1978. No children
2023 ii Helen Mann, born 20 July 1913. Married Eugene Fernsler, born 4 April 1908. No children

  1150 - STELLA(6) WOLF [John(5), Christina(4) Paulus, Daniel(3), Christina(2) Wolf, Daniel(1)]
  Stella Wolf, third child of John and Laura J. (Swallow) Wolf, was born 28 June 1898, died 7 February 1957. She married Marvin Fraze, born 5 April 1897, died 18 May 1956. They are buried in New Lisbon Cemetery, Randolph County, IN.

Child of Marvin and Stella (Wolf) Fraze:
2024 i Vernon Fraze, born 11 September 1920 in Randolph County, IN. He was a WWII veteran, serving in the northern Netherlands. Married Margery Brown, born 21 April 1921. He was employed by the Dana Corporation in Ft. Wayne, IN from which he retired. Children Carol, Dwight and Ruth

1151 - RUSSELL(6) WOLF [John(5), Christina(4) Paulus, Daniel(3),
Christina(2) Wolf, Daniel(1)]
    Russell Wolf, fourth child of John and Laura J. (Swallow) Wolf,
was born 27 July 1900. He was a WWI veteran, serving in the Indiana
31st Brigade. He married Edna Shell, born 24 December 1905. She died 9
August 1950 and Russell 20 March 1988. They are buried in New Lisbon
Cemetery, Randolph County, IN.
    Children of Russell and Edna (Shell) Wolf:
  2025   i Lawrence Wolf, born 11 November 1922, died 29 July 1988 in
            Indiana. Married 1) Edith Mae Warren, died December 1963,
            children Larry and John. He married 2) Eileen Smeltzer,
            born 11 October 1922, no children. Lawrence was an elec-
            trician, farmer and contractor
  2026   ii Harold Wolf, born 25 January 1924. Married Donna Green,
            children Catherine and Julia
  2027   iii Charles W. Wolf, born 30 July 1926, died 11 May 1984.
            Married Monetta Clements, born 31 August 1932, children
            Jamia and Beth Ann

    1161 - ADA C.(6) WHITE [Clara B.(5) Wolf, Christina(4) Paulus,
Daniel(3), Christina(2) Wolf, Daniel(1)]
    Ada C. White, first child of Frank B. and Clara B. (Wolf) White,
was born 15 August 1896 in Indiana. She married 22 July 1912 Clarence
Lutz, born 20 December 1891, died 2 February 1941.
    Children of Clarence and Ada C. (White) Lutz:
  2028   i Pauline Lutz, born 20 November 1913. Married John Ogle,
            born 18 February 1917, died 15 July 1978, no children
  2029   ii Willard Lutz, born 27 December 1919, died 24 January 1981.
            Married 30 May 1940 _____ , born 16 April 1924, children
            Terry and Becky

    1162 - INEZ L.(6) WHITE [Clara B.(5) Wolf, Christina(4) Paulus,
Daniel(3), Christina(2) Wolf, Daniel(1)]
    Inez L. White, second child of Frank B. and Clara B. (Wolf)
White, was born 12 July 1902 in Indiana. She married 11 October 1919
Joseph Smith, born 15 May 1900, died 29 March 1970.
    Children of Joseph and Inez L. (White) Smith:
  2030   i Benson D. Smith, born 10 August 1920. Married 29 October
            1942 Lilian Speres, born 21 January 1921, children Patri-
            cia, Cynthia, Susan, Rebecca, Joseph, Mary Ann, Angel and
            Christine
  2031   ii Joseph F. Smith, born 12 July 1922. Married 21 December
            1947 Marilyn Dencer, born 22 February 1928, children
            Douglas and Daniel

    1164 - LUCILLE E.(6) WHITE [Clara B.(5) Wolf, Christina(4)
Paulus, Daniel(3), Christina(2) Wolf, Daniel(1)]
    Lucille E. White, fourth child of Frank B. and Clara B. (Wolf)
White, was born 29 May 1907 in Indiana, died 30 January 1977. She
married Baker Smith.
    Children of Baker and Lucille E. (White) Smith:
  2032   i Sally Smith. Married ____ Snow
  2033   ii Dee Ann Smith. Married ____ Solt
  2034   iii Michael Smith
  2035   iv Jack Smith

    1165 - EVON C.(6) WHITE [Clara B.(5) Wolf, Christina(4) Paulus,
Daniel(3), Christina(2) Wolf, Daniel(1)]

Evon C. White, fifth child of Frank B. and Clara B. (Wolf) White, was born 2 March 1909 at Utica, OH. She married 1) 30 August 1924 Chester Monroe Black, born 2 November 1900, died 6 September 1975 and 2) 10 June 1977 Laurence Hansley. There were no children by the second marriage.

Children of Chester Monroe and Evon C. (White) Black:

2036   i Robert Eugene Black, born 14 December 1926. Married Mary Lou _____, children Bobby Lyn, Tom, Beckie, Jamie, Billie

2037   ii Richard Lee Black, born 27 July 1928. Married Joan _____, children Mike, Pat, Chris, Virginia, Barbara and Pam

2038 iii Carl Edwards Black, born 5 September 1929. Married Marg _____, children Anita, Carla and Jeff

2039   iv Charles Ray Black, born 24 November 1931. Married Nancy Ewing, children Kimberly, Kathy, Douglas and Terry

1166 - FRED W. SR(6) WHITE [Clara B.(5) Wolf, Christina(4) Paulus, Daniel(3), Christina(2) Wolf, Daniel(1)]

Fred W. White Sr, sixth child of Frank B. and Clara B. (Wolf) White, was born 20 December 1910 at Utica, OH. He married 1) 30 June 1928 Edith Harden, died 24 May 1976. They divorced and Fred married 2) 21 October 1955 at Logan, OH Gladys Eveland Harper. There were no children by this marriage.

Children of Fred W. Sr and Edith (Harden) White:

2040   i Fred W. White Jr, born 17 January 1930. Married 2 April 1950 Meredith Drum, born 5 April 1930, child Steven Allen

2041   ii Norman White, born 10 February 1932. Married 1 June 1951 Catherine Bookwalter, born 12 December 1931, children Timothy Allen, Brian and Linda

2042 iii Thelma L. White, born 29 June 1938. Married 7 June 1958 Richard Reid, born 25 January 1935, children Jennifer and James

1167 - KATHLEEN I.(6) WHITE [Clara B.(5) Wolf, Christina(4) Paulus, Daniel(3), Christina(2) Wolf, Daniel(1)]

Kathleen I. White, seventh child of Frank B. and Clara B. (Wolf) White, was born 19 September 1914 at Utica, OH. She married 28 January 1933 at Lancaster, OH Franklin A. Ayers Sr, born 27 May 1913 at Rendville, OH.

Children of Franklin A. Sr and Kathleen I. (White) Ayers:

2043   i Susan Ayers, born 17 May 1935. Married 1) Fred Fauble, children Sabrina and Celina, and 2) Victor Starkey who had daughters Vickie and Brookie by a previous marriage

2044   ii Thomas W. Ayers, born 21 July 1936. Married 10 April 1955 Patricia Burnside, born 17 March 1934, children Susan Annett, Cathy Jo and Linda Kay

2045 iii Raymond Ayers, born 20 January 1938. Married Marjorie Denman, born 28 july 1936, children Beth Holly, Brad Lee and Danny R.

2046   iv Jerry Ayers, born 23 May 1940 at Columbus, OH. Married Olive Brower, children James B. and Kathleen Louise

2047   v Kay Frances Ayers, born 23 August 1941. Married 1) 3 July 1959 Richard Springer, born 13 May 1941, children Christopher and Daffney 2) Preston Like, born in Texas, and 3) Don Lenschow.

2048   vi Franklin A. Ayers Jr, born 20 December 1942 at Baltimore, OH. Married 20 december 1964 Floranna Taggert, born 8 February 1942, children Jeffery, Craig and Jeanette

2049 vii Verne Ayers, born 29 May 1944 at Baltimore, OH. Married 3

July 1963 Betty Shrieves, born 14 December 1944 in Ohio,
child Sheri Lynette
2050 viii Michael Ayers, born 27 June 1946 at Lancaster, OH. Married
11 September 1966 Carlene Bader, born 24 December 1945,
children Nichi and Chellie

1168 - FOSTER R.(6) WHITE [Clara B.(5) Wolf, Christina(4) Paulus,
Daniel(3), Christina(2) Wolf, Daniel(1)]
Foster R. White, eighth child of Frank B. and Clara B. (Wolf)
White, was born 14 July 1916 at Utica, OH, died 21 January 1973. He
married 3 July 1937 Elinor Christ, born 18 November 1918. He served in
the navy in WWII and after the war was employed by Anchor Hocking at
Lancaster, OH.
Child of Foster R. and Elinor (Christ) White:
2051 i Elaine White, born 10 July 1939. Married 23 September 1956
Isaac Hill, born 12 March 1936, children Mark and Angela

1169 - FRANCES M.(6) WHITE [Clara B.(5) Wolf, Christina(4)
Paulus, Daniel(3), Christina (2) Wolf, Daniel(1)]
Frances M. White, ninth child of Frank B. and Clara B. (Wolf)
White, was born 18 May 1919 at Utica, OH. She married 1) 26 November
1938 at Greenup, KY Carl W. Beavers, born 9 December 1914, died 25
December 1956 and 2) 11 april 1967 Robert S. Jordan, born 23 June 1924
at Columbus, OH.
Children of Carl W. and Frances M. (White) Beavers:
2052 i Janet Beavers, born 14 April 1943 at Lancaster, OH.
Married 1) 15 June 1963 Mike Kelly, born August 1943, no
children, divorced and 2) 14 march 1972 at Cincinnati, OH
Bruce Brockman, born 20 august 1943, no children
2053 ii Patricia Beavers, born 8 April 1954. Married 7 December
1974 at Millersport, OH Scott Jamisom, born 16 November
1954, no children, divorced

1187 - EDNA(6) KELTNER [Francis M.(5), Rachel(4) Paulus,
Daniel(3), Christina(2) Wolf, Daniel(1)]
Edna Keltner, second child of Francis M. and Rebecca (_____)
Keltner, was born in 1879, died 26 May 1923 at Tampa, FL, buried in
Beech Cemetery, Muncie, Delaware County, IN. She married Philip
Deterling.
Children of Philip and Edna (Keltner) Deterling:
2054 i Francis Deterling, born at Muncie, Delaware County, IN
2055 ii Martha Deterling, born at Muncie, Delaware County, IN

1191 - RUTH(6) KELTNER [Sanford M.(5), Rachel(4) Paulus,
Daniel(3), Christina(2) Wolf, Daniel(1)]
Ruth Keltner, first child of Sanford M. and Alice May (Cockefair)
Keltner, was born 7 January 1888 at Anderson, Madison County, IN,
died 2 June 1960 at Anderson. She married Charles W. Masters, born 1
December 1884, died 15 October at Connersville, Fayette County, IN.
Child of Charles W. and Ruth (Keltner) Masters:
2056 i Mary Alice Masters, born at Connersville, Fayette County,
IN. Married Carl Sadler, divorced in 1973, children Anne
and James Charles

1193 - LAURA(6) PAULUS [Augustus Daniel(5), Henry(4), Daniel(3),
Christina(2) Wolf, Daniel(1)]
Laura Paulus, first child of Augustus Daniel and Sarah (Stom-
baugh) Paulus, was born 7 February 1881 in Paulding County, OH. She

married Grover Snellenberger.

Children of Grover and Laura (Paulus) Snellenberger:

2057   i Bernice Snellenberger, born 9 January 1909. Married Henry Bastion, born in Cornwall, England, children Barbara and John

2058   ii Gladys Snellenberger, born 31 January 1914. Married Denby Morris, born 16 April 1910, died 1951, children Carole, Janet, Constance and Valerie

1194 - OSCAR(6) PAULUS [Augustus Daniel(5), Henry(4), Daniel(3), Christina(2) Wolf, Daniel(1)]

Oscar Paulus, second child of Augustus Daniel and Sarah (Stombaugh) Paulus, was born 9 September 1882 in Paulding County, OH, died 13 July 1970. He married Virginia P. Bess, born 1 September 1885. She can trace her ancestry back to Henry Whitner of Germany who was a brother of the King of Belgium and a cousin of Queen Victoria.

Children of Oscar and Virginia P. (Bess) Paulus:

2059   i Margaret Paulus, born 8 February 1915, did not marry

2060   ii Frances J. Paulus, born 2 November 1919. Married William Legg, born 19 July 1912, children John and Robert

2061 iii Helen Paulus, born 20 February 1921. Married Stanley Mills, born 17 September 1922, child Lawrence

1195 - ADOLPH(6) PAULUS [Augustus Daniel(5), Henry(4), Daniel(3), Christina(2) Wolf, Daniel(1)]

Adolph Paulus, third child of Augustus Daniel and Sarah (Stombaugh) Paulus, was born 18 October 1884 in Paulding county, OH, died 3 March 1964. He married Isabelle Brosseau, born 13 July 1896.

Children of Adolph and Isabelle (Stombaugh) Paulus:

2062   i Raymond Paulus, born 6 April 1925. Did not marry

2063   ii Dorothy Paulus, born 29 December 1929. Married James Shipper, born 12 march 1925, children Brent, Brenda, Mark, Paul and Denise

2064 iii Jean Paulus, born 2 December 1933. Married Daniel O'Brien, born 7 October 1936, child Jennifer

1202 - EDNA E.(6) PAULUS [Lafayette(5), Henry(4), Daniel(3), Christina(2) Wolf, Daniel(1)]

Edna E. Paulus, seventh child of Lafayette and Lydia Ann (Anspach) Paulus, was born 8 November 1895, died 24 August 1942, buried in Spring Creek Cemetery, Kosciusko County, IN. She married Clifton Shira, born 18 December 1891.

Children of Clifton and Edna E. (Paulus) Shira:

2065   i Betty Rose Shira, born 10 June 1917, died 3 December 1922

2066   ii Arden Shira, born 9 September 1918. Married Katherine Ann _____, born 25 August 1919, children Linda Dianne and Arden Ann

1203 - LELA MAY(6) PAULUS [Lafayette(5), Henry(4), Daniel(3), Christina(2) Wolf, Daniel(1)]

Lela May paulus, eighth child of Lafayette and Lydia Ann (Anspach) Paulus, was born 1 October 1896. She married Owen Moore, born 1892. He taught school for 50 years.

Child of Owen and Lela May (Paulus) Moore:

2067   i Donna Allison Moore, born 24 June 1922. Married _____ Bell, children Ginger M. and Peggy Ann

1205 - ESTHER(6) PAULUS [Lafayette(5), Henry(4), Daniel(3),
Christina(2) Wolf, Daniel(1)]
     Esther paulus, tenth child of Lafayette and Lydia Ann (Anspach)
Paulus, was born 28 October 1899, died 12 December 1921. She married
Paul Shriver.
     Children of Paul and Esther (Paulus) Shriver:
  2068   i Marcella Shriver
  2069   ii Madra Shriver

     1206 - ELRA PAUL(6) PAULUS [Lafayette(5), Henry(4), Daniel(3),
Christina(2) Wolf, Daniel(1)]
     Elra Paulus, eleventh child of Lafayette and Lydia Ann (Anspach)
Paulus, was born 2 December 1900. He married Bonnie Shock.
     Child of Elra Paul and Bonnie (Shock) Paulus:
  2070   i Elloise Paulus, born 19 december 1923. Married _____
           Price, children Richard and Bonnie Rae

     1208 - WARREN AUGUSTUS(6) PAULUS [Lafayette(5), Henry(4),
Daniel(3), Christina(2) Wolf, Daniel(1)]
     Warren Augustus Paulus, thirteenth child of Lafayette and Lydia
Ann (Anspach) Paulus, was born 28 september 1903. He married Mable
Ashcraft, born 6 January 1909.
     Child of Warren Augustus and Mable (Ashcraft) Paulus:
  2071   i Janet Paulus, born 28 January 1933. Married James A.
           Roberts, born 7 April 1929, children Paulette, Amie, Tobin
           and Whitney

     1211 - SINCLAIR VIRGIL(6) PAULUS [Charles Wilbur(5), Henry(4),
Daniel(3), Christina(2) Wolf, Daniel(1)]
     Sinclair Virgil Paulus, first child of Charles Wilbur and Lovina
(Dearth) Paulus, was born 24 February 1900, died 20 October 1971. He
married 22 July 1919 Eva E. Linn, born 3 September 1901.
     Children of Sinclair Virgil and Eva E. (Linn) Paulus:
  2072   i Robert E. Paulus, born 31 January 1920. Married 19 January
           1939 Elizabeth Knox, children James Allen, Carol Ann and
           Robert M.
  2073   ii Clair Paulus. Married Virginia _____
  2074 iii Donald A. Paulus, born 26 January 1926. Married 20 Decem-
           ber 1947 Ruth E. Riggenbach, born 2 April 1928, child
           Patricia A.
  2075   iv Betty Paulus

     1213 - CHARLES WILBUR II(6) PAULUS [Charles Wilbur(5), Henry(4),
Daniel(3), Christina(2) Wolf, Daniel(1)]
     Charles Wilbur Paulus II, third child of Charles Wilbur and
Lovina (Dearth) Paulus, was born 25 March 1910 in Paulding County, OH,
died 22 August 1972. He married Elizabeth J. Lehman, born 23 February
1911.
     Children of Charles Wilbur II and Elizabeth J. (Lehman) Paulus:
  2076   i Wilbur Harlan Paulus, born 15 January 1931, killed in
           auto accident 7 January 1976
  2077   ii Floyd Henry Paulus, born 19 August 1932, died 8 March 1933

     1214 - GORDON LAFAYETTE(6) PAULUS [Charles Wilbur(5), Henry(4),
Daniel(3), Christina(2) Wolf, Daniel(1)]
     Gordon Lafayette Paulus, fourth child of Charles Wilbur and
Lovina (Dearth) Paulus, was born 24 August 1911 in Paulding County,
OH, died 8 November 1982, buried in St. Paul Lutheran Church Cemetery,

Paulding County, OH. Married Ruth E. Hart, born 8 March 1913. Gordon worked at the Studebaker plant in Ft. Wayne, IN, becoming a Journeyman Electrician.

Children of Gordon Lafayette and Ruth E. (Hart) Paulus:

2078   i   Richard Gordon Paulus, born 11 March 1932. Married Susan Amelia Gillette, born 12 February 1943, children Carol Sue, Dianna Kay and Pam Nanette

2079   ii   Shirly Paulus, born 29 August 1934. Married Robert Miller, born 15 January 1933, children Steven Robert, Mark Allen and Tina Marie

2080   iii   Sharon Lee Paulus, born 1 August 1937. Married Larry Leon Whitman, born 17 February 1937, children Brad and Bruce Lynn

1218 - GOLDIE BELLE(6) WOLFE [William Henry(5), Elma Elizabeth(4) Paulus, Daniel(3), Christina(2) Wolf, Daniel(1@]

Goldie Belle Wolfe, only child of William Henry and Hattie (Boner) Wolfe, was born 24 November 1880 in Illinois, died 9 September 1978 in Ohio. She married 10 John W. Rinehart, born 13 April 1876, died 14 September 1940 in Ohio. They operated a store, Post Office and Depot for many years in West Sonora. Goldie married 2) Warren Worley.

Children of John W. and Goldie Belle (Wolfe) Rinehart:

2081   i   Elma B. Rinehart, born 26 September 1902, died 28 May 1977 in a fire in which 158 people died.

2082   ii   Ruth Lucile Rinehart, born 1 September 1905. Married _____ Bunger, child Russell

2083   iii   John Lowell Rinehart, died 25 December 1915 at a very young age

1219 - JOHNNY D.(6) PLESSENGER [Rachel Ann(5) Paulus, Samuel(4), Daniel(3), Christina(2) Wolf, Daniel(1)]

Johnny D. Plessenger, only child of Frank and Rachel Ann (Paulus) Plessenger, was born November 1883, died 1939. He married Ethel Mills, born 1887.

Child of Johnny D. and Ethel (Mills) Plessenger:

2084   i   Donald Plessenger

1225 - LESSIE IRENE(6) HOLLEHAN [Joseph Harrison(5), Lucy Ann(4) Paulus, Daniel(3), Christina(2) Wolf, Daniel(1)]

Lessie Irene Hollehan, first child of Joseph Harrison and Delilah (DeHoff) Hollehan, was born 30 March 1882 at Greenville, OH, died 22 August 1962 at Ft. Wayne, IN. She married 31 December 1899 Lewis Arlington Ridenour, born 24 January 1876 at Paulding, OH, son of Ephraim Valentine and Sophia (Mechling) Ridenour, died 24 May 1951 at Ft. Wayne. They are buried in Lindenwood Cemetery, Ft. Wayne.

Children of Lewis Arlington and Lessie Irene (Hollehan) Ridenour:

+ 2085   i   Edith Pauline Ridenour, born 15 July 1901

2086   ii   Donald Wade Ridenour, born 23 April 1903 at Briceton, OH, died 17 August 1953 at Milwaukee, WI, buried in Lindenwood Cemetery, Ft. Wayne, IN. Married 8 May 1947 at Milwaukee Evelyn Manz. No children

+ 2087   iii   Murrell Valentine Ridenour, born 20 August 1904

+ 2088   iv   Paul Joseph Ridenour, born 24 April 1907

+ 2089   v   Dorothy Elsie Ridenour, born 14 May 1913

1240 - GEORGE ROBERT(6) BAUGHER [Elmer Calvin(5), Allen(4), Mary(3) Paulus, Christina(2) Wolf, Daniel(1)]

George Robert baugher, third child of Elmer Calvin and Mary E.

(Tague) Baugher, was born 10 October 1911 at Kokomo, Howard County, IN, died 14 September 1976. Married 5 December 1936 Velma Small, born 22 February 1919.

Children of George Robert and Velma (Small) Baugher:
2090   i   Norman Ray Baugher, born 22 November 1937
2091   ii Robert Wayne Baugher, born 20 June 1943. Wife not known, child Amanda Dee
2092   iii Sandra L. Baugher, born 6 January 1942. Married _____ Decker, children Mark Edward and Matthew David
2093   iv Terry Linn Baugher, born 19 September 1955
2094   v   Vicky Ellen Baugher, born 16 October 1960

1241 - MARIE(6) MOSS [Ida Alice(5) Baugher, Allen(4), Mary(3) Paulus, Christina(2) Wolf, Daniel(1)]
Marie Moss, first child of Flavius and Ida Alice (Baugher) Moss, was born 12 September 1889, died 30 December 1974. She married Harry Gray, born 15 February 1898, died 19 December 1965. They lived at Clearwater, FL and are buried in the Largo Cemetery.

Child of Harry and Marie (Moss) Gray:
2095   i   Gladys Gray, born 10 February 1921. Married Hugh Teague, born 3 July 1917

1243 - TIRZAH(6) MOSS [Ida Alice(5) Baugher, Allen(4), Mary(3) Paulus, Christina(2) Wolf, Daniel(1)]
Tirzah Moss, third child of Flavius and Ida Alice (Baugher) Moss, was born 14 June 1893. Married 1) Edward Hultz, and 2) Lewis Overholser

Children of Edward and Tirzah (Moss) Hultz:
2096   i   Morris Hultz. Married June _____
2097   ii Malcolm Hultz. Married Joyce _____

1246 - ROI ELLSWORTH(6) BAUGHER [Edward Elsworth(5), Allen(4), Mary(3) Paulus, Christina(2) Wolf, Daniel(1)]
Roi Ellsworth Baugher, first child of Edward Elsworth and Gertrude (McWilliams) Baugher, was born 24 February 1910 at Port Rowan, Ontario, Canada. He married 28 October 1934 Princess Virginia Finney, born 18 June 1909. Roi attended the University of Cincinnati and Indiana University-Kokomo. He worked for Delco Electronics Division, retiring in 1974. Princess attended Jordan Conservatory of Music, Butler University and Ball State Teachers College. She died 26 January 1961 and Roi married 2) Marjorie Odella Finney, sister of Princess. She was a school teacher. Roi died 9 October 1978.

Children of Roi Ellsworth and Princess Virginia (Finney) Baugher:
2098   i   Roy Ellsworth Baugher II, born 12 November 1936. Married Paige Ann Bilz, born 10 august 1940. He graduated from Purdue University and holds a Masters Degree from the University of Cincinnati and a Law Degree from Northern Kentucky University. Children John Bilz and Juliet Lyons
2099   ii Marjorie Adele Baugher, born 16 January 1941. Married 1 June 1974 Charles E. Pierson

1247 - GLADYS(6) BAUGHER [Edward Elsworth(5), Allen(4), Mary(3) Paulus, Christina(2) Wolf, Daniel(1)]
Gladys Baugher, second child of Edward Elsworth and Gertrude (McWilliams) Baugher, was born 19 December 1912. She married 16 April 1933 Joseph G. Baker, born 4 June 1908, son of Joseph J. and _____ Baker, died 1963.

Children of Joseph G. and Gladys (Baugher) Baker:
2100   i James Joseph Baker, born 24 May 1934, died 27 May 1934
2101   ii Donald E. Baker, born 2 October 1936
2102 iii David Allen Baker, born 20 February 1938
2103   iv Carol Baker. Married _____ Unger

  1248 - SYLVIAN DAVID(6) SORTOR(A) [Eva Sophronia(5) Baugher,
Allen(4), Mary(3) Paulus, Christina(2) Wolf, Daniel(1)]
    Sylvian David Sortor, adopted son of Marvin David and Eva Sophro-
nia (Baugher) Sortor, was born 27 August 1905. He married 25 October
1930 at London, England Margaret Hills Eastman, born March 1907. They
divorced.
    Child of Sylvian David and Margaret Hills (Eastman) Sortor:
2104   i Peter E. Sortor, born 2 May 1931 at Vienna, Austria.

  1250 - RAYMOND A.(6) BAUGHER [Walter Raymond(5), Allen(4),
Mary(3) Paulus, Christina(2) Wolf, Daniel(1)]
    Raymond A. Baugher, first child of Walter Raymond and Grace Marie
(Price) Baugher, was born 5 January 1915. He married Agnes Lucille
Glover.
    Children of Raymond A. and Agnes Lucille (Glover) Baugher:
2105   i Michael Charles Baugher. Married Caroline Sue _____,
           children John, Michael Ray, Brian Allen and Christina Sue
2106   ii Sandra Kay Baugher. Married 1) _____ Davis, 2) _____
           Barnes

  1254 - VIRGINIA ANN(6) BAUGHER [Walter Raymond(5), Allen(4),
Mary(3) Paulus, Christina(2) Wolf, Daniel(1)]
    Virginia Ann Baugher, fifth child of Walter Raymond and Grace
Marie (Price) Baugher, was born 1 July 1922. She married Gilbert E.
Spradlin, born 12 January 1939, died 6 July 1972.
    Children of Gilbert E. and Virginia Ann (Baugher) Spradlin:
2107   i Gilbert E. Spradlin II, born 25 October 1940. Married
           Esther Riley, born 20 december 1938, children Susan,
           Jeffery Lynn and Terry Ward
2108   ii Jerry Lynn Spradlin, born 11 November 1942
2109 iii Ronnie Lee Spradlin, born 21 June 1945. Married Beverly
           Draper, divorced, children Portia Lynn and Ronnie Lee Jr
2110   iv Gina Marie Spradlin, born 21 Deptember 1960

  1257 - AGNES MALISSA(6) SORTOR [Estella Opal(5) Baugher,
Allen(4), Mary(3) Paulus, Christina(2) Wolf, Daniel(1)]
    Agnes Malissa Sortor, third cvhild of Marvin David and Estella
Opal (Baugher) Sortor, was born 13 December 1919. She married 1)
Wendell Bubp, born 9 March 1915, they divorced. She married 2) 23
December 1950 Harold Boyd, born 21 June 1920 in Virginia.
    Child of Wendell and Agnes Malissa (Sortor) Bubp:
2111   i Larry Allen Bubp, born 16 September 1943 in Indiana
    Children of Harold and Agnes Malissa (Sortor) Boyd:
2112   i Jeffery Lynn Boyd, born 3 January 1956
2113   ii Patricia Ann Boyd, born 23 September 1958
2114 iii Stanley David Boyd, twin, born 18 March 1961
2115   iv Steven Douglas Boyd, twin, born 18 March 1961

  1258 - NORMA ALICE(6) SORTOR [Estella Opal(5) Baugher, Allen(4),
Mary(3) Paulus, Christina(2) Wolf, Daniel(1)]
    Norma Alice Sortor, fourth child of Marvin David and Estella Opal
(Baugher) Sortor, was born 27 december 1922. She married Bruce Frank

Rostinski, born 3 March 1924, died 15 October 1972.
    Children of Bruce Franf and Norma Alice (Sortor) Rostinski:
2116   i Terry Bruce Rostinski, born 14 january 1947
2117   ii Carol Sue Rostinski, born 17 August 1954

    1259 - MARVIN EARL(6) SORTOR [Estella Opal(5) Baugher, Allen(4),
Mary(3) Paulus, Christina(2) Wolf, Daniel(1)]
    Marvin Earl Sortor, fifth child of Marvin David and Estella Opal
(Baugher) Sortor, was born 30 July 1926. He married Joann Tucker, born
13 October 1926.
    Children of Marvin Earl and Joann (Tucker) Sortor:
2118   i Randy Earl Sortor, born 22 January 1944. Married 1) Joy
          Antoinette Roberts, born 31 March 1947 in Florida, child
          Camarem Marie. They divorced and Randy married 2) 10
          February 1973 at New Smyrna Beach, FL Patricia Marie
          Currie, born 6 November 1950 in New York, children Michael
          James and Christine Ann
2119   ii Cheryl Dee Sortor

    1260 - KENNETH V.(6) BAUGHER [William(5), Calvin(4), Mary(3)
Paulus, Christina(2) Wolf, Daniel(1)]
    Kenneth V. Baugher, first child of William and Minnie (Dullinger)
Baugher, was born 8 June 1895 at Leesburg, Kosciusko County, IN, died
26 March 1953. He married 19 September 1919 at Goshen, Elkhart County,
IN Faye Eyler, born 20 June 1895 at Wawaka, IN, died 1 April 1972,
daughter of Oliver C. and Minnie (Latimer) Eyler.
    Children of Kenneth V. and Faye (Eyler) Baugher:
2120   i Alice Marie Baugher, born 16 September 1922. Married
          Robert Fairfield, four children
2121   ii Alma Marie Baugher, born 23 May 1925. Married 1) Sanford
          Keim, child Esther and 2) Ray Swank
2122 iii Allen Elmer Baugher, born 6 November 1927, died 31 August
          1952 in Korea with the U.S. Armed Forces

CHAPTER No. 8

SEVENTH GENERATION

1262B - MARY JANE(7) TURMAN [Mary Turner(6) Wolf, Fred Wade(5),
Frederick Clark(4), Frederick(3), Jacob(2), Daniel(1)]
    Mary Jane Turman, second child of Earl Sims Sr. and Mary Turner
(Wolf) Turman, was born 24 December 1953 at Nashville, Davidson
County, TN. She married 25 May 1974 at San Diego, San Diego County, CA
Richard Fuller Norton Jr., born 11 November 1950 at San Diego, son of
Richard Fuller Sr. and Donna (_____) Norton.
    Children of Richard Fuller Jr. and Mary Jane (Turman) Norton,
born at Indianapolis, Marion County, IN:
  2122A   i Jennie Marie Norton, born 17 March 1979
  2122B ii Julie Elizabeth Norton, born 27 June 1980

    1262C - BENJAMIN FREDERICK(7) TURMAN [Mary Turner(6) Wolf, Fred
Wade(5), Frederick Clark(4), Frederick(3), Jacob(2), Daniel(1)]
    Benjamin Frederick Turman, third child of Earl Sims Sr. and Mary
Turner (Wolf) Turman, was born 6 April 1955 at Gallatin, Sumner
County, TN. He married 24 December 1988 at San Diego, San Diego
County, CA Lantha Louise (Hamilton) Shaw (previously married to _____
Shaw), born 13 October 1948.
    Child of _____ and Lantha Louise (Hamilton) Shaw and step-son of
Benjamin Frederick Turman:
        i Ahren Lynn Shaw, born 1 August 1978

    1262E - KENNETH MARSHALL(7) TURMAN [Mary Turner(6) Wolf, Fred
Wade(5), Frederick Clark(4), Frederick(3), Jacob(2), Daniel(1)]
    Kenneth Marshall Turman, fifth child of Earl Sims Sr. and Mary
Turner (Wolf) Turman, was born 21 September 1957 at Gallatin, Sumner
County, TN. He married 28 December 1989 Dannielle Daskam born 27
September   .
    Child of Kenneth Marshall and Dannielle (Daskam) Turman:
  2122C   i Kyle Edward Turman, born 5 March 1991 at Centralia, Lewis
            County, WA

    1263 - ALICE ANNE(7) KNABENSHUE [Kenneth(6), Anna Evalee(5)
Shroyer, Malinda Ann(4) Wolf, Frederick(3), Jacob(2), Daniel(1)]
    Alice Anne Knabenshue, first child of Kenneth and Wilma J.
(Boltenhouse) Knabenshue, was born 8 October 1920. She married 31
December 1938 Ivan McClone, died 25 October 1976.
    Child of Ivan and Alice Anne (Knabenshue) McClone:
  2123   i Kathleen Anne McClone, born 17 March 1946

    1265 - KENNETH A. II(7) KNABENSHUE [Kenneth(6), Anna Evalee(5)
Shroyer, Malinda Ann(4) Wolf, Frederick(3), Jacob(2), Daniel(1)]
    Kenneth A. Knabenshue II, third child of Kenneth and Wilma J.
(Boltenhouse) Knabenshue, was born 12 February 1924, died 30 October
1970. He married Verna Dean Black.
    Children of Kenneth A. II and Verna Dean (Black) Knabenshue:
  2124   i Kenneth A. Knabenshue III, born 14 March 1945
  2125   ii Kerry L. Knabenshue, born 27 August 1949. Married 4
            October 1975 Catherine Golpfrick

1267 - SHIRLEY ANN(7) KNABENSHUE [Kenneth(6), Anna Evalee(5)
Shroyer, Malinda Ann(4) Wolf, Frederick(3), Jacob(2), Daniel(1)]
    Shirley Ann Knabenshue, fifth child of Kenneth and Wilma J.
(Boltenhouse) Knabenshue, was born 17 September 1935. She married 12
December 1953 John G. Strauser.
    Children of John G. and Shirley Ann (Knabenshue) Strauser:
  2126   i Debra K. Strauser, born 7 December 1957
  2127   ii Victoria Ann Strauser, born 22 December 1959
  2128 iii James E. Strauser, born 5 June 1961

    1268 - NAOMI BERNICE(7) MALHAUPT [Violet Audry(6) Knabenshue,
Anna Evalee(5) Shroyer, Malinda Ann(4) Wolf, Frederick(3), Jacob(2),
Daniel(1)]
    Naomi Bernice Malhaupt, first child of Verner W. and Violet Audry
(Knabenshue) Malhaupt, was born 15 May 1920. She married 22 November
1942 at South Bend, IN Raymond Cordtz.
    Children of Raymond and Naomi Bernice (Knabenshue) Cordtz:
+ 2129   i Anne Katherine Cordtz, born 15 April 1944
+ 2130   ii Susan Marie Cordtz, born 1 March 1948
  2131 iii Michael Raymond Cordtz, born 1 December 1952

    1269 - RICHARD VERNE(7) MALHAUPT [Violet Audry(6) Knabenshue,
Anna Evalee(5) Shroyer, Malinda Ann(4) Wolf, Frederick(3), Jacob(2),
Daniel(1)]
    Richard Verne Malhaupt, second child of Verner W. and Violet
Audry (Knabenshue) Malhaupt, was born 2 November 1922. He married 12
January 1945 Dorothy Murphy.
    Children of Richard Verne and Dorothy (Murphy) Malhaupt:
+ 2132   i Richard Carl Malhaupt, born 10 June 1946
+ 2133   ii Kristine Lynn Malhaupt, born 16 January 1951

    1270 - MARJORIE F.(7) MALHAUPT [Violet Audry(6) Knabenshue, Anna
Evalee(5) Shroyer, Malinda Ann(4) Wolf, Frederick(3), Jacob(2),
Daniel(1)]
    Marjorie F. Malhaupt, third child of Verner W. and Violet Audry
(Knabenshue) Malhaupt, was born 29 September 1924. She married _____
Kinas.
    Children of _____ and Marjorie F. (Malhaupt) Kinas:
+ 2134   i Robert E. Kinas, born 27 April 1943
+ 2135   ii Ronald Dean Kinas, born 12 March 1945
+ 2136 iii Richard Douglas Kinas, born 1 October 1946
  2137   iv Margie L. Kinas, born 4 October 1952. Married 2 November
           1971 George M. Cote'

    1271 - GENEVIEVE I.(7) MALHAUPT [Violet Audry(6) Knabenshue, Anna
Evalee(5) Shroyer, Malinda Ann(4) Wolf, Frederick(3), Jacob(2),
Daniel(1)]
    Genevieve I. Malhaupt, fourth child of Verner W. and Violet Audry
(Knabenshue) Malhaupt, was born 9 March 1926. She married 13 September
1947 Gerald Shultz.
    Child of Gerald and Genevieve I. (Malhaupt) Shultz:
  2138   i Dennis P. Shultz, born 21 July 1954 at Norfolk, VA

    1272 - VERNA L.(7) MALHAUPT [Violet Audry(6) Knabenshue, Anna
Evalee(5) Shroyer, Malinda Ann(4) Wolf, Frederick(3), Jacob(2),
Daniel(1)]
    Verna L. Malhaupt, fifth child of Verner W. and Violet Audry
(Knabenshue) Malhaupt, was born 23 August 1929. She married 1 October

1949 William McElhemy.
    Children of William and Verna L. (Malhaupt) McElhemy:
+ 2139   i Sandra J. McElhemy, born 25 November 1950
  2140   ii Nancy Jo McElhemy, born 13 May 1953

    1273 - ESTHER IRENE(7) JACKMAN [Vivian Ann(6) Knabenshue, Anna
Evalee(5) Shroyer, Malinda Ann(4) Wolf, Frederick(3), Jacob(2),
Daniel(1)]
    Esther Irene Jackman, first child of Alvia and Vivian Ann (Kna-
benshue) Jackman, was born 25 October 1919. She married 16 November
1946 at Traverse City, MI Paul Arp.
    Children of Paul and Esther Irene (Jackman) Arp:
+ 2141   i Robert Leroy Arp, born 6 July 1947
  2142   ii Richard P. Arp, born 24 January 1953

    1274 - VIRGINIA M.(7) JACKMAN [Vivian Ann(6) Knabenshue, Anna
Evalee(5) Shroyer, Malinda Ann(4) Wolf, Frederick(3), Jacob(2),
Daniel(1)]
    Virginia M. Jackman, second child of Alvia and Vivian Ann (Kna-
benshue) Jackman, was born 24 January 1922. She married 5 December
1945 Ronald Deal.
    Children of Ronald and Virginia M. (Jackman) Deal:
+ 2143   i Manford Paul Deal, born 1 April 1947
  2144   ii Judith Marie Deal, born 19 February 1951. Married 15 June
            1974 Lyle G. White

    1276 - EARL WAYNE(7) JACKMAN [Vivian Ann(6) Knabenshue, Anna
Evalee(5) Shroyer, Malinda Ann(4) Wolf, Frederick(3), Jacob(2),
Daniel(1)]
    Earl Wayne Jackman, fourth child of Alvia and Vivian Ann (Knaben-
shue) Jackman, was born 12 January 1927. He married 4 June 1965 Sue
Wallace, died 22 March 1966.
    Child of Earl Wayne and Sue (Wallace) Jackman:
  2145   i Shannon Marie Jackman, born 21 July 1965

    1277 - BETTY ANN(7) JACKMAN [Vivian Ann(6) Knabenshue, Anna
Evalee(5) Shroyer, Malinda Ann(4) Wolf, Frederick(3), Jacob(2),
Daniel(1)]
    Betty Ann Jackman, fifth child of Alvia and Vivian Ann (Knaben-
shue) Jackman, was born 27 August 1930. She married 1) _____ Finnila
and 2) 14 February 1969 Kenneth Archer.
    Children of _____ and Betty Ann (Jackman) Finnila:
  2146   i Michael K. Finnila, born 13 July 1950
+ 2147   ii David R. Finnila, born 28 October 1951
+ 2148 iii Christie Lynn Finnila, born 1 April 1955

    1278 - ALTON R.(7) JACKMAN [Vivian Ann(6) Knabenshue, Anna
Evalee(5) Shroyer, Malinda Ann(4) Wolf, Frederick(3), Jacob(2),
Daniel(1)]
    Alton R. Jackman, sixth child of Alvia and Vivian Ann (Knaben-
shue) Jacklin, was born 12 April 1932. He married 5 December 1955
Shirley Stiener.
    Children of Alton R. and Shirley (Stiener) Jackman:
  2149 · i Jeffery L. Jackman, born 14 July 1956
  2150   ii Randy S. Jackman, born 22 August 1959

1280 - JOSEPH L.(7) JACKMAN [Vivian Ann(6) Knabenshue, Anna
Evalee(5) Shroyer, Malinda Ann(4) Wolf, Frederick(3), Jacob(2),
Daniel(1)]
Joseph L. Jackman, eighth child of Alvia and Vivian Ann (Knaben-
shue) Jackman, was born 26 December 1941. He married 5 May 1962 Sue
McWalters.
Children of Joseph L. and Sue (McWalters) Jackman:
2151   i Kristen N. Jackman, born 5 October 1965
2152   ii Jason Jackman, born 8 January 1971 at Dayton, OH

1282 - BARTON LEE(7) BRUGH [Alta Irene(6) Shroyer, Harvey Howard
(5), Malinda Ann(4) Wolf, Frederick(3), Jacob(2), Daniel(1)]
Barton Lee Brugh, first child of Charles Raymond and Alta Irene
(Shroyer) Brugh, was born 8 April 1942 at South Bend, St Joseph
County, IN. He married 18 July 1964 at Plymouth, IN Marilyn Fish, born
23 February 1942 at Plymouth, died 28 May 1990 at Plymouth.
Children of Barton and Marilyn (Fish) Brugh:
2153   i Bradley Brugh, born 5 September 1965 at Indianapolis, IN
2154   ii Jeffry Brugh, born 29 November 1966 at Indianapolis, IN

1283 - BARBARA ANN(7) BRUGH [Alta Irene(6) Shroyer, Harvey
Howard(5), Malinda Ann(4) Wolf, Frederick(3), Jacob(2), Daniel(1)]
Barbara Ann Brugh, second child of Charles Raymond and Alta Irene
(Shroyer) Brugh, was born 3 October 1944 at South Bend, St. Joseph
County, IN. She married 5 August 1967 at South Bend Richard Wadzin-
ski.
Children of Richard and Barbara Ann (Brugh) Wadzinski:
2155   i Scott Richard Wadzinski, born 24 June 1971 at South Bend,
           IN
2156   ii Todd Alan Wadzinski, born 22 February 1976 at South Bend,
           IN

1284 - JOANNE EVELYN(7) DAY [Mildred Lucille(6) Shroyer, Harvey
Howard(5), Malinda Ann(4) Wolf, Frederick(3), Jacob(2), Daniel(1)]
Joanne Evelyn Day, first child of Celestine Edward and Mildred
Lucille (Shroyer) Day, was born 14 August 1930 at Montreal, Quebec,
Canada. She married 26 November 1949 at Rockford, IL Theodore James
DePew, born 6 November 1929 at Zion, IL.
Children of Theodore James and Joanne Evelyn (Day) DePew:
+ 2157   i Dayna Christine DePew, born 23 November 1950
+ 2158   ii Tracy Joanne DePew, born 23 April 1953
+ 2159 iii Douglas James DePew, born 17 May 1961

1285 - RICHARD EDWARD(7) DAY [Mildred Lucille(6) Shroyer, Harvey
Howard(5), Malinda Ann(4) Wolf, Frederick(3), Jacob(2), Daniel(1)]
Richard Edward Day, second child of Celestine Edward and Mildred
Lucille (Shroyer) Day, was born 4 June 1932 at Montreal, Quebec,
Canada. He married 2 August 1952 at Love's Park, IL Dorothy Jean
Husen, born 25 January 1932.
Children of Richard Edward and Dorothy Jean (Husen) Day, born at
Rockford, IL:
2160   i Denise Lynette Day, born 19 August 1954
+ 2161   ii Diane Day, born 19 March 1957
2162 iii Dann Richard Day, born 3 May 1962. Married 10 June 1989 at
           Rockford, IL Kimberly Owens
2163   iv Tammy Marie Day, born 26 August 1964. Married 26 May 1984
           at Rockford, IL Kelly E. Nelson

1286 - CRAIG DOUGLAS(7) DAY [Mildred Lucille(6) Shroyer, Harvey Howard(5), Malinda Ann(4) Wolf, Frederick(3), Jacob(2), Daniel(1)]
     Craig Douglas Day, third child of Celestine Edward and Mildred Lucille (Shroyer) Day, was born 6 May 1934 at Mishawaka, St. Joseph County, IN. He married 26 June 1954 at Rockford, IL Betty Seymour, born 2 November 1936.
     Child of Craig Douglas and Betty (Seymour) Day:
2164   i Kelly Jean Day, born 12 April 1961 at Rockford, IL

1287 - BRIAN DEAN(7) DAY [Mildred Lucille(6) Shroyer, Harvey Howard(5), Malinda Ann(4) Wolf, Frederick(3), Jacob(2), Daniel(1)]
     Brian Dean Day, fourth child of Celestine Edward and Mildred Lucille (Shroyer) Day, was born 27 September 1944 at Rockford, IL. He married 1) 28 November 1970 at Love's Park, IL Lucille Sandra Bagley, born 23 January 1952. They divorced and Brian married 2) 9 June 1973 Sandi (Mackey) Amans, born 2 February 1942, who had married first _____ Amans.
     Child of Brian Dean and Lucille Sandra (Bagley) Day:
2165   i Brian James Day, born 20 January 1973 at Rockford, IL
     Children of _____ and Sandi (Mackey) Amans (stepchildren of Brian Dean Day), born at Rockford, IL:
2166   i Dean Amans, born 13 December 1961
2167   ii Jodi Amans, born 13 November 1963
2168   iii Katie Amans, born 18 March 1967
     Child of Brian Dean and Sandi (Mackey) (Amans) Day:
2169   i Shannon Colleen Day, born 10 June 1974 at Rockford, IL

1288 - JANICE ELAINE(7) STARKWEATHER [Norma Leora(6) Shroyer, Harvey Howard(5), Malinda Ann(4) Wolf, Frederick(3), Jacob(2), Daniel(1)]
     Janice Elaine Starkweather, first child of Walter Edward and Norma Leora (Shroyer) Starkweather, was born 17 February 1934 at Madison, WI. She married 16 October 1954 at Madison, WI Marvin Francis Van Lysel, born 29 November 1934 at Wisconsin Rapids, WI.
     Children of Marvin Francis and Janice Elaine (Starkweather) Van Lysel:
2170   i Michael Scott Van Lysel, born 8 November 1955 at Wisconsin Rapids, WI
+ 2171   ii Sally Lynn Van Lysel, born 30 March 1958
+ 2172   iii Stephen Patrick Van Lysel, born 10 March 1961

1290 - PETER EDWARD(7) STARKWEATHER [Norma Leora(6) Shroyer, Harvey Howard(5), Malinda Ann(4) Wolf, Frederick(3), Jacob(2), Daniel(1)]
     Peter Edward Starkweather, third child of Walter Edward and Norma Leora (Shroyer) Starkweather, was born 22 March 1937 at Madison, WI. He married 8 July 1961 at Oak Park, IL Frances Ann Kerrigan, born 9 March 1937 at Michigan City, IN.
     Children of Peter Edward and Frances Ann (Kerrigan) Starkweather:
2173   i Patricia Lynn Starkweather, born 16 August 1962 at Oak Park, IL. Married 3 October 1987 at Middletown, WI William Peter Hammill
2174   ii John Phillip Starkweather, born 22 December 1964 at Madison, WI
2175   iii Melinda Ann Starkweather, born 18 September 1966 at Madison, WI. Married 24 November 1989 at Madison, WI Joseph Plasterer

197

2176   iv Sandra Marie Starkweather, born 4 August 1969 at Madison, WI

1291 - LINDA ANN(7) STARKWEATHER [Norma Leora(6) Shroyer, Harvey Howard(5), Malinda Ann(4) Wolf, Frederick(3), Jacob(2), Daniel(1)]
    Linda Ann Starkweather, fourth child of Walter Edward and Norma Leora (Shroyer) Starkweather, was born 4 March 1942 at Madison, WI. She married 29 September 1962 at Madison Harley E. Spilde, born 31 January 1940 at Madison.
    Children of Harley E. and Linda Ann (Starkweather) Spilde:
2177   i Eric Andrew Spilde, born 21 October at Temple, TX
2178   ii Thor Allen Spilde, born 21 March 1967 at Madison, WI
2179   iii Kirsten Ann Spilde, born 24 February 1969 at Madison, WI
2180   iv Britta Allison Spilde, born 31 January 1974 at Madison, WI

1292 - NORBURT RAYMOND(7) SHROYER [Dean Kermit(6), Harvey Howard(5), Malinda Ann(4) Wolf, Frederick(3), Jacob(2), Daniel(1)]
    Norburt Raymond Shroyer, child of Dean Kermit and Gladys Kusmanovitch (Bordman) Shroyer, was born 31 October 1935 at Mishawaka, IN. He married 1) 2 August 1957 at Rome, Italy Leonilda Paccasassi. They divorced July 1970 and Norburt married 2) 3 March 1977 at Plainfield, IN Claudia A. _____.
    Children of Norburt Raymond and Leonilda (Paccasassi) Shroyer:
2181   i Deana L. Shroyer, born 7 May 1958 at Lakeland, FL. Married 8 July at Leavenworth, KS Douglas Price
2182   ii Lea G. Shroyer, born 10 April 1961 at Aberdeen, ND
2183   iii Marina A. Shroyer, born 26 June 1962 at El Paso, TX
2184   iv Mara M. Shroyer, born 1 September 1963 at Biloxi, MS

1293 - CHARLENE MARIE(7) SHROYER [Dalton Howard(6), Harvey Howard(5), Malinda Ann(4) Wolf, Frederick(3), Jacob(2), Daniel(1)]
    Charlene Marie Shroyer, first child of Dalton Howard and Charlotte (Pherson) Shroyer, was born 29 July 1944 at Mishawaka, IN. She married 1) 26 September 1964 at Litchfield, MN James Pearson, born 26 October 1944. They divorced in 1988 and she married 2) 25 February 1989 at Mesa, AZ James M. Kelley.
    Children of James and Charlene Marie (Shroyer) Pearson:
+ 2185   i Cheryl Marie Pearson, born 24 March 1965
  2186   ii Jeffry David Pearson, born 1 September 1966 at Grand Maria, MN. Married 29 December 1990 at Minneapolis, MN
        _____ _____

1294 - WAYNE HOWARD(7) SHROYER [Dalton Howard(6), Harvey Howard(5), Malinda Ann(4) Wolf, Frederick(3), Jacob(2), Daniel(1)]
    Wayne Howard Shroyer, second child of Dalton Howard and Charlotte (Pherson) Shroyer, was born 14 May 1946 at Mishawaka, IN. He married 1) at Minneapolis, MN Cathy Ouji. They divorced in 1977 and Wayne married 2) September 1977 Karen _____.
    Child of Wayne Howard and Cathy(Ouji) Shroyer:
2187   i Adam Wayne Shroyer, born 26 March 1971 at Minneapolis, MN

1295 - CARYN MARGARET(7) SHROYER [Dalton Howard(6), Harvey Howard(5), Malinda Ann(4) Wolf, Frederick(3), Jacob(2), Daniel(1)]
    Caryn Margaret Shroyer, third child of Dalton Howard and Charlotte (Pherson) Shroyer, was born 3 December 1948 at Mishawaka, IN. She married 1) at St. Paul, MN Roger Speck. After divorcing she married 2) at Muskegon, MI James Clifford and 3) 8 December 1990 at Mesa, AZ Paul Potter.

Children of Roger and Caryn Margaret (Shroyer) Speck:
2188   i Brian Speck, born 24 November 1967 at Grand Marie, MN
2189   ii Collette Caryn Speck, born 4 July 1970 at Muskegon, MI.
          Married 29 July 1985 at Las Vegas, NV Patrick Terpak

1296 - ROBERT(7) SHROYER [Dalton Howard(6), Harvey Howard(5),
Malinda Ann(4) Wolf, Frederick(3), Jacob(2), Daniel(1)]
    Robert Shroyer, fourth child of Dalton Howard and Charlotte
(Pherson) Shroyer, was born 29 January 1952 at Mishawaka, St. Joseph
County, IN. He married 5 June 1983 Kelly Carter. They divorced 14
December 1986.
    Child of Robert and Kelly (Carter) Shroyer:
2190   i Darrin Robert Shroyer; born 27 December 1983

1297 - LARRY(7) SHROYER [Keith Laverne(6), Harvey Howard(5),
Malinda Ann(4) Wolf, Frederick(3), Jacob(2), Daniel(1)]
    Larry Shroyer, first child of Keith Laverne and Barbara (Duck-
worth) Shroyer, was born 14 March 1948 at Mishawaka, IN. he married 17
August 1968 at South Bend, IN Suzanne Wade, born 1 March 1948 at
Peoria, IL.
    Children of Larry and Suzanne (Wade) Shroyer, born at Mishawaka,
IN:
2191   i Theresa Shroyer, born 4 November 1971
2192   ii Erica Shroyer, born 23 February 1973
2193 iii Laree Shroyer, born 1 May 1974

1298 - LAURA MAE(7) SHROYER [Keith Laverne(6), Harvey Howard(5),
Malinda Ann(4) Wolf, Frederick(3), Jacob(2), Daniel(1)]
    Laura Mae Shroyer, second child of Keith Laverne and Barbara
(Duckworth) Shroyer, was born 15 February 1949 at Kansas City, MO. She
married 7 July 1967 at Anniston, AL Thomas Avery, born 19 July 1948
at Mishawaka, IN
    Children of Thomas and Laura Mae (Shroyer) Avery:
2194   i Thomas Avery, born 23 May 1968 at South Bend, IN, died 17
          April 1978 at Mishawaka, IN
2195   ii Jennifer Avery, born 7 November 1973 at Elkhart, IN
2196 iii Suzanne Lee Avery, born 4 November 1978 at South Bend, IN
2197   iv John Avery, born 12 December 1981 at South Bend, IN
2198   v Kayleen Marie Avery, born 18 September 1983 at South Bend,
          IN

1300 - KATHLEEN(7) SHROYER [Keith Laverne(6), Harvey Howard(5),
Malinda Ann(4) Wolf, Frederick(3), Jacob(2), Daniel(1)]
    Kathleen Shroyer, fourth child of Keith Laverne and Barbara
(Duckworth) Shroyer, was born 5 October 1951 at South bend, IN. She
married 26 August 1972 Max Wright, born 4 November 1948.
    Children of Max and Kathleen (Shroyer) Wright:
2199   i Max Wright, born 7 March 1973 at Elkhart, IN
2200   ii Cassandra Wright, born 18 September 1974 at Elkhart, IN
2201 iii Aaron Wright, born 31 July 1976 at Elkhart, IN
2202   iv Melissa Wright, born 10 April 1979 at Elkhart, IN

1301 - VIRGIL(7) PYLE [Mary Alice(6) Montel, Samuel(5), Abra-
ham(4), Susan(3) Wolf, Jacob(2), Daniel(1)]
    Virgil Pyle, first child of Elmer C. and Mary Alice (Montel)
Pyle, was born 18 May 1903. He married 24 November 1927 Hazel Baker,
born 27 July 1905, daughter of George and Amy May (Flora) Baker.

Children of Virgil and Hazel (Baker) Pyle:
+ 2203   i Byron Jay Pyle, born 8 July 1929
+ 2204   ii Ina Louise Pyle, born 9 June 1933

1302 - WILBUR(7) PYLE [Mary Alice(6) Montel, Samuel(5), Abraham(4), Susan(3) Wolf, Jacob(2), Daniel(1)]
Wilbur Pyle, second child of Elmer C. and Mary Alice (Montel) Pyle, was born 23 November 1906. He married 20 november 1932 Hazel Snell, born 27 November 1912, daughter of John Amsa and Esta Mae (Kreider) Snell.
Children of Wilbur and Hazel (Snell) Pyle:
+ 2205   i Vivian Pyle, born 20 August 1933
+ 2206   ii Leonard Pyle, born 8 May 1936

1303 - ROBERT(7) PYLE [Mary Alice(6) Montel, Samuel(5), Abraham(4), Susan(3) Wolf, Jacob(2), Daniel(1)]
Robert Pyle, third child of Elmer C. and Mary Alice (Montel) Pyle, was born 19 March 1909. He married 11 October 1931 Lucile Rager.
Children of Robert and Lucile (Rager) Pyle:
  2207   i Doris Pyle, born 28 February 1933
  2208   ii Evelyn Pyle, born 9 December 1934
  2209 iii Esther Pyle, born 8 July 1936
  2210   iv Cecil Pyle, born 7 September 1937

1304 - EMERY(7) PYLE [Mary Alice(6) Montel, Samuel(5), Abraham(4), Susan(3) Wolf, Jacob(2), Daniel(1)]
Emery Pyle, fourth child of Elmer C. and Mary Alice (Montel) Pyle, was born 30 July 1911. He married 14 November 1931 Grace Moe, born 1 September 1909, died 14 May 1975, daughter of Homer and Cora (McPherson) Moe.
Children of Emery and Grace (Moe) Pyle:
+ 2211   i Helen Joan Pyle, born 6 March 1934
+ 2212   ii Loren Pyle, born 11 July 1938

1306 - HAROLD M.(7) NEHER [Elizabeth(6) Montel, Samuel(5), Abraham(4), Susan(3) Wolf, Jacob(2), Daniel(1)]
Harold M. Neher, first child of Simon P. and Elizabeth (Montel) Neher, was born 8 April 1904, died 26 October 1972. He married 28 February 1928 Fannie Bridge, born 30 April 1906, daughter of George and Lydia Margaret (Byroad) Bridge.
Children of Harold M. and Fannie (Bridge) Neher;
+ 2213   i Donald Neher, born 18 December 1928
+ 2214   ii Dean Neher, born 20 April 1930
+ 2215 iii Dale Arden Neher, born 16 October 1931

1307 - CHARLES S.(7) NEHER [Elizabeth(6) Montel, Samuel(5), Abraham(4), Susan(3) Wolf, Jacob(2), Daniel(1)]
Charles S. Neher, second child of Simon P. and Elizabeth (Montel) Neher, was born 1 March 1906. He married 20 January 1934 Iva Brock, born 1 October 1911, daughter of Luther and Ethel (Payne) Brock.
Children of Charles S. and Iva (Brock) Neher:
+ 2216   i Charles E. Neher, born 29 November 1937
+ 2217   ii Terry Eugene Neher, born 16 January 1940
+ 2218 iii Joe Allen Neher, born 25 February 1947
+ 2219   iv Kenneth Ray Neher, born 24 December 1950

1308 - ESTHER L.(7) NEHER [Elizabeth(6) Montel, Samuel(5), Abraham(4), Susan(3) Wolf, Jacob(2), Daniel(1)]

Esther L. Neher, third child of Simon P. and Elizabeth (Montel) Neher, was born 7 March 1910. She married in 1928 William Harter Hutchens, born 1 August 1906, died 4 September 1977, son of William and Oral (Wilson) Hutchens.

Children of William Harter and Esther L. (Neher) Hutchens:
2220   i Beverly Jene Hutchens, born 13 June 1929
+ 2221   ii Dianne Elizabeth Hutchens, born 27 December 1944

1309 - E. PAUL(7) NEHER [Elizabeth(6) Montel, Samuel(5), Abraham(4), Susan(3) Wolf, Jacob(2), Daniel(1)]
E. Paul Neher, fourth child of Simon P. and Elizabeth (Montel) Neher, was born 24 July 1912. He married 14 November 1936 Evelyn McKee, born 13 July 1914, daughter of Jacob M. and Lora (Thomas) McKee.

Children of E. Paul and Evelyn (McKee) Neher:
+ 2222   i Sharon Kay Neher, born 1 September 1939
+ 2223   ii Beth Diann Neher, born 13 January 1942
  2224   iii Stephen Paul Neher, born 8 July 1944

1310 - DEVERL(7) MONTEL [Charles(6), Samuel(5), Abraham(4), Susan(3) Wolf, Jacob(2), Daniel(1)]
Deverl Montel, first child of Charles and Mary C. (Freed) Montel, was born 28 July 1912, died 20 August 1980. He married 5 December 1931 Ruby (Ayres) Sellers, born 24 March 1913, daughter of Edward and Ruth (Metzger) Ayres. This was her second marriage having previously been married to _____ Sellers.

Child of _____ and Ruby (Ayres) Sellers (stepchild of Deverl Montel):
2225   i Richard Sellers, born 7 March 1931. married 29 October
             1974 Mary Belle McClouse
Children of Deverl and Ruby (Ayres) (Sellers) Montel:
+ 2226   i Carolyn Montel, born 4 July 1932
+ 2227   ii Phyllis Montel, born 4 July 1933
+ 2228   iii Larry Montel, born 28 June 1935
+ 2229   iv Robert Montel, born 14 October 1936
+ 2230   v Roger Montel, born 27 May 1938

1312 - RUBY(7) MONTEL [Charles(6), Samuel(5), Abraham(4), Susan(3) Wolf, Jacob(2), Daniel(1)]
Ruby Montel, third child of Charles and Mary C. (Freed) Montel, was born 30 October 1916. She married 19 February 1938 Hobert D. Sponhaurer, born 24 March 1915, son of Niles and Dessie (Harter) Sponhaurer.

Children of Hobert D. and Ruby (Montel) Sponhaurer:
2231   i Marvey Sponhaurer, born 28 December 1938. Married 19
             August 1962 Beverly Wysong
2232   ii Sherry Sponhaurer, born 25 July 1943. Married 5 June 1971
             Charles Dennis Todd Jr
2233   iii Charles Sponhaurer, born 10 August 1948. Married 23 August
             1969 Barbara Weaver

1315 - PHOEBE LAVON(7) METZGER [Edith(6) Montel, Samuel(5), Abraham(4), Susan(3) Wolf, Jacob(2), Daniel(1)]
Phoebe Lavon Metzger, second child of Chester Ray and Edith (Montel) Metzger, was born 4 September 1912. She married 31 March 1934 Leon Clingaman, born 10 Octobert 1906, died 17 November 1981, son of Sam and Bessie (Whitney) Clingaman.

Children of Leon and Phoebe Lavon (Metzger) Clingaman:
+ 2234   i Max Leon Clingaman, born 25 January 1939
+ 2235   ii Don Clingaman, born 1 February 1942

1316 - ELIZABETH RUTH(7) METZGER [Edith(6) Montel, Samuel(5), Abraham(4), Susan(3) Wolf, Jacob(2), Daniel(1)]
      Elizabeth Ruth Metzger, third child of Chester Ray and Edith (Montel) Metzger, was born 14 December 1914. She married 7 March 1936 Donald B. Warner, born 25 April 1912, died 17 August 1976, son of J. V. and Blanche (Bowers) Warner.
      Children of Donald B. and Elizabeth Ruth (Metzger) Warner:
+ 2236   i Beverly Sue Warner, born 17 March 1940
  2237   ii Peggy Jo Warner, born 12 April 1951

1317 - ERNEST RAY(7) METZGER [Edith(6) Montel, Samuel(5), Abraham(4), Susan(3) Wolf, Jacob(2), Daniel(1)]
      Ernest Ray Metzger, fourth child of Chester Ray and Edith (Montel) Metzger, was born 5 November 1917. He married Bonnie Schipper Meinert.
      Child of Ernest Ray and Bonnie (Schipper) Metzger:
  2238   i Tamra Ann Metzger, born 23 February 1958

1319 - GRACE M.(7) MONTEL [Albert(6), Samuel(5), Abraham(4), Susan(3) Wolf, Jacob(2), Daniel(1)]
      Grace M. Montel, first child of Albert and Bertha (Miller) Montel, was born 18 October 1910. She married 24 February 1932 Harry Albright, born 24 February 1910.
      Children of Harry and Grace M. (Montel) Albright:
  2239   i Leon Albright, twin, born 24 September 1944
  2240   ii Kenneth Albright, twin, born 24 September 1944

1320 - JOE(7) MONTEL [Albert(6), Samuel(5), Abraham(4), Susan(3) Wolf, Jacob(2), Daniel(1)]
      Joe Montel, second child of Albert and Bertha (Miller) Montel, was born 29 May 1913. He married 17 February 1940 Mildred Gephart.
      Stepchild of Joe Montel:
  2241   i Lavone Gephart, born 18 November 1936
      Child of Joe and Mildred (Gephart) Montel:
  2242   i Larry Joe Montel, born 28 November 1940

1321 - EVERETT(7) MONTEL [Albert(6), Samuel(5), Abraham(4), Susan(3) Wolf, Jacob(2), Daniel(1)]
      Everett Montel, third child of Albert and Bertha (Miller) Montel, was born 8 September 1916. He married Imogene Houser, daughter of John and Esther (Coon) Wesley.
      Children of Everett and Imogene (Houser) Montel:
  2243   i Karen Montel, born 1 September 1949
  2244   ii Norma Montel, born 18 February 1952

1322 - HAROLD RAY(7) MONTEL [Albert(6), Samuel(5), Abraham(4), Susan(3) Wolf, Jacob(2), Daniel(1)]
      Harold Ray Montel, fourth child of Albert and Bertha (Miller) Montel, was born 31 January 1919. He married 20 march 1941 Lois Evelyn Haupert, born 24 August 1919, daughter of Ross and Ada (Hubbard) Haupert.
      Children of Harold Ray and Lois Evelyn (Haupert) Montel:
+ 2245   i Margaret Shirley Montel, born 6 December 1942
+ 2246   ii Beverly Kay Montel, born 14 March 1948

2247   iii Shirley Ann Montel, born 6 April 1950. Married 16 June
         1979 Kim Ray Kuhn

   1323 - MAX ALBERT(7) MONTEL [Albert(6), Samuel(5), Abraham(4),
Susan(3) Wolf, Jacob(2), Daniel(1)]
     Max Albert Montel, fifth child of Albert and Bertha (Miller)
Montel, was born 26 July 1920. He married 24 February 1941 Nellie
Gingle.
     Children of Max Albert and Nellie (Gingle) Montel;
   2248   i Steven Montel, born 7 November 1946. Married Carolyn Davis
   2249   ii Linda Montel, born 8 September 1953

   1324 - DELBERT(7) MONTEL [Albert(6), Samuel(5), Abraham(4),
Susan(3) Wolf, Jacob(2), Daniel(1)]
     Delbert Montel, sixth child of Albert and Bertha (Miller) Montel,
was born 17 February 1924. He married 14 December 1947 Beulah Stiver.
     Children of Delbert and Beulah (Stiver) Montel:
   2250   i Stephen Montel, born 1 September 1951
   2251   ii David Montel, born 21 December 1960
   2252   iii Martha Montel, born 9 October 1962
   2253   iv Esther Montel, born 26 February 1964

   1325 - LOIS(7) MONTEL [Albert(6), Samuel(5), Abraham(4), Susan(3)
Wolf, Jacob(2), Daniel(1)]
     Lois Montel, seventh child of Albert and Bertha (Miller) Montel,
was born 8 October 1926. She married 17 October 1943 Robert Gearhart,
born 21 May 1922, son of Ralph and Edna (Brown) Gearhart.
     Children of Robert and Lois (Montel) Gearhart:
   2254   i Thomas Lyle Gearhart, born 17 September 1946. Married 10
           October 1971 Elaine K. Shambarger
   2255   ii Elaine Kay Gearhart, born 18 July 1948. Married 31 May
           1969 Daniel Drabenstat
   2256   iii Robert Kent Gearhart, born 3 February 1953. Married 16
           December 1972 Pamela Kay Hoover

   1326 - WAYNE(7) MONTEL [Albert(6), Samuel(5), Abraham(4),
Susan(3) Wolf, Jacob(2), Daniel(1)]
     Wayne Montel, eighth child of Albert and Bertha (Miller) Montel,
was born 31 March 1933. He married 23 August 1963 Karen Graff.
     Children of Wayne and Karen (Graff) Montel:
   2257   i Julie Montel, born 16 July 1964
   2258   ii Gregory Montel, born 13 July 1965
   2259   iii Jeffery Montel, born 18 March 1967

   1327 - RETHA ELIZABETH(7) MONTEL [Emery(6), Samuel(5), Abra-
ham(4), Susan(3) Wolf, Jacob(2), Daniel(1)]
     Retha Elizabeth Montel, first child of Emery and Mary Fay (Metz-
ger) Montel, was born 18 August 1917. She married 11 March 1939
Everett Ivan Jenkins, born 16 April 1911, son of Harry F. and Jessie
(Stoner) Jenkins.
     Children of Everett Ivan and Retha Elizabeth (Montel) Jenkins:
 + 2260   i Robert Lamar Jenkins, born 7 May 1940
 + 2261   ii Leonard Alan Jenkins, born 23 April 1944
 + 2262   iii Arden Ray Jenkins, born 9 September 1948
   2263   iv Carl Gene Jenkins, born 10 July 1954

   1328 - LAMOIN ALBERT(7) MONTEL [Emery(6), Samuel(5), Abraham(4),
Susan(3) Wolf, Jacob(2), Daniel(1)]

Lamoin Albert Montel, second child of Emery and Mary Fay (Metzger) Montel, was born 7 August 1919. He married 25 September 1942 Mary Mildred Callahan, born 8 August 1919, daughter of John Joseph and Ruth (Anderson) Callahan.
    Child of Lamoin and Mary Mildred (Callahan) Montel:
+ 2264   i Gary Eugene Montel, born 9 November 1943

    1329 - BLANCHE MATTIE(7) MONTEL [Emery(6), Samuel(5), Abraham(4), Susan(3) Wolf, Jacob(2), Daniel(1)]
    Blanche Mattie Montel, third child of Emery and Mary Fay (Metzger) Montel, was born 12 June 1922. She married 10 December 1941 Russel Elmer Fisher, born 4 March 1915, died 4 June 1977, son of Charles and Manda (Bentz) Fisher.
    Children of Russel Elmer and Blanche Mattie (Montel) Fisher:
  2265   i Melvin Leroy Fisher, born 30 January 1945. Married 2 March 1971 Jill Dooley, they divorced
  2266   ii James Russel Fisher, born 3 April 1949
+ 2267 iii Ann Arlene Fisher, born 11 May 1951
+ 2268   iv Paul Ray Fisher, born 11 February 1954

    1330 - JOHN IRVIN(7) MONTEL [Emery(6), Samuel(5), Abraham(4), Susan(3) Wolf, Jacob(2), Daniel(1)]
    John Irvin Montel, fourth child of Emery and Mary Fay (Metzger) Montel, was born 18 March 1924. He married 25 July 1948 Wanda Jean Bryan, born 7 May 1930, daughter of Henry and Edith (Hively) Bryan.
    Children of John Irvin Montel and Wanda Jean (Bryan) Montel:
  2269   i Brenda Sue Montel, born 4 July 1951. Married 3 July 1971 Dewayne Thomas
+ 2270   ii Barbara Jean Montel, born 7 August 1953

    1331 - MILDRED PHOEBE(7) MONTEL [Ralph(6), Samuel(5), Abraham(4), Susan(3) Wolf,Jacob(2), Daniel(1)]
    Mildred Phoebe Montel, first child of Ralph and Oznola V. (Freed) Montel, was born 19 August 1915. She married 1) William Teeter, died 8 April 1936, and 2) 30 march 1941 James C. Eads.
    Child of William and Mildred Phoebe (Montel) Teeter:
  2271   i Harold Ray Teeter, born 5 August 1933
    Child of James C. and Mildred Phoebe (Montel) (Teeter) Eads:
  2272   i Tommy Lee Eads, born 5 August 1942

    1332 - MARIE ESTHER(7) MONTEL [Ralph(6), Samuel(5), Abraham(4), Susan(3) Wolf, Jacob(2), Daniel(1)]
    Marie Esther Montel, second child of Ralph and Oznola V. (Freed) Montel, was born 19 August 1915. She married 25 October 1934 Wayne Bouse, born 14 July 1915, son of Chester and Daisy (Carr) Bouse.
    Children of Wayne and Marie Esther (Montel) Bouse:
+ 2273   i Marlene Marie Bouse, born 16 May 1935
+ 2274   ii Roberta Jean Bouse, born 25 October 1937
+ 2275 iii Terry Wayne Bouse, born 1 March 1943
+ 2276   iv Nancy Bouse, born 21 June 1945

    1333 - ELVA OZNOLA(7) MONTEL [Ralph(6), Samuel(5), Abraham(4), Susan(3) Wolf, Jacob(2), Daniel(1)]
    Elva Oznola Montel, third child of Ralph and Oznola V. (Freed) Montel, was born 20 August 1917, died 29 November 1958. She married 19 October 1935 Ira Ray Miller, born 2 May 1916, died 29 November 1958, son of Chester and Emma (Leiter) Miller.

Children of Ira Ray and Elva Oznola (Montel) Miller:
2277   i Richard Ray Miller, born 26 September 1940
2278   ii Toni Rita Miller, born 15 December 1943. Married 6 July
          1963 Terry L. Ayres, born 3 March 1944, son of Arden and
          Mary Elizabeth (Badskey) Ayres
2279 iii Robert Ryan Miller, born 4 December 1948.
2280   iv Randall R. Miller, born 14 September 1955, died 29 Novem-
          ber 1958

   1339 - MERLE D.(7) MONTEL [Ralph(6), Samuel(5), Abraham(4),
Susan(3) Wolf, Jacob(2), Daniel(1)]
   Merle D. Montel, ninth child of Ralph and Oznla V. (Freed)
Montel, was born 18 May 1939. He married 21 September 1958 Lessie Mae
Collins, born 12 April 1939.
   Children of Merle D. and Lessie Mae (Collins) Montel:
2281   i Cheryl Lynn Montel, born 19 November 1959
2282   ii Dean Ray Montel, born 6 August 1961
2283 iii Erica Gayle Montel, born 30 June 1970

   1340 - BEULAH MAY(7) MONTEL [Frank(6), Samuel(5), Abraham(4),
Susan(3) Wolf, Jacob(2), Daniel(1)]
   Beulah May Montel, first child of Frank and Mary (Burger) Montel,
was born 31 December 1919. She married 29 May 1938 David Emery Morphew, born 14 August 1916.
   Children of David Emery and Beulah May (Montel) Morphew:
  2284   i Dona Elaine Morphew, born 9 July 1943
+ 2285   ii Kathleen Sara Morphew, born 19 January 1945
+ 2286 iii Philip Lee Morphew, born 6 October 1947
  2287   iv Roger Allen Morphew, born 16 December 1949. Married Diana
          L. Sleighter

   1341 - EDWARD FRANK(7) MONTEL [Frank(6), Samuel(5), Abraham(4),
Susan(3) Wolf, Jacob(2), Daniel(1)]
   Edward Frank Montel, second child of Frank and Mary (Burger)
Montel, was born 10 March 1921. He married 15 april 1942 Hazel Jean
Werman. They divorced.
   Children of Edward Frank and Hazel Jean (Werman) Montel:
2288   i Susan Kay Montel, born 2 July 1944
2289   ii Jonathan Edward Montel, born 25 August 1948
2290 iii Dianna Jean Montel, born 8 March 1952
2291   iv Mark Montel

   1342 - ERNEST HAROLD(7) MONTEL [Frank(6), Samuel(5), Abraham(4),
Susan(3) Wolf, Jacob(2), Daniel(1)]
   Ernest Harold Montel, third child of Frank and Mary (Burger)
Montel, was born 16 May 1922. He married 10 March 1945 Enid Arleet
Puterbaugh, born 12 August 1921.
   Children of Ernest Harold and Enid Arleet (Puterbaugh) Montel:
2292   i Charlotte Montel. Married _____ Boynton, born 27 November
          1945
2293   ii Kenneth Montel, born 6 August 1948
2294 iii Barbara Jean Montel, born 25 September 1953
2295   iv Jane Ellen Montel, born 20 June 1959

   1343 - MARJORIE JANE(7) MONTEL [Frank(6), Samuel(5), Abraham(4),
Susan(3) Wolf, Jacob(2), Daniel(1)]
   Marjorie Jane Montel, fourth child of Frank and Mary (Burger)
Montel, was born 2 November 1924, died 11 April 1965. She married George

Allen Morgan, born 19 April 1919.
        Children of George Allen and Marjorie Jane (Montel) Morgan:
    2296   i Joan Kay Morgan, born 8 August 1945
    2297   ii George Joseph Morgan, 4 September 1946
    2298   iii Linda Jane Morgan, born 10 January 1948
    2299   iv Daniel Lee Morgan, 21 September 1954

        1344 - WALTER LLOYD(7) MONTEL [Frank(6), Samuel(5), Abraham(4),
Susan(3) Wolf, Jacob(2), Daniel(1)]
        Walter Lloyd Montel, fifth child of Frank and Mary(Burger)
Montel, was born 10 November 1926. He married 1947 Barbara Jean
Everts, born 23 February 1931.
        Children of Walter Lloyd and Barbara Jean (Everts) Montel:
    2300   i Sue Anne Montel, born 1 June 1948
    2301   ii Samuel Lloyd Montel, born 16 August 1950
    2302   iii Peggy Lynn Montel, born 31 March 1955

        1346 - ELIZABETH ANN(7) MONTEL [Frank(6), Samuel(5), Abraham(4),
Susan(3) Wolf, Jacob(2), Daniel(1)]
        Elizabeth Ann Montel, seventh child of Frank and Mary (Burger)
Montel, was born 2 December 1930. She married 1 June 1952 Noble Dwight
Morphew, born 26 January 1918, son of John Emery and Lena Myrtle
(Allen) Morphew.
        Children of Noble Dwight and Elizabeth Ann (Montel) Morphew:
    2303   i Timothy Kent Morphew, born 20 May 1953
    2304   ii Ryan Douglass Morphew, born 22 August 1954, died 13 May
              1956
  + 2305   iii Joseph Dwight Morphew, born 8 September 1956
    2306   iv Robert John Morphew, born 12 October 1959
    2307   v Nancy Lenore Morphew, born 10 February 1965

        1350 - RUTH ELEANOR(7) MONTEL [Frank(6), Samuel(5), Abraham(4),
Susan(3) Wolf, Jacob(2), Daniel(1)]
        Ruth Eleanor Montel, eleventh child of Frank and Mary (Burger)
Montel, was born 7 February 1934. She married 19 January 1957 James
Frederick Creighton, born 13 January 1932, son of Charles H. and Laura
E. (Wessman) Creighton.
        Children of James Frederick and Ruth Eleanor (Montel) Creighton:
    2308   i Karen Ruth Creighton, born 28 October 1957. Married 26
              April 1980 Gary Olson
  + 2309   ii Janice Leslie Creighton, born 12 May 1960
    2310   iii Stephanie Creighton, born 2 September 1961
    2311   iv James Christopher Creighton, born 5 August 1964
    2312   v Shawn Michael Creighton, born 12 May 1966
    2313   vi Kevin Francis Creighton, born 10 December 1970

        1355 - MIRIAM(7) OVERHOLSER - [Effie(6) Montel, Jacob(5), Abra-
ham(4), Susan(3) Wolf, Jacob(2), Daniel(1)]
        Miriam Overholser, second child of Howard and Effie (Montel)
Overholser, was born 4 September 1916. She married 27 December 1941
Gerald Shull, born 17 May 1913, died 19 October 1979.
        Children of Gerald and Miriam (Overholser) Shull:
  + 2314   i Helen Joyce Shull, born 22 September 1942
    2315   ii William Howard Shull, born 30 April 1944
  + 2316   iii Gerald Lamoine Shull, born 2 June 1948
  + 2317   iv Mary Ann Shull, born 8 January 1951

1361 - DELBERT MILTON(7) RHOADES [Iva Ann(6) Montel, Jacob(5), Abraham(4), Susan(3) Wolf, Jacob92), Daniel(1)]
    Delbert Milton Rhoades, first child of Sherman Alfred and Iva Ann (Montel) Rhoades, was born 28 August 1922. He married 12 October 1945 Hattie Jane Grossnickle, born 10 June 1927, daughter of Chester and Lula (Frederick) Grossnickle.
    Children of Delbert Milton and Hattie Jane (Grossnickle) Rhoades:
    2318   i Eugene Rhoades, born 25 November 1951. Married Elizabeth
              Chapman
    2319   ii David Milton Rhoades, born 27 June 1957. Married 1) 11
              June 1977 Cheryl Wrightsman, 2) 1981 Delynde Lynn Lightle
  + 2320 iii Steven Earl Rhoades, born 15 July 1960

    1362 - LEANNA MAY(7) RHOADES [Iva Ann(6) Montel, Jacob(5), Abraham(4), Susan(3) Wolf, Jacob(2), Daniel(1)]
    Leanna May Rhoades, second child of Sherman Alfred and Iva Ann (Montel) Rhoades, was born 13 May 1924. She married 31 December 1950 Delbert Adam Johnson, born 13 October 1908, died 16 July 1980, son of Marcellus E. and Sarah Elizabeth (Burns) Johnson.
    Children of Delbert Adam and Leanna May (Rhoades) Johnson:
    2321   i Terry Lynn Johnson, born 31 January 1952. Married 24 May
              1971 Pamela Bashore
    2322   ii Randy Johnson, born 23 November 1955

    1363 - WAYNE LOWELL(7) RHOADES [Iva Ann(6) Montel, Jacob(5), Abraham(4), Susan(3) Wolf, Jacob(2), Daniel(1)]
    Wayne Lowell Rhoades, third child of Sherman Alfred and Iva Ann (Montel) Rhoades, was born 1 September 1926, died 4 May 1978. He married 12 February 1954 Martha Toy, born 20 October 1920, daughter of Homer Toy.
    Children of Wayne Lowell and Martha (Toy) Rhoades:
    2323   i Michael Wayne Rhoades, born 29 February 1956. Married 30
              June 1978 Susan Leffel
    2324   ii Joyce Ann Rhoades, born 6 February 1960

    1364 - EVA KATHLENE(7) RHOADES [Iva Ann(6) Montel, Jacob(5), Abraham(4), Susan(3) Wolf, Jacob(2), Daniel(1)]
    Eva Kathlene Rhoades, fourth child of Sherman Alfred and Iva Ann (Montel) Rhoades, was born 13 April 1927. She married 6 December 1947 Donald Leroy Slater, born 30 July 1929, son of Harley and Miriam (Miller) Slater.
    Children of Donald Leroy and Eva Kathlene (Rhoades) Slater:
  + 2325   i Sue Anne Kay Slater, born 13 May 1949
    2326   ii Gregory Jay Slater, born 11 May 1952
    2327 iii Jerilyn Jo Slater, born 11 June 1954

    1365 - DORSEY HURL(7) RHOADES [Iva Ann(6) Montel, Jacob(5), Abraham(4), Susan(3) Wolf, Jacob(2), Daniel(1)]
    Dorsey hurl Rhoades, fifth child of Sherman Alfred and Iva Ann (Montel) Rhoades, was born 24 November 1931. He married 21 June 1957 Janet Edna Smith, born 19 October 1938, daughter of Virgil and Beulah (_____) Smith.
    Children of Dorsey Hurl and Janet Edna (Smith) Rhoades:
  + 2328   i Marla Jo Rhoades, born 16 January 1958
    2329   ii James Dorsey Rhoades, born 17 March 1960
  + 2330 iii Lisa Ann Rhoades, born 27 November 1961
    2331   iv John David Rhoades, born 5 April 1971

1367 - BERNICE IRENE(7) MONTEL [Artemus(6), Jacob(5), Abraham(4), Susan(3) Wolf, Jacob(2), Daniel(1)]
Bernice Irene Montel, second child of Artemus and Bertha V. (Beight) Montel, was born 3 August 1925. She married 19 July 1944 Charles Fisher Jr, born 8 May 1921, son of Charles and Amanda (Bentz) Fisher.
Children of Charles Jr and Bernice Irene (Montel) Fisher:
+ 2332   i Janet Kay Fisher, born 8 March 1945
+ 2333   ii Becky Sue Fisher (adopted), born 26 June 1946
  2334 iii Janice Rae Fisher, born and died 21 November 1947

1368 - FRANCIS EARL(7) MONTEL [Artemus(6), Jacob(5), Abraham(4), Susan(3) Wolf, Jacob(2), Daniel(1)]
Francis Earl Montel, third child of Artemus and Bertha V. (Beight) Montel, was born 7 July 1926. He married 11 January 1948 Phyllis Eileen Bolinger, born 8 December 1927, daughter of Alvin and Orpha (Weller) Bolinger.
Children of Francis Earl and Phyllis Eileen (Bolinger) Montel:
+ 2335   i Karen Sue Montel, born 24 January 1949
+ 2336   ii Kathy Ann Montel, born 28 December 1952

1369 - BETTY ANN(7) MONTEL [Artemus(6), Jacob(5), Abraham(4), Susan(3) Wolf, Jacob(2), Daniel(1)]
Betty Ann Montel, fourth child of Artemus and Bertha V. (Beight) Montel, was born 11 april 1928. She married 12 October 1946 Joseph Wilmer Yoder, born 19 July 1923, son of Joseph and Dorothy Kathryn (Dorse) Yoder.
Children of Joseph Wilmer and Betty Ann (Montel) Yoder:
+ 2337   i Laura Ann Yoder, born 24 June 1948
  2338   ii James Allen Yoder, born 3 February 1950. Married 8 Febru-
             ary 1975 Lois Ann Yoder, born 18 August 1953, daughter of
             Sanford Amos and Shirley Bernice (Cooper) Yoder
+ 2339 iii Edwin Ray Yoder, born 22 October 1953
+ 2340   iv Margaret Sue Yoder, twin, born 29 April 1959
  2341   v Mary Lou Yoder, twin, born 29 April 1959. Married 16
             August 1979 Jeffery P. Douglas, born 29 January 1957, son
             of Halard and Gertrude (Wilson) Douglas

1370 - BARBARA J.(7) MONTEL [Artemus(6), Jacob(5), Abraham(4), Susan(3) Wolf, Jacob(2), Daniel(1)]
Barbara J. Montel, fifth child of Artemus and Bertha V. (Beight) Montel, was born 30 December 1937. She married 1) 25 August 1957 S. Rudolph Harley, born 22 November 1938, died 29 September 1957, son of Samuel A. and Elsie (Hollen) Harley and 2) 23 december 1960 W. Gene Rarick, born 12 November 1938, son of Dane W. and Hazel I. (Weybright) Rarick.
Child of S. Rudolph and Barbara J. (Montel) Harley:
  2342   i Jonel Anne Harley, born 20 February 1958. Married 4 August
             1979 William S. Fawley
Children of W. Gene and Barbara J. (Montel) Rarick:
  2343   i Risa Marie Rarick, born 17 December 1962
  2344   ii Philip Alan Rarick, born 23 January 1965
  2345 iii Lynette Sue Rarick, born 5 October 1968

1371 - MELVIN(7) WYATT [Mary Magdeline(6) Metzger, Susanna(5) Montel, Abraham(4), Susan(3) Wolf, Jacob(2), Daniel(1)]
Melvin Wyatt, son of Frank and Mary Magdeline (Metzger) Wyatt, was born 5 May 1919. He married 29 November 1949 Gwen Ellen Yatckoska,

daughter of _____ and _____ (Miller) Yotckoska.
    Children of Melvin and Gwen Ellen (Yatckoska) Wyatt:
    2346   i Harold Wyatt, born 9 December 1951. Married Betty _____
    2347   ii James Wyatt, born 20 april 1954. Married Cindy _____
    2348 iii Karen Wyatt, born 3 July 1957, died 24 march 1977. Married
            Charles Deneen
    2349   iv Patricia Wyatt, born 7 january 1966

    1380 - KATHRYN ELIZABETH(7) METZGER [Irvin(6), Susanna(5) Montel,
Abraham(4), Susan(3) Wolf, Jacob(2), Daniel(1)]
    Kathryn Elizabeth Metzger, daughter of Irvin and Ella Pearl
(Warner) Metzger, was born 19 August 1912. She married 10 November
1934 Lowell Brown, born 4 September 1904, son of Jacob and Laura Belle
(Kinteigh) Brown.
    Children of Lowell and Kathryn Elizabeth (Metzger) Brown:
+ 2350   i Phillip Brown, born 29 July 1936
+ 2351   ii Thomas Brown, born 9 November 1944

    1382 - ROBERT DEAN(7) GRIMES [Susanna(6) Metzger, Susanna(5)
Montel, Abraham(4), Susan(3) Wolf, Jacob(2), Daniel(1)]
    Robert Dean Grimes, second child of Arthur Harley and Susanna
(Metzger) Grimes, was born 12 October 1920, died 17 March 1975. He
married 25 May 1945 Rae Johnston.
    Children of Robert Dean and Rae (Johnston) Grimes:
    2352   i Virginia Lou Grimes, adopted, born 23 December 1939
    2353   ii Elise Ann Grimes, born 17 February 1946

    1383 - JOAN BETH(7) GRIMES [Susanna(6) Metzger, Susanna(5)
Montel, Abraham(4), Susan(3) Wolf, Jacob(2), Daniel(1)]
    Joan Beth Grimes, third child of Arthur Harley and Susanna
(Metzger) Grimes, was born 1 March 1924. She married 3 June 1944
George T. Robinson, born 26 August 1922.
    Children of George T. and Joan Beth (Grimes) Robinson:
    2354   i Michael Allen Robinson, born 1 January 1955
    2355   ii Steven David Robinson, born 31 March 1956
    2356 iii Lisa Ann Robinson, born 3 November 1959

    1390 - LOUISE(7) WALTHER [Nellie(6) Butterbaugh, William H.(5),
Sarah(4) Montel, Susan(3) Wolf, Jacob(2), Daniel(1)
    Louise Walther, first child of Glen and Nellie (Butterbaugh)
Walther, was born 5 March 1913. She married 10 October 1937 Blaine
Bowen.
    Children of Blaine and Louise (Walther) Bowen:
+ 2357   i Karen Bowen, born 1940
    2358   ii Todd Allan Bowen

    1391 - MAURICE(7) WALTHER [Nellie(6) Butterbaugh, William H.(5),
Sarah(4) Montel, Susan(3) Wolf, Jacob(2), Daniel(1)]
    Maurice Walther, second child of Glen and Nellie (Butterbaugh)
Walther, was born 12 September 1914. He married 30 January 1938 Vivian
Brecht, born 16 September 1917.
    Child of Maurice and Vivian (Brecht) Walther:
    2359   i Linda Lou Walther, born 25 January 1941. Married 1 Febru-
            ary 1960 Leonard Pyle. See #2206

    1392 - DOSCAS IRENE(7) WALTHER [Nellie(6) Butterbaugh, William
H.(5), Sarah(4) Montel, Susan(3) Wolf, Jacob(2), Daniel(1)]
    Doscas Irene Walther, third child of Glen and Nellie (Butter-

baugh) Walther, was born 24 December 1917. She married Arden Warner, son of Glen and Marie (Ulrey) Warner.
        Children of Arden and Doscas Irene (Walther) Warner:
+ 2360   i Annie Jeanine Warner, born 18 March 1942
+ 2361   ii Sue Elaine Warner, born 4 February 1945

        1393 - MAX DONALD(7) WALTHER [Nellie(6) Butterbaugh, William H.(5), Sarah(4) Montel, Susan(3) Wolf, Jacob(2), Daniel(1)]
        Max Donald Walther, fourth child of Glen and Nellie (Butterbaugh) Walther, was born 2 February 1925. He married Leona Fleck.
        Children of Max Donald and Leona (Fleck) Walther:
+ 2362   i Donald Dean Walther, born 1944
+ 2363   ii Jerry Lee Walther, born 1946
  2364   iii David Glen Walther, born 5 September 1952, died 20 Febru-
                ary 1965
+ 2365   iv Dennie Lynn Walther, born 8 October 1955

        1394 - MARY BLANCHE(7) TRIDLE [Elvin Peter(6), George III(5), Adaline(4) Montel, Susan(3) Wolf, Jacob(2), Daniel(1)]
        Mary Blanche Tridle, adopted daughter of Elvin Peter and Ella (Ulrey) Tridle, was born 14 January 1903, died 25 January 1983. She married 28 August 1927 Fred Walgamuth, born 11 March 1902, son of Charles and Rosa (Haines) Walgamuth.
        Children of Fred and Mary Blanche (Tridle) Walgamuth:
+ 2366   i Arden Dee Walgamuth, born 20 February 1937
+ 2367   ii Terry Lee Walgamuth, born 17 September 1939

        1395 - KEITH EMERSON(7) ROSS [Lizzie(6) Tridle, George III(5), Adaline(4) Montel, Susan(3) Wolf, Jacob(2), Daniel(1)]
        Keith Emerson Ross, first child of Elmer C. and Lizzie (Tridle) Ross, was born 23 April 1909. He married 21 June 1936 Helen Marie Eikenberry, daughter of Amos R. and Elizabeth Rosetta (Wagoner) Eikenberry.
        Child of Keith Emerson and Helen Marie (Eikenberry) Ross:
  2368   i Margaret Ann Ross, born 2 March 1942. Married 12 June 1965
                Howard R. Pletcher, born 31 August 1942, son of Howard W.
                and Betty (Buchanan) Pletcher

        1397 - HAROLD WAYNE(7) ROSS [Lizzie(6) Tridle, George III(5), Adaline(4) Montel, Susan(3) Wolf, Jacob(2), Daniel(1)]
        Harold Wayne Ross, third child of Elmer C. and Lizzie (Tridle) Ross, was born 9 April 1918. He married 30 June 1950 Mary Elizabeth Brandenburg, born 1 July 1920, daughter of Albert and Tressa (Frantz) Brandenburg.
        Children of Harold Wayne and Mary Elizabeth (Brandenburg) Ross:
+ 2369   i Linda Diane Ross, born 20 August 1955
  2370   ii Beth Ann Ross, born 16 June 1961

        1398 - DOROTHA MAXINE(7) ROSS [Lizzie(6) Tridle, George III(5), Adaline(4) Montel, Susan(3) Wolf, Jacob(2), Daniel(1)]
        Dorotha Maxine Ross, fourth child of Elmer C. and Lizzie (Tridle) Ross, was born 15 August 1921. She married 1) 25 December 1941 Merle Newby Jr, born 5 February 1921, died 26 June 1944, son of Merle Sr and Linn (_____) Newby. She married 2) 19 October 1946 Paul Winford Rider, born 22 January 1920, son of William S. and Mabel (Cave) Rider.
        Child of Merle Jr and Dorotha Maxine (Ross) Newby:
+ 2371   i Joyce Ann Newby, born 10 September 1944

Child of Paul Winford and Dorotha Maxine (Ross) Rider:
+ 2372   i Connie Sue Rider, born 10 September 1948

1399 - LOREN LEROY(7) TRIDLE [Glenn(6), George III(5), Adaline(4)
Montel, Susan(3) Wolf, Jacob(2), Daniel(1)]
    Loren Leroy Tridle, first child of Glenn and Mattie (Pfleiderer)
Tridle, was born 4 April 1914. He married 24 November 1938 Mary K.
Ayres, born 30 January 1916, daughter of Edward and Ruth (Metzger)
Ayres.
    Children of Loren Leroy and Mary K. (Ayres) Tridle:
  2373   i Eddie Glenn Tridle, born 19 January 1945. Married 22
            August 1970 Elizabeth C. Billings, born 22 January 1947,
            daughter of Thomas Montgomery and Eleanor (Caldwell)
            Billings
+ 2374   ii Lorna Louise Tridle, born 26 November 1946
+ 2375 iii Kathy Ann Tridle, born 18 December 1949

1400 - EARL EUGENE(7) TRIDLE [Glenn(6), George III(5), Adaline(4)
Montel, Susan(3) Wolf, Jacob(2), Daniel(1)]
    Earl Eugene Tridle, second child of Glenn and Mattie (Pfleiderer)
Tridle, was born 16 September 1915. He married 2 June 1934 Jeanette
Newcomer, born 30 October 1918, daughter of Floyd and Marie (Fox)
Newcomer.
    Children of Earl Eugene and Jeanette (Newcomer) Tridle:
  2376   i Infant, born and died 16 August 1934
  2377   ii Harold Leroy Tridle, born 11 September 1935, died 12
            September 1935
+ 2378 iii Sara Earline Tridle, born 14 January 1938
  2379   iv Alice Anne Tridle, born 11 February 1946

1401 - VERA LAVON(7) HEETER [Viola(6) Tridle, George III(5),
Adaline(4) Montel, Susan(3) Wolf, Jacob(2), Daniel(1)]
    Vera Lavon Heeter, daughter of Rolla and Viola (Tridle) Heeter,
was born 11 October 1912, died 8 October 1980. She married 18 October
1930 George William Spann, born 15 February 1910, son of Jesse and
Odessa (Spitler) Spann.
    Children of George William and Vera Lavon (Heeter) Spann:
+ 2380   i Connie Spann, born 9 November 1931
+ 2381   ii Teddy Lee Spann, born 15 February 1933

1403 - JOSEPHINE(7) OYLER [Joseph Raymond(6), Josephine Flo-
rida(5) Wolfe, Simon P.(4), Jacob Jr(3), Daniel(1)]
    Josephine Oyler, first child of Joseph Raymond and Myrtle Olive
(Peter) Oyler, was born 20 October 1908 in Cass County, IN. She
married 18 October 1928 in Cass County Donald Edgar Fitzer, born 7
September 1907 at Walton, IN, son of Millard and Pearl (Walker)
Fitzer.
    Child of Donald Edgar and Josephine (Oyler) Fitzer:
  2382   i Richard L. Fitzer. Married 25 December 1950 at Logansport,
            IN Judith Mae Shedran, born 29 July 1930 at Walton, IN,
            daughter of Ben Omar and Donna Genevieve (Widener) Shedran

1417 - JESS WARREN(7) MONTEITH [Paul Everett(6), Caroline Bar-
bara(5) Wolfe, Simon P.(4), Jacob Jr(3), Jacob(2), Daniel(1)]
    Jess Warren Monteith, first child of Paul Everett and Nellie
Enola (Warren) Monteith, was born 26 May 1915 at Springfield, Clark
County, OH. He married 19 April 1946 Phyllis Imogene (Ebersole)
Armstrong, born 26 January 1921 in German Township, Clark County, OH,

daughter of Oron Roy and Hazel Marie (Callison) Ebersole. She had
married 1) 22 November 1939 Lawrence L. Armstrong, died 16 September
1943 in Belgium, WW II. Jess was in the U.S. Navy from October 1939
until October 1945. He served as a member of the crew of the light
cruiser USS Omaha, which was on patrol in the South Atlantic prior to
the U.S. entry into WWII.
      Child of Lawrence L. and Phyllis Imogene (Ebersole) Armstrong:
+ 2383   i Marcia Armstrong, born 12 September 1941
      Children of Jess Warren and Phyllis Imogene (Ebersole) (Arm-
strong) Monteith:
+ 2384   i Cheryll Ann Monteith, born 24 August 1948
+ 2385   ii Deborah Kay Monteith, born 24 October 1951
+ 2386 iii Beverly Jo Monteith, born 18 July 1953

      1418 - VIRGIL EUGENE(7) MONTEITH [Paul Everett(6), Caroline
Barbara(5) Wolfe, Simon P.(4), Jacob Jr(3), Jacob(2), Daniel(1)]
      Virgil Eugene Monteith, second child of Paul Everett and Nellie
Enola (Warren) Monteith, was born 24 October 1916 at Springfield,
Clark County, OH. He married 31 August 1939 at Springfield Clara
Mildred Kadel, born 19 September 1917, daughter of George Rhinehart
and Clara Edith (Ulrey) Kadel.
      Children of Virgil Eugene and Clara Edith (Ulrey) Monteith:
+ 2387   i Darryl Kent Monteith, born 3 August 1941
+ 2388   ii Gary Eugene Monteith, born 18 April 1945

      1430 - MILTON CHARLES SR(7) CALDWELL [Emmet Edmunds(6), Margaret
Jane(5) Wolfe, Simon P.(4), Jacob Jr(3), Jacob(2), Daniel(1)]
      Milton Charles Caldwell Sr, first child of Emmet Edmunds and Ina
Belle (Hylander) Caldwell, was born 17 January 1914 at Springfield,
Clark County, OH. He married 18 January 1934 at Dayton, OH Julia Betty
White, born 19 January 1911 at Camargo, KY, daughter of Juniper Thomas
and Clemmie (Curtis) White.
      Children of Milton Charles Sr and Julia Betty (White) Caldwell:
+ 2389   i Judith Ann Caldwell, born 28 September 1940
+ 2390   ii Milton Charles Caldwell Jr, born 28 July 1944

      1431 - MARTHA FRANCES(7) CALDWELL [Emmet Edmunds(6), Margaret
Jane(5) Wolfe, Simon P.(4), Jacob Jr(3), Jacob(2), Daniel(1)]
      Martha Frances Caldwell, second child of Emmet Edmunds and Ina
Belle (Hylander) Caldwell, was born 12 November 1915 at Springfield,
Clark County, OH. She married 14 February 1946 at Los Angeles, CA
Joseph Andrew Robbs, born 13 September 1916, son of Willard Drew and
Mary Ida (Robinson) Robbs.
      Children of John Andrew and Martha Frances (Caldwell) Robbs:
  2391   i Miriam Kathleen Robbs, born 16 March 1948 at Anderson, IN
  2392   ii Timothy Drew Robbs, born 28 March 1950 at Coral Gables, FL
+ 2393 iii David Caldwell Robbs, born 25 August 1952

      1433 - HERBERT EUGENE SR(7) CALDWELL [Emmet Edmunds(6), Margaret
Jane(5) Wolfe, Simon P.(4), Jacob Jr(3), Jacob(2), Daniel(1)]
      Herbert Eugene Caldwell Sr, fourth child of Emmet Edmunds and Ina
Belle (Hylander) Caldwell, was born 12 July 1919 at Newark, OH, died
10 July 1984 at Columbus, OH. He married 8 August 1945 at Columbus
Mary Evelyn Price, born 11 June 1927, daughter of Charles Herschel and
Viola Elsie (Johnson) Price.
      Children of Herbert Eugene Sr and Mary Evelyn (Price) Caldwell:
+ 2394   i Nancy Jean Caldwell, born 28 February 1947
+ 2395   ii Herbert Eugene Caldwell Jr, born 15 September 1954

1435 - DORIS VIRGINIA(7) CALDWELL [Emmet Edmunds(6), Margaret Jane(5) Wolfe, Simon P.(4), Jacob Jr(3), Jacob(2), Daniel(1)]
    Doris Virginia Caldwell, sixth child of Emmet Edmunds and Ina Belle (Hylander) Caldwell, was born 28 August 1924 at Newark, OH. She married 1 November 1947 at Los Angeles, CA Raymond Elbert Maxey, born 10 June 1920.
    Children of Raymond Elbert and Doris Virginia (Caldwell) Maxey:
+ 2396   i Douglas Ray Maxey, born 15 December 1950
+ 2397   ii Carol Susan Maxey, born 4 March 1954

1436 - PRISCILLA MAXINE(7) CALDWELL [David Milo(6), Margaret Jane(5) Wolfe, Simon P.(4), Jacob Jr(3), Jacob(2), Daniel(1)]
    Priscilla Maxine Caldwell, daughter of David Milo and Hazel Abigail (Lorton) Caldwell, was born 5 October 1921 at Springfield, Clark County, OH. She married 15 June 1949 at Springfield Edward Goodwin Gwyn, born 22 July 1916, son of Charles William and Ruth Hazel (Goodwin) Gwyn.
    Children of Edward Goodwin and Priscilla Maxine (Caldwell) Gwyn:
  2398   i Susan Elizabeth Gwyn, born 11 September 1951
  2399   ii Jennifer Caldwell Gwyn, born 24 June 1955. Married 6 June 1981 Phillip Frederick Cottrell, born 12 May 1955, son of Robert Lyman and Nancy (Sohngen) Cottrell

1437 - DOROTHY JANE(7) CALDWELL [William Arthur(6), Margaret Jane(5) Wolfe, Simon P.(4), Jacob Jr(3), Jacob(2), Daniel(1)]
    Dorothy Jane Caldwell, first child of William Arthur and Gladys Fern (Downing) Caldwell, was born 18 December 1919 at Springfield, Clark County, OH. She married 11 September 1937 at Springfield Lawrence Edgar Oyler, born 17 May 1918 at Springfield, died 24 November 1960 at Donnelsville, OH, son of Edgar Lehman and Florence (Sullivan) Oyler.
    Children of Lawrence Edgar and Dorothy Jane (Caldwell) Oyler:
+ 2400   i Terry Lynn Oyler, born 12 September 1940
+ 2401   ii Bonna Delene Oyler, born 9 August 1943
  2402 iii Larry Wayne Oyler, born at Springfield, OH. Married 21 December 1985 at Springfield Rebecca Ruth Moose

1438 - WAYNE EUGENE(7) CALDWELL [William Arthur(6), Margaret Jane(5) Wolfe, Simon P.(4), Jacob Jr(3), Jacob(2), Daniel(1)]
    Wayne Eugene Caldwell, second child of William Arthur and Gladys Fern (Downing) Caldwell, was born 13 July 1922 at Springfield, Clark County, OH. He married 1 August 1952 at Portland, ME Mary Suzanne Jameson, daughter of Colonel Frank and Edith (_____) Jameson.
    Children of Wayne Eugene and Mary Suzanne (Jameson) Caldwell:
  2403   i James Arthur Caldwell
  2404   ii Lisa Adair Caldwell
+ 2405 iii Mary Suzanne Caldwell

1440 - WILLIAM EDWARD(7) WOLFE [Clarence Leroy(6), Edward Carrol(5), Simon P.(4), Jacob Jr(3), Jacob(2), Daniel(1)]
    William Edward Wolfe, second child of Clarence Leroy and Anna Marie (Heinnickel) Wolfe, was born 25 March 1927 in Marion County, IN, died 28 May 1988 in Madison County, IN. He married, 24 July 1948 in Madison County Wilma Catherine Jessup, born 4 November 1948 in Hamilton County, IN.
    Children of William Edward and Wilma Catherine (Jessup) Wolfe:
+ 2406   i Gregory Allen Wolfe, born 21 March 1950
+ 2407   ii Patricia Lynn Wolfe, born 16 February 1953

2408   iii Donald Ray Wolfe, born 7 June 1954 in Madison County, IN.
             Married 6 August 1988 in Madison County Kristi Lee Watkins

     1441 - MIRIAM LOUISE(7) WOLFE [Clarence Leroy(6), Edward Car-
rol(5), Simon P.(4), Jacob Jr(3), Jacob(2), Daniel(1)]
     Miriam Louise Wolfe, third child of Clarence Leroy and Anna Marie
(Heinnickel) Wolfe, was born 12 September 1934 in Madison County, IN.
She married 21 August 1954 Winfried C. McGee.
     Children of Winfried C. and Miriam Louise (Wolfe) McGee:
     2409   i Gina Lynn McGee, born 26 October 1957 in Madison County,
             IN
   + 2410   ii Alane Renee McGee, born 30 June 1960
     2411   iii Jeree Patrick McGee, born 11 November 1966 in Madison
             County, IN

     1447 - WILLIAM KLINE(7) STEVENS [Charles Burton(6), Flora
Marie(5) Wolfe, Simon P.(4), Jacob Jr(3), Jacob(2), Daniel(1)]
     William Kline Stevens, first child of Charles Burton and Ruth
Rebecca (Wells) Stevens, was born 8 October 1930. He married 9 Septem-
ber 1962 Mary Lewellan.
     Children of William Kline and Mary (Lewellan) Stevens:
     2412   i Tracy Elaine Stevens, born 20 December 1968
     2413   ii Rebecca Louise Stevens, born July 1975

     1448 - SYLVIA CHARLENE(7) STEVENS [Charles Burton(6), Flora
Marie(5) Wolfe, Simon P.(4), Jacob Jr(3), Jacob(2), Daniel(1)]
     Sylvia Charlene Stevens, second child of Charles Burton and Ruth
Rebecca (Wells) Stevens, was born 29 October 1933, died 12 March 1957.
She married 14 June 1952 Joe Reed.
     Child of Joe and Sylvia Charlene (Stevens) Reed:
     2414   i Rodney Joe Reed, born 20 June 1954

   * 1449 - THELMA ELAINE(7) STEVENS [Charles Burton(6), Flora
Marie(5) Wolfe, Simon P.(4), Jacob Jr(3), Jacob(2), Daniel(1)]
     Thelma Elaine Stevens, third child of Charles Burton and Ruth
Rebecca (Wells) Stevens, was born 9 November 1945. She married 25 June
1966 Dalton L. Stewart III.
     Children of Dalton L. III and Thelma Elaine (Stevens) Stewart:
     2415   i Jill Suzanne Stewart, born 15 February 1973
     2416   ii Dale Stewart

     1451 - GORDON ARTHUR(7) STEVENS [Roy Arthur(6), Flora Marie(5)
Wolfe, Simon P.(4), Jacob Jr(3), Jacob(2), Daniel(1)]
     Gordon Arthur Stevens, second child of Roy Arthur and Phyllis
Eilene (Travis) Stevens, was born 29 July 1942. He married 7 April
1968 Sandra Sue Strauch.
     Children of Gordon Arthur and Sandra Sue (Strauch) Stevens:
     2417   i Alisa Ann Stevens, born 18 January 1971
     2418   ii Phillip Glenn Stevens, born 23 September 1972
     2419   iii Daniel Brent Stevens, born 21 November 1977

     1452 - PHYLLIS DARLENE(7) STEVENS [Roy Arthur(6), Flora Marie(5)
Wolfe, Simon P.(4), Jacob Jr(3), Jacob(2), Daniel(1)]
     Phyllis Darlene Stevens, third child of Roy Arthur and Phyllis
Eilene (Travis) Stevens, was born 17 November 1946. She married 16
September 1972 Richard Barber.
     Children of Richard and Phyllis Darlene (Stevens) Barber:
     2420   i Jillian Diane Barber, born 10 March 1981

2421   ii Allison Diane Barber, born 21 November 1953

1466 - ELIZABETH JANE(7) SMITH [John Jacob(6), Caroline Eval-
ina(5) Wolf, George Isaac(4), Jacob Jr(3), Jacob(2), Daniel(1)]
    Elizabeth Jane Smith, first child of John Jacob and Rachel
(Hynes) Smith, was born 25 April 1916 at Galveston, Cass County, IN.
She married 7 September 1941 at Galveston Gordon Edwin Haag, born 2
March 1917 at St. Joseph, IN, son of John Claude and Ethel Felina
(Gordon) Haag. Gordon was an electrician. They were members of the
Brethren Church.
    Child of Gordon Edwin and Elizabeth Jane (Smith) Haag:
    2422   i Eldon Duane Haag, born 2 December 1948 at Logansport, Cass
            County, IN

1467 - SAMUEL HYNES(7) SMITH [John Jacob(6), Caroline Evalina(5)
Wolf, George Isaac(4), Jacob Jr(3), Jacob(2), Daniel(1)]
    Samuel Hynes Smith, second child of John Jacob and Rachel (Hynes)
Smith, was born 24 August 1920 at Galveston, Cass County, IN. He
married 12 October 1946 at Monticello, White County, IN Mary Valentine
Eller, born 14 February 1922 at Kokomo, Howard County, IN , daughter
of Charlie A. and Faye Marie (_____) Eller. Samuel was a contractor
and served in the US Navy 1942-46. They were members of the Brethren
Church.
    Children of Samuel Hynes and Mary Valentine (Eller) Smith:
+ 2423   i Beverly Jean Smith, born 20 June 1949
+ 2424   ii Cynthia Lynn Smith, born 10 September 1957

1468 - DOROTHY ROSE(7) SMITH [John Jacob(6), Caroline Evalina(5)
Wolf, George Isaac(4), Jacob Jr(3), Jacob(2), Daniel(1)]
    Dorothy Rose Smith, third child of John Jacob and Rachel (Hynes)
Smith, was born 24 March 1924 at Galveston, Cass County, IN. She
married 2 June 1946 at Galveston Ethridge F. Moore, born 7 December
1920 at Muncie, Delaware County, IN, son of Hosia O. and Augusta Ann
(_____) Moore. Ethridge was a farmer and tool and die maker and served
in the US Navy 1944-46. They were members of the Brethren Church.
    Children of Ethridge F. and Dorothy Rose (Smith) Moore:
+ 2425   i Joyce Diane Moore, born 15 March 1949
  2426   ii Moore Alan Moore, born 10 October 1951 at Muncie, IN
  2427 iii Emily Jane Moore, born 25 April 1955 at Logansport,
            Delaware County, IN
  2428   iv Alice Elaine Moore, born 15 April 1961 at Logansport,
            Delaware County, IN

1469 - EDITH ANICE(7) SMITH [John Jacob(6), Caroline Evalina(5)
Wolf, George Isaac(4), Jacob Jr(3), Jacob(2), Daniel(1)]
    Edith Anice Smith, fourth child of John Jacob and Rachel (Hynes)
Smith, was born 12 January 1926. She married 1946 Claude Haag.
    Children of Claude and Edith Anice (Smith) Haag:
  2429   i Sue Marie Haag, born 1948
  2430   ii John L. Haag, born 1949
  2431 iii Donna C. Haag, born 1952
  2432   iv Sparkle D. Haag, born 1954
  2433   v Mona Lucy Haag, born 1960
  2434   vi Clint Lincoln Haag, born 1961

1470 - MAMIE ALICE(7) SMITH [John Jacob(6), Caroline Evalina(5)
Wolf, George Isaac(4), Jacob Jr(3), Jacob(2), Daniel(1)]
    Mamie Alice Smith, fifth child of John Jacob and Rachel (Hynes)

Smith, was born 12 January 1930 at Young America, Cass County, IN. She married 10 June 1951 at Galveston, Cass County, John Howard Keim, born 17 May 1928 at Chicago, Cook County, IL, son of Clarence Ray and Annie (Keim) Keim. John was a truck driver. They were members of the Brethren Church. *Mamie Alice (Smith)*

Children of John Howard and ~~Annie (Keim)~~ Keim:

2435   i   Charles Ray Keim, born 28 November 1953 at North Manchester, Wabash County, IN

2436   ii   Janis Ann Keim, born 8 December 1955 at Wabash, Wabash County, IN

2437   iii   William Edmund Keim, twin, born 18 October 1959 at Wabash, Wabash County, IN

2438   iv   Wallace Edward Keim, twin, born 18 October 1959 at Wabash, Wabash County, IN

1471 - CAROLINE EVALINA(7) HARLESS [Ida Margaret(6) Smith, Caroline Evalina(5) Wolf, George Isaac(4), Jacob Jr(3), Jacob(2), Daniel(1)]

Caroline Evalina Harless, first child of John C. (Jack) and Ida Margaret (Smith) Harless, was born 30 May 1928 at Logansport, Cass County, IN. She married 30 June 1946 at Burnettsville, White County, IN Ernest Gale Criswell, born 30 May 1926 at Logansport, son of Marcus and Ella (Boling) Criswell. Ernest was a farmer and was in military service 1944-46. They were members of the Brethren Church.

Children of Ernest Gale and Caroline Evalina (Harless) Criswell:

+ 2439   i   Cristy Sue Ann Criswell, born 9 October 1947
+ 2440   ii   Ella Kathleen Criswell, born 27 March 1949
+ 2441   iii   Kim Alan Criswell, born 14 August 1951
+ 2442   iv   Casey Mark Criswell, born 3 December 1958

1472 - ALAN JOHN(7) HARLESS [Ida Margaret(6) Smith, Caroline Evalina(5) Wolf, George Isaac(4), Jacob Jr(3), Jacob(2), Daniel(1)]

Alan John Harless, second child of John C. (Jack) and Ida Margaret (Smith) Harless, was born 7 March 1931 at Logansport, Cass County, IN. He married 10 August 1949 at Young America, Cass County Jane Ann Stafford, born 17 January 1932 at Bloomington, Monroe County, IN, daughter of Floyd and Wilma (Ridenour) Stafford. Alan was a livestock salesman and served in the armed forces in the Vietnam campaign. They were members of the Presbyterian Church.

Children of Alan John and Jane Ann (Stafford) Harless:

+ 2443   i   Marsha Ann Harless, born 28 November 1955
+ 2444   ii   Elaine Harless, born 4 February 1956
   2445   iii   Mark Alan Harless, born 13 March 1958 at Washington, IL
+ 2446   iv   Janet Lynne Harless, born 18 August 1960

1473 - RUBY EVANGELINE(7) HARNER [Martha Belle(6) Smith, Caroline Evalina(5) Wolf, George Isaac(4), Jacob Jr(3), Jacob(2), Daniel(1)]

Ruby Evangeline Harner, first child of Charles Murley and Martha Belle (Smith) Harner, was born 21 August 1926 at Chicago, Cook County, IL. She married 25 September 1949 Ernest Ralph Hanson, born 10 January 1923, son of Halge Carl and Beda Caroline (Carlson) Hanson.

Children of Ernest Ralph and Ruby Evangeline (Harner) Hanson:

2447   i   Carol Ann Hanson, born 17 August 1952. Married 14 August 1980 Daniel Mac Taylor Jr

2448   ii   Diane Sue Hanson, born 9 November 1953

2449   iii   David Alan Hanson, born 24 November 1954

2450   iv   Ronald Jeffrey Hanson, born 2 October 1957

2451   v   Sharon Kay Hanson, born 24 June 1957

1474 – MYREL EUGENE(7) HARNER [Martha Belle(6) Smith, Caroline Evalina(5) Wolf, George Isaac(4), Jacob Jr(3), Jacob(2), Daniel(1)]
Myrel Eugene Harner, second child of Charles Murley and Martha Belle (Smith) Harner, was born 7 February 1930. He married 26 October 1951 Irene Ann Holden, born 14 May 1933 at Trenton, NJ, daughter of Walter and Ann (Lewis) Holden. Myrel was in the construction business and served in the US Air Force.
Children of Myrel Eugene and Irene Ann (Holden) Harner:
+ 2452   i Martha Ann Harner, born 25 July 1952
  2453   ii Flint Lee Harner, born 27 November 1954 at Merced, CA.
          Married 13 October 1978 at Corona Del Mar, CA Terry
          Rhodes, born 25 February 1957 in California, divorced
          June1981

1475 – EVERETT DALE(7) HARNER [Martha Belle(6) Smith, Caroline Evalina(5) Wolf, George Isaac(4), Jacob Jr(3), Jacob(2), Daniel(1)]
Everett Dale Harner, third child of Charles Murley and Martha Belle (Smith) Harner, was born 2 March 1935 at Chicago, Cook County, IL. He married 24 November 1955 at Wheaton, IL Roberta St John, born 24 June 1936 at Chicago, daughter of Edward and Edna Mary (Allen) St John. Everett served in the US Air Force.
Children of Everett Dale and Roberta (St John) Harner:
  2454   i Jon Travis Harner, born 17 November 1963 at Virginia, MN
  2455   ii Katie May Harner, born 16 August 1965 at Duluth, MN –

1477 – ROSS OVID(7) SNAVELY [Vada Estella(6) Michael, Lydia Ladoskey(5) Wolf, George Isaac(4), Jacob Jr.(3), Jacob(2), Daniel(1)]
Ross Ovid Snavely, first child of Melvin Earl and Vada Estella (Michael) Snavely, was born 17 May 1909 in Cass County, IN, died 25 March 1947, buried in Galveston Cemetery, Cass County. He married 1) Ila Flagg and 2) Eve Baker. Ross served in the US Navy in WW II.
Children of Ross Ovid and Ila (Flagg) Snavely:
+ 2456   i James Edward Snavely
  2457   ii Robert Lee Snavely
  2458 iii Andrea Louise Snavely
  2459   iv Carol Snavely. Married Michael Kimmey
Child of Ross Ovid and Eve Baker Snavely:
  2460   i David Lee Snavely

1478 – IDA(7) SNAVELY [Vada Estella(6) Michael, Lydia Ladoskey(5) Wolf, George Isaac(4), Jacob Jr(3), Jacob(2), Daniel(1)]
Ida Snavely, second child of Melvin Earl and Vada Estella (Michael) Snavely, was born 2 June 1911 at Galveston, Cass County, IN. She married in Cass County Floyd Bookwalter, born 4 October 1902 at Twelve Mile, Cass County, son of Harvey and Minnie (_____) Bookwalter, his second wife as he married 1) Ruth Sheetz who died 1928. Flotd was a Railroad Foreman. They were members of the Baptist Church.
Children of Floyd and Ida (Snavely) Bookwalter:
+ 2461   i David Gene Bookwalter, born 2 March 1932
+ 2462   ii Carol Jean Bookwalter, born 13 February 1942

1479 – CLARA MONZEL(7) SNAVELY [Vada Estella(6) Michael, Lydia Ladoskey(5) Wolf, George Isaac(4), Jacob Jr(3), Jacob(2), Daniel(1)]
Clara Monzel Snavely, third child of Melvin Earl and Vada Estella (Michael) Snavely, was born 9 March 1913 in Cass County, IN, died 20 July 1949 at Metea, Cass County, buried in Metea Cemetery. She married 3 June 1934 at Metea Clarence Emerson Williamson, born 16 November 1905 in Cass County, son of Glen and Alma Ann (Carr) Williamson.

Clarence was a farmer. Church affiliation was Methodist.
    Children of Clarence Emerson and Clara Monzel (Snavely) Williamson:
+ 2463   i Shirley Lee Williamson, born 3 March 1937
+ 2464   ii Larry Joe Williamson
  2465 iii Claren Williamson, born 1 August 1947

    1480 - EDNA LEO(7) SNAVELY [Vada Estella(6) Michael, Lydia
Ladoskey(5) Wolf, George Isaac(4), Jacob Jr(3), Jacob(2), Daniel(1)]
    Edna Leo Snavely, twin, fourth child of Melvin Earl and Vada
Estella (Michael) Snavely, was born 20 November 1917 in Cass County,
IN. She married 1) 22 September 1939 at Royal Center, Cass County
Jacob (Jack) Ostheimer, born 17 September 1915 at Ft. Wayne, Allen
County, IN, son of Jacob and Henrietta (Baker) Ostheimer. They
divorced March 1962.   Edna married 2) 26 April 1970 at Buffalo, IN
Vernon Emerson, born 29 August 1931, son of Jacob and Zella (Merritt)
Emerson. There were no children by this marriage.
    Child of Jacob and Edna Leo (Snavely) Ostheimer:
+ 2466   i Marvin J. Ostheimer, born 30 November 1941

    1481 - ETHEL CLEO(7) SNAVELY [Vada Estella(6) Michael, Lydia
Ladoskey(5) Wolf, George Isaac(4), Jacob Jr(3), Jacob(2), Daniel(1)]
    Ethel Cleo Snavely, twin, fifth child of Melvin Earl and Vada
Estella (Michael) Snavely, was born 20 November 1917 in Cass County,
IN, died 19 July 1954 at Lebanon, Boone County, IN, buried in Oakhill
Cemetery, Lebanon. Married 2 July 1937 in Cass County Roy Alma.
    Children of Roy and Ethel Cleo (Snavely) Alma:
  2467   i Donna Mae Alma
  2468   ii Frances Faye Alma

    1482 - LOLA FRANCES(7) SNAVELY [Vada Estella(6) Michael, Lydia
Ladoskey(5) Wolf, George Isaac(4), Jacob Jr(3), Jacob(2), Daniel(1)]
    Lola Frances Snavely, sixth child of Melvin Earl and Vada Estella
(Michael) Snavely, was born 25 March 1926. She married 25 March 1947
Virgil Leslie Ezra, born 21 January 1911, son of Franklin Joseph and
Mitta Alma (Blackster) Ezra. Virgil was a farmer. Church affiliation
was Christian.
    Children of Virgil Leslie and Lola Frances (Snavely) Ezra:
+ 2469   i Bobbie Jo Ezra, born 5 March 1948
  2470   ii Billie Kay Ezra, born 3 December 1951. Married 7 April
            1979 Douglas Levi Kyburg
  2471 iii Virgil Lin Ezra, born 11 March 1956
  2472   iv Larin Earl Ezra, born 18 February 1960. Married 6 June
            1981 Kimberly Lynn Baker

    1483 - CORA MABEL(7) MICHAEL [Charles Franklin(6), Lydia Lados-
key(5) Wolf, George Isaac(4), Jacob Jr(3), Jacob(2), Daniel(1)]
    Cora Mabel Michael, first child of Charles Franklin and Hattie M.
E. (Teems) Michael, was born 6 January 1918 at Wabash, Wabash County,
IN. She married 5 June 1938 at South Bend, St. Joseph County, IN
Luther Lavon Walters, .born 16 October 1916 at Hicksville, Defiance
County, OH, son of James Monroe and Naoma (Humbarger) Walters. Luther
was a body draftsman. They were members of the United Brethren Church.
    Children of Luther Lavon and Cora Mabel (Michael) Walters:
+ 2473   i Sharon Kay Walters, born 15 July 1941
+ 2474   ii Michael Lee Walters, born 9 December 1944

1484 - KENNETH ROLLIE(7) MICHAEL [Charles Franklin(6), Lydia Ladoskey(5) Wolf, George Isaac(4), Jacob Jr(3), Jacob(2), Daniel(1)]
Kenneth Rollie Michael, second child of Charles Franklin and Hattie M. E. (Teems) Michael, was born 11 February 1920 at Twelve Mile, Cass County, IN. He married 6 July 1946 at Munising, Alger County, MI Naomi (Frechette) Johnson, born 2 February 1921 in Michigan, daughter of Arthur Joseph and Delisca (Viger) Frechette. Naomi had married previously _____ Johnson. Kenneth was an auto mechanic and carpenter and a veteran of WW II.
Children of _____ and Naomi (Frechette) Johnson, adopted by Kenneth Rollie Michael 18 October 1954:
  2475   i Dennis Charles Johnson, born 24 February 1938 at Manister,
          MI, died 28 May 1977 at Madison Heights, Macomb
          County, MI, buried in White Chapel Memorial Ceme-
          tary, Troy, MI. Married 28 January 1961 at Munising, Alger
          County, MI Marilyn F. Warren
  2476   ii Martha Jean Johnson, born 6 February 1941 at Munising,
          Alger County, MI. Married 10 May 1958 in Macomb County, MI
          John Robert Pickett
Children of Kenneth Rollie and Naomi (Frechette) (Johnson) Michael:
+ 2477   i Kathleen Helen Michael, born 13 February 1948
+ 2478   ii Kenneth Eugene Michael, born 11 September 1949

1485 - RUBY MAE(7) MICHAEL [George Emerson(6), Lydia Ladoskey(5) Wolf, George Isaac(4), Jacob Jr(3), Jacob(2), Daniel(1)]
Ruby Mae Michael, first child of George Emerson and Mary A. (Glassburn) Michael, was born 21 March 1925 at South Bend, St. Joseph County, IN. She married 1) 1949 at Logansport, Cass County, IN Joseph Marshall, born 29 January 1908 at Logansport, son of Frank and _____ (_____) Marshall. They divorced June 1972. Ruby married 2) 21 March 1974 at Washington, DC Thomas Green, born 8 April 1935 at Logansport.
Children of Joseph and Ruby Mae (Michael) Marshall:
  2479   i David A. Marshall, born 21 April 1950 at Peru, Miami
          County, IN. Married 30 June 1973 at Bunker Hill, Miami
          County Soledad Romos, born 15 June 1946 in the Phillipine
          Islanda, daughter of Raymundo and Matilda (Ergrelero)
          Romos. David was in the US Air Force for 12 Years
+ 2480   ii Cathy Lynn Marshall, born 10 September ____
+ 2481 iii Gary Joseph Marshall, born 3 April 1956

1486 - RAY EMERSON(7) MICHAEL [George Emerson(6), Lydia Lados-key(5) Wolf, George Isaac(4), Jacob Jr(3), Jacob(2), Daniel(1)]
Ray Emerson Michael, second child of George Emerson and Mary A. (Glassburn) Michael, was born 3 February 1932 at Mishawaka, St. Joseph County, IN. He married 1) 10 July 1954 at Logansport, Cass County, IN Gloria Shaw, born at Logansport, daughter of Marion and Pauline (Holloway) Shaw and 2) 14 November 1970 in San Francisco, CA Lynn Marie Majors, born 1945 in New Jersey, daughter of Barry and Eva (Brooks) Majors.
Children of Ray Emerson and Gloria (Shaw) Michael:
  2482   i Regina Michael, born 15 june 1957 at San Francisco, CA.
          Married 4 February 1978 at Logansport, Cass County, IN
          Randolph Alder, born at Logansport
  2483   ii Brian Keith Michael, born 6 October 1959 at Logansport,
          Cass County, IN. Married 22 March 1980 at Denver, Miami
          County, IN Scarlet Marie Looker, born 19 November 1959,
          daughter of _____ and Alva Jean (Hughes) Looker

219

1487 - RONALD LEE(7) MICHAEL [George Emerson(6), Lydia Lados-
key(5) Wolf, George Isaac(4), Jacob Jr(3), Jacob(2), Daniel(1)]
     Ronald Lee Michael, third child of George Emerson and Mary A.
(Glassburn) Michael, was born 3 November 1945 at Denver, Miami County,
IN. He married 18 January 1970 at Mexico, Miami County Patricia
Duncan, born 20 May 1948 in Virginia, daughter of Sib and Earleen
(Viers) Duncan.
     Child of Ronald Lee and Patricia (Duncan) Michael:
  2484   i Christopher George Michael, born 29 October 1976 at
            Mexico, Miami County, IN

1488 - RAYMOND CHAMP(7) MICHAEL [Earl Dewey(6), Lydia Ladoskey(5)
Wolf, George Isaac(4), Jacob Jr(3), Jacob(2), Daniel(1)]
     Raymond Champ Michael, first child of Earl Dewey and Arla Gaias
(Champ) Michael, was born 2 March 1923 at Anokia, Cass County, IN. He
married 9 April 1944 at South Bend, St. Joseph County, IN Ilene Mae
Baer, born 27 May 1924 at South Bend, daughter of D. Reviere and Ruth
Aliene (Wells) Baer. Raymond was a Quality Assurance Representative
and served in the US Army in Germany 1943-1946 during WW II.
     Children of Raymond Champ and Ilene Mae (Baer) Michael:
+ 2485   i Jerry Raymond Michael, born 17 July 1945
+ 2486   ii Dennis Reviere Michael, born 29 February 1948

1490 - ALDONNA MAXINE(7) MICHAEL [Earl Dewey(6), Lydia Lados-
key(5) Wolf, George Isaac(4), Jacob Jr(3), Jacob(2), Daniel(1)]
     Aldonna Maxine Michael, third child of Earl Dewey and Arla Gaia
(Champ) Michael, was born 17 February 1928 at Lapaz, Marshall County,
IN. She married 20 July 1946 at Mishawaka, St. Joseph County, IN
Robert Eugene Warrell, born 24 March 1924 at Mishawaka, son of Fred
and Violet (Wardlow) Warrell. Robert served in the US Army 1943-1946
during WW II.
     Child of Robert Eugene and Aldonna Maxine (Michael) Warrell:
  2487   i Jill Lynn Warrell, born 28 May 1963 at South Bend, St.
            Joseph County, IN

1491 - PHYLLIS KATHLEEN(7) MICHAEL [Earl Dewey(6), Lydia Lados-
key(5) Wolf, George Isaac(4), Jacob Jr(3), Jacob(2), Daniel(1)]
     Phyllis Kathleen Michael, fourth child of Earl Deweey and Arla
Gaia (Champ) Michael, was born 20 November 1933 at Mishawaka, St.
Joseph County, IN. She married 26 April 1952 at South Bend, St. Joseph
County Charles Albert Stuart, born 26 August 1931 at South Bend, son
of Charles Hamilton and Myrtle (Miller) Stuart.
     Children of Charles Albert and Phyllis Kathleen (Michael) Stuart:
+ 2488   i Jackie Diane Stuart, born 27 October 1952
+ 2489   ii Bruce Duane Stuart, born 20 February 1954
+ 2490   iii Gary Dean Stuart, born 29 May 1955

1492 - BOBBY CLEON(7) SUMPTER [Cleo Catherine(6) Michael, Lydia
Ladoskey(5) Wolf, George Isaac(4), Jacob Jr(3), Jacob(2), Daniel(1)]
     Bobby Cleon Sumpter, first child of Avery James and Cleo Cathe-
rine (Michael) Sumpter, was born 19 September 1927 at Nappanee,
Elkhart County, IN. He married 1) December 1945 in Indiana Rosalie
Copeland, 2) Viola Fetleg and 3) 1980 Betty _____.
     Children of Bobby Cleon and Rosalie (Copeland) Sumpter:
  2491   i Bobby Eldon Sumpter, born 24 June 1946
  2492   ii Phillip Eugene Sumpter, born 16 April ____
     Child of Bobby Cleon and Viola (Fetleg) Sumpter:
  2493   i Mark Avery Sumpter, born 20 January 1971

1493 - BOBETTA JOY(7) SUMPTER [Cleo Catherine(6) Michael, Lydia Ladoskey(5) Wolf, George Isaac(4), Jacob Jr(3), Jacob(2), Daniel(1)]
    Bobetta Joy Sumpter, second child of Avery James and Cleo Catherine (Michael) Sumpter, was born 20 November 1928 at Napponee, Elkhart County, IN. She married Ralph Robert Harter.
    Child of Bobetta Joy (Sumpter) _____:
2494   i Jerald Gene _____, born 15 March 1944. Adopted by Herbert Hughes
    Children of Ralph Robert and Bobetta Joy (Sumpter) Harter:
+ 2495   i Deanna Kay Harter, born 9 March 1949
  2496   ii Tina Rae Harter, born 29 July 1951. Married 1) Gaylon Garling, 2) unknown
+ 2497 iii Sandra Sue Harter, born 10 December 1952
  2498   iv Debra Lou Harter, born 30 April 1954
  2499   v Bonitta Ellen Harter, born 25 January 1956

1494 - OPAL NAOMI(7) SUMPTER [Cleo Catherine(6) Michael, Lydia Ladoskey(5) Wolf, George Isaac(4), Jacob Jr(3), Jacob(2), Daniel(1)]
    Opal Naomi Sumpter, third child of Avery James and Cleo Catherine (Michael) Sumpter, was born 2 January 1931 at Mishawaka, St. Joseph County, IN. She married Walter Eugene Murphy.
    Children of Walter Eugene and Opal Naomi (Sumpter) Murphy:
+ 2500   i Karen English Murphy
+ 2501   ii Terry Elaine Murphy, born 28 June ____

1495 - REAH JEANETTE(7) SUMPTER [Cleo Catherine(6) Michael, Lydia Ladoskey(5) Wolf, George Isaac(4), Jacob Jr(3), Jacob(2), Daniel(1)]
    Reah Jeanette Sumpter, fourth child of Avery James and Cleo Catherine (Michael) Sumpter, was born 28 August 1936 at Macy, Miami County, IN. She married 7 December 1957 Richard P. Autz.
    Children of Richard P. and Reah Jeanette (Sumpter) Autz:
  2502   i Koni Katherine Autz, born 13 September ____
  2503   ii Erin Sue Autz, born 18 December ____
  2504 iii Roberta Jeanette Autz, born 25 October ____
  2505   iv Effie Rachell, born 6 April ____
  2506   v Richard Michael Autz, born 30 July ____

1496 - LUCY ELLEN(7) SUMPTER [Cleo Catherine(6) Michael, Lydia Ladoskey(5) Wolf, George Isaac(4), Jacob Jr(3), Jacob(2), Daniel(1)]
    Lucy Ellen Sumpter, fifth child of Avery James and Cleo Catherine (Michael) Sumpter, was born 21 August 1938 at Macy, Miami County, IN. She married 1) Kenneth Wolfe, 2) Rex Hoffman and 3) William King.
    Children of Kenneth and Lucy Ellen (Sumpter) Wolfe:
  2507   i Sandra Jo Wolfe, born 22 August ____
  2508   ii Trina Kay Wolfe, born 2 December ____
    Child of Rex and Lucy Ellen (Sumpter) (Wolfe) Hoffman:
  2509   i Jane Ann Hoffman, born 5 December ____
    Children of William and Lucy Ellen (Sumpter) (Wolfe) (Hoffman) King:
  2510   i Kevin Lee King, born 26 July 1968
  2511   ii Clyde James King, born 26 July 1969

1497 - SHEILA JEANINE(7) SUMPTER [Cleo Catherine(6) Michael, Lydia Ladoskey(5) Wolf, George Isaac(4), Jacob Jr(3), Jacob(2), Daniel(1)]
    Sheila Jeanine Sumpter, sixth child of Avery James and Cleo Catherine (Michael) Sumpter, was born 28 May 1943 at Peru, Miami County, IN. She married Derral Paynter.

221

Child of Derral and Sheila Jeanine (Sumpter) Paynter:
2512   i Derral Avery Paynter, born 19 August 1963

1498 - DAVID ALLEN(7) MC CLOSKEY [Oscar Delmar(6), Anna Margaret(5) Wolf, George Isaac(4), Jacob Jr(3), Jacob(2), Daniel(1)]
David Allen McCloskey, first child of Oscar Delmar and Mary Iona (Peter) McCloskey, was born 27 October 1933 in Deer Creek Township, Cass County, IN. He married 19 February 1964 in Deer Creek Township Barbara May (Beckom) Hargis, born 22 February ____, daughter of William and Helen (Cedars) Beckom. Barbara had married 1) _____ Hargis.
Children of David Allen and Barbara May (Beckom) (Hargis) McCloskey:
2513   i Dean Allen McCloskey, born 2 July 1969 at Kokomo, Howard County, IN
2514   ii Judy Arnette McCloskey, born 14 October 1972 at Kokomo, Howard County, IN

1499 - DANNY LEE(7) MC CLOSKEY [Oscar Delmar(6), Anna Margaret(5) Wolf, George Isaac(4), Jacob Jr(3), Jacob(2), Daniel(1)]
Danny Lee McCloskey, second child of Oscar Delmar and Mary Iona (Peter) McCloskey, was born 15 July 1946 at Walton, Deer Creek Township, Cass County, IN. He married 26 May 1972 at Camden, Carroll County, IN Christy Marietta Wyatt, born 27 July 1947 at Logansport, Cass Coubty, IN, daughter of Bob Miller and Josephine M. (Caldwell) Wyatt.
Children of Danny Lee and Christy Marietta (Wyatt) Mc Closkey:
2515   i David Lewis McCloskey, twin, born 3 February 1976
2516   ii Daniel Lynn McCloskey, twin, born 3 February 1976

1503 - MARY ANN(7) MC KINLEY [Margaret(6) Wolf, Charles Henry(5), George Isaac(4), Jacob Jr(3), Jacob(2), Daniel(1)]
Mary Ann McKinley, first child of Stephen Edward and Margaret (Wolf) McKinley, was born 10 March 1941 at Goodland, Newton County, IN. She married 20 August 1961 at Goodland Richard Lee Rusk, born 14 February 1936 at Fair Oaks, Jasper County, IN, son of Clarence and Marie Mary (Bridget) Rusk. Richard was an Agricultural Extension Agent and served in the US Army 1960-1964. Mary Ann was a school teacher. They were members of the Methodist Church.
Children of Richard Lee and Mary Ann (McKinley) Rusk:
2517   i Deborah Lynn Rusk, born 27 May 1962 at Ann Arbor, MI
2518   ii Michelle Marie Rusk, born 13 June 1966 at Monticello, White County, IN

1505 - DELORES LORENE(7) MC KINLEY [Margaret(6) Wolf, Charles Henry(5), George Isaac(4), Jacob Jr(3), Jacob(2), Daniel(1)]
Delores Lorene McKinley, third child of Stephen Edward and Margaret (Wolf) McKinley, was born 30 April 1948 at Watseka, IL. She married 9 February 1969 at Goodland, Newton County, IN Robert LeRoy Burton, born 27 November 1945, son of Lincoln Edward and Lucille (Zuck) Burton. Robert was a Veterinarian. They were members of the Presbyterian Church.
Children of Robert LeRoy and Delores Lorene (McKinley) Burton:
2519   i Lance Robert Burton, born 27 November 1969 at Dallas, TX
2520   ii Scott Edward Burton, born 5 May 1972 at Frankfort, Germany

1510 - HELEN MAE(7) JUDY [Ora E.(6), Anna C.(5) Cree, Magdalena L.(4) Wolf, Jacob Jr(3), Jacob(2), Daniel(1)]

Helen Mae Judy, first child of Ora E. and Elizabeth (Twaits) Judy, was born 2 February 1922. She married Jack Harvey.
Child of Jack and Helen Mae (Judy) Harvey:
2521   i Max Harvey

1513 - HELEN MARIE(7) RICE [Chester L.(6), Clarissa(5) Cree, Magdalena L.(4) Wolf, Jacob Jr(3), Jacob(2), Daniel(1)]
Helen Marie Rice, first child of Chester L. and Edna (Frier) Rice, was born 1924. She married 1941 Gentry Ross.
Children of Gentry and Helen Marie (Rice) Ross:
2522   i Rondra Kay Ross, born 27 september 1941
2523   ii Patricia Lee Ross, born 4 March 1943

1515 - ROBERT(7) RICE [Luther(6), Clarissa(5) Cree, Magdalena L.(4) Wolf, Jacob Jr(3), Jacob(2), Daniel(1)]
Robert Rice, first child of Luther and Alma (Burge) Rice, was born 1929. He married 1954 Ruth James.
Child of Robert and Ruth (James) Rice:
2524   i Ronald Joe Rice, born 1955

1516 - PAULINE(7) RICE [Luther(6), Clarissa(5) Cree, Magdalena L.(4) Wolf, Jacob Jr(3), Jacob(2), Daniel(1)]
Pauline Rice, second child of Luther and Alma (Burge) Rice, was born 15 June 1930. She married 1949 Ralph Hendershot.
Children of Ralph and Pauline (Rice) Hendershot:
2525   i Unnamed infant Hendershot, born and died 1949
2526   ii Peggy Diane Hendershot, born 1952

1523 - ALBERT PAUL(7) RICE [Leo P.(6), Clarissa(5) Cree, Magdalena L.(4) Wolf, Jacob Jr(3), Jacob(2), Daniel(1)]
Albert Paul Rice was the first child of Leo P. and Edna (Saunders) Rice. He married 1944 Donna Louise Calloway, daughter of Willard Calloway.
Child of Albert Paul and Donna Louise (Calloway) Rice:
2527   i Darla Kay Rice, born 1951

1529 - MEREDITH DEAN(7) BURGE [Sarah(6) Rice, Clarissa(5) Cree, Magdalena L.(4) Wolf, Jacob Jr(3), Jacob(2), Daniel(1)]
Meredith Dean Burge, first child of John and Sarah (Rice) Burge, was born about 1929. He married Arvilla Talberry.
Children of Meredith Dean and Arvilla (Talberry) Burge:
2528   i Michael Dean Burge, born about 1954
2529   ii Pamela Ann Burge, born about 1956

1530 - MARJORIR ANN(7) BURGE [Sarah(6) Rice, Clarissa(5) Cree, Magdalena L.(4) Wolf, Jacob Jr(3), Jacob(2), Daniel(1)]
Marjorie Ann Burge, second child of John and Sarah (Rice) Burge, was born 2 April 1931. She married 10 September 1950 Wayne Dillon.
Children of Wayne and Marjorie Ann (Burge) Dillon:
2530   i Douglas Dean Dillon, born about 1952
2531   ii Sandra Kay Dillon, born 30 August 1955

1531 - AMIEL(7) SAILORS [Magdaline(6) Whipperman, Margaret(6) Cree, Magdalena L.(5) Wolf, Jacob Jr(3), Jacob(2), Daniel(1)]
Amiel Sailors, first child of Benjamin M. and Magdaline (Whipperman) Sailors, was born 12 December 1907, died 5 August 1957. He married 6 December 1934 Helen Wickersham, daughter of Donald Wickersham.

Children of Amiel and Helen (Wickersham) Sailors:
2532   i George Jay Sailors, born 22 January 1940, died 31 August
        1961. Married 8 January 1961 Roberta Jernagan
2533   ii Elaine Sue Sailors. Married Marvin Lowel Bettinger

1532 - SAMUEL(7) SAILORS [Magdaline(6) Whipperman, Margaret(5)
Cree, Magdalena L.(4) Wolf, Jacob Jr(3), Jacob(2), Daniel(1)]
    Samuel sailors, second child of Benjamin M. and Magdaline (Whip-
perman) Sailors, was born 1 May 1909, died 22 February 1969. He
married 5 February 1939 Helen Katherine Groninger, daughter of Floyd
Groninger.
    Children of Samuel and Helen Katherine (Groninger) Sailors:
2534   i Kenneth Sailors
+ 2535   ii Linda Diane Sailors

1533 - IRENE(7) SAILORS [Magdaline(6) Whipperman, Margaret(5)
Cree, Magdalena(4) Wolf, Jacob Jr(3), Jacob(2), Daniel(1)]
    Irene Sailors, third child of Benjamin M. and Magdaline (Whipper-
man) Sailors, was born 21 June 1910. She married 3 October 1931 Harry
O. Farrer, born 14 March 1911, died 1 February 1984, son of Otto and
Hanah (Vernon) Farrer.
    Child of Harry O. and Irene (Sailors) Farrer:
2536   i Jean L. Farrer

1534 - ARLO(7) SAILORS [Magdaline(6) Whipperman, Margaret(5)
Cree, Magdalena(4) Wolf, Jacob Jr(3), Jacob(2), Daniel(1)]
    Arlo Sailors, fourth child of Benjamin M. and Magdaline (Whipper-
man) Sailors, was born 21 December 1912. He married 8 September 1935
June Sharp.
    Children of Arlo and June (Sharp) Sailors:
2537   i Aleina Sue Sailors. Married 24 December 1959 Robert
        Marshall
2538   ii Rita Ann Sailors

1537 - ELMER(7) DOWNHAM [Esther(6) Whipperman, Margaret(5) Cree,
Magdalena L.(4) Wolf, Jacob Jr(3), Jacob(2); Daniel(1)]
    Elmer Downham, first child of Quincy and Esther (Whipperman)
Downham, was born 24 September 1911. He married 27 June 1933 Genevieve
Shelley.
    Children of Elmer and Genevieve (Shelley) Downham:
2539   i Barbara E. Downham. Married Glen McGary
2540   ii Joan Downham
2541   iii Janice Loren Downham

1531 - GEORGE DANIEL(7) DOWNHAM [Esther(6) Whipperman, Mar-
garet(5) Cree, Magdalena L.(4) Wolf, Jacob Jr(3), Jacob(2), Daniel(1)]
    George Daniel Downham, fifth child of Quincy and Esther (Whipper-
man) Downham, was born 28 June 1918, died 30 October 1972. He married
28 January 1945 Violet May Graf.
    Child of George Daniel and Violet May (Graf) Downham:
2542   i Linda Kay Downham

1547 - CHARLOTTE ELIZABETH(7) CREE [Walter Irving(6), George
Robert(5), Magdalena L.(4) Wolf, Jacob Jr(3), Jacob(2), Daniel(1)]
    Charlotte Elizabeth Cree, daughter of Walter Irving and Lucretia
Beatrice (Bechtol) Cree, was born 13 March 1927. She married 21 April
1945 Earnest Edward Brown, born 24 October 1922, died 13 February
1964.

Children of Earnest Edward and Charlotte Elizabeth (Cree) Brown:
2543   i James E. Brown, born 20 November 1945
+ 2544   ii Barbara A. Brown, born 22 November 1947
2545   iii Jerry Brown, born 22 July 1952
2546   iv John Brown, born 30 December 1956

1549 - WAYNE LEE(7) LANDIS [Lola Grace(6) Cree, George Robert(5),
Magdalena L.(4) Wolf, Jacob Jr(3), Jacob(2), Daniel(1)]
    Wayne Lee Landis, second child of Ardis Joseph and Lola Grace
(Cree) Landis, was born 13 November 1925. He married 7 September 1947
Geraldine Lucille Sands, born 14 January 1929.
    Children of Wayne Lee and Geraldine Lucille (Sands) Landis:
2547   i Gerald Wayne Landis, born 9 October 1949
2548   ii Douglas Evan Landis, born 3 November 1950
2549 iii Jenny Lind Landis, born 11 March 1958

1550 - DORIS RUTH(7) LANDIS [Lola Grace(6) Cree, George Rob-
ert(5), Magdalena L.(4) Wolf, Jacob Jr(3), Jacob(2), Daniel(1)]
    Doris Ruth Landis, third child of Ardis Joseph and Lola Grace
(Cree) Landis, was born 29 October 1929. She married 3 July 1947 Clyde
Allen Davis, born 26 May 1929.
    Children of Clyde Allen and Doris Ruth (Landis) Davis:
2550   i Keith Dale Davis
2551   ii Carol Elaine Davis, born 28 September 1952
2552 iii Gary Wayne Davis, born 21 September 1958
2553   iv Kay Lorraine Davis, born 13 December 1960

1551 - BETTY ARLENE(7) LANDIS [Lola Grace(6) Cree, George Rob-
ert(5), Magdalena L.(4) Wolf, Jacob Jr(3), Jacob(2), Daniel(1)]
    Betty Arlene Landis, fourth child of Ardis Joseph and Lola Grace
(Cree) Landis, was born 22 April 1933. She married 31 December 1951
Donald Eugene Huff, born 20 December 1931.
    Child of Ardis Joseph and Lola Grace (Cree) Landis:
2554   i Melody Ann Huff, born 26 February 1961

1552 - DORTHA JEAN(7) LANDIS [Lola Grace(6) Cree, George Rob-
ert(5), Magdalena L.(4) Wolf, Jacob Jr(3), Jacob(2), Daniel(1)]
    Dortha Jean Landis, fifth child of Ardis Joseph and Lola Grace
(Cree) Landis, was born 22 December 1936. She married 15 July 1955
Lyle Ervin Broughton, born 13 May 1931.
    Children of Lyle Ervin and Dortha Jean (Landis) Broughton:
2555   i Lyla Jean Broughton, born 25 June 1956
2556   ii Maria Kay Broughton, born 28 August 1959
2557 iii Jay Eric Broughton, born 22 December 1962

1557 - BILLY DEAN(7) CREE [Harold N.(6), Henry(5), Magdalena
L.(4) Wolf, Jacob Jr(3), Jacob(2), Daniel(1)]
    Billy Dean Cree, second child of Harold N. and Arlene (Barnard)
Cree, was born about 1929. His wife's name is not known.
    Child of Billy Dean and _____ (_____) Cree:
2558   i Jay Bee Cree

1559 - WAYNE BARNARD(7) CREE [Harold N.(6), Henry(5), Magdalena
L.(4) Wolf, Jacob Jr(3) Jacob(2), Daniel(1)]
    Wayne Barnard Cree, fourth child of Harold N. and Arlene (Bar-
nard) Cree, married 25 August 1951 Toyla Shepard.
    Children of Wayne Barnard and Toyla (Shepard) Cree:
2559   i Randall Wayne Cree, born about 1952

2560   ii Kenneth Eugene Cree, born about 1954

    1562 - DOROTHY IONE(7) PARROT [Mildred(6) Cree, Albert(5),
Magdalena L.(4) Wolf, Jacob Jr(3), Jacob(2), Daniel(1)]
    Dorothy Ione Parrot, first child of Walter and Mildred (Cree)
Parrot, was born about 1933. She married about 1953 Gerald Whiteman.
    Child of Gerald and Dorothy Ione (Parrot) Whiteman:
2561   i Teresa Joy Whiteman, born about 1954

    1566 - PHYLLIS ELLEN(7) PENN [Irene(6) Cree, Ezra(5), Magdalena
L.(4) Wolf, Jacob Jr(3), Jacob(2), Daniel(1)]
    Phyllis Ellen Penn, first child of Lewis and Irene (Cree) Penn,
was born about 1935. She married about 1955 Donald Myers.
    Child of Donald and Phyllis Ellen (Penn) Myers:
2562   i Donald Ray Myers

    1574 - FRIEDA MAY(7) ALLEN [Evaugn Gaston(6) Cree, Carl(5),
Malinda Jane(4) Wolf, Jacob Jr(3), Jacob(2), Daniel(1)]
    Frieda May Allen, first child of Virgil and Evaughn Gaston (Cree)
Allen, was born about 1925. She married 1) Harold Buckworth and 2)
James Reed.
    Child of Harold andFrieda May (Allen) Buckworth:
2563   i Beverly Ann Buckworth, born 6 June 19

    1618 - ALNA CHARLENE(7) PONTIUS [Charles Henry(6), Serenius(5),
John(4), Elizabeth(3) Hahn, Elizabeth(2) Wolf, Daniel(1)]
    Alna Charlene Pontius,daughter of Charles Henry and Roxanna Bell
(Hall) Pontius, was born 11 August 1921. She married 29 March 1941 at
Miamisburg, OH _____ Allen.
    Child of _____ and Alna Charlene (Pontius) Allen:
2564   i Jeanette Marie Allen, born 15 November 1951. Married 3
          July 1971 Fredric C. Weaver

    1623 - CATHERINE PAULINE(7) BAILEY [Elizabeth Idella(6) Boyer,
Alice Arretta(5) Sharritts, Samuel(4), Elizabeth(3) Hahn, Elizabeth(2)
Wolf, Daniel(1)]
    Catherine Pauline Bailey, first child of Burnett and Elizabeth
Idella (Boyer) Bailey, was born 11 September 1911 in Montgomery
County, OH, died 30 December 1971. She married 20 February 1932 Clyde
Oliver Homan.
    Child of Clyde Oliver and Catherine Pauline (Bailey) Homan:
2565   i Gerald E. Homan, born 14 March 1933 in Ohio, died 13 July
          1943

    1624 - JAMES M.(7) BAILEY [Elizabeth Idella(6) Boyer, Alice
Arretta(5) Sharritts, Samuel(4), Elizabeth(3) Hahn, Elizabeth(2) Wolf,
Daniel(1)]
    James M. Bailey, second child of Burnett and Elizabeth Idella
(Boyer) Bailey, was born 15 July 1913 in Montgomery County, OH. He
married 21 October 1933 Helen Marie Diver.
    Children of James M. and Helen Marie (Diver) Bailey:
+ 2566   i James Lee Bailey, born 13 July 1945
+ 2567   ii William Edward Bailey, born 10 April 1954

    1625 - HELEN LOUISE(7) BAILEY [Elizabeth Idella(6) Boyer, Alice
Arretta(5) Sharritts, Samuel(4), Elizabeth(3) Hahn, Elizabeth(2) Wolf,
Daniel(1)]
    Helen Louise Bailey, third child of Burnett and Elizabeth Idella

(Boyer) Bailey, was born 17 June 1919 in Montgomery County, OH. She
married 1) 27 May 1935 Chester Stupp and 2) George Tyson.
   Children of Chester and Helen Louise (Bailey) Stupp:
+ 2568   i Eugene L. Stupp, born 17 December 1935
+ 2569   ii Donna Lee Stupp, born 18 December 1938
+ 2570 iii Dale Wayne Stupp, born 22 September 1941

   1628 - MELBA MARIE(7) BORLAND [Vera(6) Wolfe, Franklin(5), Daniel
Jr(4), Daniel Sr(3), Frederick(2), Daniel(1)]
   Melba Marie Borland, first child of Raymond and Vera (Wolfe)
Borland, was born 2 December 1913 at Shannon City, Union County, IA,
died 15 May 1986 at Creston, Union County, buried at Graceland Cemetary. She married 24 November 1940 at Creston, Wood E. Fowler. Reli-
gous affiliation First United Methodist Church.
   Children of Wood E. and Melba Marie (Borland) Fowler:
+ 2571   i Rocky Lyndell Fowler, adopted, born about 1950
  2572   ii Ricky Fowler, adopted, born about 1955. Married Rose _____

   1631 - FRED DAVID(7) JACOBS [Myrtle Annie(6) Wolfe, Simon
Peter(5), Michael(4), Daniel Sr(3), Frederick(2), Daniel(1)]
   Fred David Jacobs, twin, second child of David Edwin and Myrtle
Annie (Wolfe) Jacobs, was born 5 February 1904 at Allendale, Worth
County, MO, died 8 September 1980 at King City, Worth County, buried
at Grant City , Worth County. He married 25 December 1931 at St.
Joseph, Buchanan County, MO Crystal Rose Wisecup, born 5 June 1910 at
Grant City, daughter of John William and Cora Annie (West) Wisecup.
   Children of Fred David and Crystal Rose (Wisecup) Jacobs:
+ 2573   i Delores Ann Jacobs, born 2 December 1932
+ 2574   ii John David Jacobs, born 30 October 1941
+ 2575 iii Edwin William Jacobs, born 5 September 1952

   1632 - FRANK EDWIN(7) JACOBS [Myrtle Annie(6) Wolfe, Simon
Peter(5), Michael(4), Daniel Sr(3), Frederick(2), Daniel(1)]
   Frank Edwin Jacobs, twin, third child of David Edwin and Myrtle
Annie (Wolfe) Jacobs, was born 5 February 1904 at Allendale, Worth
County, MO, died 19 November 1965 at Des Moines, Polk County, IA. He
married 5 June 1929 at Fayette, Howard County, MO Verne Opal Arnold,
born 5 May 1908 at Allendale, died 2 October 1990 at Greenfield, Adair
County, IA, daughter of Emmett Lee And Geneva Annette (Hatfield)
Arnold. They are buried in Grant City Cemetery, Worth County, MO.
   Children of Frank Edwin and Verne Opal (Arnold) Jacobs:
  2576   i Emmett Edwin Jacobs. Married 1) 29 December 1952 at
             Corning, Adams County, IA Sue Eagon, they divorced, and 2)
             17 July 1965 Dawn Anderson
+ 2577   ii Velma Rose Jacobs, born 12 April 1938

   1634 - CLAUDE(7) WOLFE [Fred Simon(6), Simon Peter(5),
Michael(4), Daniel Sr(3), Frederick(2), Daniel(1)]
   Claude Wolfe, first child of Fred Simon and Hattie Lorena (Griep)
Wolfe, was born 22 June 1907 in Union County, IA. He married about
1932 Lois Wagaman.
   Children of Claude and Lois (Wagaman) Wolfe:
+ 2578   i Edwin Wolfe, born 26 March 1937
  2579   ii Susan Wolfe, born 22 February 1945, died 19 January 1962
             of Scleraderma

   1635 - GLADYS MARIE(7) WOLFE [Fred Simon(6), Simon Peter(5),
Michael(4), Daniel Sr(3), Frederick(2), Daniel(1)]

Gladys Marie Wolfe, second child of Fred Simon and Hattie Lorena (Griep) Wolfe, was born 19 June 1910 in Union County, IA. She married 3 June 1933 at Creston, Union County J. R. (George) Kessler, born about 1910.

Children of J. R. and Gladys Marie (Wolfe) Kessler:
2580   i Daughter Kessler, died at six months of Spinal Meningitis
2581   ii Gary dean Kessler, born 9 October 1936
2582   iii Joseph R. Kessler, born May 1942
2583   iv Nancy Kessler, born 18 January 1950

1636 - DOROTHY PEARL(7) WOLFE [Fred Simon(6), Simon Peter(5), Michael(4), Daniel Sr(3), Frederick(2), Daniel(1)]
     Dorothy Pearl Wolfe, third child of Fred Simon and Hattie Lorena (Griep) Wolfe, was born 15 January 1912 in Union County, IA, died 24 August 1973 at Centerville, Appanoose County, IA. She married 20 February 1932 Marvin J. Snodgrass.
     Children of Marvin J. and Dorothy Pearl (Wolfe) Snodgrass:
+ 2584   i Carolyn Marie Snodgrass, born 25 November 1932
  2585   ii Sharon Lee Snodgrass, born 29 June 1941. Married Gary Lust

1638 - ALBERT HAROLD(7) WOLFE [Frank Peter(6), Simon Peter(5), Michael(4), Daniel Sr(3), Frederick(2), Daniel(1)]
     Albert Harold Wolfe, second child of Frank Peter and Lenora (Walker) Wolfe, was born 14 November 1910 in Union County, IA, died 12 August 1985 at Mitchellville, Polk County, IA, buried in Franklin Township Cemetery, Bondurant, IA. He married 4 August 1934 in Ringgold County, IA Stephana Margarite Kiefer, born 24 September 1917, daughter of Steve and Helen (Smith) Kiefer. Albert retired from the Iowa Department of Transportation in 1975. They were members of the Union Park Baptist Church, Des Moines, IA.
     Children of Albert Harold and Stephana Margarite (Kiefer) Wolfe:
+ 2586   i Sonya Rae Wolfe, born 18 November 1935
+ 2587   ii Stephen Frank Wolfe, born 3 August 1937
+ 2588   iii Dorcas Ann Wolfe, born 28 February 1939
+ 2589   iv Russell Alan Wolfe, born 25 February 1943
+ 2590   v Bruce Michael Wolfe, born 13 February 1952
+ 2591   vi Sara Lee Wolfe, born 29 May 1957

1642 - JOHN(7) FRANKLIN [Mae Elizabeth(6) Keedy, Howard(5), Elizabeth(4) Blecker, Tracy(3) Wolf, Frederick(2), Daniel(1)]
     John Franklin, first child of Harry and Mae Elizabeth (Keedy) Franklin, married Pat Hilger.
     Children of John and Pat (Hilger) Franklin:
2592   i Leslie Franklin
2593   ii _____ Franklin
2594   iii _____ Franklin

1643 - MARGARET(7) FRANKLIN [Mae Elizabeth(6) Keedy, Howard(5), Elizabeth(4) Blecker, Tracy(3) Wolf, Frederick(2), Daniel(1)]
     Margaret Franklin, second child of Harry and Mae Elizabeth (Keedy) Franklin, married Laverne Adams Sr.
     Children of Laverne Sr and Margaret (Franklin) Adams:
2595   i Harry Adams
2596   ii Kimberly Adams
2597   iii Laverne Adams Jr

1644 - ROGENE(7) FRANKLIN [Mae Elizabeth(6) Keedy, Howard(5), Elizabeth(4) Blecker, Tracy(3) Wolf, Frederick(2), Daniel(1)]

Rogene Franklin, third child of Harry and Mae Elizabeth (Keedy) Franklin, married Gerald Fearer.
Child of Gerald and Rogene (Franklin) Fearer:
2598   i Martha Fearer

1646 - SHIRLEY(7) LONG [Martha(6) Keedy, Frank C.(5), Elizabeth(4) Blecker, Tracy(3) Wolf, Frederick(2), Daniel(1)]
Shirley Long, first child of Eber and Martha (Keedy) Long, married Martin Kroll.
Children of Martin and Shirley (Long) Kroll:
2599   i Kevin Kroll
2600   ii Beverly Kroll

1649 - LILIAN(7) LONG [Martha(6) Keedy, Frank C.(5), Elizabeth(4) Blecker, Tracy(3) Wolf, Frederick(2), Daniel(1)]
Lilian Long, fourth child of Eber and Martha (Keedy) Long, married Robert Paul.
Children of Robert and Lilian (Long) Paul:
2601   i Darin Paul
2602   ii _____ Paul

1664 - ANNE LORRAINE(7) FORD [Kathleen Lucille(6) Gantz, Annie Virginia(5) Blecker, Jacob B.(4), Tracy(3) Wolf, Frederick(2), Daniel(1)]]
Anne Lorraine Ford, first child of Hugh A. and Kathleen Lucille (Gantz), married 12 June 1954 Glenn Hendrix.
Children of Glenn and Anne Lorraine (Ford) Hendrix:
2603   i Steven Hendrix, born 1956
2604   ii Debra Hendrix, born 1959

1665 - MARY ANN(7) GANTZ [Donald Wallace Sr(6), Jesse Berry(5), Annie Virginia(4) Blecker, Tracy(3) Wolf, Frederick(2), Daniel(1)]
Mary Ann Gantz, first child of Donald Wallace Sr and Esther Kathleen (Winfield) Gantz, was born 21 May 1936 at Boonsboro, Washington County, MD. She married Franklin Delano Lum.
Children of Franklin Delano and Mary Ann (Gantz) Lum:
2605   i Marilee Esther Lum, born 6 March 1963 at Boonsboro, Washington County, MD. Married Charles Spitzer Jr
2606   ii Franklin Calvin Lum, born 30 December 1964 at Boonsboro, Washington County, MD

1666 - DONALD WALLACE JR(7) GANTZ [Donald Wallace Sr(6), Jesse Berry(5), Annie Virginia(4) Blecker, Tracy(3) Wolf, Frederick(2), Daniel(1)]
Donald Wallace Gantz Jr, second child of Donald Wallace Sr and Esther Kathleen (Winfield) Gantz, was born 19 May 1944 at Boonsboro, Washington County, MD. He married Mary Ellen Hensen, a widow.
Child of Donald Wallace Sr and Mary Ellen (Hensen) Gantz:
2607   i Jonathan Winfield Gantz, born 21 March 1980 at Summers Point, NJ

1667 - PHILIP WILLIAM SR(7) BARDELL [Bertha Isabelle(6) Lamar, Mary Elizabeth(5) Blecker, Jacob B.(4), Tracy(3) Wolf, Frederick(2), Daniel(1)]
Philip William Bardell Sr, son of Philip Jacob and Bertha Isabelle (Lamar) Bardell, was born 14 April 1928. He married 17 January 1959 Kay Kerlin Furst, born 17 August 1934, her second marriage.

Children of the first marriage of Kay Kerlin Furst, adopted by
Philip William Bardell Sr:
  2608   i William Robison Bardell, born 17 April 1954
  2609   ii Terence Alan Bardell, born 5 June 1956
      Children of Philip William Sr and Kay (Kerlin) (Furst) Bardell:
  2610   i Philip William Bardell Jr, born 27 May 1961
  2611   ii Karen Kay Bardell, born 22 May 1964

     1669 - JOAN ELISE(7) LAMAR [Robert Fulton(6), Mary Elizabeth(5)
Blecker, Jacob B.(4), Tracy(3) Wolf, Frederick(2), Daniel(1)]
     Joan Elise Lamar, first child of Robert Fulton and Earline Elise
(Lamkey) Lamar, was born 1 July 1930. She married 21 April 1951 Walter
Fay Beckman, born 31 December 1929.
     Children of Walter Fay and Joan Elise (Lamar) Beckman:
  2612   i Bruce Robert Beckman, twin, born 4 November 1954
  2613   ii Barry Scott Beckman, twin, born 4 November 1954

     1670 - BARBARA ANN(7) LAMAR [Robert Fulton(6), Mary Elizabeth(5)
Blecker, Jacob B.(4), Tracy(3) Wolf, Frederick(2), Daniel(1)]
     Barbara Ann Lamar, second child of Robert Fulton and Earline
Elise (Lamkey) Lamar, was born 2 January 1933. She married 26 December
1951 Robert Lee Daggett, born 11 April 1930.
     Children of Robert Lee and Barbara Ann (Lamar) Daggett:
  2614   i Debra Lee Daggett, born 17 August 1954
  2615   ii Sherry Lynn Daggett, born 19 November 1957
  2616 iii Robin Ann Daggett, born 28 September 1959

     1673 - DEANNA(7) WEIPERT [Evelyn Alice(6) Young, Effie Young(5)
Blecker, Jacob B.(4), Tracy(3) Wolf, Frederick(2), Daniel(1)]
     Deanna Weipert, daughter of Ferdinand and Evelyn Alice (Young)
Weipert, was born 8 February 1937. She married William Lieber, born 15
October 1929.
     Children of William and Deanna (Weipert) Lieber:
  2617   i William Wayne Lieber, born 10 February 1956
  2618   ii Rebecca Jo Lieber, born 8 September 1957

     1674 - LEONARD EARL(7) LOWRY [Leila Emma (6) Wolf, Sherman E.(5),
Franklin(4), Simon(3), Frederick(2), Daniel(1)]
     Leonard Earl Lowry, first child of William I. and Leila Emma
(Wolf) Lowry, was born 23 February 1923 in Washington County, MD. He
married 2 April 1947 in Washington County Dorothy Cecelia Bartles,
born 6 February 1926 in Washington County, daughter of Albert and Anna
(Hamby) Bartles.
     Children of Leonard Earl and Dorothy Cecelia (Bartles) Lowry:
+ 2619   i David Earl Lowry, born 31 May 1948
  2620   ii Daniel Leonard Lowry, born 26 May 1951 in Washington
             County, MD
+ 2621 iii Carolyn Marie Lowry, born 12 January 1953

     1675 - WILLIAM ELSWORTH(7) LOWRY [Leila Emma(6) Wolf, Sherman
E.(5), Franklin(4), Simon(3) Wolf, Frederick(2), Daniel(1)]
     William Elsworth Lowry, second child of William I. and Leila Emma
(Wolf) Lowry, was born 28 October 1924 in Washington County, MD. He
married 9 April 1949 in Washington County Beatrice Lucille Myers, born
3 November 1929 in Washington County, daughter of Theodore and Helen
(Marshall) Myers.
     Children of William Elsworth and Beatrice Lucille (Myers) Lowry:
+ 2622   i Curtis Theodore Lowry, born 12 January 1951

+ 2623   ii Brenda Kay Lowry, born 3 February 1952
+ 2624   iii Charlene Rae Lowry, born 9 February 1954
+ 2625   iv Sandra Bea Lowry, born 7 September 1958

1676 - LUTHER E.(7) WOLFE [Franklin Ellsworth(6), Sherman E.(5),
Franklin(4), Simon(3), Frederick(2), Daniel(1)]
     Luther E. Wolfe, first child of Franklin Ellsworth and Esther
(Smith) Wolfe, was born 6 May 1921 at Boonsboro, Washington County,
MD, died 3 November 1945 at Hagerstown, Washington County, buried in
Boonsboro Cemetery. He married 13 June 1944 at Clearspring, Washington
County Mildred Lucille Ambrose, born 22 September 1926 at Hagerstown.
After Luther's death Mildred married 2) 5 April 1947 Richard Hamilton
Grimes.
     Child of Luther E. and Mildred Lucille (Ambrose) Wolfe:
+ 2626   i Luther Wolfe (now Luther Grimes, having taken the name of
             his step-father), born 13 January 1945

1677 - FRANKLIN EUGENE(7) WOLFE [Franklin Ellsworth(6), Sherman
E.(5), Franklin(4), Simon(3), Frederick(2), Daniel(1)]
     Franklin Eugene Wolfe, second child of Franklin Ellsworth and
Esther (Smith) Wolfe, was born 22 January 1926 at Boonsboro, Washington County, MD. He married 13 July 1945 at Boonsboro Annie Elizabeth
Higman, born 27 March 1927 at Beaver Creek, Washington County, daughter of Harold and Annie Florence (Poffenberger) Higman.
     Children of Franklin Eugene and Annie Elizabeth (Higman) Wolfe:
+ 2627   i Dennis Franklin Wolfe, born 5 February 1946
+ 2628   ii Daryl Lynn Wolfe, born 27 March 1957

1678 - WILLIAM ROSS JR(7) ADAMS [Irene Elizabeth(6) Wolf, Sherman
E.(5), Franklin(4), Simon(3), Frederick(2), Daniel(1)]
     William Ross Adams Jr, first child of William Ross Sr and Irene
Elizabeth (Wolf) Adams, was born 16 July 1934 at Middletown, Frederick
County, MD. He married 31 July 1955 at Hagerstown, Washington County,
MD Barbara Ann Sprankle, born 21 September 1934 at Hagerstown, daughter of Raymond Ellsworth and Mary Genevie (Moser) Sprankle. ·
     Children of William Ross Jr and Barbara Ann (Sprankle) Adams:
+ 2629   i Sharon Kay Adams, born 26 May 1956
+ 2630   ii William Eugene Adams, born 24 February 1958
+ 2631 iii Karen Ann Adams, born 26 June 1960
+ 2632   iv Charles Edward Adams, born 12 June 1961

1679 BARBARA(7) ADAMS [Irene Elizabeth(6) Wolf, Sherman E.(5),
Franklin(4), Simon(3), Frederick(2), Daniel(1)]
     Barbara Adams, second child of William Ross Sr and Irene Eliza-
beth (Wolf) Adams, was born 23 May 1937 at Middletown, Frederick
County, MD. She married 9 September 1962 at Middletown Thomas H.
Angleberger, born 28 March 1937 at Frederick, Frederick County, MD,
son of George Foster and Grace Amelia (Wachter) Angleberger.
     Children of Thomas H. and Barbara (Adams) Angleberger:
+ 2633   i Kelley Lynn Angleberger, born 17 April 1965
  2634   ii Randle Lee Angleberger, born 15 September 1966 at Freder-
             ick, Frederick County, MD

1680 - FRANCES(7) ADAMS [Irene Elizabeth(6) Wolf, Sherman E.(5),
Franklin(4), Simon(3), Frederick(2), Daniel(1)]
     Frances Adams, third child of William Ross Sr and Irene Elizabeth
(Wolf) Adams, was born 26 March 1945 at Middletown, Frederick County,
MD. She married 13 July 1969 at Middletown Paul Edward Eaves, born 22

October 1945 at Woodsboro, Frederick County, son of Paul Ellsworth and Louise Virginia (Kelly) Eaves.
Children of Paul Edward and Frances (Adams) Eaves:
2635   i Brian Edward Eaves, born 13 March 1971 at Frederick, Frederick County, MD
2636   ii Daniel Paul Eaves, born 9 January 1976 at Frederick, Frederick County, MD

1681 - DEBORAH JEAN(7) ADAMS [Irene Elizabeth(6) Wolf, Sherman E.(5), Franklin(4), Simon(3), Frederick(2), Daniel(1)]
Deborah Jean Adams, fourth child of William Ross Sr and Irene Elizabeth (Wolf) Adams, was born 28 July 1953 at Frederick, Frederick County, MD. She married 2 June 1975 at Middletown, Frederick County Gary Crouse, born 9 November 1952 at Frederick, son of George Franklin and Kathleen Mae (Young) Crouse.
Children of Gary and Deborah Jean (Adams) Crouse:
2637   i Heather Rochelle Crouse, born 29 May 1982 at Frederick, Frederick County, MD
2638   ii Anna Renee' Crouse, born 31 May 1988 at Frederick, Frederick County, MD

1682 - CAROLYN(7) LOHR [Ellsworth Franklin(6), Florence Estella(5) Wolf, Franklin(4), Simon(3), Frederick(2), Daniel(1)]
Carolyn Lohr, first child of Ellsworth Franklin and Dorothy Carmen (Staley) Lohr, was born 24 June 1934 at Hagerstown, Washington County, MD. She married 1) at Hagerstown William Sunderland and 2) Ronald Kline.
Children of William and Carolyn (Lohr) Sunderland:
+ 2639   i Kirk Douglas Sunderland, born 25 January 1955
  2640   ii Todd Sunderland, born November 1959 at Hagerstown, Washington County, MD

1683 - BARBARA ELLEN(7) LOHR [Ellsworth Franklin(6), Florence Estella(5) Wolf, Franklin(4), Simon(3), Frederick(2), Daniel(1)]
Barbara Ellen Lohr, second child of Ellsworth Franklin and Dorothy Carmen (Staley) Lohr, was born 3 March 1936 at Hagerstown, Washington County, MD. She married at Hagerstown Barry Lautenslager.
Children of Barry and Barbara Ellen (Lohr) Lautenslager:
2641   i Brian Lautenslager
2642   ii Rebecca Lynn Lautenslager

1684 - STEVEN ELLSWORTH(7) LOHR [Ellsworth Franklin(6), Florence Estella(5) Wolf, Franklin(4), Simon(3), Frederick(2), Daniel(1)]
Steven Ellsworth Lohr, third child of Ellsworth Franklin and Dorothy Carmen (Staley) Lohr, was born 6 January 1955 at Hagerstown, Washington County, MD. He married 3 June 1984 at Clearspring, Washington County Becky Jo Paris.
Children of Steven Ellsworth and Becky Jo (Paris) Lohr:
2643   i Christine Renee' Lohr, born 21 July 1985 at Hagerstown, Washington County, MD
2644   ii Bradley Steven Lohr, born 3 February 1989 at Hagerstown, Washington County, MD

1685 - RALPH EDWARD(7) DINKLE [Dorothy I.(6) Lohr, Florence Estella(5) Wolf, Franklin(4), Simon(3), Frederick(2), Daniel(1)]
Ralph Edward Dinkle, son of Irvin L. and Dorothy I. (Lohr) Dinkle, was born 1 January 1943 at Hagerstown, Washington County, MD. He married 30 January 1965 at Hagerstown Donna Forcino, born 30

January 1946 at Hagerstown, daughter of James and Dorothy (Fink) Forcino.
    Children of Ralph Edward and Donna (Forcino) Dinkle:
  2645   i Deborah A. Dinkle, born 29 December 1968 at Great Falls,
            MT
  2646   ii Stacea M. Dinkle, born 8 April 1972 and died 16 May 1976
            at Lake Hopatong, NJ. Buried at Rose Hill Cemetery,
            Hagerstown, Washington County, MD
  2647 iii Bradley E. Dinkle, born 10 August 1977 at Lake Hopatong,
            NJ

    1686 - CHARLES EUGENE(7) HINES [Louise Lauraetta(6) Lohr, Flo-
rence Estella(5) Wolf, Franklin(4), Simon(3), Frederick(2), Daniel(1)]
    Charles Eugene Hines, son of Charles Earl and Louise Lauraetta
(Lohr) Hines, was born 27 December 1936 at Hagerstown, Washington
County, MD. He married 6 January 1959 at Hagerstown Lana Irene Bailey
born 17 September 1941 in Maryland, daughter of _____ and Chessie
(_____) Bailey.
    Children of Charles Eugene and Lana Irene (Bailey) Hines:
+ 2648   i Kimberly Diane Hines, born 12 September 1959
+ 2649   ii Kelli Lynn Hines, born 15 February 1963
  2650 iii Kristin Lagena Hines, born 1 March 1965 at Hagerstown,
            Washington County, MD
  2651   iv Matthew Scott Hines, born 25 June 1968 at Hagerstown,
            Washimgton County, MD

    1687 - HAROLD HERMAN(7) EARLEY [Leslie Filmore(6), Nora Pearl(5)
Wolf, Franklin(4), Simon(3), Frederick(2), Daniel(1)]
    Harold Herman (Buck) Earley, first child of Leslie Filmore and
Madalene (Rhodes) Earley, was born 17 March 1930 at Hagerstwon,
Washington County, MD, died 17 February 1990 at Hagerstown, buried in
Rose Hill Cemetery at Hagerstown. He married 1 November 1952
at Hagerstown Betty Jane Cianelli, born 27 July 1931 at Hagerstown.
Buck was a star football player at Hagerstown High School and the
University of Maryland, being a member of the Maryland team that
defeated Missouri 20-7 in the Gator Bowl in 1950. He was the owner of
Norman S. Earley and Sons Inc. until retiring in 1983.
    Child of Harold Herman and Betty Jane (Cianelli) Earley:
  2652   i John Leslie Earley, born 7 December 1953 at Hagerstown,
            Washington County, MD. Married 17 August 1975 at Mexia,
            Limeston County, TX Patricia Stubbs, born 3 December 1953
            at Mexia, daughter of John Sims and Louneita (Forrest)
            Stubbs

    1689 - NORMAN SADDLER III(7) EARLEY [Norman Saddler Jr(6), Nora
Pearl(5) Wolf, Franklin(4), Simon(3), Frederick(2), Daniel(1)]
    Norman Saddler Earley III, son of Norman Saddler Jr and Mildred
May (Ruffner) Earley, was born 19 January 1951 at Hagerstown, Washington County, MD. He married 1) Ruth Ellen Reeves and 2) Nancy Louise
Athey, born 16 July 1954 at Waynesboro, Franklin County, PA, daughter
of Gerald and Helen (Aldridge) Athey.
    Children of Norman Saddler III and Ruth Ellen (Reeves) Earley:
  2653   i Rebecca Leigh Earley, born 9 October 1972 at Waynesboro,
            Franklon County, PA
  2654   ii Sean Bradford Earley, born 21 August 1975 at Waynesboro,
            Franklin County, PA
    Child of Norman Saddler III and Nancy Louise (Athey) Earley:
  2655   i Erin Nicole Earley, born 4 October 1982 at Hagerstown,

1690 - TERRY LEE(7) EARLEY [Theodore Harold(6), Nora Pearl(5) Wolf, Franklin(4), Simon(3), Frederick(2), Daniel(1)]
Terry Lee Earley, first child of Theodore Harold and Virginia Elmira (Strait) Earley, was born 11 January 1941 at Hagerstown, Washington County, MD. He married 11 May 1963 at Lebanon, Lebanon County, PA Mary Ann Hower, born 25 October 1943 at Lebanon, daughter of Ben Mark and Helen Mary (Noll) Hower.
Children of Terry Lee and Mary Ann (Hower) Earley:
2656   i Mark Bradford Earley, born 5 August 1964 at Hagerstown, Washington County, MD. Married at Virginia Beach, Princess Anne County, VA Lori Lynn Pope
2657   ii Dane Cameron Earley, born 29 May 1967 at Hagerstown, Washington County, MD. Married 12 May 1990 at Virginia Beach, Princess Anne County, VA Cynthia Gail Hamilton

1692 - DAVID ALLEN(7) EARLEY [Theodore Harold(6), Nora Pearl(5) Wolf, Franklin(4), Simon(3), Frederick(2), Daniel(1)]
David Allen Earley, third child of Theodore Harold and Virginia Elmira (Strait) Earley, was born 12 January 1946 at Hagerstown, Washington County, MD. He married 11 February 1967 in Washington County Beth Marie Sheldon, born 15 March 1946 at Sand Point, ID, daughter of Grant and Ruby (Kidd) Sheldon.
Children of David Allen and Beth Marie (Sheldon) Earley:
2658   i Leigh Ann Earley, born 6 September 1967 in Washington County, MD. Married 1 October 1988 at Hagerstown, Washington County Randy Allen Pettner, born 9 January 1966 in Washington County, son of Stephen John and Marilyn Louise (Stanfield) Pettner
2659   ii Philip James Earley, born 19 september 1972 in Washington County, MD

1693 - ROBERT RANDOLPH(7) ALTON [Pauline Mary(6) Wolfe, Truman Leo(5), Franklin(4), Simon(3), Frederick(2), Daniel(1)]
Robert Randolph Alton, first child of Edward Mealy and Pauline Mary (Wolfe) Alton, was born 24 October 1929 at Hagerstown, Washington County, MD, died 5 April 1991 at Hagerstown, buried in Boonsboro Cemetery, Washington County. He married 1) Pauline Doretos, 2) 29 June 1958 at Hagerstown Phyllis Jean (Harshman) Yeatts, born 25 November 1935 at Hagerstown, daughter of Enzie and Phyliss Elizabeth (Wilhelm) Harshman, 3) 11 October 1968 Irene (_____) Deseata, born 16 September 1923 in Maryland and 4) Helen Louise Jones, born about 1930 in Washington County, died 11 January 1989 at Hagerstown, buried in Boonsboro Cemetery, daughter of Edgar and Mary (Stull) Jones.
Children of Robert Randolph and Phyllis Jean (Harshman) Alton:
2660   i Steven Allen Alton, born 27 May 1957 at Hagerstown, Washington County, MD
2661   ii Robert Randolph Alton II, born 22 June 1961 at Hagerstown, Washington County, MD. Married 25 August at Hagerstown Shawn Renae Bittner, born 20 may 1963 at Ridgeley, Mineral County, WV, daughter of Gerald Neal and Betty Lou (Nester) Bittner

1694 - JANICE MARLENE(7) ALTON [Pauline Mary(6) Wolfe, Truman Leo(5), Franklin(4), Simon(3), Frederick(2), Daniel(1)]
Janice Marlene Alton, second child of Edward Mealy and Pauline Mary (Wolfe) Alton, was born 10 September 1934 at Hagerstown, Washing-

234

ton County, MD, died 22 July 1979 at Hagerstown, buried in Boonsboro
Cemetery, Washington County. She married 10 July 1953 at Hagerstown
Conrad Eugene Baker, born 23 February 1929 at Hagerstown.
    Children of Conrad Eugene and Janice Marlene (Alton) Baker:
+ 2662   i Alice Sue Baker, born 30 June 1955
+ 2663   ii Mark Eugene Baker, born 29 April 1959

    1695 - RICHARD LEE(7) ALTON [Pauline Mary(6) Wolfe, Truman
Leo(5), Franklin(4), Simon(3), Frederick(2), Daniel(1)]
    Richard Lee Alton, third child of Edward Mealy and Pauline Mary
(Wolfe) Alton, was born 26 July 1938 at Hagerstown, Washington County,
MD. He married 1) 14 February 1959 at Hagerstown Irene Elizabeth
Eichelberger, born 25 December 1940 at Hagerstown, they divorced 2) 4
June 1960 at Hagerstown Gloria Louella Stottlemyer, born 21 September
1934 in Maryland, they divorced, and 3) Ida Marie Trumpower.
    Child of Richard Lee and Irene Elizabeth (Eichelberger) Alton:
    2664   i Jon Alton
    Child of Richard Lee and Ida Marie (Trumpower) Alton:
    2665   ii Richard Lee Alton II, born 20 May 1970 at Hagerstown,
            Washington County, MD

    1697 - MICHAEL HENDRICKS(7) WOLF [David Earl Jr(6), David Earl
Sr(5), Franklin(4), Simon(3), Frederick(2), Daniel(1)]
    Michael Hendricks Wolf, second child of David Earl Jr and Gladys
Lee (Hendricks) Wolf, was born 3 April 1952 at Hagerstown, Washington
County, MD. He married 7 August 1976 at Roslyn, LI Catherine Marion
Hlavac, born at Mineola, NY, daughter of Edward George and Catherine
Ida (Merz) Hlavac.
    Children of Michael Hendricks and Catherine Marion (Hlavac) Wolf:
    2666   i Kyle Edward Wolf, born 16 April 1986 in West Chester
            County, NY
    2667   ii Trevor David Wolf, born 9 November 1988 in West Chester
            County, NY
    2667A iii David Lee Wolf, born 16 May 1992 in Fairfax, VA

    1699 - ANDREW ADAIR(7) WOLFE [Mary Joan(6) Ashway, Lucinda
Katheryne(5) Trone, Mary Jeannette(4) Wolf, Simon(3), Frederick(2),
Daniel(1)]
    Andrew Adair Wolfe, second child of George Adair and Mary Joan
(Ashway) Wolfe, was born 6 March 1954 at Harrisburg, Dauphin County,
PA. He married 9 June 1979 at Cincinnati, OH Gail L. Metzger.
    Children of Andrew Adair and Gail L. (Metzger) Wolfe:
    2668   i Charles Andrew Wolfe, born 7 June 1980 at Camp Hill,
            Cumberland County, PA
    2669   ii Kathryn Ashway Wolfe, born 2 March 1982 at Camp Hill,
            Cumberland County, PA

    1700 - KRISTEN TRONE(7) WOLFE [Mary Joan(6) Ashway, Lucinda
Katheryne(5) Trone, Mary Jeannette(4) Wolf, Simon(3), Frederick(2),
Daniel(1)]
    Kristen Trone Wolfe, third child of George Adair and Mary Joan
(Ashway) Wolfe, was born 31 January 1957 at Harrisburg, Dauphin
County, PA. She married 17 June 1978 at Lemoyne, Cumberland County, PA
William Charles Sauerwine.
    Children of William Charles and Kristen Trone (Wolfe) Sauerwine:
    2670   i Benjamin Adair Sauerwine, born 22 November 19   at Harris-
            burg, Dauphin County, PA
    2671   ii Grant Edward Sauerwine, born 20 May 1986 at Harrisburg,

Dauphin County, PA

1708 - JOHN MICHAEL(7) DOARNBERGER [Doris Ann(6) Schindel, Anna Ruth(5) Trone, Mary Jeannette(4) Wolf, Simon(3), Frederick(2), Daniel(1)]
John Michael Doarnberger, first child of John Adam and Doris Ann (Schindel) Doarnberger, was born 10 November 1943 at Hagerstown, Washington County, MD. He married 20 June 1970 at Hagerstown Vivian Jean Weaver, born 26 May 1944 at Hagerstown, daughter of Milford Henry and Sarah (Martin) Weaver.
Child of John Michael and Vivian Jean (Weaver) Doarnberger:
2672   i Michael Todd Doarnberger, born 11 December 1972 at Hager-
          stown, Washington County, MD

1709 - SUZANNE(7) DOARNBERGER [Doris Ann(6) Schindel, Anna Ruth(5) Trone, Mary Jeannette(4) Wolf, Simon(3), Frederick(2), Daniel(1)]
Suzanne Doarnberger, second child of John Adam and Doris Ann (Schindel) Doarnberger, was born 24 March 1946 at Hagerstown, Washington County, MD. She married Stephen Michael Absalom Sr, born 31 October 1945 at Bluefield, Mercer County, WV.
Children of Stephen Michael Sr and Suzanne (Doarnberger) Absalom:
2673   i Stephen Michael Absalom Jr, born 7 November 1969 at Las
          Vegas, NV
2674   ii Jennifer Noelle Absalom, born 14 December 1970 at Las
          Vegas, NV

1716 - SUSAN ELIZABETH(7) MILLER [Anna Elizabeth(6) Sager, Edith Mentzer(5) Harman, Ann Cora(4) Wolf, Simon(3), Frederick(2), Daniel(1)]
Susan Elizabeth Miller, twin, first child of William J. and Anna Elizabeth (Sager) Miller, was born 17 September 1944. She married 12 June 1965 Jerry L. Wilson, born 28 July 1942.
Child of Jerry L. and Susan Elizabeth (Miller) Wilson:
2675   i Ginger Samantha Wilson, born 20 August 1973

1718 - CARROLL STALEY JR(7) JAMES [Margaret Jeannette(6) Sager, Edith Mentzer(5) Harman, Ann Cora(4) Wolf, Simon(3), Frederick(2), Daniel(1)]
Carroll Staley James Jr, first child of Carroll Staley Sr and Margaret Jeannette (Sager) James, was born 21 July 1936 at Frederick, Frederick County, MD. He married 29 August 1959 at Moorestown, Burlington County, NJ Elizabeth Mathis, born 14 July 1936.
Children of Carroll Staley Jr and Elizabeth (Mathis) James:
2676   i Christine Tracy James, born 27 November 1967
2677   ii Lauren Hope James, born 2 July 1970

1719 - MARTHA HARMAN(7) JAMES [Margaret Jeannette(6) Sager, Edith Mentzer(5) Harman, Ann Cora(4) Wolf, Simon(3), Frederick(2), Daniel(1)]
Martha Harman James, second child of Carroll Staley Sr and Margaret Jeannette (Sager) James, was born 28 August 1940 at Hagerstown, Washington County, MD. She married 30 June 1962 at Hagerstown Jack Stuart Nichols, born 8 August 1938.
Children of Jack Stuart and Martha Harman (James) Nichols:
2678   i Douglas James Nichols, born 28 March 1967
2679   ii James Ryan Nichols, born 9 October 1969

1720 - RICHARD AARON(7) SAGER [Elmer Rohrer Jr(6), Edith Ment-
zer(5) Harman, Ann Cora(4) Wolf, Simon(3), Frederick(2), Daniel(1)]
    Richard Aaron Sager , first child of Elmer Rohrer Jr and Joan
(McKay) Sager, was born 23 March 1947. He married Cecile _____.
    Children of Richard Aaron and Cecile (_____) Sager:
  2680   i Sky Sager, born 1 March 1976
  2681   ii Brook Marena Sager, born 28 November 1979

1722 - JUDITH LOU(7) MC KINSEY [Morris Nevin(6), Blanche Belle(5)
Wolfe, Harvey J.(4), Simon(3), Frederick(2), Daniel(1)]
    Judith Lou McKinsey, daughter of Morris Nevin and Jane Alberta
(Kershner) McKinsey, was born 28 December 1941 at Hagerstown, Washing-
ton County, MD. She married 1) 27 May 1961 at Hagerstown William James
Hall, born 7 April 1939 at Washington, DC, they divorced 2) 24 June
1966 at Hagerstown Clarence Michael Harshman, born 16 March 1941 at
Hagerstown.
    Child of William James and Judith Lou (McKinsey) Hall:
  2682   i Stacey Hall, born 19 February 1964 at Arlington, VA.
            Married at Hagerstown, Washington County, MD Paul George
            Missud, born 11 April 1961 in New York

1723 - WILLIAM BARKDOLL JR(7) WILES [Julia Marguerite(6) McKin-
sey, Blanche Belle(5) Wolfe, Harvey J.(4), Simon(3), Frederick(2),
Daniel(1)]
    William Barkdoll Wiles Jr, son of William Barkdoll Sr and Julia
Marguerite (McKinsey) Wiles, was born 19 December 1940 at Hagerstown,
Washington County, MD. He married 17 June 1961 at Hagerstown Linda Mae
Cordell, born 28 November 1942 at Waynesboro, Franklin County, PA.
    Child of William Barkdoll Jr and Linda Mae (Cordell) Wiles:
  2683   i Craig William Wiles, born 14 October 1962 at Hagerstown,
            Washington County, MD

1724 - CAROL LOUISE(7) SMITH [Jane(6) McKinsey, Blanche Belle(5)
Wolfe, Harvey J.(4), Simon(3), Frederick(2), Daniel(1)]
    Carol Louise Smith, daughter of William Woodrow and Jane (McKin-
sey) Smith, was born 28 December 1938 at Hagerstown, Washington
County, MD. She married 1 July 1961 at Hagerstown C. Russell Long,
born 4 April 1934 at Baltimore, MD, son of A. Russell and Elizabeth
(_____) Long.
    Children of C. Russell and Carol Louise (Smith) Long:
  2684   i Bradley Russell Long, born 6 November 1962 at Baltimore,
            MD
  2685   ii Elizabeth Jane Long, born 26 January 1967 at Baltimore, MD

1725 - JODY LYNN(7) MC KINSEY [Roland Wolfe(6) McKinsey, Blanche
Belle(5) Wolfe, Harvey J.(4), Simon(3), Frederick(2), Daniel(1)]
    Jody Lynn McKinsey, first child of Roland Wolfe and Sigrid
Rebecca (Rinehart) McKinsey, was born 1 August 1951 at Hagerstown,
Washington County, MD. She married 1) 27 November 1970 at Hagerstown
Thomas Patrick Walsh, born 24 January 1952 in Maryland 2) December
1988 at Hagerstown David Beasley.
    Child of Thomas Patrick and Jody Lynn (McKinsey) Walsh:
  2686   i Steven Blaine Walsh, born 30 April 1971 at Hagerstown,
            Washington County, MD

1728 - NANCY LEE(7) BAKER [Helen Elizabeth(6) Rinehart, Fannie
Elizabeth(5) Wolfe, Harvey J.(4), Simon(3), Frederick(2), Daniel(1)]
    Nancy Lee Baker, daughter of Lester Lee and Helen Elizabeth

(Rinehart) Baker, was born 24 February 1939 at Hagerstown, Washington County, MD. She married 1) 7 January 1957 at Hagerstown Phillip Glen Moon, born 12 July 1937 at Berkeley Springs, Berkeley County, WV, son of Virgil and Esther (_____) Moon, they divorced and 2) 27 August 1971 at Funkstown, Washington County Alvin Bruce Huntsberger, born 11 November 1938 at Chambersburg, Franklin County, PA.
    Children of Phillip Glen and Nancy Lee (Baker) Moon:
2687   i Phillip Glen Moon II, born 29 May 1959 at Hagerstown, Washington County, MD. Married Karen Mae Stine
+ 2688   ii Drista Denise Moon, born 23 October 1960

    1729 - GARY LYNN(7) HARNISH [Helen Elizabeth(6) Rinehart, Fannie Elizabeth(5) Wolfe, Harvey J.(4), Simon(3), Frederick(2), Daniel(1)]
    Gary Lynn Harnish, first child of Wilbur Glen and Helen Elizabeth (Rinehart) Harnish, was born 19 September 1947 at Hagerstown, Washington County, MD. He married in 1971 at Hagerstown Barbara Andrew, born 15 September 1947 at Yonkers, NY, daughter of Marion Edgar and Louise Bernice (Radon) Andrew.
    Children of Gary Lynn and Barbara (Andrew) Harnish, all born at Denver, CO:
2689   i Mark Glen Harnish, born 9 July 1973
2690   ii Andrew Kevin Harnish, born 4 July 1975
2691   iii Jeffrey Allan Harnish, born 18 February 1978

    1730 - DEBRA DEE(7) HARNISH [Helen Elizabeth(6) Rinehart, Fannie Elizabeth(5) Wolfe, Harvey J.(4), Simon(3), Frederick(2), Daniel(1)]
    Debra Dee Harnish, second child of Wilbur Glen and Helen Elizabeth (Rinehart) Harnish, was born 12 July 1951 at Hagerstown, Washington County, MD. She married 1) 27 March 1970 at Hagerstown Isaac Russell Shanholtz, born 10 June 1949 at Hagerstown, son of Paul and Irene (_____) Shanholtz and 2) 17 June 1977 at Hagerstown Robert Frederick Socks, born 9 November 1946 at Hagerstown, son of William Frederick and Effie Mae (Gossard) Socks.
    Child of Isaac Russell and Debra Dee (Harnish) Shanholtz:
2692   i Jammie Lynn Shanholtz, born 6 November 1971 at Hagerstown, Washington County, MD
    Child of Robert Frederick and Debra Dee (Harnish) Socks:
2693   i Richard Lee Socks, born 6 March 1979 at Hagerstown, Washington County, MD

    1731 - JAMES LEE SR(7) GRANT [Thelma Marie(6) Rinehart, Fannie Elizabeth(5) Wolfe, Harvey J.(4), Simon(3), Frederick(2), Daniel(1)]
    James Lee Grant Sr, first child of Hampton Erskin and Thelma Marie (Rinehart) Grant, was born 29 December 1936 at Hagerstown, Washington County, Md. He married 1) 21 June 1956 at Huyetts, Washington County Sandra Mills, born in 1939 at Hagerstown, daughter of James Luther and _____ (Hall) Mills and 2) Patricia Ann Gaver, born 19 July 1937 at Waynesboro, Franklin County, PA, daughter of Lloyd James and Mary Matilda (Smith) Gaver.
    Children of James Lee Sr and Sandra (Mills) Grant:
+ 2694   i James Lee Grant Jr, born 14 March 1957
2695   ii Kenneth Eugene Grant, born 19 December 1958 at Hagerstown, Washington County, MD
2696   iii Thelma Marie Grant, born 22 October 1962 at Hagerstown, Washington County, MD
    Child of James Lee and Patricia Ann (Gaver) Grant:
+ 2697   i Keith Duane Grant, born 17 June 1968

1732 - BARBARA ANN(7) GRANT [Thelma Marie(6) Rinehart, Fannie Elizabeth(5) Wolfe, Harvey J.(4), Simon(3), Frederick(2), Daniel(1)]
    Barbara Ann Grant, second child of Hampton Erskin and Thelma Marie (Rinehart) Grant, was born 1 June 1939 at Hagerstown, Washington County, MD. She married 2 April 1960 at Hagerstown James Robert Franks, born 25 March 1930 at Uniontown, Fayette County, PA, son of James Chester and Zada (Lafollette) Franks.
    Child of James Robert and Barbara Ann (Grant) Franks:
    2698   i Charles Willis Franks, born 24 October 1960 at Hagerstown, Washington County, MD. Married 29 December 1983 at Staunton, Augusta County, VA Lydia Goforth

    1733 - ROBERT WAYNE(7) RINEHART [Robert Roy(6), Fannie Elizabeth(5) Wolfe, Harvey J.(4), Simon(3), Frederick(2), Daniel(1)]
    Robert Wayne Rinehart, first child of Robert Roy and Jane Naomi (Springer) Rinehart, was born 10 November 1938 at Hagerstown, Washington County, MD. He married 1) at Hagerstown Helen Waters, divorced 1967 and 2) 29 April 1967 at Fairplay, Washington County Pamela Mae Bowers, born 17 September 1947 at Hagerstown, daughter of David Calvin and Lena Mae (Gaylor) Bowers.
    Children of Robert Wayne and Helen (Waters) Rinehart:
    2699   i Richard Wayne Rinehart, born 7 July 1959 at Hagerstown, Washington County, MD. Married 28 January 1984 at San Antonio, Bexar County, TX Elizabeth Rendon, born 15 October 1960 at San Benito, Cameron County, TX, daughter of Victor and Gila (Pente') Rendon
    2700   ii Lisa Rinehart, born 10 October 1964 at Hagerstown, Washington County, MD

    1734 - JO ELLEN(7) RINEHART [Robert Roy(6), Fannie Elizabeth(5) Wolfe, Harvey J.(4), Simon(3), Frederick(2), Daniel(1)]
    Jo Ellen Rinehart, second child of Robert Roy and Jane Naomi (Springer) Rinehart, was born 22 March 1948 at Hagerstown, Washington County, MD. She married 6 August 1965 at Hagerstown Harry Angle Daley, born 2 August 1947 at Hagerstown, son of Irvin Roger and Ruth (Hornbaker) Daley.
    Children of Harry Angle and Jo Ellen (Rinehart) Daley:
    2701   i Kendra Jane Daley, born 25 July 1966 at Hagerstown, Washington County, MD. Married 19 September 1987 at Chambersburg, Franklin County, PA Daniel Sleichter
    2702   ii Leslie Ruth Daley, born 27 October 1968 at Hagerstown, Washington Copunty, MD. Married 5 May 1990 at Hagerstown Max Chester Mills
    2703   iii Ellie Jo Daley, born 16 August 1974 at Hagerstown, Washington County, MD

    1737 - CHRISTINE MARILYN(7) RINEHART - [Raymond Wolfe(6), Fannie Elizabeth(5) Wolfe, Harvey J.(4), Simon(3), Frederick(2), Daniel(1)]
    Christine Marilyn Rinehart, daughter of Raymond Wolfe and Betty Jane (Shoemaker) Rinehart, was born 12 January 1956 at Hagerstown, Washington County, MD. She married Kim Curtis Weaver.
    Children of Kim Curtis and Christine Marilyn (Rinehart) Weaver:
    2704   i Dustin Michael Weaver
    2705   ii Nathan Patrick Weaver

    1740 - STEVEN KEITH(7) RODGERS [Joanne Marie(6) Wolfe, Charles Eugene(5), Harvey J.(4), Simon(3), Frederick(2), Daniel(1)]
    Steven Keith Rodgers, second child of Robert Dean and Joanne

Marie (Wolfe) Rodgers, was born 7 January 1962 in Washington County, Md. He married 3 May 1986 at Smithsburg, Washington County Dena Lin Ray, born 25 March 1963 at Waynesboro, Franklin County, PA.

Child of Steven Keith and Dena Lin (Ray) Rodgers:
2706   i   Kaitlyn Nicole Rodgers, born 1 August 1987 at Waynesboro, Franklin County, PA

1742 - DENNIS ALAN(7) HUFFINGTON [Carlton Dale(6), Ada Blanche(5) Wolf, Carlton Emmert(4), Jacob(3), Frederick(2), Daniel(1)]
Dennis Alan Huffington, first child of Carlton Dale and Lona Mildred (Howe) Huffington, was born 22 August 1941 at Rockford, Winnebago County, IL. He married 29 November 1968 at Rockford Gail Lee Anderson, born 15 May 1945 at Rockford, daughter of Eric and Rowena (Thompson) Anderson. Dennis graduated in Mechanical Engineering from the University of Illinois.

Children of Dennis Alan and Gail Lee (Anderson) Huffington, born in Rockford:
2707   i   Leigh Maurine Huffington, born 12 August 1970
2708   ii   Eric Franklin Huffington, born 3 August 1973

1743 - ROBERT DALE(7) HUFFINGTON [Carlton Dale(6), Ada Blanche(5) Wolf, Carlton Emmert(4), Jacob(3), Frederick(2), Daniel(1)]
Robert Dale Huffington, second child of Carlton Dale and Lona Mildred (Howe) Huffington, was born 13 March 1944 at Rockford, Winnebago County, IL. He married 3 July 1970 at Rockford Mary Lou Rippberger, born 24 February 1944 at Freeport, IL, daughter of Charles Leon and Alta Elizabeth (Dreier) Rippberger.

Children of Robert Dale and Mary Lou (Rippberger) Huffington, born at Rockford:
2709   i   Christopher Dale Huffington, born 19 March 1977
2710   ii   Dana E. Huffington, born 11 July 1980

1744 - CAROL DIANE(7) HUFFINGTON [Carlton Dale(6), Ada Blanche(5) Wolf, Carlton Emmert(4), Jacob(3), Frederick(2), Daniel(1)]
Carol Diane Huffington, third child of Carlton Dale and Lona Mildred (Howe) Huffington, was born 20 June 1946 at Rockford, Winnebago County, IL. She married 1) 10 August 1968 at Rockford Dennis Martin Jobe, born 12 December 1945 at Milwaukee, WI, son of Martin Lawrence and Ruth Inez (Wills) Jobe, divorced 24 November 1974 and 2) 6 July 1985 at Rockford Vern Miller, born 21 September 1974 at Rockford.

Child of Dennis Martin and Carol Diane (Huffington) Jobe:
2711   i   Matthew Dennis Jobe, born 2 November 1972 at Rockford
Children of Vern Miller, step-children of Carol Diane (Huffington) (Jobe) Miller:
2712   i   Stephanie Miller, born 21 September 1974
2713   ii   Nancy Miller, born 13 March 1977

1745 - RICHARD WILLIAM(7) HUFFINGTON [Carlton Dale(6), Ada Blanche(5) Wolf, Carlton Emmert(4), Jacob(3), Frederick(2), Daniel(1)]
Richard William Huffington, fourth child of Carlton Dale and Lona Mildred (Howe) Huffington, was born 30 June 1949 at Rockford, Winnebago County, IL. He married 6 October 1973 at Rockford Judy A. Dahlstrom, born 17 June 1951 at Rockford, daughter of Paul G. and Beverly J. (Johnson) Dahlstrom.

Children of Richard William and Judy A. (Dahlstrom) Huffington:
2714   i   Andrew R. Huffington, adopted, born 9 March 1982 at Aurora, IL

2715   ii Sarah J. Huffington, adopted, born 12 August 1988 at
            Sterling, IL

    1746 - JAMES FRANKLIN(7) HUFFINGTON [Carlton Dale(6), Ada
Blanche(5) Wolf, Carlton Emmert(4), Jacob(3), Frederick(2), Daniel(1)]
    James Franklin Huffington, fifth child of Carlton Dale and Lona
Mildred (Howe) Huffington, was born 17 June 1951 at Rockford, Winne-
bago County, IL. He married 1) 6 July 1974 at Rockford Sally Joan
Bradley, born 23 October 1951 at Rockford, daughter of Charles M. and
Joan (Drane) Bradley, divorced July 1978, 2) 8 August 1981 at Rockford
Heidi Heeb, born 22 November 1960 at Milwaukee, WI. There were no
children by the first marriage.
    Children of James Franklin and Heidi (Heeb) Huffington, born at
Rockford:
    2716   i Jami Marie Huffington, born 30 January 1983
    2717   ii Nicholas James Huffington, born 31 December 1985
    2718 iii Phillip David Huffington, born 22 May 1987

    1747 - JOANNE LEE(7) HUFFINGTON [Carlton Dale(6), Ada Blanche(5)
Wolf, Carlton Emmert(4), Jacob(3), Frederick(2), Daniel(1)]
    Joanne Lee Huffington, sixth child of Carlton Dale and Lona
Mildred (Howe) Huffington, was born 14 December 1953 at Rockford,
Winnebago County, IL. She married 19 November 1988 at Oswego, Kendall
County, IL Roy Murphy.
    Child of Roy Murphy, step-child of Joanne Lee (Huffington)
Murphy:
    2719   i Ray Murphy

    1748 - JEFFREY MEADE(7) HUFFINGTON [Carlton Dale(6), Ada
Blanche(5) Wolf, Carlton Emmert(4), Jacob(3), Frederick(2), Daniel(1)]
    Jefrey Meade Huffington, seventh child of Carlton Dale and Lona
Mildred (Howe) Huffington, was born 14 December 1953 at Rockford,
Winnebago County, IL. He married 17 September 1978 at Palatine, IL
Kathleen Ann Landcaster, born 26 February 1955, daughter of John
Kenneth and Mary Ellen (McGrath) Landcaster.
    Children of Jeffrey Meade and Kathleen Ann (Landcaster) Huffing-
ton:
    2720   i Melissa K. Huffington, born 6 January 1981 at Rockford
    2721   ii Erin V. Huffington, born 31 January 1983 at Palatine, IL
    2722 iii Brittany L. Huffington, born 23 September 1985 at Palatine
    2723   iv Brendon J. Huffington, born 10 September 1987 at Palatine

    1751 - SUSAN FLEET(7) HIGHBARGER [Paul George W.(6), Harry Luther
Sr.(5), Catherine(4) Wolf, Jacob(3), Frederick(2), Daniel(1)]
    Susan Fleet Highbarger, child of Paul George W. and Ruth Eliza-
beth (Fleet) Highbarger, was born 11 August 1946 at Hagerstown,
Washington County, MD. She married 1) at Hagerstown Donald Lee Burkett, born 2 January 1944 at Hagerstown, 2) 2 February 1967 at Hagerstown Robert Lester Pardue, born 3 April 1944 in Arkansas and 3) 23
November 1973 at Hagerstown Larry George Trumpower, born 25 July 1946
at Hagerstown, died 6 October 1985 at Hagerstown, son of Victor and
Betty (Kuhn) Trumpower, buried in Cedar Lawn Memorial Park, Hagerstown.
    Children of Donald Lee and Susan Fleet (Highbarger) Burkett:
+ 2724   i Lauri Ann Burkett, born 10 December 1962
    2725   ii Lisa Annette Burkett, born 29 May 1964 at Hagerstown, died
            31 May 1964 at Hagerstown, buried in Boonsboro Cemetery,
            Washington County, MD

Child of Robert Lester and Susan Fleet (Highbarger) (Burkett)
Pardue:
2726   i Robert Lester Pardue II, born 16 September 1967

1752 - WILLIAM VICTOR(7) ROBINSON [Ruth Anne(6) Hebscher, Maude
May(5) Wolf, John Albaugh(4), Jacob(3), Frederick(2), Daniel(1)]
    William Victor Robinson, first child of Victor Norman and Ruth
Anne (Hebscher) Robinson, was born 13 April 1947 at Bakersfield, Kern
County, CA. He married 12 May 1984 at Fresno, Fresno County, CA Cheryl
Lynn Bishop, born 18 July 1954, daughter of James T. and _____ (Smi-
ley) Bishop.
    Children of William Victor and Cheryl Lynn (Bishop) Robinson,
born at Fresno, Ca:
2727   i Jana Patrice Robinson, born 30 November 1986
2728   ii Sara Robinson, born 19 April 1990

1753 - JOHN ALEC SR(7) ROBINSON [Ruth Anne(6) Hebscher, Maude
May(5) Wolf, John Albaugh(4), Jacob(3), Frederick(2), Daniel(1)]
    John Alec Robinson Sr., second child of Victor Norman and Ruth
Anne (Hebscher) Robinson, was born 10 July 1949 at Roslyn Heights,
Long Island, NY. He married 1) 24 August 1968 at Bakersfield, Kern
County, CA Brenda Jannene Latham, born 17 May 1950 at Bakersfield and
2) 26 July 1980 at Virginia City, NV Martha Jane Jones, born 9 April
1949 at Athens, TN.
    Children of John Alec Sr. and Brenda Jannene (Latham) Robinson,
born at Bakersfield:
2729   i John Alec Robinson Jr., born 25 April 1970
2730   ii Dustin Wayne Robinson, born 24 January 1972

1754 - KOYYA ANN(7) ROBINSON [Ruth Anne(6) Hebscher, Maude May(5)
Wolf, John Albaugh(4), Jacob(3), Frederick(2), Daniel(1)]
    Koyya Ann Robinson, third child of Victor Norman and Ruth Anne
(Hebscher) Robinson, was born 13 February 1954 at Bakersfield, Kern
County, CA. She married 9 June 1972 at Baltimore, MD Robert Lee Pugh,
born 14 April 1952 at Bakersfield.
    Children of Robert Lee and Koyya Ann (Robinson) Pugh, born at
Bakersfield:
2731   i Robert Paul Pugh, born 13 April 1975
2732   ii Victoria Nichole Pugh, born 18 October 1978

1756 - JOSEPH WAYNE SR(7) WOLF [John Franklin Bernard(6), Harry
Edwin(5), John Albaugh(4), Jacob(3), Frederick(2), Daniel(1)]
    Joseph Wayne Wolf Sr.,only child of John Franklin Bernard and Eva
Glenview (Ebersole) Wolf, was born 8 November 1937 at Hagerstown,
Washington County, MD. He married 1) Carol Ann White, born 1943, died
22 November 1967, daughter of Hurxtel and _____ (_____) White and 2)
Hazel Carson, born 3 June 1955, daughter of Dealus and Nannie (Byrge)
Carson.
    Child of Joseph Wayne Sr. and Carol Ann (White) Wolf:
2733   i Joseph Wayne Wolf Jr., born and died 22 November 1967
    Children of Joseph Wayne Sr. and Hazel (Carson) Wolf:
2734   i Bradford Wayne Wolf, adopted, step-son of Joseph, born 27
           March 1975 at Jacksboro, TN
2735   ii Byron Franklin Wolf, born 19 April 1980 at Jacksboro, TN

1757 - BARBARA LOUISE(7) WOLF [Charles Coulson(6), Charles
Welty(5), John Albaugh(4), Jacob(3), Frederick(2), Daniel(1)]
    Barbara Louise Wolf, first child of Charles Coulson and Julia

Cornelia (Foreman) Wolf, was born 11 January 1943 at Hagerstown, Washington County, MD although her parents were at the time living at Cumberland, Allegany County, MD. She married 29 December 1961 at Charlestown, WV Robert Clark Kight Sr., born 13 September 1941 at Hagerstown, son of Linwood Starr and Evelyn (Hill) Kight.

Children of Robert Clark Sr. and Barbara Louise (Wolf) Kight:
+ 2736   i Stephanie Coulson Kight, born 21 October 1962
  2737   ii Lindley Hill Kight, born 15 January 1964 at Silver Spring, Montgomery County, MD. Married 17 June 1989 at Crofton, Anne Arundel County, MD Vincent Joseph Bucci, born 6 May 1963 at Pittsburgh, PA, son of Emidio Felix and Johanna Rita (Lison) Bucci
  2738 iii Robert Clark Kight Jr., born 29 October 1968 at Silver Spring, Montgomery County, MD

1758 - MARY JULIA(7) WOLF [Charles Coulson(6), Charles Welty(5), John Albaugh(4), Jacob(3), Frederick(2), Daniel(1)]

Mary Julia Wolf, second child of Charles Coulson and Julia Cornelia (Foreman) Wolf, was born 18 March 1946 at Hagerstown, Washington County, MD although her parents were living at the time at Cumberland, Allegany County, MD. She married 5 September 1970 at Hagerstown John Lawrence Good, born 4 May 1947 at Philadelphia, PA, son of James John Davis and Anna (Alferio) Good.

Children of John Lawrence and Mary Julia (Wolf) Good:
  2739   i Katharine Anne Good, born 2 October 1974 at Silver Spring, Montgomery County, MD
  2740   ii Margaret Emily Good, born 24 November 1978 at College Park, Prince Georges County, MD
  2741 iii Claire Julia Good, born 22 June 1982 at Broomall, Delaware County, PA

1759 - REUEL AUGUSTINE III(7) WIEBEL [Betty Ann Reece(6) Wolf, Charles Welty(5), John Albaugh(4), Jacob(3), Frederick(2), Daniel(1)]

Reuel Augustine Wiebel III, first adopted child of Reuel Augustine Jr. and Betty Ann Reece (Wolf) Wiebel, was born 19 December 1957 at Charlottesville, Albemarle County, VA. He married 1) 14 November 1981 Leah Anna Parker, born 4 July 1957 at Camden, NJ, they divorced January 1982 and he married 2) 3 August 1984 at Charlottesville Nancy Fay Bourne, born 14 February 1963 at Charlottesville, daughter of Donald Wade and Fay (Richardson) Bourne.

Child of Reuel Augustine III and Nancy Fay (Bourne) Wiebel:
  2742   i Reuel Augustine Wiebel IV, born 18 December 1988 at Charlottesville, Albemarle County, VA

1762 - KIM ELIZABETH(7) RHOADS [Donald Wolf(6), Mary Ellen(5) Wolf, John Albaugh(4), Jacob(3), Frederick(2), Daniel(1)]

Kim Elizabeth Rhoads, second child of Donald Wolf and Jane Marie (Dambach) Rhoads, was born 9 June 1956 at Buffalo, NY. She married 23 November 1979 Mark Thomas Spence, born 17 January 1956.

Children of Mark Thomas and Kim Elizabeth (Rhoads) Spence:
  2743   i Mark Alan Spence, born 11 December 1982
  2744   ii Robert Rhoads Spence, born 27 October 1985
  2745 iii Michael Jacob Spence, born 15 September 1987

2020 - MERRITT WENDELL(7) WOLFE [Arthur Wendell(6), Henry(5), Christina(4) Paulus, Daniel(3), Christina(2) Wolf, Daniel(1)]

Merritt Wendell Wolfe, child of Arthur Wendell and Celia (Robinson) Wolfe, was born 10 May 1920 in Grant County, IN. He married 6 May

1946 Catherine Elizabeth Wimmer, born 27 August 1922. Merritt is an engineer and retired in 1985 from Goodyear Tire and Rubber Company.
    Children of Merritt Wendell and Catherine Elizabeth (Wimmer) Wolfe:
+ 2746   i Wayne Wendell Wolfe, born 30 June 1950
  2747   ii Juanita Jayne Wolfe, born 6 September 1954. Married 2 October 1977 John Burt Frank, born 19 July 1954

    2085 - EDITH PAULINE(7) RIDENOUR [Lessie Irene(6) Hollehan, Joseph Harrison(5), Lucy Ann(4) Paulus, Daniel(3), Christina(2) Wolf, Daniel(1)]
    Edith Pauline Ridenour, first child of Lewis Arlington and Lessie Irene (Hollehan) Ridenour, was born 15 July 1901 at Briceton, OH, died 15 February 1969 at Ft. Wayne, IN. She married 16 July 1927 at Ft. Wayne Edward William Witte, born 28 April 1893 at Ft. Wayne, died 30 December 1979 at Ft. Lauderdale, FL. They are buried at Ft. Wayne.
    Children of Edward William and Edith Pauline (Ridenour) Witte:
+ 2748   i Joanne Arlyn Witte, born 19 April 1930
  2749   ii Janet Marie Witte, born 7 February 1936 at Ft. Wayne, IN

    2087 - MURRELL VALENTINE(7) RIDENOUR [Lessie Irene(6) Hollehan, Joseph Harrison(5), Lucy Ann(4) Paulus, Daniel(3), Christina(2) Wolf, Daniel(1)]
    Murrell Valentine Ridenour, third child of Lewis Arlington and Lessie Irene (Hollehan) Ridenour, was born 20 August 1904 at Briceton, OH, died 23 March 1966 at Nitro, WV. He married 13 October 1928 Fanny Marvin.
    Child of Murrell Valentine and Fanny (Marvin) Ridenour:
  2750   i John Marvin Ridenour, born 19 September 1930. Married 27 May 1967 Janet Seymore

    2088 - PAUL JOSEPH(7) RIDENOUR [Lessie Irene(6) Hollehan, Joseph Harrison(5), Lucy Ann(4) Paulus, Daniel(3), Christina(2) Wolf, Daniel(1)]
    Paul Joseph Ridenour, fourth child of Lewis Arlington and Lessie Irene (Hollehan) Ridenour, was born 24 April 1907 at Briceton, OH, died 7 April 1948 and is buried at Ft. Wayne, IN. He married Juanita Leeth.
    Children of Paul Joseph and Juanita (Leeth) Ridenour:
  2751   i Lois Renee Ridenour, born 11 October 1937 at Ft. Wayne, IN
+ 2752   ii Lewis Garfield Ridenour, born 2 September 1946

    2089 - DOROTHY ELSIE(7) RIDENOUR [Lessie Irene(6) Hollehan, Joseph Harrison(5), Lucy Ann(4) Paulus, Daniel(3), Christina(2) Wolf, Daniel(1)]
    Dorothy Elsie Ridenour, fifth child of Lewis Arlington and Lessie Irene (Hollehan) Ridenour, was born 14 May 1913 at Briceton, OH, died August 1979 at North Ft. Myers, FL, and is buried at Ft. Wayne, IN. She married 14 September 1935 at Ft. Wayne Arnold White.
    Children of Arnold and Dorothy Elsie (Ridenour) White:
+ 2753   i Barbara Marie White, born 10 June 1941
  2754   ii Judith Anne White, born 2 August 1944 at Ft. Wayne, IN. Married Jay Maltz

CHAPTER No. 9

EIGHTH GENERATION

2129 - ANNE KATHARINE(8) CORDTZ [Naomi Bernice(7) Malhaupt,
Violet Audry(6) Knabenshue, Anna Evalee(5) Shroyer, Malinda Ann(4)
Wolf, Frederick (3), Jacob(2), Daniel(1)]
    Anne Katharine Cordtz, first child of Raymond and Naomi Bernice
(Malhaupt) Cordtz, was born 15 April 1944. She married 27 July 1963
Michael Harman.
    Children of Michael and Anne Katharine (Cordtz) Harman:
  2755   i Christopher Harman, born 18 September 1968
  2756   ii Katherine Anne Harman, born 6 January 1972

    2130 - SUSAN MARIE(8) CORDTZ [Naomi Bernice(7) Malhaupt, Violet
Audry(6) Knabenshue, Anna Evalee(5) Shroyer, Malinda Ann(4) Wolf,
Frederick (3), Jacob(2), Daniel(1)]
    Susan Marie Cordtz, second child of Raymond and Naomi Bernice
(Malhaupt) Cordtz, was born 1 March 1948. She married 30 August 1969
Ronald Lee May.
    Children of Ronald Lee and Susan Marie (Cordtz) May:
  2757   i Jennifer May, born 7 October 1970
  2758   ii Karon May, born 4 January 1975

    2132 - RICHARD CARL(8) MALHAUPT [Richard Verne(7), Violet
Audry(6) Knabenshue, Anna Evalee(5) Shroyer, Malinda Ann(4) Wolf,
Frederick (3), Jacob(2), Daniel(1)]
    Richard Carl Malhaupt, first child of Richard Verne and Dorothy
(Murphy) Malhaupt, was born 10 June 1946. His wife's name is not
known.
    Child of Richard Carl and _____ (_____) Malhaupt:
  2759   i William Richard Malhaupt, born 18 February 1967 at South
           Bend, IN

    2133 - KRISTINE LYNN(8) MALHAUPT [Richard Verne(7), Violet
Audry(6) Knabenshue, Anna Evalee(5) Shroyer, Malinda Ann(4) Wolf,
Frederick (3), Jacob(2), Daniel(1)]
    Kristine Lynn Malhaupt, second child of Richard Verne and Dorothy
(Murphy) Malhaupt, was born 16 January 1951. She married 9 December
1972 at South Bend, IN Curtis Weiand.
    Child of Curtis and Kristine Lynn (Malhaupt) Weiand:
  2760   i Heather Ann Weiand, born 14 December 1977

    2134 - ROBERT E.(8) KINAS [Marjorie F.(7) Malhaupt, Violet
Audry(6) Knabenshue, Anna Evalee(5) Shroyer, Malinda Ann(4) Wolf,
Frederick (3), Jacob(2), Daniel(1)]
    Robert E. Kinas, first child of _____ and Marjorie F. (Malhaupt)
Kinas, was born 27 April 1943. He married 2 June 1962 Nora O'Banion.
    Children of Robert E. and Nora (O'Banion) Kinas:
  2761   i Roxanna L. Kinas, born 17 October 1963
  2762   ii Vicky L. Kinas, born 22 January 1965
  2763 iii Kathleen M. Kinas, born 11 March 1966
  2764   iv Robert E. Kinas, born 24 December 1971

    2135 - RONALD DEAN(8) KINAS [Marjorie F.(7) Malhaupt, Violet

Audry(6) Knabenshue, Anna Evalee(5) Shroyer, Malinda Ann(4) Wolf,
Frederick (3), Jacob(2), Daniel(1)]

Ronald Dean Kinas, second child of _____ and Marjorie F. (Malhaupt) Kinas, was born 12 March 1945. He married 5 January 1964
Kristine Dudeck.
Children of Ronald Dean and Kristine (Dudeck) Kinas:
2765   i Angela C. Kinas, born 15 October 1965
2766   ii Stephen E. Kinas, born 16 November 1966

2136 - RICHARD DOUGLAS(8) KINAS [Marjorie F.(7) Malhaupt, Violet
Audry(6) Knabenshue, Anna Evalee(5) Shroyer, Malinda Ann(4) Wolf,
Frederick (3), Jacob(2), Daniel(1)]

Richard Douglas Kinas, third child of _____ and Marjorie F.
(Malhaupt) Kinas, was born 1 October 1946. He married 16 June 1964
Margaret O'Banion.
Children of Richard Douglas and Margaret (O'Banion) Kinas:
2767   i Richard Joseph Kinas, born 14 October 1965
2768   ii Tammy Sue Kinas, born 17 September 1969 at Goshen, IN

2139 - SANDRA J.(8) MC ELHEMY [Verna L.(7) Malhaupt, Violet
Audry(6) Knabenshue, Anna Evalee(5) Shroyer, Malinda Ann(4) Wolf,
Frederick (3), Jacob(2), Daniel(1)]

Sandra J. McElhemy, first child of William and Verna L. (Malhaupt) Mc Elhemy, was born 25 November 1950. She married 15 November
1969 Donald Collins.
Children of Donald and Sandra J. (McElhemy) Collins:
2769   i Tracy Collins
2770   ii Michael Collins

2141 - ROBERT LEROY(8) ARP [Esther Irene(7) Jackman, Vivian
Ann(6) Knabenshue, Anna Evalee(5) Shroyer, Malinda Ann(4) Wolf,
Frederick (3), Jacob(2), Daniel(1)]

Robert Leroy Arp, first child of Paul and Esther Irene (Jackman)
Arp, was born 6 July 1947. He married 5 October 1968 Kathleen J.
Wallace.
Children of Robert Leroy and Kathleen J. (Wallace) Arp:
2771   i Gary Allen Arp, born 2 August 1971
2772   ii Michael Paul Arp, born 24 July 1975

2143 - MANFORD PAUL(8) DEAL [Virginia M.(7) Jackman, Vivian
Ann(6) Knabenshue, Anna Evalee(5) Shroyer, Malinda Ann(4) Wolf,
Frederick (3), Jacob(2), Daniel(1)]

Manford Paul Deal, first child of Ronald and Virginia M. (Jackman) Deal, was born 1 April 1947. He married 5 October 1969 Nancy
Kintz.
Children of Manford Paul and Nancy (Kintz) Deal:
2773   i Ronald Joseph Deal, born 5 January 1972
2774   ii Jennifer R. Deal
2775 iii Michael Paul Deal

2147 - DAVID R.(8) FINNILA [Betty Ann(7) Jackman, Vivian Ann(6)
Knabenshue, Anna Evalee(5) Shroyer, Malinda Ann(4) Wolf, Frederick(3),
Jacob(2), Daniel(1)]

David R. Finnila, second child of _____ and Betty Ann (Jackman)
Finnila, was born 28 October 1951. He married Judy _____.
Child of David R. and Judy (_____) Finnila:
2776   i David Allen Finnila

2148 - CHRISTIE LYNN(8) FINNILA [Betty Ann(7) Jackman, Vivian Ann(6) Knabenshue, Anna Evalee(5) Shroyer, Malinda Ann(4) Wolf, Frederick (3), Jacob(2), Daniel(1)]
Christie Lynn Finnila, third child of _____ and Betty Ann (Jackman) Finnila, was born 1 April 1955. She married 28 December 1974 David Coats.
Child of David and Christie Lynn (Finnila) Coats:
2777   i Angela L. Coats

2157 - DAYNA CHRISTINE(8) DE PEW [Joanne Evelyn(7) Day, Mildred Lucille(6) Shroyer, Harvey Howard(5), Malinda Ann(4) Wolf, Frederick(3), Jacob(2), Daniel(1)
Dayna Christine DePew, first child of Theodore James and Joanne Evelyn (Day) DePew, was born 23 November 1950 at Rockford, IL. She married 1) 30 September 1978 at Sierra Vista, AZ Larry Harpster. They divorced at Spokane, WA and she married 2) 4 February 1989 at Morrow Bay, CA Jack Drake.
Child of Larry and Dayna Christine (DePew) Harpster:
2778   i Danielle Christine Harpster, born 21 March 1980 at Spokane, WA
Child of Jack and Dayna Christine (DePew) (Harpster) Drake:
2779   i Connors James Drake, born 27 February 1991

2158 - TRACY JOANNE(8) DE PEW [Joanne Evelyn(7) Day, Mildred Lucille(6) Shroyer, Harvey Howard(5), Malinda Ann(4) Wolf, Frederick(3), Jacob(2), Daniel(1)]
Tracy Joanne DePew, second child of Theodore James and Joanne Evelyn (Day) DePew, was born 23 April 1953 at Pasadena, CA. She married 4 August 1975 at Spokane, WA Timothy O'Brien Robbins.
Children of Timothy O'Brien and Tracy Joanne (DePew) Robbins:
2780   i Tyler O'Brien Robbins, born 31 July 1978 at San Mateo, CA
2781   ii Tiana Day Robbins, born 10 March 1980 at Spokane, WA
2782   iii Travis Joe Robbins, born 6 October 1982 at Spokane, WA

2159 - DOUGLAS JAMES(8) DE PEW [Joanne Evelyn(7) Day, Mildred Lucille(6) Shroyer, Harvey Howard(5), Malinda Ann(4) Wolf, Frederick(3), Jacob(2), Daniel(1)]
Douglas James DePew, third child of Theodore James and Joanne Evelyn (Day) DePew, was born 17 May 1961 at Kansas City, KS. He married December 1984 Susan Breman.
Children of Douglas James and Susan (Breman) DePew:
2783   i Shannan Katherine DePew, born 29 September 1988 at Santa Mavia, CA
2784   ii Shelby Joanne DePew, born 28 February 1991

2160 - DENISE LYNETTE(8) DAY [Richard Edward(7), Mildred Lucille(6) Shroyer, Harvey Howard(5), Malinda Ann(4) Wolf, Frederick(3), Jacob(2), Daniel(1)]
Denise Lynette Day, first child of Richard Edward and Dorothy Jean (Husen) Day, was born 19 August 1954 at Rockford. IL. She married 30 April 1983 Stevens Perkins, born 29 December 1947.
Child of Stevens and Denise Lynette (Day) Perkins:
2785   i Stephanie Denise Perkins, born 31 October 1983

2161 - DIANE(8) DAY [Richard Edward(7), Mildred Lucille(6) Shroyer, Harvey Howard(5), Malinda Ann(4) Wolf, Frederick (3), Jacob(2), Daniel(1)]
Diane Day, second child of Richard Edward and Dorothy Jean

(Husen) Day, was born 19 March 1957 at Rockford, IL. She married 1) 8 February 1975 Fred Galetti. They divorced 6 June 1977 and she married 2) 16 January 1982 Tom M. Fay, born 24 November 1954. They divorced 19 December 1986.

Child of Fred and Diane (Day) Galetti:
2786   i Michael David Galetti, born 15 September 1975 at Rockford, IL. Adopted by his step-father Tom M. Fay

Child of Tom M. and Diane (Day) (Galetti) Fay:
2787   i Jennifer Fay, born 1 October 1984

2166 - DEAN(8) AMANS [Brian Dean(7) Day, Mildred Lucille(6) Shroyer, Harvey Howard(5), Malinda Ann(4) Wolf, Frederick (3), Jacob(2), Daniel(1)]

Dean Amans, child of _____ and Sandi (Mackey) Amans and step-son of Brian Dean Day, was born 13 December 1961 at Rockford, IL. He married 3 August 1985 at West Bend, WI Darlene Mae Wahl.

Children of Dean and Darlene Mae (Wahl) Amans:
2788   i Amanda Amans, born 17 March 1988
2789   ii James Dean Amans, born 12 June 1990

2168 - KATIE(8) AMANS [Brian Dean(7) Day, Mildred Lucille(6) Shroyer, Harvey Howard(5), Malinda Ann(4) Wolf, Frederick (3), Jacob(2), Daniel(1)]

Katie Amans, child of _____ and Sandi (Mackey) Amans and step-daughter of Brian Dean Day, was born 18 March 1967 at Rockford, IL. She married 25 September 1985 at Montello, WI Thomas O'Malley.

Child of Thomas and Katie (Amans) O'Malley:
2790   i Megan Marie O'Malley, born 26 February 1986

2171 - SALLY LYNN(8) VAN LYSEL [Janice Elaine(7) Starkweather, Norma Leora(6) Shroyer, Harvey Howard(5), Malinda Ann(4) Wolf, Frederick (3), Jacob(2), Daniel(1)]

Sally Lynn Van Lysel, second child of Marvin Francis and Janice Elaine (Starkweather) Van Lysel, was born 30 March 1958 at Wisconsin Rapids, WI. She married 5 January 1979 at Sun Prairie, WI Arthur R. Anderson, born 13 March 1957.

Children of Arthur R. and Sally Lynn (Van Lysel) Anderson, born at Madison< WI:
2791   i Angela Marie Anderson, born 27 July 1979
2792   ii Amy Leah Anderson, born 11 November 1982
2793 iii Andrew James Anderson, born 23 April 1988

2172 - STEPHEN PATRICK(8) VAN LYSEL [Janice Elaine(7) Starkweather, Norma Leora(6) Shroyer, Harvey Howard(5), Malinda Ann(4) Wolf, Frederick (3), Jacob(2), Daniel(1)]

Stephen Patrick Van Lysel, third child of Marvin Francis and Janice Elaine (Starkweather) Van Lysel, was born 10 March 1961 at Madison, Dane County, WI. He married 20 September 1986 at Madison Karen Hanson, born 9 February 1962 at Madison.

Children of Stephen Patrick and Karen (Hanson) Van Lysel:
2794   i Matthew Lee Van Lysel, twin, born 21 June 1991 at Madison
2795   ii Neil Allen Van Lysel, twin, born 21 June 1991 at Madison

2185 - CHERYL MARIE(8) PEARSON [Charlene Marie(7) Shroyer, Dalton Howard(6), Harvey Howard(5), Malinda Ann(4) Wolf, Frederick (3), Jacob(2), Daniel(1)]

Cheryl Marie Pearson, first child of James and Charlene Marie (Shroyer) Pearson, was born 24 March 1965 at South Bend, IN. She

married 8 February 1987 at Orlando, FL David M. Budimir.
Child of David M. and Cheryl Marie (Pearson) Budimir:
2796   i Jennifer Marie Pearson, born 29 October 1980 at Grand
           Maria, MN, adopted 22 November 1988 by David Budimir

2203 - BYRON JAY(8) PYLE [Virgil(7), Mary Alice(6) Montel,
Samuel(5), Abraham(4), Susan(3) Wolf, Jacob(2), Daniel(1)]
Byron Jay Pyle, first child of Virgil and Hazel (Baker) Pyle, was
born 8 July 1929. He married 16 July 1950 Jackie Surgey, born 17
October 1930.
Children of Byron Jay and Jackie (Surgey) Pyle:
2797   i Jana Rae Pyle, born 22 January 1952
2798   ii Becky Susan Pyle, born 10 August 1953
2799 iii Tonia Lee Pyle, born 27 August 1956
2800   iv Barton Jay Pyle, born 22 October 1966

2204 - INA LOUISE(8) PYLE [Virgil(7), Mary Alice(6) Montel,
Samuel(5), Abraham(4), Susan(3) Wolf, Jacob(2), Daniel(1)]
Ina Louise Pyle, second child of Virgil and Hazel (Baker) Pyle,
was born 9 June 1933. She married 17 April 1955 _____ Warrington.
Children of _____ and Ina Louise (Pyle) Warrington:
2801   i Timothy Duane Warrington, born 7 June 1957
2802   ii Ted Arthur Warrington, born 3 December 1960
2803 iii Mark Allen Warrington, born 28 February 1962

2205 - VIVIAN(8) PYLE [Wilbur(7), Mary Alice(6) Montel, Sam-
uel(5), Abraham(4), Susan(3) Wolf, Jacob(2), Daniel(1)]
Vivian Pyle, first child of Wilbur and Hazel (Snell) Pyle, was
born 20 August 1933. She married 2 May 1951 William Walgamuth Jr.,
born 29 May 1926, son of William Sr. and Vista (_____) Walgamuth.
Children of William Jr. and Vivian (Pyle) Walgamuth:
2804   i Sherry Ann Walgamuth, born 25 February 1955. Married 12
           April 1980 Charles Fruit
2805   ii Thomas Eugene Walgamuth, born 18 October 1957
2806 iii Randy Walgamuth, born 5 July 1960
2807   iv John William Walgamuth, born 20 December 1962

2206 - LEONARD(8) PYLE [Wilbur(7), Mary Alice(7) Montel, Sam-
uel(5), Abraham(4), Susan(3) Wolf, Jacob(2), Daniel(1)]
Leonard Pyle, second child of Wilbur and Hazel (Snell) Pyle, was
born 8 May 1936. He married 1 February 1960 Linda Lou Walther (#2359),
born 25 January 1941, daughter of Maurice and Vivian (Brecht) Walther.
Children of Leonard and Linda Lou (Walther) Pyle:
2808   i Jeffrey Lee Pyle, born 14 August 1961
2809   ii Michael Jon Pyle, born 14 June 1963
2810 iii Kirk Loyne Pyle, born 3 August 1966

2211 - HELEN JOAN(8) PYLE [Emery(7), Mary Alice(6) Montel,
Samuel(5), Abraham(4), Susan(3) Wolf, Jacob(2), Daniel(1)]
Helen Joan Pyle, first child of Emery and Grace (Moe) Pyle, was
born 6 March 1934. She married 20 March 1954 Gene C. Metzger, born 12
March 1931, son of Dorsey and Georgia (Christman) Metzger.
Children of Gene C. and Helen Joan (Pyle) Metzger:
2811   i Douglass C. Metzger, born 27 July 1957
2812   ii Daniel L. Metzger, born 15 October 1960

2212 - LOREN(8) PYLE [Emery(7), Mary Alice(6) Montel, Samuel(5),
Abraham(4), Susan(3) Wolf, Jacob(2), Daniel(1)]

Loren Pyle, second child of Emery and Grace (Moe) Pyle, was born 11 July 1938. He married Edith Sloan, born 29 July 1942.
Child of Loren and Edith (Sloan) Pyle:
2813   i Lori Ann Pyle, born 13 September 1968

2213 - DONALD(8) NEHER [Harold M.(7), Elizabeth(6) Montel, Samuel(5), Abraham(4), Susan(3) Wolf, Jacob(2), Daniel(1)]
Donald Neher, first child of Harold M. and Fannie (Bridge) Neher, was born 18 December 1928. He married 28 February 1953 Jean Seidler, born 14 November 1931, foster daughter of Clifford and Ina (_____) Glass.
Children of Donald and Jean (Seidler) Neher:
2814   i Lee Roger Neher, born 21 November 1953
2815   ii Duane Kent Neher, born 19 November 1954
2816 iii Gail Lynn Neher, born 13 October 1956
2817   iv Brenda Neher, born 22 November 1966

2214 - DEAN(8) NEHER [Harold M.(7), Elizabeth(6) Montel, Sam-uel(5), Abraham(4), Susan(3) Wolf, Jacob(2), Daniel(1)]
Dean Neher, second child of Harold M. and Fannie (Bridge) Neher, was born 20 April 1930. He married 1) 12 March 1956 Jean Juilleret, born 25 July 1937, daughter of Orville and Chloe (_____) Juilleret and 2) 31 July 1971 Shelba Bechtold.
Child of Dean and Jean (Juilleret) Neher:
2818   i Darryl Neher, born 22 January 1966

2215 - DALE ARDEN(8) NEHER [Harold M.(7), Elizabeth(6) Montel, Samuel(5), Abraham(4), Susan(3) Wolf, Jacob(2), Daniel(1)]
Dale Arden Neher, third child of Harold M. and Fannie (Bridge) Neher, was born 16 October 1931. He married 18 August 1957 Maxine Sands, daughter of Glenn and Maude (Archer) Sands.
Children of Dale Arden and Maxine (Sands) Neher:
2819   i Larry Neher, born 11 November 1960
2820   ii Chris Neher, born 2 November 1965

2216 - CHARLES E.(8) NEHER [Charles S.(7), Elizabeth(6) Montel, Samuel(5), Abraham(4), Susan(3) Wolf, Jacob(2), Daniel(1)]
Charles E. Neher, first child of Charles S. and Iva (Brock) Neher, was born 29 November 1937. He married Nancy Weinberger, daugh-ter of Walter and Ruth (_____) Weinberger.
Children of Charles E. and Nancy (Weinberger) Neher:
2821   i Timothy Mark Neher, born 23 October 1958
2822   ii Shelley Kay Neher, born 18 September 1964
2823 iii Andrew Dean Neher, born 27 May 1968

2217 - TERRY EUGENE(8) NEHER [Charles S.(7), Elizabeth(6) Montel, Samuel(5), Abraham(4), Susan(3) Wolf, Jacob(2), Daniel(1)]
Terry Eugene Neher, second child of Charles S. and Iva (Brock) Neher, was born 16 January 1940. He married 25 October 1958 Linda Lee Thompson.
Children of Terry Eugene and Linda Lee (Thompson) Neher:
2824   i Jeffrey Michael Neher, born 27 November 1959
2825   ii Heather Lynn Neher, born 26 September 1969
2826 iii Christopher Grant Neher, born 13 May 1971

2218 - JOE ALLEN(8) NEHER [Charles S.(7), Elizabeth(6) Montel, Samuel(5), Abraham(4), Susan(3) Wolf, Jacob(2), Daniel(1)]
Joe Allen Neher, third child of Charles S. and Iva (Brock) Neher,

was born 25 February 1947. He married 1 October 1967 Bobbi Jean Sennik, born 28 December 1948.
    Child of Joe Allen and Bobbi Jean (Sennik) Neher:
 2827   i Eric Simon Neher, born 10 January 1975

    2219 - KENNETH RAY(8) NEHER [Charles S.(7), Elizabeth(6) Montel, Samuel(5), Abraham(4), Susan(3) Wolf, Jacob(2), Daniel(1)]
    Kenneth Ray Neher, fourth child of Charles S. and Iva (Brock) Neher, was born 24 December 1950. He married Susan Gail Murphy.
    Child of Kenneth Ray and Susan Gail (Murphy) Neher:
 2828   i Jennifer Susanne Neher, born 28 November 1973
 2829   ii Craig Allen Neher, born 7 December 1976

    2221 - DIANNE ELIZABETH(8) HUTCHENS [Esther L.(7) Neher, Elizabeth(6) Montel, Samuel(5), Abraham(4), Susan(3) Wolf, Jacob(2), Daniel(1)]
    Dianne Elizabeth Hutchens, second child of Wiliam Harter and Esther L. (Neher) Hutchens, was born 27 December 1944. She married 24 July 1965 Eric Lehman Peterson.
    Children of Eric Lehman and Dianne Elizabeth (Hutchens) Peterson:
 2830   i Eric William Peterson, born 15 November 1967
 2831   ii Heather Peterson, born 11 November 1969
 2832 iii Daniel James Peterson, born 7 July 1974

    2222 - SHARON KAY(8) NEHER [E. Paul(7), Elizabeth(6) Montel, Samuel(5), Abraham(4), Susan(3) Wolf, Jacob(2), Daniel(1)]
    Sharo Kay Neher, first child of E. Paul and Evelyn (McKee) Neher, was born 1 September 1939. She married 11 December 1960 Elvin G. Zook, born 21 March 1937, son of Glen and Ruth (Barton) Zook.
    Children of Elvin G. and Sharon Kay (Neher) Zook:
 2833   i Tara Elizabeth Zook, born 6 November 1963. Married 6
            August 1988 at Springfield, IL George Lee Bennett, born 5
            May 1965, son of Lee and Margie (_____) Bennett
 2834   ii Leigh Ann Zook, born 3 November 1967
 2835 iii Nichole Lynn Zook, born 24 July 1970

    2223 - BETH DIANN(8) NEHER [E. Paul(7), Elizabeth(6) Montel, Samuel(5), Abraham(4), Susan(3) Wolf, Jacob(2), Daniel(1)]
    Beth Diann Neher, second child of E. Paul and Evelyn (McKee) Neher, was born 13 January 1942. She married 1) 1 September 1962 Lynn J. Tanner, born 9 August 1941, son of Lee and Catherine (Oppel) Tanner and 2) 18 July 1978 David Boswell, born 5 July 1930.
    Children of Lynn J. and Beth Diann (Neher) Tanner:
 2836   i Carrie Beth Tanner, born 3 July 1964. Married 7 May 1988
            at Kalamazoo, MI Kim Jeffrey Gloyston, born 1 March 1957,
            son of Floyd and Virginia (_____) Gloyston
 2837   ii Andrew Lee Tanner, born 15 July 1967
 2838 iii Sarah Kay Tanner, born 30 July 1969

    2226 - CAROLYN(8) MONTEL [Deverl(7), Charles(6), Samuel(5), Abraham(4), Susan(3) Wolf, Jacob(2), Daniel(1)]
    Carolyn Montel, first child of Deverl and Ruby (Ayres) (Sellers) Montel, was born 4 July 1932. She married 9 September 1951 Dean Eberly, born 22 September 1931, son of Levi and Mary (Mishler) Eberly.
    Children of Dean and Carolyn (Montel) Eberly:
+ 2839   i Marvin Eberly, born 28 August 1952
+ 2840   ii Pamela Sue Eberly, born 9 November 1954

2227 - PHYLLIS(8) MONTEL [Deverl(7), Charles(6), Samuel(5), Abraham(4), Susan(3) Wolf, Jacob(2), Daniel(1)]
Phyllis Montel, second child of Deverl and Ruby (Ayres) (Sellers) Montel, was born 4 July 1933. She married 2 January 1953 Lon Price.
Child of Lon and Phyllis (Montel) Price:
2841   i Cynthia Jean Price. Married 2 July 1977 Delton Ray Keener, son of Raymond Keener

2228 - LARRY(8) MONTEL [Deverl(7), Charles(6), Samuel(5), Abraham(4), Susan(3) Wolf, Jacob(2), Daniel(1)]
Larry Montel, third child of Deverl and Ruby (Ayres) (Sellers) Montel, was born 28 June 1935. He married 10 July 1964 LaVerne Garber, born 28 February 1933, daughter of Blaine and Effie (Amberg) Garber.
Children of Larry and LaVerne (Garber) Montel:
2842   i Brent Lee Montel, born 3 August 1965
2843   ii Rhonda Jo Montel, born 8 May 1966

2229 - ROBERT(8) MONTEL [Deverl(7), Charles(6), Samuel(5), Abraham(4), Susan(3) Wolf, Jacob(2), Daniel(1)]
Robert Montel, fourth child of Deverl and Ruby (Ayres) (Sellers) Montel, was born 14 October 1936. He married 22 December 1959 Linda Clark, born 27 January 1940, daughter of Cyril and Marie (Williams) Clark.
Children of Robert and Linda (Clark) Montel:
2844   i Douglas Montel, born 19 October 1960. Married Debra Drudge, daughter of Donald and Barbara (Earl) Drudge
2845   ii Ricky Montel, born 29 December 1961
2846   iii Lori Montel, born 3 April 1971
2847   iv Michael Montel, born 23 December 1972

2230 - ROGER(8) MONTEL [Deverl(7), Charles(6), Samuel(5), Abraham(4), Susan(3) Wolf, Jacob(2), Daniel(1)]
Roger Montel, fifth child of Deverl and Ruby (Ayres) (Sellers) Montel, was born 27 May 1938. He married 1) 15 October 1958 Karen Elaine Bowen and 2) 30 September 1972 Linda Sue Linn, born 26 June 1940, daughter of Merl and Elsie (Robbins) Linn.
Children of Roger and Karen Elaine (Bowen) Montel:
2848   i Tamara Sue Montel, born 21 April 1959
+ 2849   ii Timothy Roger Montel, born 12 July 1960
2850   iii J. Todd Montel, born 17 August 1961

2234 - MAX LEON(8) CLINGAMAN [Phoebe Lavon(7) Metzger, Edith(6) Montel, Samuel(5), Abraham(4), Susan(3) Wolf, Jacob(2), Daniel(1)]
Max Leon Clingaman, first child of Leon and Phoebe Lavon (Metzger) Clingaman, was born 25 January 1939. He married 13 November 1960 Janis Mishler.
Children of Max Leon and Janis (Mishler) Clingaman:
2851   i Wende Clingaman, born 18 January 1964
2852   ii Rodney Clingaman, born 25 July 1967

2235 - DON(8) CLINGAMAN [Phoebe Lavon(7) Metzger, Edith(6) Montel, Samuel(5), Abraham(4), Susan(3) Wolf, Jacob(2), Daniel(1)]
Don Clingaman, second child of Leon and Phoebe Lavon (Metzger) Clingaman, was born 1 February 1942. He married 12 March 1961 Kathy Perry.
Children of Don and Kathy (Perry) Clingaman:
2853   i Tony Clingaman, born 27 November 1962
2854   ii Brent Clingaman, born 20 April 1966

2855   iii Dana Clingaman, born 12 February 1970

2236 - BEVERLY SUE(8) WARNER [Elizabeth Ruth(7) Metzger, Edith(6) Montel, Samuel(5), Abraham(4), Susan(3) Wolf, Jacob(2), Daniel(1)]
Beverly Sue Warner, first child of Donald B. and Elizabeth Ruth (Metzger) Warner, was born 17 March 1940. She married 26 June 1960 DeWayne Brubaker.
Children of DeWayne and Beverly Sue (Warner) Brubaker:
2856   i Jeffery Wayne Brubaker, born 23 February 1963
2857   ii Timothy William Brubaker, born 26 March 1966
2858   iii Susan Lynn Brubaker, born 30 November 1969

2245 - MARGARET SHIRLEY(8) MONTEL [Harold Ray(7), Albert(6), Samuel(5), Abraham(4), Susan(3) Wolf, Jacob(2), Daniel(1)]
Margaret Shirley Montel, first child of Harold Ray and Lois Evelyn (Haupert) Montel, was born 6 December 1942. She married Larry Cox, born 7 December 1941.
Children of Larry and Margaret Shirley (Montel) Cox:
2859   i Scottie Ray Cox, born 22 April 1964
2860   ii Debbie Jean, born 18 October 1968

2246 - BEVERLY KAY(8) MONTEL [Harold Ray(7), Albert(6), Samuel(5), Abraham(4), Susan(3) Wolf, Jacob(2), Daniel(1)]
Beverly Kay Montel, second child of Harold Ray and Lois Evelyn (Haupert) Montel, was born 14 March 1948. She married Harold Dean Ferrell, born 10 May 1947.
Child of Harold Dean and Beverly Kay (Montel) Ferrell:
2861   i Tricia Kay Ferrell, born 22 July 1969

2260 - ROBERT LAMAR(8) JENKINS [Retha Elizabeth(7) Montel, Emery(6), Samuel(5), Abraham(4), Susan(3) Wolf, Jacob(2), Daniel(1)]
Robert Lamar Jenkins, first child of Everett Ivan and Retha Elizabeth (Montel) Jenkins, was born 7 May 1940. He married 12 January 1964 Grace Hull, born 25 March 1943.
Children of Robert Lamar and Grace (Hull) Jenkins:
2862   i Lena Kay Jenkins, born 20 January 1965
2863   ii Troy Martin Jenkins, born 19 November 1969
2864   iii Sonya Sue Jenkins, born 3 July 1973

2261 - LEONARD ALAN(8) JENKINS [Retha Elizabeth(7) Montel, Emery(6), Samuel(5), Abraham(4), Susan(3) Wolf, Jacob(2), Daniel(1)]
Leonard Alan Jenkins, second child of Everett Ivan and Retha Elizabeth (Montel) Jenkins, was born 23 April 1944. He married 26 June 1963 Susan Hipskind, born 12 April 1944.
Children of Leonard Alan and Susan (Hipskind) Jenkins:
2865   i Aileen Jenkins, born 12 April 1970
2866   ii Jennifer Lynn Jenkins, twin, born 5 February 1972
2867   iii Anthony Joseph Jenkins, twin, born 5 February 1972

2262 - ARDEN RAY(8) JENKINS [Retha Elizabeth(7) Montel, Emery(6), Samuel(5), Abraham(4), Susan(3) Wolf, Jacob(2), Daniel(1)]
Arden Ray Jenkins, third child of Everett Ivan and Retha Elizabeth (Montel) Jenkins, was born 9 September 1948. He married Trecca Lancaster.
Children of Arden Ray and Trecca (Lancaster) Jenkins:
2868   i Scott Richard Jenkins, adopted, born 30 March 1966
2869   ii Garth Ray Jenkins, born 25 September 1969
2870   iii Heath Rynn Jenkins, born 21 March 1972

2871   iv Clinton Roary Jenkins, born 22 December 1974

2264 - GARY EUGENE(8) MONTEL [Lamoin Albert(7), Emery(6), Sam-
uel(5), Abraham(4), Susan(3) Wolf, Jacob(2), Daniel(1)]
    Gary Eugene Montel, first child of Lamoin Albert and Mary Mildred
(Callahan) Montel, was born 9 November 1943. He married 5 June 1965
Areldean Marie Reckard, born 16 August 1946, daughter of Dean and
Elsie (Wine) Reckard.
    Children of Gary Eugene and Areldean Marie (Reckard) Montel:
2872   i Beth Marie Montel, born 17 August 1966
2873   ii Barth Eugene Montel, born 26 November 1968

2267 - ANN ARLENE(8) FISHER [Blanche Mattie(7) Montel, Emery(6),
Samuel(5), Abraham(4), Susan(3) Wolf, Jacob(2), Daniel(1)]
    Ann Arlene Fisher, third child of Russel Elmer and Blanche Mattie
(Montel) Fisher, was born 11 May 1951. She married 25 February 1974
Gary Eugene Cole.
    Children of Gary Eugene and Ann Arlene (Fisher) Cole:
2374   i Jennifer Lynn Cole, born 18 October 1974
2875   ii Kelly Elizabeth Cole, twin, born 8 May 1978
2876   iii Kimberly Ann Cole, twin, born 8 May 1978
2877   iv Lori Lee Cole, born 7 March 1981

2268 - PAUL RAY(8) FISHER [Blanche Mattie(7) Montel, Emery(6),
Samuel(5), Abraham(4), Susan(3) Wolf, Jacob(2), Daniel(1)]
    Paul Ray Fisher, fourth child of Russel Elmer and Blanche Mattie
(Montel) Fisher, was born 11 February 1954. He married 6 March 1977
Tammie Jolene Hites, born 23 October 1959.
    Child of Paul Ray and Tammie Jolene (Hites) Fisher:
2878   i Paulette Raene Fisher, born 10 February 1980

2270 - BARBARA JEAN(8) MONTEL [John Irvin(7), Emery(6), Sam-
uel(5), Abraham(4), Susan(3) Wolf, Jacob(2), Daniel(1)]
    Barbara Jean Montel, second child of John Irvin and Wanda Jean
(Bryan) Montel, was born 7 August 1953. She married 5 July 1975 Duane
Watson.
    Child of Duane and Barbara Jean (Montel) Watson:
2879   i Nichole Maria Watson, born 30 October 1976

2273 - MARLENE MARIE(8) BOUSE [Marie Esther(7) Montel, Ralph(6),
Samuel(5), Abraham(4), Susan(3) Wolf, Jacob(2), Daniel(1)]
    Marlene Marie Bouse, first child of Wayne and Marie Esther
(Montel) Bouse, was born 16 May 1935. She married in 1955 John Reed,
born 31 March 1930.
    Children of John and Marlene Marie (Montel) Reed:
2880   i J. Gregory Reed, born 22 April 1958
2881   ii Teresa Reed, born 13 October 1959
2882   iii Scott Reed, born 1961
2883   iv Judi Reed, born 8 may 1964

2274 - ROBERTA JEAN(8) BOUSE [Marie Esther(7) Montel, Ralph(6),
Samuel(5), Abraham(4), Susan(3) Wolf, Jacob(2), Daniel(1)]
    Roberta Jean Pouse, second child of Wayne and Marie Esther
(Montel) Bouse, was born 25 October 1937. She married in 1956 Larry
Tucker, born 4 December 1936.
    Children of Larry and Roberta Jean (Bouse) Tucker:
2884   i Debra Tucker, born 5 June 1957
2885   ii Timothy Tucker, born 12 January 1959, died 4 December 1961

2886   iii Dennis Tucker, born 28 December 1960
2887   iv Cynthia Tucker, born 29 November 1963
2888   v Jeffrey Tucker, born 21 September 1966

   2275 - TERRY WAYNE(8) BOUSE [Marie Esther(7) Montel, Ralph(6),
Samuel(5), Abraham(4), Susan(3) Wolf, Jacob(2), Daniel(1)]
   Terry Wayne Bouse, third child of Wayne and Marie Esther (Montel)
Bouse, was born 1 March 1943. He married in 1967 Susan Wolfe, born 26
November 1945.
   Children of Terry Wayne and Susan (Wolfe) Bouse:
2889   i DeNae Bouse, born 16 September 1970
2890   ii Shanda Bouse, born 3 June 1974
2891 iii Tyler Bouse, born 11 November 1975
2892   iv Ashlee Bouse, born 5 June 1980

   2276 - NANCY(8) BOUSE [Marie Esther(7) Montel, Ralph(6), Sam-
uel(5), Abraham(4), Susan(3) Wolf, Jacob(2), Daniel(1)]
   Nancy Bouse, fourth child of Wayne and Marie Esther (Montel)
Bouse, was born 21 June 1945. She married in 1968 George Wayne Krom
III, born 4 June 1945.
   Children of George Wayne III and Nancy (Bouse) Krom:
2893   i Kristina Krom, born 7 October 1969
2894   ii Kimberly Krom, born 4 January 1972
2895 iii George Wayne Krom IV, born 25 December 1975
2896   iv Ivy Krom, born 3 June 1980

   2285 - KATHLEEN SARA(8) MORPHEW [Beulah May(7) Montel, Frank(6),
Samuel(5), Abraham(4), Susan(3) Wolf, Jacob(2), Daniel(1)]
   Kathleen Sara Morphew, second child of David Emery and Beulah May
(Montel) Morphew, was born 19 January 1945. She married 25 February
1967 Dale Francis Stephenson Jr., born 11 December 1945.
   Children of Dale Francis Jr. and Kathleen Sara (Morphew) Stephenson:
2897   i David Dale Stephenson, born 20 July 1971
2898   ii Amber Lynn Stephenson

   2286 - PHILIP LEE(8) MORPHEW [Beulah May(7) Montel, Frank(6),
Samuel(5), Abraham(4), Susan(3) Wolf, Jacob(2), Daniel(1)]
   Philip Lee Morphew, third child of David Emery and Beulah May
(Montel) Morphew, was born 6 October 1947. He married 12 June 1972
Catherine Elaine Birt, born 20 September 1946, daughter of Clifford W.
and Lilly Elizabeth (Durbin) Birt.
   Child of Philip Lee and Catherine Elaine (Birt) Morphew:
2899   i Louis Charles Morphew

   2305 - JOSEPH DWIGHT(8) MORPHEW [Elizabeth Ann(7) Montel,
Frank(6), Samuel(5), Abraham(4), Susan(3) Wolf, Jacob(2), Daniel(1)]
   Joseph Dwight Morphew, third child of Noble Dwight and Elizabeth
Ann (Montel) Morphew, was born 8 September 1956. He married 8 May 1976
Diana Ruth Marie Kuszmaul, born 13 May 1957.
   Children of Joseph Dwight and Diana Ruth Marie (Kuszmaul) Mor-
phew:
2900   i Joshua Joseph Morphew, born 19 January 1977
2901   ii Johanna Elizabeth Morphew, born 19 November 1980

   2309 - JANICE LESLIE(8) CREIGHTON [Ruth Eleanor(7) Montel,
Frank(6), Samuel(5), Abraham(4), Susan(3) Wolf, Jacob(2), Daniel(1)]
   Janice Leslie Creighton, second Child of James Frederick and Ruth
Eleanor (Montel) Creighton, was born 12 May 1960. She married 14 July

1979 David Slachciak.
Child of David and Janice Leslie (Creighton) Slachciak:
2902   i Jessica Lynn Slachciak, born 24 July 1980

2314 - HELEN JOYCE(8) SHULL [Miriam(7) Overholser, Effie(6)
Montel, Jacob(5), Abraham(4), Susan(3) Wolf, Jacob(2), Daniel(1)]
Helen Joyce Shull, first child of Gerald and Miriam (Overholser)
Shull, was born 22 September 1942. She married James Hartog.
Children of James and Helen Joyce (Shull) Hartog:
2903   i Michael James Hartog, born 23 April 1967
2904   ii Mark Allen Hartog, born 28 November 1972

2316 - GERALD LAMOINE(8) SHULL [Miriam(7) Overholser, Effie(6)
Montel, Jacob(5), Abraham(4), Susan(3) Wolf, Jacob(2), Daniel(1)]
Gerald Lamoine Shull, third child of Gerald and Miriam (Over-
holser) Shull, was born 2 June 1948. He married Jane Smith.
Child of Gerald Lamoine and Jane (Smith) Shull:
2905   i Elyssa Anne Shull, born 5 November 1980

2317 - MARY ANN(8) SHULL [Miriam(7) Overholser, Effie(6) Montel,
Jacob(5), Abraham(4), Susan(3) Wolf, Jacob(2), Daniel(1)]
Mary Ann Shull, fourth child of Gerald and Miriam (Overholser)
Shull, was born 8 January 1951. She married 3 November 1973 Michael
O'Neil.
Children of Michael and Mary Ann (Shull) O'Neil:
2906   i John Carl O'Neil, born 5 July 1978
2907   ii David Gerald O'Neil, born 7 December 1979

2320 - STEVEN EARL(8) RHOADES [Delbert Milton(7), Iva Ann(6)
Montel, Jacob(5), Abraham(4), Susan(3) Wolf, Jacob(2), Daniel(1)]
Steven Earl Rhoades, third child of Delbert Milton and Hattie
Jane (Grossnickle) Rhoades, was born 15 July 1960. He married Sue Ann
Raber, born 3 January 1958.
Children of Steven Earl and Sue Ann (Raber) Rhoades:
2908   i Jeff Allen Rhoades, born 21 June 1978
2909   ii Amanda Nicole Rhoades, born 14 August 1979

2325 - SUE ANNE KAY(8) SLATER [Eva Kathlene(7) Rhoades, Iva
Ann(6) Montel, Jacob(5), Abraham(4), Susan(3) Wolf, Jacob(2),
Daniel(1)]
Sue Anne Kay Slater, first child of Donald Leroy and Eva Kathlene
(Rhoades) Slater, was born 13 May 1949. She married 25 September 1971
Donald Undell Immel.
Children of Donald Undell and Sue Anne (Slater) Immel:
2910   i Brian James Immel, born 28 January 1972
2911   ii Cory Lynn Immel, born 5 April 1973
2912 iii Dawn Elizabeth Immel, born 25 May 1974
2913   iv Daniel Wesly Immel, born 21 August 1975
2914   v Barbara Ann Immel, born 17 November 1976

2328 -MARLA JO(8) RHOADES [Dorsey Hurl(7), Iva Ann(6) Montel,
Jacob(5), Abraham(4), Susan(3) Wolf, Jacob(2), Daniel(1)]
Marla Jo Rhoades, first child of Dorsey Hurl and Janet EDna
(Smith) Rhoades, was born 16 January 1958. She married Gary Yentes.
Child of Gary and Marla Jo (Rhoades) Yentes:
2915   i Aaron Scott Yentes

2330 - LISA ANN(8) RHOADES [Dorsey Hurl(7), Iva Ann(6) Montel, Jacob(5), Abraham(4), Susan(3) Wolf, Jacob(2), Daniel(1)]
   Lisa Ann Rhoades, third child of Dorsey Hurl and Janet Edna (Smith) Rhoades, was born 27 November 1961. She married James Aust.
   Child of James and Lisa Ann (Rhoades) Aust:
 2916   i Amanda Aust

   2332 - JANET KAY(8) FISHER [Bernice Irene(7) Montel, Artemus(6), Jacob(5), Abraham(4), Susan(3) Wolf, Jacob(2), Daniel(1)]
   Janet Kay Fisher, first child of Charles Jr. and Bernice Irene (Montel) Fisher, was born 8 March 1945. She married 26 September 1964 Everett G. Maurer.
   Children of Everett G. and Janet Kay (Fisher) Maurer:
 2917   i Tammy Lynn Maurer, born 5 December 1965
 2918   ii Teresa Ann Maurer, born 11 September 1969

   2333 - BECKY SUE(8) FISHER [Bernice Irene(7) Montel, Artemus(6), Jacob(5), Abraham(4), Susan(3) Wolf, Jacob(2), Daniel(1)]
   Becky Sue Fisher, adopted daughter of Charles Jr. and Bernice Irene (Montel) Fisher, was born 26 June 1946. She married 12 March 1966 Frederick Mack.
   Children of Frederick and Becky Sue (Fisher) Mack:
 2919   i Stan Ray Mack, born 12 June 1966
 2920   ii Eric J. Mack, born 27 July 1970

   2335 - KAREN SUE(8) MONTEL [Francis Earl(7), Artemus(6), Jacob(5), Abraham(4), Susan(3) Wolf, Jacob(2), Daniel(1)]
   Karen Sue Montel, first child of Francis Earl and Phyllis Eileen (Bolinger) Montel, was born 24 January 1949. She married 12 July 1967 David Ellis Caudill, born 10 March 1948.
   Children of David Ellis and Karen Sue (Montel) Caudill:
 2921   i Rachelle Lynn Caudill, born 24 February 1968
 2922   ii Gregory Scott Caudill, born 4 September 1973

   2336 - KATHY ANN(8) MONTEL [Francis Earl(7), Artemus(6), Jacob(5), Abraham(4), Susan(3) Wolf, Jacob(2), Daniel(1)]
   Kathy Ann Montel, second child of Francis Earl and Phyllis Eileen (Bolinger) Montel, was born 28 December 1952. She married 12 August 1972 Robert Lee Allen.
   Children of Robert Lee and Kathy Ann (Montel) Allen:
 2923   i Chad Eric Allen, born 23 May 1975
 2924   ii Amy Jo Allen, born 8 February 1977

   2337 - LAURA ANN(8) YODER [Betty Ann(7) Montel, Artemus(6), Jacob(5), Abraham(4), Susan(3) Wolf, Jacob(2), Daniel(1)]
   Laura Ann Yoder, first child of Joseph Wilmer and Betty Ann (Montel) Yoder, was born 24 June 1948. She married 16 October 1971 Charles Robert Holloway Jr., born 4 October 1940, son of Charles Robert Sr. and Chrystal (Darling) Holloway.
   Child of Charles Robert Jr. and Laura Ann (Yoder) Holloway:
 2925   i Kimberly Michelle Holloway, born 23 June 1976

   2339 - EDWIN RAY(8) YODER [Betty Ann(7) Montel, Artemus(6), Jacob(5), Abraham(4), Susan(3) Wolf, Jacob(2), Daniel(1)]
   Edwin Ray Yoder, third child of Joseph Wilmer and Betty Ann (Montel) Yoder, was born 22 October 1953. He married 15 September 1973 Teresa Lynette Rymon, born 8 August 1953, daughter of Glen Devon and Janet Elaine (Swihart) Rymon

Child of Edwin Ray and Teresa Lynette (Rymon) Yoder:
2926   i Don Christopher Yoder, born 5 June 1974

2340 - MARGARET SUE(8) YODER [Betty Ann(7) Montel, Artemus(6),
Jacob(5), Abraham(4), Susan(3) Wolf, Jacob(2), Daniel(1)]
    Margaret Sue Yoder, twin, fourth child of Joseph Wilmer and Betty
Ann (Montel) Yoder, was born 29 April 1959. She married 2 February
1980 Bud Barnell,born 9 March 1946, son of Cleo and Esther (Reed)
Barnell.
    Child of Bud and Margaret Sue (Yoder) Barnell:
2927   i Todd Allen Barnell, born 5 January 1968

2350 - PHILLIP(8) BROWN [Kathryn Elizabeth(7) Metzger, Irvin(6),
Susanna(5) Montel, Abraham(4), Susan(3) Wolf, Jacob(2), Daniel(1)]
    Phillip Brown , first child of Lowell and Kathryn Elizabeth
(Metzger) Brown, was born 29 July 1936. He married 29 June 1958 Jo
Ellen Gerdes, born 1 March 1936, daughter of Brice and Mary (Winger)
Gerdes.
    Children of Phillip and Jo Ellen (Gerdes) Brown:
2928   i Katrinka Brown, born 17 May 1964
2929   ii Amanda Brown, born 18 May 1968

2351 - THOMAS(8) BROWN [Kathryn Elizabeth(7) Metzger, Irvin(6),
Susanna(5) Montel, Abraham(4), Susan(3) Wolf, Jacob(2), Daniel(1)]
    Thomas Brown, second child of Lowell and Kathryn Elizabeth
(Metzger) Brown, was born 9 November 1944. He married 18 June 1965
Eloise Harold, born 7 June 1943, daughter of Howard and Frances
(Graff) Harold.
    Children of Thomas and Eloise (Harold) Brown:
2930   i Mikel Brown, born 22 June 1966
2931   ii Stephen Brown, born 27 August 1971
2932 iii Ryan Brown, born 20 March 1977

2357 - KAREN(8) BOWEN [Louise(7) Walther, Nellie(6) Butterbaugh,
William H.(5), Sarah(4) Montel, Susan(3) Wolf, Jacob(2), Daniel(1)]
    Karen Bowen, first child of Blaine and Louise (Walther) Bowen,
was born in 1940. She married 1) Roger Mold and 2) Dick Dawson.
    Children of Roger and Karen (Bowen) Mold:
2933   i Tamara Mold, born 1959
2934   ii Timmie Mold, born July 1960

2360 - ANNIE JEANINE(8) WARNER [Doscas Irene(7) Walther, Nel-
lie(6) Butterbaugh, William H.(5), Sarah(4) Montel, Susan(3) Wolf,
Jacob(2), Daniel(1)]
    Annie Jeanine Warner, first child of Arden and Doscas Irene
(Walther) Warner, was born 18 March 1942. She married 1) Larry Drudge
and 2) William Rudig.
    Child of Larry and Annie Jeanine (Warner) Drudge:
2935   i Lausie Ann Drudge, born 17 June 1962
    Child of William and Annie Jeanine (Warner) (Drudge) Rudig:
2936   i Steven Trace Rudig

2361 - SUE ELAINE(8) WARNER [Doscas Irene(7) Walther, Nellie(6)
Butterbaugh, William H.(5), Sarah(4) Montel, Susan(3) Wolf, Jacob(2),
Daniel(1)]
    Sue Elaine Warner, second child of Arden and Doscas Irene (Wal-
ther) Warner, was born 4 February 1945. She married 11 June 1966
Randolph Wagner.

Children of Randolph and Sue Elaine (Warner) Wagner:
2937   i Julie Wagner, born 27 January 1968
2938   ii Janet Elaine Wagner, born 29 June 1970

2362 - DONALD DEAN(8) WALTHER - [Max Donald(7), Nellie(6) Butter-
baugh, William H.(5), Sarah(4) Montel, Susan(3) Wolf, Jacob(2),
Daniel(1)]
Donald Dean Walther, first child of Max Donald and Leona (Fleck)
Walther, was born in 1944. He married 25 October 1964 Joyce Darlene
Brown.
Children of Donald Dean and Joyce Darlene (Brown) Walther:
2939   i Wicki Sue Walther, born 11 November 1965
2940   ii Rhonda Kay Walther, born 3 May 1967

2363 - JERRY LEE(8) WALTHER [Max Donald(7), Nellie(6) Butter-
baugh, William H.(5), Sarah(4) Montel, Susan(3) Wolf, Jacob(2),
Daniel(1)]
Jerry Lee Walther, second child of Max Donald and Leona (Fleck)
Walther, was born in 1946. He married 17 December 1964 Melody Tucker.
Children of Jerry Lee and Melody (Tucker) Walther:
2941   i Michael Alan Walther, born 9 September 1967
2942   ii Kasi Lynn Walther, born 27 April 1971

2365 - DENNIE LYNN(8) WALTHER [Max Donald(7), Nellie(6) Butter-
baugh, William H.(5), Sarah(4) Montel, Susan(3) Wolf, Jacob(2),
Daniel(1)]
Dennie Lynn Walther, fourth child of Max Donald and Leona (Fleck)
Walther, was born 8 October 1955. He married 18 December 1974 Ruth Ann
Bucher.
Children of Dennie Lynn and Ruth Ann (Bucher) Walther:
2943   i Melissa Walther, born 1975
2944   ii Jonathan Daniel Walther, born 30 January 1980

2366 - ARDEN DEE(8) WALGAMUTH [Mary Blanche(7) Tridle, Elvin
Peter(6), George III(5), Adaline(4) Montel, Susan(3) Wolf, Jacob(2),
Daniel(1)]
Arden Dee Walgamuth, first child of Fred and Mary Blanche
(Tridle) Walgamuth, was born 20 February 1937. He married 14 June 1958
Sandra Van Lue, born 20 September 1940, daughter of Mark and Catherine
(Personett) Van Lue.
Children of Arden Dee and Sandra (Van Lue) Walgamuth:
2945   i Mark Frederick Walgamuth, born 3 March 1960
2946   ii Kristen Kay Walgamuth, born 30 December 1962
2947 iii Mary Catherine Walgamuth, born 14 August 1965

2367 - TERRY LEE(8) WALGAMUTH [Mary Blanche(7) Tridle, Elvin
Peter(6), George III(5), Adaline(4) Montel, Susan(3) Wolf, Jacob(2),
Daniel(1)]
Terry Lee Walgamuth, second child of Fred and Mary Blanche
(Tridle) Walgamuth, was born 17 september 1939. He married 19 June
1959 Judith Ann Rosenbury, born 20 June 1940, daughter of Harry and
Helen (Lowe) Rosenbury.
Children of Terry Lee and Judith Ann (Rosenbury) Walgamuth:
2948   i Terri Lynn Walgamuth, born 22 December 1960. Married 12
           June 1982 Michael G. Vicceli, born 7 November 1956, son
           ofJoseph and Mary (Anagaran) Vicceli
2949   ii Patrick R. Walgamuth, born 29 January 1962
2950 iii Tamara Sue Walgamuth, born 9 April 1963

2369 - LINDA DIANE(8) ROSS [Harold Wayne(7), Lizzie(6) Tridle, George III(5), Adaline(4) Montel, Susan(3) Wolf, Jacob(2), Daniel(1)]
Linda Diane Ross, first child of Harold Wayne and Mary Elizabeth (Brandenburg) Ross, was born 20 August 1955. She married 24 April 1982 Johnnie Ray Hanger, born 1 July 1957, son of Ray and Mary (Wyatt) Hanger.
Child of Johnnie Ray and Linda Diane (Ross) Hanger:
2951   i Theresa Ann Hanger, adopted from Johnnie Ray's first
          marriage, born 19 July 1977

2371 - JOYCE ANN NEWBY(8) RIDER [Dorotha Maxine(7) Ross, Lizzie(6) Tridle, George III(5), Adaline(4) Montel, Susan(3) Wolf, Jacob(2), Daniel(1)]
Joyce Ann Newby Rider, first child of Merl Jr. and Dorotha Maxine (Ross) Newby and step-daughter of Paul W. Rider, was born 10 september 1944. She married 20 August 1966 Dennis Jay Grothrian, born 27 January 1944, son of Oscar and Lora (Werling) Grothrian.
Children of Dennis Jay and Joyce Ann (Newby) (Rider) Grothrian:
2952   i Sarah Jo Ann Grothrian, born 13 May 1972
2953   ii Grechen Sue Grothrian, born 18 October 1975

2372 - CONNIE SUE(8) RIDER [Dorotha Maxine(7) Ross, Lizzie(6) Tridle, George III(5), Adaline(4) Montel, Susan(3) Wolf, Jacob(2), Daniel(1)]
Connie Sue Rider, first child of Paul Winford and Dorotha Maxine (Ross) Rider, was born 10 September 1948. She married 23 August 1969 Stanley C. Phillips, born 3 October 1947, son of Carrol R. and Evelyn L. (Greek) Phillips.
Children of Stanley C. and Connie Sue (Rider) Phillips:
2954   i Jason Bradley Phillips, born 7 June 1973
2955   ii Blair Rider Phillips, born 25 March 1978

2374 - LORNA LOUISE(8) TRIDLE [Loren Leroy(7), Glenn(6), George III(5), Adaline(4) Montel, Susan(3) Wolf, Jacob(2), Daniel(1)]
Lorna Louise Tridle, second child of Loren Leroy and Mary K. (Ayres) Tridle, was born 26 November 1946. She married 23 February 1974 Alfred Don Klein, born 10 June 1944, son of Richard S. and Mary (Nicholson) Klein.
Children of Alfred Don and Lorna Louise (Tridle) Klein:
2956   i Christopher Loren Klein, born 28 March 1977
2957   ii Ruth Louise Klein, born 4 January 1980

2375 - KATHY ANN(8) TRIDLE [Loren Leroy(7), Glenn(6), George III(5), Adaline(4) Montel, Susan(3) Wolf, Jacob(2), Daniel(1)]
Kathy Ann Tridle, third child of Loren Leroy and Mary K. (Ayres) Tridle, was born 18 December 1949. She married 24 February 1973 Stephen William Kinney, born 4 August 1947, son of Edgar A. and Frances Jane (Smith) Kinney.
Children of Stephen William and Kathy Ann (Tridle) Kinney:
2958   i Megihann Kathryn Kinney, born 23 May 1978
2959   ii Rebecca Jane Kinney, born 14 April 1980

2378 - SARA EARLINE(8) TRIDLE [Earl Eugene(7), Glenn(6), George III(5), Adaline(4) Montel, Susan(3) Wolf, Jacob(2), Daniel(1)]
Sara Earline Tridle, third child of Earl Eugene and Jeanette (Newcomer) Tridle, was born 14 January 1938. She married 18 March 1961 Philip Harry Joseph, born 13 January 1934, son of Harry M. and Hannah R. (Rosenthal) Joseph.

Child of Philip Harry and Sara Earline (Tridle) Joseph:
2960   i Tresa Lynn Joseph, born 6 October 1962

2380 - CONNIE(8) SPANN [Vera Lavon(7) Heeter, Viola(6) Tridle,
George III(5), Adaline(5) Montel, Susan(3) Wolf, Jacob(2), Daniel(1)]
    Connie Spann, first child of George William and Vera Lavon
(Heeter) Spann, was born 9 November 1931. She married 11 June 1950
Donald L. Hyde, son of Miller Hyde.
    Children of Donald L. and Connie (Spann) Hyde:
2961   i Randy Todd Hyde, born 18 February 1954
2962   ii Gerrianne Hyde, born 14 May 1956

2381 - TEDDY LEE(8) SPANN [Vera Lavon(7) Heeter, Viola(6) Tridle,
George III(5), Adaline(5) Montel, Susan(3) Wolf, Jacob(2), Daniel(1)]
    Teddy Lee Spann, second child of George William and Vera Lavon
(Heeter) Spann, was born 15 February 1933. He married9 February 1956
Shirley Carol Albritton.
    Child of Teddy Lee and Shirley Carol (Albritton) Spann:
2963   i Donald Lee Spann, born 9 September 1957

2383 - MARCIA ARMSTRONG(8) MONTEITH [Jess Warren(7), Paul Ever-
ett(6), Caroline Barbara(5) Wolfe, Simon P.(4), Jacob Jr(3), Jacob(2),
Daniel(1)]
    Marcia Armstrong Monteith, child of Lawrence L. and Phyllis
Imogene (Ebersole) Armstrong , step-daughter of and adopted by Jess
Warren Monteith, was born 12 September 1941 at Springfield, Clark
County, OH. She married 27 November 1965 Ronald Dick Snow, born 17
January 1939 at Springfield, son of Larned and Lavanda (Stanton) Snow.
    Children of Ronald Dick and Marcia Armstrong (Monteith) Snow,
born at Springfield, Clark County, OH:
2964   i Steven Dick Snow, adopted, born 9 February 1959
2965   ii Douglas Laren Snow, born 3 February 1973

2384 - CHERYLL ANN(8) MONTEITH [Jess Warren(7), Paul Everett(6),
Caroline Barbara(5) Wolfe, Simon P.(4), Jacob Jr(3), Jacob(2),
Daniel(1)]
    Cheryll Ann Monteith, first child of Jess Warren and Phyllis
Imogene (Ebersole) (Armstrong) Monteith, was born 24 August 1948 at
Springfield, Clark County, OH. She married 1) 5 September 1969 Ronald
Jay Jenkins, born 25 November 1946 at Springfield, son of Norman and
Norma (McWilliams) Jenkins. They divorced 18 March 1976 and 18 June
1976 Cheryll legally changed her name to Amanda Jeanne Jenkins. She
married 2) 23 August 1977 in Newton County, AR Jerry Keith Ashworth.
    Child of Ronald Jay and Cheryll Ann (Monteith) Jenkins:
2966   i Nathan Christopher Jenkins, born 18 August 1973 at Spring-
            field, Clark County, OH

2385 - DEBORAH KAY(8) MONTEITH [Jess Warren(7), Paul Everett(6),
Caroline Barbara(5) Wolfe, Simon P.(4), Jacob Jr(3), Jacob(2),
Daniel(1)]
    Deborah Kay Monteith, second child of Jess Warren and Phyllis
Imogene (Ebersole) (Armstrong) Monteith, was born 24 October 1951 at
Springfield, Clark County, OH. She married 25 September 1971 at
Springfield Michael Roy Miller, born 17 October 1949 at Springfield,
son of Roy and Darlene (McClain) Miller.
    Children of Michael Roy and Deborah Kay (Monteith) Miller, born
at Springfield, Clark County, OH:
2967   i Ty Michael Miller, born 17 April 1975

2968   ii Jenna Lynn Miller, born 26 November 1977

     2386 - BEVERLY JO(8) MONTEITH [Jess Warren(7), Paul Everett(6),
Caroline Barbara(5) Wolfe, Simon P.(4), Jacob Jr(3), Jacob(2),
Daniel(1)]
     Beverly Jo Monteith, third child of Jess Warren and Phyllis
Imogene (Ebersole) Monteith, was born 18 July 1953 at Springfield,
Clark County, OH. She married 25 September 1976 Richard Leonard
Easter, born 26 December 1950 at Springfield, son of Robert and Helen
(Williams) Easter.
     Children of Richard Leonard and Beverly Jo (Monteith) Easter,
born at Springfield, Clark County, OH:
  2969   i Ashley Jo Easter, born 6 March 1981
  2970   ii Aaron Richard Easter, born 22 August 1982

     2387 - DARRYL KENT(8) MONTEITH [Virgil Eugene(7), Paul Ever-
ett(6), Caroline Barbara(5) Wolfe, Simon P.(4), Jacob Jr(3), Jacob(2),
Daniel(1)]
     Darryl Kent Monteith, first child of Virgil Eugene and Clara
Mildred (Kadel) Monteith, was born 3 August 1941. He married 1) 20
December 1965 Jo Ann McCall, born 23 November 1946, daughter of Carlos
and Jerry (_____) McCall, 2) 2 May 1975 Penny (_____) Henry, born 7
September 1950 and 3) 3 August 1986 Sandra Kay Young, daughter of
_____ and Erma (Marquis) Young.
     Children of Darryl Kent and Jo Ann (McCall) Monteith:
  2971   i Michael Kent Monteith, born 11 September 1967. Married 28
            June 1986 Sandra Kay Farmer
  2972   ii Douglas Edward Monteith, born 27 March 1970
     Child of _____ and Penny (_____) Henry:
  2973   i Paul Henry Monteith, adopted by Darryl Monteith after his
            marriage to Penny Henry
     Child of Darryl Kent and Penny (_____) (Henry) Monteith:
  2974   i Daniel Joseph Monteith, born 18 February 1976

     2388 - GARY EUGENE(8) MONTEITH [Virgil Eugene(7), Paul Ever-
ett(6), Caroline Barbara(5) Wolfe, Simon P.(4), Jacob Jr(3), Jacob(2),
Daniel(1)]
     Gary Eugene Monteith, second child of Virgil Eugene and Clara
Mildred (Kadel) Monteith, was born 18 April 1945. He married 3 April
1964 Darlene Louise Sayers, born 13 July 1946, daughter of Paul and
Martha (Loocher) Sayers.
     Children of Gary Eugene and Darlene Louise (Sayers) Monteith:
  2975   i Cherise Kay Monteith, born 6 July 1967
  2976   ii Greg Edward Monteith, born 28 March 1971

     2389 - JUDITH ANN(8) CALDWELL [Milton Charles Sr(7), Emmet
Edmunds(6), Margaret Jane(5) Wolfe, Simon P.(4), Jacob Jr(3),
Jacob(2), Daniel(1)]
     Judith Ann Caldwell, first child of Milton Charles Sr and Julia
Betty (White) Caldwell, was born 28 September 1940 at Newark Hospital,
Newark, OH. She married 31 January 1959 at Dayton, OH William Ray
Highley Sr, son of Eddie and Edith Irene (Willis) Highley.
     Children of William Ray Sr and Judith Ann (Caldwell) Highley,
born at Good Samaritan Hospital, Dayton, OH:
+ 2977   i Julie Lynn Highley, born 22 January 1961
  2978   ii Janet Elaine Highley, born 1 September 1963
  2979 iii Rae Jean Highley, born 5 July 1969
  2980   iv William Ray Highley Jr, born 16 April 1971

2390 - MILTON CHARLES JR(8) CALDWELL [Milton Charles Sr(7), Emmet Edmunds(6), Margaret Jane(5) Wolfe, Simon P.(4), Jacob Jr(3), Jacob(2), Daniel(1)]
Milton Charles Caldwell Jr, second child of Milton Charles Sr and Julia Betty (White) Caldwell, was born at M. V. Hospital, Dayton, OH. He married 17 October 1970 at Greenville, OH Mary Ann Lantz, born at Greenville, daughter of Rome and Frances (Hough) Lantz.
Children of Milton Charles Jr and Mary Ann (Lantz) Caldwell, born at Greenville Hospital, Greenville, OH:
  2981   i Matthew Charles Caldwell, born 22 October 1971
  2982   ii Brock Lantz Caldwell, born 19 January 1976
  2983 iii Megan Elizabeth Caldwell, born 23 April 1981

2393 - DAVID CALDWELL(8) ROBBS [Martha Frances(7) Caldwell, Emmet Edmunds(6), Margaret Jane(5) Wolfe, Simon P.(4), Jacob Jr(3), Jacob(2), Daniel(1)]
David Caldwell Robbs, third child of John Andrew and Martha Frances (Caldwell) Robbs, was born 25 August 1952. He married 1 April 1972 Deborah Thomas.
Children of David Caldwell and Deborah (Thomas) Robbs, born at Canfield, OH:
  2984   i Joshua William Robbs,born 28 November 1974
  2985   ii Jemimah Drew Robbs, born 3 July 1981
  2986 iii Jon David Robbs, born 1986

2394 - NANCY JEAN(8) CALDWELL [Herbert Eugene(7), Emmet Edmunds(6), Margaret Jane(5) Wolfe, Simon P.(4), Jacob Jr(3), Jacob(2), Daniel(1)]
Nancy Jean Caldwell, first child of Herbert Eugene and Mary Evelyn (Price) Caldwell, was born 28 February 1947. She married 24 August 1974 Stephen Powell Skaggs, born 13 June 1951, son of Herbert and Doris (Ward) Skaggs.
Children of Stephen Powell and Nancy Jean (Caldwell) Skaggs:
  2987   i Amy Marianne Skaggs, born 6 November at Columbus, OH
  2988   ii Adam Powell Skaggs, born 10 May 1984 at Columbus, OH
  2989 iii Alexander Lance Skaggs, born 1986 in California

2395 - HERBERT EUGENE JR(8) CALDWELL [Herbert Eugene Sr(7), Emmet Edmunds(6), Margaret Jane(5) Wolfe, Simon P.(4), Jacob Jr(3), Jacob(2), Daniel(1)]
Herbert Eugene Caldwell Jr., second child of Herbert Eugene Sr. and Mary Evelyn (Price) Caldwell, was born 15 September 1954. He married 16 December 1973 Melanie Sue Haggard, born 30 October 1951 at Lexington, KY, daughter of Clark Lewis and Anna Margaret (Lightener) Haggard.
Children of Herbert Eugene Jr and Melanie Sue (Haggard) Caldwell, born at Columbus, OH:
  2990   i Aubrey Lynne Caldwell, born 17 December 1974
  2991   ii Gretchen Marie Caldwell, born 29 October 1979
  2992 iii Herbert Andrew Caldwell, born 17 January 1985

2396 - DOUGLAS RAY(8) MAXEY [Doris Virginia(7) Caldwell, Emmet Edmunds(6), Margaret Jane(5) Wolfe, Simon P.(4), Jacob Jr(3), Jacob(2), Daniel(1)]
Douglas Ray Maxey, first child of Raymond Elbert and Doris Virginia (Caldwell) Maxey, was born 15 December 1950. He married 31 December 1977 Judi Lungren, born 30 November 1953.

Children of Douglas Ray and Judi (Lungren) Maxey:
2993   i Rose Virginia Maxey, born 30 December 1979
2994   ii Belle Regina Maxey, born 16 March 1985

2397 - CAROL SUSAN(8) MAXEY, Doris Virginia(7) Caldwell, Emmet
Edmunds(6), Margaret Jane(5) Wolfe, Simon P.(4), Jacob Jr(3),
Jacob(2), Daniel(1)]
    Carol Susan Maxey, second child of Raymond Elbert and Doris
Virginia (Caldwell) Maxey, was born 4 March 1954. She married 1
September 1973 Robert John Groves, born 9 April 1952.
    Children of Robert John and Carol Susan (Caldwell) Groves:
2995   i Kelly Michelle Groves, born 18 April 1974
2996   ii Joseph Ryan Groves, born 6 September 1978

2400 - TERRY LYNN(8) OYLER [Dorothy Jane(7) Caldwell, William
Arthur(6), Margaret Jane(5) Wolfe, Simon P.(4), Jacob Jr(3), Jacob(2),
Daniel(1)]
    Terry Lynn Oyler, first child of Lawrence Edgar and Dorothy Jane
(Caldwell) Oyler, was born 12 September 1940 at Springfield, OH, died
29 August 1977 at Kernersville, NC. He married 1 August 1965 at
Middletown, OH Marilyn Josephine Bell, born 1 April 1938, died 15 June
1969, daughter of Robert and Hazel (_____) Bell.
    Child of Terry Lynn and Marilyn Josephine (Bell) Oyler:
2997   i Sarah Elizabeth Oyler, born 13 January 1967

2401 - BONNA DELENE(8) OYLER [Dorothy Jane(7) Caldwell, William
Arthur(6), Margaret Jane(5) Wolfe, Simon P.(4), Jacob Jr(3), Jacob(2),
Daniel(1)]
    Bonna Delene Oyler, second child of Lawrence Edgar and Dorothy
Jane (Caldwell) Oyler, was born 9 August 1943 at Springfield, OH. She
married 5 February 1966 Gary Allen Brown, born 9 April 1944, son of
Charles and Nellie Louise (Downing) Brown.
    Children of Gary Allen and Bonna Delene (Oyler) Brown:
2998   i Timothy Ray Oyler, born 5 November 1960
+ 2999   ii Dana Rene' Brown, born 22 January 1966
3000   iii Christopher Allen Brown, born 17 March 1969
3001   iv Todd Allen Brown, born 29 January 1970

2405 - MARY SUZANNE(8) CALDWELL [Wayne Eugene(7), William
Arthur(6), Margaret Jane(5) Wolfe, Simon P.(4), Jacob Jr(3), Jacob(2),
Daniel(1)]
    Mary Suzanne Caldwell was the third child of Wayne Eugene and
Mary Suzanne (Jameson) Caldwell. She married Noel Peterson.
    Children of Noel and Mary Suzanne (Caldwell) Peterson:
3002   i Chase Peterson
3003   ii Jessica Peterson

2406 - GREGORY ALLEN(8) WOLFE [William Edward(7), Clarence
Leroy(6), Edward Carrol(5), Simon P.(4), Jacob Jr(3), Jacob(2),
Daniel(1)]
    Gregory Allen Wolfe, first child of William Edward and Wilma
Catherine (Jessup) Wolfe, was born 21 March 1950 in Madison
County, IN. He married 25 August 1972 in Madison County Kathy Jo
Montgomery, born 1 October 1952 in Tippecanoe County, IN, daughter of
Harold August and Mardabeth (Redford) Montgomery.
    Children of Gregory Allen and Kathy Jo (Montgomery) Wolfe, born
in Madison County, IN:
3004   i Michelle Renee Wolfe, born 2 July 1976

3005   ii Daniel Scott Wolfe, born 1 June 1979

2407 - PATRICIA LYNN(8) WOLFE [William Edward(7), Clarence
Leroy(6), Edward Carrol(5), Simon P.(4), Jacob Jr(3), Jacob(2),
Daniel(1)]
     Patricia Lynn Wolfe, second child of William Edward and Wilma
Catherine (Jessup) Wolfe, was born 16 February 1953 in Madison County,
IN. She married 4 August 1973 in Madison County Stephen Kent Fisher,
born 6 March 1962 in Madison County.
     Children of Stephen Kent and Patricia Lynn (Wolfe) Fisher:
3006   i Jonathan David Fisher, born 8 August 1978 in Champaign
            County, IL
3007   ii Benjamin Earl Fisher, born 17 April 1981 in Adams County,
            IL

2410 - ALANE RENEE(8) MC GEE [Miriam Louise(7) Wolfe, Clarence
Leroy(6), Edward Carrol(5), Simon P.(4), Jacob Jr(3), Jacob(2),
Daniel(1)]
     Alane Renee McGee, second child of Winfried C. and Miriam Louise
(Wolfe) McGee, was born 30 June 1960 in Madison County, IN. She
married 5 November 1988 James Edward Connery.
     Children of James Edward and Alane Renee (McGee) Connery:
3008   i Amanda Nicole Connery
3009   ii Nicholas Paul Connery

2423 - BEVERLY JEAN(8) SMITH [Samuel Hynes(7), John Jacob(6),
Caroline Evalina(5) Wolf, George Isaac(4), Jacob Jr(3), Jacob(2),
Daniel(1)]
     Beverly Jean Smith, first child of Samuel Hynes and Mary Valen-
tine (Eller) Smith, was born 20 June 1949 at Logansport, Cass County,
IN. She married 29 December 1971 at Peru, Miami County, IN Thomas Lee
Ramer, born 31 July 1949 in Miami County, son of Harold Eugene and
Nellie Jean (Truitt) Ramer. They are members of the Methodist Church.
     Children of Thomas Lee and Beverly Jean (Smith) Ramer, born at
Kokomo, Howard County, IN;
3010   i Tamara Lynn Ramer, born 3 August 1972
3011   ii Beth Anne Ramer, born 27 August 1976

2424 - CYNTHIA LYNN(8) SMITH [Samuel Hynes(7), John Jacob(6),
Caroline Evalina(5) Wolf, George Isaac(4), Jacob Jr(3), Jacob(2),
Daniel(1)]
     Cynthia Lynn Smith, second child of Samuel Hynes and Mary Valen-
tine (Eller) Smith, was born 10 September 1957 at Logansport, Cass
County, IN. She married 2 July 1977 at Kokomo, Howard County, IN
Robert Wayne Beckom, born in Howard County, son of Harold Wayne and
Alice Lucille (Radliff) Beckom. They are members of the Brethren
Church.
     Child of Robert Wayne and Cynthia Lynn (Smith) Beckom:
3012   i Amanda Lynn Beckom, born 11 August 1981 at Kokomo, Howard
            County, IN

2425 - JOYCE DIANE(8) MOORE [Dorothy Rose(7) Smith, John
Jacob(6), Caroline Evalina(5) Wolf, George Isaac(4), Jacob Jr(3),
Jacob(2), Daniel(1)]
     Joyce Diane Moore, first child of Ethridge F. and Dorothy Rose
(Smith) Moore, was born 15 March 1949 at Muncie, Delaware County, IN.
She married 23 August 1969 at Indianapolis, Marion County, IN Robert
R. Boyd Jr., born 2 July 1948, son of Robert R. Boyd Sr.

Child of Robert R. Jr. and Joyce Diane (Moore) Boyd:
3013   i John Brandon Boyd, born 29 May 1974 at Indianapolis,
         Marion County, IN

    2439 - CRISTY SUE ANN(8) CRISWELL [Caroline Evalina(7) Harless,
Ida Margaret(6) Smith, Caroline Evalina(5) Wolf, George Isaac(4),
Jacob Jr(3), Jacob(2), Daniel(1)]
    Cristy Sue Ann Criswell, first child of Ernest Gale and Caroline
Evalina (Harless) Criswell, was born 9 October 1947 at Logansport,
Cass County, IN. She married 16 November 1967 at Benson, AZ David
Moore, born 25 November 1946 at Longview, WA, son of Louis Amiel and
Ethel (Griffin) Moore.
    Children of David and Cristy Sue Ann (Criswell) Moore:
 3014   i Richard Galen Moore, born 16 December 1965 at Benson, AZ
 3015   ii Heath Devin Moore, born 16 October 1968 at San Bernadino,
         CA

    2440 - ELLA KATHLEEN(8) CRISWELL [Caroline Evalina(7) Harless,
Ida Margaret(6) Smith, Caroline Evalina(5) Wolf, George Isaac(4),
Jacob Jr(3), Jacob(2), Daniel(1)]
    Ella Kathleen Criswell, second child of Ernest Gale and Caroline
Evalina (Harless) Criswell, was born 27 March 1949 at Logansport, Cass
County, IN. She married 7 June 1969 at Benson, AZ Mark Suagee, born 23
May 1948 at Washington, DC, son of Jay Tennyson and Ruth Benton
(Settle) Suagee.
    Children of Mark and Ella Kathleen (Criswell) Suagee:
 3016   i Rachel Elizabeth Suagee, born 16 January 1975 at Havre, MT
 3017   ii Dylan Suagee, born 14 January 1978 at Boulder, CO

    2441 - KIM ALAN(8) CRISWELL [Caroline Evalina(7) Harless, Ida
Margaret(6) Smith, Caroline Evalina(5) Wolf, George Isaac(4), Jacob
Jr(3), Jacob92), Daniel(1)]
    Kim Alan Criswell, third child of Ernest Gale and Caroline
Evalina (Harless) Criswell, was born 14 august 1951 at Monticello,
White County, IN. He married 28 May 1976 at Boswell, Benton County, IN
Donna Kay Nern, born 1 October 1953 at Lafayette, Tippecanoe County,
IN, daughter of Robert Eugene and Phyllis L. (Fiksoal) Nern.
    Child of Kim Alan and Donna Kay (Nern) Criswell:
 3018   i Brandon Gale Criswell, born 2 November 1979 at Lafayette,
         Tippecanoe County, IN

    2442 - CASEY MARK(8) CRISWELL [Caroline Evalina(7) Harless, Ida
Margaret(6) Smith, Caroline Evalina(5) Wolf, George Isaac(4), Jacob
Jr(3), Jacob(2), Daniel(1)]
    Casey Mark Criswell, fourth Child of Ernest Gale and Caroline
Evalina (Harless) Criswell, was born 3 December 1958 at Monticello,
White County, IN. He married 2 February 1980 at Monticello Peggy Sue
Buntenhoff, born 23 January 1959 at Madison, WI, daughter of Clarence
Harold and Carole Sue (Frie) Buntenhoff.
    Child of Casey Mark and Peggy Sue (Buntenhoff) Criswell:
 3019   i Jasmine Lee Criswell, born 16 September 1980 at Logan-
         sport, Cass County, IN

    2443 - MARSHA ANN(8) HARLESS [Alan John(7), Ida Margaret(6)
Smith, Caroline Evalina(5) Wolf, George Isaac(4), Jacob Jr(3),
Jacob(2), Daniel(1)]
    Marsha Ann Harless, first child of Alan John and Jane Ann (Staf-
ford) Harless, was born 28 November 1955 at Washington, IL. She

married 6 April 1974 at Washington David George Reisse, born 11 August 1953 at Peoria, IL, son of George and Eva (Roderick) Reisse.

Children of David George and Marsha Ann (Harless) Reisse, born at Peoria, IL:

3020   i Amanda Jayne Reisse, born 6 April 1979
3021   ii Scott David Reisse, born 28 October 1980

2444 - ELAINE(8) HARLESS [Alan John(7), Ida Margaret(6) Smith, Caroline Evalina(5) Wolf, George Isaac(4), Jacob Jr(3), Jacob(2), Daniel(1)]

Elaine Harless, second child of Alan John and Jane Ann (Stafford) Harless, was born 4 February 1956 at Washington, IL. She married 13 November 1976 at Washington Barry Mack Miller, born 3 April 1955 at Carlsbad, NM, son of Melvin L. and Pauline (Wheeler) Miller.

Children of Barry Mack and Elaine (Harless) Miller:

3022   i Shana Leigh Miller, born 27 March 1978 at Artesia, NM
3023   ii Sean Mack Miller, born 20 August 1981 at Andrews, TX

2446 - JANET LYNNE(8) HARLESS [Alan John(7), Ida Margaret(6) Smith, Caroline Evalina(5) Wolf, George Isaac(4), Jacob Jr(3), Jacob(2), Daniel(1)]

Janet Lynne Harless, fourth child of Alan John and Jane Ann (Stafford) Harless, was born 18 August 1960 at Washington, IL. She married 25 August 1979 at Washington Walter Doyle Frakes, born 13 February 1957 at Peoria, IL, son of Walter Dean and Beverly Ann (Barch) Frakes.

Children of Walter Doyle and Janet Lynne (Harless) Frakes, born at Peoria, IL:

3024   i Stephanie Jean Frakes, born 15 June 1980
3025   ii Robert Walter Frakes, born 12 July 1981

2452 - MARTHA ANN(8) HARNER [Myrel Eugene(7), Martha Belle(6) Smith, Caroline Evalina(5) Wolf, George Isaac(4), Jacob Jr(3), Jacob(2), Daniel(1)]

Martha Ann Harner, first child of Myrel Eugene and Irene Ann (Holden) Harner, was born 25 July 1932 at Merced, CA. She married 18 May 1971 at Kathleen, GA Matthew Eric Weslow, born 9 February 1947 at New York City, NY.

Children of Matthew Eric and Martha Ann (Harner) Weslow:

3026   i Aaron Frost Weslow, born 13 July 1972 at Altus, OK
3027   ii Lisa Ann Weslow, born 25 April 1975 at Fort Collins, CO

2456 - JAMES EDWARD(8) SNAVELY [Ross Ovid(7), Vada Estella(6) Michael, Lydia Ladoskey(5) Wolf, George Isaac(4), Jacob Jr(3), Jacob(2), Daniel(1)]

James Edward Snavely was the son of Ross Ovid and Ila (Flagg) Snavely. He married Shirley Jackson.

Children of James Edward and Shirley (Jackson) Snavely:

3028   i Melonie Snavely
3029   ii Ross Snavely

2461 - DAVID GENE(8) BOOKWALTER [Ida(7) Snavely, Vada Estella(6) Michael, Lydia Ladoskey(5) Wolf, George Isaac(4), Jacob Jr(3), Jacob(2), Daniel(1)]

David Gene Bookwalter, first child of Floyd and Ida (Snavely) Bookwalter, was born 2 March 1932 at Twelve Mile, Cass County, IN. His wife's name is not known.

Children of David Gene Bookwalter:
3030   i Shirley Ann Bookwalter, born 21 August 1960. Married Gene
         Dayberry
3031 ii Dale Eugene Bookwalter, born 1962
3032 iii Michael Kent Bookwalter, born 1966
3033 iv Glen Bookwalter

2462 - CAROL JOAN(8) BOOKWALTER [Ida(7) Snavely, Vada Estella(6)
Michael, Lydia Ladoskey(5) Wolf, George Isaac(4), Jacob Jr(3),
Jacob(2), Daniel(1)]
    Carol Joan Bookwalter, second child of Floyd and Ida (Snavely)
Bookwalter, was born 13 February 1947 at Gary, Lake County, IN. She
married 27 August 1965 at Merrellville, Lake County, IL Gary Charles
Brandt, born 28 November 1945 at Blue Island, IL, son of Henry and
Lorane (Wilck) Brandt.
    Child of Gary Charles and Carol Joan (Bookwalter) Brandt:
3034   i Dawn Renee' Brandt, born 14 March 1967 at Blue Island, IL

2463 - SHIRLEY LEE(8) WILLIAMSON [Clara Monzel(7) Snavely, Vada
Estella(6) Michael, Lydia Ladoskey(5) Wolf, George Isaac(4), Jacob
Jr(3), Jacob(2), Daniel(1)]
    Shirley Lee Williamson, first child of Clarence Emerson and Clara
Monzel (Snavely) Williamson, was born 3 March 1937 at Twelve Mile,
Cass County, IN. She married 15 May 1954 in Cass County Kenneth Levon
Packard, born 27 June 1936 in Cass County, son of Samuel K. and
Margarette E. (Grassmeyer) Packard.
    Children of Kenneth Levon and Shirley Lee (Williamson) Packard:
+ 3035   i Cynthia Lynn Packard, born 5 December 1954
+ 3036 ii Terry Quentin Packard, born 20 February 1957

2464 - LARRY JOE(8) WILLIAMSON [Clara Monzel(7) Snavely, Vada
Estella(6) Michael, Lydia Ladoskey(5) Wolf, George Isaac(4), Jacob
Jr(3), Jacob(2), Daniel(1)]
    Larry Joe Williamson was the second child of Clarence Emerson and
Clara Monzel (Snavely) Williamson. He married 1) Nancy _____ and 2)
unknown.
    Child of Larry Joe and Nancy (_____) Williamson:
3037   i Kay Ann Williamson

2466 - MARVIN J.(8) OSTHEIMER [Edna Leo(7) Snavely, Vada
Estella(6) Michael, Lydia Ladoskey(5) Wolf, George Isaac(4), Jacob
Jr(3), Jacob(2), Daniel(1)]
    Marvin J. Ostheimer, first child of Jack and Edna Leo (Snavely)
Ostheimer, was born 30 November 1941 at Monticello, White County, IN.
He married 4 June 1960 at Monticello Cynthia Frances Wilson, born 21
June 1942 at Oak Park, IL, daughter of Virgil Raymond and Elvira R.
(Formaggis) Wilson.
    Children of Marvin J. and Cynthia Frances (Wilson) Ostheimer,
born at Chicago, IL:
3038   i David Kevin Ostheimer, born 30 March 1962. Married 9 July
         1982 at Oklahoma City, OK Kelly Jane Bowers
3039 ii Diane Karen Ostheimer, born 13 January 1965

2469 - BOBBIE JO(8) EZRA [Lola Frances(7) Snavely, Vada
Estella(6) Michael, Lydia Ladoskey(5) Wolf, George Isaac(4), Jacob
Jr(3), Jacob(2), Daniel(1)]
    Bobbie Jo Ezra, first child of Virgil and Lola Frances (snavely)
Ezra, was born 5 March 1948 at Indianapolis, Marion County, IN. She

married 18 May 1974 Kenneth Fussichen.
    Children of Kenneth and Bobbie Jo (Ezra) Fussichen:
  3040   i Matthew Christopher Fussichen, born 27 May 1976
  3041   ii David Kyle Fussichen, born 14 may 1977
  3042 iii Vanessa Rene Fussichen, born 13 december 1980

    2473 - SHARON KAY(8) WALTERS [Cora Mabel(7) Michael, Charles
Franklin(6), Lydia Ladoskey(5) Wolf, George Isaac(4), Jacob Jr(3),
Jacob(2), Daniel(1)]
    Sharon Kay Walters, first child of Luther Lavon and Cora Mabel
(Michael) Walters, was born 15 July 1941 at South Bend, St. Joseph
County, IN. She married 11 June 1960 at South Bend Aaron Andrew White,
born 13 February 1941 in Lauderdale County, AL, son of George Andrew
and Glidis J. (Johnson) White.
    Children of Aaron Andrew and Sharon Kay (Walters) White, born at
South Bend, St. Joseph County, IN:
  3043   i Michael Andrew White, born 25 April 1969
  3044   ii Scott Alan White, born 9 December 1971

    2474 - MICHAEL LEE(8) WALTERS [Cora Mabel(7) Michael, Charles
Franklin(6), Lydia Ladoskey(5) Wolf, George Isaac(4), Jacob Jr(3),
Jacob(2), Daniel(1)]
    Michael Lee Walters, second child of Luther Lavon and Cora Mabel
(Michael) Walters, was born 9 December 1944 at South Bend, St. Joseph
County, IN. He married 10 December 1965 at South Bend Suzanne Elliott,
born 28 February 1947 at South Bend, daughter of C. Devon and Merlin
Delilah (Shirk) Elliott.
    Children of Michael Lee and Suzanne (Elliott) Walters:
  3045   i Renee Lynn Walters, born 4 November 1968 at South Bend,
            St. joseph County, IN
  3046   ii Marc Jason Walters, born 13 February 1971 at Ft. Wayne,
            Allen County, IN

    2477 - KATHLEEN HELEN(8) MICHAEL [Kenneth Rollie(7), Charles
Franklin(6), Lydia Ladoskey(5) Wolf, George Isaac(4), Jacob Jr(3),
Jacob(2), Daniel(1)]
    Kathleen Helen Michael, first child of Kenneth Rollie and Naomi
(Frechette) (Johnson) Michael, was born 13 February 1948 at Munising,
Alger County, MI. She married 1) 13 January 1966 in Macomb County, MI
William Harris, born 21 January 1944 in Michigan. They divorced 5 July
1973 and she married 2) 2 November 1973 Harold William Snider, born 29
July 1947 at Utica, Macomb County, MI.
    Children of William and Kathleen Helen (Michael) Harris:
  3047   i Jennifer Jane Harris, born 28 July 1966 at Ferndale,
            Oakland County, MI
  3048   ii William Robert Harris, born 8 October 1968 at Royal Oak,
            Oakland County, MI
    Child of Harold William and Kathleen Helen (Michael) (Harris)
Snider:
  3049   i Christine Anne Snider, born 22 March 1974 at Warren, MI

    2478 - KENNETH EUGENE(8) MICHAEL [Kenneth Rollie(7), Charles
Franklin(6), Lydia Ladoskey(5) Wolf, George Isaac(4), Jacob Jr(3),
Jacob(2), Daniel(1)]
    Kenneth Eugene Michael, second child of Kenneth Rollie and Naomi
(Frechette) (Johnson) Michael, was born 11 September 1949 in Michigan.
He married 1) 20 November 1970 at Panama City, CA Stephanie Piaro,
born 1930. They divorced in 1974, no children, and he married 2) 24

July 1976 at Las Vegas, NV Karen Ann Boley, born 3 July 1955. Kenneth served in the army in the Vietnam War.

Children of Kenneth Eugene and Karen Ann (Boley) Michael:
3050   i Michelle Suzanne Michael, born 16 February 1977 at Van Nuys, CA
3051   ii Steven Kenneth Michael, born 11 March 1981 at Mission Hills, CA

2480 - CATHY LYNN(8) MARSHALL [Ruby Mae(7) Michael, George Emerson(6), Lydia Ladoskey(5) Wolf, George Isaac(4), Jacob Jr(3), Jacob(2), Daniel(1)]
Cathy Lynn Marshall, second child of Joseph and Ruby Mae (Michael) Marshall, was born 10 September _____ at Logansport, Cass County, IN. She married 22 May 1971 at Logansport James David Andry, born 28 April 1952 at Logansport, son of James and _____ (Aborn) Andry. They have Methodist church affiliation.

Children of James David and Cathy Lynn (Marshall) Andry, born in Indiana:
3052   i James Matthew Andry, born 2 November 1971
3053   ii Chrystal Lynn Andry, born 28 January 1974
3054 iii Michael Aaron Andry, born 18 November 1976

2481 - GARY JOSEPH(8) MARSHALL [Ruby Mae(7) Michael, George Emerson(6), Lydia Ladoskey(5) Wolf, George Isaac(4), Jacob Jr(3), Jacob(2), Daniel(1)]
Gary Joseph Marshall, third child of Joseph and Ruby Mae (Michael) Marshall, was born 3 April 1956 at Logansport, Cass County, IN. He married 28 February 1976 at Logansport Teena Sedam, born 20 January 1956 at Logansport, daughter of William and _____ (Wells) Sedam.

Children of Gary Joseph and Teena (Sedam) Marshall, born in Indiana:
3055   i Jason Alan Marshall, born 19 September 1977
3056   ii Jeanell Lee Marshall, born __ September 1981

2485 - JERRY RAYMOND(8) MICHAEL [Raymond Champ(7), Earl Dewey(6), Lydia Ladoskey(5) Wolf, George Isaac(4), Jacob Jr(3), Jacob(2), Daniel(1)]
Jerry Raymond Michael, first child of Raymond Champ and Ilene Mae (Baer) Michael, was born 17 July 1945 at South Bend, St. Joseph County, IN. He married 3 May 1969 at South Bend Edith Kathleen Hanson, born 4 June 1947 at South Bend, daughter of Fred and Mabel (Freel) Hanson.

Child of Jerry Raymond and Edith Kathleen (Hanson) Michael:
3057   i Shannon Patrice Michael, born 13 November 1974 at South Bend, St. Joseph County, IN

2486 - DENNIS REVIERE(8) MICHAEL [Raymond Champ(7), Earl Dewey(6), Lydia Ladoskey(5) Wolf, George Isaac(4), Jacob Jr(3), Jacob(2), Daniel(1)]
Dennis Reviere Michael, second child of Raymond Champ and Ilene Mae (Baer) Michael, was born 29 February 1948 at South Bend, St. Joseph County, IN. He married 2 May 1970 at South Bend Mary Ellen Horvath, born 6 May 1948 at South Bend, daughter of Mathew and Helen (Moon) Horvath.

Children of Dennis Reviere and Mary Ellen (Horvath) Michael, born at South Bend, St. Joseph County, IN:
3058   i Kari Lynn Michael, born 5 December 1970

3059   ii Jeffrey Scott Michael, born 25 September 1976

    2488 - JACKIE DIANE(8) STUART [Phyllis Kathleen(7) Michael, Earl
Dewey(6), Lydia Ladoskey(5) Wolf, George Isaac(4), Jacob Jr(3),
Jacob(2), Daniel(1)]
    Jackie Diane Stuart, first child of Charles Albert and Phyllis
Kathleen (Michael) Stuart, was born 27 October 1952 at South Bend, St.
Joseph County, IN. She married 17 February 1973 at Osceola, St. Joseph
County Stephen Neal Darr, born 16 August 1951 at South Bend, son of
Victor Neal and Beverly Jewell (Grose) Darr.
    Children of Stephen Neal and Jackie Diane (Stuart) Darr, born at
South Bend, St. Joseph County, IN:
  3060   i Charles Neal Darr, born 15 December 1975
  3061   ii Kimberly Ann Darr, born 21 August 1977

    2489 - BRUCE DUANE(8) STUART [Phyllis Kathleen(7) Michael, Earl
Dewey(6), Lydia Ladoskey(5) Wolf, George Isaac(4), Jacob Jr(3),
Jacob(2), Daniel(1)]
    Bruce Duane Stuart, second child of Charles Albert and Phyllis
Kathleen (Michael) Stuart, was born 20 February 1954 at South Bend,
St. Joseph County, IN. He married 2 November 1974 at South Bend
Theresa Marie Smanda, born 25 February 1954 at South Bend, daughter
of Louis and Ruth Mary (O'Neill) Smanda.
    Children of Bruce Duane and Theresa Marie (Smanda) Stuart, born
at South Bend, St. Joseph County, IN:
  3062   i Sean Louis Stuart, born 26 August 1975
  3063   ii Shane Michael Stuart, born 6 October 1979

    2490 - GARY DEAN(8) STUART [Phyllis Kathleen(7) Michael, Earl
Dewey(6), Lydia Ladoskey(5) Wolf, George Isaac(4), Jacob Jr(3),
Jacob(2), Daniel(1)]
    Gary Dean Stuart, third child of Charles Albert and Phyllis
Kathleen (Michael) Stuart, was born 29 May 1955 at South Bend, St.
Joseph County, IN. He married 14 June 1975 at South Bend Deborah Ann
Pawlok, born 31 August 1952 in St. Joseph County, daughter of Walter
Stanley and Mary Ann (_____) Pawlok.
    Children of Gary Dean and Deborah Ann (Pawlok) Stuart, born at
South Bend, St. Joseph County, IN:
  3064   i Rodney Allen Stuart, born 16 May 1977
  3065   ii Brian Anthony Stuart, born 24 January 1980

    2495 - DEANNA KAY(8) HARTER [Bobetta Joy(7) Sumpter, Cleo Cathe-
rine(6) Michael, Lydia Ladoskey(5) Wolf, George Isaac(4), Jacob Jr(3),
Jacob(2), Daniel(1)]
    Deanna Kay Harter, first child of Ralph Robert and Bobetta Joy
(Sumpter) Harter, was born 9 March 1949. She married 1) David Wall and
2) unknown.
    Children of David and Deanna Kay (Harter) Wall:
  3066   i Shirley Wall
  3067   ii Tonya Wall

    2497 - SANDRA SUE(8) HARTER [Bobetta Joy(7) Sumpter, Cleo Cathe-
rine(6) Michael, Lydia Ladoskey(5) Wolf, George Isaac(4), Jacob Jr(3),
Jacob(2), Daniel(1)
    Sandra Sue Harter, third child of Ralph Robert and Bobetta Joy
(Sumpter) Harter, was born 10 December 1951. She married Jack Kidwell.
    Children of Jack and Sandra Sue (Harter) Kidwell:
  3068   i La Chelle Renee Kidwell

```
3069   ii Todd Kidwell
3070  iii Tammy Kidwell
```

2500 - KAREN ENGLISH(8) MURPHY [Opal Naomi(7) Sumpter, Cleo Catherine(6) Michael, Lydia Ladoskey(5) Wolf, George Isaac(4), Jacob Jr(3), Jacob(2), Daniel(1)]
    Karen English Murphy, first child of Walter Eugene and Opal Naomi (Sumpter) Murphy, married David Max Hannon.
    Child of David Max and Karen English (Murphy) Hannon:
3071   i Daun Avera Hannon, born 7 November 1970

2501 - TERRY ELAINE(8) MURPHY [Opal Naomi(7) Sumpter, Cleo Catherine(6) Michael, Lydia Ladoskey(5) Wolf, George Isaac(4), Jacob Jr(3), Jacob(2), Daniel(1)]
    Terry Elaine Murphy, second child of Walter Eugene and Opal Naomi (Sumpter) Murphy, married James Prebil.
    Child of James and Terry Elaine (Murphy) Prebil:
3072   i Christina Rachelle Prebil

2535 - LINDA DIANE(8) SAILORS [Samuel(7), Magdaline(6) Whipperman, Margaret(5) Cree, Magdalena L.(4) Wolf, Jacob Jr(3), Jacob(2), Daniel(1)]
    Linda Diane Sailors was the second child of Samuel and Helen Katherine (Groninger) Sailors. She married 22 May 1965 Theodore Stanton Williams.
    Child of Theodore Stanton and Linda Diane (Sailors) Williams:
3073   i John Williams

2544 - BARBARA A.(8) BROWN [Charlotte Elizabeth(7) Cree, Walter Irving(6), George Robert(5), Magdalena L.(4) Wolf, Jacob Jr(3), Jacob(2), Daniel(1)]
    Barbara A. Brown, second child of Ernest Edward and Charlotte Elizabeth (Cree) Brown, was born 22 November 1947. She married 14 March 1964 James Richard Banter, born 24 March 1940.
    Child of James Richard and Barbara A. (Brown) Banter:
3074   i Robert Banter, born 26 October 1964

2566 - JAMES LEE(8) BAILEY [James M.(7), Elizabeth Idella(6) Boyer, Alice Arretta(5) Sharritts, Samuel(4), Elizabeth(3) Hahn, Elizabeth(2) Wolf, Daniel(1)]
    James Lee Bailey, first child of James M. and Helen Marie (Diver) Bailey, was born 13 July 1945 at Santa Fe, NM. He married 13 July 1975 Judith Ann Decicco.
    Children of James Lee and Judith Ann (Decicco) Bailey, born in Connecticut:
3075   i Elizabeth Diver Bailey, born 5 April 1981
3076   ii Sara Frances Bailey, born 8 March 1985

2567 - WILLIAM EDWARD(8) BAILEY [James M.(7), Elizabeth Idella(6) Boyer, Alice Arretta(5) Sharritts, Samuel(4), Elizabeth(3) Hahn, Elizabeth(2) Wolf, Daniel(1)]
    William Edward Bailey, second child of James M. and Helen Marie (Diver) Bailey, was born 10 April 1954 in Montgomery County, OH. He married 19 November 1977 Karyl Elizabeth Rammel.
    Children of William Edward and Karyl Elizabeth (Rammel) Bailey:
3077   i Ian Matthew Bailey, born 19 January 1981 in Arkansas
3078   ii Aileen Marie Bailey, born 13 December 1983 in Michigan

2568 - EUGENE L.(8) STUPP [Helen Louise(7) Bailey, Elizabeth
Idella(6) Boyer, Alice Arretta(5) Sharritts, Samuel(4), Elizabeth(3)
Hahn, Elizabeth(2) Wolf, Daniel(1)]
   Eugene L. Stupp, first child of Chester and Helen Louise (Bailey)
Stupp, was born 17 December 1935 in Ohio. He married Harriet Wright.
   Child of Eugene L. and Harriet (Wright) Stupp:
   3079   i David Eugene Stupp, born 22 March 1970 in Ohio

   2569 - DONNA LEE(8) STUPP [Helen Louise(7) Bailey, Elizabeth
Idella(6) Boyer, Alice Arretta(5) Sharritts, Samuel(4), Elizabeth(3)
Hahn, Elizabeth(2) Wolf, Daniel(1)]
   Donna Lee Stupp, second child of Chester and Helen Louise
(Bailey) Stupp, was born 18 December 1938 in Ohio. She married 1)
Larry Nagle and 2) Ralph Coolridge.
   Child of Larry and Donna Lee (Stupp) Nagle:
   3080   i Patti Jo Nagle, born 26 June 1957 in Ohio
   Child of Ralph and Donna Lee (Stupp) (Nagle) Coolridge:
   3081   i Ralph J. Coolridge, born 25 June 1961 in Ohio

   2570 - DALE WAYNE SR(8) STUPP [Helen Louise(7) Bailey, Elizabeth
Idella(6) Boyer, Alice Arretta(5) Sharritts, Samuel(4), Elizabeth(3)
Hahn, Elizabeth(2) Wolf, Daniel(1)]
   Dale Wayne Stupp Sr., third child of Chester and Helen Louise
(Bailey) Stupp, was born 22 September 1941 in Ohio. He married 1)
Sandy Lyons , 2) Karen Spiegel and 3) unknown.
   Child of Dale Wayne Sr and Sandy (Lyons) Stupp:
   3082   i Dale Wayne Stupp II, born 23 April 1962
   Child of Dale Wayne Sr and Karen (Spiegel) Stupp:
   3083   i Dean Stupp, born __ September 1969

   2571 - ROCKY LYNDELL(8) FOWLER(A) [Melba Marie(7) Borland,
Vera(6) Wolfe, Franklin(5), Daniel Jr(4), Daniel Sr(3), Frederick(2),
Daniel(1)]
   Rocky Lyndell Fowler, adopted son of Wood E. and Melba Marie
(Borland) Fowler, was born about 1950. He married 1 September 1974 at
Creston, Union County, IA Sherry Lynn Genners, born about 1950,
daughter of Arthur F. and _____ Genners.
   Child of Rocky Lyndell and Sherry Lynn (Genners) Fowler:
   3084   i Lacey Lynn Fowler, born about 1978

   2573 - DOLORES ANN(8) JACOBS [Fred David(7), Myrtle Annie(6)
Wolfe, Simon Peter(5), Michael(4), Daniel Sr(3), Frederick(2),
Daniel(1)]
   Dolores Ann Jacobs, first child of Fred David and Crystal Rose
(Wisecup) Jacobs, was born 2 December 1932 at Grant City, Worth
County, MO. She married 9 May 1952 at Grant City Billie Leonard Owens,
born 31 January 1929, died 5 December 1985 and buried 10 December
1985, all at Grant City, son of Arthur Leslie and Leota Crystal
(Wilson) Owens.
   Children of Billie Leonard and Dolores Ann (Jacobs) Owens:
 + 3085   i Leslie David Owens, born 15 August 1953
 + 3086   ii Sharon Ann Owens, born 11 October 1954
 + 3087 iii Carrol Lynn Owens, born 24 November 1956
 + 3088   iv Leonard Douglas Owens, born 15 December 1958

   2574 - JOHN DAVID(8) JACOBS [Fred David(7), Myrtle Annie(6)
Wolfe, Simon Peter(5), Michael(4), Daniel Sr(3), Frederick(2),
Daniel(1)]

John David Jacobs, second child of Fred David and Crystal Rose (Wisecup) Jacobs, was born 30 October 1941 at Grant City, Worth County, MO. He married 11 August 1961 at King City, Gentry County, MO Wilma Kay Van Meter, born 15 April 1942 at Helena, Andrew County, MO, daughter of Joseph Justin and Leona Fern (Neiderhauser) Van Meter.

Children of John David and Wilma Kay (Van Meter) Jacobs, all born at King City, Gentry County, MO:

```
 3089    i Joseph David Jacobs, born 5 June 1962
+ 3090   ii John Eric Jacobs, born 27 June 1966
 3091  iii Kristi Kay Jacobs, born 23 May 1970
```

2575 - EDWIN WILLIAM(8) JACOBS [Fred David(7), Myrtle Annie(6) Wolfe, Simon Peter(5), Michael(4), Daniel Sr(3), Frederick(2), Daniel(1)]

Edwin William Jacobs, third child of Fred David and Crystal Rose (Wisecup) Jacobs, was born 5 September 1952 at Mt. Ayr, Ringold County, MO. He married 1) 25 December 1971 at Sheridan, Worth County, MO Sherry Marie Rowe, born 30 December 1952 at Sheridan, daughter of Roy Lee and Marian Ruth (Foster) Rowe and 2) 26 May 1985 at Bedford, Ringold County Loretta Faye Foster, born 2 October 1955 at Bethany, Harrison County, MO, daughter of Larry Jack and Doris Faye (Price) Foster.

Children of Edwin William and Sherry Marie (Rowe) Jacobs, born in Ringold County, MO:

```
3092    i David Edwin Jacobs, born 15 July 1972
3093   ii Julie Ann Jacobs, born 1 August 1977
```

2577 - VELMA ROSE(8) JACOBS [Frank Edwin(7), Myrtle Annie(6) Wolfe, Simon Peter(5), Michael(4), Daniel Sr(3), Frederick(2), Daniel(1)]

Velma Rose Jacobs, second child of Frank Edwin and Verne Opal (Arnold) Jacobs, was born 12 April 1938 at Albany, Gentry County, MO. She married 15 September 1957 at Corning, Adams County, IA Donald Arthur Riegel.

Children of Donald Arthur and Velma Rose (Jacobs) Riegel:

```
3094    i Daniel Arthur Riegel, born 1962
3095   ii Melody Renee Riegel, born 1967. Married Gregory Abbott
3096  iii Wendy Eileen Riegel, born 1969
```

2578 - EDWIN(8) WOLFE [Claude(7), Fred Simon(6), Simon Peter(5), Michael(4), Daniel Sr(3), Frederick(2), Daniel(1)]

Edwin Wolfe, first child of Claude and Lois (Wagaman) Wolfe, was born 26 March 1937. He married Frances _____, born 18 July 1937.

Children of Edwin and Frances (_____) Wolfe:

```
3097    i Tamara Sue Wolfe, born 26 October 1957. Married 10 Febru-
           ary 1979 Terry Killian
3098   ii Julie Ann Wolfe, born 30 September 1958. Married 3 Septem-
           ber 1977 Charles Hoisington
3099  iii Sandra Kay Wolfe, born 20 November 1962. Married 13
           December 1986 Raymond Hunter
3100   iv Amy Lynn Wolfe, born 20 February 1970
```

2584 - CAROLYN MARIE(8) SNODGRASS [Dorothy Pearl(7) Wolfe, Fred Simon(6), Simon Peter(5), Michael(4), Daniel Sr(3), Frederick(2), Daniel(1)]

Carolyn Marie Snodgrass, first child of Marvin J. and Dorothy Pearl (Wolfe) Snodgrass, was born 25 November 1932. She married 1 April 1961 Alfred B. Bauman.

Children of Alfred B. and Carolyn Marie (Snodgrass) Bauman:
3101   i Michael James Bauman, born 7 May 1963. Married 21 October
            1989 Tina Renae Cool
3102   ii Martha Diane Bauman, born 7 August 1967

2586 - SONYA RAE(8) WOLFE [Albert Harold(7), Frank Peter(6),
Simon Peter(5), Michael(4), Daniel Sr(3), Frederick(2), Daniel(1)]
     Sonya Rae Wolfe, first child of Albert Harold and Stephana
Margarite (Kiefer) Wolfe, was born 18 November 1935. She married Elvin
Vernon Bailey, born 16 October 1931.
     Children of Elvin Vernon and Sonya Rae (Wolfe) Bailey:
+ 3103   i Boyce Enoch Bailey, born 22 April 1959
  3104   ii Jonathan Bailey, born and died 1961
+ 3105 iii Vernon Albert Bailey, born 2 October 1964
  3106   iv Helen Lenore Bailey, born 24 September 1970

2587 - STEPHEN FRANK(8) WOLFE [Albert Harold(7), Frank Peter(6),
Simon Peter(5), Michael(4), Daniel Sr(3), Frederick(2), Daniel(1)]
     Stephen Frank Wolfe, second child of Albert Harold and Stephana
Margarite (Kiefer) Wolfe, was born 3 August 1937. He married Evangeline Cava Black, born 23 October 1948.
     Children of Stephen Frank and Evangeline Cava (Black) Wolfe:
3107   i Ronald Cava Wolfe, born 26 April 1969
3108   ii Mari Fe'y Luz Wolfe, adopted, born 3 October 1969
3109 iii Leland Cava Wolfe, born 11 January 1972
3110   iv Kirstine Cava Wolfe, born 13 January 1976

2588 - DORCAS ANN(8) WOLFE [Albert Harold(7), Frank Peter(6),
Simon Peter(5), Michael(4), Daniel Sr(3), Frederick(2), Daniel(1)]
     Dorcas Ann Wolfe, third child of Albert Harold and Stephana
Margarite (Kiefer) Wolfe, was born 28 February 1939.
     Child of Dorcas Ann Wolfe:
3111   i .Brent Lane Wolfe/Ring, born 22 February 1963, died 15
            August 1972

2589 - RUSSELL ALAN(8) WOLFE [Albert Harold(7), Frank Peter(6),
Simon Peter(5), Michael(4), Daniel Sr(3), Frederick(2), Daniel(1)]
     Russell Alan Wolfe, fourth child of Albert Harold and Stephana
Margarite (Kiefer) Wolfe, was born 25 February 1943. He married
Marilyn Lou Sharp, born 1943.
     Children of Russell Alan and Marilyn Lou (Sharp) Wolfe:
3112   i Mark Alan Wolfe, born 1968
3113   ii Stephanie Jean Wolfe, born 1970

2590 - BRUCE MICHAEL(8) WOLFE [Albert Harold(7), Frank Peter(6),
Simon Peter(5), Michael(4), Daniel Sr(3), Frederick(2), Daniel(1)]
     Bruce Michael Wolfe, fifth child of Albert Harold and Stephana
Margarite (Kiefer) Wolfe, was born 13 February 1952. He married Sue
Elaine Young, born 31 July 1953.
     Children of Bruce Michael and Sue Elaine (Young) Wolfe:
3114   i Tricia Sue Wolfe, born 15 October 1972
3115   ii Shane Michael Wolfe, born 19 July 1978

2591 - SARA LEE(8) WOLFE [Albert Harold(7), Frank Peter(6), Simon
Oeter(5), Michael(4), Daniel Sr(3), Frederick(2), Daniel(1)]
     Sara Lee Wolfe, sixth child of Albert Harold and Stephana Marga-
rite (Kiefer) Wolfe, was born 29 May 1957. She married 1) _____
Orfanos, 2) _____ Betts and 3) Stephen Eugene Chambers, born 9 Febru-

ary 1950.
Child of _____ and Sara Lee (Wolfe) Orfanos:
3116   i Brent Anthony Orfanos, born 4 December 1975
Children of Stephen Eugene and Sara Lee (Wolfe) (Orfanos) (Betts) Chambers:
3117   i Torrence Eugene Chambers, born 19 March 1982
3118   ii Jacob Ryan Chambers, born 6 March 1985

2619 - DAVID EARL(8) LOWRY [Leonard Earl(7), Leila Emma(6) Wolf, Sherman E.(5), Franklin(4), Simon(3), Frederick(2), Daniel(1)]
David Earl Lowry, first child of Leonard Earl and Dorothy Marie (Bartles) Lowry, was born 31 May 1948 in Washington County, MD. He married 18 October 1968 in Washington County Mara Marie Barnhart, born 27 February 1949 at Nova, Franklin County, PA, daughter of Sam Elwood and Joan Metcalfe (Scott) Barnhart.
Children of David Earl and Mara Marie (Barnhart) Lowry, born in Washington County, MD:
3119   i Penni Sue Lowry, born 17 March 1970
3120   ii David Wayne Lowry, born 10 November 1971
3121   iii Timothy Scott Lowry, born 15 January 1975

2621 - CAROLYN MARIE(8) LOWRY [Leonard Earl(7), Leila Emma(6) Wolf, Sherman E.(5), Franklin(4), Simon(3), Frederick(2), Daniel(1)]
Carolyn Marie Lowry, third child of Leonard Earl and Dorothy Marie (Bartles) Lowry, was born 12 January 1953 in Washington County, MD. She married 12 August 1978 in Washington County Jeffrey Lynn Crist, born 22 April 1954 in Washington County.
Children of Jeffrey Lynn and Carolyn Marie (Lowry) Crist:
3122   i Stacie Nicole Crist, born 12 September 1983 in Washington
              County, MD
3123   ii Ashley Marie Crist, born 18 January 1987 at Waynesboro,
              Franklin County, PA

2622 - CURTIS THEODORE(8) LOWRY [William Elsworth(7), Leila Emma(6) Wolf, Sherman E.(5), Franklin(4), Simon(3), Frederick(2), Daniel(1)]
Curtis Theodore Lowry, first child of William Elsworth and Beatrice Lucille (Myers) Lowry, was born 12 January 1951 in Washington County, MD. He married 27 June 1975 at Hagerstown, Washington County, MD Robyn J. Powell, born 24 November 1948 in New Zealand.
Child of Curtis Theodore and Robyn J. (Powell) Lowry:
3124   i Theodore Curtis Lowry, born 12 May 1981 at Bethesda,
              Montgomery County, MD

2623 - BRENDA KAY(8) LOWRY [William Elsworth(7), Leila Emma(6) Wolf, Sherman E.(5), Franklin(4), Simon(3), Frederick(2), Daniel(1)]
Brenda Kay Lowry, second child of William Elsworth and Beatrice Lucille (Myers) Lowry, was born 3 February 1952 in Washington County, MD. She married 28 June 1974 at Hagerstown, Washington County Lon Neal Solomon, born 24 August 1948 in Virginia, son of Benjamin and Hermine (_____) Solomon.
Children of Lon Neal and Brenda Kay (Lowry) Solomon:
3125   i James Benjamin Solomon, born 3 June 1977 at Washington, DC
3126   ii Justin William Solomon, born 6 January 1981 at Fairfax,
              VA
3127   iii Jonathan Neal Solomon, 26 February 1985 at Fairfax, VA

276

2624 - CHARLENE RAE(8) LOWRY [William Elsworth(7), Leila Emma((6)
Wolf, Sherman E.(5), Franklin(4), Simon(3), Frederick(2), Daniel(1)]
    Charlene Rae Lowry, third child of William Elsworth and Beatrice
Lucille (Myers) Lowry, was born 9 February 1954 in Washington County,
MD. She married 10 July 1976 at Hagerstown, Washington County Dane
West, born 11 September 1955 in Texas, son of Roger West.
    Children of Dane and Charlene Rae (Lowry) West, born at Fairfax,
VA:
  3128   i Brian Michael West, born 25 May 1982
  3129   ii Jeremiah Richard West, born 18 June 1984
  3130 iii Bradley Joseph West, born 29 March 1989

2625 - SANDRA BEA(8) LOWRY [William Elsworth(7), Leila Emma(6)
Wolf, Sherman E.(5), Franklin(4), Simon(3), Frederick(2), Daniel(1)]
    Sandra Bea Lowry, fourth child of William Elsworth and Beatrice
Lucille (Myers) Lowry, was born 7 September 1958 in Washington County,
MD. She married 28 June at Hagerstown, Washington County Lance Sparks,
born 27 March 1958. Sandra died 18 September 1985 at Briarcliff, NY
and is buried at Cedar Lawn Cemetery, Hagerstown.
    Child of Lance and Sandra Bea (Lowry) Sparks:
  3131   i Allen William Sparks, born 26 October 1984 at New York, NY

2626 - LUTHER E. JR(8) WOLFE [Luther E. Sr(7), Franklin Ells-
worth(6), Sherman E.(5), Franklin(4), Simon(3), Frederick(2),
Daniel(1)]
    Luther E. Wolfe Jr., son of Luther E. Sr. and Mildred Louise
(Ambrose) Wolfe, was born 13 January 1945 in Washington County, MD.
After the death of his father and the remarriage of his mother he took
the name of his stepfather, Grimes. He married 28 August 1966 in
Washington County Vickie Darlene Zimmerman, born 15 September 1945 in
Washington County, daughter of George and Larue (Tansill) Zimmerman.
    Children of Luther E. Jr. and Vickie Darlene (Zimmerman)
Wolfe/Grimes, born in Washington County, MD:
  3132   i Jay Todd Grimes, born 4 May 1969
  3133   ii Brandy Lynn Grimes, born 25 September 1970

2627 - DENNIS FRANKLIN(8) WOLFE [Franklin Eugene(7), Franklin
Ellsworth(6), Sherman E.(5), Franklin(4), Simon(3), Frederick(2),
Daniel(1)]
    Dennis Franklin Wolfe, first child of Franklin Eugene and Annie
Elizabeth (Higman) Wolfe, was born 5 February 1946 at Boonsboro,
Washington County, MD. He married 6 October 1979 at Hancock, Washing-
ton County Linda Jean Swain, born 11 August 1958, in Washington
County, daughter of Franklin C. and Lula (Shoemaker) Swain.
    Child of Dennis Franklin and Linda Jean (Swain) Wolfe:
  3134   i Kelli Luanne Wolfe, born 20 September 1982 in Washington
            County, MD

2628 - DARYL LYNN(8) WOLFE [Franklin Eugene(7), Franklin Ells-
worth(6), Sherman E.(5), Franklin(4), Simon(3), Frederick(2),
Daniel(1)]
    Daryl Lynn Wolfe, second child of Franklin Eugene and Annie
Elizabeth (Higman) Wolfe, was born 27 March 1957 at Boonsboro, Washington county, MD. He married 16 April 1983 at Boonsboro Shana Kay
Siponen (her second marriage), born 3 March 1958 in Washington County,
daughter of Frederick John and Beulah Virginia (Kadle) Siponan.

Children of Daryl Lynn and Shana Kay (Siponen) Wolfe, born in
Washington County, MD:
3135   i Erin Christine Wolfe, born 8 January 1985
3136   ii Matthew Evan Wolfe, born 17 May 1989

2629 - SHARON KAY(8) ADAMS [William Ross Jr(7), Irene Eliza-
beth(6) Wolf, Sherman E.(5), Franklin(4), Simon(3), Frederick(2),
Daniel(1)]
    Sharon Kay Adams, first child of William Ross Jr. and Barbara Ann
(Sprankle) Adams, was born 26 May 1956 at Hagerstown, Washington
County, MD. She married 2 July 1983 at Jefferson, Frederick County, MD
Nelson Thomas Hipkins.
    Children of Nelson Thomas and Sharon Kay (Adams) Hipkins:
3137   i Amanda Kate Hipkins, born 18 August 1986
3138   ii Seth Michael Hipkins, born 23 June 1989

2630 - WILLIAM EUGENE(8) ADAMS [William Ross Jr(7), Irene Eliza-
beth(6) Wolf, Sherman E.(5), Franklin(4), Simon(3), Frederick(2),
Daniel(1)]
    William Eugene Adams, second child of William Ross Jr. and
Barbara Ann (Sprankle) Adams, was born 24 February 1958 at Frederick,
Frederick County, MD. He married 30 November 1988 at Frederick Lynann
McMullen.
    Children of William Eugene and Lynann (McMullen) Adams:
3139   i Matthew William Adams, born 29 April 1989
3140   ii Kimberly Michelle Adams, born 1 June 1990

2631 - KAREN ANN(8) ADAMS [William Ross Jr(7), Irene Elizabeth(6)
Wolf, Sherman E.(5), Franklin(4), Simon(3), Frederick(2), Daniel(1)]
    Karen Ann Adams, third child of William Ross Jr. and Barbara Ann
(Sprankle) Adams, was born 26 June 1960 at Frederick, Frederick
County, MD. She married 18 June 1983 at Middletown, Frederick County
Thomas Ray Sullivan.
    Childen of Thomas Ray and Karen Ann (Adams) Sullivan:
3141   i Joshua Thomas Sullivan, born 24 May 1988
3142   ii Juli Ann Sullivan, born 13 December 1989

2632 - CHARLES EDWARD(8) ADAMS [William Ross Jr(7), Irene Eliza-
beth(6) Wolf, Sherman E.(5), Franklin(4), Simon(3), Frederick(2),
Daniel(1)]
    Charles Edward Adams, fourth child of William Ross Jr. and
Barbara Ann (Sprankle) Adams, was born 12 June 1961 at Frederick,
Frederick County, MD. He married 18 May 1985 at Maplewood, NJ Nancy
Jane Wilderotter.
    Child of Charles Edward and Nancy Jane (Wilderotter) Adams:
3143   i Jaclyn Marie Adams, born 31 December 1989

2633 - KELLEY LYNN(8) ANGLEBERGER [Barbara(7) Adams, Irene
Elizabeth(6) Wolf, Sherman E.(5), Franklin(4), Simon(3), Frederick(2),
Daniel(1)]
    Kelley Lynn Angleberger, first child of Thomas H. and Barbara
(Adams) Angleberger, was born 17 April 1965 at Frederick, Frederick
County, MD. She married 7 June 1986 at Jefferson, Frederick County
Lance Brian Hood.
    Child of Lance Brian and Kelley Lynn (Angleberger) Hood:
3144   i Jesse Thomas Hood, born 8 September 1990 at Frederick,
         Frederick County, MD

2639 - KIRK DOUGLAS(8) SUNDERLAND [Carolyn(7) Lohr, Ellsworth
Franklin(6), Florence Estella(5) Wolf, Franklin(4), Simon(3), Freder-
ick(2), Daniel(1)]
    Kirk Douglas Sunderland, first child of William and Carolyn
(Lohr) Sunderland, was born 25 January 1955 at Hagerstown, Washington
County, MD. He married 1) 2 June 1974 at Hagerstown Donna Sue Jones,
born 30 November 1954 in Maryland and 2) 19 June 1982 at Hagerstown
Ivy Lee Littman, born 22 October 1943 in New York.
    Child of Kirk Douglas and Donna Sue (Jones) Sunderland:
  3145   i Sean Sunderland, born about 1976

    2648 - KIMBERLY DIANE(8) HINES [Charles Eugene(7), Louise Laur-
aetta(6) Lohr, Florence Estella(5) Wolf, Franklin(4), Simon(3),
Frederick(2), Daniel(1)]
    Kimberly Diane Hines, first child of Charles Eugene and Leana
Irene (Bailey) Hines, was born 12 September 1959 at Hagerstown,
Washington County, MD. She married 21 November 1979 at Hagerstown
William Mills, born 6 July 1954 at Patterson, NJ.
    Children of William and Kimberly Diane (Hines) Mills, born at
Hagerstown, Washington County, MD:
  3146   i Natalie Marie Mills, born 5 March 1981
  3147   ii Danielle Louise Mills, born 9 September 1986

    2649 - KELLI LYNN(8) HINES [Charles Eugene(7), Louise Laur-
aetta(6) Lohr, Florence Estella(5) Wolf, Franklin(4), Simon(3),
Frederick(2), Daniel(1)]
    Kelli Lynn Hines, second child of Charles Eugene and Leana Irene
(Bailey) Hines, was born 15 February 1963 at Hagerstown, Washington
County, MD. She married 22 November 1980 at Hagerstown Michael Byers,
born 28 January 1962 at Williamsport, Washington County.
    Children of Michael and Kelli Lynn (Hines) Byers, born at Hager-
stown, Washington County, MD:
  3148   i Dustin Michael Byers, born 28 February 1982
  3149   ii Jeremy Lynn Byers, born 30 March 1984

    2662 - ALICE SUE(8) BAKER [Janice Marlene(7) Alton, Pauline
Mary(6) Wolfe, Truman Leo(5), Franklin(4), Simon(3), Frederick(2),
Daniel(1)]
    Alice Sue Baker, first child of Conrad Eugene and Janice Marlene
(Alton) Baker, was born 30 June 1955 at Hagerstown, Washington County,
MD. She married 31 August 1973 at Hagerstown Gaylord Edward Decker,
born 28 January 1953 at Neschoppen, PA, son of Jack N. and Flora Ann
(Rohrbacker) Decker.
    Children of Gaylord Edward and Alice Sue (Baker) Decker, born at
Hagerstown, Washington County, MD:
  3150   i Ami Sue Decker, born 6 March 1974
  3151   ii Kelli Brooke Decker, born 8 September 1976
  3152 iii Timothy Edward Decker, born 30 December 1977
  3153   iv Douglas Mark Decker, born 2 April 1982
  3154   v Joshua Nathaniel Decker, born 12 July 1983

    2663 - MARK EUGENE(8) BAKER [Janice Marlene(7) Alton, Pauline
Mary(6) Wolfe, Truman Leo(5), Franklin(4), Simon(3), Frederick(2),
Daniel(1)]
    Mark Eugene Baker, second child of Conrad Eugene and Janice
Marlene (Alton) Baker, was born 29 April 1959 at Hagerstown, Washing-
ton County, MD. He married 30 January 1988 at Clearspring, Washington
County Sandra Lee Repp, born 20 March 1963 at Hagerstown., daughter of

David Allen and Donna (Egolf) Repp.
    Child of Mark Eugene and Sandra Lee (Repp) Baker:
3155   i Atlee Tyler Baker, born 3 June 1989 at Hagerstown, Wash-
        ington County, MD

    2688 - DRISTA DENISE(8) MOON [Nancy Lee(7) Baker, Helen Eliza-
beth(6) Rinehart, Fannie Elizabeth(5) Wolfe, Harvey J.(4), Simon(3),
Frederick(2), Daniel(1)]
    Drista Denise Moon, second child of Phillip Glen and Nancy Lee
(Baker) Moon, was born 23 October 1960 at Hagerstown, Washington
County, Md. She married 1) 8 December 1978 at Hagerstown Charles
Patrick Neville Jr., born 3 May 1961, son of Charles Patrick Sr. and
Catherine (_____) Neville. They divorced and Drista married 2) at
Hagerstown Theron Ray Sowers, born 7 June 1958 at Hagerstown.
    Children of Theron Ray and Drista Denise (Moon) Sowers, born at
Hagerstown, Washington County, MD:
3156   i Richard Lee Sowers, born 25 July 1980
3157   ii Robert Wayne Sowers, born 21 March 1984

    2694 - JAMES LEE JR(8) GRANT [James Lee Sr(7), Thelma Marie(6)
Rinehart, Fannie Elizabeth(5) Wolfe, Harvey J.(4), Simon(3), Freder-
ick(2), Daniel(1)]
    James Lee Grant Jr., first child of James Lee Sr. and Sandra
(Mills) Grant, was born 14 March 1957 at Pensacola, Santa Rosa County,
FL. He married 1) 20 September 1975 at Hagerstown, Washington County,
MD Anna Marie Baker, born 3 March 1957 at Hagerstown, 2) Kimberly Sue
Way, born 30 April 1963 at Hagerstown and 3) Jacqueline Kay Mason,
born 20 January 1961 in Maryland.
    Child of James Lee Jr. and Anna Marie (Baker) Grant:
3158   i Jamie Marie Grant

    2697 - KEITH DUANE(8) GRANT [James Lee Sr(7), Thelma Marie(6)
Rinehart, Fannie Elizabeth(5) Wolfe, Harvey J.(4), Simon(3), Freder-
ick(2), Daniel(1)]
    Keith Duane Grant, fourth child of James Lee Sr. and Patricia Ann
(Gaver) Grant, was born 17 June 1968 at Waynesboro, Franklin County,
PA. He married Carilyn Elizabeth Chambers, born February 1968 in
Maine.
    Child of Keith Duane and Carilyn Elizabeth (Chambers) Grant:
3159   i Kelly Marie Grant, born 11 April 1990 in Germany

    2724 - LAURI ANN(8) BURKETT [Susan Fleet(7) Highbarger, Paul
George W.(6), Harry Luther Sr(5), Catherine(4) Wolf, Jacob(3), Freder-
ick(2), Daniel(1)]
    Lauri Ann Burkett, first child of Donald Lee and Susan Fleet
(Highbarger) Burkett, was born 10 December 1962 at Hagerstown, Washington County, MD. She married 8 April 1983 at Hagerstown Kenneth
Joseph Galbus Jr., born 18 April 1961 at Hagerstown, son of Kenneth
Joseph Galbus Sr.
    Children of Kenneth Joseph Jr. and Lauri Ann (Burkett) Galbus,
born at Hagerstown, Washington County, MD:
3160   i Derek Paul Galbus, born 14 November 1983
3161   ii Alisha Ann Galbus, born 17 February 1988

    2736 - STEPHANIE COULSON(8) KIGHT [Barbara Louise(7) Wolf,
Charles Coulson(6), Charles Welty(5), John Albaugh(4), Jacob(3),
Frederick(2), Daniel(1)]
    Stephanie Coulson Kight, first child of Robert Clark and Barbara

Louise (Wolf) Kight, was born 21 October 1962 at Washington, DC. She
married 26 November 1988 at Crofton, Anne Arundel County, MD John
Anthony Haley, born 6 November 1962 at Staten Island, NY, son of John
Edward and Mary Catherine (Walsh) Haley.
    Child of John Anthony and Stephanie Coulson (Kight) Haley:
  3161A   i Meghan Hill Haley, born 10 August 1992 at Silver Spring,
            Montgomery County, MD

    2746 - WAYNE WENDELL(8) WOLFE [Merritt Wendell(7), Arthur Wen-
dell(6), Henry (5), Christina(4) Paulus, Daniel(3), Christina(2) Wolf,
Daniel(1)]
    Wayne Wendell Wolfe, first child of Merritt Wendell and Catherine
Elizabeth (Wimmer) Wolfe, was born 30 June 1950. He married Shelly Ann
Pifer, born 20 July 1950.
    Child of Wayne Wendell and Shelly Ann (Pifer) Wolfe:
  3162   i Jennifer Rebecca Wolfe, born 28 August 1979

    2748 - JOANNE ARLYN(8) WITTE [Edith Pauline(7) Ridenour, Lessie
Irene(6) Hollehan, Joseph Harrison (5), Lucy Ann(4) Paulus, Daniel(3),
Christina(2) Wolf, Daniel(1)]
    Joanne Arlyn Witte, first child of Edward William and Edith
Pauline (Ridenour) Witte, was born 19 April 1930 at Ft. Wayne, IN,
died 15 August 1985, buried in Lindenwood Cemetery, Ft. Wayne. She
married 12 July 1952 at Ft. Wayne Keith Eugene Schinbeckler.
    Children of Keith Eugene and Joanne Arlyn (Witte) Schinbeckler:
+ 3163   i Homer David Schinbeckler, born 20 February 1953
  3164   ii Thomas Edward Schinbeckler, born 17 December 1958

    2752 - LEWIS GARFIELD(8) RIDENOUR [Paul Joseph(7), Lessie
Irene(6) Hollehan, Joseph Harrison(5), Lucy Ann(4) Paulus, Daniel(3),
Christina(2) Wolf, Daniel(1)]
    Lewis Garfield Ridenour, second child of Paul Joseph and Juanita
(Leeth) Ridenour, was born 2 September 1946. He married 8 June 1968
Elizabeth Smith.
    Children of Lewis Garfield and Elizabeth (Smith) Ridenour:
  3165   i Anne Renee Ridenour, born 17 July 1972 at Berlin, Germany
  3166   ii Paul Joseph Ridenour, born 17 December 1980

    2753 - BARBARA MARIE(8) WHITE [Dorothy Elsie(7) Ridenour, Lessie
Irene(6) Hollehan, Joseph Harrison(5), Lucy Ann(4) Paulus, Daniel(3),
Christina(2) Wolf, Daniel(1)]
    Barbara Marie White, first child of Arnold and Dorothy Elsie
(Ridenour) White, was born 10 June 1941 at Ft. Wayne, IN. She married
21 January 1960 Lewis Grignol.
    Children of Lewis and Barbara Marie (White) Grignol, born at
Erie, PA:
  3167   i Kathryn Sue Grignol, born 12 September 1961
  3168   ii Leslie Jane Grignol, born 4 October 1962
  3169 iii Kimberly Ann Grignol, born 18 October 1963

CHAPTER No. 10

NINTH GENERATION

2839 - MARVIN(9) EBERLY [Carolyn(8) Montel, Deverl(7),
Charles(6), Samuel(5), Abraham(4), Susan(3) Wolf, Jacob(2), Daniel(1)]
    Marvin Eberly, first child of Dean and Carolyn (Montel) Eberly,
was born 28 August 1952. He married 26 October 1979 Debra Montique.
    Child of Marvin and Debra (Montique) Eberly:
3170   i Brad Micheal Eberly, born 13 April 1981

2840 - PAMELA SUE(9) EBERLY [Carolyn(8) Montel, Deverl(7),
Charles(6), Samuel(5), Abraham(4), Susan(3) Wolf, Jacob(2), Daniel(1)]
    Pamela Sue Eberly, second child of Dean and Carolyn (Montel)
Eberly, was born 9 November 1954. She married 24 June 1973 John Nixon.
    Child of John and Pamela Sue (Eberly) Nixon:
3171   i Ted Ryon Nixon, born 2 February 1976

2849 - TIMOTHY ROGER(9) MONTEL [Roger(8), Deverl(7), Charles(6),
Samuel(6), Abraham(4), Susan(3) Wolf, Jacob(2), Daniel(1)]
    Timothy Roger Montel, second child of Roger and Karen Elaine
(Bowen) Montel, was born 12 July 1960. He married 27 October 1980
Rebecca Elaine Fowler, born 1 January 1962.
    Child of Timothy Roger and Rebecca Elaine (Fowler) Montel:
3172   i Adam Trent Montel, born 24 July 1981

2977 - JULIE LYNN(9) HIGHLEY [Judith Ann(8) Caldwell, Milton
Charles Sr(7), Emmet Edmunds(6), Margaret Jane(5) Wolfe, Simon P.(4),
Jacob Jr(3), Jacob(2), Daniel(1)]
    Julie Lynn Highley, first child of William Ray Sr. and Judith Ann
(Caldwell) Highley, was born 22 January 1961 at Good Samaritan Hospi-
tal, Dayton, OH. She married 6 September 1980 at Dayton James C.
Clapp, born 17 October 1960, son of James Coulson and Joan (Murray)
Clapp.
    Child of James C. and Julie Lynn (Highley) Clapp:
3173   i Jodi Suzanne Clapp, born 6 October 1984 at Dayton, OH

2999 - DANA RENE'(9) BROWN [Bonna Delene(8) Oyler, Dorothy
Jane(7) Caldwell, William Arthur(6), Margaret Jane(5) Wolfe, Simon
P.(4), Jacob Jr(3), Jacob(2), Daniel(1)]
    Dana Rene' Brown, second child of Gary Allen and Bonna Delene
(Oyler) Brown, was born 22 January 1966. She married James Anthony
Staccis.
    Child of James Anthony and Dana Rene' (Brown) Staccis:
3174   i Tony Allen Staccis

3035 - CYNTHIA LYNN(9) PACKARD [Shirley Lee(8) Williamson, Clara
Monzel(7) Snavely, Vada Estella(6) Michael, Lydia Ladoskey(5) Wolf,
George Isaac(4), Jacob Jr(3), Jacob(2), Daniel(1)]
    Cynthia Lynn Packard, first child of Kenneth Levon and Shirley
Lee (Williamson) Packard, was born 5 December 1954 at Logansport, Cass
County, IN. She married 28 May 1972 Michael Alan Hardy.
    Children of Michael Alan and Cynthia Lynn (Packard) Hardy:
3175   i Jeremy Alan Hardy, born 11 December 1972
3176   ii Christopher Michael Hardy, born 26 June 1976

3036 - TERRY QUENTIN(9) PACKARD [Shirley Lee(8) Williamson, Clara
Monzel(7) Snavely, Vada Estella(6) Michael, Lydia Ladoskey(5) Wolf,
George Isaac(4), Jacob Jr(3), Jacob(2), Daniel(1)]
    Terry Quentin Packard, second child of Kenneth Levon and Shirley
Lee (Williamson) Packard, was born 7 May 1974 at Monticello, White
County, IN. He married 31 July 1972 Cynthia Dianne Ashby.
    Child of Terry Quentin and Cynthia Dianne (Ashby) Packard:
  3177   i Jessica Marie Packard, born 7 May 1979, died 28 March
            1982, a crib death

3085 - LESLIE DAVID(9) OWENS [Dolores Ann(8) Jacobs, Fred
Jacob(7), Myrtle Annie(6) Wolfe, Simon Peter(5), Michael(4), Daniel
Sr(3), Frederick(2), Daniel(1)]
    Leslie David Owens, first child of Billie Leonard and Dolores Ann
(Jacobs) Owens, was born 15 August 1953 at St. Joseph, Buchanan
County, MO. He married 1 March 1976 at Grant City, Worth County, MO
Garland May Wake, born 30 June 1952 at Maryville, Nodaway County, MO,
daughter of Stanton Carlyle and Elaine Beverely (Cordell) Wake.
    Children of Leslie David and Garland May (Wake) Owens:
  3178   i Christy Michelle Wake Owens, adopted, born 28 December
            1973 at Mt. Ayr, Ringgold County, IA
  3179   ii Arthur Ray Owens, born 8 April 1978 at San Francisco, San
            Francisco County, CA

3086 - SHARON ANN(9) OWENS [Dolores Ann(8) Jacobs, Fred David(7),
Myrtle Annie(6) Wolfe, Simon Peter(5), Michael(4), Daniel Sr(3),
Frederick(2), Daniel(1)]
    Sharon Ann Owens, second child of Billie Leonard and Dolores Ann
(Jacobs) Owens, was born 11 October 1954 at Grant City, Worth County,
MO. She married 5 September 1973 at Grant City Robert Leslie Supinger,
born 27 May 1954 at Maryville, Nodawy County, MO, son of James and
Sarah Edith (Thompson) Supinger.
    Children of Robert Leslie and Sharon Ann (Owens) Supinger, born
at Albany, Gentry County, MO:
  3180   i Audrey Elaine Supinger, born 23 July 1974
  3181   ii Robert Alan Supinger, born 13 February 1978
  3182 iii Jessica Rene' Supinger, born 5 November 1980

3087 - CARROL LYNN(9) OWENS [Dolores Ann(8) Jacobs, Fred
David(7), Myrtle Annie(6) Wolfe, Simon Peter(5), Michael(4), Daniel
Sr(3), Frederick(2), Daniel(1)]
    Carrol Lynn Owens, third child of Billie Leonard and Dolores Ann
(Jacobs) Owens, was born 24 November 1956 at Yuma, Yuma County, AZ.
She married 1)   28 May 1976 at Isadora, Worth County, MO Royce Lee
Farr, no children. They divorced and she married 2) 13 October 1979 at
St. Joseph, Buchanan County, MO Douglas Michael Duy Sr., born 1
September 1954 at Kansas City, Wyandotte County, KS, son of Herbert
Donald and Dorothy Emily (Knolte) Duy.
    Children of Douglas Michael and Carrol Lynn (Owens) (Farr) Duy,
born at Tucson, Pima County, Az:
  3183   i Douglas Michael Duy Jr., born 13 April 1984
  3184   ii William Alexander Duy, born 13 February 1986
  3185 iii Andrew Christian Duy, born 11 January 1988

3088 -LEONARD DOUGLAS(9) OWENS [Dolores Ann(8) Jacobs, Fred
Jacob(7), Myrtle Annie(6) Wolfe, Simon Peter(5), Michael(4), Daniel
Sr(3), Frederick(2), Daniel(1)]
    Leonard Douglas Owens, fourth child of Billie Leonard and Dolores

Ann (Jacobs) Owens, was born 15 December 1958 at Yuma, Yuma County, AZ. He married 1) 20 May 1977 at Grant City, Worth County, MO Almeda Marie Morrow, born 23 January 1960, they divorced; 2) 19 June 1981 Gabriele Eisenbeis, born 12 December 1962, they divorced; 3) 22 September 1988 at Thibadoux, Lafourche Parish, LA Debra Ann Tatro, born 7 October 1957 at Burlington, Chittenden County, VT.
    Child of Leonard Douglas and Almeda Marie (Morrow) Owens:
  3186   i Christopher Ryan Owens, born 14 December 1977
    Child of Leonard Douglas and Gabriele (Eisenbeis) Owens:
  3187   i Jeremie Wayne Owens, born 16 March 1983 at Lawton, Comanche County, OK
    Child of Leonard Douglas and Debra Ann (Tatro) Owens:
  3188   i Jeffery Owens, born 29 September 1988 at Thibadoux, Lafourche Parish, LA

    3090 - JOHN ERIC(9) JACOBS [John David(8), Fred Jacob(7), Myrtle Annie(6) Wolfe, Simon Peter(5), Michael(4), Daniel Sr(3), Frederick(2), Daniel(1)]
    John Eric Jacobs, second child of John David and Wilma Kay (Van Meter) Jacobs, was born 27 June 1966 at King City, Gentry County, MO. He married 3 July 1987 at King City Margery Ann Schlosser, born 8 November 1969 at Torrence, CA, daughter of Robert Anthony and Linda Joyce (Armagost) Schlosser.
    Child of John Eric and Margery Ann (Schlosser) Jacobs:
  3189   i Valerie Renee Jacobs, born 19 December 1986 at St. Joseph, Buchanan County, MO

    3103 - BOYCE ENOCH(9) BAILEY [Sonya Rae(8) Wolfe, Albert Harold(7), Frank Peter(6), Simon Peter(5), Michael(4), Daniel Sr(3), Frederick(2), Daniel(1)]
    Boyce Enoch Bailey, first child of Elvin Vernon and Sonya Rae (Wolfe) Bailey, was born 22 April 1959. He married Michele Thompson, born 11 September 1960.
    Children of Boyce Enoch and Michele (Thompson) Bailey:
  3190   i Nicholas Bailey, born 27 November 1981
  3191   ii Amanda Bailey, born 8 October 1984
  3192 iii Dawn Marie Bailey, born 20 March 1989

    3105 - VERNON ALBERT(9) BAILEY [Sonya Rae(8) Wolfe, Albert Harold(7), Frank Peter(6), Simon Peter(5), Michael(4), Daniel Sr(3), Frederick(2), Daniel(1)]
    Vernon Albert Bailey, third child of Elvin Vernon and Sonya Rae (Wolfe) Bailey, was born 2 October 1964. He married Teresa Warner.
    Child of Vernon Albert and Teresa (Warner) Bailey:
  3193   i Nichole Bailey, born 28 September 1986

    3163 - HOMER DAVID(9) SCHINBECKLER [Joanne Arlyn(8) Witte, Edith Pauline(7) Ridenour, Lessie Irene(6) Hollehan, Joseph Harrison(5), Lucy Ann(4) Paulus, Daniel(3), Christina(2) Wolf, Daniel(1)]
    Homer David Schinbeckler, first child of Keith Eugene and Joanne Arlyn (Witte) Schinbeckler, was born 20 February 1953. He married Katherine Klatte.
    Child of Homer David and Katherine (Klatte) Schinbeckler:
  3194   i Logan Jarrett Schinbeckler, born 20 October 1980

#76 George Isaac and Margaret (Tolen) Wolf

Robert and #79 Magdalena L. (Wolf) Cree

#87 Hiram William and #50 Malinda Ann (Wolf) Shroyer Family
Irene, Carl, Nellie, Evalee, Harvey, Alice, Harry

Crystal Rose (Wisecup) Jacobs, seated right,
widow of #1631 Fred David Jacobs, on the occasion
of the celebration of her 80th birthday
Children #2573 Delores Ann (Jacobs) Owens,
#2575 Edwin William and #2574 John David Jacobs

Louisiana (Treon) and #192 Daniel Paulus

Jacob and #198 Christina (Paulus) Wolf

Children of #538 Samuel Delbert and Lola Augusta
(Wilkerson) Paulus: (standing) #1069 Leon Virgil,
#1068 Jay Woodrow, #1065 Lawrence Bernarr Sr.,
#1072 Russell Weldon: (seated) #1067 Thelma Esther
Reed, #1070 Evangeline K. Baker, #1066 Helen C. Hickman
(1979)

About 1880

About 1923

With his second wife Ella
Mary (Fridley), widow of his
brother #180 Carlton Emmert
Wolf on the occasion of
their marriage.

Holding two of his grand-
sons, #1022 Charles C. and
#1021 John F. Bernard Wolf.

#182 John Albaugh Wolf

293

#178 Van Luther and Jane L. (Fry) Wolf

#180 Carlton Emmert and Ella Mary (Fridley) Wolf

#182 John Albaugh and Ella Mary (Fridley) Wolf
with daughter #498 Mary Ellen (Wolf) and
Jacob Krauss Rhoads and son #1024 Donald Wolf Rhoads

#181 Catherine (Wolf) Highbarger

#496 Charles Welty Wolf

#222 Fred Wade and Jennie (Nickel) Wolf

Earl Sims Sr. and #683 Mary Turner (Wolf) Turman

Julia Cornelia (Foreman) Wolf, wife
of #1022 Charles Coulson Wolf

#1022 Charles Coulson Wolf, picture
taken 1978 during a golf trip to Scotland.

#1757 Barbara Louise (Wolf) Kight

Family of #1757 Barbara (Wolf) Kight. #2738 Robert Jr.,
#2736 Stephanie (Kight) Haley, Barbara, Robert Clark
Kight, #2737 Lindley (Kight) Bucci

#1758 Mary Julia (Wolf) Good

Family of #1578 Mary Julia (Wolf) Good. John L. Good,
#2740 Margaret Emily, # 2741 Claire Julia, #2758 Mary
Julia (Wolf) Good, #2739 Katharine Anne.

Tombstones of #28 Tracy (Wolf) Blecker and
#29 Sarah (Wolf) Stinger in Schang
Church Cemetery, Boonsboro, Washington Co., MD

Tombstones of #32 Jacob and Mary Ellen (Albaugh)
Wolf in Boonsboro Cemetery, Washington Co., MD

Tombstone of #5 Frederick Wolf in old
Reformed Church Cemetery, Boonsboro,
Washington Co., MD

Tombstone of Magdalene (Schmidt) Wolf, wife of
#5 Frederick, in Schang Church Cemetery,
Boonsboro, Washington Co., MD

House on property of #1Daniel Wolf
in Frederick County, MD 1784-1800.
Picture taken in 1985

INDEX

A few notes of clarification will be appropriate to aid in the use of this index.

The index includes only the names of direct descendants of Daniel Wolf (#1) and their spouses. No locations, events, etc. are included.

Although several surnames have had multiple spellings over the years, the index has been prepared using a single spelling (the most common), thus both Wolf and Wolfe appear under the Wolf listing. The same principle applies to other surname variations.

Females have been listed under both their married and maiden names, when the maiden name is known.

For each direct descendant the unique number assigned to that individual in the text is shown in the index.

A Supplemental Index follows the original Index containing names inadvertently omitted from the original Index.

BEAVERS, Patricia(2053) 186
BECKOM, Amanda Lynn(3012) 265
BECKOM, Cynthia Lynn(2424) 265
BECKOM, Robert Wayne 265
BECHTOL, Lucretia Beatrice 145
BECHTOLD, Shelba 250
BECK, Bruce 90
BECK, Eva(782) 90
BECKER, Albert M. 97
BECKER, Bessie Luceal(902) 97
BECKER, Viola 148
BECKMAN, Barry Scott(2613) 230
BECKMAN, Bruce Robert(2612) 230
BECKMAN, Joan Elise(1669) 230
BECKMAN, Walter Fay 230 .
BECKOM, Barbara May 222
BEEN, Bernice 145
BEERS, Mary 80
BEIGHT, Bertha V. 132
BELL, Donna Allison(2067) 187
BELL, Elizabeth(400) 62
BELL, Ginger M. 187
BELL, Marilyn Josephine 264
BELL, Peggy Ann 187
BENCHOFF, Dorothy Louise 160
BENCHOFF, Edith Marie(486) 106
BENCHOFF, James C. Jr.(1010) 106
BENCHOFF, James Carroll Sr. 106
BENCHOFF, Phillip Edwin(1738) 161
BENCHOFF, Phyllis Elaine(1012) 106
BENCHOFF, Theron E.(1011) 106, 160
BENNETT, Elizabeth 39
BENNETT, George Lee 251
BENNETT, Henry(406) 62
BENNETT, John 62
BENNETT, Pheby 36
BENNETT, Tara Elizabeth(2833) 251
BERKLEY, Cora(893) 96
BERRY, Eunice Loretta(1933) 176
BERRY, Rowena May(1932) 176
BESS, Virginia P. 187
BETTINGER, Elaine Sue(2533) 224
BETTINGER, Marvin Lowel 224
BETTS, Sara Lee(2591) 275
BIERSWORTH, Harry 52
BIERSWORTH, Ludie Alice(235) 53
BILLINGS, Elizabeth C. 211
BILZ, Paige Ann 190
BIRT, Catherine Elaine 255
BISHOP, Cheryl Lynn 242
BISMAN, Jacob 41

BISMAN, Magdalena(130) 41
BITTNER, Shawn Renae 234
BLACK, Anita 185
BLACK, Barbara 185
BLACK, Beckie 185
BLACK, Bobby Lyn 185
BLACK, Carl Edwards(2038) 185
BLACK, Carla 185
BLACK, Charles Ray(2039) 185
BLACK, Chester Monroe 185
BLACK, Chris 185
BLACK, Douglas 185
BLACK, Emily Elizabeth 116
BLACK, Evon C.(1165) 185
BLACK, James 185
BLACK, Jeff 185
BLACK, Joan 185
BLACK, Kathy 185
BLACK, Kimberly 185
BLACK, Marg 185
BLACK, Mary Lou 185
BLACK, Michael 185
BLACK, Nancy 185
BLACK, Pam 185
BLACK, Pat 185
BLACK, Richard Lee(2037) 185
BLACK, Robert Eugene(2036) 185
BLACK, Terry 185
BLACK, Thomas 185
BLACK, Verna Dean 193
BLACK, Virginia 185
BLACK, William 185
BLACKHURST, Katherine G. 145
BLECKER, Alice Virginia 66
BLECKER, Ann C. 43
BLECKER, Annie Virginia(469) 66, 101
BLECKER, Daniel Henry 43
BLECKER, Effie Young(472) 67, 102
BLECKER, Elizabeth(148) 43, 66
BLECKER, Elizabeth Ann 43
BLECKER, Emma Tracy(468) 66
BLECKER, George Dallas 43
BLECKER, Jacob 43
BLECKER, Jacob B.(152) 43, 66
BLECKER, John(151) 43
BLECKER, Josiah 43
BLECKER, Katie May(470) 66
BLECKER, Magdalena(150) 43
BLECKER, Mary Ann(149) 43, 66
BLECKER, Mary Catharine 43
BLECKER, Mary Elizabeth 43

BLECKER, Mary E.(471) 67, 101
BLECKER, Tracy(153) 43
BLECKER, Tracy(28) 43
BLECKER, William 43
BLOOM, Barbara Ann 169
BOBILYA, Carolyn Sue(1822) 168
BOBILYA, Douglas Kent 168
BOBILYA, George Victor 168
BOGGS, Belle Myrtle(930) 99
BOGGS, Bertha(931) 99
BOGGS, DeWitt Clinton 99
BOGGS, Mary Catherine(425) 99
BOLEY, Karen Ann 270
BOLINGER, Phyllis Eileen 208
BOLTENHOUSE, Wilma J. 127
BONER, Hattie 122
BOOKER, Malinda(859) 94
BOOKWALTER, Carol J.(2462) 217, 268
BOOKWALTER, Catherine 185
BOOKWALTER, Dale Eugene(3031) 268
BOOKWALTER, David G.(2461) 217, 267
BOOKWALTER, Floyd 217
BOOKWALTER, Glen(3033) 268
BOOKWALTER, Ida(1478) 217
BOOKWALTER, Michael Kent(3032) 268
BOOKWALTER, Ruth 217
BOOKWALTER, Shirley Ann(3030) 268
BOPE, Christina M. 76
BORDMAN, Gladys Kusmanovitch 129
BORLAND, Melba Marie(1628) 150, 227
BORLAND, Mildred(1629) 150
BORLAND, Raymond 150
BORLAND, Vera(917) 150
BOSWELL, Beth Diann(2223) 251
BOSWELL, David 251
BOURNE, Nancy Fay 243
BOUSE, Ashlee(2892) 255
BOUSE, DeNae(2889) 255
BOUSE, Marie Esther(1332) 204
BOUSE, Marlene Marie(2273) 204, 254
BOUSE, Nancy(2276) 204, 255
BOUSE, Roberta Jean(2274) 204, 254
BOUSE, Shanda(2890) 255
BOUSE, Susan 255
BOUSE, Terry Wayne(2275) 204, 255
BOUSE, Tyler(2891) 255
BOUSE, Wayne 204
BOWEN, Blaine 209
BOWEN, Karen(2357) 209, 258
BOWEN, Karen Eliane 252
BOWEN, Louise(1390) 209

BOWEN, Todd Allan(2358) 209
BOWERS, Kelly Jane 268
BOWERS, Pamela Mae 239
BOWMAN, Helen E. 179
BOYD, Agnes Malissa(1257) 191
BOYD, Ardith R. 167
BOYD, Harold 191
BOYD, Jeffery Lynn(2112) 191
BOYD, John Brandon(3013) 266
BOYD, Joyce Diane(2425) 3265
BOYD, Patricia Ann(2113) 191
BOYD, Robert R. Jr. 265
BOYD, Stanley David(2114) 191
BOYD, Steven Douglas(2115) 191
BOYER, Albert(901) 97, 150
BOYER, Alice Arretta(376) 97
BOYER, Arthur Samuel(904) 97
BOYER, Bessie Luceal(902) 97
BOYER, Charles Laird(900) 97, 150
BOYER, Dorothy(1622) 150
BOYER, Earl(1620) 150
BOYER, Edna Pauline(903) 97
BOYER, Elizabeth I.(905) 97, 150
BOYER, Florence V.(378) 61
BOYER, Irvin(899) 97
BOYER, Orlando 97
BOYER, Ray(1621) 150
BOYER, Ruth 150
BOYNTON, Charlotte(2292) 205
BRADFORD, Acil 118
BRADFORD, Lola Dale 117
BRADFORD, Margaret 115
BRADLEY, Sally Joan 241
BRANDENBURG, Mary Elizabeth 210
BRANDT, Carol Joan(2462) 268
BRANDT, Dawn Renee'(3034) 268
BRANDT, Gary Charles 268
BRECHT, Vivian 209
BREEDLOVE, James 79
BREEDLOVE, Malissa 79
BREMAN, Susan 247
BREWER, Grace Maude 84
BRICKEN, Lois Mildred(1633) 151
BRICKEN, Nolan 151
BRIDGE, Fannie 200
BRIGGS, Arlene June(1790) 166
BRIGGS, Clarence Thomas(1596) 148
BRIGGS, Franklin 148
BRIGGS, Harry(1595) 148
BRIGGS, Mabel(842) 148
BRIGGS, Patricia Mae(1597) 148

DOARNBERGER, Doris Ann(991) 157
DOARNBERGER, Gretchen C.(1710) 157
DOARNBERGER, Jeffery S.(1712) 157
DOARNBERGER, John Adam 157
DOARNBERGER, John M.(1708) 157, 236
DOARNBERGER, Michael Todd(2672) 236
DOARNBERGER, Nancy Ann(1711) 157
DOARNBERGER, Suzanne(1709) 157, 236
DOARNBERGER, Vivian Jean 236
DODSON, Dorothy Helen(1251) 125
DODSON, William 125
DONOVAN, Ada Elizabeth(748) 88
DONOVAN, Matilda 52
DONOVAN, Smith 88
DOOLEY, Jill 204
DORETOS, Pauline 234
DORSEY, Dr. Allen T. 54
DORSEY, Emma Jane(275) 54
DOTSON, Elmo 147
DOTSON, Mary Thelma(836) 147
DOTSON, Raymona(1587) 147
DOTSON, Raymond(1586) 147
DOUB, Doris Ann 170
DOUB, Esther Irene 170
DOUB, James Lee Roy 170
DOUB, Laura Irene(1849) 170
DOUB, Linda Lou 170
DOUB, Margaret Alice 170
DOUB, Marion Delbert 170
DOUGLAS, Jeffery P. 208
DOUGLAS, Mary Lou(2341) 208
DOWNHAM, Alvina Marie(1544) 145
DOWNHAM, Barbara E.(2539) 224
DOWNHAM, Bernadine Ardil(1538) 144
DOWNHAM, Elmer(1537) 144, 224
DOWNHAM, Esther(818) 144
DOWNHAM, Genevieve 224
DOWNHAM, George D.(1541) 145, 224
DOWNHAM, Ione(1540) 145
DOWNHAM, Jane Ellen 146
DOWNHAM, Janice Loren(2541) 224
DOWNHAM, Joan(2540) 224
DOWNHAM, Linda Kay(2542) 224
DOWNHAM, Lucretia(1539) 145
DOWNHAM, Mary Margaret(1543) 145
DOWNHAM, Otho Carl(1542) 145
DOWNHAM, Quincine Juanita(1545) 145
DOWNHAM, Quincy 144
DOWNHAM, Violet May 224
DOWNING, Gladys Fern 138
DOWNING, Mary Melinda 136

DOYLE, Kimberly Lynn 161
DRABENSTAT, Daniel 203
DRABENSTAT, Elaine Kay(2255) 203
DRAKE, Connors James(2779) 247
DRAKE, Dayna Christine(2157) 247
DRAKE, Jack 247
DRAPER, Beverly 191
DREHR, Margaret(865) 95, 149
DREHR, Sarah(350) 95
DREW, G. E. 181
DREW, Kathryn(2007) 181
DRILL, Myrtle O. 104
DRUDGE, Annie Jeanine(2360) 258
DRUDGE, Debra 252
DRUDGE, Larry 258
DRUDGE, Lausie Ann(2935) 258
DRUM, Meredith 185
DUCKWORTH, Barbara 129
DUDECK, Kristine 246
DULANEY, Dennis 54
DULANEY, Emma Jane(275) 54
DULLINGER, Minnie 126
DUNCAN, Patricia 220
DUNLAP, Marcell 169
DUY, Andrew Christian(3185) 284
DUY, Carrol Lynn(3087) 284
DUY, Douglas Michael Jr.(3183) 284
DUY, Douglas Michael Sr. 284
DUY, William Alexander(3184) 284

EADS, James C. 204
EADS, Mildred Phoebe(1331) 204
EADS, Miriam Donna(1337) 131
EADS, Tommy Lee(2272) 204
EAGLE, Bernice Ellen(1422) 137
EAGLE, Roger 137
EAGON, Sue 227
EARLEY, Beth Marie 234
EARLEY, Betty Jane 233
EARLEY, Beverly Ann(1688) 155
EARLEY, Cynthia Gail 234
EARLEY, Dane Cameron(2657) 234
EARLEY, David Allen(1692) 156, 234
EARLEY, Erin Nicole(2655) 233
EARLEY, Harold Herman(1687) 155, 233
EARLEY, John Leslie(2652) 233
EARLEY, Leigh Ann(2658) 234
EARLEY, Leslie Filmore(979) 103, 155
EARLEY, Lori Lynn 234
EARLEY, Madalene 155
EARLEY, Mark Bradford(2656) 234

GRIMES, Joan Beth(1383) 133, 209
GRIMES, Luther E.(2626) 231, 277
GRIMES, Mary Ann(1384) 133
GRIMES, Mildred Lucille 231
GRIMES, Rae 209
GRIMES, Richard Hamilton 231
GRIMES, Robert Dean(1382) 133, 209
GRIMES, Susanna(724) 133
GRIMES, Vickie Darlene 277
GRIMES, Virginia Lou(2352) 209
GROBY, Arlina(876) 95
GROFF, Edna 53
GROFF, Franklin 65
GROFF, Malinda 65
GRONINGER, Helen Katherine 224
GROSS, Jaqueline Jeanne(1424) 137
GROSS, Pearl 97
GROSS, Rev. Ernest Jr. 137
GROSSE, Barbara Louise 169
GROSSE, Linda Louise 169
GROSSE, Lisa Anne 169
GROSSE, Wilbur Scott 169
GROSSNICKLE, Gorman 133
GROSSNICKLE, Hattie Jane 209
GROSSNICKLE, Susanna(724) 133
GROTHRIAN, Dennis Jay 260
GROTHRIAN, Grechen Sue(2953) 260
GROTHRIAN, Joyce Ann N.(2371) 260
GROTHRIAN, Sarah Jo(2952) 260
GROVES, Carol Susan(2397) 263
GROVES, Joseph Ryan(2996) 263
GROVES, Kelly Michelle(2995) 263
GROVES, Robert John 263
GUCKIEN, Marilyn(1571) 146
GWYN, Edward Goodwin 213
GWYN, Jennifer Caldwell(2399) 213
GWYN, Priscilla Maxine(1436) 213
GWYN, Susan Elizabeth(2398) 213

HAAG, Claude 215
HAAG, Clint Lincoln(2434) 215
HAAG, Donna C.(2431) 215
HAAG, Edith Anise(1469) 215
HAAG, Eldon Duane(2422) 215
HAAG, Elizabeth Jane(1466) 215
HAAG, Gordon Edwin 215
HAAG, John L.(2430) 215
HAAG, Mona Lucy(2433) 215
HAAG, Sparkle D.(2432) 215
HAAG, Sue Marie(2429) 215
HAAS, Ada Irene 174

HAAS, Ardella Azella 113
HAAS, Arthur Lee(1947) 176
HAAS, Barbara Ellen(543) 73, 112
HAAS, Bertha Marie(552) 74, 114
HAAS, Bess 172
HAAS, Betty Viola(1872) 172
HAAS, Blanch I.(1931) 176
HAAS, Catherine Elizabeth(193) 73
HAAS, Clara 112
HAAS, Clara Viola(547) 73
HAAS, Dale Eugene(1867) 172
HAAS, Daniel Virgil(542) 73, 112
HAAS, Danny 172
HAAS, David Alan(1900) 174
HAAS, Dennis E. 172
HAAS, Donnie Lee(1936) 176
HAAS, Dorothy Ann(1943) 176
HAAS, Dorothy M.(1873) 172
HAAS, Edith May(1088) 113, 173
HAAS, Ernest Welcome(1080) 112, 171
HAAS, Ervine Ray(1938) 176
HAAS, Eunice Loretta(1933) 176
HAAS, Evelyn Lucile(1945) 2176
HAAS, Fred Jay(1941) 176
HAAS, Gertrude Ellen 174
HAAS, Gertrude M.(1935) 176
HAAS, Glenn Martin(1099) 113, 176
HAAS, Grace I. 113
HAAS, Grace M. 172
HAAS, Harry James(1868) 172
HAAS, Hattie Elizabeth 113
HAAS, Hazel Violet(1078) 112, 170
HAAS, Helen Irene(1101) 113, 176
HAAS, Herbert Seymore(1934) 176
HAAS, Herman Henry(1100) 113
HAAS, Homer Jennings(1098) 113, 176
HAAS, Jesse James 172
HAAS, Joan E. 172
HAAS, Joann M.(1871) 172
HAAS, Joseph Daniel(1081) 112, 172
HAAS, Joseph Eugene(1870) 172
HAAS, Joseph Henry 73
HAAS, Joseph Henry Jr.(548) 113
HAAS, Karen Jean(1901) 174
HAAS, Kay Yvonne(1946) 176
HAAS, Kenneth Dean(1897) 174
HAAS, Lena Arvilla(1076) 112
HAAS, Lenora H. 172
HAAS, Lulu Lurene(1079) 112, 171
HAAS, Lyle Jennings(1937) 176
HAAS, Mable Esther(1075) 112, 170

HENDERSHOT, Ralph 223
HENDERSON, Richard E. 172
HENDRICKS, Clarence 132
HENDRICKS, Dessie(1357) 132
HENDRICKS, Gladys Lee 156
HENDRIX, Debra(2604) 229
HENDRIX, Glenn 229
HENDRIX, Anne Lorraine(1664) 229
HENDRIX, Steven(2603) 229
HENRY, Bertha(779) 90, 139
HENRY, Essie(780) 90
HENRY, Eva(782) 90
HENRY, Iva(781) 90
HENRY, Penny 262
HENRY, Sarah C.(301) 90
HENRY, William 90
HENSEN, Mary Ellen 229
HERRON, Mary J. 168
HESS, Jannette Sue(1893) 173
HESS, Phillip 144
HIATT, Bessie May(1235) 124
HIATT, John 124
HICKMAN, Carolyn Sue(1822) 168
HICKMAN, Charles Emil 168
HICKMAN, Helen Christena(1066) 168
HICKMAN, Lois June(1823) 168
HICKMAN, Lola Ann(1820) 168
HICKMAN, Mary Lou(1821) 168
HICKS, Alfred Jr.(2006) 181
HICKS, Alfred Sr. 181
HICKS, Cladola(1140) 181
HICKS, Kathryn(2007) 181
HIGHBARGER, Ada May 107
HIGHBARGER, Ada May(493) 69
HIGHBARGER, Carol C.(492) 69
HIGHBARGER, Catherine(181) 69
HIGHBARGER, George W. 69
HIGHBARGER, David E.(1749) 162
HIGHBARGER, Harry L. Sr.(491) 69, 107
HIGHBARGER, H. L. Jr.(1017) 107, 161
HIGHBARGER, Jessie 69
HIGHBARGER, June A. 162
HIGHBARGER, Paul G. W.(1018) 107, 162
HIGHBARGER, Ruth Elizabeth 162
HIGHBARGER, Susan F.(1751) 162, 241
HIGHBARGER, Vincent(1750) 162
HIGHLEY, Janet Elaine(2978) 262
HIGHLEY, Judith Ann(2389) 262
HIGHLEY, Julie Lynn(2977) 262, 283
HIGHLEY, Rae Jean(2979) 262
HIGHLEY, William Ray Sr. 262

HIGHLEY, William Ray Jr.(2980) 262
HIGMAN, Annie Elizabeth 231
HILGER, Pat 228
HILL, Angela 186
HILL, Elaine(2051) 186
HILL, Georgetta 70
HILL, Isaac 186
HILL, Lois Beth(1528) 144
HILL, Lucretia(1539) 145
HILL, Mark 186
HILL, Michael J. 144
HILL, Robert 145
HINDS, Erdeen(737) 135
HINDS, L. Alice(1402) 135
HINDSLEY, Alice(577) 117
HINDSLEY, Elsie Mabel(1153) 118
HINDSLEY, Estella(1157) 118
HINDSLEY, Esther 118
HINDSLEY, Franklin P. 117
HINDSLEY, Joseph Foster(1155) 118
HINDSLEY, Lottie(1154) 118
HINDSLEY, Nelson(1158) 118
HINDSLEY, Ross(1156) 118
HINES, Charles Earl 155
HINES, Charles Eugene(1686) 155, 233
HINES, Kelli Lynn(2649) 233, 279
HINES, Kimberly Diane(2648) 233, 279
HINES, Kristin Lagena(2650) 233
HINES, Lana Irene 233
HINES, Louise Lauraetta(978) 155
HINES, Matthew Scott(2651) 233
HINKLE, Minerva Belle(877) 96
HINTON, Elaine Sybil(1909) 174
HIPKINS, Amanda Kate(3137) 278
HIPKINS, Nelson Thomas 278
HIPKINS, Seth Michael(3138) 278
HIPKINS, Sharon Kay(2629) 278
HIPP, Dora 94
HIPPLE, Andrew J.(355) 60, 95
HIPPLE, Arlina(876) 95
HIPPLE, Celia(869) 95
HIPPLE, Charles(873) 95
HIPPLE, Daniel(356) 60, 95
HIPPLE, Elizabeth Helena(107) 60
HIPPLE, Ella(362) 60
HIPPLE, Flossie(875) 95
HIPPLE, Grover(868) 95
HIPPLE, Henry(874) 95
HIPPLE, John I.(360) 60
HIPPLE, Julia(870) 95
HIPPLE, Lydia(871) 95

HIPPLE, Mary(361) 60
HIPPLE, Minerva(358) 60, 96
HIPPLE, Salome(357) 60, 96
HIPPLE, William L.(359) 60
HIPPLE, Wilson(872) 95
HIPSKIND, Susan 253
HITCH, Janet May(1956) 177
HITES, Tammie Joline 254
HLAVAC, Catherine Marion 235
HODGES, Ardella Azella 113
HOFFMAN, Allen Schindel(1707) 157
HOFFMAN, Barbara Ann(1706) 157
HOFFMAN, Dudley Curtis 157
HOFFMAN, Dudley Curtis Jr.(1705) 157
HOFFMAN, Jane Ann(2509) 221
HOFFMAN, Lucy Ellen(1496) 221
HOFFMAN, Patricia Lynn 157
HOFFMAN, Raymond Stevens 157
HOFFMAN, Rex 221
HOFFMAN, Sarah Jeannette(990) 157
HOISINGTON, Charles 274
HOISINGTON, Julie Ann(3098) 274
HOKE, Bessie May(1235) 124
HOKE, Goldie Arnetta(1234) 124
HOKE, Lucy Anna(643) 124
HOKE, William 124
HOLDEN, Irene Ann 217
HOLLAND, C. L. 64
HOLLAND, Maude Agnes(432) 64
HOLLEHAN, Clara 78
HOLLEHAN, Daniel B.(623) 78
HOLLEHAN, Delilah 123
HOLLEHAN, James Thomas(626) 78
HOLLEHAN, John 78
HOLLEHAN, John(1226) 123
HOLLEHAN, John Francis(622) 78
HOLLEHAN, Joseph H.(621) 78, 123
HOLLEHAN, Lessie Irene(1225) 123, 189
HOLLEHAN, Lucy Ann(205) 77
HOLLEHAN, Peter(625) 78
HOLLEHAN, Sally 78
HOLLEHAN, Sarah Ella(627) 78, 123
HOLLEHAN, William(624) 78
HOLLOPETER, Charles 71
HOLLOPETER, Emma Alace(519) 71
HOLLOWAY, Charles Robert Jr. 257
HOLLOWAY, Kimberly Michelle(2925) 257
HOLLOWAY, Laura Ann(2337) 257
HOOVER, Pamela Kay 203
HOLTRY, Catherine 37
HOMAN, Catherine Pauline(1623) 226

HOMAN, Clyde Oliver 226
HOMAN, Gerald E.(2565) 226
HONEYWELL, Allie May(1031) 109
HONEYWELL, Clarence 109
HONEYWELL, Ellen Martha(512) 109
HONEYWELL, Elmer(1030) 109
HONEYWELL, Flora Bell(1028) 109
HONEYWELL, Fred(1029) 109
HONEYWELL, Lucinda 109
HONEYWELL, Minnie(1032) 109
HONEYWELL, Perry C, 109
HOOD, Jesse Thomas(3144) 278
HOOD, Lance Brian 278
HOON, Alice F. 125
HOOVER, Pamela Kay 203
HORVATH, Mary Ellen 270
HOSLER, Marie(564) 115
HOSLER, Maxine(1117) 115, 178
HOSLER, Otis 115
HOSTETTLER, Fern Madeline(1890) 173
HOUCHIN, Arthur E. 122
HOUCHIN, Norma(1212) 122
HOUSER, Imogene 202
HOWARD, Melba 179
HOWE, Lona Mildred 161
HOWER, Mary Ann 234
HUBBARD, Eliza Jane 122
HUFF, Betty Arlene(1551) 225
HUFF, Donald Eugene 225
HUFF, Melody Ann(2554) 225
HUFF, Wilma Lucile 176
HUFFINGTON, Ada Blanche(489) 106
HUFFINGTON, Andrew R.(2714) 240
HUFFINGTON, Brendon J.(2723) 241
HUFFINGTON, Brittany(2722) 241
HUFFINGTON, Carlton D.(1015) 106, 161
HUFFINGTON, Carol D.(1744) 161, 240
HUFFINGTON, Christopher D.(2709) 240
HUFFINGTON, Dana E.(2710) 240
HUFFINGTON, Dennis A.(1742) 161, 240
HUFFINGTON, Eric Franklin(2708) 240
HUFFINGTON, Erin V.(2721) 241
HUFFINGTON, Frank 106
HUFFINGTON, Gail Lee 240
HUFFINGTON, Heidi 241
HUFFINGTON, James F.(1746) 161, 241
HUFFINGTON, Jami Marie(2716) 241
HUFFINGTON, Jeffrey M.(1748) 161, 241
HUFFINGTON, Joanne Lee(1747) 161, 241
HUFFINGTON, Judy A. 240
HUFFINGTON, Kathleen Ann 241

HUFFINGTON, Leigh Maurine(2707) 240
HUFFINGTON, Lona Mildred 161
HUFFINGTON, Mary Lou 240
HUFFINGTON, Maurine E.(1014) 106, 161
HUFFINGTON, Melissa K.(2720) 241
HUFFINGTON, Nicholas James(2717) 241
HUFFINGTON, Phillip David(2718) 241
HUFFINGTON, Richard W.(1745) 161, 240
HUFFINGTON, Robert D.(1743) 161, 240
HUFFINGTON, Sally Joan 241
HUFFINGTON, Sarah J.(2715) 241
HUGHES, Herbert 221
HUGHES, Jerald Gene(2494) 221
HUGHES, Mabel 93
HUFFMAN, Matilda 58
HULL, Grace 253
HULL, Roxanna Bell 149
HULTZ, Edward 190
HULTZ, Joyce 190
HULTZ, June 190
HULTZ, Malcolm(2097) 190
HULTZ, Morris(2096) 190
HULTZ, Tirzah(1243) 190
HUNTER, Raymond 274
HUNTER, Sandra Kay(3099) 274
HUNTSBERGER, Alvin Bruce 238
HUNTSBERGER, Nancy Lee(1728) 238
HUSEN, Dorothy Jean 196
HUSTED, Cinie 55
HUSTED, Elizabeth Exie 88
HUTCHENS, Beverly Jene(2220) 201
HUTCHENS, Diane E.(2221) 201, 251
HUTCHENS, Esther L.(1308) 201
HUTCHENS, William Harter 201
HYDE, Connie(2380) 261
HYDE, Donald L. 261
HYDE, Gerrianne(2962) 261
HYDE, Randy Todd(2961) 261
HYLANDER, Ina Belle 137
HYNES, Rachel 140

ILER, Alice E.(523) 72, 110, 115
ILER, Carrie(1035) 109, 163
ILER, Elizabeth 109
ILER, Emerson(1036) 109
ILER, Ezra G.(522) 72, 109
ILER, John S.(520) 72, 109
ILER, Joshua 72
ILER, Margaret(1039) 110, 163
ILER, Mariah(190), 72
ILER, Mary 109

ILER, Maude(1037) 110
ILER, Mazie 109
ILER, Robert(521) 72, 109
ILER, Ruth(1034) 109
IMMEL, Barbara Ann(2914) 256
IMMEL, Brian James(2910) 256
IMMEL, Cory Lynn(2911) 256
IMMEL, Daniel Wesly(2913) 256
IMMEL, Dawn Elizabeth(2912) 256
IMMEL, Donald Undell 256
IMMEL, Sue Anne Kay(2325) 256
INGRAM, Ann Agnes 62
INSLEY, Mary 56
IRWIN, Edith Olive(434) 64
IRWIN, Louis 64
IRWIN, Mary Elizabeth(471) 101
IRWIN, Paul Blecker(962) 101, 153
IRWIN, William L. 101
IRWIN, William Paul(1667) 153
IRWIN, Zelma 153
ISENBARGER, Retha May 166
IZOR, Barbara 35

JACKMAN, Alton R.(1278) 128, 195
JACKMAN, Alvia 128
JACKMAN, Betty Ann(1277) 128, 195
JACKMAN, Earl Wayne(1276) 128, 195
JACKMAN, Esther Irene(1273) 128, 195
JACKMAN, Jason(2152) 196
JACKMAN, Jeffery L.(2149) 195
JACKMAN, Joseph L.(1280) 128, 196
JACKMAN, Kristen N.(2151) 196
JACKMAN, Randy S.(2150) 195
JACKMAN, Robert Vance(1275) 128
JACKMAN, Shannon Marie(2145) 195
JACKMAN, Shirley 195
JACKMAN, Shirley J.(1279) 128
JACKMAN, Sue 195, 196
JACKMAN, Virginia M.(1274) 128, 195
JACKMAN, Vivian Ann(686) 128
JACKSON, Georgia Ann 169
JACKSON, Malinda A. 65
JACKSON, Shirley 267
JACOBS, Alfred Clark(1630) 151
JACOBS, Clara(911) 98
JACOBS, Crystal Rose 227
JACOBS, David Edwin 151
JACOBS, David Edwin(3092) 274
JACOBS, Dawn 227
JACOBS, Dolores Ann(2573) 227, 273
JACOBS, Edwin William(2575) 227, 274

KRETZER, Gladys Mae(983) 103
KRETZER, William 103
KRIEDER, Alfred Ray 118
KRIEDER, Mayme(1160) 118
KROLL, Beverly(2600) 229
KROLL, Kevin(2599) 229
KROLL, Martin 229
KROLL, Shirley(1646) 229
KROM, George Wayne III 255
KROM, George Wayne IV(2895) 255
KROM, Kimberly(2894) 255
KROM, Kristina(2893) 255
KROM, Nancy(2276) 255
KUHL, Ella(612) 77
KUHN, J. Edward(879) 96
KUHN, Kim Ray 203
KUHN, Louella(880) 96
KUHN, Minerva(358) 96
KUHN, Shirley Ann(2247) 203
KUNKLE, Arleva Belle(518) 72
KURTZ, Charles Edward 177
KURTZ, Gary Lynn(1960) 177
KURTZ, Janet May(1956) 177
KURTZ, Larry Dean(1959) 177
KURTZ, Rosemary(1958) 177
KURTZ, Vivian Jean(1957) 177
KURTZ, Virginia Mae(1106) 177
KUSZMAUL, Diana Ruth Marie 255
KYBURG, Billie Kay(2470) 218
KYBURG, Douglas Levi 218
KYES, Donna Jean(1835) 169
KYES, Lewis 169

LACHER, Joyce A.(1883) 173
LAHR, Cecil 132
LAMAR, Barbara Ann(1670) 154, 230
LAMAR, Bertha Isabelle(963) 102, 153
LAMAR, Earline Elise 153
LAMAR, Joan Elise(1669) 154, 230
LAMAR, Mary Elizabeth(471) 101
LAMAR, Robert Fulton(964) 102, 153
LAMAR, William Bishop 101
LAMBERT, Ella(381) 61
LAMBERT, Nancy Helen(1948) 176
LAMKEY, Earline Elise 153
LANCASTER, Trecca 253
LANDCASTER, Kathleen Ann 241
LANDIS, Ardis Joseph 145
LANDIS, Betty Arlene(1551) 145, 225
LANDIS, Doris Ruth(1550) 145, 225
LANDIS, Dortha Jean(1552) 145, 225

LANDIS, Douglas Evan(2548) 225
LANDIS, Eugene(1548) 145
LANDIS, Gerald Wayne(2547) 225
LANDIS, Jenny Lind(2549) 225
LANDIS, Lola Grace(821) 145
LANDIS, Geraldine Lucille 225
LANDIS, Wayne Lee(1549) 145, 225
LANE, Catherine E.(1096) 175
LANE, Claudia 167
LANE, Esther Virginia(1055) 167
LANE, Jennie 167
LANE, Lawrence 167
LANE, Mary Jane 78
LANE, Max Leroy(1807) 167
LANE, Neil Arden(1806) 167
LANE, Ulta M.(1925) 175
LANE, Walter Jennings 175
LANE, Wilbur M. 167
LANTZ, Mary Ann 263
LARIMORE, Delbert 91
LARIMORE, Nellie Belle(800) 91
LATHAM, Brenda Jannene 242
LAUTENSLAGER, Barbara Ellen(1683) 232
LAUTENSLAGER, Barry 232
LAUTENSLAGER, Brian(2641) 232
LAUTENSLAGER, Rebecca Lynn(2642) 232
LAVERING, Anna 72
LAVERING, Mazie 109
LAWRENCE, Beverly(1651) 152
LAWRENCE, Carl(1650) 152
LAWRENCE, Carolee 152
LAWRENCE, Pearl(950) 152
LAWRENCE, William 152
LAYKAUF, Maude(1037) 110
LAYKAUF, Otto 110
LEE, Charles 83
LEE, Charles D.(682) 83
LEE, Elmer 83
LEE, Emma(681) 83
LEE, Eva Sophronia(652) 125
LEE, Harry 83
LEE, Margaret(1249) 125
LEE, William Albert 125
LEEPER, Herbert Lee 170
LEEPER, Lewis Duane 170
LEEPER, Marvin Gene 170
LEEPER, Richard Russell 170
LEEPER, Violet Estella(1850) 170
LEETH, Juanita 244
LEFFEL, Susan 207
LEGG, Frances J.(2060) 187

MACK, Becky Sue(2333) 257
MACK, Eric J.(2920) 257
MACK, Frederick 257
MACK, Stan Ray(2919) 257
MACKEY, Charles Henry 124
MACKEY, L:illian May(644) 124
MACKEY, Mabel Violla(1236) 124
MACKEY, Sandi 197
MAHOY, Bessie(941) 100
MAHOY, Ralph 100
MAJORS, Lynn Marie 219
MAKEMSON, Lillie 94
MALHAUPT, Dorothy 194
MALHAUPT, Genevieve I.(1271) 128, 194
MALHAUPT, Kristine L.(2133) 194, 245
MALHAUPT, Marjorie F.(1270) 127, 194
MALHAUPT, Naomi B.(1268) 127, 194
MALHAUPT, Richard Carl(2132) 194, 245
MALHAUPT, Richard V.(1269) 127, 194
MALHAUPT, Verna L.(1272) 128, 194
MALHAUPT, Verner W. 127
MALHAUPT, Violet Audry(685) 127
MALHAUPT, William Richard(2759) 245
MALTZ, Jay 244
MALTZ, Judith Anne(2754) 244
MANGUSON, Catherine E. 178
MANGUSON, Deanne 178
MANGUSON, Donald E. 178
MANGUSON, Douglas M. 178
MANGUSON, Lori 178
MANGUSON, Maxine(1117) 178
MANGUSON, Robert(1977) 178
MANGUSON, Terrance 178
MANGUSON, Terry(1978) 178
MANGUSON, Thomas 178
MANGUSON, Timothy 178
MANGUSON, Vicky(1979) 178
MANGUSON, Victor 178
MANN, Cora(1149) 183
MANN, Frank E. 183
MANN, Harold E.(2022) 183
MANN, Helen(2023) 183
MANN, Retha 183
MANULA, Shirley J.(1921) 175
MANZ, Evelyn 189
MARKS, Agnes Pearl(1083) 172
MARKS, Clyde J. 172
MARKS, Harold J.(1876) 173
MARKS, Helen P.(1877) 173
MARKS, June Eleanore(1878) 173
MARKS, Marvel L.(1875) 172

MARSH, Mary E. 171
MARSHALL, Aleina Sue(2537) 224
MARSHALL, Cathy Lynn(2480) 219, 270
MARSHALL, Cora 123
MARSHALL, David A.(2479) 219
MARSHALL, Gary Joseph(2481) 219, 270
MARSHALL, Jason Alan(3055) 270
MARSHALL, Jeanell Lee(3056) 270
MARSHALL, Joseph 219
MARSHALL, Robert 224
MARSHALL, Ruby Mae(1485) 219
MARSHALL, Soledad 219
MARSHALL, Teena 270
MARTIN, Elta(778) 139
MARTIN, Harold E. 141
MARTIN, Harry F. 139
MARTIN, Kathern D.(1476) 141
MARTZ, Annie A. 45
MARTZ, Laura Henrietta 67
MARTZ, Mary 61
MARVIN, Fanny 244
MASON, Jacqueline Kay 280
MASTERS, Charles W. 186
MASTERS, Mary Alice(2056) 186
MASTERS, Ruth(1191) 186
MATHIS, Elizabeth 236
MAURER, Everett G. 257
MAURER, Janet Kay(2332) 257
MAURER, Sarah 13
MAURER, Tammy Lynn(2917) 257
MAURER, Teresa Ann(2918) 257
MAXEY, Belle Regina(2994) 264
MAXEY, Carol Susan(2397) 213, 264
MAXEY, Doris Virginia(1435) 213
MAXEY, Douglas Ray(2396) 213, 263
MAXEY, Raymond Elbert 213
MAXEY, Judi 263
MAXEY, Rose Virginia(2993) 264
MAY, Jennifer(2757) 245
MAY, Karon(2758) 245
MAY, Ronald Lee 245
MAY, Susan Marie(2130) 245
MAZAK, Effie(898) 96
MC ALISTER, Joseph E. 65
MC ALISTER, Margaret(449) 65
MC ALISTER, Maria(142) 65
MC ALISTER, Nettie(448) 65
MC CALEB, Sarah M. 98
MC CALL, Jo Ann 262
MC CAULEY, Carolyn M. 63
MC CLONE, Alice Anne(1263) 193

MILLER, Merrit 152
MILLER, Michael Roy 261
MILLER, Nancy(2713) 240
MILLER, Phyllis Jean(1407) 135
MILLER, Randall R.(2280) 205
MILLER, Richard Ray(2277) 205
MILLER, Robert 189
MILLER, Robert E. 172
MILLER, Robert J. 172
MILLER, Robert Ryan(2279) 205
MILLER, Ruth(1385) 134
MILLER, Sandra Sue 172
MILLER, Sean Mack(3023) 267
MILLER, Shana Leigh(3022) 267
MILLER, Shirley(2079) 189
MILLER, Stanley 164
MILLER, Stephanie(2712) 240
MILLER, Steven Robert 189
MILLER, Susan E.(1716) 158, 236
MILLER, Tina Marie 189
MILLER, Toni Rita(2278) 205
MILLER, Ty Michael(2967) 261
MILLER, Vern 240
MILLER, Viola Maude(756) 88
MILLER, William J. 158
MILLS, Barbara Dawn 171
MILLS, Betty Lou 171
MILLS, Carol Ann 171
MILLS, Cherie Bradean 171
MILLS, Danielle Louise(3147) 279
MILLS, Donald Leroy(1862) 171
MILLS, Donna Lurene 171
MILLS, Dorothy Esther(1861) 171
MILLS, Dorothy J. 171
MILLS, Ethel 189
MILLS, Evelyn Louise 171
MILLS, Fred Raymond(1863) 171
MILLS, Helen(2061) 187
MILLS, Kathleen D. 171
MILLS, Kimberly Diane(2648) 279
MILLS, Lawrence 187
MILLS, Leslie Ruth(2702) 239
MILLS, Lois Ann 171
MILLS, Lulu Lurene(1079) 171
MILLS, Margie Ellen 171
MILLS, Martha J. 171
MILLS, Max Chester 239
MILLS, Mary E. 171
MILLS, Natalie Marie(3146) 279
MILLS, Otis Gene(1860) 171
MILLS, Otis Otto 171

MILLS, Robert Virgil(1864) 171
MILLS, Sandra 238
MILLS, Sandra K. 171
MILLS, Stanley 187
MILLS, Stephanie F. 171
MILLS, Virginia 171
MILLS, Virginia M. 171
MILLS, William 279
MISHLER, Janis 252
MISSUD, Paul George 237
MISSUD, Stacey(2682) 237
MITCHELL, Ethel 149
MITCHELL, Irene(957) 101
MOE, Grace 200
MOHLER, Arthur Maurice 160
MOHLER, Elena Sue 160
MOHLER, Evelyn Mae(1008) 160
MOHLER, Keith Duane(1735) 160
MOHLER, Kevin Lynn(1736) 160
MOLD, Karen(2357) 258
MOLD, Roger 258
MOLD, Tamara(2933) 258
MOLD, Timmie(2934) 258
MONTEITH, Anna Ruth(1423) 137
MONTEITH, Bernice Ellen(1422) 137
MONTEITH, Beverly Jo(2386) 212, 262
MONTEITH, Byron Ellsworth(1419) 136
MONTEITH, Caroline Barbara(282) 87
MONTEITH, Charles O.(742) 87, 136
MONTEITH, Cherise Kay(2975) 262
MONTEITH, Cheryll Ann(2384) 212, 261
MONTEITH, Clara Mildred 212
MONTEITH, Cleo 136
MONTEITH, Daniel Joseph(2974) 262
MONTEITH, Darlene Louise 262
MONTEITH, Darryl Kent(2387) 212, 262
MONTEITH, Deanna Kay(1426) 137
MONTEITH, Deborah Kay(2385) 212, 261
MONTEITH, Donald Edgar(1421) 137
MONTEITH, Douglas Carter(1425) 137
MONTEITH, Douglas Edward(2972) 262
MONTEITH, Florence Alice 137
MONTEITH, Frank Allen(746) 87, 136
MONTEITH, Gary Eugene(2388) 212, 262
MONTEITH, Greg Edward(2976) 262
MONTEITH, Harold John(740) 87, 136
MONTEITH, Homer Francis(1413) 136
MONTEITH, Howard Casper(1412) 136
MONTEITH, Hugh Simon(743) 87
MONTEITH, Ira Edgar(744) 87
MONTEITH, Jaqueline Jeanne(1424) 137

PAULUS, Mazie(530) 72
PAULUS, Melvin Lawrence(516) 72
PAULUS, Nicholas Andrew 168
PAULUS, Norma(1212) 122
PAULUS, Norma Lynn(1840) 170
PAULUS, Oliver L.(634) 78, 123
PAULUS, Oscar(1194) 121, 187
PAULUS, Pam Nanette 189
PAULUS, Patricia A. 188
PAULUS, Peggy D. 167
PAULUS, Phillip(599) 76
PAULUS, Rachel(200) 48, 76
PAULUS, Rachel Ann(609) 77, 122
PAULUS, Ralph(1215) 122
PAULUS, Ray(641) 79
PAULUS, Raymond(1199) 121
PAULUS, Raymond(2062) 187
PAULUS, Ressette(613) 77
PAULUS, Richard(1071) 112
PAULUS, Richard Gordon(2078) 189
PAULUS, Robert Clayton Jr. 167
PAULUS, Robert Clayton Sr.(1813) 167
PAULUS, Robert E.(2072) 188
PAULUS, Robert M. 188
PAULUS, Rose(539) 73
PAULUS, Rose Etta(1818) 168
PAULUS, Roy(1230) 123
PAULUS, Ruby(1233)124
PAULUS, Russell Weldon(1072) 112, 169
PAULUS, Ruth E. 188, 189
PAULUS, Samuel(204) 48, 77
PAULUS, Samuel Charles(1837) 169
PAULUS, Samuel Delbert(538) 73, 111
PAULUS, Sarah 121
PAULUS, Sarah(206) 48, 78
PAULUS, Sarah Jane 71
PAULUS, Sharon Lee(2080) 189
PAULUS, Shirley(2079) 189
PAULUS, Simeon(34) 29, 49
PAULUS, Simon Flavius(515) 72
PAULUS, Simon Peter(195) 47, 74
PAULUS, Sinclair V.(1211) 122, 188
PAULUS, Stella(639) 79
PAULUS, Stephen Keith 169
PAULUS, Susan Amelia 189
PAULUS, Taresa 168
PAULUS, Terry L. 167
PAULUS, Thelma Esther(1067) 112, 168
PAULUS, Tracy Yvonne 169
PAULUS, Trenton(1204) 121
PAULUS, Velma(1042) 110

PAULUS, Vera(1231) 123
PAULUS, Vickie Leonna(1836) 169
PAULUS, Virginia 187, 188
PAULUS, Virginia P. 187
PAULUS, Warren Augustus(1208) 121, 188
PAULUS, Wilbur Harlan(2076) 188
PAULUS, William Allen(513) 72
PAULUS, William Daniel 168
PAULUS, William Francis(645) 79
PAULUS, William H.(611) 77
PAULUS, William H.(633) 78, 123
PAULUS, William J.(1229) 123
PAVEY, Barbara L.(1853) 171
PAVEY, Charles E. 171
PAVEY, Laura J. 171
PAVEY, Nancy Beth 171
PAVEY, Phillip Dennis 171
PAVEY, Roger Allen 171
PAWLOK, Deborah Ann 271
PAYNTER, Derral 221
PAYNTER, Derrel Avery(2512) 222
PAYNTER, Sheila Jeanine(1497) 221
PEACOCK, Annie 153
PEARSON, Charlene(1293) 198
PEARSON, Cheryl Marie(2185) 198, 248
PEARSON, James 198
PEARSON, Jeffry David(2186) 198
PEFFLY, Jane(368) 60
PENCE, Mary A. 137
PENN, Dale(1568) 146
PENN, Gerald Allen(1567) 146
PENN, Irene(829) 146
PENN, Jane Ellen 146
PENN, Janice(1569) 146
PENN, Larry(1570) 146
PENN, Lewis 146
PENN, Linda Fae 146
PENN, Marilyn(1571) 146
PENN, Mary Lou(1572) 146
PENN, Phyllis Ellen(1566) 146, 226
PENN, Roselyn(1573) 146
PERKINS, Denise Lynette(2160) 247
PERKINS, Stephanie Denise(2785) 247
PERKINS, Steven 247
PERKINS, Vivian Fay 183
PERRINE, Gladys(1063) 111
PERRINE, Lester 111
PERRY, Alvin 134
PERRY, Ellouise(1389) 134
PERRY, Hazel(731) 134
PERRY, Kathy 252

PESHBAUGH, Margaret(865) 149
PETER, Mary Iona 142
PETER, Myrtle Olive 135
PETERSON, Chase(3002) 264
PETERSON, Daniel James(2832) 251
PETERSON, Dianne Elizabeth(2221) 251
PETERSON, Eric Lehman 251
PETERSON, Eric William(2830) 251
PETERSON, Heather(2831) 251
PETERSON, Jessica(3003) 264
PETERSON, Mary Suzanne(2405) 264
PETERSON, Noel 264
PETTNER, Leigh Ann(2658) 234
PETTNER, Randy Allen 234
PFEIDERER, Mattie 134
PHEISTER, Ilene(1052) 111
PHEISTER, Lester 111
PHERSON, Charlotte 129
PHILLIPS, Blair Rider(2955) 260
PHILLIPS, Connie Sue(2372) 260
PHILLIPS, Jason Bradley(2954) 260
PHILLIPS, Stanley C. 260
PIARO, Stephanie 269
PICKETT, John Robert 219
PICKett, Martha Jean(2476) 219
PIERSON, Charles E. 190
PIERSON, Marjorie Adele(2099) 190
PIFER, Shelly Ann 281
PIPPENGER, Phyllis J.(1881) 173
PLANK, Burt(768) 89
PLANK, Charles(769) 89
PLANK, Clara(770) 89
PLANK, Clarissa Adelaide(294) 56
PLANK, Conrad 55
PLANK, Ella(771) 89
PLANK, Elmer(772) 89
PLANK, Frances(75) 55
PLANK, Frank(773) 89
PLANK, George C.(297) 55
PLANK, John J.(295) 55, 89
PLANK, Louanna(774) 89
PLANK, Louella F. 89
PLANK, Malinda Alice(296) 55
PLANK, Mary Elizabeth(767) 89
PLANK, Pearl(775) 89
PLANK, Rose(776) 89
PLASTERER, Joseph 197
PLASTERER, Melinda Ann(2175) 197
PLATZ, Floyd Emerson 113
PLATZ, Kenneth J.(1103) 114
PLATZ, Margaret Maycapitolia(551) 114

PLATZ, Martha Elizabeth(549) 113
PLATZ, Mildred May(1104) 114
PLATZ, Otto Clyde 114
PLATZ, Virginia Emma(1102) 114
PLESSENGER, Donald(2084) 189
PLESSENGER, Ethel 189
PLESSENGER, Frank 122
PLESSENGER, Johnny D.(1219) 122, 189
PLESSENGER, Rachel Ann(609) 122
PLETCHER, Howard R. 210
PLETCHER, Margaret Ann(2368) 210
PLUMMER, Sarah Jane 71
POCKMIER, Louise Ann(598) 76
POCKMIER, Warren 76
PONTIUS, Allen(353) 60
PONTIUS, Alna Charlene(1618) 149, 226
PONTIUS, Amanda(347) 60, 94
PONTIUS, Charles Henry(864) 95, 149
PONTIUS, Ellen(352) 60, 95
PONTIUS, John 60
PONTIUS, John(354) 60
PONTIUS, Malinda(349) 60
PONTIUS, Mary Magdalena(106) 60
PONTIUS, Milton, (866) 95
PONTIUS, Minerva 95
PONTIUS, Roxanna Bell 149
PONTIUS, Samuel(351) 60, 95
PONTIUS, Sarah(350) 60, 95
PONTIUS, Serenius(348) 60, 95
POPE, Lori Lynn 234
POTTER, Caryn Margaret(1295) 198
POTTER, Paul 198
POWELL, Robyn J. 276
PRASS, Nancy 180
PRASS, Odessa(1993) 180
PREBIL, Christina Rachelle(3072) 272
PREBIL, James 272
PREBIL, Terry Elaine(2501) 272
PRESSLER, Betty(1769) 164
PRESSLER, Emaline(533) 110
PRESSLER, Emerson 110
PRESSLER, Harlan E.(1043) 110, 164
PRESSLER, J. D.(1768) 164
PRESSLER, John Dee 164
PRESSLER, Mildred 164
PRESSLER, Pearl J. 164
PRESSLER, Ralph A.(1044) 110, 164
PRESSLER, Ralph A. Jr. 164
PRESSLER, Ronald Jay 164
PRESSLER, Ursula 164
PRESSLER, Virginia R.(1770) 164

INDEX

REED, James 226
REED, Joe 214
REED, John 254
REED, Judi(2283) 254
REED, Kiley Lane 168
REED, Marlene Marie(2273) 254
REED, Mary Ellen 168
REED, Nelletta 168
REED, Paula Jane(1827) 169
REED, Richard Allen(1824) 168
REED, Richard Leon 168
REED, Rita Mary(1828) 169
REED, Robert E. 182
REED, Rodney Joe(2414) 214
REED, Roger Lee(1825) 168
REED, Scott(2882) 254
REED, Sylvia Charlene(1448) 214
REED, Tamarah Ann 168
REED, Teresa(2881) 254
REED, Thelma Esther(1067) 168
REED, Thomas Raymond II 169
REED, Thomas Raymond(1826) 168
REED, Yvonne Irene 169
REEVES, Margaret(1405) 135
REEVES, Ruth Ellen 233
REHM, Rachel E. 136
REID, James 185
REID, Jennifer 185
REID, Richard 185
REID, Thelma L.(2042) 185
REISSE, Amanda Jayne(3020) 267
REISSE, David George 267
REISSE, Marsha Ann(2443) 267
REISSE, Scott David(3021) 267
RENAS, Hattie Elizabeth 113
RENDON, Elizabeth 239
REPP, Sandra Lee 279
RHOADE, Elaine Sybil(1909) 174
RHOADE, Gerald Roger(1912) 175
RHOADE, James Lee(1910) 175
RHOADE, Mary Lou(1911) 175
RHOADE, Raymond W. 174
RHOADE, Violet Marie(1093) 174
RHOADES, Amanda Nicole(2909) 256
RHOADES, Betty Elizabeth(1108) 177
RHOADES, Cheryl 207
RHOADES, Darl Wayne(1964) 177
RHOADES, David Milton(2319) 207
RHOADES, Delbert M.(1361) 132, 207
RHOADES, Delynde Lynn 207
RHOADES, Dorsey Hurl(1365) 132, 207

RHOADES, Elizabeth 207
RHOADES, Eugene(2318) 207
RHOADES, Eva Kathlene(1364) 132, 207
RHOADES, Hattie Jane 207
RHOADES, Iva Ann(717) 132
RHOADES, James Dorsey(2329) 207
RHOADES, Janet Edna 207
RHOADES, Jeff Allen(2908) 256
RHOADES, John David(2331) 207
RHOADES, Joseph 177
RHOADES, Joyce Ann(2324) 207
RHOADES, Leanna Mae(1362) 132, 207
RHOADES, Lisa Ann(2330) 207, 257
RHOADES, Marla Jo(2328) 207, 256
RHOADES, Martha 207
RHOADES, Michael Wayne(2323) 207
RHOADES, Patricia Ann(1965) 177
RHOADES, Sherman Alfred 132
RHOADES, Steven Earl(2320) 207, 256
RHOADES, Sue Ann 256
RHOADES, Susan 207
RHOADES, Wayne Lowell(1363) 132, 207
RHOADS, Donald Wolf(1024) 108, 163
RHOADS, Evelyn Mae 163
RHOADS, Jacob Krauss 108
RHOADS, Jane Marie 163
RHOADS, Jeffrey Scott(1761) 163
RHOADS, Kim Elizabeth(1762) 163, 243
RHOADS, Mary Ellen(498) 108
RHOADS, Ruth Elizabeth 145
RHODES, Madalene 155
RHODES, Terry 217
RICE, Albert 91
RICE, Albert Paul(1523) 144, 223
RICE, Alma 143
RICE, Arla Rose 161
RICE, Berlie A. 57
RICE, Bonnie Ruth 144
RICE, Carolyn Sue(1518) 144
RICE, Carrol Elmer(1527) 144
RICE, Chester L.(811) 91, 143
RICE, Clarissa(314) 91
RICE, Darla Kay(2527) 223
RICE, Delsinia Lilly(321) 57
RICE, Donna Louise 223
RICE, Edna 143, 144
RICE, Freda Marie(1514) 143
RICE, Gloria Ann 144
RICE, Helen Marie(1513) 143, 223
RICE, Jessie(813) 91
RICE, John Edward(1524) 144

349

ROBBS, Martha Frances(1431) 212
ROBBS, Miriam Kathleen(2391) 212
ROBBS, Timothy Drew(2392) 212
ROBERTS, Amie 188
ROBERTS, Annabelle Lou(1074) 170
ROBERTS, Carol Ann(1846) 170
ROBERTS, Christopher Brian 170
ROBERTS, James A. 188
ROBERTS, Janet(2071) 188
ROBERTS, Joy Antoinette 192
ROBERTS, Matthew Allen 170
ROBERTS, Paul Olney 170
ROBERTS, Paulette 188
ROBERTS, Randall Scott(1844) 170
ROBERTS, Rebecca Ellen 64
ROBERTS, Richard Paul(1845) 170
ROBERTS, Sharon Sue(1847) 170
ROBERTS, Shirley Anne 170
ROBERTS, Tobin 188
ROBERTS, Whitney 188
ROBERTSON, Charles 114
ROBERTSON, Duward(1109) 114
ROBERTSON, Martha Ellen(562) 114
ROBINSON, Brenda Jannene 242
ROBINSON, Celia 182
ROBINSON, Charles Victor(1755) 162
ROBINSON, Cheryl Lynn 242
ROBINSON, Dustin Wayne(2730) 242
ROBINSON, George T. 209
ROBINSON, Jana Patrice(2727) 242
ROBINSON, Joan Beth(1383) 209
ROBINSON, John Alec Jr.(2729) 242
ROBINSON, John A. Sr.(1753) 162, 242
ROBINSON, Koyya Ann(1754) 162, 242
ROBINSON, Lisa Ann(2356) 209
ROBINSON, Martha Jane 242
ROBINSON, Michael Allen(2354) 209
ROBINSON, Ruth Anne(1019) 162
ROBINSON, Sara(2728) 242
ROBINSON, Steven David(2355) 209
ROBINSON, Victor Norman 162
ROBINSON, William V.(1752) 162, 242
ROBSON, Janice Leah(1831) 169
ROBSON, Thomas R. 169
RODGERS, Dena Lin 240
RODGERS, James Allen(1741) 161
RODGERS, Joanne Marie(1013) 161
RODGERS, Kaitlyn Nicole(2706) 240
RODGERS, Kimberly Lynn 161
RODGERS, Robert Dean Jr.(1739) 161
RODGERS, Robert Dean Sr. 161

RODGERS, Steven Keith(1740) 161, 239
ROGGEE, Edna Pauline(903) 97
ROGGEE, Irvin 97
ROMOS, Soledad 219
RONK, Bessie Louella(848) 94
RONK, Earnest Lee(849) 94
RONK, Eva Lucille(845) 94, 148
RONK, Forrest Cree(847) 94, 148
RONK, Gladys Marie(846) 94
RONK, Goldalee(323) 94
RONK, Shirley May(1607) 148
RONK, Thelma 148
RONK, Thomas G. 94
ROSE, Anne(565) 74
ROSE, Bertha Marie(552) 114
ROSE, Betty Elizabeth(1108) 114, 177
ROSE, Carl W. K.(1107) 114, 177
ROSE, Dale Leroy(1105) 114, 176
ROSE, Ed 74
ROSE, Ernestine M. 177
ROSE, Hiram W. K. 114
ROSE, Jack D.(1954) 177
ROSE, Jerry Dean(1962) 177
ROSE, Kathleen Sue(1961) 177
ROSE, Pearl(885) 96
ROSE, Richard Allen(1955) 177
ROSE, Thelma V. 177
ROSE, Virginia Mae(1106) 114, 177
ROSENBURY, Judith Ann 259
ROSS, Beth Ann(2370) 210
ROSS, Dorotha Maxine(1398).134, 210
ROSS, Elmer C. 134
ROSS, Everett Max(1396) 134
ROSS, Gentry 223
ROSS, Harold Wayne(1397) 134, 210
ROSS, Helen Marie 210
ROSS, Helen Marie(1513) 223
ROSS, Keith Emerson(1395) 134, 210
ROSS, Linda Diane(2369) 210, 260
ROSS, Lizzie(734) 134
ROSS, Margaret Ann(2368) 210
ROSS, Mary Elizabeth 210
ROSS, Patricia Lee(2523) 223
ROSS, Rondra Kay(2522) 223
ROSS, Ruby(1233) 124
ROSS, Winfield 124
ROSTINSKI, Bruce Frank 191
ROSTINSKI, Carol Sue(2117) 191
ROSTINSKI, Norma Alice(1258) 192
ROSTINSKI, Terry Bruce(2116) 192
ROUSE, Carolee 152

SHAFER, Anna R. 57
SHAFFNER, Elizabeth Ann 71
SHAGLEY, Freda Marie(1514) 143
SHAMBARGER, Elaine K. 203
SHANHOLTZ, Debra Dee(1730) 238
SHANHOLTZ, Isaac Russell 238
SHANHOLTZ, Jammie Lynn(2692) 238
SHANK, Jacob 54
SHARP, June 224
SHARP, Marilyn Lou 275
SHARP, Shirley Martha 167
SHARRITT, Aaron(380) 61, 97
SHARRITT, Alice Arretta(376) 61, 97
SHARRITT, Amanda(367) 60
SHARRITT, Anna(894) 96
SHARRITT, Ann Agnes 62
SHARRITT, Bruce(910) 97
SHARRITT, Catherine(366) 60, 96
SHARRITT, Charles(883) 96
SHARRITT, Charles Edward(375) 61
SHARRITT, Clara(884) 96
SHARRITT, Clarence(890) 96
SHARRITT, Cleveland(889) 96
SHARRITT, Clyde(891) 96
SHARRITT, Cora(386) 61
SHARRITT, Daniel 38
SHARRITT, Daniel(120) 39
SHARRITT, Daniel Jr. (115) 38, 62
SHARRITT, David(888) 96
SHARRITT, David C.(387) 61
SHARRITT, Dolly(370) 60
SHARRITT, Edward(404) 62
SHARRITT, Edwin(384) 61
SHARRITT, Elizabeth 61
SHARRITT, Elizabeth(123) 39
SHARRITT, Elizabeth(21) 37
SHARRITT, Elizabeth H.(107) 38, 60
SHARRITT, Ella(381) 61
SHARRITT, Elwood(881) 96
SHARRITT, Emma(382) 61
SHARRITT, Florence M.(388) 61
SHARRITT, Florence V.(378) 61
SHARRITT, Francis(886) 96
SHARRITT, Frank(371) 60
SHARRITT, George(365) 60, 96
SHARRITT, Harley(405) 62
SHARRITT, Harvey(403) 62, 97
SHARRITT, Henry(364) 60, 96
SHARRITT, Hiram(113) 38, 61
SHARRITT, Horace Clayton(377) 61
SHARRITT, Ida(389) 52

SHARRITT, Isabel 61
SHARRITT, Jacob(116) 38, 62
SHARRITT, Jane(368) 60
SHARRITT, Joel 39
SHARRITT, John(108) 38, 60
SHARRITT, John(892) 96
SHARRITT, L. Jesse(392) 62
SHARRITT, Laura(383) 61
SHARRITT, Leah(121) 39
SHARRITT, Lemuel L.(379) 61
SHARRITT, Leonard(111) 38, 61
SHARRITT, Lester(882) 96
SHARRITT, Margaret 61
SHARRITT, Margaret(119) 39
SHARRITT, Martha(402) 62
SHARRITT, Mary 51
SHARRITT, Mary(24) 39
SHARRITT, Mary Elizabeth(373) 61
SHARRITT, Mary Magdalene(106) 38, 60
SHARRITT, Melazina 61
SHARRITT, Minerva(887) 96
SHARRITT, Minnie May(390) 62
SHARRITT, Monroe(372) 60
SHARRITT, Oma(391) 62
SHARRITT, Paul(907) 97
SHARRITT, Pearl 97
SHARRITT, Pearl(885) 96
SHARRITT, Peter(363) 60, 96
SHARRITT, Rachel(122) 39
SHARRITT, S. 61
SHARRITT, Sally(385) 61
SHARRITT, Samuel(109) 38, 60
SHARRITT, Sarah(112) 38
SHARRITT, Sarah(374) 61
SHARRITT, Savilda(369) 60
SHARRITT, Sophia(114) 38, 62
SHARRITT, Walter(908) 97
SHARRITT, William(110) 38, 61
SHAW, Ahren Lynn 193
SHAW, Gloria 219
SHAW, Kathleen Sue(1961) 177
SHAW, Lantha Louise 193
SHAW, Martha E. 70
SHEDRAN, Judith Mae 211
SHEETS, Carl 165
SHEETS, Elizabeth Catherine(1780) 165
SHEETS, Karla Kristine 165
SHEETS, Rodney C. 165
SHEETS, Roger Lesco 165
SHEETZ, Ruth 217
SHELDON, Beth Marie 234

SILER, William M.(591) 75
SILER, Winnie(1170) 119
SIMMONS, Mary 109
SINGLE, Irene(1981) 179
SINGLE, Malinda Maude(1119) 179
SINGLE, William F. 179
SIPONEN, Shana Kay 277
SKAGGS, Adam Powell(2988) 263
SKAGGS, Alexander Lance(2989) 263
SKAGGS, Amy Marianne(2987) 263
SKAGGS, Nancy Jean(2394) 263
SKAGGS, Stephen Powell 263
SKINNER, Bernard(1773) 164
SKINNER, Eugene(1772) 164
SKINNER, Gary 164
SKINNER, Wilda(1045) 164
SLACHCIAK, David 256
SLACHCIAK, Janice Leslie(2309) 256
SLACHCIAK, Jessica Lynn(2902) 256
SLATER, Donald Leroy 207
SLATER, Eva Kathlene(1364) 207
SLATER, Gregory Jay(2326) 207
SLATER, Jerilyn Jo(2327) 207
SLATER, Sue Anne Kay(2325) 207, 256
SLEICHTER, Daniel 239
SLEICHTER, Kendra Jane(2701) 239
SLEIGHTER, Diana L. 205
SLOAN, Edith 250
SMALL, Velma 190
SMANDA, Theresa Marie 271
SMELTZER, Eileen 184
SMITH, Abraham 90
SMITH, Alma Iva(787) 90
SMITH, Alvin Isaac(786) 90
SMITH, Angel 184
SMITH, Annabelle Lou(1074) 112, 170
SMITH, Archie Lee(1073) 112, 170
SMITH, Baker 184
SMITH, Benson D.(2030) 184
SMITH, Beverly Jean(2423) 215, 265
SMITH, Carol Louise(1724) 159, 237
SMITH, Caroline Evalina(302) 90
SMITH, Christena Marie(541) 112
SMITH, Christene 184
SMITH, Cora(386) 61
SMITH, Cynthia 184
SMITH, Cynthia Lynn(2424) 215, 265
SMITH, Daniel 184
SMITH, Daniel Lee(790) 90
SMITH, Deanna Mae 90
SMITH, Dee Ann(2033) 184

SMITH, Dorothy Louise 160
SMITH, Dorothy Rose(1468) 140, 215
SMITH, Douglas 184
SMITH, Edith Anise(1469) 140, 215
SMITH, Elizabeth 89, 281
SMITH, Elizabeth Jane(1466) 140, 215
SMITH, Ella(401) 62
SMITH, Elsie Armetta(783) 90
SMITH, Esther Viola 154
SMITH, Frances Evelyn 180
SMITH, Harley Monroe 112
SMITH, Henry 123
SMITH, Henry Abraham(791) 90
SMITH, Ida Margaret(785) 90, 140
SMITH, Inez L.(1162) 184
SMITH, Jack(2035) 184
SMITH, Jane 256
SMITH, Jane(1000) 159
SMITH, Janet Edna 207
SMITH, Janice Louise(1843) 170
SMITH, John Jacob(784) 90, 140
SMITH, Joseph 54, 184
SMITH, Joseph F.(2031) 184
SMITH, Kenneth 180
SMITH, Lilian 184
SMITH, Lucille E.(1164) 184
SMITH, Lydia(1228) 123
SMITH, Mamie Alice(1470) 140, 215
SMITH, Marilyn 184
SMITH, Mark 180
SMITH, Martha Belle(787) 90, 140
SMITH, Mary 179
SMITH, Mary Alice(789) 90
SMITH, Mary Ann 184
SMITH, Mary Helen 90
SMITH, Mary Valentine 215
SMITH, Marylin Sue(1842) 170
SMITH, Michael(2034) 184
SMITH, Mike 180
SMITH, Nadia Geraldine 170
SMITH, Oda(272) 54
SMITH, Patricia 184
SMITH, Rachel 140
SMITH, Rebecca 184
SMITH, Reuben 39
SMITH, Ruth(1995) 180
SMITH, Sally 78
SMITH, Sally(2032) 184
SMITH, Samuel Hynes(1467) 140, 215
SMITH, Sarah Ellen(627) 123
SMITH, Susan 184

SMITH, Susannah 17
SMITH, Viola 100
SMITH, Virgil(1227) 123
SMITH, William Woodrow 159
SNAPP, Molly 101
SNAVELY, Andrea Louise(2458) 217
SNAVELY, Carol(2459) 217
SNAVELY, Clara Monzel(1479) 141, 217
SNAVELY, David Lee(2460) 217
SNAVELY, Edna Leo(1480) 141, 218
SNAVELY, Ethel Cleo(1481) 141, 218
SNAVELY, Eve 217
SNAVELY, Ida(1478) 141, 217
SNAVELY, Ila 217
SNAVELY, James Edward(2456) 217, 267
SNAVELY, Lola Frances(1482) 141, 218
SNAVELY, Melonie(3028) 267
SNAVELY, Melvin Earl 141
SNAVELY, Robert Lee(2457) 217
SNAVELY, Rose Ovid(1477) 141, 217
SNAVELY, Ross(3029) 267
SNAVELY, Shirley 267
SNAVELY, Vada Estella(793) 141
SNELL, Hazel 200
SNELLENBERGER, Bernice(2057) 187
SNELLENBERGER, Gladys(2058) 187
SNELLENBERGER, Grover 187
SNELLENBERGER, Laura(1193) 187
SNIDER, Christine Anne(3049) 269
SNIDER, Harold William 269
SNIDER, Kathleen Helen(2477) 269
SNODGRASS, Carolyn M.(2584) 228, 274
SNODGRASS, Dorothy Pearl(1636) 228
SNODGRASS, Marvin J. 228
SNODGRASS, Sharon Lee(2585) 228
SNOEBERGER, Esther(806) 92
SNOEBERGER, Tony 92
SNOOK, Catharine 54
SNOW, Douglas Laren(2965) 261
SNOW, Flora(958) 101
SNOW, Marcia Armstrong(2383) 261
SNOW, Ronald Dick 261
SNOW, Sally(2032) 184
SNOW, Steven Dick(2964) 261
SNYDER, Anna E. 105
SNYDER, Bertha(617) 122
SNYDER, Dale 122
SNYDER, Kenneth(1220) 122
SNYDER, Mary Lou 137
SOCKS, Debra Dee(1730) 238
SOCKS, Richard Lee(2693) 238

SOCKS, Robert Frederick 238
SOLOMON, Brenda Kay(2623) 276
SOLOMON, James Benjamin(3125) 276
SOLOMON, Jonathan Neal(3127) 276
SOLOMON, Justin William(3126) 276
SOLOMON, Lon Neal 276
SOLT, Dee Ann(2033) 184
SORTOR, Agnes Malissa(1257) 126, 191
SORTOR, Camarem Marie 192
SORTOR, Cheryl Dee(2119) 192
SORTOR, Christine Ann 192
SORTOR, Estella Opal(654) 125
SORTOR, Eva Sophronia(652) 125
SORTOR, Joann 192
SORTOR, Joy Antoinette 192
SORTOR, Margaret Hills 191
SORTOR, Marvin David 125
SORTOR, Marvin Earl(1259) 126, 192
SORTOR, Michael James 192
SORTOR, Norma Alice(1258) 126, 191
SORTOR, Patricia Marie 192
SORTOR, Paul Allen(1256) 126
SORTOR, Peter E.(2104) 191
SORTOR, Randy Earl(2118) 192
SORTOR, Sina Delight(1255) 126
SORTOR, Sylvian David(1248) 125, 191
SOWERS, Drista Denise(2688) 280
SOWERS, Richard Lee(3156) 280
SOWERS, Robert Wayne(3157) 280
SOWERS, Theron Ray 280
SPANN, Connie(2380) 211, 261
SPANN, Donald Lee(2963) 261
SPANN, George William 211
SPANN, Shirley Carol 261
SPANN, Teddy Lee(2381) 211, 261
SPANN, Vera Lavon(1401) 211
SPARKS, Allen William(3131) 277
SPARKS, Lance 277
SPARKS, Lucinda 109
SPARKS, Sandra Bea(2625) 277
SPECK, Brian(2188) 199
SPECK, Caryn Margaret(1295) 198
SPECK, Collette Caryn(2189) 199
SPECK, Roger 198
SPEECE, Linda 168
SPENCE, Kim Elizabeth(1762) 243
SPENCE, Mark Alan(2743) 243
SPENCE, Mark Thomas 243
SPENCE, Michael Jacob(2745) 243
SPENCE, Robert Rhoads(2744) 243
SPERES, Lilian 184

SPICHER, Gertrude Ellen 174
SPIEGEL, Karen 273
SPIELMAN, Catherine Tracy(162) 45
SPIELMAN, Ellen Sophia(160) 45
SPIELMAN, Emory Allen(164) 45
SPIELMAN, Georgina Frances(159) 45
SPIELMAN, John Calvin(156) 45
SPIELMAN, John Jr. 44
SPIELMAN, John Luther Wolf(163) 45
SPIELMAN, Lawson(155) 45
SPIELMAN, Lizzie 45
SPIELMAN, Margaret Elizabeth(165) 45
SPIELMAN, Mary Magdalene(157) 45
SPIELMAN, Robert(161) 45
SPIELMAN, Sarah Ann 45
SPIELMAN, Sarah Elizabeth(158) 45
SPIELMAN, Sophia(30) 44
SPILDE, Britta Allison(2180) 198
SPILDE, Eric Andrew(2177) 198
SPILDE, Harley 198
SPILDE, Kirsten.Ann(2179) 198
SPILDE, Linda Ann(1291) 198
SPILDE, Thor Allen(2178) 198
SPITZER, Charles Jr. 229
SPITZER, Marilee Esther(2605) 229
SPONHAURER, Barbara 201
SPONHAURER, Beverly 201
SPONHAURER, Charles(2233) 201
SPONHAURER, Hobert D. 201
SPONHAURER, Marvey(2231) 201
SPONHAURER, Ruby(1312) 201
SPONHAURER, Sherry(2232) 201
SPRADLIN, Beverly 191
SPRADLIN, Esther 191
SPRADLIN, Gilbert E. 191
SPRADLIN, Gilbert E. II(2107) 191
SPRADLIN, Gina Marie(2110) 191
SPRADLIN, Jeffery Lynn 191
SPRADLIN, Jerry Lynn(2108) 191
SPRADLIN, Portia Lynn 191
SPRADLIN, Ronnie Lee(2109) 191
SPRADLIN, Ronnie Lee Jr. 191
SPRADLIN, Susan 191
SPRADLIN, Terry Ward 191
SPRADLIN, Virginia Ann(1254) 191
SPRANKLE, Barbara Ann 231
SPRECHER, Ada (944) 100
SPRECHER, Alice(457) 100
SPRECHER, Guy(943) 100
SPRECHER, Sam 100
SPRINGER, Christopher 185

SPRINGER, Daffney 185
SPRINGER, Jane Naomi 160
SPRINGER, Kay Frances(2047) 185
SPRINGER, Richard 185
ST JOHN, Roberta 217
STACCIS, Dana Rene'(2999) 283
STACCIS, James Anthony 283
STACCIS, Tony Allen(3174) 283
STAFFORD, Jane Ann 216
STALEY, Dorothy Carmen 155
STARKEY, Brookie 185
STARKEY, Susan(2043) 185
STARKEY, Vickie 185
STARKEY, Victor 185
STARKWEATHER, David Walter(1289) 129
STARKWEATHER, Frances Ann 197
STARKWEATHER, Janice (1288) 129, 197
STARKWEATHER, John Phillip(2174) 197
STARKWEATHER, Linda A.(1291) 129, 198
STARKWEATHER, Melinda Ann(2175) 197
STARKWEATHER, Norma Leora(694) 128
STARKWEATHER, Patricia Lynn(2173) 197
STARKWEATHER, Peter E.(1290) 129, 197
STARKWEATHER, Sandra Marie(2176) 198
STARKWEATHER, Walter Edward 129
STARLIPER, David Russell 157
STARLIPER, Gretchen Carroll(1710) 157
STAUBLIN, Arla Rose 161
STAUBLIN, Gerald David 161
STAUBLIN, Jeanne Margaret 161
STAUBLIN, Maurine Ella(1014) 161
STAUBLIN, Percy Wayne 161
STEINHILLER, Carol J.(1899) 174
STEPHENSON, Amber Lynn(2897) 255
STEPHENSON, Dale Francis Jr. 255
STEPHENSON, David Dale(2896) 255
STEPHENSON, Kathleen Sara(2285) 255
STETLER, Margaret 61
STETTLER, Margaret(865) 149
STETTLER, William(1619) 150
STEVENS, Alisa Ann(2417) 214
STEVENS, Amye Frances(761) 88
STEVENS, Charles Burton(759) 88, 139
STEVENS, Daniel Brent(2419) 214
STEVENS, Flora Marie(290) 88
STEVENS, Glen Alva(760) 88
STEVENS, Gordon Arthur(1451) 139, 214
STEVENS, Kathleen Rose(1453) 139
STEVENS, Mary 214
STEVENS, Phillip Glenn(2418) 214
STEVENS, Phyllis D.(1452) 139, 214

TRIDLE, Ella 134
TRIDLE, Elvin Peter(733) 86, 134
TRIDLE, George II 54
TRIDLE, George III(267) 54, 86
TRIDLE, Glenn(735) 86, 134
TRIDLE, Harold Leroy(2377) 211
TRIDLE, Jeanette 211
TRIDLE, Kathy Ann(2375) 211, 260
TRIDLE, Lizzie(734) 86, 134
TRIDLE, Loren Leroy(1399) 135, 211
TRIDLE, Lorna Louise(2374) 211, 260
TRIDLE, Margaret(266) 54
TRIDLE, Mary Blanche(1394) 134, 210
TRIDLE, Mary K. 211
TRIDLE, Mattie 134
TRIDLE, Sarah 86
TRIDLE, Sara Earline(2378) 211, 260
TRIDLE, Viola(736) 86, 135
TRINE, Acil 118
TRINE, Alfred H. 118
TRINE, Charles A.(1159) 118
TRINE, Lucy(578) 118
TRINE, Mayme(1160) 118
TRONE, Anna Ruth(481) 67, 104
TRONE, Charles Alfred 67
TRONE, Lucinda K.(480) 67, 104
TRONE, Mary Jeannette(173) 67
TROTTER, Audie 181
TRUMPOWER, Ida Marie 235
TRUMPOWER, Larry George 241
TRUMPOWER, Susan Fleet(1751) 241
TUCKER, Cynthia(2887) 255
TUCKER, Debra(2884) 254
TUCKER, Dennis(2886) 255
TUCKER, Jeffrey(2888) 255
TUCKER, Joann 192
TUCKER, Larry 254
TUCKER, Melody 259
TUCKER, Roberta Jean(2274) 254
TUCKER, Timothy(2885) 254
TURMAN, Benjamin F.(1262C) 127, 193
TURMAN, Dannielle 193
TURMAN, Earl Sims Jr.(1262A) 127
TURMAN, Earl Sims Sr. 127
TURMAN, Kenneth M.(1262E) 127, 193
TURMAN, Kyle Edward(2122C) 193
TURMAN, Lantha Louise 193
TURMAN, Mary Jane(1262B) 127, 193
TURMAN, Mary Turner(683) 127
TURMAN, Robert Edward(1262D) 127
TWAITS, Elizabeth 143

TYSON, George 227
TYSON, Helen Louise(1625) 227

ULREY, Ella 134
ULREY, Sarah 86
ULRICH, George Jacob 13
ULRICH, Maria Elizabetha 13
UNGER, Carol(2103) 191
URSCHEL, Alice Arretta(376) 97
URSCHEL, Charles B. 97
URSCHEL, Mary Viola(906) 97

VAN BEBBER, Nora 131
VAN DYNE, Della(912) 98
VAN LUE, Sandra 259
VAN LYSEL, Janice Elaine(1288) 197
VAN LYSEL, Karen 248
VAN LYSEL, Marvin Francis 197
VAN LYSEL, Matthew Lee(2794) 248
VAN LYSEL, Michael Scott(2170) 197
VAN LYSEL, Neil Allen(2795) 248
VAN LYSEL, Sally Lynn(2171) 197, 248
VAN LYSEL, Stephen P.(2172) 197, 248
VAN METER, Wilma Kay 274
VAN OSDOL, Dale(1443) 138
VAN OSDOL, Denny(1444) 139
VAN OSDOL, Karen(1445) 139
VAN OSDOL, Ralph Hillis 138
VAN OSDOL, Ruth Catherine(758) 138
VAN OSDOL, Wilma(1446) 138
VANITOR, Delores 165
VANITOR, Denise 165
VANITOR, Erma(1047) 165
VANITOR, Gary 165
VANITOR, Gayle 165
VANITOR, Glen Allen(1786) 165
VANITOR, Glenda Rae 165
VANITOR, Jane 165
VANITOR, Janet 165
VANITOR, Jill 165
VANITOR, Mary Alice 165
VANITOR, Mary Alice(1787) 165
VANITOR, Michael Ray 165
VANITOR, Nancy 165
VANITOR, Ray G.(1785) 165
VANITOR, Stanley 165
VANITOR, Thomas(1784) 165
VANITOR, Vickie 165
VICCELI, Michael G. 259
VICCELI, Terri Lynn(2948) 259
VOGEL, Bessie Vonvor(431) 64

VOGEL, William 64
VOGT, Benjamin(895) 96
VOGT, Catherine(366) 96
VOGT, Effie(898) 96
VOGT, Glenn(896) 96
VOGT, Lester(897) 96

WADE, Suzanne 199
WADE, Sarah 51
WADZINSKI, Barbara(1283) 196
WADZINSKI, Richard 196
WADZINSKI, Scott Richard(2155) 196
WADZINSKI, Todd Alan(2156) 196
WAGAMAN, Lois 227
WAGLEY, Billy Dean(1904) 174
WAGLEY, Dennis Dale(1908) 174
WAGLEY, Donald Eugene(1903) 174
WAGLEY, Jack Lee(1905) 174
WAGLEY, Jeannette E.(1906) 174
WAGLEY, Nettie Almira(1092) 174
WAGLEY, Orville 174
WAGLEY, Richard Lewis(1907) 174
WAGNER, Janet Elaine(2938) 259
WAGNER, Julie(2937) 259
WAGNER, Mary Anna 55
WAGNER, Randolph 258
WAGNER, Ruth 152
WAGNER, Sue Elaine(2361) 258
WAHL, Darlene Mae 248
WAHL, Harry Frederick 179
WAHL, Kirk S. 179
WAHL, Margaret(1987) 179
WAHL, Robert 179
WAHL, Robert T. 179
WAHL, Tanya Marie 179
WAKE, Garland May 284
WALGAMUTH, Arden Dee(2366) 210, 259
WALGAMUTH, Fred 210
WALGAMUTH, John William(2807) 249
WALGAMUTH, Judith Annn 259
WALGAMUTH, Kristen Kay(2946) 259
WALGAMUTH, Mark Frederick(2945) 259
WALGAMUTH, Mary Blanche(1394) 210
WALGAMUTH, Mary Catherine(2947) 259
WALGAMUTH, Patrick R.(2949) 259
WALGAMUTH, Randy(2806) 249
WALGAMUTH, Sandra 259
WALGAMUTH, Sherry Ann(2804) 249
WALGAMUTH, Tamara Sue(2950) 259
WALGAMUTH, Terri Lynn(2948) 259
WALGAMUTH, Terry Lee(2367) 210, 259

WALGAMUTH, Thomas Eugene(2805) 249
WALGAMUTH, William Jr. 249
WALKER, Elsie May 135
WALKER, James Otto 115
WALKER, Lenora 151
WALKER, Lydia(570) 115
WALKER, May(1126) 116, 179
WALKER, Otto(1127) 116
WALKER, Stella(1125) 116
WALL, David 271
WALL, Deanna Kay(2495) 271
WALL, Shirley(3066) 271
WALL, Tonya(3067) 271
WALLACE, Allen(1973) 178
WALLACE, Anne(565) 74
WALLACE, Arlene 178
WALLACE, Bess(566) 74
WALLACE, Bessie 114
WALLACE, Brenda Kay 177
WALLACE, Carl Dean(1968) 177
WALLACE, Carla Sue 177
WALLACE, Carol 178
WALLACE, Cecil(1112) 114, 178
WALLACE, Charles M.(1110) 114, 177
WALLACE, Clarence(563) 74, 114
WALLACE, Dawn 178
WALLACE, Dixie 177
WALLACE, Dorothy 178
WALLACE, Edna(1111) 114
WALLACE, Eleanor 165
WALLACE, Emeline(197) 74
WALLACE, Fern(1114) 114
WALLACE, Gary Eugene 177
WALLACE, Gene Charles(1969) 177
WALLACE, Glenn(1975) 178
WALLACE, Jake(561) 74
WALLACE, James Conrad 178
WALLACE, Jeanna Lynn 178
WALLACE, Jeannette 177
WALLACE, Jennifer Lynn 177
WALLACE, Jerry(1974) 178
WALLACE, John 74
WALLACE, Jon Eugene(1966) 177
WALLACE, Joyce Marie(1967) 177
WALLACE, Judith 178
WALLACE, Julie Lynn 178
WALLACE, Karen(1972) 178
WALLACE, Kathleen J. 246
WALLACE, Kimberly Jo 178
WALLACE, Lila 178
WALLACE, Marie(564) 74, 115

WOLF, Russell(1151) 117, 184
WOLF, Russell Alan(2589) 228, 275
WOLF, Ruth(343) 59
WOLF, Ruth Ann(497) 70
WOLF, Ruth Catherine(758) 88, 138
WOLF, Samantha(409) 63
WOLF, Sandra Jo(2507) 221
WOLF, Sandra Kay(3099) 274
WOLF, Sarah 51
WOLF, Sarah C.(301) 56, 90
WOLF, Sarah Catherine(1134) 116, 180
WOLF, Sarah E. 33
WOLF, Sarah E.(473) 67
WOLF, Sarah Eleanor 57
WOLF, Sarah Ellen(568) 75, 115
WOLF, Sarah J.(90) 36
WOLF, Sara Lee(2591) 228, 275
WOLF, Sarah M. 97
WOLF, Sarah Margaret 91
WOLF, Sarah(11) 23, 35
WOLF, Sarah(124) 41, 62
WOLF, Sarah(29) 29, 44
WOLF, Shana Kay 277
WOLF, Shane Michael(3115) 275
WOLF, Shannon Mae 156
WOLF, Shelly Ann 281
WOLF, Sherman E.(474) 67, 102
WOLF, Simon P.(74) 35, 55
WOLF, Simon Peter(411) 63, 98
WOLF, Simon(131) 41
WOLF, Simon(31) 29, 45
WOLF, Sonya Rae(2586) 228, 275
WOLF, Sophia 33, 63
WOLF, Sophia(30) 29, 44
WOLF, Sophia(45) 33
WOLF, Stella(1150) 117, 183
WOLF, Stephana Margarite 228
WOLF, Stephanie Jean(3113) 275
WOLF, Stephen Frank(2587) 228, 275
WOLF, Steve 182
WOLF, Steven(1506) 143
WOLF, Sue Elaine 275
WOLF, Susan 255
WOLF, Susan(9) 23, 34
WOLF, Susan(44) 33
WOLF, Susan(94) 36
WOLF, Susan(2579) 227
WOLF, Susanna 17
WOLF, Synthia Sue 183
WOLF, Tamara Sue(3097) 274
WOLF, Theodore(679) 83

WOLF, Thomas Ashway(1698) 156
WOLF, Tracy(28) 29, 43
WOLF, Trevor David(2667) 235
WOLF, Tricia Sue(3114) 275
WOLF, Trina Kay(2508) 221
WOLF, Truman Leo(477) 67, 103
WOLF, Uarda May 106
WOLF, Van Luther(178) 46, 68
WOLF, Velma L. 179
WOLF, Vera(917) 98, 150
WOLF, Vera Margaret(926) 99
WOLF, Viola Maude(756) 88
WOLF, Violet E.(1781) 165
WOLF, Virginia Mae 179
WOLF, Vivian Fay 183
WOLF, Walter Cleveland(483) 68, 104
WOLF, Washington Clark(49) 33, 52
WOLF, Washington M.(226) 51
WOLF, Wayland(919) 99
WOLF, Wayne Wendell(2746) 244, 281
WOLF, Willadene 183
WOLF, William Alfred(286) 55
WOLF, William Carlton(172) 45
WOLF, William Edward(1440) 138, 213
WOLF, William Harvey(1776) 165
WOLF, William Henry(604) 77, 122
WOLF, William M.(418) 64
WOLF, Willis(913) 98
WOLF, Wilma Catherine 213
WOLF, Wilma Delight 181
WOLPERS, Frank 62
WOLPERS, Martha(402) 62
WOODS, Fern(1313) 130
WOODS, Richard 130
WOODWARD, Laura(394) 62
WOOTEN, Florence Irene 169
WORLEY, Goldie Belle(1218) 189
WORLEY, Warren 189
WORTH, Esther 118
WRIGHT, Aaron(2201) 199
WRIGHT, Cassandra(2200) 199
WRIGHT, Edgar 73
WRIGHT, Harriet 273
WRIGHT, Kathleen(1300) 199
WRIGHT, Leona 135
WRIGHT, Max 199
WRIGHT, Max Jr.(2199) 199
WRIGHT, Melissa(2202) 199
WRIGHT, Rose(539) 73
WRIGHTSMAN, Cheryl 207
WYATT, Betty 209

WYATT, Christy Marietta 222
WYATT, Cindy 209
WYATT, Frank 133
WYATT, Gwen Ellen 208
WYATT, Harold(2346) 209
WYATT, James(2347) 209
WYATT, Karen(2348) 209
WYATT, Mary Magdeline(719) 133
WYATT, Melvin(1371) 133, 208
WYATT, Patricia(2349) 209
WYNCOTTE, George F. 132
WYNCOTTE, Glenora June(1352) 132
WYSONG, Beverly 201
WYSONG, Hazel Marie 141

YARBOUGH, Blanch I.(1931) 176
YATCKOSKA, Gwen Ellen 208
YEATTS, Phyllis Jean 234
YEISLEY, Helen Lucile 107
YENSON, Douglas James 163
YENSON, Mary Rebecca(1760) 163
YENTES, Aaron Scott(2915) 256
YENTES, Gary 256
YENTES, Marla Jo(2328) 256
YODER, Betty Ann(1369) 208
YODER, Don Christopher(2926) 258
YODER, Edwin Ray(2339) 208, 257
YODER, James Allen(2338) 208
YODER, Joseph Wilmer 208
YODER, Laura Ann(2337) 208, 257
YODER, Lois Ann 208
YODER, Margaret Sue(2340) 208, 258
YODER, Marion Nathan 136
YODER, Mary Lou(2341) 208
YODER, Teresa Lynette 257
YODER, Zona Artis(1410) 136
YOST, Alfred Roy(1951) 176
YOST, Dale Eugene(1949) 176
YOST, Danalene Antoinette(1952) 176
YOST, Helen Irene(1101) 176
YOST, Joyce Alfreda(1950) 176
YOST, Kenneth 176
YOUNG, Alice Virginia 66
YOUNG, Edith 66
YOUNG, Effie Young(472) 102
YOUNG, Evelyn Alice(966) 102, 154
YOUNG, Helen Bertha 154
YOUNG, Polly 56
YOUNG, Sandra Kay 262
YOUNG, Simon Luther 102
YOUNG, Steven Alan(1672) 154

YOUNG, Sue Elaine 275
YOUNG, Wallace Brian(1671) 154
YOUNG, Walter Luther(965) 102, 154
YOUNGS, Eldina M.(1898) 174
YOUNKER, Samuel Earl Jr. 105
YOUNKER, Vivian Genevieve(1007) 105
YOUNT, Sarah Ann 54

ZECHER, Elizabeth 61
ZELLERS, Anna(1663) 153
ZELLERS, Annie 153
ZELLERS, Annie(461) 101
ZELLERS, Betty(1662) 153
ZELLERS, Donald(1658) 152
ZELLERS, Doris(1660) 152
ZELLERS, Dorothy(1652) 152
ZELLERS, Edward(952) 101
ZELLERS, Ella 152
ZELLERS, Ernest(953) 101, 152
ZELLERS, Florence(1659) 152
ZELLERS, Floyd(954) 101, 152
ZELLERS, Karl(955) 101, 152
ZELLERS, Katheryn 152
ZELLERS, Keith(1656) 152
ZELLERS, Laurence(1661) 152
ZELLERS, Laverne(1655) 152
ZELLERS, Lillian Barr 102
ZELLERS, Lola(1653) 152
ZELLERS, Martin 101
ZELLERS, Mary 152
ZELLERS, Robert(1657) 152
ZELLERS, Royal(1654) 152
ZELLERS, Ruth 152
ZELLERS, Wilbur(956) 101, 153
ZENTZ, Ada Irene 174
ZIMMERMAN, Vickie Darlene 277
ZIMMERMAN, William 146
ZIMMERMAN, Wilma Jean(1556) 146
ZOLMAN, Sondra 131
ZOOK, Elvin G. 251
ZOOK, Leigh Ann(2834) 251
ZOOK, Nichole Lynn(2835) 251
ZOOK, Sharon Kay(2222) 251
ZOOK, Tara Elizabeth(2833) 251

www.ingramcontent.com/pod-product-compliance
Lightning Source LLC
Chambersburg PA
CBHW070543270326
41926CB00013B/2182